Seeing Canada Whole

A Memoir

Seeing Canada Whole

A Memoir

J.W. Pickersgill

Fitzhenry & Whiteside

© 1994 J.W. Pickersgill

Published by Fitzhenry & Whiteside
195 Allstate Parkway
Markham, Ontario L3R 4T8

Editor: Theresa Griffin
Design: McCalla Design Associates
Typesetting: ISIS Communications

Printed and bound in Canada

Canadian Cataloguing in Publication Data

Pickersgill, J. W., 1905-
    Seeing Canada Whole

Includes index.
ISBN 1-55041-069-5

1. Pickersgill, J. W., 1905-   . 2. Canada —
Politics and government — 1963-1968.*   3. Canada —
Politics and government — 1957-1963.*   4. Canada —
Politics and government — 1935-1957.*   5. Cabinet
ministers — Canada — Biography.   6. Politicians —
Canada — Biography.   7. Liberal Party of Canada —
Biography.   I. Title.

FC611.P5A3 1994   971.064'3'092   C94-931100-6
F1034.3.P53A3 1994

Contents

1 A Homesteading Childhood

First Years

Birth in Ontario

I was born in the county of Norfolk, Ontario, on 23 June 1905 in a large, handsome red-brick farmhouse built in 1886. My father was born on the same farm in 1879 in an earlier and more modest house. The farm was close to a crossroads, where there was a general store owned by my grandfather. A post office called Wyecombe was located in the store. There was a Methodist church a short distance away. The post office was closed years ago and the church more recently. The name Wyecombe has not appeared on the map since the church was closed.

My grandfather, Thomas Pickersgill, was born in Yorkshire in 1835. He came with his parents and grandparents to Canada West, now Ontario, in 1841. They eventually settled on a farm at Bookton, Norfolk County. In due course my grandfather acquired a farm of his own at Wyecombe and prospered substantially both as a farmer and as a general storekeeper. He was a managing type. No man should have to work himself, he boasted, if he was good at organizing the work of others. My grandfather certainly organized the lives of his sons and gave them little scope for making decisions on their own. My father's two older brothers, John and Walter, were sent to high school and both became schoolteachers.

1

Grandfather later had John give up teaching to manage the general store at Wyecombe. When John died, Walter was conscripted to run the store. Grandfather decided that my father, Frank, probably because he was strong and a hard worker, was the son best suited to operate the farm and eventually to take it over.

My father, therefore, instead of going to high school, was kept at home to learn how to be a farmer. His one great adventure while growing up was a trip to Manitoba on a harvest excursion. Until the Great Depression the grain harvest on the prairies required extra seasonal labour and offered a way for teenagers to be paid for seeing a new part of the world.

My mother, Sara Smith, was born in 1877 on a farm adjacent to the village of Port Rowan, at the landward end of Long Point Bay on Lake Erie. Port Rowan was 14 miles south of Wyecombe. Her family life was very different from that of the Pickersgills. Her father died when she was two. Her brother, John, was seven years older. Her mother was left with a good farm, which was cultivated for her by a farmer who lived in a house on the property built for farm labourers or tenants.

Birthplace of J.W.P. Thomas Pickersgill's red brick farmhouse built in 1886 at Wyecombe, Norfolk County. All persons in picture are family members.

J.W.P.'s grandparents, Mr. and Mrs. Thomas Pickersgill.

Mother received a high school education. Her cousin, Dr Annie Backus, many years her senior and one of the early women medical doctors in Ontario, told me that Mother was the best student who ever attended the Port Rowan high school. She went on to the model school at Simcoe, the county town, and became a schoolteacher. After teaching for four years she had saved enough from her salary of $300 a year to pay her way through the nursing school of the Toronto General Hospital. She graduated in 1903 with the highest standing in that distinguished school.

Fourteen miles was a long way in the days of the horse and buggy, and it is unlikely Mother would ever have met the Pickersgill family if one of her mother's sisters, her favourite aunt, had not married a cousin of Grandfather Pickersgill, who also lived at Wyecombe. As a girl Mother often visited her aunt, and on those visits she encountered members of the Pickersgill family. My father's brother John, 'paid attention' to Mother, but he died at the age of 26 of typhoid fever, a frequent cause of death in those days. My father, a year and a half younger than Mother, she barely noticed on her visits to Wyecombe.

It was in Toronto that my father first became interested in my mother. One day he and a friend bicycled the 100 miles to

Brick house — birthplace of J.W.P.'s mother.

Frank Allan Pickersgill with son J.W.P. 1905.

Toronto on a sightseeing holiday. His friend knew Mother well and persuaded my father to go with him to visit her at the hospital. The next day my father went back, alone. It is said that he never looked at another girl afterwards. The courtship developed rapidly, and my father soon proposed marriage. At about the same time Mother, who had graduated and was doing special nursing, was offered the position of superintendent of the hospital at Dawson City, in the Klondyke. She was greatly tempted by the offer, but marriage won out.

Sara C. Smith, graduate nurse, Toronto General Hospital 1903. Married Frank A. Pickersgill of Wyecombe, Ontario, Nov. 25, 1903.

My parents were married on 25 November 1903, and, inevitably, went to Niagara Falls for their honeymoon. They had a ready-made home of their own, as my father's parents had migrated to Manitoba to settle at Cartwright earlier in 1903, and my father had taken over the farm at Wyecombe, where I was born in a larger and finer house than any I have lived in since then.

My father early developed an interest in public affairs. He was elected to the township council before he was 25. Both my parents were keen and articulate Conservatives. My mother's family had much deeper North American roots than my father's. All her Canadian ancestors had been in Norfolk County before 1800, and all but one family were Loyalists. From the start of the Long Point settlement her ancestors had been magistrates and other officials of the local 'family compact' and, of course, opposed to William Lyon Mackenzie and the Reformers. With that heritage I had a long way to go to become a Liberal.

The Liberal party had been in office in Ontario for 35 years when an election was held in 1905. One of the earliest political cartoons of the time was of a tired, broken-down horse with a decrepit rider. It appeared day after day in a Tory paper in Toronto with the slogan 'Thirty-five Years in the Saddle; It's Time for a Change.' The Conservatives won a decisive victory under the leadership of J.P. Whitney.

My own political life began early. Four or five months before I was born, my father said that the son my parents were expecting should be given Whitney as his middle name. My Tory name caused occasional surprise and amusement after I became a practising Liberal politician nearly half a century later.

I have no recollection of living in rural Ontario because my parents moved to Manitoba in the spring of 1907, when I was not yet two years old, and my earliest memories are of the prairies of southern Manitoba. Mother often told me that I learned to talk before I learned to walk, contrary to the more usual practice. That may have been a forecast of my lifelong backwardness in physical activity.

The move to Manitoba

I never discovered why my parents decided to join the rest of my father's immediate family in Manitoba in 1907. There was a restless spirit in southwestern Ontario in those years and a large migration to Manitoba. My father's brother Walter, who managed Grandfather's general store, had felt the urge to go west to make a fortune growing wheat. Grandfather Pickersgill sold the store and set up Uncle Walt as a farmer in the prairies in 1903. My grandparents settled three miles from his farm in the village of Cartwright, on the southernmost branch of the CPR, six miles north of the North Dakota border.

Cartwright had three grain elevators, two or three general stores, the inevitable barber shop and poolroom, a cobbler, a brick hotel, a medical doctor, a Chinese laundry, and a livery stable with horse-drawn vehicles. There were no motorcars. The village had three churches — Presbyterian, a frame building, Methodist, brick, and Church of England, the smallest, built of stone. My great-grandmother from the Hebrides, a devout Presbyterian, brought up her children to believe the Presbyterian was the true church, though she attended the Methodist church, the only church at Wyecombe, where she spent her married life. The Pickersgill children had been baptized there, as I had been. But in Cartwright the 'true church' asserted itself, and my grandparents attended the Presbyterian. When we reached Cartwright, Mother, whose family were Baptists, and my father, a Methodist, were ushered by Grandmother into the Presbyterian church, as was I and, in due course, my brothers and sister.

Instead of acquiring a farm in Manitoba we lived in the village, where my father started a retail lumber business and also became manager of a grain elevator belonging to a farmers' cooperative.

Cartwright was where I first became aware of the world around me. Grandfather Pickersgill died in 1908, when I was three. I can still see him lying in bed during his last illness. I had never before seen a man with a beard. That is the first memory I can date. I do not remember the birth of my brother Tom, in 1907. For me, he was always there. I do remember the birth of my sister, Bessie, and her twin, Walter, in January 1909; what impressed the event on my memory was that it took place the night the village poolroom burned down. My recollections of our four years at Cartwright are spotty, but my first impression of the prairie landscape is as fresh as ever.

Discovering that I was a Canadian was a gradual experience. No one is born conscious of belonging to a particular place, much less a country. For children, definition of their environment is a gradual and imperceptible process. But if my discovery of Canada was not a sudden revelation, my discovery that there was another country that was not mine, where people were not Canadians, was abrupt. Six miles south of the North Dakota border was a village called Hansboro. In 1910 a young lawyer, a friend of our family, acquired the first motorcar in Cartwright. One day that summer he invited my parents to drive to Hansboro with him, and as the eldest in the family I was taken too. I was told before we went that Americans were not like us, and that we were Canadians. Hansboro looked like Cartwright. The first difference I noticed was that it had four grain elevators, whereas Cartwright had only three. But what made the visit memorable was to see that there were churches in Hansboro. I was shocked; my grandmother had told me the Americans were heathens. I could hardly wait to get home to put her straight.

That summer King Edward VII died. I did not know what a king was or what he did. But the attitude of my parents and others to his death gave me the idea that a king must be very important.

Until January 1911 my physical environment was limited to a few square miles of relatively flat prairie without many trees, my uncle's wheat farm, our village, built along the railway, my father's lumberyard and the grain elevator he managed.

In 1911 my parents decided the time had come to go back 'down east' to visit our numerous relatives.

The journey of 48 hours between Winnipeg and Toronto, the first train journey I can remember, was exciting, and going to bed a great adventure. Tom and I slept in an upper berth with our father, the twins in a lower with Mother. Travelling in sleeping cars with sheets and blankets, I found out later, was luxury. Most settlers travelled in colonist cars, with wooden seats which could be transformed into bunks and of course no bedding. And Norfolk County, Ontario, even in the dead of winter, was still more exciting. The villages were larger, the houses more spacious and comfortable, and the trees much taller and growing everywhere. Mother had told me it was a land where apples, pears, peaches, plums and cherries grew on trees, and where rivers of maple syrup flowed in the spring. I still remember the thrill of seeing one frozen apple on a tree in the village of Port Rowan. It convinced me that apples did not just come out of barrels. Of course I did not know anything yet about provinces, but 'down east' was clearly different from the prairies, and the visit marked a great expansion of the horizons of a five-year-old.

For many Canadians of my generation in western Canada, the motherland was somewhere in the British Isles or in Europe; for our family in Manitoba, the real motherland was Ontario, invariably called 'down east.'

Ashern

Homesteading

When Manitoba was carved out of the former Hudson's Bay Territory, the crown lands were owned and administered by the federal government. The American system of surveying the land into townships six miles square was adopted for the Canadian prairies and ultimately for all the unoccupied lands in what became the provinces of Manitoba, Saskatchewan and Alberta.

Construction of the first stage of a railway to Hudson Bay had started in 1905 and had been completed as far as Oak Point on Lake Manitoba, 50 miles northwest of Winnipeg, when the builders ran out of funds. The Canadian Northern Railway acquired the line in 1910, when a gypsum deposit was discovered 100 miles north of Oak Point. The railway began to extend the line northwards to carry the gypsum from the prospective mine to the market in Winnipeg.

Until 1910 the only residents of the country north of Oak Point were the Icelandic settlers along the shore of Lake Manitoba and the Indians on two reserves, one at Dog Creek, 30 miles north of Oak Point, the other at Fairford, where the railway was to cross the Fairford River.

The area north of Oak Point, like the prairies, was surveyed into townships of 36 sections of a square mile each. The sections were divided into quarter sections, and those were the units of settlement: a homestead was a quarter section of land, and it was free, except for a $10 registration fee. To get clear title one had to build a house, clear and cultivate 30 acres and still be in residence after three years.

Once railway construction had begun north of Oak Point, settlers came in a steady stream until 1914. Some were from 'down east' but most were from the British Isles and continental Europe. Free land so close to Winnipeg was a great attraction.

In the years at Cartwright my father's lumberyard did not prosper, and his remuneration for managing the farmers' elevator was small. By 1910 he was yearning for greener pastures. During a visit to an old friend from Wyecombe who ran a grocery store in Winnipeg, my father met a cousin of the friend also from Ontario, who was looking for a place to settle in Manitoba. His name was W.H. (Bert) Hyde. The two men struck up a friendship and decided to go north together to look for homesteads on the new rail line already under construction.

There were sidings every seven or eight miles, where identical townsites were surveyed by the railway. That summer my father and Bert Hyde went as far as the seventh siding, about 110 miles north of Winnipeg, looking for a likely spot to homestead. Each of them filed on a quarter section close to the seventh siding, where a few buildings had already been started on the townsite. In addition to taking up homesteads they planned to operate a general store at the siding.

Bert Hyde had already moved to the seventh siding and built a small log house on his homestead before we left Cartwright, in June 1911. At Winnipeg we changed trains from the CPR to the

Canadian Northern. Our journey from Winnipeg started at about 4 p.m. on a regular passenger train that went as far as Oak Point. There we had supper at the small country hotel, and we four children were bedded down until nearly midnight, when the construction train was to leave.

Once a week passengers were carried north of Oak Point in an ordinary freight caboose at the end of the construction train. On that June night the caboose was packed until the train reached the fourth siding, Eriksdale, at about 4 a.m. We children were asleep on the floor in a corner. Our father stood over us as protection from an uproarious but good-natured drunk, who marched up and down singing 'King George he was, King George he was,' in honour of the recent coronation of King George V. After the train left the fourth siding we were almost alone for the last 25 miles, which the train took three more hours to travel. As we neared our destination, my parents were standing on the back platform of the caboose. Mother asked whether the rails were not supposed to be nailed to every tie. My father said he had hoped she wouldn't notice, and added that the casual way the rails were laid accounted for the lack of speed and for at least one derailment on almost every trip. We reached the seventh siding safely, however.

On the morning of our arrival my first impression was that there were trees and bush everywhere. Except for the hay meadows along the lake, the country north of Oak Point on the Lake Manitoba side of the interlake country was a land of bush and muskegs very different from the prairie we had left, except that it too was flat. There were almost no streams and therefore little drainage except into the innumerable sloughs. Moreover, as the settlers were soon to find out, the land was poor and stony. The stones were never all picked — a new crop appeared every spring. The growing season was short, with greater risk of late spring and early fall frosts than in southern Manitoba. It was not the promised land many of the settlers had hoped for when it was surveyed.

There were small trees, poplars and spruce and jack pine, and, as we soon learned, substantial stands of tamarack, which made the best firewood. Tamarack burned slowly, and the logs were so straight they were easy to split; that mattered a great deal to my brothers and me a few years later. There were sloughs, muskegs and willow-runs parallel to Lake Manitoba at irregular intervals. Because of the lack of drainage, the water lasted well into the summer.

We were met at the train by Bert Hyde, and moved into his small log house, where we lived for six weeks while a two-storey house was built on our homestead. The house was 16 feet by 22 feet, about the dimensions of our present-day living room. The frame was covered with shiplap, tar paper and siding on the outside, with bare two-by-four studs on the inside — no plaster or wallboard. The downstairs was divided into a kitchen and a dining-living room. In addition to a kitchen stove, a sideboard, a table, six straight chairs and two rocking chairs the room contained a desk-secretary with three glass-fronted bookshelves above a desk with cubbyholes and three drawers below. The top drawer was filled with family photographs we often looked at, particularly when we had visitors. There were cement foundations, but the cellar was merely a hole in the ground reached from a trapdoor and a ladder. The upstairs had two bedrooms. The larger was occupied by my parents and the two-and-a-half-year-old twins, who slept in a large crib bed. Tom and I slept in a double bed in the smaller room. There was of course no electricity, no telephone, no running water and no plumbing. There was a two-seater outhouse attached to the granary about 50 feet from the house. So Mother would not have to use the outhouse in the winter, my father built a wooden box in the clothes cupboard off the large bedroom to cover a large metal pail, which had to be emptied often. Our guest room, often occupied, was the living room, with sleeping accommodation on a Toronto couch — a couch by day with a second set of springs that could be pulled out to make a double bed or two single beds. The accommodation was primitive and crowded but comfortable, better than the housing of most of our neighbours.

As well as the granary, the farm buildings consisted of a log barn with a loft for hay and a concrete structure partitioned to provide shelter for chickens and pigs. The section for the chickens had all glass windows on the south side. The well was half way between the house and the barn. Adjacent to the well was a water trough for the livestock. The water was hard in that limestone country but beautifully clear and good to drink.

We never had to depend exclusively on the homestead for our livelihood. There were two general stores at the siding when we arrived. A company called the Lake Manitoba Trading Company opened a store at each siding north of Oak Point as soon as the railway reached it. The other store, in a warehouse on the railway right-of-way with direct access from the boxcars, belonged to a man named Hardisty, who wanted to sell it. My father and Bert Hyde bought it and called the business Hyde and Pickersgill. Hardisty was also postmaster, so a replacement was needed. My father was known as an active Conservative, and since the post office was in the store, he was the obvious choice. When I was a little older and had learned to read, I loved to help sort the mail. My father received other minor appointments, both federal and provincial; he registered vital statistics, for example, and compiled the voters' list for provincial elections.

Ashern, Manitoba, main street 1912. Hyde/Pickersgill building first on left.

In 1912 Hyde and Pickersgill built a two-storey building at the southwest corner of Main Street and Railway Avenue, the first two streets at the siding. The main floor was store and post office. The first tenant of the upper floor was Safiolis, a Greek, who established a hotel there. The hotel prospered, and he built his own three-storey building after a year or two. Hyde and Pickersgill's upper storey then became the magistrates' court.

Since my father was busy in the general store and the post office, we hired labourers for clearing land and ploughing and cultivating the fields. The first were Indians from the Dog Creek Reserve. I had never seen Indians before, and probably had never heard of their existence, and I was very curious. Smoking by women was unheard of at that time, and I still recall my astonishment when I saw an old Indian woman smoking a cigar. During the summers until about 1918, Indians ranged the countryside digging seneca root, locally called snake root, for which there was a ready cash market in the United States, where it was used in some pharmaceutical products.

Despite the overcrowding in our house we nearly always had a hired girl. The first two, and the best, were Icelandic girls, who remained our friends as long as we lived in Manitoba. In 1912 we added a lean-to as a summer kitchen. The addition had a bedroom partitioned off it; it was winterproofed in 1913, and reduced our overcrowding substantially. The house was heated and the cooking done exclusively with wood as fuel; we never had a piece of coal in the house. We needed a good supply of wood — poplar for the cook stove and tamarack or spruce for the box stove for heating. We always bought the wood in tree lengths, so cutting, splitting and piling was one of the heavy chores.

We had a good team of horses and several cows, a lumber wagon and a democrat, a buggy, a bobsleigh and a cutter. Since most of the settlers started with a yoke of oxen, a lumber wagon and a bobsleigh, we felt ourselves privileged to have a team of good horses and a variety of conveyances, as well as farm implements, including a horse-drawn plough, harrows, a hay mower, a hay rake and, ultimately, a self-binder to cut oats and barley. We never tried to grow wheat.

In 1911 we managed to get one acre of land broken, which was seeded to alfalfa, the first grown in the interlake country. We also had a garden plot broken in time to grow a few vegetables. In 1912 our garden extended to nearly half an acre. Mother was a knowledgeable and enthusiastic gardener, and every year we tried some new experiment with varying degrees of success. Our garden provided all our summer vegetables, and potatoes and root vegetables for the winter as well. After a year or two I became the number two gardener. Once I had learned to read, I could hardly wait each spring to study the seed catalogues.

The garden was north of the house and well fenced to keep out the farm animals. The house and yard were surrounded by a five-foot-high page-wire fence with a hedge of small spruce trees along the road allowance in front of the house. By 1913 we already had a good lawn in front of the house. One evening that summer Mother, who had gone to bed early, heard a crash in front of the window and, looking out, saw a moose, which had jumped the fence, and was lying quite still on the ground. She dressed quickly and hurried over to the store, where my father was just closing for the night. He rushed home and stabbed and bled the moose. We had a supply of good meat for a week or two, as did several neighbours. The blood killed the grass: the dark spot on the lawn lasted for years, as we could get no grass to grow where the moose had fallen.

There was a similar page-wire fence at each side of the railway right-of-way. One day in 1913 or 1914, when Bessie and I were going to Winnipeg by train with our father, a moose jumped the railway fence, fell and broke its neck just as the train was passing. The train was stopped. My father was handed a butcher knife that the crew used in preparing their meals in the baggage car. He was the only passenger willing to approach the animal, which might still have been alive. He bled it on the spot, and the carcass was lifted into the baggage car and cut up into pieces of meat, with one given to each passenger.

In that empty land there was an abundance of wild game. Moose and elk were plentiful. Unlike many of the settlers, my father never shot those animals out of season, but gifts of moose meat or elk, which was much tastier, often found their way to our dinner table. The elk were soon depleted. As the settlement advanced, the moose retreated farther into the unsurveyed land to the east. It was then that the deer first appeared; they survived for many years as the game laws came to be better respected. There were plenty of partridges and prairie chickens and wild ducks in season.

Because of poor drainage the sloughs were filled with water until late summer. June was the great month for mosquitoes. The first year we were unprepared for their onslaught. Tom, who was a fat child, was so badly bitten that his eyes were completely closed for two or three days.

It was some compensation that late June and early July was also the season of the wild strawberry. Strawberries were abundant and were an important part of the diet of all the settlers. We ate them once a day during the growing season, and preserved 40 or 50 quarts so that we could have enough for every Sunday dinner throughout the year.

I did not like to pick strawberries and much preferred to work in the garden. We all did chores willingly but without enthusiasm. Being the eldest I started the soonest; my first chore was to wash the dishes, for which I was paid 25 cents a week. When I had saved two dollars there was a disaster. I had a new pair of shoes, which got soaked when I walked through a water-filled slough. Mother told me to open the oven door and put the shoes on the door to dry. I failed to pay attention and put them in the oven and closed the door. They were shrunken beyond repair. I had to buy the replacements with my two dollars. It took a lot more dishwashing to restore my hoard of savings.

The first real money I made in my life was from raising ducks. Mrs Dodd, a neighbour, had given me a setting of duck eggs, on which one of our hens sat. Only three eggs hatched, a drake and two ducks. At Mrs Dodd's suggestion I named them Jacob, Leah and Rachel. The next year I had 10 ducks altogether and decided to sell them and go out of business.

My father refused to buy them in his store, so I went across the street to what in those less sensitive days we called the Jew store. Jake Serkau, who ran the store for his brother, was a kind and friendly fellow. He bought all my ducks for a little more than eight dollars. I have never again felt so rich.

There were 99-foot road allowances surveyed between each two sections, but no roads along them. In 1911, from our siding, there were only two trails, one leading south to Dog Lake and the other west to Lake Manitoba, known respectively as the Dog Lake trail and the Moosehorn Bay trail.

My father often took me with him when he was delivering lumber or on other trips into the countryside. On one trip we picked up a homesteader and his son walking south on the Dog Lake trail. They communicated with my father mostly by signs, supplemented by a few English words, but the man talked to his son in a strange gibberish. I was completely baffled and could hardly wait until we dropped them at their homestead to ask my father what those strange sounds were. He told me they were speaking another language called German and explained that everyone in the world did not speak our language. That was the first time I realized the language we spoke was English and that there were other languages. For a while I thought any language that wasn't English was German.

The first Icelandic girl Mother hired spoke English to us but Icelandic to her family. Not long afterwards I encountered Danish, when I went with my father to take a family, just arrived from Denmark, to their homestead nearly five miles along the Moose-horn Bay trail. They already spoke good English and did not seem at all foreign. The older girl, Clara, was the first woman other than Mother and Grandmother Pickersgill I ever shared a bed with. It happened this way. George Dodd, the homesteader immediately east of us, was a veteran of the South African War and for that reason had an extra quarter section free. His wife loved children but had none of her own. I became one of her favourites, and so did Clara Birnbaum. Mrs Dodd invited both of us to stay over one night. They had only one spare bedroom with a double bed, in which Clara, 17 or 18, and I, 6 or 7, both slept. It was not an educational experience. The younger daughter, Ingeborg, was even more beautiful than Clara. Her picture was used for one of the illustrations in Eaton's catalogue — a source of some excitement at the siding.

Many of the settlers seemed much more foreign than did the Icelanders or Danes. One family, who stayed only a few years, were called Bohemians; I assume they were Czechs. There were a number of Galician families, as everyone then called Ukrainians. There were also German families, some from Germany and others from German-speaking settlements in Russia, and one or two Polish families. We also had French immigrants from France and two or three French-Canadian families, one of them half breeds, as Métis were then called. To add to the multicultural mix we lived in long before the word was invented, there was a Scottish half breed named Billy Sutherland, who helped build our house. One day Bessie and Walter, not yet three, climbed the ladder to the roof where Billy was working. With great skill and patience he talked them down and probably saved them from a bad fall. As long as he lived at the siding, Billy Sutherland was a close friend of the family.

As the country filled up the settlement at the siding also grew. More and more people began to call it Ashern, not 'the siding,' and to refer to a visit to the siding as a trip to town. There were only five or six buildings when we arrived. A year or so later there were a farm implement dealer's warehouse on Main Street, a livery stable on First Avenue South, an Anglican church on First Avenue North and two or three private houses. By 1914 there were a second hotel run by French Canadians and inevitably called the French House, a poolroom and barber shop, a butcher shop and several more houses. With the outbreak of war the growth of the village virtually ceased except for the establishment of a creamery to make butter for sale in Winnipeg. The creamery was started in 1917 and contributed a solid base to the local economy. Rural settlement also stopped with the outbreak of war. The period of real homesteading was over.

All my adult life I have appreciated the wonderful experience it was to put down roots in soil that had never before been settled or cultivated in the history of the world. That homestead on the edge of Ashern is where my real roots have been for 80 years.

Developing a community

Our family home was at Ashern from 1911 to 1926, and during those fifteen years the population of the 'town' never exceeded 100. By 1914 most of the homesteads between the railway and Lake Manitoba had been taken up. East of the railway, settlement was more scattered, and stopped altogether less than 10 miles from the track. There was no population farther east, where the land was poorer. It should have been difficult to transform the heterogeneous elements in Ashern into an integrated community, but it was not. Thinking back, I can see that the public school was the main instrument of integration. At school I recall no tension, social, religious or even political. The half dozen Métis children, whether English- or French-speaking, were accepted, like all the others, on their individual merits.

Not that Ashern was an egalitarian community. Most of the homesteaders were poor, some of them almost destitute when they arrived. Certainly no one was rich. But there were recognized degrees of affluence. Our family never considered itself poor. The English-speaking settlers, whether Canadians from 'down east' or British immigrants, took the lead in developing the community. My parents were among the leaders. They had brought a tradition of public service with them from rural Ontario. Conservative politicians, Protestant clergy and other prominent visitors were almost always invited to our house. Even when there were visitors, we children were at the dinner table. Though we were not encouraged to take part in conversation, we were expected to listen. I loved those visits. On such occasions, as the eldest child I felt that I was part of the adult world, and I began to learn about public affairs, provincial, national and even international.

Our family had another advantage shared by almost no other in the community: my father's mother and sister lived in Winnipeg. When my father went there on business, several times a year, he usually took at least one of us with him. For the first year or two I was favoured as the eldest. The visits to Winnipeg gave us an awareness of the world beyond our local community.

Ashern itself had certain amenities that helped to transform what was a settlement of strangers into a community. Of those the Canadian Northern Railway was important. It was the only link with the outside world. Though many of the settlers and their children never took the train again after their arrival, the railway brought us supplies without which we could not have lived, and soon provided an outlet for some excess produce. The railway also provided the only link by telegraph and, later, telephone with Winnipeg and beyond. There were no private or business telephones, but the railway telephone could be used by the public in emergencies. It cost a dollar to Winnipeg, an immense sum in those days, to use it, but it was a comfort to know it was there.

The first graded roads were started only in 1914, and no roads were gravelled for many years. The first motorcar got through from Winnipeg in 1915, and the first car owned in Ashern arrived in 1917. A return journey to any place further than 15 miles away was practically impossible in a single day. Until the end of the war local travel for the fortunate was by horse and buggy in the summer and horse and cutter in the winter. It was quite usual during spells of wet weather, especially in the spring, for a horse and buggy or even a team pulling a farm wagon to be stuck in the muskeg or the mud. Most homesteaders depended on oxen for both farm work and trips to the siding for groceries and supplies.

The virtual impossibility of long-distance travel by road enhanced the importance of the passenger train. We had mixed trains, one coach on a freight train, three times a week as early as 1912. By 1914 we had a passenger train with a regular schedule. As long as our family lived in Ashern, the whistle of the steam locomotive was the voice of the outside world.

The train to Winnipeg left early in the morning, but the north-bound train in the afternoon attracted all the children and most of the adults in the village. Only a quarter mile away, we were nevertheless not 'town kids,' and we were not allowed to go to the village without Mother's permission. Permission was not given for idle pursuits like watching a train arrive.

The settlement at the end of the railway was named Gypsumville. The transport of gypsum and, later, of limestone quarried out of Lake Manitoba at Steep Rock made that particular branch of the Canadian Northern one of its most profitable for many years. The carriage of settlers and their effects and the subsequent transport out of the new region of their produce — fish in the winter, cream and, later, butter in the summer, and livestock mainly in the fall — were merely a welcome addition to the main traffic. One summer, probably in 1914, my father arranged to have me take a basket of vegetables from our garden to the train crew from time to time. I became friends with the crew, and one day they took me as their guest in the baggage car to Gypsumville for the night. I felt very important.

The railway was not the only amenity. Post offices had been established at every siding even before the construction of the railway was completed, and as settlement progressed, a network of country post offices grew up in homesteaders' houses about five or six miles apart. Those country post offices received mail once a week. Before my father ceased to be postmaster, in 1916, there were seven or eight of those offices dependent on Ashern; the farthest was 20 miles away on Lake Manitoba. The post office was the only real link between the government of Canada and the homesteaders once they had received title to their land. In those days crown lands in the prairies belonged to Canada, not to the provinces. Until homesteaders got title to their land, the Dominion Land Office and its travelling homestead inspector constituted a formal presence. We had a homestead inspector residing in Ashern from 1914 for several years.

The Church also contributed to the development of the community from its beginning. Though we had no resident clergy in my time at Ashern, we were well served by student missionaries, both Anglican and Presbyterian. Theological students stayed in the district all summer and, once there was regular train service, came out from Winnipeg for weekends during the college terms. Ordained clergymen of both churches visited Ashern two or three times during the year to hold Communion services. The Anglican church had a student missionary in the area in 1911, who served more than one settlement. I remember services that summer in the boardinghouse kept by an English family at the siding. The dining room was large enough to hold the small congregation, which always included my parents and me though we were not Anglicans. In 1912 the Anglicans built a small church.

That summer a Presbyterian student missionary visited the district. We had been Presbyterians in Cartwright, and my father persuaded the Anglicans to let the Presbyterians hold services in the Anglican church. Because student missionaries served two or three settlements, it was easy to arrange to have the Anglican and Presbyterian services on alternate Sundays. Our family attended both. The arrangement continued until my father went to the war. Then there was some kind of dispute, and the Presbyterians built a church of their own, which they called the Union Church in anticipation of the union that would give birth to the United Church in 1925. Mother was the driving force in organizing an interdenominational Sunday school, which was attended by all Protestant children. She succeeded in keeping one Sunday school for several years after there were two church buildings. The Sunday school continued to meet in the Anglican church, until the membership became so large it was moved to the larger Union church.

Mother had the Sunday school use the Methodist Sunday school papers, which she thought more interesting than the Anglican or the Presbyterian. The Methodist paper for older children, which I read every week, was called *Onward*. I was proud when *Onward* published a story about the first field of wheat at Long Point, Norfolk County, which told how our Dedrick ancestors had sown an acre of wheat in the spring and shared their first crop with settlers who arrived in the fall.

Onward had a column for children's letters. A letter from a boy in Newfoundland caught my fancy; I wrote to him, and we became pen pals for some time. That was my first contact with Newfoundland. It would not have happened if we had not used Methodist papers, because the Methodist church in Newfoundland was even then an integral part of the Methodist Church of Canada. The Anglican and Presbyterian churches in Newfoundland had no connection with Canada.

The Scandinavian and Icelandic Lutherans did not have their own church in Ashern in our time. The few who lived in or near the village went to the Sunday school and the Union Church. Today the Lutheran is the largest church in Ashern. There are no longer services in the Anglican church, which has been moved to another site and is preserved as a heritage building in a small park.

The few Catholics in Ashern and the surrounding area were mostly French-speaking. Shortly before the war they built a church half a mile east of the siding; they had no resident priest but were visited about once a month by a priest from a settlement more than 30 miles south of Ashern. There was no ecumenical fraternization, except at school, between Protestants and Catholics, but we were friendly neighbours. Our parents taught us that Catholics were also Christians, even if they had a few regrettable superstitions.

For the first two years after we arrived in Ashern we had no resident medical doctor and no health services of any kind. Mother, as a graduate nurse from the Toronto General Hospital, was always willing to help anyone who had a bad accident or a serious illness or a baby to deliver. Some mornings we woke up to find Mother absent and my father or the hired girl getting breakfast. There was no question of payment for Mother's services, though frequently we were given a piece of moose meat or a brace or two of partridges, prairie chickens or wild ducks.

In 1913 a French-Canadian doctor from Montreal, who had just graduated from medical school, opened a practice at Ashern. Dr

Prévost was a delightful young man and a frequent visitor to our house. He was the first French Canadian we knew well, and his charm predisposed us to like French Canadians in general. Shortly after the war broke out, he joined the army, went off to the war and was killed. He was succeeded by Dr C.R. Bunn. Dr Bunn was married, and we did not see him so often in our house. In 1916 he too went to the war, and Ashern was again without a doctor, until 1919. Once more Mother's services were called on, and because my father was away at the war, Mother insisted that those needing her services at night bring someone to look after the house and the children. By 1916 there was a doctor at Lundar, 40 miles away, and good passenger train service, which made him available for serious cases. But Mother was still called for emergencies and births.

Ashern had no municipal government until 1917. The few roads we had were built by the provincial government. Fortunately we had a Conservative member of the legislature, until the Liberal government was elected in 1915, when we returned a Liberal member. There was not much road work during the war, but at least Ashern was not punished for voting the wrong way.

We did have self-government in one area. The public school system of Manitoba was modelled on the Ontario system, with each one-room school having its own school district governed by three elected trustees. My father was a trustee from the start. The Ashern school was opened early in 1912 at the geographical centre of the district, two-and-a-half miles northwest of the siding. The school building was the centre of social activity, with dances, concerts and box socials, and as such played a major role in the transformation of the settlement into a community. By 1917 more than half the pupils in the Ashern school were from the village or, like us, from a farm on the edge of the village. That year the school district was divided, and a new Ashern school built on the edge of the townsite.

Ashern had no resident police, but by 1913 or 1914 we had a justice of the peace, who had been in the Irish constabulary. I doubt if Sam Browne knew much law, but he had an imposing presence, and for us children he was the very embodiment of law and order. Fortunately there was no crime and little disorder in those pre-1914 days.

The annual 1 July picnic was important to our sense of community. The first was held in 1912 on a three- or four-acre flat meadow on our homestead. At the edge of the meadow the bush had been cleared to make a half-mile racetrack, where horse races were run for a year or two. In 1914 the local blacksmith fell off his horse and was so badly injured that he died a few hours later. The tragedy ended the races, which would have found few participants in any case after the war took away most of the young men. The picnics continued on our homestead until 1918. People brought their own lunches; no meals were served, but there was always someone selling ice cream cones and lemonade. In 1919 the picnic was moved to a more convenient site on the new school grounds, where a baseball diamond was marked out and a small grandstand built. The picnics were really sports days, and almost everyone for miles around attended, from babies to grandparents. There were footraces for children. I never won a race, but Bessie was a champion. Once travel became a little easier and the motorcar more common, there were baseball tournaments between settlements throughout the summer.

The comparative isolation of each village before the end of the First World War stimulated self-reliance in the settlers. There was almost universal readiness to cooperate in social activities, and in times of trouble homesteaders counted on the spontaneous help of neighbours. In spite of the diverse origins and backgrounds of the settlers, a genuine sense of community existed by the time the war broke out.

School, the war and politics

My first two years at school, the outbreak of war in 1914 and my discovery of politics are so mixed up together that I cannot sort out how much each contributed to my early education.

I was with my father, on the wagon, when he delivered lumber to the site for the Ashern school in 1911. When the school opened in January 1912, I was six-and-a-half years old, but I didn't start school until my seventh birthday. Mother, who had taught in one-room schools in Ontario for four years, considered it a burden on the teacher to send children to school before they could read. There were no children of school age to walk with me, and my parents thought I was too young to walk two-and-a-half miles to school by myself. When I started school on my seventh birthday, it was summer, and I could read.

I was a thin, timid child with no aptitude for sports and no appetite for fistfighting. All my life I have been awkward and poorly coordinated. Before I started school, my father's mother told me I would be teased and called names by the older children. She advised me to pay no attention. If I took no notice, she said, the others would soon tire of teasing me, but if I cried or fought back, it would never end. To compensate for my physical disadvantages I did have the faculty of listening to advice and, if it seemed good, following it rigidly. No advice given me in my life has helped me so much as that warning from my grandmother. I followed it, and it worked. In my later life people have commented on my apparent indifference to the attacks and abuse directed at me while I was in public life. But no ridicule or attack has ever been half as hard to take as that in those first few weeks at school in the summer of 1912.

There were still no children in the village of school age with whom I could walk. My father bought a pony, which he expected me to ride bareback. I could not mount the pony without help; once we were out of sight of the house, the pony paid no attention to my directions and preferred to stall. After a few days my father bought a fine new saddle so I could mount by myself, but that did not make me the boss. I was strictly forbidden to put on the saddle until I had taken the halter off and put the bridle on. The pony disliked the bridle, and I was afraid she might bite me, so one day I broke the rule and put the saddle on first. When I took off the halter, the pony bolted out of the barn door I had foolishly left open and disappeared into the woods. Mother helped me look for her. We found her standing in water about a foot deep in a slough, and there was no way to get her out. The slough thereafter was known as the pony slough. The hired man was sent to bring her home, which he did, but the saddle was gone and never seen again. I was contrite but also relieved; now I would be able to walk to school. Despairing of making me a horseman, my father sold the pony.

About half way to the school an Irish family named McCandless had settled. They had three children at school, and I liked to be able to join them, but if they were not out in plain sight, I often made a detour so as not to be seen by their collie dog, which barked furiously. They assured me the dog would not bite me, but I was not sure anyone had told the dog.

My progress was better in school than on the road. Within a week I was moved up one grade, so I was not behind others of my age. Occasionally I got a lift with a homesteader. Once in 1913 a man of 30 or 40 gave me a lift. Somehow I found out that although English was his mother tongue, he had never learned to read. I felt so sorry for him that I read the whole of the grade two reader to him during the two-and-a-half-mile trip. At the end of the summer of 1913 the teacher got married. Qualified teachers were scarce in Manitoba, and none could be found for Ashern, so the school had to close until January 1914.

In the late fall, my parents became worried about the interruption of my education. To have a school to go to I was taken to Winnipeg to live with my grandmother. For six weeks I attended the Greenway school on St Matthews Avenue. I was kept in grade two on the theory that children from the country were backward. In fact I had already completed the work of that grade and I learned nothing new in the classroom during those six weeks. If I had known the word, I would probably have said I was bored. I missed the one-room school, where I could give most of my attention to the lessons of those in the higher grades. I have never got over the feeling that for a bright child, a one-room school with a good teacher is better than a schoolroom where all the pupils are in the same class. I learned nothing in the Greenway schoolyard either, for though I was bright in class, I was timid about making advances to other children.

But living in Winnipeg was exciting. I was never homesick. My grandmother was a good companion, always thinking of interesting things for me to do. Aunt Hattie and her Scottish husband were kind to me, and their bright eight-month-old child flattered me by learning my name, Jack, as her first word. I tended to be a solitary child and to prefer adults to other children as company. The policeman on Portage Avenue became my friend. I often walked with him on his beat, feeling very important. If I did not learn much at school in those six weeks in Winnipeg, I learned a great deal about city life. Electric lights, indoor plumbing, bread from the bakery, milk from bottles, street cars, the toy department at Eaton's, at first true wonders, soon became part of a familiar world. I saw my first picture show, to which the price of admission was five cents. The film was a pie-throwing comedy. I did not think it very funny and never really learned to like movies. But real people acting on stage excited me from the start. My grandmother took me to the Walker Theatre to see *The Wizard of Oz*, and I was fascinated. I saw Eaton's Santa Claus parade for the first time. I was still a true believer, and my expectations were not disappointed. By the time I went home for Christmas the Winnipeg of that autumn had become my measure of a real city. To some degree Winnipeg itself still is.

My grandmother died just after Christmas. I probably would not have gone back to Winnipeg anyway, because the Ashern school trustees had found a teacher, a young Irishman named Jack Nelson, who had immigrated to Canada to become a Presbyterian minister. He had been the student missionary at Ashern the previous year and was well liked by everyone. A shortage of funds and a waning vocation had led him to give up his theological studies at Manitoba College. Since no professional teacher was available, the school board got a permit for Nelson to teach. He was born to the task and we learned far more from him than was contained in the schoolbooks. Nelson's permit was not renewed because in the summer of 1914 another crop of professional teachers graduated from the normal school in Winnipeg. Our new teacher was a young woman, Ethel Dicks, who had never taught before. She was young and pretty with a wonderful disposition, but we quickly found out that she was the boss and would stand no nonsense. Like Nelson, she was a born teacher, and we were lucky enough to keep her at Ashern until Christmas, 1916.

In September 1914 I was in grade four. One of my classmates was a boy named Timothy Webster, who was at least as bright as I was. We competed, and I am sure both made greater progress than either would have without the other. He should have gone to high school and university as I did, but his parents lacked the ambition for him that my parents had for me. I shall never forget the eagerness with which Tim and I attacked geography in grade four. When we started grade five, each of us devoured the English history textbook during the first weekend. When we finally reached Canadian history in grade six, we both found it exciting. The textbook was biased: the French in New France were always right, and the English colonists wrong. From the American Revolution on, the Americans were the enemy, and the Canadians invariably on the side of right. When the school district was divided in 1917, Tim remained in the old school, and I went to the new one in the village. The end of our competition was a loss for both of us.

Today a two-and-a-half-mile walk to school would be an intolerable hardship, but we never felt it was, except in the coldest weather. In September 1914 there were eight children from the town in the school, counting my brother Tom and me. Three of them belonged to a Norwegian family. The father was the foreman of the section gang that maintained the railway right-of-way. Two of them were pretty girls who were the life of the 'town kids' as we were called. We walked together in the spring and fall. On most days we had a wonderful time. In the winter we travelled by horse and cutter. For three winters there were two cutters, ours and one other. We often had races, even though Mother had forbidden them. The last winter I was considered old enough to drive. Our cutter won the race whenever I could get started ahead of the other, but it was no special credit to me. Our horse, Old Nell, would rarely allow the other horse and cutter to pass her. She was very cunning about blocking the way, and the other cutter was occasionally upset. I usually got started first because an older boy helped me harness the horse and hitch her to the cutter. On days when I was left to myself I rarely got started first, and getting ahead was not easy, as Old Nell would not pass unless it was quite safe. I was the driver only by courtesy; Old Nell was really in charge, and she was completely trustworthy. Getting to school was much less fun when the new school opened five minutes away.

My closest friend was a boy named Morgan Self, who was a year older and one year ahead of me in school. He had a small collection of Henty books, which supplemented his geography and history. He lent them to me, and they filled my imagination with visions of adventures in far-off places. The Henty books had titles such as *With Wolfe in Canada* and *With Clive in India*. I was particularly fascinated by the book about the black uprising in Haiti led by Toussaint L'Ouverture. Morgan should have gone on to higher education too, and would have had there been opportunities in those days. His parents did believe in education.

The outbreak of war in 1914 made both geography and history real to me. At the age of nine I knew that in addition to Canada and the United States there were other countries in the world, but even the British Isles were still a vague place. I remember my father discussing Home Rule for Ireland with an Irish Protestant visitor, who claimed that Home Rule would mean Rome Rule. My father was not impressed; he thought Ireland should have Home Rule and shocked me by saying that if he lived in England, he would be a Liberal.

I learned gradually to connect the many languages spoken in our settlement with countries on the map. Germany was the first European country that really entered my consciousness, because early in 1914, before the war started, my father named a calf Kaiser Wilhelm. He made it clear that was not meant as a compliment to the German emperor. As I think back on those years, I am astonished how well-informed my father was about the outside world despite his limited formal education. He was keenly and actively involved in politics. In many ways my father deferred to

Mother's greater booklearning, but his breadth of interest and his awareness of public affairs were greater than hers.

At our dinner table there was rarely any gossip about the neighbours but everything in the newspapers was regularly discussed. My parents eagerly welcomed opportunities for talk with our frequent visitors and the few neighbours who were aware of a larger world than our settlement. The day the news reached Ashern that Archduke Franz Ferdinand had been assassinated at Sarajevo, on 28 June 1914, my father read the account in the newspsper, turned to Mother and said, 'There is going to be a war.' I don't believe such a reaction was common on Canadian farms at the time. On the three days a week that the train brought the newspapers the crisis was followed closely. I did not know what war was, but my father told me which countries were involved, and that it was our war because Canada was a part of the British Empire, and we were British. In 1914 my parents made no distinction between the interests of Canada and those of the Empire; they took it for granted that the interests were identical. And, of course, I did too.

Since geography began at school in grade four, in my case a month after war broke out, it is small wonder that it became a living thing for me. I had, of course no doubt that 'we' would win the war. Looking at all the red patches on the map of the world I thought how wonderful it would be when the Germans lost their colonies in Africa, and there would be an unbroken strip of red from Cairo to the Cape.

The outbreak of war and geography at school expanded the world for me. At about that time I also became interested in politics. I was dimly aware there had been an election in 1911, and that Robert Borden was prime minister. But my real interest was provincial politics, largely because, after 1911, the elections until 1917 were provincial. Early in 1914 there was a by-election in Gimli constituency that was watched throughout Manitoba because of the growing weakness of the Tory government. My father, as one of the party organizers, drove the Conservative candidate around the Ashern area and introduced him to as many voters as possible. The candidate, E.L. Taylor, was the first politician I ever met and I was thrilled when he won. He held Gimli in the general election later in the year. The Conservatives retained a bare majority in the legislature. My father worked day and night in the campaign, and I felt he was responsible for the victory. I had no idea what the issues were; all I knew was that the Liberals were the enemy.

In 1915 it was different. A succession of scandals led the lieutenant-governor to dismiss the government of Sir Rodmond Roblin and to invite the Liberal leader, without a majority in the legislature, to form a government and call an election. I knew nothing about the scandals, but I did know that the Liberal premier, T.C. Norris, promised, if he won the election, to give votes to women and to introduce prohibition. In 1914 Gimli had been divided into two constituencies. Ashern was in the new constituency of St George. My father worked hard for Paul Reykdal, the Conservative candidate. When Reykdal visited us at home I spontaneously proposed that we drink his health in raspberry vinegar, a popular soft drink at the time. I don't know where I learned about toasts. That was the first one I ever proposed, and I felt very grown up.

Because the Liberals favoured prohibition, I assumed my father was against it. I was able to persuade four or five boys to let me harangue them on the evils of prohibition and votes for women — the only issues I knew about — and the superiority of the Conservative party. I converted two of them to Toryism; they must have been the only two Conservative converts in Manitoba in 1915. Their fathers were Liberals and complained to my father. I was forbidden to talk politics at school, but my zeal was not easily discouraged. I interpreted that order to apply to the school grounds and persuaded the boys to go out into the bush at lunchtime, swore them to secrecy and continued my political propaganda. I was devastated when the Conservatives were overwhelmingly defeated. I have never since then been so blindly partisan.

In the summer of 1915 we had a visit from a cousin of my father's from Brantford, Ontario. After visiting us he was going on to Cartwright to visit Uncle Walt and Aunt Annie. It was arranged that I should go with him and stay for two or three weeks. I was to come home by myself — another sign I was no longer a mere child. The visit to Cartwright not only refreshed my memory of living on the prairie, it gave me my first real notion of the wheat economy. The crop was obviously good by late August, and wheat for the first time was a dollar a bushel. On the strength of that good fortune Uncle Walt had bought a Tin Lizzie, as the model 'T' Fords were called. The 1915 model was the first with a magneto that controlled the lights; the 1914 model had oil lamps for headlights. The lights were much better in 1915, but if the car stalled or the motor stopped for any reason, the lights went out, which was a problem on a dark night. Uncle Walt also had a telephone, and I learned to use it. But the greatest thrill for this 10-year-old adult was to go by train from Cartwright to Winnipeg on his own. Before the visit to Cartwright I was a fussy, picky eater. I came home with a huge appetite, much to Mother's relief. During that visit I discovered *Waghorn's Guide*, published monthly for five cents. It listed all the passenger train timetables in the prairie provinces. I bought the *Guide* regularly for several years; it started my lifelong interest in railways. That visit to Cartwright was a milestone in my education.

I later found another way to expand my knowledge of geography and of railways. The new Liberal government published an excellent map of Manitoba, which was free. We got one and put it on our dining room wall. I assumed that, if the government of Manitoba published a map, the governments of other provinces probably did too. By 1917 I had written to all the provincial capitals and had maps of all the provinces pasted on the walls of our bedroom. In 1919, when I started to collect stamps, I was attracted by the Newfoundland ones, and it occured to me that Newfoundland probably had a free map too. In response to a letter, the government of Newfoundland sent me a splendid one and half a dozen publications about the colony, all of which I read avidly. At the age of 14, I was an expert on the educational system of Newfoundland.

The War Comes Home

The departure of a soldier

The outbreak of war affected the Ashern district at once. Immigration stopped, homesteading practically ceased, and for a year or two the village stopped growing. A substantial number of the young men in the Ashern area were unmarried, and most of the single men of British ancestry, whether immigrant or Canadian-born, enlisted in 1914 and 1915.

In 1916 the MP for Selkirk became a 'political' colonel. He began at once to raise the 108th (Selkirk) Battalion. The first stage of training took place in separate platoons in the local villages so that the men would not have to leave home until the early summer. By 1916, older men, some of them married, were also enlisting.

My father, who was almost 37, enlisted on 26 February. I naturally believed his motive was pure patriotism. Looking back, I have no reason to doubt that patriotism and genuine concern about the outcome of the war were elements in the decision. But I learned later that there were other, less noble, considerations. The general store was not a financial success. Rather than pledge the farm as security, as the creditors demanded, my father in 1914 had given up his share in the partnership to Bert Hyde, who had no children and was willing to risk his homestead. My father continued as postmaster until he enlisted in 1916.

During 1915 he had been active in the provincial election campaign and had derived some income from his duties as registrar of the voters for a considerable part of St George constituency. He also had some income from minor provincial public functions, which ceased after the Liberals won the election. Though none of us children realized it, our family was in straitened circumstances by the beginning of 1916. Enlistment in the army offered my father a small but regular income as well as allowances for the rest of the family.

He continued to live at home after he enlisted. Instead of going to the post office in the morning, he went to an improvised drill hall in the farm implement warehouse in the village to train with his platoon. The whole battalion was not assembled until late spring.

Though my father's being a soldier did not at first disturb our family life, that life almost ended in March 1916. Mother and all of us children came down with scarlet fever. In those days houses where the disease broke out were severely quarantined. My father took a room in the Greek hotel and went on with his military training. He came home morning and evening to look after the livestock, to do other farm chores and to make sure we had groceries and other provisions as well as plenty of firewood. Mother was very ill. My father had a trained nurse come out from Winnipeg to take care of her. An unmarried family friend, well liked by all of us, kept house. For three days Mother was on the brink of death, and the doctor had almost given up hope. Once she passed that crisis, she recovered quickly, but it was several weeks before she could take charge of the household. The period of quarantine was prolonged because I did not get the fever until the rest of the family had almost recovered.

In 1915 my parents' last child was born at Grace Hospital in Winnipeg. We children were allowed to suggest a name for the baby, and we agreed on Frank, after our father. When we were stricken with scarlet fever Frank was about 10 months old and could crawl but not walk. His illness did not seem severe, and he got little attention. When the fever abated, he had a period of severe earache followed by ear trouble and deafness that lasted the rest of his life.

While we were in bed with scarlet fever, we narrowly escaped another disaster. The kitchen, which had been added to the main house, was only one storey high. One morning the far side of the kitchen caught fire. Fortunately my father was still at home finishing the chores. The only way to put out the fire was with water, and the only water was in a well with a hand-operated pump. The pails were all mobilized, the ladder was put in place, and my father carried pail after pail of water as fast as he could to the fire while the housekeeper pumped steadily. The fire was put out, but it was a close call. No one told Mother, but one of us, looking out the window, wondered out loud why our father was running between the well and the house with pails of water. When the housekeeper came to her room later, Mother asked calmly how bad the fire had been. The housekeeper was astonished and wondered how Mother had found out. I was left with a lasting fear of fire.

By April those trials were over, and our family life was restored to normal until our father went off for summer training with his whole battalion at Camp Hughes, in a sandy area near the present Camp Shilo. Mother went to Brandon for a weekend to visit him in midsummer, but we children did not see him again until late September, when he came home for final leave before going overseas.

It was already apparent, in 1916, that my brother Tom, who was not yet nine, and my brother Walter, who was only seven, were going to be better at splitting wood, milking cows, harnessing horses and using tools and machinery than I would ever be. They also had at least an average aptitude for playing games, and Bessie was better at games than any of us. I realized that my lack of physical skill was a disappointment to my father. He was never unkind about it, but he could not understand a boy who did not measure up to his standards of manliness. It pleased him, however, that I took an interest in everything he said and rarely forgot anything he told me. He was also impressed by my sense of direction. I rarely forget, even today, how to find my way over any road I have once travelled. I remember, when the family was on a Sunday drive in May 1916, how thrilled I was when my father said that anyone with my sense of direction should be a civil engineer. Until that time the only kind of engineer I had heard of was the driver of the steam locomotive on the railway. My father gave me a simple explanation of what civil engineers did, and until a few weeks before I enrolled in university I planned to become an engineer.

During that summer I decided to try something 'manly.' The only thing I could think of that I might have any aptitude for was swearing. It was not hard to acquire a large vocabulary of profanity and foul language at school in a homesteading settlement. Apart from an occasional 'damn' from my father, my parents never used any bad language, and I knew they would disapprove. But I started rehearsing as I brought the cows home from pasture in the evenings. By September I felt I could hold my own with the toughest boys in the school. I daresay my language would have been really manly in a few weeks if the whole project had not been brought to an abrupt halt.

The afternoon our father took the train to go overseas the family naturally was at the station to say goodbye. Shortly before train time he took me off by myself, and we sat down side by side at the far end of the platform. He told me that when he left, I would be head of the family and would have the responsibility of helping Mother to keep the farm going. I would be expected to be a man. He said he hoped I would never do anything Mother did not approve of and warned me particularly against using bad language. I believe it was almost 10 years before I used even the faintest 'damn' again.

Family group on front lawn Ashern 1916. Frank Pickersgill carried a print of this photo in the trenches of France in 1917. Children left to right: Bessie, J.W.P., Walter, Tom.

I was tremendously proud of the confidence my father showed in me and eager to accept all the responsibility I could. From that day I considered myself an adult. I suppose the feeling of self-importance compensated for my feelings of inadequacy in other directions, but it undoubtedly made me even less one of the gang. From that September afternoon the war being fought in France was also my war. I read all the war news in the newspapers we received from Winnipeg, studied the maps, particularly the western front, and became increasingly indignant over the neutrality of the United States.

My father spent the winter of 1916-17 in training in England. Early in 1917 a draft from the 108th Battalion was sent to France to reinforce the 16th Canadian Scottish. During the eight months my father served in France and was in the trenches, the war seemed to touch us even more. I was thrilled by the story of the battle of Vimy Ridge. In due course we received a vivid account of action at the front in a letter from my father that somehow had escaped the censors. He had actually been at Vimy. When a telegram reached us that he had been wounded — it was at Hill 70 — we waited with anxiety until we heard from him that the wound was slight. He was back in action in time to settle down into the mud of Passchendaele, from which he emerged in November seriously ill with nephritis. He was in various military hospitals in England from November 1917 until May 1918, when he returned to military duty in reserve in England. He was invalided home in October 1918.

The war on the home front also made an impression on our family. We children enlisted enthusiastically in the campaign to conserve food and avoid waste. Seventy years later it still pains me to leave anything uneaten on my plate.

In the summer of 1917 we children made a teepee-shaped house, draped with the branches of poplar trees, in the woods west of the farm buildings. One evening Mother agreed to let the older four of us sleep there for the night. During the night there was a thunderstorm and a downpour. We were drenched to the skin, and the others wanted to go back to the house. But I insisted that our hardship was nothing compared to what our father was enduring in the trenches in France and shamed them into staying until the first light of dawn. Mother had lit a lamp and put it in the upstairs window facing west, expecting us to give up once the storm started. When I explained why we had stayed she did not laugh or say we had been silly.

That same summer I discovered *The Swiss Family Robinson*, the book that fascinated me most during my childhood. I decided to share my pleasure with the other children and arranged four sticks of tamarack wood in a circle and had Bessie, Tom and Walter sit on those stools while I read the book for what seemed like an hour. They stayed put, but I could soon see that they were not entranced, and that their minds were elsewhere. I could not get them to agree to a second instalment and had to keep my pleasure to myself.

There was another wartime activity, of which I am not proud. As the campaign for the army intensified, I joined in the popular game of drawing up lists of 'slackers' who should have been in uniform. I got no encouragement from Mother. She did, however, support conscription, and so of course did I. During the 1917 election campaign I first became aware of Sir Wilfrid Laurier, the Liberal leader who opposed conscription; to me he was almost a traitor. In that election many of our German-speaking neighbours had been disenfranchised by the Wartime Elections Act. There were rumours that there might be a riot on election night, but in fact there was not the slightest disturbance. When the Parliament Building in Ottawa burned down in 1916, I readily believed the widespread rumour that it was the work of German spies. There were also rumours that some of our German-speaking neighbours were spies, which I half believed because it seemed exciting. But when members of a particular family, who were friends, were included, I believed no longer. When war broke out in 1939 those memories came back to me, and I resolved to do what I could to avoid a repetition of such rumours. Happily, so far as German Canadians were concerned, there was no similar reaction during the Second World War.

A creamery was established at Ashern in 1917, and Mother decided to start building up our herd of cattle. By the fall of 1918 the revenue from cream and the sale of yearlings was beginning to be an appreciable supplement to the family income. We began to raise more pigs. As each of us had allotted chores, the farm work went relatively smoothly, though we found plenty of other things to quarrel about. One day in 1918 I had trouble beating Tom in a fight and knew he might win the next one. That was our last fight; from then I practised diplomacy.

In 1917 my progress at school was unspectacular. The teacher at the old school was ineffective, and none of us learned very much. She left one day before the term was supposed to end, without giving the pupils any notice. When we town kids arrived at school and found no teacher, we were really annoyed and wrote a number of uncomplimentary things about her on the blackboard. Later, after we had gone home, a couple of older boys who lived beyond the school arrived late and added one or two obscenities. One of the trustees blamed me for this outrage and called a meeting to confront Mother with my crime. She convinced them, by showing them my handwriting, that I had not written the offensive words, and that the accusation was false, but no apology was offered. To this day I resent the injustice.

The new school opened in September 1917. The first teacher was not first rate. Fortunately for me my cousin, Mabel Pickersgill, who was teaching at Beauséjour, near Winnipeg, came to Ashern to spend Christmas with us. After questioning me closely about school, she told me I should be in grade eight and should write the 'entrance' in June. She urged me to speak to the teacher, who said, rather indifferently, that I could go into grade eight if I wanted to. The 'entrance' was a province-wide examination at the end of grade eight. The papers were examined in Winnipeg, and those who passed were admissible to high school. I had a lifelong debt to Mabel, as I might otherwise have drifted along and wasted a year. Instead, in September 1918 I was ready for grade nine, the first year of high school. There was no high school nearer than Winnipeg, but the good-natured teacher allowed me and one or two other pupils to do our grade nine classes in the one-room school.

The return and death of a veteran

My father returned from the war in October 1918, as a disabled soldier. He reached Ashern by train at the end of the afternoon, still in uniform, wearing the kilt of his regiment. My brother

J.W.P.'s father in uniform of 16th Canadian Scottish which he was wearing on his return home in 1918.

Frank, almost three-and-a-half years old and without recollection of his father, went into our parents' bedroom the following morning and asked, 'Are you really my father?' The answer was 'yes.' Frank then asked, 'If you are my father, will you please wear pants?'

Though still in the army our father was on indefinite leave. After the armistice he was soon discharged. Fortunately he was awarded a small monthly pension, because his long illness had left some disability.

For Ashern the armistice ushered in a short-lived boom. In 1917 the village had begun to grow again. In addition to the school, a third general store was started by two Icelandic Canadians. More important was the creamery. Butter quickly became the single most important product of the settlement. That year too Ashern became the headquarters of the newly established rural municipality of Siglunes, which for many years was to be the most northerly municipal government between the lakes. The armistice was soon followed by the opening of a law office, a branch of the Standard Bank and a lumberyard. The butcher shop became the front for the local bootlegger, whose business flourished once it was clear that prohibition would be continued in Manitoba after the war. Mother was greatly relieved when Ashern once more had a doctor, one who had been an army medical officer and expected his patients to prove they were really ill and not just 'swinging the lead,' a wartime term for soldiers' pretending to be ill. What sustained the boom for a couple of years was a veritable flood of returned soldiers settled on homesteads by the Soldiers' Settlement Board, established to assist in the demobilization and reestablishment of veterans. The best land had been settled before 1914, and the soldier settlers were located on less productive homesteads, mainly east of the railway. Most of the veterans had never farmed before. By the end of 1921 many of them had abandoned their homesteads and gone off to Detroit or California or, at least, Winnipeg. But while it lasted, the boom was good for the lumber business and the sales of farm machinery.

My father's health was never good again. Clearly he could not undertake full-time farm work and needed a job. He was lucky enough to be chosen to manage the lumberyard, part of a small new chain with its head office in Winnipeg, appropriately named the Victory Lumber Company. The lumberyard was busy all through 1919. During the summer I helped full time and learned the rudiments of the business.

I had completed grade nine in June. There was an annual prize, $50 I believe, for the boy or girl who got the highest mark in the province in the Canadian history examination. I was the winner in 1919, and the Department of Education sent a telegram to announce my good fortune. My father was inordinately proud of me. Though I was of little use at farm work requiring any skill, here was evidence that I was good at something. Mother took my success more calmly. She expected me to do well and, I believe, simply took the result for granted. In any case there was no doubt that I would continue at school.

In the fall of 1919 we had a new teacher, who put new life into the one-room school. He readily agreed to let me go on to grade 10, though I was alone in the class. My father was ill so often that I had to stay away from school days at a time to look after the lumberyard. In mid-October he suggested that I postpone grade 10 for a year and help him full time. I was proud to be needed for a man's work. By March 1920 my father was absent from work oftener than he was present. At the beginning of May he went off to Winnipeg to the hospital. The lumber company let me look after the yard for the whole month of May, but at the beginning of June they decided my father would never be well enough to resume work at the yard, and found a new manager. My father was operated on in mid-June, and cancer was found. Mother called me to come to Winnipeg, where I arrived on the morning of 15 June. I spent most of the day at the hospital with my parents and went back to Ashern on the train on 16 June. I had barely reached home before word came from Mother that our father had died.

From the time I began to help my father in the lumberyard, I learned something about operating a small retail business, but more about the big world in which my father lived. Life as a soldier in England and France, with a long leave in Scotland, had broadened his horizons. He looked at Canada with new eyes. He loved to discuss the conduct of public affairs with visitors to Ashern and a few close friends with similar interests. I listened avidly to those conversations, especially to my father's opinions, though I did not always agree with them.

In fact I was sometimes profoundly shocked. One day, out of the blue, my father said that if he had to choose between Canada and the Empire, he would choose Canada. The possibility that there could be such a choice had never occurred to me, and I wondered what he had gone to war for. I was even more shocked when, at the time of Sir Wilfrid Laurier's death early in 1919, my father said that if he had had to choose between Bob Rogers and Laurier, he would have supported Laurier. I knew almost nothing about the Hon. Robert Rogers except that he had a reputation for political corruption in Manitoba. But after all, he was a Conservative!

At the end of the war there was growing support in rural areas of Manitoba for an agrarian movement in politics. Though he had never been a full-time farmer in Manitoba, my father was a farmer in his outlook. I was not surprised by the sympathy he expressed for the farmers' movement in politics. Had he lived, I am sure he would have joined the United Farmers of Manitoba when they became a provincial party after the 1920 election. Many former Conservatives could not bring themselves to become Liberals, and some of them undoubtedly joined the farmers in politics in the hope of defeating the Liberal government, an objective the United Farmers achieved in 1922. But paternal deviations from this true gospel failed to shake my Conservative imperialism.

On his deathbed my father admonished me not to make a fool of myself about politics, as he had done. By that statement I suppose he meant he had devoted time to politics that he might have used better in providing for his family. I did not think he had made a fool of himself, and that was one admonition I did not heed. On the contrary I became more absorbed than ever in the political scene, though without any thought of becoming a politician myself.

Manitoba was in the midst of an exciting provincial election campaign in the summer of 1920. Ashern was in the new constituency of Fairford, where the political situation was confused. Three candidates claimed to be official Liberals supporting the Norris government; one old man called himself an Independent Liberal; and a fifth candidate called himself an Independent Farmer and was suspected of being a crypto-Conservative. The Conservatives did not bother to nominate a candidate of their own.

Early in 1920, at my father's suggestion, I had written to the *Winnipeg Telegram* to ask that paper to appoint me its local correspondent, and the paper had done so. The confused political situation in Fairford excited more than local interest. The political meetings were lively, with plenty of personal abuse among the candidates. I went to as many meetings as I could and reported them at some length. It was fun for me, and the *Telegram* paid well; I made about $30 in two months. Unfortunately, soon after the election, the *Telegram* disappeared. There was no room in Manitoba for a Tory paper, and the *Telegram* was acquired by the independent *Winnipeg Tribune*. In the face of that disaster I applied to the *Manitoba Free Press* to become its correspondent and was accepted. The rate of pay was lower, and I was rather ashamed to write for a Liberal paper, but at least it did not go broke.

A single-parent family

At the age of 15, when my father died, I considered myself an adult, but I was in no sense the head of the family. Mother resumed that role, which she had filled during the war, and which all of us children accepted without question. Our parents had been devoted to each other and had loved each other's company. I cannot remember a harsh word between them, much less a quarrel; there always appeared to be harmony and mutual respect. It never occurred to us that one of our parents had greater authority than the other.

Mother was over five feet nine inches, with a fine figure, neither stout nor thin. She stood straight and had a horror of round shoulders. Her face was handsome, with beautiful blue eyes and naturally pink cheeks. When she was a tall high-school girl, an Anglican parson had told her she was 'divinely tall and divinely fair' and never to stoop to reduce her height. My father was heavy-set and very strong, but only five feet seven inches. He never showed any embarrassment that Mother was taller. He was intelligent and quick to learn. His lack of formal education was not a serious handicap. From my earliest days I recall his deference to Mother's greater knowledge and his readiness to benefit from it. But one thing he did not share. In her old age Mother confessed to me that my father had not kept her informed about the finances of the family, and that she never knew how they stood until after he went overseas. That was unfortunate, as she was a good manager and could have looked after the family finances as well before my father died as she did afterwards.

Mother never in any way acted like a dependent woman. She had a natural and easy air of authority that commanded respect. The role of head of the household was perhaps easier for Mother than for some women, because her father had died when she was an infant, and her mother had remained a widow. As I remember her, that grandmother was austere, demanding attention and respect but lacking an appreciation of the ridiculous, a faculty which mother had in abundance. No doubt Mother's experience as a teacher in a one-room school and as a nurse helped her head a family on her own. She had a great capacity for organization and an ability to get her own way unobtrusively and without raising her voice.

As we grew older and could be of more help, the operation of the farm expanded. When the creamery provided an outlet for our cream, the weekly cream cheque became the base of our farm income. The male calves were allotted to each of us children in turn and, when sold, became the main source of the bank accounts we managed ourselves, from 1920 on. The creamery was a quarter mile away, and buttermilk was readily available, free to be taken away. It became the major element in the diet of our pigs. We had a flock of good hens and even a few ducks, though the ducks were really pets, never very productive of income.

When he came home, my father bought three horses, so we were able to cultivate our own fields with a minimum of hired labour. We experimented with fodder corn, with indifferent success because of the frost hazard, and gradually increased the amount of land we devoted to sweet clover, which was becoming the main field crop in the Ashern district.

At the end of the war my father had taken up a soldier grant of a quarter section of land five miles northeast of our homestead. It contained a large slough with fine natural grass. In the summer of 1920, after my father's death, I undertook to make hay on the soldier grant and arranged to board with a family on the adjoining homestead. The summer was sunny, hot and dry. The haymaking was a great success, and several tons were well cured and stacked ready to bring home for the winter. In mid-August the whole countryside was swept with bush fires. To bring home the first

Family group in 1920 south of farmhouse and beside tent where children slept in summer. Walter and Tom sitting at back. J.W.P., Frank and Mother at front. Tomatoes ripening on rack beside the tent.

load of hay I had to cross a wide slough that had been swept by the fire and was still smouldering. I waited about an hour until the wind died down and then stood on the wagon tongue ready to unhitch the horses if a spark set the hay on fire. That hay got home without harm, but the rest of my hay went up in smoke the next day.

Losing the hay was bad enough, but one day near the end of the haymaking operation one of our three horses strayed off and was never seen again. We reluctantly concluded that she must have been stolen. I enjoyed the haymaking and was not lonely working by myself, but I had little liking for most farm work, and the summer's disappointments did nothing to encourage me to consider farming as a career.

In September I resumed grade 10, which had been interrupted so early the year before. The teacher was concerned about having a class of one pupil in grade ten. He talked the problem over with Mother and me, and we agreed on a plan whereby I would teach the beginners to read, write and do a little arithmetic, and he would help me with any problems I found in doing the grade 10 work by myself. The plan worked out well. I discovered both an aptitude and a liking for teaching and found it easy to study by and for myself. My difficulties were saved until the end of the day, and the teacher helped me with them after the regular school hours. Any problems he could not solve were referred to Mother. We children had found out long before that Mother preferred schoolwork, particularly mathematics, to housework. It was easy to entice her into helping us with arithmetic, algebra, geometry and English grammar.

French presented another problem. There was no public examination in French until grade 11, but I could not matriculate without passing the provincial examination in one of French or Latin. Neither Mother nor the teacher knew any French. Mother had the rudiments of the Ontario high school Latin but wanted me to do French, as I did. The butter maker at the creamery, an Acadian, had a sister keeping house for him. She had been a schoolteacher in New Brunswick. We sold milk to them, as to many of the families in the village, for 10 cents a quart; I delivered it after supper. Mother offered to provide free milk for the Belliveaus in exchange for a half-hour lesson in French each evening. It was an excellent arrangement. When I went to Winnipeg for grade 11, I was far ahead of the other pupils, who had already taken two years of French. I had no thought at that time how useful a knowledge of French would be throughout my life. For me in 1920, French was merely the passport to university, where Mother was determined I should go.

The French requirement for university was to be a more serious problem for my siblings. I was able to go to Winnipeg for the final year of high school, but Tom, Walter and Bessie did not have that advantage. Ashern by their time had a two-room school, and the generous teacher of the higher grades permitted them to do grade 11 there. But no French was taught. Tom's problem was solved by his doing the exercises in French grammar and sending them to me in Winnipeg for correction. For the French authors we had a concentrated reading course during the Christmas holidays. Tom did not learn a great deal of French, but he managed to pass the examination. As for Walter and Bessie, I went home for the summer of 1924 and spent part of every afternoon giving them French lessons. They were not as serious workers as Tom had been, and both failed the examination in September. During the school year they put in enough work to squeak through in June 1925. It was not an ideal way to learn French, but we all got into university.

It would be wrong to give the impression that we could have lived comfortably on the income from the farm; it is doubtful if it would have provided us with subsistence. The backbone of the family income was the pension for widows of veterans. Mother was kept in suspense for several weeks while the pension board decided whether or not father's death was really the result of his military service. If the decision had been adverse, we would have been destitute. The security given to Mother by the widow's pension enabled me to stay in school and go on to university instead of looking for a job. Ever since then I have appreciated how great an opportunity that measure of social security gave our whole family. I later came to believe that all families, not just veterans' families, should have similar security.

Matriculation

The decision that I should go to Winnipeg to high school in the fall of 1921 was Mother's. I don't recall any strong ambition to continue my education; Mother was the driving force. She had longed to go to the University of Toronto but had lacked encouragement and the means. Training as a nurse in Toronto was all she had been able to manage. As a nurse she had been fascinated by surgery and had regretted she could not study medicine. I have had the good fortune to know many people of exceptional intelligence during my life. But I believe no one I have known had a finer intelligence than Mother's. She was fascinated by mathematics and had a preference for facts over faith. Fortunately for us Mother did not live exclusively for her children but to a great extent in a world of her own. We were lucky that she encouraged us to be self-reliant and to use whatever initiative we had, and that she was determined we should get all the education we could.

Mother didn't think I could get through grade 11, as I had through grade 10, in the one-room school. My father's sister, Aunt Hattie, and her family lived in Norwood, the English-speaking section of St-Boniface. Norwood had a small high school, with only three teachers, housed in a part of an elementary school building. Mother arranged to have me board with Aunt Hattie so that I could attend Taché High School. I had a couple of hundred dollars of my own savings, but my year at high school must have cost Mother something out of her meagre income.

I was lucky to go to a small high school, where the transition from a one-room school was easier than it would have been in a major high school in Winnipeg. At Taché the classes were small, and I could compare myself with my classmates. I needed to know where I stood scholastically. I soon realized that in many subjects I was more advanced, and that as a learner I was the equal of any of them.

My one hope of getting to university was to win a scholarship. The most likely prospect was the bursary offered by the IODE to assist children of veterans who had been killed in battle or had died as a result of military service. In the provincial examinations in June 1922 I had first place in Taché school, and soon afterwards I learned I had won the bursary. It was $250 a year for four years, and the holders were given free tuition at university. I was assured of four years to work for a BA degree.

When I started at Taché, the school principal told me that pupils from the country were less advanced than city pupils, especially in languages. I wanted to take Latin as well as French, but he insisted that I do physics instead of Latin. I had no aptitude for physics. The principal's decision, I believe, cost me an Isbister scholarship. The Isbister scholarships were awarded each year to 10 or so grade 11 pupils who got the highest standing in the provincial examinations. I narrowly missed one.

Although I liked most of my classmates, I made no lasting friends. My lack of skill in playing games, no matter how hard I tried, was no help. Aunt Hattie was concerned that I should get enough physical exercise and encouraged me to join the YMCA, where I went for three evenings a week. The exercises I hated, but I did learn to swim, though not gracefully. It was about two miles to the Y from Norwood, and my walk both ways certainly gave me enough exercise. Never since then have I felt anything colder than the walk across the Norwood Bridge over the Red River at −30°(F).

Aunt Hattie's husband, Thomas Roberts, was a Scottish immigrant educated at Heriot's, one of the best private schools in Edinburgh. I learned a great deal from him about many subjects, including the middle-class Edinburgh attitude to life. He was interested in theology and introduced me to Catholic apologetics, which I found clever but unconvincing. Until then I had not been interested in theology, nor much interested in sectarian differences. Mother had taught me to accept nothing on faith but to insist on proof. She applied that principle to everything except religion, but I did not stop there. I found myself, while still a child, listening to sermons with a critical attitude and often finding they were not credible. I did not like emotional evangelism. Austere Presbyterianism was much more to my liking, though when I began to learn about it, Calvinist theology repelled me.

In Norwood the Presbyterian minister was an unintellectual muscular Christian, named Daniel McIvor, who had a large popular following. He later moved to Fort William and in 1940 distinguished himself by defeating the Tory leader, Robert Manion, and becoming a member of Parliament. McIvor did not appeal to Uncle Tom, who was much more attracted to the Anglican church and its restrained and intellectual parson. Uncle Tom also liked the greater participation of the congregation, the ritual and particularly the music. He joined the church choir. The whole family attended the Anglican church, and for the year I lived with them, so did I. The parson was a congenial man, and we became friends. There was a Boy Scout troop attached to St Philip's Church, and I became a Boy Scout at the late age of 16. I was poor at tying knots and remained a tenderfoot.

One lasting benefit of my living in Norwood was a result of its being part of the city of St-Boniface. Many Winnipeggers lived their lives without being aware of the French-Canadian city across the river. Uncle Tom and I went to high mass in the St-Boniface cathedral on Easter Sunday. I had never before attended a Catholic church service or even been in a Catholic church, and I was impressed. During my time in Norwood I became dimly aware of the dual nature of Canada.

As soon as I was installed at school, I went to call at the head office of the lumber company my father had worked for. The general manager, who remembered I had worked with my father in 1920, received me warmly. I told him it would be a tremendous help to me if I could have a part-time job. He agreed to let me work on Saturdays. To give me a specific job to do they saved the week's correspondence for me to file. The office closed on Saturdays at noon, but I was allowed to stay in the afternoon until my work was done. I felt important and responsible, and the $2.50 a day was a great help. Before the end of the school year I asked the general manager if they could give me a job for the summer. He decided that I could fill in for other members of the staff while they were on holidays, and I earned a little more money for the next year. During my first university year I continued to work part time for the lumber company, but unfortunately, by the spring of 1923 the lumber business had declined so much that I was told there would be no work for me in the fall.

Aunt Hattie and her family spent the summer of 1922 at a cottage on Lake Winnipeg, so I had to find somewhere else to live. Uncle Walt, my father's only surviving brother, and Aunt Annie, his wife, lived in the western suburb of Deer Lodge. They readily accepted me as a boarder at five dollars a week. I continued to live with them happily for most of my first three years at university.

A federal election took place in the late fall of 1921. The Conservatives were in office, and Arthur Meighen was prime minister. The government was opposed by the Liberal party led by Mackenzie King and also by a newly formed farmer party called the Progressives, who had a candidate in the historic constituency of Provencher, which included St-Boniface. The Progressive leader, T.A. Crerar, spoke at a meeting in Norwood; it was the first time I saw him. Even at that time I did not think political parties should base themselves on farmers or the members of any other vocational group.

My hereditary antipathy to the Liberal party was as strong as ever, and I had a great admiration for Arthur Meighen, though I was not to see him or hear him speak until 1925. The 1921 election results, especially the defeat of Meighen in Portage la Prairie, disappointed me. The results were tabulated on a board on the front of the *Manitoba Free Press* building on a bitterly cold election night in December. J.S. Woodsworth won an overwhelming victory as a Labour candidate in Winnipeg Centre. He was given a tremendous reception and lifted high above the enthusiastic crowd. He spoke briefly, shaking his fist at the building and denouncing the *Free Press*, which had opposed him bitterly during the general strike in 1919. Woodsworth was wearing a handsome beaver coat that I thought inappropriate for a socialist.

When I went home for Christmas, I had a painful shock in learning that Mother had voted Progressive. Meighen had visited Ashern and addressed a public meeting, and she had found him arrogant and unfeeling about the problems of ordinary people. Though far from convinced by the program of the Progressive party, she had felt the Meighen government should be defeated. I was more upset than I would have been if Mother had told me she was no longer a Christian; I did not understand how she could have repudiated her proud Loyalist tradition.

The election of 1921 introduced me to federal political parties and their programs. I discovered that issues in federal politics were wider and more interesting than the provincial politics of Manitoba. Without actually seeing any more of Canada I was beginning to be more Canadian.

In July of 1922, while I was working at the office of the lumber company in Winnipeg for the summer, Mother's life changed abruptly with the sudden death of her only brother. After his marriage my grandmother had lived with him and his family at Port Rowan. But there was no question after Uncle John died of her staying on with her daughter-in-law. Mother took Frank with her to Port Rowan to bring her mother back to live in Ashern. Until then Mother had planned to move to Winnipeg so that Tom, Walter and Bessie could go to high school, and I could live at home while attending university. She intended to resume working as a nurse. Because her mother, as long as she lived, needed constant care, that plan had to be abandoned.

2 Student Years at Home and Abroad

Winnipeg

The University of Manitoba

Our grandmother Pickersgill, who died in 1913, made it possible for all of us to go to university. She left $250 to each of her five grandchildren, the four of us and Aunt Hattie's daughter, Jean Roberts. Our legacies were invested in victory bonds during the war. By the time any of us had to use the money, the legacies had more than doubled in value. I would not have had enough in scholarships and earnings to pay my way through university without grandmother's bounty. Thanks to my summer job and part-time employment with the lumber company I did not draw on the legacy until the end of my second year; it was all gone, however, by the time I became a bachelor of arts.

In September 1922 I registered in the first year of the course leading to the BA degree. Until about two weeks earlier I had intended to begin the course in civil engineering. I can't remember who persuaded me that that would be a mistake, but I have always been grateful it never happened.

During the fall term I applied myself assiduously and got first-class standing in the Christmas exams. It was a shock when I dropped to second class in the spring examinations and actually failed English composition, in which I had scored over 90 percent at Christmas. Despite the humiliation of having to write a supplemental examination in September, I did not work very hard in my second year. During that year I learned to play bridge.

There was as yet no distinction in Manitoba between honours and pass degrees; every BA student took the four-year course. In the third and fourth years there was specialization in two or three subjects. In my case there was no doubt one would be history. In my third year the other two subjects were political economy, as economics was then called, and French. I was determined to learn to read French easily — a goal I achieved that year. The fourth year I concentrated on history and political economy.

Our history professors, Chester Martin and D.C. Harvey, both Maritimers and Rhodes scholars, were excellent teachers. Though I was not a slave to my studies, I really became a student in my final two years, and I won the Isbister scholarship in history in my third year. I was fascinated by classical economic theory, taught by Professor A.B. Clarke as ultimate truth. My doubts about free trade were aroused long before 1988. In my fourth year I did very well in the final examinations and was awarded the Sir Daniel McMillan Fellowship of $500, which enabled me to go on for another year to become a master of arts.

The Legislative Building was across Broadway from the university, and I soon began to frequent the gallery of the legislature. In 1922 the United Farmers defeated the Liberal government. The Farmers, who had no leader, chose John Bracken, the president of the Agricultural College, to be their leader, and he became premier. Bracken was a Presbyterian, and the Presbyterians were the largest denomination in Manitoba. Nevertheless, there was some lifting of eyebrows when the press reported that every member of Bracken's first cabinet was Presbyterian. As he gained political experience, Bracken found it expedient to expand the denominational base of his government, though in his 20 years as premier the government never entirely lost its Presbyterian flavour or its thrifty attitude to the public purse. Bracken's two immediate successors were former Presbyterians (by then in the United Church) and just as careful of public money.

In the 1920s the dominant element in the Manitoba population was almost exclusively British in origin. The settlers from Ontario and their children largely determined the character of the province socially and politically. At the university the mother tongue of most of the students was English. A few Icelandic students, most of them born in Manitoba, had found their way there. A growing Jewish minority of students in my day kept largely to themselves, though I recall no overt anti-Semitism. Otherwise the immigrant population was almost entirely unrepresented among the students. There was one Ukrainian in my first year. The main reasons for there being almost no students of immigrant background were the lack of access to high schools, and poverty.

There was still prohibition in Manitoba in 1922. Among students, drinking was rare; in the Arts faculty it was confined to a very few. We heard stories of 'depraved' behaviour on the part of engineering and medical students, but the predominant tone was puritanical.

Formality was normal. Women students were always addressed as Miss by the men, who called one another by their surnames unless and until they were close friends. Men and women rarely sat side by side in the classroom, or at the same table in the library. The sexes mixed at occasional class parties and larger social functions, but those affairs were not much help to me, as I never learned to dance. After four years I had few women student friends, but my circle of men friends had grown steadily.

The long summer vacations contributed as much to my development as my studies did. A good friend I made in first year, Norval Hunter, was the son of the general manager of the Swift Canadian meat-packing plant. R.B. Hunter knew the manager of the pulp and paper mill at Kenora, Ontario, at the outlet of the Lake of the Woods. Norval's father got him and me jobs for that first summer in a timber-cruising operation with the Keewatin

Lumber Company, which owned the paper mill. While we were waiting to be called to Kenora, the company gave me a temporary job as a labourer at a small box factory in Norwood, where I worked for three-and-a-half days at 20 cents an hour and had my only experience at punching a time clock. I was vastly relieved when we received our summons from Kenora.

Norval and I and the timber cruiser, a man named Mark Sauerbrau, spent much of the summer cruising the large islands in the southern expanse of the Lake of the Woods. Our final month was spent travelling through a long series of lakes just east of the Lake. The American interests in Minneapolis who owned the Keewatin Lumber Company and its timber limits were considering building a railway from Kenora to Fort Frances, opposite International Falls, Minnesota, where they had another mill. On that final job we did no timber cruising but moved camp almost every two days and climbed hills to look at the character of the country. The whole summer was splendid.

I had not been out of Manitoba since I was five years old, and I found the scenery almost overwhelming in its beauty. No doubt the novelty of my being in that setting invested it with a special quality for me. To this day the Lake of the Woods area remains in my eyes the most beautiful inland country in Canada.

When we returned to Winnipeg at the end of August, Canada had a wonderful new dimension for me. I had also saved practically all the $35 a month we were each paid. The only thing I remember buying was a safety razor, which I used on my 18th birthday for my first shave. I really had no whiskers, just a hint of fuzz, but shaving made me feel I was a man. I had a little money to add to my IODE bursary, and I was certainly going to need it, as I no longer had part-time work.

A year of shock

Mother had asked me not to look for a job in the summer of 1924 but to come home to the farm, to teach the twins French. After her mother came to live at Ashern, the house was terribly cramped. She felt an addition to the original house was necessary. I helped her with the plan, and I did some of the farm work and so enabled us to cultivate our own fields that year. That was the last time I lived in Ashern. I enjoyed my summer at home, but clearly it was financially important that I get a summer job in 1925.

Tom completed grade 11 successfully that June, though he did not do well enough to get an IODE bursary. So there was no question of his starting at university for at least another year.

Frank, left with ear trouble as a result of his scarlet fever, quite suddenly in January 1925 became very ill with a high fever. Mother left my grandmother, who was by then completely bed-ridden, in the care of the older children and brought Frank to Winnipeg. By great good fortune she had been advised to consult Dr F.D. McKenty, one of the leading specialists in Winnipeg, who put Frank into the St-Boniface Hospital at once. Dr McKenty told Mother Frank had badly infected mastoids and would likely die. The only hope was a new type of operation, which he had never done, and which, so far as he knew, had been done only once before. He put the chances of success at one in a thousand, but

Front of farmhouse at Ashern showing addition built in 1924.

Mother did not hesitate. Though the actual operation was miraculously successful, Frank continued to lie in bed with a fever, hovering between life and death, for three weeks. By that time Dr McKenty had decided, despite Frank's fever and weakness, to operate on the other ear, which was also badly infected. The second operation was equally successful. Within two weeks Frank was out of the hospital and able to go home to Ashern. It was a terribly anxious time for Mother.

In the midst of that near tragedy I received a personal blow. I had lived amicably with Uncle Walt and Aunt Annie for more than two-and-a-half years. My uncle was an asthmatic and very taciturn, but always kind and considerate; my aunt loved to talk and, I believed, enjoyed my company. From earliest childhood I had considered her a friend, almost a second mother. I was totally unprepared, therefore, for what happened the day before Frank was to have his second operation. When I returned from the hospital and was reporting on Frank's precarious condition, Aunt Annie suddenly turned on me and said I should be ashamed of myself for staying on at the university when I should be working and earning money to help Mother. She added that I did not appear to be taking my studies seriously, and that she doubted anyone so indolent would ever achieve anything. A year earlier the criticism might have been justified, but in the third year I was working steadily and had done well in the Christmas exams.

I did not attempt to defend myself but said I could not go on living in her house if she felt as she did, and would make other arrangements as soon as possible. Later that day I told Mother what had happened and asked her if she felt I should leave university and get a job. If I did, she said, it would break her heart. And she thought it would be good for me to be living on my own. The next day I found an attic room in a house on Broadway, near the university. The rent was four dollars a month; the room was large enough for four or five people to sit in and had two chairs, a bed, a small table. There were no cooking facilities. I bought a toaster and was able to get my breakfast and a cold lunch in my room and had only dinner to eat in a restaurant. Five or six of my friends were good enough with invitations that most weeks I had at least two and often three dinners with one or other of their families. Friends, in turn, often lunched with me in my room, where vast quantities of soda biscuits, cheese and jam were consumed for the rest of the year. In my diary I somewhat extravagantly described the day of my aunt's onslaught as 'the most uncomfortable day in my life' but I soon discovered life had become much more agreeable.

Because it cost me more to live, finding a job for the summer was all the more important. James Tod, who for a couple of years after the war had been a school inspector stationed at Ashern, was a friend. In 1925 he was living in Winnipeg. When I mentioned a summer job, he said that there was a shortage of schoolteachers in the province, and that senior students were occasionally given permits to teach in remote areas where qualified teachers were not willing to go, and where the schools were generally open only in the spring, summer and early fall. Such schools usually had residences for the teachers, who could get their own meals and live cheaply. The pay was good at $2.75 a day. He recommended to the Department of Education that I be given a permit.

The term went smoothly after Mother and Frank returned to Ashern. My room on Broadway became a sort of clubroom, with too much bridge and other frivolity. I seem to have attended every theatrical show in what was a good season. In spite of the distractions and the wonderful hospitality of the families of friends I managed to get more academic work done than I had in the first two years. I went home to Ashern for a study week and did a solid review preparing for the exams. On 8 May 1925 I left for my summer job as a schoolteacher. When I received the exam results, I learned that my marks ranged from 80 to 88, and that I had won the Isbister scholarship for history. The $100 would be useful.

Teaching school

The school, called McMaster, where I was to teach was in the interlake country 100 miles north of Winnipeg and 12 miles east of Hodgson, the terminus of another branch of the CN. Hodgson was only 30 miles east of Ashern, but there was no road between them.

My friend and classmate Frank Garland had a permit to teach at a school seven miles east of Broad Valley, two stations short of Hodgson. On 8 May Garland and I left Winnipeg by train. He got off at Broad Valley, and I went on to Hodgson, where I spent the night at the local hotel. The next day a man drove me as far as the road to the school was passable for motorcars; there a widow lived who put me up for the night. The following morning Pete Brown, who lived nearby, took me and my effects, with a team of horses and a wagon, the last four miles along a trail that crossed two large muskegs. Pete Brown was a Métis whose children attended the school.

The school was built of logs, and the residence was a shack with a small bedroom at one end. The main room contained a cook stove, a table, three or four chairs and a Toronto couch. There was a real bed in the bedroom. Once I had stowed my clothes away, found a shelf for my books and unpacked the food I had brought, I went for a walk to the nearest homestead, which was half a mile east of the school. There I found three teenage children, who spoke English, playing cards. They could read the section for children in the weekly *Free Press Prairie Farmer*, the only literature in the district except Eaton's catalogue, which was the introduction to Canadian culture for thousands of immigrants.

McMaster school and teacher's residence, 1925.

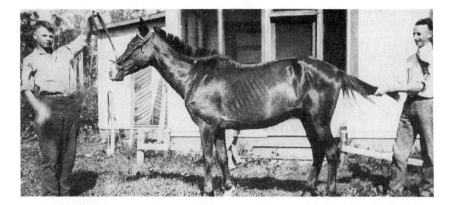

Horse owned by J.W.P. and Frank Garland at the door of Frank's Barrie school residence, 1925.

The teenagers were shy, but I was able to make arrangements to have their families supply me with milk and homemade butter, which the children could bring with them to school.

McMaster school district was half way between Lake Winnipeg and Lake Manitoba. No one lived north of the school. The last homestead was a mile east of the school. There was no population beyond, until the shore of Lake Winnipeg, 30 or 40 miles away. Settlement stretched southwards, with homesteads every half mile or so.

Apart from the Brown family the population of the school district consisted almost exlusively of Ukrainian and Polish peasants who had homesteaded there in 1913, and who eked out a bare existence. Only two adults in the district, Pete Brown and the German husband of one Ukrainian woman, could read or write in any language. The school had not been open every summer, but often enough that the older children had learned to read a little English.

On Monday morning, before I had breakfast, between 15 and 20 children arrived to wait for classes to start at 9. I emerged at one minute to 9, and all the children disappeared to the far side of the school. One or two heads appeared around the corner to watch me. I went into the school for the bell, came to the door and rang it. Slowly and shyly the children came in and took seats. I started to ask their names. Everyone spoke in a whisper, and several names had to be repeated more than once before I caught them. I managed to get the surname right because the oldest child in each family could write it for me, but I was baffled by some of the given names. One or two were so obscure that, ignoring their culture, I gave the children English names, which they retained for the rest of their lives, as I found out 29 years later.

For the next two weeks not one of the pupils spoke out loud, and I found the silence oppressive. I started in at once visiting the homesteads after school and meeting the parents. Most of them spoke little English. Even those who did had been isolated in the bush so long that the range of topics for conversation was quickly exhausted. The two teenage boys I had met that first Sunday came to visit me about one evening a week. I had recently taken up golf in Winnipeg and had brought a putter with me. I improvised a rough green in the schoolyard to practice putting, at which the boys were soon more skillful than I ever became.

There was almost no cash in the district, and the children could not buy the pencils or scribblers that seemed to me essential if they were to learn very much. I solved the problem by buying a supply of pencils and scribblers from Eaton's at my own expense. I sold pencils for two eggs each and scribblers for three. For several weeks I had eggs three times a day. Happily the wild strawberries ripened. The tariff was a cup of strawberries picked and hulled for either a pencil or a scribbler. My cups were in demand at all recesses and lunch periods. For several weeks no meal was complele without both strawberries and eggs. With the ripening of the wild raspberries and the saskatoons my diet was more varied. The saskatoon is a berry that tastes like the blueberry when raw, but is woody and unpleasant when cooked, unless rhubarb is added.

The teaching made no great demands as there was no pupil beyond grade four. For the younger children the main task was to teach them English. I made it a rule that they must all speak English on the school grounds. Though there were occasional lapses, I refused to permit tattling. The older children were so proud of their English that I believe they 'rammed it down the throats' of the younger children. One six-year-old, who had never been to school, burst into tears whenever I spoke to him. I spoke to him only about once a week, feeling it was wiser to let him ripen in his own time.

Gradually I gained the confidence of the parents, who came to me to write letters for them and to explain things that puzzled them. I became quite expert at treating minor wounds with iodine and bandaids and even at operating on ingrown toenails.

I was saved from loneliness because Frank Garland's school was only about 15 miles away. By one means or another we managed to spend most weekends together. I had had my bicycle sent from Ashern, and Garland and I invested $35 in a horse, estimated to be about 20 years old, a rather decrepit buggy and a saddle. The logistics were complicated. The horse could barely trot, but we managed somehow. The first time I went to visit Garland I discovered that an Icelandic family lived six miles south of my school. When I stopped to ask directions, I felt right at home. The coffee pot was on the stove, and there was plenty to talk about; I might almost have been at home in Ashern. I drank a lot of coffee with that family in the summer of 1925.

One week in mid-August Garland went home to Winnipeg. I went on my bicycle 25 miles to Arborg, where I had an introduction to an Icelandic family named Danielson who had relatives in Ashern. When Mrs Danielson and I discovered that we had each received the prize for the highest mark in the province in Canadian history, a real bond was established between us. On Saturday afternoon the Danielsons took me off by motorcar to Winnipeg Beach, a popular resort on Lake Winnipeg, where I had my first and last experience on a roller coaster.

The one really disagreeable feature was the persistent rainy weather. Nineteen twenty-five had the wettest summer for a long time. The school was surrounded by muskegs, which had the greatest swarms of mosquitoes I have ever seen. The school walls were full of cracks, and the screens on the windows were old and decrepit. Even some cotton material I bought to reinforce them did not help much. Day after day the mosquitoes inside the school became unbearable, and the pupils had to be dismissed for short periods while the room was smoked out with a smudge of damp grass burned in a metal pail.

By the end of May my brother Frank no longer needed bandages on his ears. He went to Winnipeg to see the doctor for a final examination and then came to stay with me until the end of July. In order to keep him busy while I was in school I taught him French. He loved to learn and was a wonderful pupil. By the end of the summer, at the age of 10, he had completed grade 11 French.

I had other visitors. The first was Norval Hunter's seven-year-old brother, Dick, who arrived in Hodgson by train on 1 July. In mid-August James Tod, the school inspector, came for a day. He seemed pleased with the way I was performing. He let the children go home at noon as there was a meeting in the afternoon of ratepayers, most of whom found it hard to pay their taxes. They assured him that if I could come, they would welcome me back the next summer.

The summer at McMaster was my first and only experience of living in a relatively homogeneous homesteading community. I did not see McMaster school again for 29 years. In 1954 I was campaigning in a federal by-election in the Selkirk riding and visited the school with the Liberal candidate. The log building was gone, and a modern frame building in its place. The windows had good screens, and the teacher did not have to empty the room twice a day and make a smoky smudge to clear out the mosquitoes. There was a new four-room residence, and there was electricity. I went into the school; class was in session. The children looked like my pupils, but there were three differences: they all spoke out loud, they could all speak English, and every child wore shoes.

I asked the teacher to tell me the names of the children but then decided to name them myself. I identified the family name of all but one of them, because they looked so much like their parents.

In the one case where I was wrong I had given the mother's maiden name instead of the father's name. The children were astonished. For the first time I realized that once immigration ceased with the First World War, the rural population of Manitoba had become as stable as any in Canada and more stable than most. In 1954 McMaster district was still not prosperous and still on the edge of settlement, but it had lost its pioneer look.

Three more Pickersgills at the university

Before the university term started, I went home to Ashern for a short visit. Bessie and Walter had passed grade 11 in June. Tom had been working for more than a year. Mother decided that all three of them should enter university and, for their first year, supplement what savings they had by drawing from grandmother's legacies. Tom and Bessie both went into the students' residence at the Manitoba Agricultural College, Tom in agriculture and Bessie in home economics, both five-year courses. Walter had a job on a farm in southern Manitoba. He was to enter first-year Arts and to share a housekeeping room with me. Mother would have loved to move to Winnipeg that fall. She did not look forward to being alone with her mother, whose memory had failed, and with only Frank for company. But she had a good house at Ashern and could not possibly afford to live in Winnipeg while Grandmother needed constant care. She decided she could no longer do any farming, and disposed of most of the livestock and the machinery.

The four of us children maintained a sort of family life in Winnipeg through the academic year. For Walter and me I found a housekeeping room on Vaughan Street, only a short distance from the university. The room had a gas cook stove, two beds, a table and three or four chairs. It was not luxurious, but it cost only $12 a month. Walter and I cooked most of our meals. Our living costs were low. Ours was not a well-balanced diet except on Sundays, when Tom and Bessie usually came from the Agricultural College to spend the day in town, and Bessie prepared one and sometimes two decent meals.

All four of us attended Knox Church every Sunday. The minister, F.W. Kerr, had visited Ashern more than once and impressed all of us. After much soul searching and growing skepticism about the doctrines of the church, I became a member of the United Church, to which all the Presbyterian churches in Winnipeg belonged after church union. My decision to become a member was based on the belief that the Church was a valuable moral and social institution.

There was a federal election in the fall of 1925. I went to the Winnipeg rink with Stanley Laing to hear Arthur Meighen speak. I was still a Conservative, but I noted in my diary, 'Like his style and the man, not policy.' I remember telling Stan, whose father was an active and ardent Liberal, that I favoured Liberal policies but did not see how I could support a party whose leader was the grandson of a rebel. A few days later Stan and I went to hear Mackenzie King. He made, I noted, 'a splendid defence of his policies but leaving several loopholes for attack.' The twenty-ninth of October was election day. Stan Laing's father had arranged, through the South Winnipeg Liberal Association, that at a poll on River Avenue the deputy returning officers, poll clerks, Liberal scrutineers and even a constable were members of our class at the university, many of them neither Liberal nor anything else. The Tory scrutineers did not know what to make of us, but obviously none of us was stuffing ballot boxes or doing anything irregular. The Liberals lost that poll, and, as I noted of the national result, the 'Conservatives almost made a cleanup.' Though the Liberals had only 101 members to 116 Tories, nothing in my diary refers to Mackenzie King's unexpected decision to remain in office until Parliament met.

On 6 November I became quite ill and, after lectures, went to bed in our room. Stan came in during the afternoon, carried me off to their house and got a doctor. My temperature was over 102. I stayed at the Laings until mid-November, where I was given wonderful care, and I have never ceased to be grateful for the friendship that inspired it. Stan's father was a widower. He had a housekeeper, who brought me tea to wake me in the morning —

the first time I encountered that English custom. I had always disliked tea, which we were not allowed to drink as children on the theory that it stunted one's growth. I did not want to offend the housekeeper, and drank the tea free of milk and sugar. After 10 days I was an addict for life.

Later in November Professor Chester Martin invited me to tea to discuss my future. He advised me to apply for the Sir Daniel McMillan Scholarship in history. He felt my chances for an overseas scholarship would be greater if I received the scholarship and an MA degree. Professor Martin's interest stirred my ambition to continue my education.

The Christmas exams went smoothly. Mine were over on 19 December and I intended to go right home to Ashern. That day Tom telephoned me early in the morning. He was too ill to write his exam and decided to go home with me. I persuaded him instead to get in touch with Dr McKenty, who advised him he needed a mastoid operation. The date was set for 24 December. Mother arrived from Ashern the morning before the operation, and Bessie went home the same day to look after Grandmother and Frank. Tom's operation went well. He was released from hospital on 28 December and went home with Mother two days later. I was already there. On New Year's Eve we received our examination results. Mine were all high A's, and Tom and Bessie had respectable B's. Walter had a miserable average between 51 and 52, with failures in three subjects.

All of us were back in Winnipeg by 6 January. That day Mother telephoned to say that Grandmother had died, and that she and Frank would take her body to Port Rowan for burial. She planned to stay in Ontario for two months. When she got back in early March, she spent several days in Winnipeg having her credentials as a trained nurse brought up to date. Mother's plan was to leave the homestead and look for work in Winnipeg later in the year. While she was still there, I went to see the deputy minister of education, who promised me a school for the summer. I told him I would like one with a residence large enough that Mother and Frank could spend the summer with me.

My permit to teach was for a school called Happy Lake, in the Duck Mountains 30 miles due north of Roblin. The nearest railway station was at Togo, just across the boundary in Saskatchewan. As soon as my exams were over, I went on the overnight train to Togo where, according to my diary, I was thrilled to find myself half a mile into another province. In the afternoon I was driven by motorcar over passable roads to the school, a standard one-room building with a good cottage residence. There was a lake with good swimming a mile away, and a cold creek near the house with water wonderful for drinking. The creek was also a good place for storage of perishable food — a ready-made refrigerator.

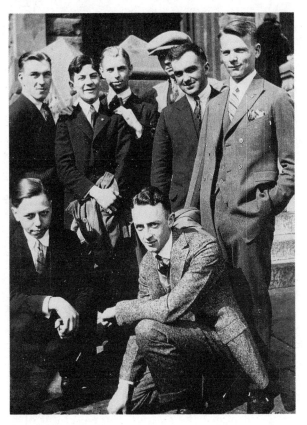

A group of classmates (J.W.P. on right) in front of University Arts building Winnipeg, 1926.

J.W.P. as BA, Manitoba, 1926.

Happy Lake, like McMaster, was at the very margin of settlement, six miles north of the nearest post office, Boggy Creek.
Their isolation was the only point of similarity between the two
school districts. Happy Lake school was well built of lumber and
had good screens. The house had three rooms and adequate
furniture. There were mosquitoes and flies, but in moderation.

The countryside was pleasant, with wooded hills, frequent streams and good drainage.

I started teaching on 10 May and got the pupils sorted out and classes started before I went back to Winnipeg for graduation. I travelled overnight by day coach. When the train from Winnipeg met ours in the early morning, I bought a newspaper giving the examination results. All my friends had clear passes and would get their degrees except for Sam Hayakawa. Despite his failure to get his BA and his having to write a supplemental examination, Hayakawa was to have a long and distinguished academic career in the United States and later in life to become a Republican U.S. senator for California. I had been awarded the McMillan Scholarship, which assured me a year in which to do the MA course.

Summer at Happy Lake

After convocation Mother and Frank came back with me to Happy Lake. Mother was charmed with the teacher's residence, and Frank was thrilled by the swimming. School resumed the next morning. We had a wonderful summer.

Mother was keen to have more to do than cook and read and sew. She had some background in high school Latin but not enough to complete her matriculation. I still regretted beinq deprived of Latin in grade 11. We decided to do Latin during the summer, correct each other's exercises and write the grade 11 supplemental exams in September. We enjoyed pitting our minds against each other and did very well in the examinations.

The population of the Happy Lake district was as heterogeneous as that of McMaster had been homogeneous. The French-speaking Métis family across the creek were friendly, the children attractive, well mannered and bright. There were several Mennonite families who had moved from the colonies in southern Manitoba. A family of poor white Anglo-Saxons from Ontario lived in a primitive fashion about a mile away. Strangest of all were a couple of families of hillbillies originally from the Cumberland Gap region on the border of Virginia and Kentucky. According to gossip they had left the east because one of the men had shot and killed a neighbour in a feud. They had moved to North Dakota and then, as civilization began to encroach, had migrated to the Duck Mountains. They lived in one-room log cabins with sod floors. The men reputedly derived their cash income from making moonshine and supplemented the food they bought with game shot in and out of season. The women, who could read and write a little, had made contact with the Salvation Army in Winnipeg as their source of clothes. The children were well behaved at school, though their attendance was irregular, and punctuality rare. I doubt if the families bothered with clocks. There was no language problem at the school. All the children understood and spoke English, and one or two had reached grade seven. I enjoyed teaching, but it was not stimulating as there were no really bright pupils and none with a passion to learn.

In 1926 there was still no radio broadcasting to rural areas. For news we depended on the daily *Manitoba Free Press*, which we received in a bundle in the weekly mail. I had read somewhere about a Hudson's Bay factor who received the *Times* of London once a year and read it methodically day by day one year later. Mother and I decided to have a daily paper by reading each day's paper one week late. The arrangement worked well until the end of June, when the King-Byng crisis arose, and we began scanning the papers as soon as they arrived.

That political crisis marked a turning point in my life. My diary records that on 2 July we received the *Free Press* with a report on the 'defeat of King government: no dissolution; Meighen's shadow cabinet.' On 9 July I noted, 'Byng granted Meighen a dissolution — unparalleled constitutional issue.'

When I had heard Meighen in 1925, I had been impressed by his eloquence but repelled by his policies, particularly the brick-for-brick tariff proposed against the United States, which offended against the classical economics I was absorbing at university. My political allegiance was shaken.

I did not believe a prime minister had an automatic right to be granted a dissolution whenever he asked for it, but neither did I believe a governor general had a constitutional right to refuse a dissolution and choose a new prime minister, unless the new prime minister had an assurance of the support of a majority in Parliament — which Meighen did not have. In such a situation the Crown, I believed, would inevitably be drawn into political controversy, and responsible government would be in jeopardy. Meighen's acceptance of office gave me sufficient reason to leave the Tory party.

The Meighen government was defeated in Parliament two days after it was formed. Parliament was dissolved at once, and an election called. I had reached my 21st birthday that June and had a vote. I wanted to cast my first vote for the Liberal-Progressive candidate in Dauphin constituency. In 1925, Tory candidates had been elected in Manitoba, with a minority of the votes, because there were both Liberal and Progressive candidates in most rural ridings. Early in 1926 the Liberals and the Progressives had worked out alliances in most constituencies and nominated Liberal-Progressive candidates. In Dauphin the candidate was W.J. Ward. One of his canvassers called on us and promised to return on election day to drive Mother and me to the poll which was 12 miles away. He never turned up. By 4 p.m., when school was over, it was too late for me to get to the poll on my bicycle before it closed at 6, so I lost my first chance to vote. But I had overcome my aversion to Mackenzie King's ancestry and become a Liberal.

On 20 August Mother and Frank left for Ashern to close up the homestead. After that they went to Winnipeg to find an apartment and get Frank started at school. My school remained open until 24 September. It began to snow on 22 September and continued all the next day, and no one turned up for school. Some of the pupils came by bobsleigh with their parents on 24 September for the prize giving.

Before going back to Winnipeg I made a short tour in Saskatchewan. In Regina I visited a family named Pickersgill who were English immigrants. That visit was the start of a lifetime of spasmodic research into the Pickersgill name and family. Regina did not impress me; their legislative building I considered a poor copy of ours in Winnipeg. I also spent two or three days with the family of one of Mother's cousins, who had a large farm south of Moose Jaw. The Lannings were in the midst of threshing. On that large-scale wheat farm I saw harvesting on the prairies for the first time. In those days grain was cut by a horse-drawn self-binder, which tied the cut grain into sheaves. Hand labour was used to stand 8 or 10 sheaves together in bundles called stooks, where the grain dried for several days. When the grain was ready, a threshing machine was moved into a convenient place near a road. A horse-drawn, hayrack-mounted wagon picked up the sheaves from the stooks. To speed up the operation, the driver was usually assisted by a 'field pitcher,' who moved from one wagon to another and worked steadily. At the threshing machine the wagon driver was assisted by a 'spike pitcher' in tossing the sheaves into the thresher. Field and spike pitching were the hardest jobs and the best paid. I spent half a day field pitching and the rest of the day spike pitching. The next morning I was so stiff I could barely lift my arms. I was astonished at the hugeness of the operation and the contrast with our small-scale farming in interlake Manitoba.

I met Tom at Woodrow, in the southwestern corner of Saskatchewan where he had been working on a farm, and we went back to Winnipeg by train. A new dimension was added to my image of Canada by the long journey through southern Saskatchewan.

The family in Winnipeg

Tom and I reached Winnipeg at the end of September, to find Mother and Frank installed in the Rozel apartments on Clarke Street, just off River Avenue. There Walter, Frank and I were to live with Mother for the next year. Bessie and Tom returned to the residence at the Agricultural College.

When Mother and Frank left Happy Lake I suggested to her that she find an apartment in the area served by Earl Grey Junior High School, which had a deservedly high reputation. Because Frank was only 11 years old and from the country, the school authorities insisted that he go into grade six at the nearby Fort Rouge school. Knowing how advanced he was, I felt sure grade six would be a wasted and discouraging experience. I went to see J.S. Little, the principal of Earl Grey, and asked him to let Frank into grade seven, the first year of junior high school. He told me our apartment was not really in the Earl Grey district and added that parents from all over the city were trying to get their children into Earl Grey. When he specifically mentioned the president of the university, I asked him whether he had accepted the president's son. When he answered yes, I asked why the son of the president should have preference over my brother. It was evidently the right question. He agreed to admit Frank for two weeks' trial. If he was not equal to the work, he would return to the Fort Rouge school in grade six. I accepted the challenge without hesitation. Frank was at the top of his class for each of his three years at Earl Grey.

During the academic year 1926-27 I completed the work for my MA and also did the first-year Arts course in Latin without attending classes. My regular routine was to spend most of every day in researching for my thesis, reading for examination courses and doing exercises in first-year Latin. I worked hard in the daytime and kept the evenings free for family and friends, with a lot of bridge and frequent visits to the theatre. I worked every night from midnight until 2 a.m. and did not get up until 10. Since we had a small apartment, this arrangement gave us all more privacy and assured me two solid hours' work at night without distraction or interruption.

When the time came to apply for scholarships, Chester Martin told me he was well satisfied with my work, but he advised me not to apply for the Rhodes scholarship because I played no games, and because he felt sure I would be awarded the IODE overseas scholarship. He felt Ross McLean was more likely to be elected Rhodes scholar. Martin was chairman of the selection committee, and I felt sure he would support Ross. In the event each of us was successful, and we both went to Oxford in the autumn of 1927, Ross to Balliol and I to New College. The IODE scholarship permitted me to go to any British university, but it did not occur to me to apply anywhere except at Oxford, and I have never had any regrets.

Indian motorbike, 1927 at Cartwright. Used for peddling door to door a one-volume encyclopedia and later for travelling from Winnipeg to Ingersoll, Ontario enroute to Oxford.

After receiving the MA in May I had the summer to spend before leaving for Oxford. I knew I should try to earn something to supplement my scholarship. I forget how I met the man who had the Manitoba concession for the sale of a one-volume encyclopedia of which I can no longer remember the name. He assured me that a good, hard-working salesman might earn $300 or $400 in three months and persuaded me that I had the talent needed. I started out enthusiastically enough. I bought a motorcycle and sidecar for $150. With a small tent I owned, I was sure I could live and travel cheaply and keep nearly every cent I earned. My territory was west of the Red River and south of the main line of the CPR. I travelled several hundred miles, developed a knowledge of the geography and ethnography of that section of Manitoba and met a number of interesting people. But I was almost invariably persuaded by the counterarguments of prospective customers. I could not convince myself or them that their lives would be greatly enriched by owning the encyclopedia. The few copies I sold were, I believe, bought on compassionate grounds by people who wanted to help me with my expenses at Oxford. I earned barely enough to pay for the gasoline. As a salesman I was hopeless.

Oxford

A motorcycle journey and a crossing

Late in July 1927 I set out for Oxford on my motorcycle. Frank went with me as far as Toronto. We started enthusiastically, but it was soon evident that the motor bike was not strong enough to carry Frank, the tent, the blankets and luggage in the sidecar. We made a stop for repairs at almost every garage between Winnipeg and Detroit.

In 1927 there was no continuous road in northern Ontario, and few roads of any kind, so travelling through the United States was the only way. For most Canadian motorists from the prairies 'the States' was simply a corridor to southern Ontario.

For me the greatest adventure of the trip was riding the motorbike through Chicago on Michigan Avenue, then still on the lakefront. When we crossed from Detroit to Windsor, where a cousin of Mother's put us up, I had the motorbike completely overhauled. When we left Windsor the machine seemed to have new life, but we got only as far as Ingersoll before it broke down again. We left the bike at a garage and hitchhiked to Port Rowan to stay with Mother's cousin Dr Annie Backus. A few days later I went back to Ingersoll and sold the bike for $25. After visits to various relatives we went on our own to Niagara Falls for a day, and then to Toronto, where Frank took the train back to Winnipeg.

From Toronto I went back to Port Rowan to stay with Dr Annie Backus. She had a close friendship with Brigadier General

Blacklock and his Canadian wife. That English general had retired to Port Rowan after service in the British Army. He gave me a letter of introduction to his parents, who lived near Banbury, about 20 miles from Oxford. Later, when I presented my letter to his parents, they gave me an open invitation to stay with them, and I often did.

In late September I left for Montreal. My first sight of Ottawa was during a brief afternoon stop on a rainy day. From Montreal I boarded the CP steamship *Minnedosa*.

We had beautiful weather down the St Lawrence and through the Gulf. We passed Belle Isle at about 4 p.m., after my first sight of the island of Newfoundland. By 6 p.m. we were in a raging equinoctial storm. I went in to supper and had a bite or two of fish, and left hastily for the washroom and my cabin, where I stayed for the next two days praying the ship would sink. Finally, when the steward asked me if I wanted to get over my seasickness, I agreed to try anything. He brought me a large neat brandy, told me to swallow it as fast as possible and warned me it would make me even sicker than I had been but that would be the end. And it was. That neat brandy was my first acquaintance with hard liquor, and I have never since then been so grateful for a drink.

The storm abated on the third day, and the rest of the voyage was pleasant. On board there were a number of students who had been harvesting in Saskatchewan, among them two South African medical students returning to Edinburgh University. I arranged to meet them there at Christmas.

We disembarked at Liverpool early in the morning. I took the ferry across the Mersey to Birkenhead and the Great Western Railway to Oxford. The day was sunny, and I shall never forget how beautiful I found the English countryside on that journey. The landscape, the train and the towns were at the same time strange and familiar, but I felt no sense that it was the land of my ancestors, as I had felt in southwestern Ontario. I did not feel that day, and never came to feel, that England was my country.

Before leaving home I had resolved to try to adapt myself to the customs of the country. My first big step was to drink beer with my lunch on the train. Apart from a tentative experiment with Dr Annie's home-made beer that step was my introduction to real beer drinking. I did not like the beer, but without much persever-ance I acquired a taste for it. I decided, quite deliberately and very foolishly, to start smoking cigarettes. It took me several days to learn to draw instead of blowing, but eventually I succeeded, though I never did inhale, except by accident. One of my regrets is the money wasted on thousands of cigarettes until I gave up smoking at the age of 40.

I had read so much about Oxford and looked at so many pictures that its appearance contained few surprises that first day. Ross McLean was already there, and we had arranged to meet. Fortunately, as soon as I arrived, I was able to occupy my rooms at New College. I then found my way to Balliol to see Ross. After dinner he took me to Eugene Forsey's rooms for the evening. Forsey had come to Oxford the year before as a Rhodes scholar from McGill. He told me he had a job waiting for him at McGill but that eventually he would be fired because of his radical views. He obviously relished the prospect.

Forsey and I got into an animated controversy over the King-Byng affair. He had already combined his socialist views with ardent ad-miration for Arthur Meighen. When I told him Byng and Meighen had made me a Liberal, he was incredulous and rather contemptu-ous. A lifelong difference over the question did not inhibit our friendship. I met Eugene on Parliament Hill during the 1968 election campaign. He greeted me by saying I would be astonished to learn that Pierre Trudeau had made him a Liberal. I replied that his conversion raised my first doubt about being a Liberal myself.

The first term did not begin for another week, so the day after I reached Oxford, Ross and I went to London. Ross had been in London earlier and took me to see all the sights he had already seen. Westminster Abbey, the Houses of Parliament, the Tower of London, St Paul's and other famous buildings looked just as I expected them to, but London, unlike Oxford, did not look famil-iar and was full of amazing surprises. The succession of different boroughs and the many green-clad squares seemed to make it several cities, not one. During those few days I learned to find my way about and had my first taste of the theatre, which became my chief delight in London.

Life at New College

In mid-October 1927 I took up residence at New College to read modern history for a BA degree. Chester Martin and D.C. Harvey had advised Ross McLean and me to become undergraduates instead of attempting to begin postgraduate work, which they felt would take us out of the mainstream of university life. I suspect they also felt, certainly with reason in my case, that we lacked the historical background and the maturity desirable for postgraduate work.

One of the history tutors at New College was David Ogg, a lowland Scot, who was a fellow of the college. Another was E.L. Woodward, a fellow of All Souls and, for me, a much more interested and interesting tutor. Woodward suggested I try a few lectures and shop around to see what interested me; Ogg said lectures had become obsolete with the invention of printing but that, fortunately for him, the authorities at Oxford had not yet discovered that evident truth. I sampled a good many lecture courses but stuck with very few; in my second year I rarely attended any lectures. Tutorials, on the other hand, I took very seriously.

Chester Martin had a modified tutorial system in Manitoba, but the number in each seminar was large, and no one got to read more than one essay a term. At New College there were just two undergraduates at each tutorial. Maurice Ashley and I were in the same one and read essays to our tutors and to each other. With Woodward it was almost always a stimulating experience, and David Ogg's occasional dry observations were sometimes rewarding. Though Ashley was younger, it was soon obvious he was academically better prepared, and his essays better written. While we were still at Oxford, he began to work with Winston Churchill on the life of Marlborough and was already laying the foundation for his career as a distinguished historian.

In 1927, luckily for me, the IODE decided to renew the overseas scholarships for a second year in some cases. I embarked on the two-year BA program hoping mine would be renewed. I was in suspense until mid-term, when I became the first IODE scholar appointed for a second year. The stipend was $1200 a year. The $2000 received by Rhodes scholars was no more than adequate, and I soon realized I would have difficulty getting by.

At New College one of the fellows of the college was assigned to each undergraduate as what was called a moral tutor. Mine was a shy, friendly South African, Charles Manning, who somehow found out my straitened circumstances and offered to recommend that the college give me a loan. The loan made life bearable, though I had to exercise the greatest economy, especially during vacations.

Partly because I did not play outdoor sports, I made friends rather slowly, though I found bridge a great help after I had sorted out my contemporaries during the second term. Nearly every afternoon in the first year I walked when most undergraduates were playing games. One or two friends usually joined me, and we visited almost every village church within walking distance. Many others more distant we reached by motorbike. William Luttrell, one of my first friends, shared my growing interest in medieval architecture. He had a motorbike and, clinging to him on the rear seat, I widened the radius of my explorations. For me Oxford and its environs were a visual textbook of English history. In my second year I forced myself to get up early enough to run three miles every morning before breakfast. Running was not fun, but I seemed to thrive on the discipline.

That year I was drawn into more activities. In the first term I was chosen secretary of the college debating society, and in the second term became president. I could not afford to join the Oxford Union, but often friends who were members took me when leading public men were debating. Kenneth Younger, then a very proper young Tory, took me to hear Prime Minister Stanley Baldwin. We were not impressed. Many years later, when Younger was junior minister in the Attlee government, I asked him if Baldwin's performance at the Union that night was the beginning of his disillusionment with the Tory party. He recalled the occasion but said the real beginning of his conversion to the Labour party came after the formation of the National Government by Ramsay MacDonald and Baldwin. In the subsequent election Kenneth campaigned for the National Government. He told me that while canvassing in the East End of London he began to feel the policies he was supporting were irrelevant to the poor people he was appealing to, and increasingly unconvincing to him. He joined the Labour party not long afterwards. In 1945 he was elected to Parliament and became the junior minister in the foreign office. Kenneth was one of the few lasting British friends I made at Oxford.

I was active in the Stubbs Society, which had members from several colleges who read papers to one another on historical subjects. I belonged as well to an informal group that met for a preprandial drink every evening before dining in hall. I also became a member of the University Liberal Club and took a minor part in the 1929 general election campaign in one of the suburbs of Oxford. I was, in fact, a mediocre and undistinguished junior member of the university. The second-class honours I received in the final history examinations were a proper measure of my achievement.

Apart from Ross McLean and Eugene Forsey I do not recall meeting any Canadians in my first year. I called once on a classmate from Manitoba, Ruth Herriot, who was at St Hugh's. I had admired her from afar in Winnipeg and once plucked up enough courage to walk home with her from a class party. At Oxford she met Escott Reid, a Rhodes scholar from Toronto, whom she married soon after they left Oxford. Escott was appointed to External Affairs shortly after I was.

I made several Canadian friends in the second year. David Turnbull was the 1928 Manitoba Rhodes scholar. He was at St John's College, where he shared a sitting room with James Sinclair, the Rhodes scholar from British Columbia. There I first met Jimmy, little suspecting we would later be close political associates. Turnbull was quiet and rather strait-laced. Jimmy, on the other hand, was a hearty, with friends such as Sandy Skelton, with whom he shared occasional binges. Skelton I barely knew at Oxford, but our association in Ottawa was close in the war and postwar years. Albert (Bud) Trueman was a 1928 IODE scholar. I saw a good deal of him that year. Our subsequent careers led us to a close association when Trueman became head of the National Film Board and, later, director of the Canada Council. The two most outstanding Rhodes scholars from Canada in 1928 were Ronald Martland, from Alberta, and George Curtis, from Saskatchewan. Both distinguished themselves in the law school in two successive years, outclassing all others in the examinations, a harbinger of their subsequent careers: Martland became a judge of the Supreme Court of Canada, and Curtis, the first dean and virtual founder of the law faculty of the University of British Columbia. Both have been lifelong friends of mine.

On a few occasions during my second summer term I was persuaded to accompany the college cricket team, ostensibly as scorekeeper, to play local teams in the neighbourhood. I did not understand the game, but at Blenheim Palace one of our players failed to turn up, and I was pressed into service. I was the eleventh man at bat, and though I did not hit the ball myself, I kept at bat long enough for the team to win by a single run. The players on the Woodstock team claimed I made them laugh so much that I really won the game. Both teams retired to the local pub, where I was treated to so many half pints of beer that I returned to college exuberant and insisted on going around the front quad shaking hands with everyone I met, including several undergraduates I had never spoken to before. I felt rather foolish next morning, but that cricket game was the one athletic triumph of my life.

The examinations went on for a week, and I felt I had done reasonably well. Just afterwards I got word that I had been appointed to a lectureship at Wesley College in the University of Manitoba. It was a great relief. I was to replace Albert Cooke, who had found a better position elsewhere. Cooke, who had been an IODE scholar at Oxford, was a history lecturer and a friend in Winnipeg. I assumed I owed my appointment to Wesley to a

J.W.P. in costume for BA examinations.

recommendation by Cooke to the president. The salary was $2200. I accepted eagerly.

By the end of June I was so short of funds that I feared I would have to borrow to pay my way home. That problem was solved soon afterwards. In 1912 or 1913 Mother had been at the founding meeting of the Manitoba Women's Institute, where she had met Dr Black, then president of the Manitoba Agricultural College, who later became head of the colonization department of the Canadian National Railways. CN in 1929 was still sponsoring the immigration to Canada of groups of boys to work on farms. Mother wrote to Dr Black, who arranged for me to escort one of those groups. On 27 June I had word I would get a free passage home sailing from Liverpool at the end of July.

There were nearly three weeks to put in between the written examinations and the viva, as the oral examination was called. Ross McLean and I went on a walking tour and were back in Oxford for the viva on 17 July. I went to the examination 'schools' at 9:30 a.m. With four others I was told to come back at 10. When I realized I was not to have an individual viva, I lost hope of a first class.

Vacation travel

At Oxford there was a vacation at Chrismas and one at Easter, each of about six weeks, and a long summer vacation from the end of June to the middle of October. During the Christmas

J.W.P. in a punt in the Cherwell, Oxford.

J.W.P. and a group of residents at the Maison Canadienne of the Cité Universitaire in Paris, Easter vacation, 1928. J.W.P.'s first visit to the continent of Europe.

vacation of 1927-28 I carried out the arrangement I had made to visit Edinburgh, where I stayed in the same lodgings as the two medical students I had met on board ship. I was not at all prepared for the stunning topography or the unique architecture. Edinburgh fascinated me, and I found the Scots in general more like Canadians than were the English.

I left Edinburgh on January 2 and for the rest of that first vacation, I stayed with families in England.

I was determined to spend as much of subsequent vacations as I could afford on the Continent. Ross McLean and I decided to go to Paris for Easter. That first visit was an unending delight. We had comfortable rooms at the Maison Canadienne. We visited the monuments and museums, heard our first opera, and sampled the Comédie Française. I could speak enough French to find my way around, but I understood very little even at the end of our six weeks, partly because we spoke English at the Maison. All the residents there were men and Canadian, but there was almost no fraternizing between English and French Canadians.

We visited the Louvre conscientiously, but most of the time we walked and explored the city. Ever since then I have been able to walk farther and longer in Paris than in any other city. Of night life we could afford little; Mistinguette and Maurice Chevalier and one venture to the top of Montmartre were the limit. Occasionally we spent part of an evening and the price of two beers at the Dôme in Montparnasse, from which we could walk back to the Maison. When we got back to England I felt I knew Paris and would never tire of it, and I never have.

The long summer vacation was a financial challenge. Luttrell, my closest English friend at Oxford, a loner, a Liberal and an amateur of architecture and antiquities, agreed to go with me on a six weeks' holiday on the Continent, some of which we spent camping and some in cheap hotels. We crossed the channel to Dunkirk and made our way to Ostend, from which we took a train into the westernmost village in Holland so that I could say I had set foot in that country. We visited Bruges, Ghent and Brussels and then took the train to Aachen. From there we went to Cologne and then by boat up the Rhine to Coblenz and Mainz and then on by train to Frankfurt. The medieval centre of Frankfurt fascinated us. From there we went to Heidelberg for a day and on to Nuremburg for two days. We camped and walked in the Bohmerwald, wandering back and forth across the German-Czech frontier without interference; it was less guarded than the border between Manitoba and Minnesota, with no intimation of the tragedy of 10 years later, when the Sudetenland was the first Nazi

Rhodes scholars with J.W.P. (an IODE scholar), Easter week in Rome, 1929. Left to right: Ronald Martland (Alberta — later a judge of the Supreme Court of Canada), Clark (Saskatchewan), George Curtis (Saskatchewan — later first dean of British Columbia law school), J.W.P., David Turnbull (Manitoba — later business consultant, Toronto and Montreal).

land grab. We went by train from Pilsen to Prague, where we spent a couple of days. From Prague we went to Budapest. The general aspect of Budapest was pleasing, but I was surprised there were no buildings from before the 18th century and few from before the 19th; as a confirmed medievalist I was disappointed. We took the boat up the Danube to Vienna, where we saw all the regular sights, and from there we went to Munich, where at last I tasted dark beer. The food, the beer and the cheer in the beer cellars were a delight. From Munich we took a local train to Garmisch-Partenkirchen, whence we walked up the mountains, through a high pass and down into the Tyrol. We spent a night at Innsbruck and the next day took the train through the Brenner pass, which was the Italian frontier after 1919. We got off at the first station in the Italian Tyrol to do some walking in the mountains, where rain forced us to take shelter in a hut with two Fascist militiamen, who had stopped to warn us off military territory. Next, on to Verona, Milan and, through the Simplon tunnel, Lausanne, near which Luttrell had arranged for us to stay at the chalet of some friends. The six weeks of travel had cost me only about $100 for everything and was to prove a wonderful apprenticeship for teaching European history.

I spent a couple of pleasant days with Luttrell's friends in Switzerland, a country I would not visit again until 1970. One reason for avoiding Switzerland was the high cost of living. For young idealists, it was the fashion to make the pilgrimage to Geneva to the seat of the League of Nations — the hope of the future. I could not afford it and took a perverse satisfaction for years in saying I had never been to Geneva.

Dave Turnbull and I spent the Easter vacation of 1929 in Italy. We travelled by stages across France and northern Italy, stopping in Paris long enough for an evening at the Folies Bergères. We visited Avignon, Monte Carlo, Pisa, Rome, Naples, Florence, Venice, and Verona. We returned from Italy through Germany by way of Munich, where we spent two or three days drinking dark beer. I got back to Oxford penniless.

Vacations with families

From my arrival at Liverpool in 1927 until my departure from the same port in 1929, 22 months elapsed. I resided in college for only the required 12 months and spent the other 10 in vacations. There was not much leeway to economize during terms in college, though in my second year I stopped having breakfast in the junior common room and made my own in my sitting room. Vacations were different. I would have run out of money altogether if I had not received a good deal of hospitality. In addition to Bill Luttrell's family, four families in particular were very generous in having me stay with them.

Soon after I arrived in Oxford, Brigadier General Blacklock's parents invited me for a weekend. The host, who had been crippled in a hunting accident years before, and his wife, an inveterate gardener, were a typically upper-middle-class family

J.W.P. in gondola, Venice, Easter, 1929.

and very kind to me. That weekend was my introduction to butlers, to having my suitcase unpacked and my clothes (such as they were) laid out, to dressing for dinner and to all the ritual of country house life. I spent the end of the first Christmas vacation with the Blacklocks and enjoyed other short visits later.

My first visits to two other families were arranged through an organization headed by Lady Frances Ryder which had recruited a large number of families willing, during the holidays, to receive undergraduates from the Dominions — visits designed to cement

The residence of Sir Charles and Lady Mander, "The Mount", visited in January 1928 and Christmas of the same year.

the bonds of Empire. How successful the visits were in achieving that objective is questionable, but they were certainly a godsend to impecunious students like me.

In January 1928 I spent a week with Sir Charles and Lady Mander at their spacious house called The Mount. There were other house guests, and thanks to bridge I was able to fit into the party without too much difficulty. Lady Mander organized expeditions in her Rolls Royce to Chester, Shrewsbury, and many smaller places. The Manders had a substantial business at Wolverhampton in the manufacture of paint. The family had a connection with Canada. Two Mander cousins had visited Halifax years before and had met and married two sisters named Paint whose father was an MP from Cape Breton. Lady Mander had never gone back to Nova Scotia, but she was one of those Haligonians who could put the English in their place. She never spoke on the telephone and never carried a watch, expecting others to remind her of the hour when necessary. The Manders had an unmarried middle-aged daughter, Daisy, a fox-hunting type and a traveller, who was proud of her Canadian connection and had been in every county in Nova Scotia except Guysborough, and also had been fox-hunting in Virginia and Ohio. She was particularly kind to me on that first visit, and before I left England, we became good friends. I developed a friendly relationship also with the Manders' younger son, Gerald, who was interested in history and archeology, his wife, Nancy, and their children, Daphne and Philip. I made at least three visits to the Gerald Manders. During one of them Gerald offered to finance a third year at Oxford for me. I was grateful for the evidence of friendship and tempted to accept, but with the assurance of a job at Wesley College I decided I could not. Later, when I discovered how hard it would have been to find a job in 1930, I was glad I had returned home in 1929.

My most memorable visit to The Mount was for Christmas, 1928. The highlight began on a Sunday, when some of the house guests accompanied Lady Mander to church, where there was a new curate who had not made a good impression. On the way back Lady Mander asked me if, as a lark, I would impersonate the curate. I agreed, and she told the other guests she had invited the curate to dinner later in the week. When the day arrived, she reported that the curate's wife was ill, and the curate was coming by himself. Shortly before dinner I went to my room after explaining that I felt unwell and would not be down for dinner. One of those in the conspiracy had found me a high stiff collar and a piece of black cloth to cover my shirt front. I dressed in my dinner jacket with the collar reversed and the black bib, put on dark glasses because the curate's eyes were supposed to be poor, rumpled my hair and, just before dinner, slipped out a side door and appeared at the front door. Sir Charles and two of the older guests were not in on the secret. At dinner I talked a lot in a loud voice, pretending I was a socialist who wanted to wipe out class distinctions, increase welfare and get rid of the colonies. I was in favour of almost everything the conservative company did not approve. I paid obvious attention to Daphne from time to time. I was told later that Sir Charles had turned to the guest next to him and growled that that bounder was being too familiar with his granddaughter. It was a real triumph when the butler, who was in on the secret, began to titter while filling Lady Mander's glass and had to withdraw, coughing loudly. After dinner I excused myself early on account of my sick wife and my poor eyes. After a suitable interval I came downstairs, thanked Lady Mander for the chicken broth sent to my room, and said my headache had quite disappeared. I listened sympathetically to the indignant account of the appalling behaviour of the curate from Sir Charles and two of the elderly lady guests. One of them, Mrs Goodwin, who had a real sense of humour, was let in on the secret. But no one ever dared to tell the other guest or the host that they had been tricked.

My third family lived in Montgomeryshire, in Wales. I had been introduced to them also by the Ryder organization. Walter Buckley-Jones was a native of Wales, and his wife was English with a Canadian connection. In her youth Mrs Buckley-Jones, whose maiden name was Covernton, had visited cousins in Norfolk county, Ontario. The connection with my native county created a bond between us. It was my first time in Wales, and we went on frequent excursions, once or twice into remote villages where the children spoke only Welsh. During my visit a group of young people including Nigel Heseltine, a grandson, came to stay. One evening they put on amateur theatricals in which I took the part of Boots, a servant who shined shoes. Thereafter Boots was my name in that family.

But the family with whom I established the longest and deepest friendship was not English but French. I was determined to improve my French and was advised to stay with a family in France, preferably in the country, where there would be no opportunity to use English. Luttrell's mother had a friend who lived in a château in the Somme. She wrote to her friend, Vicomtesse Henry de France, who agreed to accept me as a paying guest for a month in the summer. After leaving Luttrell in Switzerland at the end of our European tour and stopping for a few days in Paris, I took the train to Rue, north of Abbeville, where the de Frances met me.

Chateau d'Arry, Somme, residence of Henry de France. J.W.P. first visited the family in August 1928 and frequently thereafter.

I liked the family from the first day. Mme de France, though slightly austere in manner, was kindness itself. Her husband, Vicomte Henry de France, was the epitome of the country gentleman. He had a passion for fly-fishing and had once been president of the Casting Club of France. His consuming interest was water divining, which he considered a science and about which he had written several books and pamphlets. He was well educated and deeply interested in history and politics. Nominally a Royalist, he was enough of a realist and a moderate not to accept the extreme views of the Royalist journal *Action française*. The Château d'Arry was a typical 18th-century country house; with a fine park with formal paths through the woods. During visits extending from 1928 to 1937 I must have walked more than a hundred miles on those paths with Henry de France, listening and gradually talking more and more. Fortunately for me he spoke slowly and calmly; I never saw him excited. At the end of the First World War he had been a widower with two sons; by 1928 they were both adults living on their own. Madame de France was the widow of another vicomte de France, a younger cousin of Henry. Her first

J. Ross McLean, Rhodes scholar, Manitoba, 1927 with J.W.P. during a visit to Arry, 1929.

husband had been killed on active service in 1914, before their son, Paul, was born, on 1 January 1915. The widower and the widow were married sometime after the war and had a daughter, Colette, who was five years old in 1928, when I first visited Arry. Paul was a tall, thin, red-haired boy with a ready smile and an open friendly manner; he welcomed me sympathetically, and I had no doubt we would become friends. By the end of my visit Paul was almost like a younger brother. Our friendship lasted with undiminished warmth until his death 60 years later. The family relationship was further complicated by the presence of Henry de France's stepmother, who lived in Paris in the winter and spent every summer at Arry. She was a formidable dowager who dominated the dinner table and talked very rapidly.

During that first visit to the de France family I took almost no part in general conversation. I still had to translate anything I wanted to say from English into French, and by the time I had done so, it was rarely relevant. Eventually I could make myself understood in French and had no problems in shopping and travel, but I was not capable of sustained conversation. The effort had been a strain. When I got back to London I found myself making up questions in French and then realizing I was in England.

I stayed with the de Frances for three weeks in January 1929, and on the way to Italy at Easter Dave Turnbull and I stopped at the château for a couple of days. I was no longer a paying guest and was never to be so again with that family. Our relationship has extended into a second generation for the Pickersgills and a third for the de France family, with no sign of waning.

Farewell to England

For the three weeks between the written exams at the end of June and the oral exams in mid-July, I decided a tour west and south of Oxford would be interesting and cheap. What was supposed to be a walking and camping tour with Ross McLean had little camping and even less walking, and frequent buses and trains. But we saw a good deal of Somersetshire, which I thought had the most beautiful countryside I had yet seen in England, and we followed the coast of the English Channel from Exeter to Folkestone. There we took the ferry to Boulogne, for a visit to the de Frances for me, while Ross went on a farewell visit to Paris.

Afterwards I went to London to stay for a weekend with a friend from New College and then returned to Oxford for the viva. Later on the day of the exam I went to Banbury to say goodbye to the Blacklocks, and from there I went on to Wolverhampton to stay with the Gerald Manders, where I found a letter from Oxford with my marks. All B plus except one. I noted that I had 'kept a pretty even level, just not the best, And that is the end of that.'

I stayed with the Manders until the morning of 26 July, when I left for Liverpool to board the *Doric*. After we sailed I went down to the third class to visit my charges, five boys. The next day we picked up five more boys from Northern Ireland and, in the evening, three more at Greenock. The following morning, out in the open Atlantic, I visited my charges; most of them had been seasick; and it was rather gruesome. I found some games for them, and by evening they had begun to cheer up. I visited the boys every day and did my best to keep them from being home-sick. They were a good lot, some from Yorkshire. At Quebec I landed my party and left them safely in charge of the port reception officer, promising to see them again in Montreal, which I did.

3 From Academe to Ottawa
Home from Oxford

Lecturer in history

I enjoyed the voyage up the St Lawrence as much as I had enjoyed going down river in 1927. It was Canada, beautiful, but oddly enough I did not feel at home until I got off the overnight train from Montreal in Toronto and went to Child's restaurant for a breakfast of pancakes and maple syrup. Child's had been a regular haunt during my student years.

After a brief visit to Dr Annie Backus in Port Rowan, I took the train from Toronto to Winnipeg, where Frank met me. Mother, he told me, had seized a rare chance to go with friends for a brief motor holiday in Minnesota, so after a day in Winnipeg Frank and I decided to go to Ashern for a couple of days. When we began walking over our old homestead, I felt for the first time I was back in the place where my roots were. We walked along every cowpath, examined every slough and looked nostalgically at the old picnic ground. We were amazed at the tall spruce trees, which had been the spruce hedge planted in front of our house in 1912, and which had grown very slowly during the 14 years our family lived at Ashern. We went to Silver Bay on Lake Manitoba and camped for a night on the familiar beach in the same small tent we had used on the motorcycle trip to Ontario in 1927. Frank was almost fully grown at 14 and had developed a great deal mentally as well as physically. I was happy to find we were as compatible as ever. We went back to Winnipeg in time to meet Bessie on her return from a summer working in Banff. She too had developed a great deal in the two years I had been away, but she had the same independent spirit and an even greater sense of fun. I thought she compared very favourably with any young woman I had met in England.

A day or two later Mother returned from her holiday. She seemed quite unchanged, the same upstanding, beautiful woman, at home in any company and equal to any situation. But I had changed a great deal, and I knew some of the changes would not please her. She was sorry I smoked, because she disapproved of smoking. I explained at the first opportunity that I also drank moderately and intended to go on doing so at home. If she could not accept that I would have to find a place of my own to live.

That was the first and the most serious decision we made about the organization of our family. The basic decision had to be made quickly. In the fall of 1928 Mother had moved to an apartment on Broadway, nearer her work and more convenient for my brother Walter, who had a job in the Portage Avenue branch of the Bank of Montreal, and for Frank, who was to start at Kelvin High School that fall. The apartment was too small to hold another person, and if I was to live with the rest of the family we would have to get a larger place.

One other adjustment we had to make was about attending church. Before I left for Oxford I had become a member of Knox United Church. When Mother and Frank moved to Winnipeg in 1926, Knox became the family church, and we all attended regularly. I found that Tom, Walter and Bessie had become desultory in their attendance. I was resolved as a matter of principle not to attend any church regularly, even though I feared church attendance might be expected of a member of the faculty of a college affiliated with the United Church. The question was never raised by the college. Mother accepted that decision without discussion, but I knew it had distressed her.

Once Mother realized I intended to live my own life, that I really wanted to live with the family and was ready to pay whatever was necessary, we decided to find a house. We settled on one at 202 Walnut Street, for $60 a month. Mother was to pay the same amount she was already spending to run the household. Walter, who received the princely salary of $475 a year at the Bank of Montreal, could not pay any more than he had been paying. I would pay the rest, whatever it turned out to be. Tom and Bessie were still at the Agricultural College for another year.

My first year back at home was a real culture shock. I did not fully recover until I had been back to Europe for the summer of 1930 and came home to an environment that, the second time, seemed really my own. I became conscious that my own manner of speaking had changed. I had not deliberately tried to speak like the English, but I had tended to adopt the English vocabulary where it differed from the Canadian. Many of my friends in Winnipeg, I noticed, considered my speech and manner affected. It took some time for the veneer to wear off.

Winnipeg and Manitoba had changed too. I was shocked to find respectable women, including my sister, wearing lipstick; almost no woman at the university had done so in 1927. Women's smoking in public I had accepted in England, but it was a surprise in Winnipeg. Furthermore, nearly everyone had a radio, though it was not until two years after my return that we bought one. But what I found most difficult to accept was the outward intellectual conformity and the still rather puritanical attitudes — a real contrast to the greater tolerance of dissent and eccentricity in England.

I had accepted the hierarchical structure of English life, but it did not take me long to appreciate the greater openness of Canadian society and the much lower resistance to outsiders who were striving to improve their lot in life. Some resistance to all but Anglo-Saxons was still present. Though passage upward was easier, there were strata in Winnipeg society. Part of the explanation for the relative openness, I realized, was the absence of any marked accents. In Canada there was a more or less standard speech in English from coast to coast, and no marked difference in speech between the products of private schools and those of public schools.

I had grown accustomed to English upper-middle-class life and standards and in many ways had found that life agreeable. My first two years at home required some readaptation, which took longer because I was not returning to the old environment of a student but to a new environment as a member of the faculty of a college with a different atmosphere and background from those of the university proper.

In my days as an undergraduate Wesley College had been regarded by the students at the rest of the university as a 'hick' college that drew most of its students from the country and many from Methodist parsonages. Its academic standards were, most unfairly, regarded as lower. In my five years before going to Oxford I believe I entered the doors of Wesley only once, and the sole friend I had there was Albert Cooke, my predecessor as lecturer in history.

In late September 1929 I began my career as a lecturer. I was not at all apprehensive; I knew I liked to teach. The Department of History at Wesley consisted of Arthur R.M. Lower, who was professor and head, and me as a lecturer. We were both new to the college, and the two of us gave all the courses taught by four members of the history department in the university Arts faculty — about 18 hours of classes each and every week.

Lower and I shared an office for eight years and worked together in complete harmony, though we did not always have the same views. He was the greatest teacher I encountered in academic life, and he taught me more Canadian history than anyone else did. We quickly became friends, and we continued such until his death at the age of 98. Lower was always forthright in expressing his opinions and in disagreeing with the views of others. Many found his vigourous way of expressing himself offensive, or at least not persuasive. His approach often shocked the good students, but it also stimulated them to appreciate that conventional ways of looking at the past and the present needed critical examination. After a time the good students were gener-

The faculty at Wesley College, 1930 — J.W.P. front row right.

ally devoted to him, the poorer ones often confused and sometimes frustrated.

I gave my first lecture to the second-year students. When I
walked into the room, one of the students told me the freshman
class was next door. Probably I looked a little lost. Certainly I did
not look my 24 years and I might have passed as a late teenager.
By the end of the first lecture I hoped the students were convinced
I was old enough to teach, but to make sure, I began at once to
grow what became a pale and sparse moustache, which I continued to sport until I was well into my forties.

Despite my youthful appearance I had little difficulty imposing
myself on my classes. I enjoyed teaching from the first day. That
first year, however, was hard work. For many a lecture I was just
one jump ahead of the class. It became clearer to me every week
how sketchy was my knowledge of the subjects I was pretending
to expound. During my absence in Oxford, the honours degree in
Arts had been instituted in Manitoba. I had two fifth-year honour
students, one of them Gerald Riddell, the son of the college
president. Riddell was a competent and thorough student, though
not brilliant. I gave the two honour students one seminar a week

J.W.P. at Winnipeg, 1930-31.

at home in my library, where they took turns reading essays. I found that the most enjoyable part of my work.

I had one seminar a week with the students in each year. The classes were small enough that almost every student had a chance to read one essay to the class at some time during the year. I read all their essays conscientiously and spent more time correcting the English than criticizing the history, especially in the first and second years. I was appalled at the ignorance of many of the first-year students. I did not expect them to know much, if any, history, but I did think they would know who was the premier of Manitoba and who was the prime minister of Canada and have opinions on public questions. Many of them seemed totally unaware of the political world around them and quite indifferent to it. It was a pleasure to find students with opinions and prejudices however wrong-headed I sometimes felt they were. I have to confess I devoted most of my attention to the minority who cared.

I had to work so hard that first year that I had little time for any outside activities. I did play bridge occasionally with one or two of my classmates who were still in Winnipeg, and I resumed my close friendship with Stanley Laing, who had married or was about to marry Gertrude Amies. Gertrude was to serve years later on the bilingual and bicultural commission. Norval Hunter was working at the newsprint mill at Pine Falls, and I spent several weekends with him. Those weekends were a life-saving respite from the steady grind. Our friendship remained close until his relatively recent death. At Pine Falls I first met King Gordon, who was the United Church minister there and shared a house with Norval.

Among colleagues in the faculty Arthur Phelps, head of the English department, was a sheer delight and a stalwart friend in good times and bad. Louis Moffit, like Phelps, was a one-time Methodist parson. He had done postgraduate work at Edinburgh and was the professor of economics. He was a confirmed Tory, an Orangeman and a protectionist, not a great scholar but a splendid human being. Our antipathetic views did nothing to inhibit a close friendship I cherished as long as he lived. With most of the other members of the faculty my relations were pleasant, though few of them became close.

The history department at the university had changed radically. Chester Martin had gone to the University of Toronto as head of the department there. D.C. Harvey had left to become head of the Nova Scotia Archives. They had been succeeded by Noel Fieldhouse, an Englishman who ended his career at McGill, and R.O. MacFarlane, who became a close friend. MacFarlane had a distinguished career in Manitoba as a professor and later as deputy minister of education. He completed his career as head of the School of Public Administration at Carleton University in Ottawa. My best friend on the university faculty was Lloyd Wheeler, of the Department of English.

Another friend during my years at Wesley was Norman Young, who had established and become headmaster of Ravenscourt School for boys. Young had been in his final year when I was a freshman and had been the one senior who paid any attention to me. Shortly after term began in 1929 Norman and his wife, Grace, Maryon Pearson's sister, invited me to play bridge. I spent many happy evenings at Ravenscourt.

I am astonished to recall how little attention I paid to public affairs during my first year at home. I was barely conscious of the stock exchange crash in October r 1929 and totally unperceptive of its overwhelming social and political consequences. I was vaguely aware of R.B. Bennett, the Tory leader of the Opposition, and was unimpressed by his views, which I found naive. I was unenthusiastic about Mackenzie King but thought him an adequate prime minister. I had little time to follow provincial affairs, though I did resume a friendship, from Ashern days, with Stuart Garson, who was in the legislature. The thought of a political or even a bureaucratic career never entered my mind.

When I resumed my diary on 21 May 1930, for the first time since the entry of 20 September 1929, I wrote that I would not attempt to recount the happenings of my first year as a university lecturer or as a repatriated Canadian. I noted, 'on the whole I enjoyed the former and found adjustment to the latter none too easy. I am sure next year will be much easier.' I added, 'the greatest blessing has been my colleague, Dr A.R.M. Lower of Toronto University, the Royal Navy and Harvard. He has been very kind to me, and we have been rather brothers-in-arms than superior and inferior.'

Summer in Europe

Before leaving Oxford in 1929, I had arranged to work towards a B Litt degree in 19th-century French history, and I learned that if

I resided at Oxford for six weeks of one term, I could then get leave of absence to do the rest of my research in Paris, where all the documents I needed were housed. I left Winnipeg to return to Europe as soon as I finished marking the examination papers at the beginning of May 1930.

I would have to exercise the most rigid economy all summer, and I was fortunate to get a free passage to Montreal. Norval's father, R.B. Hunter, offered me a place on a livestock train in charge of a carload of hogs. A colonist car was attached to each train of livestock, and one free passage given for each car of hogs or cattle. When I asked what my duties would be, R.B. said that whenever the train stopped long enough, I should go and look at the hogs but not make any comments. He forgot I was a farm boy! From the outside a colonist car looked like an ordinary passenger car. Inside it had hard wooden seats that could be extended to become bareboard beds. Passengers had to provide their own bedding and food. There was a coal stove for cooking at one end of the car. I foolishly left without any food, thinking the train would stop at divisional points where I could eat at CPR lunch counters. We passed Kenora before I woke up in the morning, and by the time we reached Ignace at 1 p.m. and discovered there was no lunch counter I was starving.

The passengers on the car were a collection of Jewish horse dealers, English hoboes, Nova Scotia farmers, and a young Englishman, Bernard Radley, an ex naval sublieutenant later employed by Sassoon's in Bombay, who was travelling from Vancouver to look for a better job in Montreal. Radley later settled in business in Toronto, and we maintained a casual acquaintance for several years. He was the only other 'hogherd' on the train. We became travelling partners for the rest of the journey. At the general store at Ignace we laid in a stock of food, two knives and two cups. We used tobacco tins as plates and got our own meals. Radley was a good and ingenious cook, and we fared well.

After four days and five nights we reached Montreal just too late for the Canadian Pacific ship *Duchess of Bedford*. I had reserved an alternative passage on the *Doric*, the White Star liner on which I had come home in August 1929 in first class, travelling free. In May 1930 I was in steerage as a paying passenger. The accommodation was not bad, but the passengers were mostly uninteresting, and the voyage uneventful. But the rail journey from Liverpool to Oxford was memorable. The English spring was at its very best, and I realized how much I had missed the beautiful countryside, especially the trees.

I looked up my friends, dined in hall at New College and began to arrange to work for a B Litt in a highly irregular fashion. With help from E.L. Woodward I got my application ready and arranged to have six weeks recognized as the one term of compulsory residence and was granted leave of absence to work in Paris for the rest of the period of research. I worked out a theme for my thesis with Woodward. He had read a book by Jean Maurain on the influence of the Catholics on the politics of the Second Empire in France until 1869. He suggested I continue that study for the final year of the Second Empire, until Napoleon III went into exile. Woodward wrote to Maurain and arranged to have him supervise my research. It proved an ideal arrangement. I saw Maurain once or twice that summer and again in 1931 and 1932. I continued to see Maurain every summer I was in Paris. He was a keen alpinist, and when he was killed mountain climbing, I lost a friend.

While waiting for approval of my plan I enjoyed Oxford. Bill Luttrell, another friend and I were taken up in an Avro plane for ten minutes' view of the city — I had flown! I worked fairly hard at general reading of my period of research and had a good deal of social activity as well. On the last day of June, which ended the period of my required residence at Oxford, I went to London, where I spent two days visiting friends, and on 2 July to France. I stayed until 14 July with the de France family and then went on to Paris.

I found a room in a genuine slum, at 40, rue des Écoles, opposite the Collège de France. The next day I checked in at the Canadian legation, the library of the Institut Catholique and the Bibliothèque Nationale. Late in the evening I encountered by chance my friend and a former classmate from Manitoba, Victor

Leathers. He was in Paris pursuing his French studies, which were to lead ultimately to a long career at Wesley College and the University of Winnipeg. Victor introduced me to several restaurants, which he declared clean and cheap. We often went to the state theatres, with their inexpensive seats. Despite a sober and almost puritanical manner, Victor had a lively sense of humour, and his company was always welcome.

George Curtis was in Paris a little later in the summer, and we spent many pleasant evenings together. He introduced me to a table d'hôte in an apartment at 5, avenue du Maine, just off the Boulevard Montparnasse, where the lunches were substantial, of good plain quality and not expensive. One of the other patrons was Simone Routier, a girl from Quebec City who copied documents for the Public Archives in Ottawa, and who wrote poetry in her spare time. Curtis and I often spent evenings with Simone who was, I suppose, the first French-speaking Canadian I got to know well.

George and I spent the evening of the Canadian election, 28 July 1930, together. I had paid so little attention to federal politics in my first year at home that I did not realize unemployment was a political concern. I took it for granted that the Liberal government of Mackenzie King would win. My hunch seemed to be confirmed by the first returns in the evening paper, and I began to drink to victory while George, who was a Tory, started to drown his sorrows. At about 1 a.m., when the first morning paper appeared, Bennett's victory was reported and we reversed our roles. Neither of us really regarded the result as a momentous event, but once I got home, I discovered there had been a profound change of policy. I never again took federal politics casually.

I worked hard and by the late summer was beginning to make sense of the topic for my thesis. At Oxford I had read enough to be aware of the sharp division between the Liberal Catholics and the ultramontanes, and of the latent hostility of the Royalists to Napoleon III and the Second Empire. Most of my research that summer consisted of reading newspapers, of which the ultramontane *L'Univers* was the most useful. It was not until 1931 that I began to examine relevant documents in the Archives Nationales and elsewhere. Reading the newspaper gave me some insight into French politics in general.

I had a few days in England with the Manders before embarking from Liverpool on the *Baltic*, one of the oldest ships in the White Star fleet. The ship bumped into the dock the day we reached Liverpool, and the sailing was delayed for 24 hours. The White Star line put the passengers up for the night and assigned the steerage passengers to a mouldy old hotel. I decided not to stay there and went to the company office to complain that I did not mind their third class but refused to stay in a slum. They asserted that every other hotel in Liverpool was full, but promised to pay the bill if I could find a room. I walked up the street to the Adelphi, then the leading hotel in Liverpool, and got one. When I presented the bill the next day after explaining I had found a fairly good pub called the Adelphi, the White Star official was visibly shocked, but he paid. I fear that after that there was no profit for the company on my passage.

I bought all the Edgar Wallace paperbacks in Woolworths and read them on the way home. The third class was full of returning English wives of Canadian veterans who had been 'home' after some years in Canada. There were children crying from morning to night and some sort of piped-in music, which played 'Spring-time in the Rockies' incessantly. I cannot bear the sound of that tune to this day. When we docked in Montreal, I was happy to be in Canada again.

Family years in Winnipeg

Before I left Winnipeg Louis Moffit and I had agreed to meet in the late summer in Ottawa, where he would be doing research, and to drive back to Winnipeg together. That was for me the first of a long series of motor trips in the 1930s using the United States as a corridor between Winnipeg and Ontario, which route I had travelled originally by motorbike in 1927.

I arrived in Ottawa just in time to witness the opening of the new Parliament. Standing outside the Parliament Building watching the governor general drive up to the main door for the opening ceremony, I realized that someone beside me was claiming my attention. It was Charles Stacey, who had been at Oxford when I was. His first words were 'Pickersgill, did you ever see a sloppier looking body of men?' He was referring to the Governor General's Footguards. Two or three years earlier, when Stacey and I were riding on the rear platform of a Paris bus, we had passed some conscripts marching by in shabby First World War uniforms. Stacey had embarrassed me by saying in a loud voice, 'Pickersgill, did you ever see a sloppier looking body of men?' In those days I tended to regard Stacey as what I called a militaromaniac, little guessing he was destined to be one of the most distinguished historians of Canada's part in the Second World War.

Moffit and I had an afternoon in the gallery of the House of Commons looking at the triumphant Tory government and the bombastic prime minister, Bennett, and the dispirited Liberal Opposition led by Mackenzie King. We argued back and forth on the way to Winnipeg about the contents of the Speech from the Throne and Bennett's boast that to reduce unemployment he would 'blast his way into the markets of the world' by raising tariffs to unprecedented heights that would stimulate manufacturing in Canada. In the election campaign he had promised to 'end unemployment or perish in the attempt.' Politically, perish he did.

No one yet realized the magnitude unemployment would reach as the depression deepened. I regarded the high tariff policy as sheer madness; Moffit, who was a protectionist as well as a Tory, thought it might reduce unemployment. He admired Bennett for his sincerity and was quite shocked when I retorted that the sincerest people were in insane asylums. Our differences were always friendly, and we had a pleasant trip, with none of the mishaps and repair stops of my trip on the motorbike in 1927.

At home our family organization changed in the fall of 1930. Bessie and Tom had graduated from the university in the spring. Tom was doing postgraduate work and being paid for assistance in a soil survey. Though he worked at the Agricultural College, he lived at home and paid a share of the household costs, thereby relieving me a little. By great good fortune Bessie had found a position in the diet kitchen of the Winnipeg General Hospital. The job provided her with a room at the nurses' residence. She came home every day for dinner and made a small financial contribution to the running of the house. For seven years we maintained the household with little friction and a great deal of enjoyment. Mother could not manage the housekeeping as well as her work as a nurse, and in the fall of 1931 we had the good fortune to find an efficient and pleasant young Danish girl to live in as housekeeper. For $15 a month, raised later to $18, Hedwig managed our house and did all the housework and most of the cooking, though Bessie generally helped with dinner. Hedwig remained with us until the family broke up. That fall too we moved from the house on Walnut Street to a better-planned one at the end of Broadway, which was heated with steam piped from a central steam plant about a mile away and had no furnace to stoke. We loved that house from the start and more each year.

In the late summer of 1932 Mother fell ill, really suffering from exhaustion, and had to give up working. We persuaded her to go to Barbados for the winter of 1932-33 instead of being confined to the house in the cold weather. During her absence and later Hedwig took all the housekeeping in stride. We realized she was the pivot of the household.

Although we became increasingly aware of the depression with each passing year, none of us was ever unemployed. Indeed, with prices falling we were probably marginally better off, even though our incomes did not rise. My own salary from Wesley College originally was $2200; and in the second year it was increased to $2300. In subsequent years the salaries of all faculty members were reduced by a share of the college deficit. From one year to the next I never knew what my income would be. On my salary I was able to live comfortably, go to Europe every summer until 1934 and meet the monthly deficit on the housekeeping account, after the others paid their fixed shares.

In 1932 we decided that we could afford to buy a second-hand Chevrolet sedan. The car served us well until 1937; we all deriveda great deal of pleasure from it, and we used it in a practical way for essential transportation. Also, shortly after we moved to Broadway, we had broken down and bought a radio. I think back with nostalgia to the New York Philharmonic on Sunday afternoons and later the Metropolitan Opera on Saturdays. At that time we did not expect anything Canadian, even national news. I learned to operate the radio, but the car presented problems. Tom did his best to teach me to drive, but I was a slow learner, and it was not until 1934 that I felt comfortble at the wheel on Portage Avenue or any main highway. During the early learning stage I was driving on a country road when an approaching car appeared on the horizon. I stopped the car, told Tom I could not stand the nervous strain of all that traffic and waited until the car passed. I was never allowed to forget that incident.

By 1931 I had fallen back into a semipaternal, semifraternal relationship with Frank. He completed grade 11 at Kelvin in June, and it was clear he could not afford to go on to university without a substantial scholarship. Frank was born after our grandmother's death, so he did not have the legacy the rest of us had had, which was our financial foundation at university. The obvious goal to strive for was the IODE bursary. I advised Frank to take grade 12 and delay applying for the IODE, which was for four years. If he completed grade 12, the scholarship would enable him to take the BA honours course. He was duly awarded the IODE bursary, which was worth $300 a year, and which the university supplemented with free tuition. He also won another scholarship worth $100. Altogether, when he entered the university in the fall, he could feel free of financial worries for the next four years.

When Frank started at university the arts students in the junior years were still at the old downtown Broadway campus, and he spent his first year there. But from the fall of 1933 he had to travel out to the Fort Garry campus, five miles away, and the problem of transport arose. We agreed that if he could find three or four paying passengers to travel with him, he could use the car. He did so, for the next three years, having had no trouble finding passengers.

Like all the rest of us Frank was encouraged to invite his friends to our house. Sunday evenings were enlivened by a group of bright young men and women, most of whom became friends of the whole family. Altogether we had a lively time socially during the years we lived on Broadway.

Thanks to Mother's pension as a veteran's widow the financial consequence of her stopping work was not crippling. When she returned to Montreal from Barbados in early May 1933, Bessie, Frank and I were there to meet her and were happy to find her restored in health and spirits.

We had been renting out our farm at Ashern for several years at a steadily declining rent. By 1933, rents for city houses were also falling. Shortly after my return from Europe the rental agency approached me about renewing our lease. I offered to renew at $40 per month instead of the $60 we had been paying, intending to haggle a little and agree to $45. The agent pretended to be insulted by my offer. When I told him the rent we received from our property had gone down 50 percent he sneered that he supposed it was farm property. I replied that city property also was going down, and he could take or leave my offer. When he telephoned to seek a compromise, I suggested he look for another tenant. I was confident he would not find one because the cost of heating the house was nearly $300 a year, very high for those days. I guessed that all we needed to do was to show any prospective tenant the heating bills. In fact only two parties turned up to look at the house. But as 1 October approached, Mother began to worry that we would find ourselves on the street. Just before the last day the agent telephoned again and offered the house at $45. I said my $40 offer stood. On the last day of the month he called again and asked me to come to his office to sign a lease at $40. The reduction in rent helped substantially to keep down the cost of running the house.

We continued to live on Broadway until 1 October 1935. By then it seemed that the family might be scattered during the coming year. Our landlord insisted on a full year's lease, which we were not prepared to sign. We found a house on Dorchester Avenue, not nearly as attractive but with a little more room. The rent was the same, and the house could be rented on a month-to-month basis. We moved reluctantly. Though it was in a more fashionable neighbourhood, the new house never had the same atmosphere.

Other interests

During my eight years at Wesley College teaching occupied most of my time, but after two years, preparations for lectures became easier, and I had leisure for other activities.

I was very proud of a college organization I founded at Lower's suggestion — the History Club, organized on the same basis as Professor G.M. Wrong's history club at the University of Toronto, to which Lower had belonged. Membership was limited, and members were selected from the senior years. One member read a paper at each meeting. Meetings were held in private houses. Several of the college governors and other distinguished citizens acted as hosts. It was considered a great honour to belong.

I loved the theatre, which still functioned, or at least hung on, in Winnipeg, until after I left for Oxford. In the two years I was away the professional theatre had almost disappeared, though one or two stock companies tried to carry on for a season at a time. The Little Theatre, however, was flourishing. Bessie and I attended almost every show, though we had no part except as spectators. By the time the Winnipeg Auditorium had been completed as an unemployment relief project, the Winnipeg Symphony Orchestra was established, with Bernard Naylor as conductor. Bessie and I rarely missed a concert.

I have never been much of a 'joiner,' but I was persuaded by Lower to become a member of two organizations that helped widen my horizons. One was a small luncheon club called the

National Club. Its objective was to encourage the development of a stronger sense of Canadian nationhood and to uphold the view that in its relations with the rest of the world, Canada should act exclusively in its own interest. Most of the members were veterans of the First World War and had been deeply affected by it. I was the youngest member. Apart from Lower, those I remember best were James H. Stitt, the conservative MP for Selkirk, later a member of the Civil Service Commission in Ottawa; R.K. Finlayson, a lawyer, who subsequently went to Ottawa as private secretary to Prime Minister Bennett; C. Rhodes Smith, a Rhodes scholar, a lawyer, later a member of the legislature and attorney general, a senior official in Ottawa and finally a judge; and Rev. Clark Lawson, a United Church minister of wide interests and sound judgment. He was the father of W.R. Lawson, who became a deputy governor of the Bank of Canada, and of two daughters, Bea, married to Gordon Robertson, and Margaret, married to Douglas Fraser, both men distinguished public servants in Ottawa. The National Club did not have outside speakers; it was a discussion club, with talk that was not exciting but serious and often penetrating.

The other organization was the Winnipeg Branch of the Canadian Institute of International Affairs, of which J.W. Dafoe, the editor of the *Winnipeg Free Press*, was the presiding genius. Two of the most prominent members were Edgar J. Tarr and James B. Coyne. All three became close friends of mine and had a profound influence on the development of my outlook on public affairs, both national and international. The Institute was able to enlist as a speaker almost every important visitor to Winnipeg, of whom there were many in those days of rail travel. Because its proceedings were confidential, members frequently were exposed to information not available to the public and to candid opinions on important questions. The branch also had study groups that examined international problems in some depth. A deliberate attempt was made to enlist members from the whole spectrum of public attitudes. Dafoe once said no one was too far to the right to be unacceptable nor too far to the left to be unwelcome.

During my eight years in academic life I did not participate actively in any political organization, but I made no secret of the fact I was a Liberal federally, and that I supported the Progressive government of John Bracken provincially. Perhaps because I never suffered personally from the depression, I took a somewhat detached view of the panaceas offered for the suffering, which I increasingly recognized was real and deeply wounding, but which, I believed, had complex causes for which there were no simple remedies. I was greatly attracted by the pragmatism of the Roosevelt New Deal and impressed by the Liberals, who had organized the Port Hope Conference to give a new direction to Canadian Liberalism. During the short period in 1935 when the *Canadian Forum* was under Liberal direction, I contributed an article entitled 'The Decay of Liberalism' setting out views that became the foundation of my political faith. In the election held in October 1935 I was a firm if not enthusiastic supporter of Mackenzie King and the Liberal party. Though I had never believed in occupational or class foundations for political parties, I recognized that Bracken's government was not simply agrarian but had broadened its base. The first vote I cast in my life was for his government, in 1927. I was pleased when the provincial Liberal and Progressive parties united in 1932. My friendship and admiration for Stuart Garson added to the solidity of my support for Bracken's Liberal-Progressive government, but I did not associate myself in any way with the party organization. I took little or no interest in municipal government. It seemed to me that Winnipeg as a city was well managed, regardless who was mayor, or who dominated the council.

I never lacked definite views on public questions. I believed in political parties as instruments of government, but throughout those eight years in Winnipeg I was content with the role of citizen and had not the slightest thought that I would ever become an active politician.

Three summers of European travel

In 1931 I sailed to Europe from New York on the Red Star liner *Westernland*. On board I met several charming Americans who remained my friends for many years. Among them were Dr Sanford Larkey and his wife, Geraldine. Larkey was a Rhodes scholar the same year as Arnold Heeney, who later became a colleague of mine in the public service. Both he and his wife were Californians from San Francisco. We were constant companions on the voyage. After landing we went to Oxford together for two or three days during the boat races. Also on board were a beautiful girl named Dorothy Cassard and her mother, Southerners living in Washington, and another charming girl, Nancy Terrell, who was being chaperoned by a Frenchwoman in her late thirties named Zette. Zette needed a chaperone more than Nancy did. They apparently slept all day and stayed up most of the night, so I was able to be attentive to Dorothy in the daytime and to Nancy in the late evening without either meeting me with the other. Up until that time I had been almost without a romantic interest in women, and I was not eager to develop one as I felt my financial circumstances made marriage out of the question. But my caution did not stop me from being attracted to these two American women. I maintained a desultory correspondence with Dorothy Cassard for several years and actually met her briefly in Washington twice. I saw much more of Nancy, later in the summer in France; I was greatly attracted to her. But despite the distractions I made good progress with my work. At the end of the summer I went to the de Frances and made one or two short visits in England before returning to New York.

By 1932 there were no further increases in salary, but prices had gone down so much that I had no hesitation that summer in travelling tourist on CP *Duchess* ships both ways. I settled down in Paris to complete the research for my thesis and had done so by the end of July. Cyril Meredith-Jones of the French department of the University of Manitoba and I decided to make a short visit to Moscow and Leningrad. We were held up for a week in Berlin, waiting for Soviet visas, so we decided to cancel the Russian trip and go to Scandinavia instead. We visited Copenhagen, Malmö, Stockholm, Trondjem and Oslo. We found the evidence of the Viking heritage in Oslo fascinating. My overall impression was that Scandinavia was more like North America than Europe in atmosphere and outlook — the least rewarding part of Europe for a Canadian seeking the exotic but the most rewarding if one wanted to feel at home.

The summer of 1933 was somewhat more memorable. I booked a passage from New York on the German liner *Bremen* and a return on the *Empress of Britain*. I learned that the Beatties, from Winnipeg, were also sailing on the *Bremen* to visit their Rhodes scholar son, Bob, in Oxford and, once he got his degree, to make a family tour of the British Isles. I feared it might be boring to have to be nice to Bob's little sister, but in fact I found Margaret delightful and spent most of my waking hours on the voyage in her company.

Before we reached Southampton, Mr Beattie invited me to join them on a motor trip to Land's End before they went to Oxford. After meeting his family at Southhampton, Bob had to return to Oxford to complete his exams. I accepted with alacrity; my thesis was complete and ready for presentation, and I had to stay in England until the examination. We had a lovely week or so in the west country, during which I made the most of my self-appointed role as guide. Later I stayed in London at the same bed and breakfast place in Bayswater as the Beatties; it was an Oxford Canadian haunt. I took every excuse I could find to show Margaret the sights, but I took care not to display any romantic interest, which I felt would be cradle-snatching.

The Lowers were in Oxford when I went there to defend my thesis. I was accepted for the B Litt degree but did not feel I could afford the required £20 fee to receive the degree. Arthur Lower suggested I join him on a visit to Russia. Remembering the futile experience of the year before, I was reluctant to accept. But when he asked if I would have refused a chance to visit Paris during the French Revolution, I changed my mind. I made arrangements to meet him in Riga.

I crossed from London to Hamburg on a Soviet ship and took the train from there to Riga, through the Danzig corridor, where I looked with interest at the new town of Gdynia, which the Poles had built to give them a window on the sea. From the train, Gdynia looked like a raw small city in the American or Canadian west. Riga was unexciting. The tension between the Latvian and German-speaking population could be felt, though they were clearly united by a common fear of Russia.

Lower and I went from Riga to Moscow, which I found drab and depressing. There was an obvious shortage of consumer goods, and we had the impression we were being shadowed. One day we lunched at the British embassy where William Strang, later permanent under-secretary at the foreign office, was chargé d'affaires. There were several journalists present. The other Canadian guest was Robert Cromie, publisher of the *Vancouver Sun*, who asked Strang repeatedly what lesson the Soviets had for Canada. Finally, in exasperation, Strang replied shortly but politely, 'I would say, Mr Cromie, absolutely none.'

From Moscow Lower went on to Leningrad and through Finland to Stockholm to join his wife, and I went south to Odessa via Kiev. Everyone I spoke to at the embassy was astonished that I had got a ticket to travel south; no foreigners had been allowed to visit Ukraine during that year of the great famine. I was on my own for 40 hours on the train, a hot and exhausting journey. From the train I could see no evidence that anyone was actually starving, but at one station I threw a rock-hard dry roll on to the platform, and there was a mad scramble for it. As I gazed over the Ukrainian steppes, I realized for the first time how the Canadian prairies must have appeared to immigrants from other parts of Europe, who had no sentimental association with prairie landscape. I also realized why it had been so easy for Ukrainians to adapt to western Canada.

From Odessa I took an Italian ship to Greece. There were two other passengers on board; a Soviet official of some kind in first class, and a Jewish American born in Russia with me in the lower class. He had visited relatives in Russia. He opined that despite the famine, the harsh conditions and the repression, there would be no resistance to the regime unless and until economic condiions improved and life became easier. I have often reflected on that prophetic view. The ship put into Istanbul, where I went ashore and was overwhelmed by what seemed, in relative terms, the almost obscene luxury of the city. The next evening the ship reached Piraeus, and I was soon installed in a comfortable hotel in the middle of Athens. After Russia Greece felt free.

One evening at New College before leaving for Russia, I had played bridge with two recent graduates of Trinity College, Toronto, Jim McMullen of Vancouver, and Swotty Wotherspoon, of Ottawa. They told me a third classmate, Bob Dale Harris, was to join them for a motor trip through France, Italy, Austria and Germany. We arranged to meet in Vienna. We did so, and drove on to Salzburg. When we crossed the border just beyond Salzburg, the contrast between Austria and Germany, where there were signs of the Nazi regime, struck me forcibly. We had a leisurely trip through southern Germany; after two or three days sightseeing and beer drinking in Munich, we went on to Ingolstadt, Nuremburg, Heidelberg, Frankfurt and Mainz and up the Moselle to Bernkastel. From there we drove to Luxembourg, Reims and Ypres. Outside Ypres we discovered a place where an enterprising proprietor had refused to have his property restored after the war and was doing a thriving business showing tourists the authentic trenches. Two years later Bessie and I discovered that the Belgian revenue department had caught up with him and was making him collect 'amusement tax.' By the time we reached Calais, McMullen, Dale Harris, Wotherspoon and I were all fast friends. Unhappily I never saw McMullen again; he was killed in the Second World War. But Bob and Swotty remained my friends for the rest of their lives.

The remainder of the summer was relatively uneventful, with a visit to the de Frances and a few days in London before I sailed on the *Empress of Britain*. The Beatties had left on an earlier crossing, but Bob was still staying in London. One evening after dinner he chanced to say that his mother had been born in Port Rowan, Ontario. I was astonished and said that if his family had been in or near Port Rowan for more than a century, we were almost certainly cousins. When I got back to Winnipeg, I told Mother, who phoned Mrs Beattie. In no time they discovered they were second cousins. The discovery resulted in a close relationship between our two families. We had started off rather inauspiciously. In 1922, as a freshman, I had opened a savings account at the Bank of Commerce on Portage Avenue, opposite Eaton's. One day I went in to draw out some money and was asked to see the manager. He told me that I was writing too many cheques on my account, and that the bank lost money on such accounts. The manager was J.T. Beattie. I was so affronted that I went down the street to the Huron and Erie Mortgage Corporation and asked them if they had any limit on the number of cheques that could be drawn. They replied that they had not as long as there was balance enough to cover them. I returned to the Bank of Commerce and drew out all my money. I have not had a Bank of Commerce account since that day.

My next encounter with a member of the Beattie family was in the fall of 1929, after Bob had been awarded the Rhodes scholarship for Manitoba. He came to see me to talk about choosing a college and other aspects of life at Oxford, and I liked him very much. We met again in the early summer of 1931 at Oxford, and the next summer we were both staying at the Maison Canadienne in Paris. After I had finished my research, I went with Bob and two of his friends on a short motor trip through Belgium and Holland and up the Rhine to Cologne. That same fall of 1932 back in Winnipeg, a friend of Bob's and mine from Oxford was passing through the city. He had dinner with the Beatties, and I was invited also. That was the day I first met Margaret, so we were not complete strangers when we met on the *Bremen* at the beginning of the eventful summer of 1933.

New directions

A year of change

Six things happened in 1934 that changed my outlook on Canada and my own pattern of life. Early in the new year I decided not to go to Europe for the summer. That decision resulted in the offer of a teaching post in the university summer school for July and August. The appointment added modestly to my income for the year and so enabled Bessie and me to build a cottage. Arthur Lower invited me to join him and his wife on a motor trip deep into the United States and subsequently to accompany him to Montreal for the annual meetings of the Learned Societies. And I fell in love.

After I presented my B Litt thesis at Oxford in 1933, I was far from sure what direction any further research should take. I had to make up my mind within a year or two if I was to remain in academic life; I had no thought or prospect of any other way to earn my living. I was beginning to realize that by going off to Europe every summer I was missing an essential part of Canadian life. My decision to spend the summer of 1934 in Canada was influenced by the opening of the highway between Winnipeg and Kenora. It was still possible to buy property a few miles west of Keewatin on the shores of Clearwater Bay of the Lake of the Woods.

Bessie and I explored sites there. When the chance came to teach in the summer school, the financial problem was solved and the property was bought. Our lot had no beach, and a sloping cliff rose from the shore. We had no choice but to build at the brow of the hill, about 300 feet from the water at an elevation of 80 feet. There was no road into the lot, but from the highway a trail about a mile long led to a shack owned by a man named Harper. We rented his shack for a month, to have a place to sleep in until our building was sufficently advanced to provide shelter. Furniture and supplies were carried in on the trail by hand from the highway. We decided to use the best BC finished lumber, which was dirt cheap in 1934. We had all the building materials brought in by boat from Kenora and dumped on the shore at the foot of the hill, and we carried the lumber, shingles and cement up the 300 feet on our shoulders, hard work and made harder by mosquitoes.

Uncle Walt, who had been the principal clerk in a law firm in Winnipeg since he retired from his farm in 1919, was a victim of the depression and without a job that spring. He was a highly accomplished amateur carpenter, and we persuaded him to be the master builder. Except for the masons hired to build a massive fireplace, all the rest of the labour was voluntary. We enlisted a number of students, one of whom was Margaret Beattie, for varying periods. Various members of the family helped too, but the main job was done by Uncle Walt. When I last visited the cottage briefly over 30 years later, it looked as solid and level as when it was built.

The height above the lake gave a magnificent view, and inevitably we called the place Highbrow House. The cottage had a spacious living room stretching its whole length, with two bedrooms and a kitchen opening off the back. The total cost of materials, labour, furniture and furnishings was $1100. The cottage gave the family and many of our friends great pleasure for years, until we sold it reluctantly in 1941, after I had become established in Ottawa, and Bessie had moved to Calgary. No one got greater joy out of Highbrow than Mother. Like several million other Canadians we soon took it for granted that owning a cottage on a lake was essential to living in Canada.

Between 1927 and 1933 I had made frequent trips between Winnipeg and Toronto, through the 'Canadian corridor' of the states of Minnesota, Wisconsin, Illinois, Indiana and Michigan. I had also been in New York two or three times. But those experiences had given me no impression of the magnitude or the complexity of the United States. Furthermore, I had never studied American history, I knew less of American politics than I did of the politics of Britain or France, and I had little understanding of the geography or the economy of the United States. Arthur Lower felt that most Canadians knew next to nothing about the country that had the most influence on their country. I eagerly fell in with his suggestion that I motor south with him and his wife in May. Our trip took us down the Mississippi to St Louis, and on to a small city called Ste Genevieve, 60 miles further south. There everyone on the streets spoke French, and the architecture was like Quebec's, and the convents and schools were painted the same grey; I had never realized so vividly how culturally resistant the French are, wherever they go. We then crossed the Mississippi into southern Illinois, Lincoln country, and from there we crossed the Ohio River and continued through what was perceptively the South: across Kentucky and Tennessee, a mile or two into Alabama near the Chattanooga battlefield, east into the mountains and a mile or two into northwestern Georgia. We then turned north through the Smoky Mountains of North Carolina and Virginia and across Virginia to Jamestown, where continuous English settlement began in 1607, and to nearby Yorktown, where the colonial period ended. From there we went to Washington, my first visit.

I saw both Houses of the Congress in session and was appalled by the informality and apparent confusion. R.B. Bennett's brother-in-law, W.D. Herridge, was the Canadian minister in Washington. Canada had established diplomatic relations with the United States but had only a legation with a minister until the end of the Second World War, when the status was raised to that of embassy with an ambassador. Neither Lower nor I had met Herridge, but he received us cordially and offered to 'throw a party' for us, a phrase I had never heard before. I was sorry our limited time prevented us from staying.

From Washington to Montreal the scenery and atmosphere were more familiar, but the differences from Canada struck me forcibly, even in the northeast. I came home impressed, oppressed and bewildered. The United States was so immense, the problems so vast, the means of dealing with them so seemingly inadequate and the possibility of the individual citizen having any real influence on the course of events so remote that I felt individual Americans were politically at sea. Nearly 60 years later I have not lost that feeling.

On the return trip from Montreal to Winnipeg I travelled by bus through Detroit, Chicago and Minneapolis. I looked at the familiar Canadian corridor with new eyes. The United States would never again be for me a narrow fringe of people south of the border.

The meeting of the Learned Societies made an equally lasting impression. There in a single room in Montreal were most of those Canadians thinking about the country's political problems and many of those dealing with them. The attendance was predominantly English-speaking, but there were a few French-speaking Canadians. It was possible to know personally nearly all the Canadians who concerned themselves seriously with public affairs. I realized then as I never had before that life in Canada was small and intimate enough that an individual Canadian could really hope to influence the course of national life.

By the Labour Day weekend Highbrow House was officially open, and we managed several weekends during the fall before it was closed for the winter. One of the guests that first weekend was Beatrice Young. I had first seen her early in the year literally across a crowded room at a Sunday afternoon tea party and been attracted by her. Frank, who was also at the party, knew her and identified her from my description later in the day. Bea was the daughter of Dr F.A. Young, a war veteran and a member of the medical staff of the veterans' hospital. She was born on 3 April 1913, and had a sister, Katherine, born in 1920 after her father returned from overseas. Her mother had died several years before, and her father was a widower when I first met him. Later, in the summer of 1935, Dr Young married Lana Fisher, the manager of the book department of Eaton's. Frank and I knew her well, and she often let us know of bargains. Frank arranged a meeting between Bea and me, and I contrived to meet her three or four times before taking courage and inviting her to Highbrow. I saw her three or four times during the fall, and by the end of the year I was infatuated.

We traditionally had a dinner party at our house on New Year's Eve and then went on to the ball at the main office of the Bank of Montreal, at which we were sponsored by Walter. In 1934 I invited Bea, and at about midnight I told her I was in love with her. For the next four months I pressed my suit.

Bea came to Highbrow in April along with Dick Hunter, Mother and me for an enjoyable weekend. Before I left for Europe at the beginning of May, I felt she was beginning to care, and we agreed to correspond during the summer. Bea received her BA that spring; in the fall she was to enter the library school at the University of Toronto. We arranged to meet in Toronto in September while I was on my way home from Europe.

I went to Europe in 1935 with no very clear decision about future research. I continued to examine the influence of the Catholics in French politics into the period after 1870, but I was not deeply interested. I had few friends left in Paris and was glad I was not staying for the whole summer. Bessie was coming to Europe for the first time and wanted to spend most of the summer in England and Scotland. She landed at Cherbourg, where I met her, and we had a few days in France and Belgium before going on to England. At Oxford I bought a second-hand car for £10; Bessie and I drove it from Land's End to John O'Groats and back to London and had a wonderful time. R.O. MacFarlane was in Europe that summer and travelled with us, sharing expenses. At the end of the summer I sold the car to Lady Mander's butler for £5.

Bessie and I returned to Montreal on the *Empress of Britain*. She rushed home to work in Winnipeg; I went to Toronto to see Bea. Bea met me at the train in Toronto on 1 September, and I stayed in the city for a week. During that time Bea told me she reciprocated my feelings. We agreed to correspond regularly and see what our feelings were in the spring.

In the fall of 1935 there were several signs that our corporate family life probably would not last more than another year. We could not maintain the establishment unless Tom and Walter were at home. There were growing intimations that the bank might transfer Walter away from Winnipeg. Tom and Margaret Wilkinson had been attached to one another since 1926, and they obviously meant to be married as soon as Tom could support them; by 1935 his prospects had improved. Frank would graduate in 1936, with hopes of the Rhodes scholarship or the IODE; in any event he was unlikely to be in Winnipeg for long after graduation. We decided we could not lease our house for another year, and the landlord refused to keep us on after 1 October on a monthly basis, so the family moved at the end of September from the

Broadway house to a house at 909 Dorchester Avenue, which we occupied until May 1936.

I had found an excuse for being in Toronto in May and June 1936. When Bea and I had met in Toronto the previous September, Bea had been staying with two of her mother's unmarried sisters, Florence and Gertrude Wright. Gertrude had just acquired a piece of land on the banks of the Credit River near the village of Terra Cotta on which she planned to build a summer cottage. On the strength of my experience with Highbrow I offered to come to Toronto early in May to supervise the construction until the building was completed early in July. In exchange the Wright sisters were to provide me with a room and bed and some of my meals.

Bea was to complete her year at the library school in late June. I wanted to persuade her that we should get married right afterwards, and by the middle of May I had done so. The wedding was to be in Toronto after her examinations were over. The earliest possible date on which her father, stepmother and sister could attend the wedding proved to be 3 July.

During that May-June period I also went to Ottawa for the meetings of the Learned Societies, where I read a report of a symposium of the Winnipeg branch of the Institute of International Affairs. Shortly after I got back to Toronto, Mother and Bessie arrived in our car from Winnipeg. The family had decided to give the car to Bea and me as a wedding present.

The wedding itself was simple. Professor George B. King of the theology department of United College officiated. The ceremony was in the austere chapel of Emmanuel College, Victoria University. The only guests were Bea's family and other close relatives and my mother. Bob Beattie came from Ottawa to be best man. The wedding was at noon, and Dr Young had a luncheon for the guests. We left in the early afternoon for a weekend at Long Point.

On 21 July Bea and I set out on a motor tour. We had an old tent, a folding double bed, red Hudson's Bay blankets, which we rarely needed, and a one-burner coal oil (kerosene) stove for cooking. We intended to camp out every night we were on the road and do our cooking in the open trunk of the car. Fortunately there was good weather during most of the trip. On most nights,

J.W.P. married Beatrice Landon Young of Winnipeg on July 3, 1936 in Toronto; she died Ottawa January 17, 1938.

we found a secluded spot to put up our bed and slept under the stars. Our route took us through New England to Boston, and then on up the Atlantic coast to New Brunswick and Nova Scotia and back west by the south shore of the St Lawrence — all new country to both of us. Approaching the Maritime provinces for the first time from Boston rather than Montreal served the purpose of portraying graphically the competing magnetic attractions for Maritimers of what they traditionally called Upper Canada and the Boston States. We saw a great deal of New Brunswick and Nova Scotia in the first two weeks of August, at the end of which we drove up the south shore of the St Lawrence to St-Roch, just west of Pocatière. The next day was Monday, 17 August 1936 — election day in the province of Quebec. That evening in Quebec City we watched the delirious celebrations of the Union Nationale supporters, who had ended 39 years of Liberal government. The Duplessis era had begun. We drove from Quebec City to St-Jerome and north to Mont Laurier and west to Maniwaki, once again in an unconventional direction. After two lovely days at Blue Sea Lake with the Dale Harrises, we drove south to Ottawa in the rain. My first impression of the Gatineau River and Valley was misty, and I was not enthusiastic, except for the beautiful curve of the shore at Wakefield. We had a day in Toronto and a short visit to Bea's aunts, and a day with Mother and Dr Annie at Port Rowan. From Toronto to Winnipeg, the country was familiar and the trip uneventful. We reached Winnipeg at the end of August.

Before we were married, I had told Bea exactly what my financial situation was, and how frugally we would have to live. Having had no emergencies, we had managed so far to live within our means. From our departure for the Maritimes on 21 July to our arrival in Winnipeg 1 September we had travelled 5655 miles and spent $180 on gas, oil, repairs and maintenance of the car and $99.43 on our living and other expenses. We had been 42 nights on the trip. Deducting 16 nights for which we found longer-term accommodation or were given hospitality, we were on the road 26 nights and had to seek accommodation only 7 times. The other 19 times we had slept in the open. Canada had a new dimension for both Bea and me.

The last year in Winnipeg

Our first task when Bea and I arrived in Winnipeg was to find a place to live. We were lucky to find an apartment within easy walking distance of the college, in the lower half of a house on Chestnut Street. The rent was only $35 because I undertook to look after the furnace for the whole house. Fortunately Frank and I had had an apprenticeship with stoking a furnace at the Dorchester house the previous year, and the chore did not prove a great burden. We set a target of $30 a month for housekeeping expenses, and we rarely exceeded it by more than $5. We lived very frugally but were comfortable and had plenty of society. Many of our friends were already friends of both of us.

The Pickersgills had already scattered. The Bank of Montreal had transferred Walter to Fort William. Tom had found a room in a fraternity house to live in until he and Margaret Wilkinson were married in the fall. Frank had failed to get the Rhodes or the IODE but had been awarded a two-year research scholarship to work for an MA degree at the University of Toronto. Tom and Bessie were the only other Pickersgills left in Winnipeg.

Tom and Margaret were married on 14 November 1936. They had a small apartment near ours, and we saw them often. Bessie arranged to dine with us whenever she had no engagement; in exchange she contributed a little to our meagre income.

Bea fitted well into the academic community and readily enough found other activities beyond housekeeping. One friend we frequently saw was Margaret Beattie. She and Bea had been close friends from childhood, had walked to school together every day for years and had been at the university at the same time.

My interests in politics grew that year. Stuart Garson became provincial treasurer. I became more concerned than ever about provincial financing and federal-provincial relations, particularly during and after the federal government, at Garson's request, sent Sandy Skelton, John Deutsch and Bob Beattie of the Bank of Canada to examine the provincial financial situation and advise both governments. That undertaking was the origin of the long preoccupation of Canadian politics with federal-provincial financial and constitutional relations, which culminated 20 years later in the process of equalization now embodied in the Constitution.

I saw Skelton, Deutsch and Beattie two or three times while

they were in Winnipeg. Beattie had been married in January 1937 and had been obliged to cut short his honeymoon to come to Winnipeg. He had dinner with Bea and me one evening, the first time we had seen him since he was best man at our wedding. My admiration for his superb intellect increased, as it did with every meeting during the rest of his life.

We looked forward to my continuing in academic life indefinitely. But I soon discovered that two could not live as cheaply as one, and that there seemed to be no prospect of any improvement in academic salaries, even though by 1936 there had been a little recovery in the economy since the depths of the depression. But I might not have taken a step to improve my situation if a friend had not urged me strongly to write the civil service examinations for entry into the Department of External Affairs. All the papers, except the essay, were on subjects I was teaching. I could obviously choose an essay topic I knew something about. The examinations were on 14 and 15 October 1936. I did not find them difficult and felt I had done reasonably well. I heard nothing about them for many months and settled into the routine of the academic year. I still loved teaching and had no real desire to do anything different.

I felt I should get at some new research in the summer of 1937 and decided on a study of the recent general election in France. Bea was keen about a possible visit to Europe, and we began to work out the means to get there. I applied to the American Social Science Research Council for a research grant and received one of $500. We sold the car and a few bonds Bea had. Word came that I had passed the written examinations for External Affairs and must be in Ottawa for the oral exam late in April. That meant leaving Winnipeg before the university examinations were completed. It was arranged that Bea would do my share of supervision. My colleagues in the history department generously agreed to read my share of the examination papers as well as their own.

Most of my few days in Ottawa I spent with Bob Beattie, who gave me moral support. I found the oral no apparent strain and felt I was making a fair impression especially as one of the examiners, Laurent Beaudry, the assistant under-secretary, asked me a number of questions in French to which luckily I had ready answers. When I left the room I suddenly went limp and could barely walk. Evidently the tension had been far greater than I had realized.

As we would be away from Canada all summer, I wanted to know whether on our return I would be going back to teaching in Winnipeg or to a new job in Ottawa. Fortunately, J.H. Stitt, one of the civil service commissioners, and a friend from National Club days in Winnipeg, was one of the examiners. When I confided my anxiety to him, he told me in confidence that I would be appointed to the department, but that the formalities would be delayed because O.D. Skelton, the under-secretary, was going off to London with Mackenzie King for the coronation of George VI and the imperial conference. I decided not to worry, and met Bea in Toronto. We reached New York on 1 May and sailed the next day.

On to Ottawa

Europe and Ottawa

Bea and I had booked third-class passages on the Italian liner *Saturnia*, which sailed from New York on 2 May and was due in Venice, after many stops, on 16 May. We could afford to travel on the *Saturnia* because the transatlantic service was so competitive that Canadian Pacific could sell us a ticket to Venice and give us a railway ticket from Turin to Southampton and a return on the *Empress of Britain* for about $20 more than a straight return from Montreal to England. The railway journey was supposed to be taken without stopovers, but the CP agent in Winnipeg found a way to arrange stopovers for us in both Paris and London. For the additional $20 we had an extra week on board ship, a free railway journey from Italy to England that gave us a chance to do a tour of Italy before settling down in Paris for the summer's work on my research grant, and a holiday in England.

Apart from seasickness on the overnight trip from New York to Boston, the voyage was a delight. We went ashore in the Azores and at Lisbon, Gibraltar, Algiers, Palermo, Naples, and Patras and sailed up the Gulf of Cattaro, on the Adriatic coast, before landing at Venice in glorious morning sunshine. Our Italian tour included Rimini, San Marino, Assisi, Sienna, Rome, Florence, Rapallo and Milan. We reached Paris on 3 June and the same day found a two-room furnished flat with a kitchen in a slum in the rue Thouin, behind the Panthéon. I set to work at once and through June and most of July worked conscientiously until the project was completed.

There were distractions. We were at the Canadian Pavilion of the International Exposition on 1 July when Mackenzie King made the opening speech, a few days after his notorious visit to Hitler. The speech caused a good deal of controversy at home based on conflicting reports as to what he had said. According to one press report he had said that Canada would fight if the existence of Britain was at stake, and according to another, if freedom was at stake. I had noticed that freedom was the word he used. I knew that even the correct statement would get a mixed reception at home.

I had a small part at an international conference in Paris as a representative of the Canadian Institute of International Affairs. Edgar Tarr of Winnipeg was head of the Canadian delegation at the conference, and there, for the first time, I met John Baldwin, who had just completed his Rhodes scholarship at Oxford. I liked him at once but could not have guessed how much our careers would be linked.

Bea and I had two or three small parties in our apartment for visiting Canadians and one or two Parisians I knew. Helen Magill was in Europe; she came over from London to stay with us for a week or two in July and accompanied us on a short expedition to visit the châteaux of the Loire. Our most frequent visitor was Paul de France, who was in Paris in June as a student. We saw him again at the end of July, when we visited his parents for 24 hours at the Château d'Arry while on our way to England.

We spent three weeks in England before sailing home. In London, like most Canadian transients, we used Canada House as our postal address. Ross McLean, Vincent Massey's secretary, was very helpful. One day he introduced me to Lester B. Pearson, who was number three in the high commissioner's office. Mike already knew I had been a successful candidate for External Affairs and told me a little about the scope of the work. I had never met him before, and my first impression was very favourable.

We visited the Gerald Manders at Wolverhampton, and shortly before sailing we hired a car for a week. Helen Magill shared our tour and expenses. We spent a couple of days in Montgomeryshire with the Buckley-Joneses, who at my suggestion also invited Helen. While we were there, Mrs Jones invited Senator Rupert Davies and his son, Robertson, to tea one afternoon. Robertson was then at Oxford and an obvious aesthete. I was more interested in his father, who knew 'Mitch' Hepburn well and entertained me with stories about behind-the-scenes Ontario politics. Rupert Davies was a native of Montgomeryshire and had recently bought a country house near his birthplace.

We landed in Montreal on 28 August with barely enough money left to get us home to Winnipeg. By almost incredible restraint we had managed to make the whole trip and live for four months for a total cost of $1105.55. From Montreal Bea went direct to Toronto to stay with her aunts; I went to Ottawa to find out about my job. I called on the under-secretary, who told me that the college had been in touch with him and that he had told Dr J.H. Riddell, the president, to find a successor for me, as I would be appointed to External Affairs on my return from Europe. I thought I might have been consulted but was not dissatisfied with the decision.

I explained to Skelton that I would have no income after 31 August but would have to return to Winnipeg to pack up our furniture and close the apartment. After spending the winter in Florida Mother had returned to Winnipeg to occupy our apartment. She was already planning to go to Port Rowan for a visit and later to winter in Florida again. I told Skelton we could probably get along without going into debt if I was appointed by the end of September, but would be willing to come earlier. He promised to write to me in Winnipeg, and I went off to join Bea in Toronto.

By great good fortune one of Bea's aunts, Dorothy Wright, who lived in New York, was in Toronto on holidays and offered Bea and me a free ride to Winnipeg and back. In Winnipeg we packed up our furniture and other possessions and shipped them to Ottawa. Dr and Mrs Riddell had a farewell party for us at their home, and the college gave us a watercolour by W.J. Phillips which I still treasure. There had been no letter from Skelton, and I was beginning to feel uneasy.

When we reached Toronto, Bea decided to stay with her aunts while I went to Ottawa. Dorothy was to return to New York through the Adirondacks and drove me as far as the first ferry across the St Lawrence. I hitchhiked from there to Brockville, where I tried to get another lift to Ottawa but ended up taking the train. The next day I called at Skelton's office to learn that he had been seriously ill for several weeks and could not be disturbed with minor matters such as the employment of a penniless third secretary.

I saw Jimmy Stitt at the Civil Service Commission, who told me it would not be easy to have an appointment made until Skelton could authorize it. He offered me shelter, however, at their summer home at Aylmer, which in those days was reached by the Hull Street Railway from its terminal below Wellington Street, beside the Rideau Canal. I spent several days there, but it became very cold. I had no money to buy a top coat and no way of heating the cottage.

I consulted Norman Robertson of External Affairs, who could do nothing about the appointment but assured me it would not be delayed very long. He generously offered to lend me some money, an offer I declined, and advised me to look for an apartment. Meanwhile I took a room on Cooper Street by the day and without difficulty persuaded Bea to join me. Thanks to Bob Beattie, who lent us his car, we soon found an apartment, on Oak Hill off Beechwood in Rockcliffe, in a building that had been Harry Southam's old stables. The stables had been converted into four apartments and had the advantage of being less than 100 feet from a stop on the Lindenlea streetcar line.

Nearly 10 days in October had elapsed, and still there was no sign of Skelton. Finally Stitt called Beaudry, the acting under-secretary, and told him he had heard the prime minister was disturbed about the delay in making new appointments — which I believe was stretching the truth. On 13 October, I received word to report to the East Block for work the next morning. That date, 14 October, was precisely one year after the examination — an indication of the pace at which government moved in those prewar years. The fourteenth of October 1937 was the end of the only period of unemployment in my life. It was a month or two before we recovered from the six weeks without income.

To give some idea of the finances of junior academics and of public servants on probation, I have looked at my income tax returns for 1936 and 1937. For 1936 my gross income was $2185 on which my federal and provincial taxes were $61.98. For 1937 my gross income was only $1720.32 because of the six weeks of unemployment. I paid no federal or Ontario tax, but the Mani-toba wage tax was $24.60. That income was supplemented by the research grant of $500 and the proceeds of the sale of the car and Bea's bonds, but the total could not have been much greater than $2600. On that we had been from Winnipeg to Europe for four months and then back to Winnipeg to pack and ship our furniture to Ottawa. We had found and rented an apartment before I was actually appointed to External Affairs. The first instalment of my $2280-a-year salary came none too soon. The appointment was on probation, but I had no fear that it would not be confirmed. I still feel it was a tribute to our Manitoba thrift and our good health that we had survived financially on that income.

External Affairs

When I joined the Department of External Affairs I had only the haziest ideas of its functions and almost no knowledge of its structure. The prime minister was also the secretary of state for external affairs. I soon learned he did not concern himself with the administration of the department, which he left entirely to Skelton, the under-secretary. Skelton also supervised the administration of the Prime Minister's Office. The functions of the Privy Council Office were purely formal, concerned only with the handling of orders-in-council and other official documents. Mackenzie King consulted Skelton about every problem of government, domestic as well as external. Skelton felt free to involve senior officers of External in dealing with any problem on which he felt they could provide informed or expert assistance.

The number of senior officials was small, and within a month or so I not only knew all of those who were in Ottawa but had friendly relations with most. Laurent Beaudry, the assistant under-secretary, was in charge of the department when I started work. I never worked closely with him, but we had established a genuine rapport during my oral examination. He was a man of great charm and unfailing courtesy but was not an expert in any particular field. Third in command was John Read, the legal advisor. He was a learned legal scholar who had been dean of the Dalhousie law school. I soon realized that though he was apparently austere and even stern at times, he was basically a teacher always ready to guide an interested pupil.

Next in the hierarchy was Loring Christie. Like John Read, Christie was a Nova Scotian and a lawyer, but his career had been very different. As a young man fresh from Harvard, he had been secretary to Prime Minister Borden, throughout the First World War. He had continued in External Affairs while Meighen was prime minister and had served for a short time under Mackenzie King. He left because King, regarding him as a Tory, never trusted him. Christie had returned to the department near the end of the period when Bennett was prime minister. There was initially some concern on Mackenzie King's part about retaining Christie, but Skelton was able to overcome his reluctance and soon convinced the prime minister of Christie's value. By good fortune I performed my first research task under Christie's supervision. I shared his outlook on Canada's place in the world and was eager to learn about his experiences in Borden's wartime government.

We soon became fast friends. During my first two years in Ottawa I learned more from Christie than from anyone else.

At the next level in Ottawa were Hugh Keenleyside, Scott Macdonald and Norman Robertson, all three first secretaries. Keenleyside I had met in late 1936 when he spoke at an Institute meeting in Winnipeg, soon after I had written the examinations. He was recently home from serving in the legation in Japan, and his performance that evening impressed me. I had an encouraging talk with him after the meeting. He and his wife were very kind to us when we first arrived in Ottawa. Though we rarely worked on the same problems, my relations with Keenleyside remained friendly as long as he served in Ottawa.

Scott Macdonald, a war veteran, had been a civil servant in another department before entering External Affairs through a competitive examination. He had in some ways a more typical civil service attitude than did other diplomatic officers. He also had some of the quirks of the largely self-educated person, and an original outlook on many questions. He was helpful at the outset in explaining the routines of the department, sometimes with a touch of cynicism. One of the main tasks of novice third secretaries was to decode routine telegrams, most of them from the Dominions Office in London. Macdonald advised me never to decode the daily batch of telegrams until I had first read the *New York Times*, assuring me I would find most of their contents in that paper. It was good advice, not because it really helped with the telegrams, but because it made me realize that the *New York Times* was essential reading for a would-be diplomat.

Scott Macdonald and his wife, Ruth, were lifelong friends, though our paths seldom crossed after the outbreak of the war in 1939. He was serving in the legation in Paris before the fall of France in 1940, and I never ceased to be grateful for his many kindnesses to my brother Frank. Macdonald was ambassador in Vienna when I was there about the Hungarian refugee emergency in 1956; it was my only direct contact with him during his service abroad.

Norman Robertson was younger than Macdonald and Keenleyside and only a year and a half older than I. But he had already begun to have a reputation for brilliance and wisdom, and it would increase with the years. Though I had first met him only when I came to Ottawa for my oral, and though I saw little of him while he was away in Washington during most of my first year, our lives were to be mixed up together as long as he lived. He was one of a few friends with whom communication was almost total. We could pick up conversations on specific matters after months of interruption, and go right on from the point where we had left off. My admiration and affection for Norman grew steadily with time.

There were only two of the junior foreign service officers at Ottawa in 1937, H.F. (Temp) Feaver, also a lawyer and a Nova Scotian, and Léon Mayrand, a Montrealer who had come into the department in the promotion of 1934, the last one before my own. Temp and I soon became friendly, but our relations were primarily social. Mayrand and I became close friends in the next year or so, before he was posted abroad. He introduced me to the small circle of French Canadians in Ottawa with intellectual and artistic interests. We had frequent discussions of the relations between English- and French-speaking Canadians that helped to fill many gaps in my understanding of the country.

I recall one occasion, quite soon after I started to work in the department, when I expressed surprise that there were so few French Canadians in senior posts in Ottawa. Mayrand asked me how well I could work and how happy I would be if I had to write all my memoranda and other documents in French and communicate with most of my fellow workers in a language that was not my own. The question had never occurred to me before. In a flash I realized the disability under which one-third of the population had to operate if they wished to be successful in the public service of their own country. I could read French practically as easily as I could English and could understand most spoken French and make myself understood, but I was not fluent. As for writing in the language, the result was laboured, unidiomatic and slow to be produced. Even before coming to Ottawa I had been convinced that Canadians could not have a good future until most learned to treat English- and French-speaking Canadians as equals and the two languages with equal respect. But the practical problem of equality at work was new to me. I resolved that very day to do whatever I could to help solve it. I like to believe that when I retired from the public service 35 years later, I had kept that resolution.

As well as External Affairs, the East Block on Parliament Hill at that time housed the Cabinet Chamber, the Privy Council Office, the Prime Minister's Office, a small suite of rooms for the govenor general, the Department of Finance and the gold reserve. The government of Canada had not yet become big business.

In 1937, in addition to the office of the Canadian high commissioner in London, which dated from the 19th century, Canada had diplomatic missions only in the United States, France and Japan and an office at the headquarters of the League of Nations in Geneva. We accordingly depended mainly on the British government for official information about the rest of the world.

The work of a junior officer in External Affairs at that time was not onerous. We were left to ripen, half-forgotten, in the attic of the East Block. We were expected to be in our offices by 10 a.m. and not to leave before 4 p.m., with generous time off for lunch. The one regular task we all shared was the decoding of routine telegrams. Most of those were from the Dominions Office in London, which passed on as much of the reports from Britain's world-wide diplomatic service as it felt would be useful to Canada.

In addition to decoding, each third secretary from time to time was assigned specific tasks by senior officers. I recall very few of the tasks I was called on to perform. I made a summary of the information about a subsidized steamship service between Canada and New Zealand, which, I concluded, was not worth the cost. The service was later suspended and never resumed. I was also asked to study the file about a protest made by Senator William Duff of Lunenburg, who had been charged duty on his ships' stores by Newfoundland customs because one of his schooners had stayed too long in St John's on the way to the Labrador coast. I recall meeting the senator in the Parliament Building, introducing myself and asking him why a schooner needed only one roll of toilet paper for the summer voyage to Labrador. He explained graphically and then asserted in a loud voice that none of us in External Affairs was any damned good 'from Skelton right down to you.' He added that as a Liberal and a free trader he did not believe in customs duties.

As I had received the highest marks in the examinations, I was the first new secretary appointed in 1937. Max Wershof was appointed about a month later, and Jean Chapdelaine in December. Chapdelaine was assigned the other desk in the room I was in and a day or two afterwards came to our apartment for dinner. We quickly became close friends, though we shared the office for barely a week.

One morning in mid-December Read, who was Acting undersecretary, appeared at the door of our room. Chapdelaine was out, and I was alone. Read looked at me sternly and said, 'You are sacked; you are fired.' I was shocked but said nothing. During the brief silence that followed I asked myself what dreadful offence I might have committed to warrant such drastic action. I consoled myself with the reflection that if I was going to fire someone, I would not go to his room but summon him to mine. When he realized he had produced no visible effect, Read explained that he had just received a telephone call from Skelton, who was staying in Florida with Mackenzie King. Skelton directed him to assign me to the Prime Minister's Office on loan. I was to go there the next morning and report to Edward Pickering, the assistant private secretary, who would be supervising my work. I must have appeared unenthusiastic because Read hastened to assure me that the assignment would not interfere with my career. He predicted that I would not last more than six months in the Prime Minister's Office, because nobody else from External had.

Read explained that I was to replace Norman Robertson, who had been seconded to the Prime Minister's Office only a month before. Skelton wanted Norman back in the department and had persuaded Mackenzie King that it was essential that Robertson go to Washington to assist in negotiating a revision and expansion of the 1935 trade agreement with the United States. The prime minister had agreed, but only if another officer from External replaced Robertson, and Skelton had offered me.

I had never met the prime minister, and he had never seen me to identify me. I had mixed feelings. I was really more interested in politics than diplomacy and felt it might be interesting to find out at first hand how a prime minister performed. But I expected to spend the rest of my life in the diplomatic service and could not see how such an assignment would help me to become proficient in my career. The idea of objecting never occurred to me. The depression was still on, and there was no bargaining about the terms of employment. I had no idea that after only two months my diplomatic career had terminated forever, much less that I would still be in the Prime Minister's Office when Mackenzie King retired 11 years later.

Bea's death

By mid December Bea and I had settled down to a pleasant, if not very exciting, life in Ottawa. In addition to the circle of members of the department and their wives, we began with a small circle of friends: Bob Beattie and his wife, Kay; Clare Dudley, a Winnipeg friend of Bea's, and her husband, Jim, who was in the National Housing Administration; Swotty Wotherspoon, with whom I had travelled in Europe in 1933, and who was practising law in Ottawa, and his wife, Enid; and Ross Tolmie and his wife, Hélène. I had met Ross once or twice in Oxford and once in Winnipeg when he was staying with Jim Coyne while on his way to Ottawa to a legal position in the income tax department. All of them were to remain friends of mine.

At Christmas my brother Frank, who was at the University of Toronto as a postgraduate student, came to spend the holiday with us. Jim Coyne was in Ottawa before joining the staff of the Bank of Canada in the new year. Bea and I had encountered Jim in London in August, and he had taken us to dinner at Simpson's in the Strand. We were happy to reciprocate by having him to dinner on Christmas Day.

Bea had decided to learn to ski and had bought a new pair of boots. Early in January one of the boots rubbed her heel and broke the skin, but the scratch did not seem at all serious. On Thursday 13 January she began to feel unwell and feverish. We had not yet needed a doctor and did not even have a thermometer. As the fever continued on Friday, I telephoned Hélène Tolmie for advice. She walked with her baby daughter, Anne, the mile from the Tolmies' apartment to ours to bring her thermometer. Ross telephoned his friend Dr Plunkett, who saw Bea. The doctor thought she had a bad case of flu. When she became delirious on Saturday night and was still delirious on Sunday morning, I was seriously alarmed and got in touch with the doctor, who agreed to come to the house. He did not arrive until mid-afternoon but promptly called an ambulance and moved Bea to the Civic Hospital. She never regained consciousness, and on Monday 17 January, at about 6 p.m. she died.

I was numb with shock. I telephoned Dr Young at once and we quickly decided that the funeral should be in Winnipeg, and that Bea should be buried beside her mother in the family plot at Kildonan Cemetery. When I called Mother in Florida she offered to come to Ottawa at once, but I suggested she wait and come to spend the summer with me.

The train arrived in Winnipeg early in the morning of 20 January, a bitterly cold day. The funeral, at St Stephens—Broadway Church, was conducted by the minister, Dr Woodside, and by Professor King, who had married us only 18 months before. The icy north wind that day at Kildonan Cemetery fitted my spirit. I have never ceased to be thankful that Bea and I pushed our resources to the very limit to make the most of our short life together.

The morning after Bea's death I received a telegram from Winnipeg from Coyne, who was on the point of moving to Ottawa, inviting me to share his apartment with him. I accepted his offer at once as I did not want to go on living alone in an apartment full of memories. No brother could have been kinder or more thoughtful than Jim was during those months in 1938, from January until May, when Mother came from Florida and I moved with her into my own apartment for the summer. Jim and I decided to take a larger apartment on the ground floor of the Mayfair at the beginning of October. We lived there until June 1939. Not only did we survive that test of our friendship, our friendship grew steadily closer. Nothing I could ever do could repay Jim for the help and understanding he gave me during the hardest months of my life.

4 In the Prime Minister's Office

The scope of the government of Canada in 1937

Half a century later it is hard to realize how limited the scope of the federal government was before the Second World War, and how few ministers and senior officials were concerned with more than routine administration. There was at least one minister in the federal cabinet from every province, though from time to time the minister from Prince Edward Island was in fact from another province. Some ministers were little more than reporters on the political weather in their province or region.

After 1935, when Mackenzie King returned to office, the two ministers with the greatest influence and prestige were Ernest Lapointe, the minister of justice, and Charles A. Dunning, the minister of finance. Lapointe was in all but name the deputy prime minister; his position as first lieutenant did not depend on the portfolio he held. Lapointe's primacy was due to his position as the leading spokesman of French Canada in Parliament, the affection he inspired in the Liberal caucus, the respect accorded him by MPs of all parties and, above all, the high degree of confidence the prime minister had in him.

Dunning did not owe his prestige to the prime minister's affection, but to his reputation in financial circles. His health was already impaired in 1937. For nearly a year before the war he was absent from his office, and J.L. Ilsley, the minister of national revenue, was acting minister. I cannot remember how I came to meet Ilsley, but I quickly formed a great respect for his mind. In 1938 we occasionally went for walks together and discussed public affairs. My admiration for him grew steadily with the years.

The functions of the Department of Finance were relatively narrow before the war. The primary duties of the minister were to recommend to Parliament the level of taxation, to keep down expenditures and to balance the budget. Through the customs tariff Finance provided protection for some Canadian industries. No attempt was made to influence the economy through fiscal policy, and almost none through monetary policy. Indeed, monetary policy did not really exist before the Bank of Canada was established in 1934.

Next to O.D. Skelton, the under-secretary of state for external affairs, W.C. Clark, the deputy minister of Finance, was the most influential public servant. He and Skelton had been mainly responsible for persuading Prime Minister Bennett to have the Bank of Canada established. In its early stages the Bank was what would later have been called a think tank. Clark was almost a think tank in himself, and Skelton the prime minister's main adviser on the whole range of government activity.

Though depression and prairie drought had generated massive unemployment and widespread penury, there was no federal welfare department. Old age pensions of $20 a month were paid by the provincial governments to paupers over 70, and to those pensions the federal treasury made a 75-percent contribution. The total federal budget was a half billion dollars a year, including grants to provincial governments to assist in the relief of the unemployed and of destitute farmers in the prairies.

The federal government had the responsibility for external relations and for the defence of the country. The prime minister was the secretary of state for external affairs, but the Prime Minister's Office had no role in external affairs. Mackenzie King dealt direct with Skelton. Their primary concern was to try to see that Britain did not drag Canada into another European war and, above all, to avoid having another Canadian expeditionary force.

Defence policy, to the extent that one existed, was rudimentary and unrealistic. In 1939 one of the strategic plans still in the files of the Department of National Defence dealt with the means of resisting invasion from the United States. Once the country had dismantled its military machine after the First World War, the defence forces were negligible, and their equipment soon became obsolete. Bennett's Conservative government had even abolished the air force. Though the air force had been restored by Mackenzie King, and there were minor increases in expenditures for defence, Canada did not, in 1937, have 10,000 men permanently under arms in all three services. Ian Mackenzie, the defence minister, took almost no interest in the department.

The Department of Pensions and National Health was an out-growth of the First World War. In 1937 there were still many pensioners, several veterans' hospitals and active public support for the welfare of veterans. There was no national health service except for veterans, and no unemployment insurance. There were no federal welfare services of any kind. The minister of pensions and national health, C.G. (Chubby) Power, was a political organ-izer of high and deserved reputation and a genuine small-*l* liberal in a philosophical sense. He had negligible administrative duties until war came.

The traditional departments were the Post Office and Public Works. The Post Office was more efficient then than it is today. Canada was about to become a pioneer in the development of air mail. The public works department was notoriously inefficient. Its main function was to build public buildings, wharves and break-waters in the right constituencies and to employ the right contrac-tors. Its total expenditures were small.

Once the Judicial Committee of the British Privy Council, which was still the final court of appeal for Canada, had decided that the words 'trade and commerce' in the BNA Act did not have their dictionary meaning, the Department of Trade and Com-

merce had little to do except take the decennial census, advertise
Canadian bacon in Britain and try to sell wheat. The Bennett
government had made wheat marketing a public function, a
difficult task during a world depression.

The minister of mines and resources had a grab-bag department with an odd name, since the provincial legislatures had
jurisdiction over mines and most other resources. But the minister
did administer the national parks and had jurisdiction over Indians and immigration. Since we pretended the Indians did not
exist and there was no immigration in the 1930s, he was not very
busy.

The really dynamic departments in 1937 were Transport, Labour and Agriculture, with slight signs of activity in the relatively
new separate Department of Fisheries. C.D. Howe, still a novice in
public life, was the minister of transport. He had a large program:
reorganizing the administrative structure of Canadian National
Railways and establishing the Canadian Broadcasting Corporation, the National Harbours Board and a national air line. Entirely
without ideology, Howe, while greatly expanding public ownership, would have repudiated any suggestion that he was Canada's
first practising socialist. Norman Rogers, the minister of labour,
an intelligent and imaginative man, was almost overwhelmed by
the great volume of unemployment and discouraged because
most of his colleagues, including the prime minister, still considered unemployment primarily a provincial responsibility.
Mackenzie King's government had no choice but to continue
Bennett's policy of sharing the financial burden of relief for
unemployment, which was administered by provincial and municipal governments. The one positive initiative of the federal
government was to seek the agreement of the provincial governments to a constitutional amendment to permit a national system
of unemployment insurance. Agreement was not achieved until
1940. The minister of agriculture, James G. Gardiner, was struggling manfully to restore the economy of the prairies, ravaged by
depression and drought, and, through Prairie Farm Rehabilitation
to lay the foundations for a better future.

So in 1937 Canada was still plagued by unemployment of manpower and resources, with little but local welfare to relieve poverty and want. The government of Canada had no part in education, health care or road-building, and apart from efforts to stimulate international trade, almost no constructive policy to stimulate the economy. Many of the ministers and the prime minister realized there was widespread discontent, but most of them believed there was little that government, especially the federal government, could do to end what the political mavericks of that day denounced as 'poverty in the midst of plenty.' There was plenty of worry but little real work in carrying on government.

The Prime Minister's Office before the war

The limited scope of government was reflected in the limited and simple structure of the Prime Minister's Office.

When I reported for duty in mid-December 1937, the nominal head of the Prime Minster's Office was the private secretary, H.R.L. Henry. The most influential members of the staff were Edward Pickering, Walter Turnbull and Édouard Handy. Of them, only Pickering, the assistant private secretary, was on the office payroll. Turnbull had been seconded from the post office department, and Handy from another government agency. Neither had any formal rank or title.

The French language was almost totally ignored. Except for one stenographer, Handy was the sole French-speaking member of the prime minister's staff, and he had no regular contact with the public. He served devotedly as Mackenzie King's personal secretary until King's death in 1950. Among other duties Handy recorded the greater part of the now-famous Mackenzie King diary in shorthand. Mackenzie King often failed to look at the diary as typed. Handy's office was at Laurier House, where the prime minister spent much of his time, except when Parliament was sitting. In the summer Mackenzie King lived at Kingsmere, and Handy usually joined him there, on weekdays, on many long evenings and even occasionally on Sundays.

It was some time before I discovered what Turnbull's duties were, and it would not have been easy to define them. When Parliament was in session, he spent every afternoon and some evenings in the prime minister's House of Commons office. One of his functions was to keep too many intruders, including members and even cabinet ministers, from taking up the time of the prime minister. Many visitors learned they could tell Turnbull what they wanted the prime minister to hear and be sure their message would be passed on. Turnbull was invaluable in gathering political information, much of it gossip, which facilitated the prime minister's management of Parliament. Turnbull often helped, by his advice to the prime minister, to determine parliamentary tactics. Mackenzie King valued his advice and trusted his discretion.

I had been directed to report to Pickering and undertake the duties he assigned to me. I soon discovered that Mackenzie King used Pickering as his normal channel of communication with the rest of the staff and with other departments of government. Pickering was expected to direct research into current problems and report his findings in memoranda suggesting lines of action and occasionally offering advice on policy. He was also expected to gather material to help the prime minister in preparing speeches and often to submit first drafts of public announcements and speeches.

From the end of January 1938 Parliament was in session, and I immersed myself in assisting Pickering with all his activities. I had no contact whatever with the prime minister. My recollection is that he spoke to me only four times in the first six months I was on his staff. I was not quite sure whether he was aware of my existence, nor did I care. I soon had plenty of work to do, and I found it all interesting.

The first assignment I was given was to follow closely the proceedings of the Royal Commission on Dominion-Provincial Relations. The commission had been appointed in the summer of 1937. The first chairman was Chief Justice N.W. Rowell of Ontario, and the commission was usually referred to as the Rowell Commission. When Rowell resigned because of ill health, he was succeeded as chairman by the French-speaking commissioner, Joseph Sirois, and the commission thereafter was generally called the Rowell-Sirois Commission. The most dynamic member was J.W. Dafoe, the great editor of the *Winnipeg Free Press*. I had met Dafoe when I joined the Winnipeg branch of the Institute of International Affairs, of which he was chairman, and I became an admirer and later a friend. He had been a sponsor of my application to enter External Affairs. Dafoe was a close friend of Jim Coyne's father, and nearly every time Dafoe was in Ottawa he saw Jim and me, often for lunch, and gave us his views of the work of the commission and public affairs in general.

No assignment could have pleased me more than following the work of the Rowell-Sirois Commission. I brought with me from Winnipeg a deep interest in constitutional reform and in the financial relations between the provincial and federal governments. Living in Manitoba during the depression, I had realized that it was not possible to raise enough in provincial taxes to pay for basic provincial functions. Drastic change in federal and provincial financial responsibilities was essential.

The Rowell-Sirois Commission was responsible for the most extensive study ever undertaken of the Canadian economy in the broadest sense of that term, and it was exciting to have a ringside seat. But for the first three years I was in the Prime Minister's Office I do not recall a single request from Mackenzie King for information about the commission. Late in 1940, when its report was actually being considered by the government, I was probably as well informed about its work and its recommendations as anyone who had not actually participated in its activities.

I would have followed the commission's work closely whether or not I was paid to do it. Its hearings were well reported in the press. The academics and professionals who were doing important studies for the commission worked mainly in Ottawa. Coyne and I gradually got to know many of them. I had met John Deutsch in Winnipeg in 1937 and got to know him well when he was assistant secretary of the commission. Over the years, I learned a great deal from him about public finance and government.

My immediate work involved only one aspect of federal-provincial relations. On 5 November 1937 Mackenzie King had written to the provincial premiers seeking the approval of their governments and legislatures for an amendment to the BNA Act to give Parliament exclusive legislative jurisdiction over unemployment insurance. He undertook, if this authority were secured, to have unemployment insurance established. The letter to the premiers had been drafted by Loring Christie of External Affairs, but when the replies began to come in, I was entrusted with drafting the further correspondence. The task did not consume much time, but it taught me a good deal about the way the various premiers operated and about their attitudes to Ottawa and to Mackenzie King.

What took more of my time was a bitter controversy between Mackenzie King and Premier Hepburn of Ontario, who was seeking federal permission to have Ontario Hydro export power to the United States. The export of hydroelectric power had been expressly forbidden by an act of Parliament in 1907. Characteristically, Mackenzie King did not bluntly refuse to agree to Hepburn's proposal, but replied instead that no export could be permitted without the approval of Parliament. A stream of letters and public statements had to be drafted, legislation prepared for Parliament, and notes for speeches and comments on the legislation worked out for use by the prime minister. I became an expert on the subject and did what I thought was an excellent job of preparing alternative and mutually exclusive lines of argument in support of government policy. I was disconcerted when Mackenzie King indicated he intended to use both arguments. It was a challenge to reconcile the irreconcilable, but I did so by introducing a large dose of verbal obscurity. I never again offered Mackenzie King alternative arguments. In the end the issue petered out, and my arguments were never used.

During the first half of 1938 I began to realize that I was drafting most of the written material submitted to the prime minister, though it was always scrutinized carefully and frequently revised by Pickering. As I was to discover later, I had an unsuspected talent for drafting in a style Mackenzie King was comfortable with, though I rarely produced anything he did not revise.

In the late spring of 1938 Pickering resigned and he left the office on 1 July. The prime minister, who had been in Toronto for a day or two at the beginning of July, returned one day on the late afternoon train. Turnbull told me that the prime minister wanted to see me in his private car at the railway station before he went to Kingsmere. Turnbull warned me I would probably be asked to take on Pickering's work on a temporary basis and advised me strongly to accept. To my intense surprise Mackenzie King opened the interview by saying that he knew I had been doing most of the written work in the office, and that he had found it very helpful. He wanted me to take on Pickering's work until he could find a suitable successor.

He complained that in all the years he had been prime minister he had never had an adequate and competent staff or a suitable head of his office, but that at last he had high hopes of finding the ideal secretary. He was greatly attracted to the son of his old friend, Canon Bertal Heeney of Winnipeg, and he was going shortly to make a proposal to him. I had just missed meeting Arnold Heeney at the University of Manitoba. He had been selected as Rhodes scholar when I was a freshman, but had not returned from Oxford to live in Winnipeg. I knew a good deal about him and his family from common friends. As I had no ambition to stay in the Prime Minister's Office, I welcomed the prospect, which I thought might speed up my return to External Affairs.

For the next two months I was really in charge of the office. As it was summer and Parliament had risen at the beginning of July, there was not a great deal of work. I busied myself inquiring into the functions of every member of the staff and trying to improve the organization of the office, a task I found more to my liking than I had expected.

I also had my first experience of drafting a major speech for the prime minister. He and President Roosevelt were to meet to open the Thousand Islands Bridge across the St Lawrence at Ivy Lea. Mackenzie King was understandably keen to make a speech as good as Roosevelt's. We worked hard on the draft, through innumerable revisions. It was my initiation into a process that was to continue for another 10 years. From August 1938 until Mackenzie King retired as prime minister he almost never made a speech from a written text, with the exception of a few on external affairs that Skelton drafted, to which I did not make some contribution.

In late August Mackenzie King concluded his negotiations with Arnold Heeney, who wisely insisted on putting the terms of his employment as principal secretary into an exchange of correspondence. His having done so was to stand him in good stead on more than one occasion. When the deal was concluded, Mackenzie King brought Heeney to the East Block for a tour of the office. After introducing me he said, 'I will expect you to explain to Arnold what his duties are, and how I like material prepared for me.' I confess I thought it a trifle ironical that a probationary third secretary at $2280 a year was being directed to teach the new principal secretary with the princely salary of $7000 how to do his job.

Arnold at the time was secretary to the provincial Royal Commission on Protestant Education in Quebec. Mackenzie King agreed that Heeney could continue in that position on a part-time basis until the report of the commission was completed. When he took up his duties in September 1938, Arnold advised the staff that I would be his second-in-command and would act for him whenever he was absent. As a result I continued to have direct access to the prime minister, though on a less regular basis — a situation that had both pluses and minuses. Arnold and I worked together comfortably and happily from the first day. I do not recall a single instance of lack of harmony between us, though we certainly did not always agree about public issues or the best way to deal with problems. Arnold was to be one of my dearest friends for the rest of his life.

Rebuilding my own life

Developing outside interests

The Prime Minister's Office did not occupy all my time in 1938 and 1939. As spring approached in 1938, and I began to emerge from the numbing shock of Bea's death, I started to develop interest in activities outside my work. Every day we were both free, Jim Coyne and I had lunch together. He took the initiative in having others join us, and I began to make a few more friends. Next to Jim, the friend who was to have the most influence on my life before the war was Donald Buchanan.

Donald had a job with the CBC and soon aroused in me an active interest in public broadcasting. I had welcomed the first halting steps in public broadcasting by the Bennett government but paid little attention to the structure of the CBC when it was established by Parliament in 1936. Through Donald I came to know Alan Plaunt. He, with Graham Spry, led the campaign for a public broadcasting system modelled on the BBC. Plaunt had advised the government about the structure of the new CBC and became a member of its board of directors. I shared his conviction that there should be rigid safeguards against public broadcasting becoming a propaganda tool of the government in office. That has remained a prime concern for me.

Donald's job with the CBC was to organize broadcasts on public affairs. The CBC had a rule that both sides of an issue should be presented in such broadcasts. He discussed themes for confrontations with me. One broadcast I remember well. The president of Canadian Pacific, Sir Edward Beatty, was an advocate of a private railway monopoly. I had got to know R.J. Deachman, the MP for Huron, an old-fashioned laisser-faire liberal and a strong believer in competition. At my suggestion Donald got Deachman to debate with Beatty. Deachman was so effective that Beatty asked for extra time in which to reply. I felt reassured when the CBC showed no hesitation in turning down his request. Plaunt and his wife, Bobby, became friends of mine. Through them I met Gladstone Murray, the CBC president, a useful acquaintance but never a friend.

Donald's interests extended far beyond broadcasting. Canadian painting was his greatest love. In Winnipeg I had first become aware of the Group of Seven. Through Bernard Radley, my hog-train friend who had settled in Toronto, I met a circle of artists, friends of his, including two women sculptors, Florence Wyle and Frances Loring, whose work I admired. But it was Donald who introduced me to the whole range of Canadian painting. Through Donald I met Pegi Nicol, Carl Shaeffer and A.Y. Jackson. The Plaunts had a Lawren Harris sketch of the shore of Lake Superior hanging in their living room. On my first visit I could not take my eyes off that sketch. Years later, when Bobby was away for the summer, she lent it to us. That fall I told her I could not live without it, and she sold it to me for $100. The Lawren Harris has remained one of our treasures. In the 1950s, when I was the minister responsible for the National Gallery, I met Harris and persuaded him to become a member of the Board. In my eyes Lawren Harris is the greatest of Canadian painters.

Jim and I became members of the Ottawa branch of the Canadian Institute of International Affairs. The atmosphere in the Ottawa branch was different from that in the Winnipeg branch; there was less candour in the discussions and, we were to learn, much less respect for confidentiality. After one meeting, when Jim and I had expressed ourselves freely in response to opinions of senior and more conservative members, we were summoned to meet the executive. A senior member had complained that he had encountered several nonmembers who expressed shock at the kind of discussions they heard were going on at the institute. It was clear that that member of the executive wanted us to be disciplined. I reminded him that our meetings were confidential and pointed out that anyone who was not a member could have heard about our discussions only from a member who had not respected that confidentiality. I suggested that at the next meeting members be reminded that our discussions were strictly confidential. My response might not have had much effect had it not been supported warmly and eloquently by Mr Justice George Sedgwick, then chairman of the Tariff Board. Before his appointment to the bench Judge Sedgwick had been an active, partisan Conservative. But he demonstrated to me that day that he knew what freedom meant. Later Jim and I were invited to the Sedgwicks' for dinner. There I met their daughter, Anne, for whose intelligence and knowledge I developed an admiration that has been lifelong.

In the early summer there was a family reunion. Mother arrived from Florida at the beginning of May, and I moved back to the apartment on Oak Hill for the summer. Bessie came from Winnipeg for a holiday in late May and early June, and Walter joined her on the train at Fort William. Frank had completed his second year in Toronto and received his MA in May. He had not been able to find a job. I was able to lend him some money, and he decided to go to France in June to continue his education. Before he left, Mother got word that Dr Annie Backus was very ill and likely to die soon. She went to Port Rowan to care for her and was still there when Frank left for Europe. None of us dreamed we would never see him again.

Mother returned to Ottawa after Dr Annie's death, and we had a happy summer together. Buchanan, who was to be absent for the summer, lent me his car, and we made many pleasant excursions. One excursion was to the St Lawrence to look at the new Thousand Islands Bridge, which Roosevelt and Mackenzie King were to open officially soon afterwards. I felt some local colour might help me with my draft of the prime minister's speech. We hired a boat and were rowed under the bridge among the islands in what seemed like a fairy land. I submitted the first expense account of my career, 50 cents for hire of the boat, to Agnes McCloskey, the External Affairs accountant, who also kept the accounts of the Prime Minister's Office. She was an unmarried woman, often a lot of fun, but she did not think expense accounts funny and jealously guarded the public purse. She 'was not amused' by my frivolous claim, but grimaced and paid.

Tom and Margaret came east for a brief visit to Ottawa and New York. They went from New York to Philadelphia to see Mother off on the ship that in mid-September was to take her through the Panama Canal to winter in southern California.

The lease of my Rockcliffe apartment expired at the end of September, and I moved back with Coyne into a more commodious apartment at the Mayfair. In addition to a kitchen and two comfortable bedrooms it had a living room extending the whole length of the apartment. It was ideal for modest hospitality, which we offered a good deal of during the next nine months.

Grant Dexter, the Ottawa correspondent of the *Winnipeg Free Press*, was an occasional guest and became a valued friend. On one occasion he brought his colleague and closest friend, Bruce Hutchison of Victoria. I had listened with pleasure to Bruce's broadcasts on the CBC about a mythical place he called Scrub Oak Hollow. From that first meeting I felt he was a kindred spirit. Until his death in 1992, Bruce was a cherished friend.

My contact with French Canadians in Ottawa, which began with Laurent Beaudry, and Léon Mayrand, expanded when Mayrand introduced me to Léopold Richer, who was in the parliamentary press gallery for *Le Devoir*, which I read every day. I had frequent political discussions with Richer. While still in Winnipeg I had developed a growing interest in French-Canadian nationalism in Quebec. I was repelled by the position of the extreme nationalists but greatly attracted by the views of Henri Bourassa in his later years, as expressed in Parliament during the Bennett regime. I regretted his defeat in the election of 1935. The most interesting new friends I made among French Canadians were Jules Léger and his wife, Gaby. Jules was Jean Chapdelaine's closest friend. Jean introduced me to Jules, who had recently joined the editorial staff of the newspaper *Le Droit*. In 1940 Jules was to become a secretary in the Prime Minister's Office. Those early months in Ottawa confirmed my view that the future of Canada depended upon mutual respect on both sides for the equal status of the English and French languages.

Margaret Beattie

The most important thing that happened to me in the summer of 1938 was Margaret Beattie's visit to Ottawa. She came there to visit her brother Bob and his wife, Kay. Margaret had been

J.W.P. married Mary Margaret Beattie June 23, 1939 in Ottawa. Left to right J.W.P.'s mother, Margaret, J.W.P. and Margaret's mother.

working on the editorial staff of the *Winnipeg Free Press* for four years. She returned to Winnipeg from Ottawa for the summer and then went to Toronto in September as private secretary to the headmaster of the Preparatory School of Upper Canada College. Once she was in Toronto we met nearly every weekend in either Toronto or Ottawa. By Christmas she had agreed to marry me as soon as the school year ended, and she could decently leave her new job. Our parents were present for our marriage, at St Bartholemew's Church in Ottawa on 23 June 1939, my 34th birthday and the anniversary of Margaret's parents' wedding 30 years earlier.

Shortly before we were married we bought a Chevrolet car and made plans to drive to the Lake of the Woods and Winnipeg for our honeymoon. We left Ottawa in mid-afternoon, after a wedding luncheon at the Bob Beatties for family and friends. Our trip took us to Algonquin Park, through Muskoka and along Georgian Bay to Tobermory, whence we crossed to Manitoulin Island and went on to Sault Ste Marie, Duluth, Fort Frances, Margaret's birthplace, and Kenora. We saw a lot of Canada we had never seen before, all of it beautiful. We spent part of our time at Highbrow, on the Lake of the Woods, and the rest of the time in Winnipeg.

Before we were married, we agreed to take over the Mayfair apartment early in the fall, once Jim was installed in a smaller apartment in the same building. Ross Tolmie's wife, Hélène, had gone to Vancouver for the summer. We arranged to occupy the Tolmies' apartment. Ross meanwhile would replace me in the Mayfair apartment with Jim. That summer was very hot, and we felt the heat acutely in the Tolmies' small apartment. We were grateful when Norman Robertson suggested that we move into their house in Rockcliffe, where there was more breeze and shade. Norman's wife, Jetty, had gone home to Holland for the summer, and Norman went to visit his parents in Vancouver. In mid-August, when war seemed imminent, Norman returned to Ottawa, and we stayed on with him until we moved to the Mayfair.

All that shifting around was hard on Margaret, who had to start keeping house in places not our own. She had little help from me because I was occupied fully in the daytime and often in the evenings as war approached and then broke out. So it was a great relief to get into our own place in the Mayfair, where we stayed until after Jane was born, 27 September 1941. We then found a house on the Russell Road, close to the Rideau River, at $35 a month. We could have bought the house for $3600 if we had had any hope of raising such a sum. One of the main attractions of the house was that the Tolmies lived in a fine old stone house next door. Our house was only two miles from Parliament Hill, but in Overbrook, not then part of Ottawa. We had no household mail delivery, and the post office was a quarter mile down the road. Though not without charm, the house was badly built. It was hard to heat, and the roof leaked, but we managed to survive there without real hardship for four years. One advantage was that the rent was frozen — just as well, as salaries were frozen too.

The view from the Prime Minister's Office

When the House of Commons was sitting, I was in the official gallery every day for the opening proceedings. I stayed during any debates in which the prime minister took part and often during others. I looked at Hansard every day and read everything likely to be useful as background. Such was to be my routine until June 1952. After I became secretary to the cabinet, I continued to follow Hansard but stopped going to the official gallery.

I knew a few MPs before the war started. J.T. Thorson and Ralph Maybank I had met several times in Winnipeg. I had marked my first federal ballot for Maybank in Winnipeg South Centre in 1935. I soon got to know W.G. (Gib) Weir, another MP from Manitoba. Bill Taylor, the member for my native county of Norfolk, I met occasionally, as he was chief Liberal whip. Walter Tucker, MP for Rosthern, Saskatchewan, a native of Manitoba, soon attracted my attention. In a different sense, so did Jean-François Pouliot, the clown of the House. One member I admired was Agnes MacPhail, the only woman elected to Parliament up to that time. Originally a Progressive, when the CCF was formed she became a member. J.S. Woodsworth, the CCF leader, and his daughter Belva were friends of Bessie's in Winnipeg. An older daughter, Grace, had been a contemporary of mine at the University of Manitoba. Through Grace I met her husband, Angus MacInnis, an MP from Vancouver. I became friendly with Grant MacNeill, another CCF member from Vancouver, a war veteran who like me thought Canada should not take part in another European war and unlike me expressed his opinion in public. MacNeill was defeated in the 1940 election by my Oxford friend Jimmy Sinclair.

I do not recall meeting any Tory MP before the war started. I watched Bennett, the former prime minister, and his surviving cabinet colleagues filled with frustration on the Opposition front bench. In 1938 Bennett resigned as party leader, and a Conservative convention held in Ottawa chose Robert Manion as his successor. Manion was a Catholic, and his wife was a French Canadian. The choice was designed to give the party an opening in the province of Quebec. The convention took place in Ottawa. On the night Manion was chosen I went to watch the proceedings from the back of the hall. The contest was bitter, and it was obvious then that an anglophone Protestant wing of the party, mainly from Ontario, would never be loyal to Manion.

The MPs I had most frequent contact with were the cabinet ministers, and the one I got to know best was Lapointe, who was acting prime minister whenever Mackenzie King was absent from Ottawa. I had known T.A. Crerar, the senior minister in precedence, in Winnipeg in my university days. Crerar took a mild and benevolent interest in me in Ottawa. Rogers, the minister of Labour, and I had many common academic friends. He had been in the Prime Minister's Office before 1930. Once we met, we quickly developed a rapport, and I admired him greatly. I have already referred to my acquaintance with Ilsley. I never met Dunning, the minister of finance. He collapsed in the House during the budget debate in 1938 and did not regain his health, and Ilsley was acting minister for nearly a year. I recall one occasion when Ilsley expressed irritation that Dunning could not make up his mind whether to return to work or to resign. That question was not resolved until the outbreak of war. Howe I had spoken to only once before the war started.

The only other minister I knew before the war was C.G. Power. Every one in Ottawa referred to him as Chubby, even those who like me did not address him that way. Chubby had an extraordinary capacity to elicit loyal and even enthusiastic support from many who would not have tolerated some of his weaknesses in anyone else. In the dying days of August 1939, when the wartime organization for government was being planned, Chubby Power was in the thick of the planning, as I was. His irreverence and wit appealed to me, and I soon learned that they were merely the outward screen of a thoughtful and philosophical mind with shrewd judgment of the character and capacity of others. We became very good friends.

I knew a good deal at second hand about Gardiner, who became minister of agriculture in 1935. Gardiner had succeeded

Dunning as premier of Saskatchewan in 1926, when Dunning joined the cabinet in Ottawa. The day after Gardiner became premier Professor Chester Martin told our history class that Gardiner had been one of three members of the first class he taught in the University of Manitoba. Gardiner's professor of political economy had also been mine. Our common connection with the University of Manitoba created a social bond between us despite the great difference in our ages but we never became friends. His narrow sectarian Liberalism and his machine politics had no appeal for me. Like many other Manitoba Liberals in 1926, I had seen the salvation of the party in an alliance with the erstwhile Progressives. As I observed Gardiner in the years from 1938 to 1957, I concluded he was a poor judge of issues and an arrogant leader of people. But his forceful personality and his dogged determination ensured him long political survival.

During the summer of 1939 I became mildly involved with the work of a commission of inquiry into a Bren gun contract, which the Conservatives, inspired by George Drew, the leader of the Opposition in Ontario, had tried to turn into a scandal. J.L. Ralston was counsel for the commission. On one or two occasions he sought, through the Prime Minister's Office, information he needed from the government. As Heeney was away with the prime minister, those requests came to me, and I had several conversations with Ralston. I liked him at once. His simple, direct manner, courtesy and charm attracted me. That brief acquaintance stood me in good stead when he joined the government as minister of finance at the outbreak of war.

Apart from Skelton, the only deputy minister I had much contact with before the war was Clark, in Finance. He had a wonderful way with junior civil servants, as he had probably had earlier with students. The prime minister asked me to consult him from time to time on particular matters, and we soon got into discussion of other questions in which I was interested. While still living in Manitoba I had come to feel strongly that the government of Canada should have the primary responsibility for dealing with unemployment and the main if not the total burden of providing relief for the unemployed. I prepared a memorandum making the case for federal responsibility. Clark prepared a detailed, point-by-point rebuttal of my arguments. I was flattered that a busy man would give so much time to the views of a novice in the public service. I continued to deal with Clark as long as he remained in office. Our intellectual and official association was one of the joys of my life. In his last years, when he lived in a house across the street from ours our friendship became even closer. He was one of our greatest public servants.

In the two years before the outbreak of war, thanks to my position in the Prime Minister's Office I had begun to find my way around official and political Ottawa and to differentiate between those who mattered and those who did not.

I realized that the most important and influential minister was Ernest Lapointe. From the gallery I saw that he was a splendid parliamentarian, effective in debate and obviously well liked on both sides of the House. He was a big man physically but even bigger politically, and the dean of the House of Commons. He had been elected first in 1904, a young country lawyer with little knowledge of English. Thirty-five years later he was the unchallenged leader of French Canada in Parliament and equally effective in either language. A large banquet was organized in February 1939 in Quebec City to celebrate the anniversary of his election. Mackenzie King was of course to be one of the main speakers. He went to Quebec City in his private railway car and took Norman Rogers with him. I asked him to take me as well. It was a feast of oratory. P.J.A. Cardin, the minister of public works, was even more eloquent than Lapointe, but the speaker who impressed me most was Adélard Godbout, Liberal Opposition leader in the Quebec legislature. He was as great an orator as Cardin, and his speech had more substance. The occasion gave me a new look at the politics of Quebec and of Canada.

The royal visit gave me the opportunity to know Lapointe well. Mackenzie King had arranged to have King George VI and Queen Elizabeth visit Canada in 1939 and to tour the country from coast to coast. He accompanied them as minister in attendance on the

King throughout the tour and also during the royal visit to the United States. Heeney, Turnbull and Handy accompanied the prime minister. I had no part in the royal visit except to help Mackenzie King draft the speeches of the King and Queen. I was left in charge of the Prime Minister's Office. Lapointe was acting prime minister, and with Parliament in session I saw him almost every working day. He was far more accessible than Mackenzie King and became something of a hero to me. I felt he liked and trusted me, and our discussions were easy and frank. From his day-to-day direction of the government I learned a great deal about how cabinet government really functions more than I had learned from Mackenzie King. I also began to see how the process of keeping French- and English-speaking Canadians together in a single political party actually worked.

The Shadow of War

When Mackenzie King returned to Ottawa after the departure of the King and Queen from Halifax, he began to make plans for a general election. On 22 June, at the first cabinet meeting after his return, he found the whole cabinet in favour. His tentative plan was to have Parliament dissolved in mid-September, with an election later in the fall. But firm plans were not possible under the shadow of war, which the prime minister hoped and half believed might be averted. The prime minister invited Margaret and me to dinner at Kingsmere on 15 August. Norman Rogers and his wife were also there. Mrs Pattison, whom we met that day for the first time, acted as hostess. The prime minister had Margaret and me come earlier than the other guests so that he could have a short talk with me.

He told me he was seriously considering an autumn election and, if he decided to have one, would like me to work closely with him on the campaign, particularly to assist him with his speeches. He was flattering about my abilities and altogether very persuasive. He had hoped that Heeney would perform the task, but Arnold was not willing to do so. He had invoked the written exchange between them, which clearly showed (to Heeney but not to Mackenzie King) that his position as principal secretary was to be official and nonpartisan and was to lead eventually to appointment as secretary to the cabinet if such a position was established. The prime minister left no doubt that he resented Heeney's attitude but realized he had to accept his decision or lose him altogether.

I told the prime minister that I was flattered by his request, and in fact I was. I asked for 24 hours in which to consider whether or not I felt I could do the job. I was quite confident I could. What I really wanted the time for was to consult Skelton about its implications for my future. My status was that of a civil servant on loan. I knew that civil servants were not permitted to engage in most forms of partisan activity, and I did not want to jeopardize my livelihood and Margaret's. Skelton pointed out that as long as I was in the Prime Minister's Office I was expected to serve the prime minister in whatever way he requested, and that such service could not be considered partisan unless I made speeches or engaged in any other form of campaigning in my own name. He assured me that Mackenzie King would never ask me to do that.

I had no worry on that score. The prime minister felt that members of his staff should, like children, be seen as little as possible and never heard. Once I had talked to Skelton, I was eager enough if an election came, to take on the task. I lost no time the next day in letting the prime minister know I was willing. In retrospect I believe that decision sealed my fate.

That evening at Kingsmere after dinner, Mackenzie King discussed with Rogers and me the pros and cons of calling an election. The only question in his mind was whether war might break out. He retained some hope that it might not because of a secret proposal he had received from the German consul-general for an exchange of German and Canadian young people in the autumn. Rogers and I both wondered out loud if that was not merely a blind or ruse. That evening Mackenzie King decided to consult Chamberlain, the British prime minister, about the probabilty of war. Within two weeks Hitler, not Chamberlain, had answered his question. Instead of an election we faced war. I had been conscripted not for an election but for service with the prime minister during six years of war and beyond.

The shadow of war had been on the horizon before Mackenzie King was returned to office in 1935, but it increased greatly with Hitler's claim that the Aryan Germans were a master race, and that all racial Germans everywhere should be under German sovereignty. In the summer of 1938 the Nazis claimed that the population of the western tip of Czechoslovakia, the Sudetenland, was mainly German and should be part of Germany. That claim was a gross distortion of fact: the population was partly German but equally Czech. When Czechoslovakia was created, Britain and France had solemnly undertaken to preserve its integrity and independence, by force if necessary. At Munich on 27 September 1938 the British and French governments repudiated their undertaking and left Czechoslovakia a choice between fighting alone or surrendering the territory Hitler had demanded. The Czechoslovakian government submitted.

The craven abandonment of Czechoslovakia by Britain and France shocked most liberal-minded people in the West, including me. But Canada was not a party to the guarantee, and I remained convinced that Canada had no vital interest at stake in a European war. Mackenzie King feared that Canada would have been deeply divided if the crisis over Czechoslovakia had not ended at Munich. I shared that fear and felt that every year that passed without war would make it less difficult for Canadians to recognize their real interest was to stay out of a European war. The British prime minister claimed that Munich assured 'peace in our time.' By the time Parliament met in January 1939, Mackenzie King was losing confidence in Chamberlain's prediction.

The prime minister's speech at the opening of the parliamentary session contained one sentence pointing to possible Canadian participation if war came. He repeated Laurier's statement 'if England is at war we are at war and liable to attack,' and added Laurier's further statement that the degree of Canadian participation would be decided by Parliament. He said Laurier's statement was still Liberal policy. Nationalists in Quebec and some Liberal MPs from Quebec were disturbed. There was open criticism by one or two Liberal MPs.

On 20 March 1939, when Hitler, in a total breach of the Munich pact, seized the rest of Czechoslovakia, there was widespread public indignation in Britain and France. The indignation found echoes in Canada that were heard in the cabinet, where a statement by the prime minister was hastily prepared for presentation in the House of Commons. The most important passage read: 'If there were a prospect of an aggressor launching an attack on Britain, with bombers raining death on London, I have no doubt what the decision of the Canadian people and of Parliament would be. We would regard it as an act of aggression, menacing freedom in all parts of the British Commonwealth. If it were a case, on the other hand, of a dispute over trade or prestige in some far corner of the world, that would raise quite different considerations.' There was no suggestion of liberating Czechoslovakia, and Mackenzie King added that there was no reason to despair of peace, nor scarcely anything he would not sacrifice for peace, but that he would never surrender the liberty we enjoyed. The prime minister read the statement at the opening of the House, and the leader of the Opposition started to reply. Mackenzie King then realized he had not read the page containing the reference to the possible bombing of London. He had left page five on his desk in the East Block. He interrupted Manion and explained what had happened, and the House agreed to go on to other business until he could get the missing page five and read his full statement. The interruption lasted about a half hour and embarrassed Mackenzie King greatly. When Hansard appeared, there was no reference to the interruption, which had been widely reported in the press. A Tory member raised an objection that the Hansard report was not complete. Mackenzie King and Manion had agreed to the omission and were both disconcerted.

Ten days later, on 30 March, the prime minister made a long speech on external affairs that contained the pledge that if Canada became involved in war, there would be no conscription for service beyond Canada. Manion gave a similar pledge on behalf of the Conservative party.

After Hitler had taken over the whole of Czechoslovakia, I assumed there would be no resistance by Britain and France to Nazi aggression anywhere in Eastern Europe. I was aghast when Britain and France guaranteed the integrity of Poland. It was hard to believe that they would 'rat' on that guarantee as they had on their guarantee of Czechoslovakia. If Hitler attacked and Poland resisted, the guarantee would almost certainly bring Western Europe into the war.

In early 1939 I felt the prime minister was moving the country step by step closer to a war it should not be in. One of the steps in my view was the royal visit. I felt the irony of having to share in drafting the speeches of the King and Queen. Mackenzie King was horrified by the tone and substance of the draft of the speech the King was to make from Canada to the Empire. It was the only one originally drafted in London. He and I redrafted it completely. All the other royal speeches were drafted in Canada, and in all of them I had a hand. I was amused when in a burst of colonial sentiment the *Ottawa Journal* commended the form and style of the royal speeches, which it found far above Canadian capabilities.

I believe Mackenzie King always realized that if Britain was involved in a European war, many Canadians would want Canada to rush to Britain's side. The one hope was to keep Britain out of war, and that hope seemed almost gone after the guarantee to Poland.

Canada goes to war

Parliament decides

Barely a week after the prime minister had asked me to assist him in a possible election campaign, the nonaggression pact between Hitler and Stalin ended any possibility for an election and removed the last doubt that an attack on Poland was imminent. That day the government started to organize for the outbreak of war.

I was convinced by then that if Mackenzie King's government had tried to keep the country out of a war in which Britain was involved, the government would not survive. The probable alternative was a government pledged to support Britain and to impose conscription. In my view such a government could not maintain national unity and might be faced with civil disorder. The government of Mackenzie King, I believed, was the only one that might keep the country united, and it was my duty to continue to serve the prime minister. Having reached that conclusion I had little time to brood about it. An attack on Poland seemed inevitable. Unless Poland gave up without a fight, Britain was almost certain to go to war. In response to the Hitler-Stalin pact, the government's first step was to bring the War Measures Act of 1914 into force by proclamation and to use the extraordinary powers under the act before a shot had been fired anywhere in actual combat.

On Thursday, 31 August, I worked in the Office in the East Block until about 11 p.m. Before going back to the Robertson's house for the night I stopped at the Canadian Press office on Sparks Street to look at the latest news on the wires. In Europe it was already the early morning of Friday, 1 September. The first item on the wire was a report that the German army had crossed the Polish frontier. It was no surprise, but the certainty was a shock. When I got to the house John F. MacNeill of the Department of Justice and Norman Robertson were sitting at the dining room table. As soon as I gave them the news, they told me they had been going over the police lists of suspected Nazi agents and sympathizers in Canada to decide which should be recommended for internment.

Norman called Skelton immediately. Skelton felt there was no point in disturbing the Prime Minister, who was at Kingsmere, until morning. When Skelton called him at 6 a.m., Mackenzie King summoned the cabinet for 8. I recall walking from Rockcliffe to Parliament Hill that Friday. It was a beautiful, fresh, sunny summer morning. Ottawa looked profoundly peaceful, and it was hard to realize that war was already raging in Eastern Europe, and that Canada almost certainly would be in that war.

The cabinet decided to have Parliament called into session on 7 September, the earliest date feasible in those days before air travel. The armed forces were placed on alert, but no other action would be taken until France and Britain indicated what they would do about their guarantee. The theoretical option of nonparticipation still existed. The government, or more correctly the prime minister, still insisted that Parliament would decide, but precisely what it would decide he never defined.

On Sunday, 3 September, France and Britain declared war on Germany. That was a day of feverish activity in Ottawa. The prime minister decided to give a national broadcast in mid-afternoon, to be repeated in French immediately afterwards by Lapointe. I was summoned to Laurier House to help prepare the broadcast. I suggested that I bring Jean Chapdelaine to translate the text into French, page by page, so it would be ready for Lapointe. Mackenzie King, who never realized that translations were not instantaneous, said that that was not necessary, but unknown to him I had Chapdelaine come to Laurier House to work in a back room.

The English text was barely finished when Mackenzie King had to leave for the CBC studio in the Château Laurier. On arrival he found he had left page five behind, and the chauffeur was sent back for it. There seemed to be something fatal about page five. I took the missing page to the studio and had the car return to Laurier House for Chapdelaine and the French text. Page five and I arrived less than a minute before Mackenzie King was due to start his broadcast.

Lapointe frantically demanded the French text. I did my best to assure him it would arrive in time. He was not convinced, and neither was I. Fortunately Norman Rogers was also at the studio, to broadcast an announcement that a Wartime Prices and Trade Board had been established to prevent profiteering and hoarding. There were already reports that sugar was being hoarded, and that merchants were raising prices. Chubby Power was to repeat in French the announcement by Rogers.

As Mackenzie King was nearing his conclusion and the French translation had not yet arrived, I sent a note to the CBC general manager, Gladstone Murray, who was in the studio with the prime minister, to put Rogers on after the prime minister, and to announce that French translations of both speeches would follow immediately. Rogers had barely started when Chapdelaine arrived with the French text. Lapointe had read it hurriedly before his turn came to broadcast. He read the text calmly and in as natural a tone as if he had composed it himself. Power then followed in his own inimitable French.

Mackenzie King announced that when Parliament met on 7 September, the government would recommend that Canada go to war at Britain's side. Even that categorical announcement was received by some political opponents and newspapers with skepticism. The procedure was resented indignantly by the ultra-imperialists, who felt that Canada was already, automatically, at war. There were minor protests from nationalists in Quebec, but the great majority of Canadians seemed to concur without enthusiasm in the government's decision. There was none of the excited jubilation of August 1914, that as a nine-year-old I had shared.

The next few days were filled with preparations for Parliament, plans for the wartime organization of the cabinet and cabinet committees, and a host of other problems. At one point I prepared a memorandum for Skelton in which I referred to the vacuum at the centre of government. He seemed to agree with me and was surprisingly receptive. By vacuum I meant the lack of any mechanism for recording decisions made by the prime minister and the cabinet and for making sure they were carried out.

A chart of cabinet organization was prepared, mainly by Power. At the centre was an Emergency Committee, which after 10 September was called the War Committee. The War Committee quickly filled the vacuum, thanks largely to the appointment of Arnold Heeney as its secretary. Heeney hated disorder and untidiness. He had studied carefully the organization of the British cabinet in the First World War, and he adapted its procedures, frequently with resistance from Mackenzie King, who disliked being bound by decisions almost as much as he did by commitments. In the light of the elaborate organization of the Privy

Council Office today, it is hard to believe that before 1939, except for formal orders-in-council, there was no record of decisions of the government. From the outset, full minutes were kept of the proceedings of the War Committee, and follow-up machinery put in place to make sure decisions were carried out by ministers and departments and agencies of government. A couple of weeks or more after the Canadian declaration of war on 10 September, I mentioned to Loring Christie the concern I felt about the administrative confusion in the face of war. He said that we had been well prepared, that the confusion was superficial and would be quickly dispelled. He added that I should have been in Ottawa, as he was, in August 1914.

Most of my working time in those early days of September was spent either with the prime minister in revising various documents for his use or in drafting documents for him to revise. While the House of Commons was sitting, I was in the gallery watching proceedings and seeking to anticipate material Mackenzie King might need in debate. That was to remain one of my functions for the rest of the war.

I had helped to draft the Speeches from the Throne opening and closing the regular session of Parliament in 1939 and had a large part in drafting those for the special wartime session which opened 7 September. From 1939 until Parliament was dissolved in 1957, I was to have a part in drafting every Speech from the Throne.

Far more important than the Speech from the Throne was the prime minister's own speech justifying Canadian participation in the war and forecasting the general lines of action the government would propose to Parliament. Much of the original draft was prepared by Skelton and others in External Affairs, but I helped the prime minister with the final revision and adaptation to his views and vocabulary. I have since then taken particular satisfaction that a paragraph I wrote about the defence of Newfoundland was included precisely as I drafted it. In speeches I made after I became a member of Parliament from Newfoundland I referred to that paragraph frequently.

The members who were to move and second the Address in Reply to the Speech from the Throne were both veterans of the First World War. Helping movers and seconders with their speeches was a task I performed for the first time. Th prime minister always wanted to be sure the backbenchers chosen for that honour said the right thing and, especially, said nothing embarrassing to the government. They proved quite amenable to including Mackenzie King's suggestions, which I passed on to them. I performed that task many more times and did not always find the members so ready to accept help or advice.

Manion, the leader of the Opposition, gave full approval to the decision of the government and reiterated for the Conservatives the pledge he had made in March 1939, not to support the use of conscription for service outside Canada. The prime minister in replying to Manion repeated for the government the pledge not to resort to conscription.

The most dramatic incident that day was the speech by Woodsworth. He did not speak as leader of the CCF but for himself alone, and he repeated, in moving terms, his lifelong conscientious pacifism. He was listened to in intense and respectful silence. The way Woodsworth's speech was received gave me hope that Canada might avoid much of the domestic acrimony and bitterness of the 1917 conscription crisis, which had left such a legacy of disunity. The deputy leader of the CCF, M.J. Coldwell, stated the official policy of the party, which advocated less than full-scale participation.

In his speech the prime minister failed to inform the House precisely of the way in which Parliament would make its decision. I pointed out the omission and gave him a draft statement, which he revised slightly. At the opening of the sitting next day he announced that a vote of approval of the Speech from the Throne would be taken as approval of a declaration of war. It was characteristic of Mackenzie King that the King was asked not to declare war on Germany on behalf of Canada but to declare that a state of war existed between Canada and the German Reich.

The most influential speech of the special session was made by Lapointe. It was addressed to French Canada and was an appeal for Canadian unity.

When the vote was called on Saturday evening, only two members stood up, instead of the five required by the rules if the votes of individual members were to be recorded. The virtual unanimity of the parliamentary decision had been assured by Lapointe's eloquent and persuasive speech. On Sunday morning, 10 September, the King's declaration was made. By the decision of our own Parliament Canada was at war.

The last two days of the war session were taken up with approval of a war appropriation of $100 million and legislation to establish a department of Munitions and Supply, to be set up whenever the government felt it expedient.

Before the session ended Manion asked the prime minister to give an undertaking that Parliament would not be dissolved until it had met again. Mackenzie King gave the undertaking readily enough, but he lived to regret it, in January 1940.

The war effort and the Quebec election of 1939

Early in September Jim Coyne moved to another apartment in the Mayfair. Margaret and I at last had a home of our own, at apartment 10, the Mayfair, though in those early days of war I was rarely there except to sleep.

From Margaret's point of view worse was to follow. One day shortly after the war session of Parliament ended, I went into Arnold's office. He looked up and said, 'You are staring in two different directions; you'd better go home.' I then realized the right side of my face was paralyzed. Terrified, I went to the doctor as soon as possible. He diagnosed the malady as Bell's palsy and assured me that the paralysis usually lasted only a week or two and generally disappeared completely. But my recovery was not total, and I was left with permanent deafness in my right ear. Until the paralysis ended, I was unable to read and expected Margaret to do it for me. Instead of being grateful, I am ashamed to say, I was irritable and critical.

Once the parliamentary session closed in mid-September 1939, the government concentrated on organizing what soon came to be called the 'war effort.' The first step was a cabinet shuffle. Mackenzie King realized that Ian Mackenzie could not remain minister of defence. He decided to relegate him to the minor portfolio of Pensions and Health and to replace him with Chubby Power. After a good deal of soul-searching he felt that, because Power had a drinking problem, the risk would be too great. He chose Norman Rogers, the minister of labour, instead, and made Power postmaster general, with the understanding that he would assist Rogers and act for him at National Defence whenever necessary. Rogers, like Power, was a veteran of the Great War. He was an effective minister, and Power supported him with loyalty and wisdom.

Mackenzie King would have liked to limit the growth of the army and to avoid organizing an expeditionary force, which he feared would arouse fear of conscription. But the expeditionary force of 1914-18 was Canada's only military tradition, and a large section of the public, especially veterans, demanded one. The defence department did not have plans for anything else. Mackenzie King yielded to the pressure and agreed to the establishment of one army division for service overseas if required.

Shortly after that decision was announced, the British prime minister, Neville Chamberlain, proposed that a Commonwealth air training program be established in Canada. Mackenzie King received the proposal for joint air training with genuine enthusiasm. He believed that air power would be the most important factor in fighting the war, and that Canadians had a special aptitude for flying. There would never be conscription of pilots and other airmen.

Mackenzie King sensed much sooner than most of his ministers that the war would be long and fierce, and that Canada could not hope to limit the war effort. I did not share Mackenzie King's view, because I could not believe Nazi Germany was stronger than France and Britain combined. I continued to nourish my illusion until the collapse of the western front in May and June 1940.

Mackenzie King was also one of the first and most convinced exponents in the cabinet of war production on a large scale; he believed more effective armaments would reduce the loss of human lives. Despite his unwavering support for the expansion of air power and war production, he never succeeded in restraining the growth of the army.

The attention of ministers turned to the political arena when Premier Maurice Duplessis on 25 September had an election called in the province of Quebec. Duplessis did not question the right of the federal Parliament to decide whether or not Canada should go to war. Instead, he made an issue of the use of the War Measures Act to override the normal provincial jurisdiction of the Quebec and other legislatures. Duplessis's challenge was regarded both by his opponents and the Canadian public generally as an attempt to prevent effective prosecution of the war. The federal ministers from Quebec, Lapointe, Cardin and Power, decided to participate actively in the provincial campaign in support of Adélard Godbout, the Liberal leader. They announced that if Duplessis won the election, they would all resign and leave Quebec without representation in the Cabinet at Ottawa. The claim was that they would be more effective in preventing conscription than any provincial premier would be. Mackenzie King felt their threat was too bold, but he was unable to dissuade them. Godbout won the election in a landslide.

The Liberal victory in Quebec was widely misinterpreted in the rest of Canada as wholehearted support by French Canadians for participation in the war. I did not share that illusion. My French-Canadian friends, particularly Philéas Côté, the associate secretary of the National Liberal Federation, who had worked closely with Power during the campaign, warned me that the Liberal victory, far from indicating support for an all-out war effort, really signified a belief that keeping Lapointe, Cardin and Power in office was a safer insurance against conscription and other extreme measures than a victory for Duplessis.

Shortly after the Quebec election, Mackenzie King made two broadcasts that had gone through endless revisions. After the first broadcast he lamented to me that if he had had only one more day for preparation, it would have been better — a cry I was to hear after almost every broadcast for the next nine years.

Mackenzie King realized that his speeches did not electrify the country, and he was resolved to find someone who could draft speeches that would. At that time the finest phrase-making orator in Canada was L.W. Brockington of Winnipeg. Brockington was persuaded to join the prime minister's staff in an ill-defined capacity. In those days politicians still pretended they wrote their own speeches. No one was shameless enough to describe a secretary as a speechwriter, but that was what Brockington was expected to be. I already knew Brockington slightly. He was counsel for the Northwest Line Elevator Association, in charge of their public relations. My brother Tom was his assistant in Winnipeg. I welcomed Brockington's appointment, and we quickly became fast friends. Unfortunately he proved completely unsuited to the task he was expected to perform, and his relationship with Mackenzie King deteriorated. Brockington joined the staff shortly before the end of 1939. My active collaboration with him in preparing speeches began when a federal election was called in late January 1940.

Late in 1939 I had an early speechwriting experience that threw some light on Mackenzie King's character. The CBC had asked Ralston to give a national broadcast. He sought my advice about whether or not he should, and what he should say. I made some suggestions and offered to prepare a draft. I soon learned that he too was an inveterate reviser, but the broadcast turned out well and received favourable press comment. I had specifically asked Ralston not to mention my part to the prime minister. Either Ralston forgot my request or thought I really wanted to be given some credit; in any event he did speak to Mackenzie King, who in turn told me that he would have been glad to offer my services to Ralston, but that my duty was to him. His reaction confirmed my feeling that my god was a jealous god.

After Poland was defeated and carved up by Nazi Germany and Soviet Russia, the anticipated attack on France and Britain did not come. Late September 1939 to April 1940 was the period of the phony war. During that time Mackenzie King did not concentrate exclusively on the war effort. Late in 1937 he had tried to get the provincial governments to agree to a constitutional amendment to give Parliament exclusive jurisdiction over unemployment insurance. Quebec, Alberta and New Brunswick had refused. After the Quebec election Mackenzie King learned from Power that Premier Godbout was in favour of federal unemployment insurance. Accordingly, the prime minister tried again to persuade the premiers of the three provinces to agree to the amendment.

In March Premier Dysart of New Brunswick resigned; he was replaced by John B. McNair, who readily agreed. Mackenzie King used his own blandishment to get agreement from Premier Aberhart of Alberta. The way was then clear to seek the unemployment insurance amendment to the BNA Act from the British Parliament. The necessary amendment was made automatically at Westminster on 10 July 1940. I was really pleased that the constitutional amendment on which I had worked had been achieved. Unemployment insurance on a national scale was established without delay.

5 Conscripted for the Duration

The wartime election

When the year 1940 began Mackenzie King began to regret his promise to Manion that Parliament would meet again before an election. The normal life of Parliament would expire in 1940, and Mackenzie King felt it would be desirable to have the disruption of an election over before actual combat began in western Europe. Because of growing criticism in Tory circles, especially in Ontario, that the government was not doing enough to prepare for Nazi aggression, the prime minister anticipated an unpleasant session.

Mackenzie King was considering ways to limit the session to a minimum when the premier of Ontario unwittingly played into his hand. The Ontario legislature was already in session, and one day Premier Hepburn asked Drew, the Tory leader, to second a motion censuring the federal government for its inadequate war effort. Drew eagerly accepted, and the motion quickly passed, with 10 Liberal backbenchers opposing it.

Mackenzie King saw at once that censure by the Ontario legislature provided the pretext he needed to shorten the session and hold an election. At first he thought the session might run for a week, but on the morning of the opening day, 25 January, instead of going to a cabinet meeting, he had Heeney and me come to Laurier House. Pacing up and down the library like a caged tiger, he told us that he had decided Parliament would be dissolved that day. It was the most dramatic display I ever saw of the forceful and almost violent will of that man generally considered weak and mild. Heeney and I were overawed and scarcely uttered a word.

Long afterwards I wondered whether he had been using us as guinea pigs to test probable public reaction. He told us he had dictated to the King's Printer the necessary passage to be inserted in the Speech from the Throne. He directed me to go to the Printing Bureau and check the speech to be sure it was correct. He said he would have someone telephone to give me the final okay once he had seen the governor general and shown him the revisions in the speech. While we were still in the library, he telephoned Lapointe, who was presiding at the cabinet, told him what he had decided and authorized him to inform the ministers after warning them there must be no leak. He told Heeney to go right back to the East Block and repeat the warning.

When I received the okay from the prime minister, I told the King's Printer to complete the official text for the governor general but to hold up the actual printing of copies for distribution until he had further word from me. I feared the prime minister might decide on some further change. He did. There was not time to reprint the official copy. I made the changes in handwriting. It may have been the only time the governor general read a Speech from the Throne with a handwritten insertion.

The copies for distribution were printed with the corrections, but the usual custom of distributing copies to the press in advance was not followed. The news had not been leaked to anyone before the speech was read in the Senate, shortly after 3 p.m. The press copies were not distributed until the governor general had finished reading the speech in English. In those days the whole speech was read first in English, and then in French.

When the members returned to the House of Commons chamber, there was something approaching pandemonium. Manion succeeded in catching the Speaker's eye. He was so indignant I feared he might have apoplexy. The Opposition kept up the protest until 6 p.m., when the House rose for dinner. The cabinet met at once and authorized the prime minister to recommend an immediate dissolution to the governor general. Before 8, when the House would normally have resumed its sitting, there was a notice on the door that Parliament had been dissolved.

The election date was set for Tuesday, 26 March, the day after Easter Monday. Most of the press was highly critical. The Opposition denounced the dissolution as an outrage and a breach of the commitment to have a session of Parliament. The actual words used by the prime minister in reply to Manion on 12 September 1939 had been as follows: 'It is my intention to have Parliament called again in January. . . . At that time we will be in a position to consider what steps may be most necessary with regard to developments that may ensue meanwhile.' Mackenzie King's pointing out that he had undertaken merely to have Parliament meet, not to have a session, was described as trickery unworthy of a prime minister and an insult to Parliament.

His own conscience was not altogether clear. For almost half the campaign his speeches contained lengthy statements to justify the dissolution. One morning Power looked into my room in the East Block after a cabinet meeting and saw me writing furiously. He said he supposed I was still trying to justify the dissolution. I was thoroughly bored with the subject. I said being a frank unbeliever was sometimes preferable to having a Presbyterian conscience, to which he replied, 'Or being like me, saying to myself, Chubby Power, you know what you are going to do is wrong, but you are going to do it just the same.'

It was clear that radio would be a large feature of the election campaign. Before the war started a plan had been worked out by the CBC with the party representatives for free broadcasting for each of the parties represented in the House of Commons, time, on a limited scale during an election campaign. There would be no paid broadcasting. But after consultation with Howe, Gladstone Murray announced to a meeting of the party representatives that, as a war measure, the plan would be set aside, and paid broadcasting permitted. The spokesmen of the Opposition parties expressed outrage. Senator Norman Lambert, the president of the National Liberal Federation, was even more indignant at what was obviously a clumsy attempt to stack the cards in favour of the government. Lambert urged me to express his deep concern to the prime minister, and I did so, and added my own.

Mackenzie King understood at once that the government would be charged with fascism. He authorized Lambert to have a protest made to the CBC in the name of the Liberal party. He also had Howe speak to Murray. Spokesmen for all four party organizations arranged to meet Murray jointly. To the astonishment of the representatives of the other parties, Walter Herbert, the secretary of the Liberal Federation, made the strongest protest of all. Murray then told the meeting the original plan would be followed.

Mackenzie King announced that a prime minister should be absent from Ottawa in wartime as rarely as possible, and that he would limit his travelling to a visit to Prince Albert for his nomination as Liberal candidate, and a meeting in Winnipeg on the way. That brief tour was to be in mid-February. Except for that absence he would campaign by radio.

Brockington and I were to work with him on his broadcasts. Brockington had been the first chairman of the CBC and was assumed to be an expert in preparing broadcasts. Certainly he was a superb broadcaster, but writing for someone else he could not do. For the first broadcast I waited for him to prepare a draft based on notes from the prime minister. Nothing was ready for days. Mackenzie King became more and more impatient, complaining not to Brockington but to me. As the deadline came closer, I prepared a draft myself and showed it to Brock. I did not like to seem to be undercutting him by submitting it to Mackenzie King, but finally in desperation I felt obliged to.

At the last moment Brock submitted a draft, which did not in the least resemble Mackenzie King's style, and paid little attention to his suggestions. Meanwhile the prime minister had produced a draft of his own, with no plan and almost no form. He and I then spent several hours trying to put all three drafts together. When we had finally worked out a single composite draft containing almost nothing Brock had written, he was called in to a three-way revision session. He was obviously hurt that his superior material, with its fine phrases and rhetorical flights, had barely survived. He had difficulty concealing his distaste for Mackenzie King's own phrases, which were often banal when they were not turgid. Mackenzie King's instinct in rejecting language he did not feel comfortable with was sound. In my drafts I tried to use phraseology that was second nature to him.

The same process repeated itself, with variations, for each broadcast. Between Brockington's procrastination and Mackenzie King's passion for revision the broadcasts were never completed more than an hour or two before they had to be delivered. I found the process exhausting. One evening when I was late for dinner as usual, Margaret made some exasperated remark to me. I retorted that I had to put up with two prima donnas at work and I could not stand another at home. Happily she was amused.

Despite the strain my personal relations with Brockington remained good, and a close friendship developed. I learned a great deal from him in addition to being vastly entertained by his brilliant wit and inspired by his truly tolerant and generous spirit. Half Welsh and half highland Scot, he belonged to two minorities. His sage observation that majorities quickly forget setbacks and even defeats, but minorities never forget slights, has been a guide to me ever since.

The Tory strategy was based on an undertaking that if Manion won the election he would form a National Government. They actually described their candidates not as Conservatives, but as National Government candidates. Far from winning votes, the name recalled bitter memories of the Union Government of the First World War and the fear of conscription.

Mackenzie King's broadcasts became progressively more effective, particularly after he stopped justifying the dissolution and addressed himself to the National Government issue. Poor Manion proved himself manifestly incapable of leadership, and the fire-eaters in the Tory party were increasingly disloyal to him.

Whatever feelings there may have been of Mackenzie King's deficiencies as a war leader, he was seen to be surrounded by capable ministers. Ralston's enlistment in the cabinet as soon as the war started was a special source of strength, particularly among veterans. Lapointe's enhanced prestige after the defeat of Duplessis was an equal source of confidence. By mid-February, when Mackenzie King went to Prince Albert, the tide was clearly running in favour of the government.

For the visit to Prince Albert I was in charge of the prime minister's entourage, which consisted of my assistant, William Paterson, who had been my most brilliant student at United College, and another young Winnipeger, Deane Russell, a stenographer who had been recently hired to assist Handy at Laurier House. The party of course included Handy, and also John Nicol, whose rank was confidential messenger but who in function was Mackenzie King's personal servant. We stopped for a day in Winnipeg, where the prime minister was to speak in the evening. The speech was far from ready when we arrived in the morning and installed ourselves in the Fort Garry Hotel. I was assailed by a half dozen reporters seeking advance copies of the speech. I explained that it was not ready and would be so sooner if they would leave me free to work on it with the prime minister. I asked the youngest of the reporters, John Bassett, to keep the press at bay. He did so with flourish and success, and I have had a soft spot for John from that time. Prince Albert was a new experience for me. The nomination was carried out like clockwork, and Mackenzie King made a rousing impromptu speech. Required to be little more than an observer, I watched the political hangers-on vying for the prime minister's notice, each seeking to assert his own role as the main architect of the coming local victory, clearly never in doubt. In 1940 Saskatchewan was still basically Liberal.

On the return trip Paterson and Russell asked me if they could stay over in Winnipeg for 24 hours to visit their families, pointing out that they could still be at the office in Ottawa Monday morning. I thought the prime minister was tiring of having them around with nothing to do and put the request to him in their presence. He agreed readily and I thought, cheerfully. My brother Tom met the train, and once he had been introduced to the prime minister, we went off to have a beer. After the train left Winnipeg, Mackenzie King, Handy and I had a pleasant dinner. I thought he was relieved not to have Paterson and Russell at the table. Before we retired he asked me if I would do a first draft of the next broadcast, and to the draft I devoted most of Saturday morning. Handy was busy with dictation all morning, so I had to enlist the CN telegraph operator accompanying us to type my draft.

Shortly before lunch, Mackenzie King asked to see me, and I presented the draft. He put it aside, apparently surprised that it was ready, turned to me and said no one had embarrassed him so much in his life as I had done in Winnipeg when I had put Paterson and Russell's request to him in their presence, He added that he had been unable to refuse without appearing heartless, but that their conduct was almost equivalent to desertion in the face of the enemy. I replied that I had thought he would be relieved not to have them around, and that I was exceedingly sorry he had been displeased. I then picked up a newspaper and began to read. I knew he sensed my indignation; not a word more was said until after we were summoned to lunch. The prime minister thereupon tried to start up a conversation. To each initiative I replied politely in a fashion that closed that subject. At one point he said of Tom, 'a fine-looking young man, your brother,' to which I replied 'Yes, isn't he?' When I took a piece of bread, he reached over and put some butter on my plate — at which point I had trouble not to burst out laughing but was able to remain respectfully taciturn.

I had watched the way Mackenzie King bullied others and turned some members of his staff into doormats, and I was determined he would not do the same to me. I realized this was the acid test. I must have reacted in the right way, because as long as he was in office, he never again tried to intimidate me.

Margaret and I were invited to Laurier House with the Heeneys and the Pattisons to listen to the broadcast of election returns on 26 March. Manion did not win his own seat, and the Tories elected no more members than in 1935. The Liberals had another landslide, with a few more seats than in 1935, and for the first and only time the Liberals under Mackenzie King had more than 50 per cent of the popular vote. Even in the hour of his greatest political triumph Mackenzie King's enjoyment was not complete: his victory broadcast was being revised and revised.

The Prime Minister's Office after the election

On the eve of the election Heeney had been appointed clerk of the Privy Council and also the first secretary to the cabinet in Canadian history. A decision would have to be made as to who would preside over the Prime Minister's Office in his place. I had acted for Heeney whenever he was absent, and I might have seemed the obvious successor, even on a temporary basis.

Self-interest might have prompted me to stay in Ottawa, but instead I asked the prime minister if I could take a week off to rest. I was exhausted, and Margaret, though not really ill, was far from well. Her parents, who were in Florida, had generously offered to meet us in Washington and to take Margaret back with them for a holiday. We accepted with gratitude and invited Jean Chapdelaine to drive to Washington with us so that I would have company on the way home. We spent the night before arrival near Baltimore, and were up early and checked into a Washington hotel as soon as we reached the city. Margaret and Jean went sightseeing, and I went to bed to try to sleep. Within a minute or two a morning newspaper was slipped under my bedroom door, and I picked it up to look at the headlines. It was 9 April, and I read that the Nazis had occupied Denmark and invaded Norway. I never did get to sleep.

By coincidence that day had been chosen to proclaim the act establishing the Department of Munitions and Supply. The news announcement made it appear that the government in Ottawa had reacted promptly to the attack in Scandinavia. For the Allies the brutal and totally unprovoked attack still failed to dispel all illusions.

Chamberlain announced that by invading Norway Hitler had missed the boat. In a week or two it was clear that it was the unfortunate Chamberlain who had missed the boat.

When I returned to Ottawa two or three days later, I learned that Mackenzie King had appointed Turnbull acting principal secretary. I would have been hardly human if I had not felt a little chagrin, but I think I succeeded in hiding it. My relations with Turnbull remained as good as ever.

It was understood from the outset that our responsibilities would be sharply defined: Turnbull would be responsible for administering the office, dealing with the public, attending on the prime minister in the East Block and the Parliament Building, and I would deal direct with the prime minister about all the written work, correspondence, memoranda and speeches. We organized the office so that Turnbull, Handy and I would always be informed about what the others were doing for the prime minister, and no matter whose responsibility it was, we would not be caught napping when he wanted something in a hurry. We got through the whole war without recrimination and with a high degree of harmony. Long before the war ended I was grateful that Turnbull and not I had been chosen as acting principal secretary. I doubt whether I could have survived had I had to manage the office, in addition to assisting the prime minister with speech-writing and correspondence.

The French presence was still very small in the Prime Minister's Office, but there had been a marked improvement over 1937. Heeney had finally succeeded in persuading Mackenzie King to have a French secretary added to the staff, and early in 1940 he recruited a brilliant young lawyer, Genest Trudel. Trudel was a hard worker and a splendid colleague. We worked closely together. His main task during the election was to translate the prime minister's speeches into French and to broadcast them as an anonymous voice. Unfortunately he had come for only six months and felt he had to go back to his law firm at the end of that period to support his young family. Mackenzie King agreed that he should be replaced.

Jules Léger, who had just been appointed a third secretary in External Affairs, was his replacement. Léger was my choice, and thereupon we began an official association so harmonious that when Léger resumed his diplomatic career in 1943, he told me that if he was needed again in Ottawa to work with me, he would respond to the call. He was to be needed, in 1948. Two or three weeks before he became prime minister, Louis St Laurent met Léger in London. Not long afterwards St Laurent asked me whether or not I thought Léger wold be willing to return to Ottawa to join the staff. I answered yes. During Léger's second stint in the Prime Minister's Office our official association was even closer, and he remained one of my most cherished friends until his death. But our friendship began in those dark days in the early 1940s, when Léger was, among other things, the French voice of the prime minister on broadcasts he had translated himself.

The prime minister's staff was also strengthened by James Gibson's assignment at Laurier House. Before Gibson joined the Department of External Affairs in 1938, Skelton had apparently arranged to have one of the newly appointed third secretaries seconded to the Prime Minister's Office, which had been reduced in strength by Pickering's departure. I recall being consulted as to which of the new recruits should be seconded. Though I did not yet know James well, I had been impressed by his concern for accuracy, his meticulous attention to detail and the way in which he expressed himself. I felt he could adapt himself to Mackenzie King's vocabulary and at the same time preserve clarity — a rare gift. I recommended that he be chosen. Only later did I learn that Gibson had the additional merit of being completely bilingual, a qualification not as highly valued in the Prime Minister's Office in 1938 as it became in 1940 and has remained.

Shortly after the outbreak of war Gibson, at the prime minister's request, was selected to be the keeper at Laurier House of dispatches and memoranda from External, the minutes of the War Committee of the cabinet and other secret documents. Gibson did not have a place in the office structure at the East Block; he had direct access to the prime minister and liaison with the Cabinet Office and External. Though Gibson was not in the East Block, on most Saturdays, when the prime minister 'cleaned up' accumulated correspondence and other papers on his desk, I worked with him. The clean-up took place in the library at Laurier House and involved a good deal of drudgery, with occasional interesting moments. Gibson impressed me by his wide knowledge of the prime minister's papers and his thoroughness. Mackenzie King was not an orderly worker, and Gibson was indispensable in keeping him on the rails. By his isolation at Laurier House Gibson was limited in his opportunities to work with his colleagues in External — perhaps one reason why he left the public service for academic life. Gibson is a fine scholar, and his true vocation may have been academic. The climax of his career was as president of Brock University, which was largely his creation. I feel Gibson's war service has never received adequate recognition. All of us in the East Block valued his loyal and effective cooperation as a colleague. In recent years my friendship with him has been strengthened by a common devotion to New College, our college at Oxford.

The office did not suffer from Heeney's departure to become secretary to the cabinet. He had developed an orderly administrative structure which served well without any major changes during the war and after. All the work he had been doing since the outbreak of war he took with him as secretary to the cabinet. His new office was a few doors along the corridor from Turnbull's and mine, and we had day-to-day contact.

Once the real war began my own work increased in volume and complexity. I had a wonderful assistant in my onetime student, Bill Paterson, who helped bear the burden. As the war intensified, Paterson felt he should have a more active role, and he was enticed into Sir William Stephenson's organization in New York, with which he later became disillusioned. He resigned and joined the RCAF and was killed on what was to have been his last combat mission. His death was a loss to Canada and to me.

The late E.K. Brown, who had been an academic colleague in Manitoba and was a professor at an American university, wrote to me about doing a war job in Canada. I persuaded him to come to the Prime Minister's Office for six months. It was a mistake I deeply regretted. Brown, like Brockington, had a cultivated mind and real style, but neither could get on Mackenzie King's wavelength, and their great talents were largely wasted.

In 1943 Norman Robertson wanted Léger back in External to share in the establishment of a Canadian legation in Chile. I was sorry to see him go but realized he was ideally fitted for diplomatic life and should be allowed to get on with his career. Robertson agreed to second a more junior officer, Jean-Louis Delisle, who carried on Jules's work in the Prime Minister's office effectively for the rest of the war.

Mackenzie King continued to complain that he never had an adequate staff but it remains my conviction that he was as well served as anyone of his difficult temperament could have been. Ilsley once told one of my friends that his relations with Mackenzie King were correct but not friendly, because the prime minister wanted only boot-lickers close to him. My friend asked, 'What about Pickersgill?' to which Ilsley replied, 'I suppose everyone has to have one hair-shirt.' I doubt I was really abrasive, but I never developed a taste for anyone's boots.

The wartime parliament

Many of the MPs elected in 1940 were to play a large part in my life. Among the Liberals was Ernest Lapointe's son, Hugues, universally called Bob or Bobby. He was chosen to move the Address in Reply to the Speech from the Throne in the new Parliament. He made an eloquent speech that pleased the prime minister. Bob was away from Parliament on active service in the army for most of the war years. I did not get to know him well until afterwards, when he became a minister. I was increasingly impressed by his capacity to avoid trouble and his exceptional political 'flair.' I admired even more the devotion to duty he showed in his later career by becoming lieutenant-governor of Quebec, an essential but far from agreeable post after Jean Lesage ceased to be premier. I was proud to call Bob a friend.

The new member chosen to second the address was Jimmy Sinclair. He and I had kept up a desultory but friendly relationship since our time at Oxford. Despite my coaching Sinclair delivered a fire-eating speech interpreted by the press as favouring conscription, though he did not come close to using the word. The prime minister was furious and neither forgot nor forgave. He denied Sinclair the recognition due his superb parliamentary talents. On one occasion after the war he promised him appointment as parliamentary assistant, but he did not keep the promise. I did not see Jimmy often until after the war, as he was on active service in the RCAF, but we later were colleagues in cabinet, where he was minister of fisheries. As minister from Newfoundland, more than once I owed a great deal to his loyal support.

Another newcomer was Walter Harris, who had defeated Agnes MacPhail. I had admired the first woman ever elected to Parliament, was sorry to see her go and was not disposed to look with favour on a young man so ungallant as to defeat her. Senator Lambert told me Harris was one of the ablest new members and a man to watch. I soon liked what little I saw, but he was in the army, and it was 1944 before I got to know him well. We worked closely together as long as he was in public life, and he has remained one of my dearest friends.

Two young and successful lawyers, Brooke Claxton and D.C. Abbott, were elected in Montreal. Brooke I had met once or twice; Doug I had never heard of until his election. Both were friends of Heeney, and I got to know them through him. From the time of their entry into Parliament our lives were mixed up together.

I should mention one other new member whose life was subsequently connected closely with mine, John Diefenbaker. I had never seen him until he appeared in the House of Commons. His ham acting repelled me, and the superficiality of his speeches seemed so obvious that I could not see how anyone could take him seriously. On one occasion in the 1940 session Margaret was in the gallery. When I came home to dinner, she asked me who

that man was with the fanatical eyes; she was sure he was dangerous. When I realized which member she meant, I said, 'Oh, that's
Diefenbaker, who tried more than once to unseat Mackenzie
King. He's just a phony.' I decided later that we were each half
right.

By the beginning of May 1940 the failure of the attempt to save
Norway had created a political crisis in Britain, which was resolved when Churchill replaced Chamberlain as prime minister.
Churchill created a coalition cabinet in which Labour members
were given a large place, and in which the leader of the Liberal
party was included. Churchill became prime minister on 10 May,
the very day Hitler chose to launch the blitzkrieg in the West.
From the outside, Churchill's appointment looked like Britain's
response to the Nazi onslaught.

When Canada's new Parliament met six days later, the country
was in shock, and the government itself had been severely shaken
by the speed of the Nazi advance. The political atmosphere
changed quickly; it was no longer the phony war it had seemed
to be during the election campaign. Many of the Tories and a
large number of nonpartisan English Canadians, influenced by
Churchill's example, felt Canada also should have a coalition
government. Notwithstanding their election defeat on the issue of
National Government, the Conservative Opposition once again
demanded such a measure.

Mackenzie King never wavered in his conviction that National
Government in the form of a coalition with the Opposition in
Parliament would weaken rather than strengthen the war effort.
He knew that for most French Canadians National Government
would evoke the memory of the Union Government of 1917,
which had not included a French-Canadian minister or even a
French-Canadian supporter from Quebec in the House of Commons. Many of the most vociferous advocates of National Government in 1940 did not conceal their aim of achieving a
government in which the influence of French Canada would be
diminished. For many, the first consequence of National Government would be conscription. Manion's personal defeat in the

election and the quick repudiation of his leadership that followed removed the one influential opponent of conscription in the Tory Opposition.

I felt strongly that any concession to the clamour for so-called National Government would reduce the influence of the ministers from Quebec and weaken the government without in any way increasing the war effort. Mackenzie King was hypocritically praised by the Opposition in the House and in the Tory press as a fine peacetime leader but one unsuited to lead a government in wartime. They advocated Ralston as leader of a National Government. After a couple of weeks a highly effective reply to this agitation was made by Gardiner, and the campaign petered out.

Mackenzie King never considered inviting any Conservative MPs to join the government, but he did approach two or three leading citizens with Tory backgrounds with offers of seats in the cabinet. I shared his relief when the proposals were rejected. In the end the only new face in the cabinet from outside Parliament was the popular premier of Nova Scotia, Angus L. Macdonald, who was a Liberal.

The government suffered a grievous loss on 10 June, when Norman Rogers, who was proving his worth as minister of national defence, was killed in a plane crash. His death made urgent the reorganization of the cabinet. Power had already been named minister of national defence for air. He became acting minister of defence until Ralston was moved from Finance to Defence as minister after presenting his budget. On 12 July Power became associate minister of defence as well as continuing as minister for air, and Angus Macdonald became minister for naval services.

Ilsley succeeded Ralston in Finance. While minister of national revenue, Ilsley was not well known in the country. The prime minister never found him congenial, did not appreciate his capacity, and appointed him reluctantly. When Mackenzie King discussed the possible appointment with me, I told him I believed Ilsley was seriously underrated and would be a thoroughly competent minister of finance. He proved far more than that. By the end of the war Ilsley, in the popular mind, was the ablest and strongest of all the ministers.

But in June 1940 Ilsley's appointment did not seem to add new strength to the government. Indeed, the only two ministers with substantial prestige in the public mind were Ralston and Lapointe. Howe still had his great reputation to make.

The fighting war in Europe

The fall of France

The public and Parliament were deeply stirred by the Nazi blitz-krieg and especially by the British retreat from Dunkirk. Mackenzie King felt a positive response by Parliament was needed. One sweeping measure taken was the enacting of a bill called the National Resources Mobilization Act (NRMA) under which all resources including manpower could be conscripted for the pros-ecution of the war. When that measure was introduced, the government announced that single men would be conscripted for military training for the defence of Canadian territory, but section 3 of the bill expressly provided that men conscripted for military service could not be sent outside Canada unless they subse-quently volunteered.

It is doubtful whether the NRMA added anything to the powers the government already had under the War Measures Act of 1914, but it had symbolic value as a fresh expression by Parlia-ment of its intention to support prosecution of the war whole-heartedly. In response to the fall of France and the imminent threat of invasion of Britain, the decision to conscript men for home defence was accepted calmly, if without enthusiasm, in French Canada.

For such conscription a compulsory national registration of all residents over 16 was deemed necessary. The mayor of Montreal, Camillien Houde, described the registration as a prelude to full conscription and advised people not to register. He was promptly interned under the Defence of Canada Regulations, and remained in custody without trial for the rest of the war. I was shocked by his internment; I felt there should have been a trial. Two or three years later I learned Lapointe had been advised that no jury would convict Houde, and that a show of force was essential if widespread disobedience was to be prevented. No one can be sure of the wisdom of that judgment. There was no resistance to the registration or the first call-up except by isolated individuals. The fact that Houde's internment had been recommended by a French-Canadian minister prevented it from taking on a racial overtone.

The Defence of Canada Regulations had been adopted under the War Measures Act at the beginning of the war to deal with the problem of internal security. Among other powers, the regulations authorized the government to arrest and detain persons without trial. In the summer of 1940 those arbitrary regulations were amended to make an offence of membership in the Communist party and also of membership in a number of Communist front organizations, in a cranky outfit called Technocracy and in the Jehovah's Witnesses. Power did his utmost in the cabinet to prevent the decision, and I did what I could to urge one or two ministers I knew well to oppose it. Without being asked I expressed my concern to the prime minister. Mackenzie King clearly did not like the proposals but said Lapointe felt the ban on the Communist party was politically essential in Quebec. For the prime minister, what was politically essential was to keep Lapointe in the government. I agreed with that conclusion, but I felt as unhappy as Chubby did about this illiberal and totally irrelevant decision.

Once France had fallen and the expected onslaught on Britain did not come at once, the atmosphere in Parliament became less tense. After the government was reorganized, the budget adopted, and the NRMA enacted, the parliamentary Opposition ran out of steam. Parliament was adjourned rather than prorogued so that it could resume without formality whenever needed. That was a device used generally during the war, and in recent years it has become normal practice. The session met for prorogation on 6 November 1940, and a new session began the next day. That second session of the Parliament of 1940 was not prorogued until early in 1942, and again a new session opened the next day.

Just after the evacuation from Dunkirk, Skelton showed me a telegram from the British government asking Canada to send our few obsolete destroyers to the English Channel to help defend their coast from invasion. It seemed an almost futile gesture, but the government did not hesitate. The public could not be told about the destroyers, or that Canada's army division in Britain was almost the only trained and equipped land force in the island. That what Canada was doing for Britain was more than Britain had done for France in its extremity the public could not know. That state of affairs made it all the harder for Mackenzie King to bear the taunts of the Opposition that he was a half-hearted leader.

The disastrous course of the war in Europe was a tremendous emotional strain for most Canadians. For me the fall of France had a personal aspect. I felt more attachment to France than to any country but my own. Moreover, I was increasingly anxious about the fate of my brother Frank. His last letter had been written from Paris. When the members of the Canadian legation reached England, they reported that they had lost track of him. From the middle of June until November 1940 we had no news. Not knowing whether Frank was alive or dead was very hard on the family, especially Mother. Eventually we received a letter through the Red Cross from an internment camp at St Denis. In the letter, dated 29 October, Frank wrote: 'It's great to be in Paris. My friends come to see me on my visiting days. Life here is as good as it could possibly be without liberty.' We corresponded and sent parcels through the Red Cross until 18 March 1942, when I received a cable from a friend of Frank's in the unoccupied zone of France saying, 'Your brother arrived here in good health. Try to send underwear, shoes, money, advice.' I feared a direct reply might get Frank or his friends in trouble and doubted that a message would ever reach him. Instead I spoke to the United States minister in Ottawa, Pierrepont Moffatt, and asked him to try to have the embassy at Vichy get in touch with Frank. As we learned from Frank when he reached Lisbon and freedom in late September 1942, the American embassy was very helpful.

I did not need the anxiety about Frank to convince me how wrong my judgment had been before the spring of 1940. The overwhelming success of the blitzkrieg in Belgium and Holland, the collapse of resistance and the armistice in France, and the imminent peril to Britain made it clear to me that Hitler's Germany was a direct threat to the security of Canada, the United States and the Western Hemisphere. Canada was not in the war, in Mackenzie King's phrase, merely standing at Britain's side; the country was at war to defend its own national existence.

The American reaction to Canada at war

The whole of North America held its breath that summer, waiting for the expected invasion of Britain. An increasingly bitter debate developed in the United States between the isolationists, who wanted to retreat into what they called Fortress America, and those who favoured all-out aid for Britain short of war. The supporters of Britain fortunately included President Roosevelt, whose popularity in Canada was all but universal.

Mackenzie King's objective was to promote understanding and cooperation between the United States on the one hand and Canada and Britain on the other. In mid-August Roosevelt invited him for a 24-hour meeting at Ogdensburg, New York. The prime minister drove the 50 miles accompanied only by Handy and Nicol and spent the night on the president's train. On Sunday morning, 18 August 1940 he and the president initialled the handwritten Ogdensburg Agreement pledging the two countries to mutual defence of their territory and establishing a Permanent Joint Board on Defence to advise both governments. Without waiting to submit the agreement to Parliament or even consulting the cabinet or the minister of defence, Mackenzie King joined with Roosevelt in making it public at once.

By chance I was the first in the Prime Minister's Office to learn of the Ogdensburg Agreement. At the beginning of the war we started a system whereby a secretary was on duty in the East

Block every evening until 11 and all day on Saturdays and Sundays. It was my turn that Sunday. When Mackenzie King arrived unexpectedly at the East Block, he sent at once for Skelton and then asked me to find Ralston and have him join them. Ralston was 30 miles up the Gatineau River at the Five Lakes Fishing Club, where there was no telephone, so a military car was sent to bring him back. As he was out on one of the lakes, the whole operation took more than two hours. When Ralston arrived, he approved wholeheartedly of Ogdensburg, and I never heard that any member of the cabinet had had reservations. The next day Arthur Meighen, the Tory leader in the Senate, denounced the agreement as a desertion of Britain. His criticism found no echo and was soon refuted by the exchange of bases in the British Caribbean for 50 retired American destroyers, including 6 for the Canadian navy, and by the establishment of three American military bases in Newfoundland. No one in Newfoundland was consulted about the grant of the bases, but Churchill sought and received the concurrence of the Canadian government.

Canada had assumed responsibility for the territorial defence of Newfoundland in 1939. Mackenzie King never failed to assert the priority of Canada's interest in Newfoundland, which both Roosevelt and Churchill invariably recognized. Most Canadians and Newfoundlanders realized that the United States bases were a tangible element in the common defence of North America.

My only part in those developments was to assist in the preparation of Mackenzie King's speech welcoming the destroyer-bases exchange between the United States and Britain. The broadcast was well received, and strengthened his leadership.

In September we watched the Battle of Britain with a mixture of admiration and vicarious terror. Though our air force was not engaged, many of the pilots were Canadians serving in the Royal Air Force. Their exploits enabled citizens at home to take pride in the Canadian contribution to that stupendous British victory. The excitement and tension affected me, but I have wondered since then why I never really doubted the outcome. Friends and members of the family have often described me as an unrealistic wishful thinker; that may well be the explanation.

The invasion of Britain having failed to take place, the rest of 1940 was largely a political anticlimax in Canada. The first call-up of conscripts for one month's military training took place without incident. There was increasing progress in developing the armed forces, establishing the air training organization and beginning the production of munitions on a large scale.

The political front was relatively quiet. The gravest problems faced by the government were financial. One pressing problem was the shortage of U.S. dollars. American dollars were needed to pay for Canadian purchases of munitions and supplies on Canadian account in the United States. The shortage was overcome by skilful Canadian diplomacy in Washington, which produced the Hyde Park Declaration, issued by Roosevelt and Mackenzie King on 20 April 1941. The basic point in the declaration was agreement to make the most effective use of the production facilities of North America for both local and hemispheric defence. To do so, each country would provide the other with defence articles it was able to produce quickly. It was estimated that during the next 12 months Canada could supply the United States with between $2 million and $3 million worth of such defence articles, and that payment to Canada for those articles would help meet the cost of Canadian purchases in the United States, thereby reducing the country's need for American dollars. I had nothing whatever to do with that brilliant exercise in statesmanship. After the fact, I assisted the prime minister in preparing a broadcast explaining it to the public. By that time my understanding of financial problems was growing quickly, and I was beginning to achieve a reputation among the financial bureaucrats as a popularizer of financial and economic policies.

The federal-provincial taxation problem

Another financial problem was just as difficult. If the war was to be financed effectively, some kind of fiscal arrangement had to be made with the provincial governments. Speaking broadly, what was physically possible had to be made financially possible; that was the first priority at home at the beginning of 1941. The most pressing concern was how to finance the expansion of the armed forces, the air training plan and the production of weapons.

It was essential to make full use of direct taxation, particularly income tax. The first obstacle was the existence of provincial income taxes at varying rates. It could be removed by adopting recommendations of the Royal Commission on Dominion-Provincial Relations. The commission's proposed solution to the domestic financial problem which had seemed so desperately urgent during the depression, seemed almost irrelevant in 1940 as the country moved towards full employment. The report had been ignored when it was received in 1940. Later in 1940 the report was examined seriously, as a guide to the financial relations between the government of Canada and the provincial governments for the rest of the war and beyond. The plan recommended in the report would have given Parliament permanently the exclusive power to levy income taxes on individuals and corporations in exchange for greater financial benefits to the provincial treasuries.

The cabinet, particularly the prime minister, doubted that all the provincial governments would agree to the implementation of the Rowell-Sirois plan. It was explained in the most persuasive way possible in a draft speech prepared for the prime minister. Mackenzie King was reluctantly persuaded to call a dominion-provincial conference to meet 14 January 1941.

I was involved at every stage in the planning of the conference and in the preparation of the opening speech. I was as keen on the longterm as on the short-term obectives of the plan. Of all the provincial governments, Manitoba's alone understood the recommendations of the report thoroughly. The Manitoba government was the most enthusiastic, perhaps the only unreservedly enthusiastic, provincial supporter. The premiers of Ontario, British Columbia and Alberta refused to consider the proposals, and the conference failed. The prime minister noted in his diary that

Manitobans, Brockington, Heeney and I were its keenest advocates. After the conference collapsed, he wrote that the Manitoba influence in his office was much too great.

Though the conference failed to agree on the implementation of the Rowell-Sirois plan, Ilsley had insisted in a passionate speech that federal control of personal and corporation income taxes was essential to an effective war effort. In his subsequent budget he proposed wartime tax-rental agreements, under which the provincial governments would receive payments from the national treasury in exchange for suspending their own taxes for the duration of the war and one year thereafter. Though I was disappointed at the time, I became convinced later that it was fortunate the Rowell-Sirois plan was rejected. In my judgment the postwar tax-rental arrangements and the equalization plan that would evolve from them served the purpose better than the original plan would have done.

All the provincial governments accepted the wartime tax-rental agreements that Ilsley proposed in his budget. The agreements left the federal government free to raise income taxes to uniform rates everywhere in Canada, rates that would be high enough to pay a substantial part of the cost of waging war, and that, incidentally, would serve as a brake on inflation.

Hitler attacks Russia

In early 1941 there was widespread expectation that Hitler was planning an invasion of Britain in the late spring or early summer. The expectation was reduced after 6 April 1941, when the Nazis invaded Yugoslavia and Greece. News of the fresh aggression reached us early on a Sunday morning. Mackenzie King asked me to draft a statement he could make that evening. I sent him a draft in the late morning and then went off to celebrate Margaret's birthday.

Shortly after we got home, I called the office and was told Mackenzie King wanted to speak to me. He was not satisfied with my draft. In the morning he had mentioned to me a passage he liked in a statement by 'Wild Bill' Donovan, which I had not included. Donovan was then at an early stage in his extraordinary career in military intelligence, which he began as a secret intermediary between Roosevelt and the British government in 1940 and 1941. After Pearl Harbor, Donovan created the American Office of Strategic Services, which became the Central Intelligence Agency after the war.

My failure to include Donovan's phrase was cited as a grievance. My absence during the day was hinted at as desertion of the prime minister in his hour of need, though there was no direct accusation. I felt my draft of the morning was adequate. I had steered clear of quoting Donovan because I disliked the prime minister's practice of embellishing his speeches with quotations from Churchill or Roosevelt; I felt it reflected a colonial attitude. I had drawn the line at Donovan. I had been sure Mackenzie King would not start revising his statement until evening, when I would be back from our outing. I resented the implication that I had been derelict in my duty. But we had no trouble in working out a statement in time for the national news broadcast that duly reflected Donovan's inspired words.

The 1941 parliamentary session was a relatively easy one for the prime minister. The prospect of an immediate invasion of Britain ended when Hitler attacked the Soviet Union on 22 June. On hearing the news of the attack I sat down and wrote a draft of a speech for the prime minister. Churchill was to make a broadcast in mid-afternoon, Ottawa time. Mackenzie King had me come to Laurier House to listen to Churchill. He said his own statement would be prepared right afterwards. Luckily in my draft I had taken the same general line as Churchill, and when we began revising, my draft survived with relatively few alterations.

The myth of Nazi invincibility on land was at its height in 1941. The ease and thoroughness of the conquest of Yugoslavia and Greece, the seizure of Crete, the appearance of the Germans in North Africa and the rapid advance across Russia seemed to indicate that nothing would stop them.

The prime minister's recruiting mission in western Canada

As long as Britain was not fighting on land, except briefly in Greece and in North Africa, there was no military action possible for Canada beyond the air training and naval patrols in which the country was already engaged. Recruiting for the army had slowed down, and the prime minister was urged by Ralston to join in an appeal for recruits. Mackenzie King was not enthusiastic. He never lost a feeling of guilt that he had not served in the First World War, and he was unfamiliar with ranks and badges and uncomfortable reviewing troops. At the same time he was under Tory pressure to visit Britain and demonstrate the solidarity of what many still called the Empire. Others felt he should go to London to insist on a voice in the direction of the war. He considered a tour in Canada to stimulate recruiting a lesser burden than a visit to London.

The parliamentary session was adjourned on 14 June 1941. Ten days later Mackenzie King set out by train on an inspection tour of military establishments. The tour began in Calgary and included appeals for recruits in Vancouver, Victoria, Prince Albert and Winnipeg. Conscriptionists regarded the tour as a splendid opportunity to counter the appeal for volunteers with their own campaign. Calgary seemed to them the best place in Canada for such a demonstration. Although Liberals had won both seats in Parliament in 1940, Calgary at heart was a Tory town, always demonstrative and often flamboyant.

The city was inundated with leaflets urging conscription. Mackenzie King decided to meet the defiance head on. He made an excellent speech in reply, that with unreserved gusto I had worked on with him. Since no Canadian soldiers were in action, the conscription campaign had very little popular support, and it was not repeated elsewhere on the trip. The only attraction of Calgary for me was that Bessie and her husband lived there, and it was my first chance to see them since the beginning of the war.

Before June 1941 I had never been more than a few miles west of Moose Jaw. Like almost all visitors I was impressed by the mountains and astonished by the aridity of what little I saw of the interior of British Columbia. We stopped for the weekend at Harrison Hot Springs. All the Liberal hangers-on and ward-heelers from Vancouver were there to greet the prime minister and court his favour; I did not find it a pretty sight, and neither did Mackenzie King.

On Sunday afternoon we boarded the private car and were hooked on to the train for Vancouver. Before dinner Mackenzie King, who had given up drinking for the duration of the war, turned to me and said, 'Pickersgill, would you like a scotch? I feel I need one.' I accepted with alacrity, and I am sure both of us felt better for it, though in those days I preferred rye. So far as I know that was Mackenzie King's only lapse; he resumed drinking in a very mild way after the fighting stopped in Europe.

I remember almost nothing of that first visit to Vancouver, but I do remember Victoria, where we visited all the naval and military establishments, including Work Point, where my brother Walter was in training. He had joined the army in the spring of 1941, and he served until 1946. Mother was also in Victoria that summer, for the first of several visits, but I saw her only briefly. I was not as impressed with the beauty of Vancouver and Victoria as I was to become later. British Columbia was not love at first sight, but my admiration for its beauty, though not for its politicians, has grown steadily.

The western trip did not save Mackenzie King from his visit to London. Roosevelt and Churchill had their meeting at Argentia, Newfoundland, in August 1941. Mackenzie King felt left out of the picture, and he feared the public would think he had been left out too. Shortly after the Argentia meeting Churchill again invited him to Britain, and he accepted. He had never flown and dreaded the prospect, but he felt that his political future was at stake, and that flying the Atlantic was the lesser risk.

Mackenzie King flies the Atlantic

Once the Prime Minister decided to visit Britain a flight was easy to arrange. In 1941 Liberator bombers were being ferried across the Atlantic almost every day. Arrangements were made to have a heated cabin installed in one of them, with a couch and two reclining chairs. Mackenzie King had the couch, Georges Vanier and Norman Robertson the reclining chairs. The rest of the party were equipped with flying suits and accommodated in the cold forward part of the plane or the tail.

Norman Robertson had been appointed acting under-secretary of state for external affairs when Skelton died suddenly in January 1941. Norman quickly gained the prime minister's confidence, though he never became the regular adviser on domestic matters that Skelton had been. His appointment as under-secretary was confirmed at around the end of June, as was Turnbull's as principal secretary to the prime minister. Vanier had been minister to

Mackenzie King's flight across the Atlantic in a Liberator bomber fitted up with a cabin for the Prime Minister. The entourage were fitted out with flight clothes against the cold. Left to right in the tail of the plane: J.W.P., Nicol and Handy.

France at the time France collapsed and had managed to escape to England. He had not yet received another post and was in Ottawa that summer. Mackenzie King liked Vanier and felt he would be helpful in dealing with social contacts and correspondence in London, and so he proved to be. I scarcely knew Vanier before we left, but in the close quarters of that trip we became friends. He was somewhat hesitant about going, as his wife Pauline was pregnant, as was Margaret. There was little prospect of our baby's arriving before I returned from London, but fortunately Michel Vanier was born before we left.

Turnbull, Handy, Nicol and I completed the prime minister's entourage. One or two pressmen, including Gregory Clark, accompanied us. We took off from St-Hubert airport at about noon. All of us except the prime minister and Vanier had to pack ourselves into the bomb-bay for takeoff and landing. It was quite dark there, and I cheered up everyone by saying I did not mind being killed but would like to see it happen.

We landed at Gander to refuel. That was the first time I ever set foot in Newfoundland. The immense size of the airfield astonished me, and I was told it was the largest airport in the world. Mackenzie King had an hour or so of sleep, and we took off at the end of the afternoon to fly the Atlantic.

We were met at Prestwick, in Scotland, by Vincent Massey, the high commissioner, and several members of his staff, including Charles Ritchie and George Ignatieff, neither of whom I had met before. We were taken at once to the Railway Hotel in Glasgow, where Mackenzie King promptly went to bed. The rest of us were milling around the lobby sorting out our luggage, which Nicol was assumed to have looked after. Everything had been accounted for, when Vanier asked Nicol where his leg was. Nicol said, 'Your leg, sir?' Vanier had an artificial leg and always travelled with a spare in a leather case. When he described it, Nicol said, 'I'm sorry, Colonel Vanier, I thought it was a machine gun. I told the crew to put it back in the plane.' The two WRENS who were driving us had to be sent back to Prestwick for the missing leg. We eventually got to London by train and were installed in the Dorchester Hotel, where Massey lived during the war.

My principal task in London was to help the prime minister prepare the speech he was to give at a luncheon at the Mansion House in the City. Many exhausting hours were spent on it. It proved to be a great success both in London and, more important, at home. News reports of Churchill's attentions to Mackenzie King as well as his own performance in London certainly added to what today would be called his 'image' in Canada.

When the visit was over, we took the train from Euston Station to Glasgow. Most of the luggage was taken to the train for us, but Norman Robertson carried his own bag and walked along the platform with Nicol, who was carrying one of the prime minister's bags. Nicol put it down several times to rest. When Norman remarked that the bag seemed rather heavy, Nicol replied, 'So would yours be, Mr Robertson, if it had in it pieces of the Parliament Building and Buckingham Palace.' He was referring to stones from the bombing that Mackenzie King was taking home to add to his ruins at Kingsmere.

We left Prestwick at 6 a.m. and reached Dorval at about 4 p.m. On 20 August we had left from St-Hubert airport, by 7 September Dorval airport was open. The prime minister's private car was waiting. Ernest Lapointe and Howe had flown from Ottawa to meet the prime minister, and they offered him a flight back to Ottawa, which he declined. Norman and I were offered a lift, which we gratefully accepted. We reached Ottawa at 6 p.m. after crossing the Atlantic from Prestwick entirely in daylight. For those days it was a remarkable, though not a unique, achievement.

As we drove into town from the airport, I asked Norman if he was going to meet the train when the prime minister arrived. He asked why on earth he should, and I opined that otherwise we would be deemed 'to have deserted in the face of the enemy.' He was incredulous until I explained why I thought so. I had one day said to Norman that Mackenzie King was the most complicated human being he would ever encounter, and he demurred. As I got out of the car at the Mayfair, he said, 'I agree, the most complicated.'

Once I had greeted Margaret, I asked if there was any beef in the house. There was not, so we went to the Château Laurier, where we encountered Jim Coyne's father, who treated us to a roast beef dinner. Norman did go to the train, which arrived at 10 p.m., and he was received coldly. I expected a similar reaction from the prime minister when he telephoned me the next morning. He asked if I was pleased to be home. I replied that I could hardly wait to get back, with my wife 'in that condition.' Mackenzie King hated any reference to pregnancy and related matters, and said, with obvious embarrassment, 'Oh, Pickersgill, I did not realize that,' and hastily changed the subject.

The price ceiling and wage stabilization

With full employment and much of the manufacturing capacity being used for war production, prices began to rise in 1941, and wage demands with them. The government was determined not to permit the price and wage inflation of the First World War. Officials in Finance and the Bank of Canada devised a plan for price and wage control that would be inflexible. The plan was called a price ceiling and wage stabilization. At first the cabinet and the prime minister were skeptical about the plan; the only minister completely in favour was Ilsley, who had been well briefed by Clark and by W.A. Mackintosh, who had been brought from Queen's University as a wartime assistant to Clark.

Mackintosh drafted a cabinet paper recommending the plan, and he also briefed me. I had already learned of the plan from Jim Coyne and Bob Beattie, who were among its original architects. I believed it would work if a strong enough chairman of the Wartime Prices and Trade Board could be found, and if he had the backing of a powerful minister. The prime minister was finally persuaded it was worth trying, because the alternative, of doing nothing, would be worse. He was to announce the policy, and I was commissioned to redraft the cabinet paper as a press release. Grant Dexter, the parliamentary correspondent of the *Winnipeg Free Press*, was enlisted to work with me. Mackenzie King felt that Grant and I would do better together than I would do by myself.

Dexter's opinion was that price ceiling defied the laws of political economy, but he agreed reluctantly to help make it look as plausible as possible. When the draft was completed, I was proud of our handiwork. I suggested to the prime minister that he broadcast the announcement so that the public would have the full description before it was attacked by the critics. He liked the text, and after further revisions to make it sound like him he agreed.

The broadcast was a national sensation. The fan mail was far greater than for all his previous broadcasts added together. Even the press comment was favourable.

It was an auspicious start. But the success of the plan clearly depended on its administration, and that too was settled before the plan was announced. Ilsley offered to undertake the ministerial responsibility, and his offer was accepted at once. Clark persuaded Ilsley and the prime minister that Donald Gordon, the deputy governor of the Bank of Canada, was the only man who combined intelligence and toughness in the right proportions to do the job. The governor, Graham Towers, was reluctant to release Gordon, and the prime minister had virtually to conscript him. It was an inspired choice. Gordon insisted on having Jim Coyne as deputy chairman. As a result I was always told of problems that required backing by the government and was sometimes able to stiffen the support of the prime minister. The Wartime Prices and Trade Board was one of the most effective of the war agencies. The price ceiling and wage stabilization did more to maintain morale throughout the war than any other action taken by the government.

Ernest Lapointe's death and other changes

In November 1941 the government and the prime minister suffered one of their greatest blows. Ernest Lapointe, in ill health for more than a year, died. He was Mackenzie King's closest colleague and the preeminent spokesman and leader of French Canada. He seemed irreplaceable. Arthur Cardin, the other French-Canadian minister, was a superb parliamentarian and a great orator, but Mackenzie King never really trusted him, and Cardin had no prestige in English Canada. What is more, Cardin himself did not aspire to the succession.

Shortly before Lapointe's death Mackenzie King took me with him to St-Lin, in Quebec, where Laurier's birthplace had been restored as a historic site. The prime minister and premier Godbout both spoke at the ceremony to open the site. Mackenzie King's admiration for Godbout was kindled anew. On the way back to Ottawa the prime minister made his last visit to Lapointe, in a Montreal hospital. Lapointe knew he was dying and urged Mackenzie King not to delay in replacing him.

The obvious choice was Godbout. Mackenzie King put great pressure on him at the funeral and later by telephone. Godbout wisely declined, on the triple ground that there was no one to replace him in Quebec, that his English was imperfect, and that he was unknown outside Quebec. Mackenzie King's second choice was Louis St Laurent. The prime minister barely knew St Laurent but his initial impression was good; no one expected St Laurent to be an adequate replacement for Lapointe. I was barely aware of St Laurent's existence before he became a minister, and had no inkling of the large part he was to have in my life.

Mackenzie King was also deeply affected by another change in the political scene. On 9 November 1941 Arthur Meighen, the Conservative leader in the Senate, became leader of the Tory party without being chosen by a national convention, in a kind of political putsch. He resigned his seat in the Senate, and the member for York South resigned at the same time to open a seat for Meighen in the House of Commons. Meighen lost no time in announcing that the Tory party favoured the immediate application of compulsory selective service, the latest euphemism for conscription. Mackenzie King hated and feared Meighen as he did no other man, and dreaded the prospect of facing him in Parliament. He was almost equally fearful of a direct debate on the conscription issue and began to consider ways of postponing, if not entirely avoiding, a confrontation.

On 6 December 1941 the government decided to tidy up the external situation by having war declared on Hungary, Romania and Finland, all of which had entered the war on the side of Germany. War was declared on them without reference to Parliament, though Mackenzie King consulted the other parliamentary party leaders. For some reason or none Bulgaria was not included. Months later someone in External Affairs realized that Bulgaria had been overlooked. Mackenzie King was sent a memorandum suggesting a declaration of war on Bulgaria. James Gibson and I were with him at Laurier House when he read the memorandum. He asked me why we should. There were many Canadians serving in the RAF; I suggested that one of them might be shot down over Bulgaria and, if we were not at war, might not be treated as a prisoner of war. It was the best reason I could think of, but it was not impressive. Mackenzie King said the Bulgarians would not know the difference between a Briton and a Canadian and told Gibson to file the memorandum. That is why Canada was never at war with Bulgaria.

The war in Europe becomes a world war

Pearl Harbor and Churchill in Ottawa

It was ironical that the spate of declarations of war against three European countries preceded by one day the transformation of the European war into a world war. I was in bed with a mild attack of flu on Sunday afternoon, 7 December, when Bob Bryce telephoned to ask if I had heard on the radio that the Japanese had bombed Pearl Harbor. I made a rapid recovery and went off to the East Block soon afterwards. For some inexplicable reason Mackenzie King was eager to have Canada declare war on Japan ahead of the United States and Britain. While the cabinet met and he consulted the other party leaders by telephone, I prepared a draft of a broadcast to announce that Canada was at war with Japan. The King's approval was secured, and war had been declared by midnight. The next day the prime minister wondered whether he had not been too rash, and whether after the war the Japanese might develop a special grudge against Canada.

The attack on Pearl Harbor brought the United States into war with Japan. The British feared, as Canada did, that the Americans might ignore Europe and concentrate on fighting the Japanese. There was profound relief when the United States did not hesitate to declare war on Germany as well as Japan. Churchill lost little time in going to Washington to confer with Roosevelt and do what he could to make sure the war on Germany had priority. Mackenzie King was invited to join them. The Canadian party, which included all three defence ministers and C.D. Howe left for Washington the afternoon of Christmas Day.

On Christmas morning the news reached Ottawa that Admiral Muselier of the Free French forces, who had been visiting Canada as the representative of General de Gaulle, had seized the islands of St-Pierre and Miquelon, the French colony off the coast of Newfoundland. The action produced a minor crisis. The United States government accused Canada of complicity, an accusation indignantly refuted. When we reached Washington the Americans tried to persuade Mackenzie King to have Canada remove the Free French by force if necessary and reinstate the governor, who represented Vichy. He refused, on the ground that Canadian opinion would be outraged, to comply with what had become almost an American order. The Americans then threatened to expel the Free French on their own. Mackenzie King had great difficulty in dissuading them. The St-Pierre affair took up a good deal of Mackenzie King's time in Washington — perhaps just as well, since he had very little part in the discussions between Roosevelt and Churchill. I felt Canada's position in Washington was humiliating, and the defence ministers, who had even less to do, felt the same way.

While in Washington Churchill accepted Mackenzie King's invitation to visit Ottawa to speak to a meeting of the members of both Houses of Parliament, who were called back from their Christmas recess for the occasion. The prime minister had worked out a program for Churchill's visit. Churchill's close friend and cabinet colleague, Lord Beaverbrook, was with him in Washington, and Mackenzie King wanted to have Beaverbrook consulted about the program. He asked me to go to Beaverbrook's suite in our hotel to see whether or not he thought the program would be agreeable to Churchill. I could not see why Beaverbrook's judgment would be any better than Mackenzie King's and felt the errand was demeaning, but I duly presented myself in Beaverbrook's anteroom and asked a flunky to introduce me. The flunky disappeared without a trace. About a quarter hour later another flunky appeared, who tried to ignore me. I took him by the arm and demanded to be taken in at once to see his master.

Beaverbrook was seated in the middle of the sitting room, surrounded by a court that included C.D. Howe. He did not ask me to sit but demanded to know my business. I said the prime minister wanted me to consult him about the program for Churchill's visit to Ottawa. I retailed the items one by one, to each of which he said that should be all right. He asked where I was from, and when I said Manitoba, he retorted that all the bright young Canadians were from the Maritimes. I replied that that might have been true in his day, but that now they were all from the prairies. That brilliant exchange concluded the audience, and I took my leave. I doubt if Churchill was ever told of the proposed program but his visit to Ottawa was an unqualified success and ended what for Mackenzie King, and for Canada, had been an eventful year.

For Margaret and me the most important event of 1941 was the birth of our daughter Jane.

The plebiscite

At the beginning of 1942 the fact that the United States was in the war was the only sign of hope. The speed of the Japanese advance in southeast Asia almost exceeded the pace of Nazi conquests in Europe and Africa. The loss of Hong Kong, where Churchill had persuaded the Canadian government to add two battalions to the garrison, brought the Japanese war home to Canadians. Fear in British Columbia of its Japanese residents, whether Canadian citizens or not, was hysterical and led to drastic protective measures that few Canadians look back on without a feeling of shame. Except in British Columbia the war with Germany continued to be the main Canadian preoccupation. The Nazis still had the upper hand in Russia, and also in North Africa, the only theatre where British troops were engaged. The Battle of the Atlantic grew more desperate for Britain. No one expected early victory, though after the United States was engaged, few believed that the Axis could actually conquer the world.

The direction of Allied strategy was taken over by a combined organization of the Americans and the British. The United States was even less willing than Britain to give any part in strategic planning to other Commonwealth nations. Mackenzie King did not press the claim to a voice in planning, but he was anxious for honourable mention in public announcements. The Canadian contribution was sometimes overlooked in London and especially in Washington, where Canada was regarded too often as a British colony or appendage.

In 1942 the prime minister's attention was focused most of the time on the political scene in Canada. After Meighen became Tory leader, Mackenzie King's immediate concern was to avoid a direct confrontation in Parliament over conscription. He had no personal conviction that conscription was wrong in itself. He admitted to me privately that he thought conscription the fairest system of recruitment, a view I never shared. But he was convinced that an attempt to impose conscription in French Canada would divide the country and weaken Canada's contribution to the prosecution of the war. He feared conscription would be unenforceable and might lead to civil disorder or worse.

The problem of avoiding a confrontation was complicated because St Laurent, though a minister, was not in Parliament, and a by-election would be necessary to secure him a seat. If a by-election was called to elect St Laurent, it would be virtually impossible not to call one in York South, where Meighen proposed to seek election. It had been the practice when a newly chosen party leader sought election to the House of Commons for the government in office not to contest the by-election. The government decided to follow that practice, and the Liberal party did not contest York South, though the CCF did. Mackenzie King never doubted that Meighen would be elected.

There were two other vacant seats, Welland and Montreal—Ste-Marie. Four by-elections were called for 9 February 1942. There seemed no doubt about the outcome in Montreal or in Quebec East, Lapointe's and Laurier's old constituency, where St Laurent was to be the candidate. Welland was a traditionally Liberal riding but there was always a danger of a surge of conscriptionist feeling in almost any Ontario seat. Mackenzie King heard that Humphrey Mitchell, who had been an Independent Labour MP from Hamilton in the early 1930s, might accept the Labour portfolio and the Liberal nomination in Welland. He did, was elected, and remained minister of labour for the rest of his life.

The United States adopted the draft as soon as it went to war. That development provided Meighen and conscriptionists with a powerful new argument for Canadian conscription for service outside the country. Indeed, one or two of my French-Canadian friends told me that right after the shock of Pearl Harbor, conscription might have been acceptable in French Canada. It was the only moment during the war when that might have been so. But even then it would not have been feasible without resignations from the government and a racial schism in the Liberal party. There was certainly no military argument for conscription at any time in 1942: apart from Dieppe later in the year, the Canadian army was not in action, and no action was in prospect. Large though the army had become by that time, there was no real difficulty in getting enough volunteers to keep it up to strength. From late 1940 the men called up for training in Canada under the NRMA were retained in the army. Some of those home defence conscripts volunteered for service anywhere. But many did not, and the presence of those conscripts under arms created, in one sense, two armies within one. If a real military crisis came, there was little doubt a widespread demand would arise for their employment overseas.

The conscriptionists' main argument was that there should be equality of sacrifice. In many cases what underlay this argument was the determination 'to make the French do their share.' The phony argument itself repelled me. Mackenzie King continued to believe that a decision to use the conscripts outside Canada would split the country and reduce the total war effort.

I remember well driving with him from the East Block to Laurier House just at dusk one December afternoon in 1941. He suddenly asked me what I would think of having a referendum on conscription. I had not thought of it and expressed no enthusiasm but promised to think about the pros and cons. At first I thought his idea was a simple referendum, yes or no, to decide the issue.

The next time the subject came up, his suggestion was more subtle. Instead of asking the voters whether or not there should be conscription for overseas service and accepting the decision of the majority, Mackenzie King now thought of asking the voters whether or not they would relieve the government of its pledge not to resort to conscription for service overseas. If there was a favourable majority in such a referendum, the actual decision to use the trained conscripts would be left to the government, to be made according to military needs. Mackenzie King believed that such a question could not be opposed easily by the conscriptionists but would still leave the government free to avoid sending conscripts out of the country except in an extremity.

To the best of my knowledge he had consulted no one but me until then. Before going to cabinet with his proposal the prime minister had me consult the chief electoral officer, Jules Castonguay, about the time required to hold a referendum. When Castonguay said it would take from seven to eight weeks, Mackenzie King sent for him and tried to bully him into reducing the time. I was present, and I saw Castonguay, in a wonderful demonstration of passive resistance, stick to his original answer. When he left, Mackenzie King muttered, 'Stupid fellow, Castonguay.' But I was filled with admiration for him, and subsequent contact increased it.

Mackenzie King decided to call the proposed vote a plebiscite rather than a referendum. He made the distinction that a plebiscite was not binding on a government but was a mere expression of opinion, whereas a referendum was binding. A plebiscite it became. The proposal was received without enthusiasm by most of the ministers and with vigorous opposition by Cardin, who said that regardless of the question most French Canadians would consider a 'yes' vote as a vote for conscription. How right he was.

The cabinet finally agreed, and the proposed plebiscite was announced in the Speech from the Throne opening the new session of Parliament late in January. The issue had no effect on the two by-elections in Ontario, but it aroused immediate and organized opposition in Montreal and Quebec City. Part of the Liberal organization in Quebec East stopped supporting St Laurent, and his extreme nationalist opponent, Paul Bouchard, mounted an abusive campaign. For a while the outcome seemed in doubt. St Laurent refused categorically to give any kind of pledge to oppose conscription, arguing that a government headed by Mackenzie King was the best guarantee that the views of French Canadians would be heard, and their interests protected, in Ottawa.

Mackenzie King was very tense until the by-elections were over. He was certain Meighen would be elected, and he began to fear St Laurent might not be. I heard reports that after the initial setback St Laurent was gaining ground, and that people were impressed by his candour and obvious courage. I also began to hear that Meighen might be defeated. The CCF had nominated a schoolteacher named Joseph Noseworthy, a Newfoundlander. He seemed a dull fellow, and at first no one thought he had a chance, except the CCF workers, who were surprised by the response they were getting. Federal Liberals took no part in the campaign until the Liberal premier of Ontario, Mitchell Hepburn, intervened on Meighen's behalf. Mackenzie King then agreed to have his supporters come out openly for the CCF candidate, though neither he nor any minister did. How much advantage that gave Noseworthy I do not know; I felt he was going to win anyway. I had a very small part in the campaign. I kept in close touch with David Lewis, the national secretary of the CCF, and helped draft one or two of the leaflets. David was more optimistic every day, and I heard that Howe also believed Meighen would lose.

On election day I told Mackenzie King that Meighen would not win. He said that Howe had told him the same thing, but that neither of us knew anything about politics. I have rarely seen anyone more delighted than the prime minister when we turned out to have been right about Meighen. St Laurent had won decisively. Mitchell had been elected in Welland, and the Liberal candidate, Gaspard Fauteux, had had an easy victory in Montreal.

The plebiscite was another matter. The bill to authorize it met immediate opposition in Parliament from French-speaking Liberal backbenchers, most of them not extremists. Organized opposition from the self-styled League for the Defence of Canada in Montreal grew steadily. One of the leaders of the League was Jean Drapeau, later the long-term mayor of Montreal.

When the plebiscite campaign began, I was not at all happy with the line the prime minister took. His arguments were directed to English-speaking Canadians, who would vote 'yes' anyway, when he should, in my view, have been making a strong emotional plea to French Canadians, who were likely to vote 'no.' Cardin was persuaded with difficulty to make an appeal for an affirmative vote. Though he spoke well, it was obvious he did not think any of the voters would be moved by his appeal. Nor were they.

I drafted one speech for Mackenzie King that he rejected utterly, almost with scorn. A day or two later Brooke Claxton asked me if I had anything in my waste basket that he could use for a local speech in Montreal, and I gave him the reject. The very next day the prime minister asked to look at the draft again and decided to use it. I believe it was the only time he delivered one of my draft speeches almost unchanged. I called Brooke at once to find out if he had used the speech, and to my consternation learned that not only had he used it, but hundreds of copies had already been printed for distribution in Montreal. I made him promise to burn them all. So far as I know, Mackenzie King never found out that his speech had already been delivered by someone else.

The result of the plebiscite revealed an almost complete racial split between English- and French-speaking Canada: a 'yes' majority in most constituencies outside Quebec, and a 'no' majority in all but four or five in Quebec. J.W. Dafoe said the question might almost as well have been, Are you a French Canadian?

The conscription crisis in Parliament, 1942

Parliament was in session, and the government had to decide what, if anything, to do about the outcome of the plebiscite. The logical course was to ask Parliament to repeal section 3 of the NRMA, which limited the service of conscripts to Canada, but not to make conscripts available for service overseas unless they were needed to meet an emergency. The opinion widely voiced in French Canada was that Mackenzie King's anticonscription pledge was intended only to reassure French Canadians, and that the majority of French Canadians had not released the government from that pledge.

Cardin argued that section 3 should not be repealed. Mackenzie King, like Cardin, would have preferred to do nothing, but his instinct told him that the government could not totally ignore the vote of a majority of Canadians. In direct opposition to Cardin's view, the defence ministers, surprisingly including Power, argued that the majority of Canadians had voted for conscription, and therefore that conscripts already in the army and men called up in the future should be made available at once for service anywhere. That course Mackenzie King refused to consider. Eventually the cabinet approved a bill merely to repeal section 3,which limited the service of conscripts to Canada.

When introduced in Parliament, the bill became known as Bill 80. I believe it was the first time a piece of Canadian legislation was popularly called by its number — a practice that has gradually become common, both in Parliament and in the provincial legislatures.

Cardin resigned from the cabinet and at once became the leader of the opponents of the bill in Parliament. It was soon apparent that the opposition would include all but a handful of the French-speaking Liberal backbenchers. St Laurent showed no hesitation in supporting the cabinet decision. It is probable that without his support Mackenzie King would not have been able to continue to lead the government.

Throughout the long debate on Bill 80 Parliament presented the curious spectacle of the Tory opposition supporting the most important and controversial of the government's measures while the Liberal ranks provided most of the opposition. The CCF also opposed the bill, primarily because it included no conscription of wealth. The Social Credit MPs supported it.

I laboured with Mackenzie King for weeks on the speech with which he opened the debate. He reviewed the course of Canadian action from the outbreak of war and gave an inventory of the measures taken to ensure that Canada was making a total war effort. He deplored the way the conscriptionists argued there could not be 'total war' without conscription. To justify the removal of the statutory limit on the use of conscripts while refraining from using them except in dire need, the prime minister described the government's policy as 'not necessarily conscription, but conscription if necessary.' The phrase was not original; it had been used in a *Toronto Star* editorial that I had shown Mackenzie King, who fastened on it at once and made it his own.

The speech was long and detailed. Bruce Hutchison wrote that it contained everything, 'including the kitchen sink.' Ilsley, who was rarely a friendly critic of Mackenzie King's speeches, told one of my friends that it was the finest definition of a total war effort he had seen anywhere. The speech served its main purpose, of providing arguments needed by the English-speaking Liberals in Parliament to justify the government's compromise. The strange debate was long but not really bitter. Before it concluded in early July, it was clear that the public was reasonably satisfied with the government's course.

One person who was not satisfied was Ralston, who was supported in his position by Angus Macdonald. During the debate a new issue had arisen because Mackenzie King had undertaken that the government would not send conscripts outside

Canada without a further reference to Parliament. He did not make clear what form the reference would take, and Ralston thought he meant that Parliament would be asked to approve the use of conscripts overseas. In their discussions Mackenzie King said no, Parliament would not be asked to decide, the government would decide, lay its decision before Parliament and ask for a vote of confidence. Ralston argued that in an emergency he could not agree to the delay that would be caused by a submission to Parliament.

He submitted his resignation, which the prime minister refused to accept. Mackenzie King asked St Laurent to talk to Ralston, knowing he respected St Laurent greatly. At the same time the prime minister prepared a reply to Ralston's letter, which I helped to draft, proposing that the resignation be kept in suspense as long as the situation was hypothetical but implying that it would be accepted if an emergency arose and there continued to be a difference between them. Ralston reluctantly agreed, but the relationship between them was never again the same. Fortunately Ralston had apparently told no one about his letter of resignation, and no rumours of the crisis within a crisis arose. Once Bill 80 was passed, the first conscription crisis was over. Public opinion had never been deeply aroused, even in Quebec, and political attention turned elsewhere.

For me the conscription crisis of 1942 was a lesson in practical politics from a master craftsman. I had worked closely and steadily with the prime minister, and I believed he had some confidence in my judgment.

By the end of the summer I was exhausted. Somehow I managed to get some time away from the office. Margaret and I spent a week alone at the Five Lakes Fishing Club. I recall that break as one of the happiest and most restful in my life. I associate the holiday with the point in the battle of Stalingrad when the tide seemed to be turning against the Nazis in Russia. Margaret and I had decided not to license our car that year in order to avoid using scarce gasoline and oil. We had our week at the Fishing Club thanks to Jules Léger, who lent us his car.

At the end of the summer the prime minister, under pressure from various temperance organizations, decided that a total war effort should include severe rationing of alcoholic beverages. Most of the ministers were unenthusiastic, and some were definitely opposed. I was unconvinced the measure would contribute to the prosecution of the war and would have liked not to have been involved in announcing it. I hoped it might be announced while I was at the Fishing Club. The morning after my return Mackenzie King telephoned. He told me he had put off announcing the rationing of alcoholic beverages until I got back, feeling sure I would want to be associated with it. I gritted my teeth and helped prepare a draft. I would not have been opposed to rationing if I had been convinced it was really needed to conserve manpower or supplies, but I found the argument thin and the highly moral tone of the broadcast nauseating. Following the divisive issue of conscription, the rationing of beer and spirits seemed to me a descent from the vital to the trivial.

North Africa and France

In the spring of 1942 there was political agitation in Britain to invade western Europe to relieve Nazi pressure on the Soviet Union. Churchill thought an attempt to invade Europe would be a catastrophe. As a compromise the British and Canadian governments agreed to a raid on the French port of Dieppe to test the Nazi defence. The Dieppe raid took the Canadian people by surprise, as it did me, so little was I aware in advance of planned military action. The agitation in Britain for a second front was considerably dampened by the appalling outcome of Dieppe. The controversy as to whether or not the raid on Dieppe should have been undertaken and whether or not it was properly organized did not begin immediately, but it is never likely to end.

Dieppe convinced the American military and the president that attack on Europe across the English Channel would require a long period of preparation. In the meantime the Americans and British agreed on an American landing in North Africa. The landing, when it was made, provoked the Nazi occupation of the whole of

France. Canada had continued until then to recognize the government at Vichy as the government of France. The French had maintained their diplomatic mission in Ottawa, and Pierre Dupuy of External Affairs had made several visits to Vichy. The Nazi seizure of the previously unoccupied zone of France presented Canada with an acute problem. Norman Robertson and I felt that it would be unfortunate to break off diplomatic relations with the French government at Vichy, since doing so would imply that a French government still existed. I believe I was the first one to suggest that Canada should declare that, with the occupation of the whole of France, the French government had ceased to exist. Norman liked the formula and easily persuaded Mackenzie King to adopt it.

Just before the American landing in North Africa we got word from my brother Frank that he was in Lisbon. He had been in frequent contact with the American diplomatic mission in the unoccupied zone, and I have always believed that the American authorities helped him to get out of France before the Nazis took over the whole country. There was no way I could arrange to get Frank back to Canada, but he did get a passage to England, where he was recruited at once into SOE, the organization that was parachuting secret agents into France. He completed his training in June 1943 and was dropped in France. In his last letter from England he told me what the objective of his mission was and enjoined me to tell no one else and to destroy the letter. I did that after copying out the vivid account of his first parachute jump during training. It was hard to have to tell the rest of the family, particularly Mother, that he was on a secret mission we must not talk about, and that we would probably have no more news of him until the war ended.

I watched the progress of the American invading forces in North Africa with great interest. The various expedients they had used to avoid recognition of De Gaulle as head of the French authority revolted me. I had been a wholehearted supporter of the Free French movement from the time it was started by De Gaulle in England in 1940 and was never happy about our continued recognition of Pétain as the head of government. I met the members of the Free French delegation to Ottawa late in 1941. The junior member, Alain Savary, and I became friends. Later, when I became an MP from Newfoundland, Savary was already the deputy for St-Pierre and Miquelon in the French National Assembly. I once suggested to him, in jest, that he bring St-Pierre and Miquelon into confederation with Canada and sit in Parliament as a Liberal. Savary later became Mitterand's minister of education.

I was pleased when De Gaulle was recognized at last as head of the French governing body in Algiers. Later, reading his memoirs, I could almost share his resentment of the condescending and sometimes scornful treatment he received from Churchill and to a greater extent from Roosevelt. I never wholly lost my admiration for De Gaulle, even after 1967, when he made himself a political embarrassment during his visit to Canada. It was ironical that he should have given encouragement in his later life to the reactionary element in Quebec that had opposed him and favoured Pétain, and thereby estranged many English-speaking Canadians who had supported him during the war.

The revival of party politics

Politics and postwar prospects

The prospect of victory, not discernible at the beginning of 1942, began to appear before the end of the year. The battle of Stalingrad ended the Nazi advance in Russia, and the winter of 1942-43 removed fear of Soviet collapse. The Battle of the Solomon Islands, little noticed in Canada at the time, marked the end of the Japanese advance in the Pacific. The growing might of the United States was reflected in the success of the North African landing and the speed of the American advance. At the other end of the North African front, British forces advanced steadily after the Victory at El Alamein.

Because of the hope of an early end to the war the parliamentary session of 1943 was relatively quiet. The conscription issue was dormant, if not dead. Another reason for the relative tranquillity was the change in the leadership of the Tory party. Meighen resigned at a convention held in Winnipeg late in the year to choose a new leader. At the last minute Meighen and a group of Tories persuaded John Bracken, the Liberal-Progressive premier of Manitoba, who had been in office for over 20 years, to become a candidate for the Tory leadership.

When rumours that Bracken was being courted began to circulate, Mackenzie King mentioned the subject to me. I had known Bracken in Manitoba. Our acquaintance developed in 1941, when I met several times with him and Stuart Garson during the dominion-provincial conference. I was incredulous, and said Bracken had too much common sense. Mackenzie King was sure he would try. I bet him a dollar (always my upper limit) that he would not. Mackenzie King was delighted when he won the bet. I still wonder if he would have paid had he lost. He thought Bracken would lose the nomination and even drafted a telegram of congratulation to M.A. MacPherson, the runner-up, which of course was not sent. When I met MacPherson years later, I told him about the draft telegram, and he asked me to send him a copy as a souvenir.

In 1927 I had cast the first vote of my life for the Bracken government, which I supported as long as I lived in Manitoba. Now I felt almost betrayed. Bracken made it a condition of his election as leader that the word Progressive be added to the name of the party. The change was no doubt designed to get some of his followers in the legislature to change parties with him and also to give the party a forward-looking image.

I was delighted that Stuart Garson was chosen as Bracken's successor. Garson with great skill held together the coalition cabinet of Liberal-Progressives, Conservatives and Social Crediters he took over as premier. He insisted that all the ministers remain neutral in federal politics but indicated his own sympathy for the Liberal party by stating publicly that everyone knew where he stood. Only one of the Liberal-Progressives followed Bracken into the newly baptized Progressive Conservative party. All the Conservative members of the provincial cabinet remained in office under Garson.

The new Tory leader did not seek a seat and was not in Parliament until after the general election of 1945. He substituted the milder and much younger Gordon Graydon for R.B. Hanson as house leader. Graydon, not Bracken, was therefore the leader of the Opposition. Mackenzie King's personal relations with Graydon were always good, and he had no fear of Bracken. Indeed, the prime minister began to be more concerned about the political threat of the CCF. That party was more aggressive after defeating Meighen in York South and began organizing in the more promising areas of Ontario and elsewhere in the country, offering an attractive social welfare program with little or no emphasis on traditional socialism.

My recollection is that I had a much less strenuous time in the first half of 1943 than earlier. I had no part in the discussion about dividing the Canadian army in Britain to dispatch troops to North Africa to take part in the invasion of Sicily.

By the end of 1942 I was a much more partisan Liberal. I was proud of the way the government had organized the country for war and filled with admiration for the political skill and wisdom with which the prime minister had maintained the unity of his Liberals following and during the conscription crisis and gained general public acquiescence, if not total approval. But I was discouraged by the negative attitude he and most of the ministers had about planning for the postwar period. The dread of a return to depression after the war was widespread, especially among those who had been without jobs until war came.

By 1943 Bruce Hutchison, then one of the editors of the *Vancouver Sun*, and I were corresponding from time to time about the political scene. In one letter I wrote, 'Some day this war is going to end,' and lamented: 'up to now there has been almost nothing done to get ready for the close of hostilities, and nothing sane is going to be done as long as the Liberal party sits on the sidelines as a confused spectator of the sterile debate on private enterprise à la Bracken versus state ownership à la CCF. . . . Surely anyone who thinks about it for five minutes realizes that if we have to wait for state ownership to get the peacetime economic machine going, we will all be dead waiting, and if we leave the whole job to private enterprise more than half the population will ... be on the dole or (what is more likely, when you think how widely men are instructed in the art of murder) there will be a bloody upheaval.

'Isn't it about time the Liberals, who are not committed to either side in this obsolete debate, pointed out that an expanding economy will provide plenty of room for a vast expansion of public undertakings and all the enterprise that is really enterprise, whether private, corporate or cooperative? Even the Liberal press is joining in the false and demoralizing attacks on bureaucracy. If, instead, Liberals would show real pride in the immense achievements of the so-called bureaucracy working in harmony with corporate enterprise (I haven't seen much of the private variety) and equal pride in the effective, but not stultifying, control Parliament has exercised over government during this war (a theme nobody has worked at), we might begin today to lay the foundations of confidence for an expansive future.

'The real problem, as I see it, is not to weaken, much less destroy, the economic activity of the state. The whole history of Canada from the building of the CPR (which depended entirely on the state) to the waging of this war has shown that we have had prosperity whenever the state has given direction and dynamic to the economy and stagnation and depression when it failed to do so.'

I added, 'The old-fashioned competitive market does not provide an adequate instrument for the distribution of the wealth we are already geared to produce. It will have to be supplemented by other devices which will determine politically how a large part of our productive energies are to be employed ... like for example, determining that children shall all have free milk in the same way they get free education.

'What I am really pleading for is an intelligent recognition of what has really been making our wartime economy tick, and an application of the same principles to peacetime. Apart from the PM, Mr Ilsley seems to be the only man in public life who has a glimmering of what is happening. He is miles in advance of the

CCF, and the Tories have been left behind in the dust. But the Liberals generally don't seem to know what is happening, and unless somebody gets the public to realize where we should be heading, I am afraid of the kind of future we shall have.'

My conviction was that there would be great hope 'if we could put real life into the historical Liberal traditions of this country. The dogmatic conflict between academic private enterprise and economic socialism does not belong to the history of Canada; it is a recent import from the United States. Our tradition is a healthy empiricism which accepts what our whole past demonstrates — that the state can work effectively with other groups in the community without either excluding the other from the field.'

Concluding that I might be hopelessly wrong, I said I seemed to feel 'an increasing pride in the fact that we are keeping our community on the rails and a hardening determination to continue that way. But that pride needs to be articulated; we need symbols (like our own flag) and a loosening of our national emotions. In this war no country in the world has managed its affairs (and very complicated they are) as well as we have in this country. Someone should hold a mirror up for us to look at ourselves.'

I did not have long to wait for a change in the attitude of the prime minister to postwar planning.

The Quebec Conference of 1943 and family allowances

For Mackenzie King the great event of 1943 was the Quebec Conference. He was at once thrilled and apprehensive when asked by Churchill to be host of a meeting with Roosevelt at Quebec in August. Needless to say, preparations for the visit had top priority for several weeks. Few people could be involved because of the need for secrecy. I was to accompany the prime minister to Quebec; we left on 9 August.

There was nothing but bad news for the Liberal party in August 1943. The Ontario election had been a disaster for the provincial Liberal government. The Liberals ran a poor third, and the Conservatives and the CCF were only four seats apart. George Drew, the Conservative leader, became premier of a minority government. On 9 August there were four federal by-elections, two in the west, won by the CCF, and one in the predominantly Jewish constituency of Cartier, in Montreal, won by Fred Rose, a known Communist who called himself Labour-Progressive. The fourth was in Stanstead, in the Eastern Townships, won by the Bloc Populaire, a new party developed out of the League for the Defence of Canada, which had been organized to oppose the plebiscite. The Bloc represented Quebec nationalists under a new name. The only consolation was that the Conservatives under their new leader had won none of the by-elections, and Bracken had not dared to test his fortunes in the constituency of Selkirk, in Manitoba, the province of which he had been premier for 20 years.

Once the Opposition parties were actively organizing, Mackenzie King decided that the time had come for the Liberals to abandon the nonpartisan stance they had taken after the election of 1940, begin to rebuild their party organization and work out a postwar program. Brooke Claxton, who had become his parliamentary assistant in May, had been eager for some time to get started on planning for the postwar. I was more than willing to help. Having little to do with the conference, I busied myself at Quebec with the preparation of a memorandum for the prime minister setting out a five-point postwar program that included family allowances.

The five points were:

1 A floor under farm prices (and fish prices) would give security to the farmers and fishermen.
2 Children's allowances would be the greatest single attack on poverty, insecurity and want. They would relieve the tension in the ranks of labour.
3 A nutrition program for postwar application would provide the best single form of health insurance and an assured market for a considerable part of our surplus food.
4 A housing program would be one of the most important single contributions to maximum employment, better health, and a higher standard of living after the war.

5 A public development program would go a long way to ensure an orderly demobilization at the close of hostilities.

I concluded the memorandum by saying: 'This five-point program could all be put into effect right now without interfering, in any way, with the prosecution of the war. On the contrary, it would give a new impetus to the war effort by its stimulating effect on morale. Domestically, it would put the other political parties on the defensive; internationally, it would put Canada in the forefront of social progress. It would give the future to the Liberal party.'

The prime minister, concentrating on family allowances, gave little attention to the other four points. He said no Canadian government would dare to start providing family allowances, because the political effect would be to pit English-Canadians against French-Canadians and Protestants against Catholics. He felt family allowances would be a greater threat to national unity than any other measure he could think of except conscription. I replied that almost no member of the existing House of Commons would be sure whether there were more voters in his constituency with children or without, and that it would surprise me if any member except Dr Herbert Bruce, the most extreme reactionary and a bitter French-hater, would dare to vote against them. In 1944, when the vote was taken in Parliament, I turned out to be right. Even Bruce did not vote against family allowances; he was absent when the vote was taken.

The question of family allowances came up again one day in the library at Laurier House. Mackenzie King asked me why I felt so passionate about family allowances. I told him I would not be in Ottawa on his staff if it had not been for the allowances for the children of pensioned widows of veterans. These allowances had provided my mother with enough income that I did not have to start working at 16, and was able to continue my education. He made no comment to me, but he subsequently told Handy, who repeated it to me later, that that account of our family experience had convinced him.

I was not in fact the first advocate of family allowances. W.A. Mackintosh and several other economic advisers to the government had recommended family allowances as a way of reducing the pressure on wage stabilization. With family allowances the argument that higher wages were needed for the support of children would lose its force. The government was not prepared to accept family allowances as a war measure, but some ministers began to consider them as an element in postwar social policy.

Family allowances were never popular with trade union leaders; I suppose that was why they were never advocated strongly by the CCF. One appeal of family allowances to me was that their net effect would be to increase rural incomes relatively more than they did urban incomes, whereas almost all other welfare measures, particularly unemployment insurance, had the opposite effect.

Liberal party organization

The Liberal response to party organizing by the Tories and the CCF began with a meeting of the National Liberal Federation in September 1943, the first since the election of 1940. The cabinet was sharply divided about the cause of the alarming decline in Liberal party fortunes. Several of the ministers, led by Gardiner, blamed wartime controls, shortages and rationing and advocated an easing of controls even if that led to some price increases. Ilsley, Howe and Ralston were adamantly opposed to any easing of controls, but none of them had constructive suggestions for improving morale. Mackenzie King supported their opposition to relaxing controls but felt the public needed some hope for the future.

Brooke Claxton and I had been in close touch with the public servants in the Department of Finance and the Bank of Canada engaged in planning measures to prevent a postwar depression. Once Mackenzie King was convinced a postwar program was necessary, he gave Brooke and me some encouragement to draft a submission for consideration by the Liberal Federation. He permitted us to hint that the party leader was favourably disposed. Almost the whole of our draft program , which included family allowances, was adopted by the federation.

During the summer of 1943 Mackenzie King was also rightly concerned by a wave of optimism that the war was nearly over.

He made a broadcast in September on four years of war. We laboured for days on the draft, which was designed to sober public opinion by stressing the grim task still ahead before victory could be achieved. His resolute support of the maximum war effort combined with growing emphasis on a concrete postwar program put the Liberal party on the road to recovery. His new attitude, I hoped, would make victory in a 1945 election a remote possibility.

The meeting of the Liberal Federation was a success, owing largely to a rousing, fighting, partisan speech by Mackenzie King. He placed the whole blame for the revival of partisan activity on the Tories, the CCF and the Quebec nationalists. The contribution to that speech in which I took special pleasure was my success in persuading him to describe the Bloc Populaire as the only political party whose program could be summed up in one word, *non*. I borrowed the phrase shamelessly from Frank Scott.

Mackenzie King was careful to emphasize that the program proposed by the Liberal Federation was merely advisory and did not commit the government. Much of the last two months of 1943 were devoted by the prime minister to persuading the cabinet to adopt the postwar program. Once decisions were made, Heeney, as secretary to the cabinet, could be counted on to put pressure on ministers and officials to work actively to have the necessary legislation ready for Parliament in 1944.

At the beginning of 1944 I was busy helping the prime minister work out the announcement of the postwar program to be included in the Speech from the Throne and, after Parliament met, following the progress of the legislation through the House. Three new departments of government were created. The legislation for National Health and Welfare and for Veterans Affairs was straightforward, but there were lengthy discussions, with divergent opinions among ministers and officials, about the scope of the Department of Reconstruction. It was not easy to give specific functions to that department without taking powers away from other departments. Whatever the law contained, the character of the department was likely to depend on the minister selected. The prime minister could not decide who should be minister of reconstruction in time to design a department to fit his talents. In the end its shape owed more to Howe, the minister eventually chosen, than to the legislation.

The one novel social program forecast in the Speech from the Throne was family allowances. The drafting of the bill was easy enough once cabinet had accepted the principle. Mackenzie King told me with evident satisfaction how he proceeded at the final decisive meeting of the cabinet. He realized that most of the ministers favouring family allowances were on one side of the round table and the main opponents on the other and took the unusual course of polling the ministers. He started on the side with most of the supporters. By the time he reached the strongest opponents, they were in a small minority. He then declared the cabinet was agreed, and no minister threatened to resign.

But how family allowances would be received in Parliament and by the public was a big question. From outside the House, Bracken denounced the measures as a bribe to voters. Premier Drew of Ontario, in a broadcast in which he predicted that the measure would never come into effect, attacked it as shameless catering to French Canadians. The memory of that broadcast contributed to Drew's failure later as a national party leader. When the debate on family allowances ended in the House of Commons, the government insisted on a recorded vote, and every member in the House voted for it, including the Conservatives, who were jeered by the Liberal backbenchers.

The invasion of France

Second visit to Britain and D-Day

The prime minister was away from Parliament in the spring of 1944. At Churchill's urging he agreed to a second visit to Britain. He found the invitation irresistible when Churchill told him he would be expected to speak to both Houses of the British Parliament. For the first time since the death of Lapointe, the prime minister would be away from Ottawa for a prolonged period while Parliament was in session. He was worried about who should be acting prime minister. He chose Ralston because Ralston then enjoyed a higher measure of public confidence than any other senior minister. Crerar, the senior privy councillor, never forgave the slight.

For that visit Mackenzie King did not have to fly in a converted bomber. He accepted the loan of the official plane of General Arnold, head of the United States Air Force. The accommodation was limited, and there was no room for me on the plane. I flew on a Lancaster bomber fitted up with comfortable seats and heated. It was luxury compared with the Liberator of 1941. We stopped to refuel at Goose Bay, the newly established base in Labrador.

My main duty in London was to work with the prime minister on the countless revisions of his speech to the British Parliament. The draft was declared finished late in the afternoon on the day before it was to be delivered. Mackenzie King went to visit friends, and I went off to dinner with friends of mine, confident that I would not be needed. I was wrong. Late in the evening Mackenzie King returned to the hotel, decided to take one more look at the speech and found I was absent. He was not pleased. We had a final look the next morning. I was completely satisfied with his text, but, as usual, he felt it could have been improved had there been one more day. The occasion was really impressive. Without upstaging him Churchill introduced Mackenzie King who read his speech most effectively and with great dignity.

I found time to see my brother Walter, who was then in the army in England, and one or two friends also in the army. Bob Dale-Harris brought his fiancée, Leslie (Doody) Howard, to see me at the Dorchester. During the weekend Mackenzie King was at Chequers, so I went on the Sunday to spend the day at army headquarters with Dick Hunter, who was on the staff of General Crerar, the successor to General McNaughton as army commander. I told Dick where the de France family lived in Picardy, only a quarter mile off Route Nationale no. 1. I said he might just find himself later in the summer on that road and have a chance to call in to see the family. And it happened just that way. He was either the first or second member of the army of liberation to visit my French family. They were almost incredulous when he told them he was a lifelong friend of mine.

The person I most wanted to see in London was Kay Moore, a friend of my brother Frank's from Winnipeg and Paris days. She was the first person he visited in England after his escape from internment and his months in unoccupied France. It was through Kay that he was recruited into SOE. She shared a house with Alison Grant, the niece of Mrs Vincent Massey, and a Scottish girl, Mary Mundle. They made their house Frank's home whenever he was on leave during his training before he went back to France. I managed to see them a couple of times and learned a great deal about Frank's last few months of freedom. It was a comfort to know what a wonderful time he had had with those friends. Kay told me how deeply attached to one another Alison and Frank had become.

I flew back on the same Lancaster, this time nonstop and all in daylight, from London to Dorval. Davidson Dunton was the only other passenger I knew. We had met before the war and became friends after he moved to Ottawa to the Wartime Information Board, where he performed most effectively. Our association and friendship developed during his years at the CBC and as head of Carleton University, and lasted until the end of his life.

It was no secret in London that France would be invaded early in the summer, but even Mackenzie King did not know the probable date. Surprisingly he had made no advance plan for a public announcement. I was called by telephone early on the morning of 6 June with the news of the landing in Normandy. I telephoned Mackenzie King at about 6. He decided at once that he would broadcast a statement on the 8 a.m. news. He asked me to draft something, and I did so sitting on the side of the bed before dressing. I arrived at Laurier House before 7 with the draft, which was typed at once and revised in time for the prime minister to reach the broadcasting studio by 8. For once Mackenzie King was pleased and said not a word about needing one more day. From D-Day the attention of the country was on the campaign in France.

While we were in England in May, Colonel Buckmaster of SOE had given me, in great confidence, a glowing report of the fine work Frank and his radio operator, Kenneth Macalister, were doing in France with one of the Resistance groups. As the liberation proceeded, especially after Paris was in Allied hands, I kept hoping for news of Frank. In early September I was depressed to learn that he was a prisoner of the Gestapo and had been for some time. I did not know then that he and Macalister had been taken prisoner a few days after they were dropped in France. For the next six months I clung to the faint hope that he might survive.

The Second Quebec Conference

Churchill and Roosevelt had found Quebec an agreeable place in which to confer. At Churchill's suggestion Mackenzie King arranged a second meeting for September 1944. That time I was not included in the prime minister's party but was left in Ottawa to mind the shop. There was the greatest optimism about an early end to the war in Europe. Mackenzie King was so confident that the danger of having to use conscripts had passed that he made an indiscreet speech at the Quebec Reform Club that greatly upset Ralston and almost provoked a cabinet crisis. I knew nothing about the incident until long afterwards, but I knew that Mackenzie King found the atmosphere at Quebec much less congenial than in 1943.

In August 1944 Godbout had been defeated in a general election, and Duplessis was once more premier of Quebec. During the conference Duplessis was given as much recognition as possible. All went well, but there remained the risk that if a crisis arose, there would be an unfriendly government in Quebec ready to fish in troubled waters.

After the Quebec conference of 1944 the prime minister was occupied with reorganizing the cabinet to accommodate the three new departments. The minister of Pensions and National Health, Ian Mackenzie, became the minister of veterans affairs. Brooke Claxton was taken into the government to head the new Department of National Health and Welfare. I was delighted by his appointment to the cabinet. We had worked closely during the previous three years, and I was confident that he would be dynamic and imaginative. After a great deal of to-ing and fro-ing of names by Mackenzie King, mainly those of Power and Howe, Howe was finally persuaded to become the minister of reconstruction as well as to continue as the minister of munitions and supply. The choice was a disappointment to the exponents of a brave new world, who believed great public initiatives would be needed to maintain employment when the war ended. I feared that Howe would be regarded as reactionary, and that the choice might increase support for the CCF. But it proved a wise decision, because he had a clearer vision of the probable shape of the postwar economy than did any other minister.

The life of the Parliament elected in 1940 would expire in mid-April 1945. The prime minister had an almost superstitious fear of letting a Parliament run its full term and a prudent bias against letting Parliament last into its final year. As soon as there was a prospect of the defeat of Germany before the end of 1944, Mackenzie King had preparations begun for an election to be held the moment victory came. Claxton as his parliamentary assistant devoted a good deal of time to planning publicity. To assist in preparing Liberal literature he arranged to have H.E. (Bob) Kidd assigned full time by Cockfield, Brown, an advertising agency doing a lot of work for the government. Howe had persuaded Gordon Fogo, a Nova Scotia lawyer serving in munitions and supply, to become national organizer. I acted as liaison for the prime minister with Claxton, Fogo and Kidd and was regularly involved in that preparatory work. I found it fascinating and absorbing, until all that optimistic activity was shattered by the gravest domestic political crisis of the war.

The conscription crisis

The crisis in the cabinet

On 18 October 1944, suddenly without warning after five long years of war, a crisis arose in the cabinet. Ralston, the minister of defence, returning from a visit to the Canadian army in Europe, reported that the Allied advance had been stopped, and that there was little prospect of the European war ending until sometime in 1945. Army casualties were heavier than expected, and the fighting had bogged down in Belgium and Holland. A shortage of reinforcements was forecast: it was estimated that there would be 22,000 more casualties in the infantry and only 18,000 volunteers available as reinforcements. In addition to the thousands who had volunteered for service anywhere, the army included 60,000 trained troops conscripted for service in Canada only. Ralston argued that the time had come to make the men who had been conscripted and trained in the army but whose service was limited to Canada available for service overseas to meet the anticipated shortage of reinforcements.

The prime minister, who was convinced that sending conscripts overseas would provoke deep controversy, divide the country and weaken the war effort, was adamantly opposed to the abandonment of the voluntary system. He resisted Ralston's recommendation and insisted that a further search be made for reinforcements among those who had already volunteered or could be persuaded to volunteer. He asked me to work with the staff at army headquarters to examine the numbers.

Meanwhile a debate began, first in the War Committee and later in the cabinet, which was soon divided, with the prime minister on one side and Ralston on the other. Angus L. Macdonald, the minister of defence for naval service, and Power, the associate minister of national defence, took opposite sides. Macdonald was an ardent supporter of Ralston. Power was against using conscripts, but he fell ill, had to have an operation and was present for only a few of the discussions.

After days of tense consideration in the cabinet, Mackenzie King believed that Ralston would resign unless one more appeal for volunteers was successful, and that he would insist on being given an assurance in advance that if the appeal failed conscripts would be used as reinforcements. Mackenzie King decided to consult General A.G.L. McNaughton, who had been commander of the Canadian forces in Britain for four years. McNaughton had retired reluctantly at the very end of 1943 and returned to Canada. He blamed his enforced retirement on Ralston and had been seething with indignation throughout 1944. Mackenzie King had escaped any share of McNaughton's resentment.

Mackenzie King found McNaughton opposed to sending conscripts overseas. He believed that a vigorous campaign could raise enough volunteers from the ranks of the conscripts to provide the reinforcements needed. With that reassurance the prime minister asked McNaughton whether or not he would be willing to become minister of defence if Ralston resigned. McNaughton said he would. That same afternoon Mackenzie King told the cabinet that McNaughton was willing to become minister of defence and believed a vigorous campaign for volunteers could be successful. Ralston at once offered to resign.

A myth about Ralston's resignation needs to be cleared up. His resignation during the first conscription crisis of 1942 had been held in suspense at Mackenzie King's request. That earlier resignation was mentioned by the prime minister in the cabinet, but the repeated assertions that it was the resignation he accepted are not true. After leaving the cabinet chamber Ralston told the principal secretary that he would send his written resignation later that day. Before the afternoon was over, he telephoned to ask if the letter could be delayed until the following morning, and the prime minister agreed.

A story about McNaughton's activity in that period is true. Shortly before he was approached by Mackenzie King, the Conservatives were holding secret discussions with McNaughton, seeking to have him replace Bracken as party leader. McNaughton told Mackenzie King about the approach and assured him the discussions had already been broken off. As soon as Ralston's letter of resignation was received, McNaughton was sworn in as minister, but his appointment was not announced that day. I spent the evening of that day with several Liberal organizers who were making preparations for an anticipated election campaign. They were speculating about the rumours that McNaughton might accept the Tory leadership, and I pretended to show an interest. When McNaughton's appointment was announced the next morning, one of them asked if I had known of the appointment the previous evening. When I admitted it, he said none of them would have guessed. My capacity to keep secrets may have been one of the reasons I survived with Mackenzie King.

A few days after he became minister, McNaughton spoke at a Canadian Legion meeting intended to open the vigorous campaign for volunteers. He got a hostile reception, and in fact the campaign never got off the ground.

Though none of the other ministers had resigned, there were growing rumours in the press that the cabinet was split down the middle. In case there should be a cabinet crisis, the prime minister had Parliament summoned to meet 22 November. Until that day no one doubted that the prime minister would hold firm to his determination not to send conscripts overseas.

Not until much later did I learn that during the evening before Parliament met, senior staff officers met McNaughton and told him that there would not be adequate reinforcements without the use of conscripts, and that unless the policy was changed, they would resign. McNaughton immediately did a complete about-face. The next morning he recommended to the prime minister that conscripts be used as reinforcements. Faced with the probable simultaneous resignation of conscriptionist ministers and senior army staff officers, Mackenzie King was persuaded that the government could not survive unless McNaughton's recommendation was accepted.

The change in policy would not be possible without the support of the senior minister from Quebec, and as soon as McNaughton left Laurier House, the prime minister sent for St Laurent. St Laurent was shocked, but Mackenzie King persuaded him that if the use of conscripts was not agreed to, the government would fall apart and be defeated in Parliament, and that no viable government would be able to replace it. I was shocked to learn through the office grapevine, at about noon, that the prime minister had reversed his position.

The debate in Parliament

Before Parliament met on the afternoon of 22 November, no minister except St Laurent was told of the decision. On my way to the gallery of the House of Commons I happened to encounter Ilsley, the minister of finance and a conscriptionist, who told me that the government would not last until the end of the day unless the prime minister changed his position, and that he was sure that would not happen. The reply I made was that I was never sure what the prime minister would do until he had done it and was not always sure even then. Ilsley gave me a look that convinced me he would not act precipitately.

The cabinet was not to be informed of the change in direction until a meeting in the evening, after Parliament had met and a Liberal caucus been held.

When Parliament met, the prime minister got permission from the House of Commons to allow McNaughton, the minister of defence but not yet a member of Parliament, to appear in the House the next day to make a statement and submit to questions. The Opposition, expecting to tear McNaughton and the voluntary system to shreds, readily agreed to the unprecedented procedure. Without giving the Liberal caucus the slightest hint that he had reversed his position, Mackenzie King persuaded the members to postpone discussion until they heard McNaughton the next afternoon. The cabinet had been called for a meeting at 8 p.m.

The one minister Mackenzie King feared might become leader of the Liberal members opposed to using conscripts overseas was Power. He insisted that Power come to his office at 7:45 for a private talk. I was the officer on duty that evening, waiting for the prime minister to arrive for the cabinet meeting. Sitting opposite me, also waiting for the prime minister, was Power. He had no inkling of the prime minister's change of position and expected him to stand firm in opposition to sending conscripts overseas. The government, Power said, would be defeated in Parliament, a coalition government of some sort would replace it, and that government would soon collapse in its turn. Though I knew

Power was the minister most likely to resign, I tried to show a lively interest in his predictions. I could not even hint at what I knew the prime minister would propose to the cabinet. As usual Mackenzie King was late. When he reached the office, the cabinet had already been assembled for about 10 minutes. I have sometimes wondered whether Power might have been persuaded to stay in the cabinet if there had been more time for private talk between them.

Of those present during those decisive hours on the night of 22–23 November 1944 I am the only survivor left to tell the story, and I report here all I know of what happened.

The cabinet meeting went on almost until 11. It was decided to make 16,000 of the home defence conscripts available as overseas reinforcements. After the meeting the prime minister brought into his office McNaughton and Claxton, the most junior minister, who had until a few weeks earlier been Mackenzie King's parliamentary assistant. General Maurice Pope, the prime minister's military adviser, and I were summoned to join them. McNaughton already had with him a draft speech defending reliance on the voluntary system. Claxton, Pope and I were told to rewrite it to justify sending conscripts overseas as reinforcements. It was a difficult turnabout to explain. We did not complete the task until 5 a.m. We met McNaughton at 8, who told us he was too tired to read the draft but would look at it before he read it in the House of Commons. I was dumbfounded by his response. I begged him to read at least two or three paragraphs that we all felt were essential to explain why St Laurent had agreed to the change of policy. McNaughton refused to read them but asked me to mark them and promised not to change a word in those paragraphs. They were not changed, and very little else was. Right after giving the draft speech to McNaughton I sent a copy to Mackenzie King. I learned from his diary years later that after receiving it, he telephoned McNaughton and suggested what he called 'slight but important changes.' McNaughton accepted the changes, and they agreed on 'one or two other points' that McNaughton brought up.

I cannot remember whether Mackenzie King told me after the cabinet meeting on 22 November or on the morning of 23 November that Power had said he could not support the change of policy, and that Gardiner and Alphonse Fournier were not sure they could.

For Mackenzie King 23 November was almost as critical a day as the previous one. He met the Liberal caucus at 11:30 a.m. and made a long speech, which he concluded by telling the members of the change of policy and begging them to keep it secret until he could announce it in the House. Power appeared at the caucus briefly and also at the cabinet meeting that followed. There he handed the prime minister a letter that all the ministers realized must be his resignation. Mackenzie King did not open it. Power then withdrew, and the cabinet approved an order-in-council authorizing the minister of defence to dispatch up to 16,000 conscripts overseas.

When the House of Commons met at 3 the prime minister rose at once. With only a few preliminary words he read the order-in-council. The announcement was a complete surprise to the Opposition and shook the House almost to its foundations. Liberal members were obviously divided, the Conservative Opposition bewildered, and the CCF not sure which way to turn; the Social Credit group alone seemed unperturbed. After some discussion of the unprecedented procedure McNaughton, with two senior military officers from the general staff, was admitted to the House and allowed to deliver his statement. He was questioned for the rest of that day and all the next day. The prime minister thought McNaughton acquitted himself well. I was vastly relieved.

At the end of Friday's sitting the Opposition raised the question of holding a secret session to inform members of precise details about the strength of the forces and forecasts of the number of reinforcements needed, information the government was not prepared to make public. No decision about a secret session was reached that day. The business announced for Monday, 27 November was the beginning of the debate on the prime minister's astutely worded motion 'that this House will aid the Government in its policy of maintaining a vigorous war effort.'

During the weekend several ministers tried without success to persuade Power to withdraw his resignation. When the sitting opened on Monday, Mackenzie King read Power's letter of resignation and his own reply. Power then made a statement elaborating on his reasons for refusing to share responsibility for sending conscripted men overseas. He spoke without bitterness and set the tone for moderate Liberals who intended to vote against the government.

The real danger to the government came from Liberal members. Gardiner was still considering resignation. I was told later by one of his close friends that what probably restrained him was the great kindness and consideration the prime minister had shown him at the time of his wife's tragic death a few weeks earlier. Fournier, who represented Hull, stayed out of the House for several days of uncertainty but ultimately decided not to resign. It was soon clear that of the French-speaking members from Quebec all but a handful would vote against the prime minister's motion. The position of some of the conscriptionist Liberals was still uncertain and would be decided by the debate.

My heart was with Power. Indeed, my personal position went further. I felt and still feel that compelling men to fight for freedom is a contradiction in logic and reason. But my head told me that the real world was not and could not be governed by logic and reason alone. I gradually became convinced that Mackenzie King, with reluctance and misgivings, had reached the only decision that took account of the political realities of November 1944.

On the Saturday before the debate was to begin Mackenzie King had me spend the whole evening alone with him in the library at Laurier House. He records in his diary that until 10:30 we were together in front of the fire, talking, among other things, about points to be brought out in his speech on Monday. I was surprised that he did not ask me to prepare a draft. I had then been in his service seven years and had helped him with nearly every important written speech he had made. I sensed that his speech on Monday would be the most important of them all, and I was close to the telephone all day Sunday and Monday morning but received no word from him. When he rose to speak in the House on Monday afternoon, I had no idea how he intended to proceed, or what he was likely to say.

He spoke almost without notes, and his speech was addressed mainly to the government benches. At times he turned his back on the Opposition to appeal directly to the Liberal members. It was certainly the most momentous speech of his life, and for once he was satisfied, as his diary records.

> 'I feel,' he wrote, 'that I spoke well — not referring much to notes, finding no difficulty in expressing myself and indeed being able to do so forcibly and adequately by not being tied to any manuscript.'

Mackenzie King took the whole afternoon and concluded his speech at 6 with the words 'Whatever may be the consequences; whether loss of prestige, loss of popularity or loss of power, I feel that I am in the right, and I know that a time will come when every man will render me full justice on that score.'

When the sitting resumed at 8 p.m., the leader of the Opposition, Gordon Graydon, replied. He began by saying that it was 'perhaps the most important and momentous debate that any of us who sit in this Parliament have participated in.' He concluded by moving an amendment calling for all conscripted men then in the forces or in future call-ups to be required to serve in any theatre of war — what was called 'all-out conscription.' Following the usual custom, M.J. Coldwell, as leader of the CCF, spoke next, and then John Blackmore, as leader of the Social Credit. Before the House adjourned that night it was decided that there should be a secret session the next day, 28 November, at which McNaughton should be present. Mackenzie King felt McNaughton handled it well.

When the debate resumed on 29 November, it was recognized that Ralston's attitude might determine the fate of the government. Had he supported the Tory amendment or even left his own position in doubt the conscriptionist Liberals might have followed his lead. When he announced that he would vote against Graydon's amendment and for the government, there was no longer any doubt that the government would be sustained.

Except for a handful of extremists, Liberal members from Quebec who would not vote confidence in the government spoke more in sorrow than in anger. They made it clear that they would encourage no resistance in the country. Cardin, who had resigned from the cabinet during the first conscription crisis in 1942, spoke impressively and with moderation. Joseph Jean, the parliamentary assistant to St Laurent, moved an amendment to Graydon's amendment urging the government to use to the best advantage the men serving voluntarily in Canada and overseas without resorting to conscription. Graydon asked Jean at once whether he had resigned as parliamentary assistant. He replied that he had already tendered his resignation to the prime minister. Jean was a highly respected member. The tone of his brief speech showed how it grieved him to vote against his leader and the government. St Laurent did not speak until 6 December. I was beginning to have a great admiration for him, and I was genuinely moved by his speech. I felt that it created for the Liberal members who were going to dissent on that one issue a bridge back to the side of the government.

The debate ended the next day. The first vote was on Jean's amendment, which was defeated 168 to 43. All but two or three of the votes for the amendment were from Quebec MPs. The next vote was on the Tory amendment, for all-out conscription. It was defeated by 170 to 44. Except for two or three Social Crediters, all its supporters were Tories. Every Liberal in the House voted against it, and that show of Liberal solidarity pleased Mackenzie King enormously.

After some further debate Coldwell moved a CCF amendment to strike out the words 'the policy of' in the prime minister's motion so that the motion would read, 'that this House will aid the Government in maintaining a vigorous war effort.' Mackenzie King saw instantly that by accepting Coldwell's amendment the CCF would be obliged to vote for his motion as amended. He accepted it at once. Coldwell's amendment was adopted 141 to 70, and the prime minister's motion as amended, 143 to 70. Mackenzie King noted in his diary that the Tories had put themselves in the ridiculous position of voting, along with the opponents of conscription, against 'maintaining a vigorous war effort.' The majority for the government was far greater than Mackenzie King had dared to hope. He was elated and rightly so. He had judged the issue was no longer conscription, but the maintenance of an effective government. His decision to resort to conscription had prevented the collapse of the wartime government.

Before the prime minister left the building that night I wrote a note by hand and gave it to him. It said that the debate had ended the conscription issue forever. The next day he thanked me for the note but said I was quite wrong. I was glad when it turned out that on that point events were to show I had been right.

The parliamentary crisis was over without disaster. Surviving the conscription crisis of 1944 was the most dramatic achievement in Mackenzie King's career. It meant that he would turn out to be the only head of government of a free country to last through the Second World War — the greatest of his many records of durability.

In five wartime years Mackenzie King's government had developed a superb wartime economy. Separated from combat by oceans on east and west, Canada, with only 12 million people, had stretched its manpower almost to the limit to create an industrial structure to produce munitions and build up volunteer fighting forces on land and sea and in the air. That such a crisis should have arisen at a time when the war in Europe seemed nearly over and victory assured was one of the almost incredible manifestations of the triumph of emotion over reason that from time to time have been characteristic of Canadian history.

Recovery

The parliamentary crisis was over when the House gave the government a vote of confidence on 7 December 1944 but there was apprehension in the government and the defence department of possible resistance from the conscripts by either wholesale desertion or even mutiny. A show of passive resistance at Terrace, BC, might have got out of hand had it not been handled with great skill and wisdom. A few conscripts deserted or failed to return from leave, but on the whole there was obedience and little apparent resistance.

A rumour circulated that after the first detachment of conscripts had embarked, they had thrown their rifles overboard as an act of defiance. Bracken, the Tory leader, repeated the rumour. A quick investigation showed that one conscript had done so but had received no support from the others. McNaughton, as minister, felt he must reply to Bracken. He sent for me and asked me to look at two draft statements. I read them twice very slowly before giving an opinion, because I wanted McNaughton to feel I was pondering the choice. One of the drafts was coldly factual; the other an intemperate denunciation of Bracken. I knew at once that McNaughton himself had written the second. I gave the opinion that when facts are in dispute, the first task is to establish the truth clearly and to make a statement the public will find credible. When that is done, it would do no harm to denounce the person who spread a false rumour. Without a word McNaughton tore up his own statement and used the other one, and the public, as a whole, accepted it as accurate. He wisely never went on to denounce Bracken.

Mackenzie King felt that it was essential to get McNaughton into Parliament. A by-election was arranged in North Grey, which the Liberals had held by substantial majorities in 1935 and 1940. That by-election might have been won if the CCF had not nominated a highly respected senior air force officer, Air Vice Marshal A.F. Godfrey, who received a fair number of potential Liberal votes. Despite their having a weak candidate the Conservatives won decisively, and the prestige of the government suffered accordingly.

Mackenzie King dreaded the prospect of a session of Parliament in 1945, particularly as McNaughton, having lost the by-election in North Grey, would not be in the House. But a session was necessary in order for Parliament to vote the money needed to carry on the war effort and the ordinary functions of government.

The prime minister feared there would be a long debate on the Speech from the Throne rehashing the conscription issue. He also expected the later debate on the appropriation of money for the army to be long and bitter.

The first business of a session of Parliament normally is a debate on the Speech from the Throne; under the rules at that time it could go on day after day, as long as there were members willing to speak. The debate is started by two government supporters, who propose and second a motion for the Address in Reply thanking the governor general for the Speech. The third speaker in the debate is the leader of the Opposition. I suggested that if after the mover had spoken, the seconder, without making a speech, moved that the debate be adjourned, the tactic would take the Opposition by surprise, and the adjournment would be adopted before Graydon realized what was happening; the debate on the Speech from the Throne would thereby be postponed. The tactic worked.

There was no such easy way to deal with the army appropriation. The resignations of Ralston and Power and the failure of McNaughton to win a seat left Angus Macdonald as the only defence minister with a seat in Parliament. He had been Ralston's strongest ally, and his personal relations with the prime minister were bad. If Macdonald had to pilot the army appropriation through the House, what might happen, to say the least, was worrying.

One day I asked the prime minister whether or not he was concerned by the prospect of Macdonald having to defend the army appropriation. He said he was and asked what could be done. I had thought up a plan. D.C. Abbott was well liked in the House and had already demonstrated his effectiveness in debate.

Abbott was parliamentary assistant to Ilsley. I said that if I was prime minister, I would ask Ilsley to release Abbott and I would appoint him parliamentary assistant to McNaughton. Abbott then could pilot the army appropriations through the House. Mackenzie King made no comment, and nothing happened for another couple of weeks. Then one day at the East Block he asked me into his room to discuss something. Shortly afterwards the telephone rang. The call was from Abbott. The prime minister motioned me to stay in the room. He asked Abbott to become parliamentary assistant to McNaughton and offered him time to consider, but Abbott accepted at once. Mackenzie King asked me to note that; he said men could be judged by their capacity to make up their minds. Soon after I was back in my own room, Abbott telephoned me and said, 'You've got me into this, and now you must help me do it.' I pretended not to know what he meant, and he explained briefly. He wanted to come to Ottawa on Sunday to talk the problem over with me.

I was sure that the Opposition, particularly John Diefenaker and Howard Green, would try to drag out every adverse piece of information to make it look as though the government had something to hide. My suggestion to Abbott was that we think up every question that might be embarrassing, and give the list of them to McNaughton and insist that the army staff prepare full and correct answers without regard to security. The plan was that Abbott would put the questions and the answers into his speech introducing the army appropriation. I predicted that the press reports of his speech admitting the deficiencies would look bad for one day, but that from then on the debate would be an anticlimax. Abbott agreed to the plan.

When Parliament met in mid-March, the only items of government business for the session were the appropriation of funds for the fiscal year beginning 1 April 1945 and a resolution to approve Canadian participation in the conference to be held at San Francisco to establish the United Nations. That resolution found ready acceptance because the prime minister had already agreed to have Opposition representation on the delegation.

The war appropriation debate began with the air defence estimates, but the real interest was in the army estimates, which Abbott introduced. He followed the plan we had worked out together. I enjoyed the looks of disappointment on the faces of the Opposition critics as their ammunition disappeared. Diefenbaker, replying to Abbott, pretended that he had no prepared speech, attacked the prime minister for keeping McNaughton in office after his defeat in the by-election and raised a few lame questions that Abbott dealt with in a conciliatory fashion, promising to get any information he did not have in front of him. Ralston followed Diefenbaker and congratulated Abbott on the lucidity of his statement. He then made two or three requests for further information, which Abbott promised to supply. Ralston's commendation took away what steam was left in the Tory Opposition. The debate on the army estimates continued for two and a half more days, but it was an anticlimax, with some of the time taken up by Frederic Dorion, an Independent with a Tory background, and one or two other opponents of the decision to send the conscripts overseas. Abbott's performance was a demonstration of dealing effectively with a tough situation in Parliament, and a triumph for him that bolstered his reputation as a parliamentarian. Mackenzie King was filled with admiration.

The War Appropriation Bill passed on Friday, 13 April. The life of the Parliament would expire at midnight on Monday, 16 April. Mackenzie King, superstitious about letting Parliament die of old age, managed to persuade Graydon, the leader of the Opposition, to agree that the Speech from the Throne be approved that same day without debate. By avoiding any debate it was possible to have the session ended with a closing Speech from the Throne on Monday, 16 April. Shortly after the session was prorogued, Parliament was dissolved a few hours before it would have died. It was a tidy end to the wartime Parliament. Given how close the government had been to collapse in November 1944, it was a remarkable recovery.

Before leaving for San Francisco for the conference that founded the United Nations, Mackenzie King shuffled the cabinet in preparation for a general election. Crerar, the senior minister, went to the Senate and was replaced as minister from Manitoba by J. Allison Glen, who had been Speaker of the House of Commons in the recently dissolved Parliament. Norman McLarty was replaced as secretary of state by Paul Martin. Angus Macdonald resigned as minister of defence for naval services and was replaced by Abbott. Macdonald resumed the position of premier of Nova Scotia shortly afterwards. Claxton had already been appointed, in October 1944, to the new Department of National Health and Welfare. Joseph E. Michaud, the minister from New Brunswick, had been appointed to the bench and was replaced as minister for that province by D.L. MacLaren, who had never sat in Parliament. Michaud was succeeded as minister of transport by Lionel Chevrier. Joseph Jean, despite his vote against the government on the conscription issue, became solicitor-general. James McCann succeeded Leo R. La Flèche as minister of war services. There were seven new ministers, eight if Claxton was included. Four of them were young men who had made their mark in Parliament. Mackenzie King had faced difficult choices in Quebec and Ontario. When he had appointed Claxton to the cabinet, he had regretted having to pass over Abbott. In April 1945 Abbott had an even greater claim to recognition, after his outstanding performance defending the army estimates.

The appointment of Abbott to the cabinet would mean having two English-speaking ministers from Quebec. The two Liberal MPs from Ontario with the greatest claims for promotion on merit were Lionel Chevrier and Paul Martin, both Catholics. Chevrier was totally French in ancestry, and Paul Martin mainly so. It was a convention of cabinet-making that there should be one minister from Ontario to represent the Catholic minority, and that minister usually had been an English-speaking Catholic. In discussion with the prime minister I asked whether Claxton and Abbott in Quebec could not be balanced by appointing both Chevrier and Martin in Ontario. I could see the idea had some appeal, but he hesitated for several days before defying convention. When he finally acted, he astounded me by appointing a third Catholic from Ontario, Dr James McCann. I never knew why. The quartet of Claxton, Abbott, Chevrier and Martin evoked no public criticism and a good deal of approval. All became outstanding ministers. The shuffle gave the cabinet a new look and added to its strength.

6 Postwar with the Prime Minister

Mackenzie King's last mandate

San Francisco and VE day

The general election was set for Monday, 11 June 1945. Almost simultaneously Premier Drew of Ontario called an election for the same day. To avoid confusing the voters, Drew hastily changed the date to 4 June. Holding the Ontario election a week earlier was obviously intended to help the federal Tories, but it turned out to have the opposite effect.

The prime minister, hoping and believing the fighting would by then be over in Europe, decided to begin his own election campaign as late as 16 May. Meanwhile he was to preside over the Canadian delegation at the San Francisco conference to draft the United Nations Charter. I was included in Mackenzie King's personal staff for the conference. I had nothing to do with the work of the conference; my main task was to prepare material for speeches and broadcasts for the election campaign, and my other duty was to keep in touch with the Prime Minister's Office and the Secretary to the cabinet so that Mackenzie King would be fully informed about what the government was doing in Ottawa. Ilsley, as senior minister, was acting prime minister; St Laurent was deputy head of the Canadian delegation to San Francisco.

Graydon, as leader of the Opposition in Parliament, rather than Bracken, as leader of the Tory party, was a member of the Canadian delegation, as was Coldwell, the leader of the CCF. The Social Credit party was not represented.

The delegation travelled to California by train. I was excited by the prospect of new geography. For the first time I realized graphically what I knew only academically. The American Great Plains dwarfed our Canadian prairies — another lesson in perspective. I was impressed by the glimpse from the train of Salt Lake City. The American Rockies did not compare with ours. We arrived at Oakland after travelling all night. I had therefore no impression, and still have no personal experience, of the vastness of California.

The train journey was enlivened for me by a telegram to the prime minister from the premier of Prince Edward Island, Walter Jones, demanding the immediate dismissal of the lieutenant-governor. Prince Edward Island still had prohibition in 1945, and on the initiative of the premier the legislature had just passed a bill to provide for the sale of alcoholic beverages in government stores, similar to the practice in other provinces. The lieutenant-governor, in addition to being a Tory, was a convinced 'dry' and had refused to give royal assent to the bill. I expected Mackenzie King to take a serious view of this constitutional crisis. Instead he took it very calmly. He acknowledged receipt of the message and told me to file it. He murmured something to the effect that he was too busy to deal with a crisis in Prince Edward Island.

During the journey west, newspapers were filled with lurid accounts of the gruesome horrors being revealed as the Nazi concentration camps were liberated. I read them with deepening anxiety. On the night before our arrival in San Francisco I did not sleep well. Shortly after we reached the St Francis Hotel, I stretched out on the bed and fell asleep. At about 11 a.m. Hume Wrong came into the room with a cable from Paris from Georges Vanier, who had just learned that Frank had been killed the previous September at Buchenwald. I had almost lost hope of seeing Frank alive, but it was a terrible blow to learn that he had actually been dead for months. The news was being withheld until arrangements could be made to have Mother told. Mother was at Port Rowan, on Lake Erie. My brother Tom, who had recently moved to Vancouver to take a new position with the Department of Labour, was the only member of the family who might be able to visit Mother and give her the news. The deputy minister generously arranged to have Tom travel to Ottawa for consultation and gave him enough leave for his sad mission. Outwardly Mother accepted the terrible news, as she had accepted the death of our father, but we knew that some of the light had gone out of her life forever.

I did not like San Francisco. No doubt my feelings were coloured by its association with Frank's death, but I also felt a sense of confinement and boredom. Mackenzie King was preparing a broadcast to deliver as soon as the fighting stopped in Europe. He was apt to want to work on the speech with me at almost any hour: I had to be on hand and had little free time. When not working on the broadcast I busied myself with preparation of speech material for the election campaign. The atmosphere in the hotel was dismal, and when I got out occasionally for a walk, the city seemed unreal, like a stage set. When we left for Vancouver on the train, Mackenzie King remarked that the absence of trees had depressed him, and I suddenly realized that it had bothered me too.

We laboured so long over the VE day broadcast that I feared we would squeeze any life out of it. It turned out to be one of the prime minister's better scripts. It was very well delivered on VE day, 8 May. All reports indicated that the public reception in Canada was unusually favourable, and the tone was set for the election campaign.

One day during preparation of the broadcast the prime minister paused suddenly and asked whether I thought the Canadian Red Ensign should be flown over the Parliament Building on VE day. I was enthusiastic but stupidly added, 'Once you put it up, you will never be able to take it down.' As his diary shows, Mackenzie King considered that a piece of impudence, and he rebuked me sharply. Even before he replied, I realized I had made an error in tactics. I should have waited until the next day and then said very tentatively, 'Mr King, I have been thinking about the flag and wondering whether you might be able to resolve the whole problem by having the Red Ensign proclaimed as the flag of Canada on a day when no one would dare to criticize.' If I had done that I believe the flag problem might have been solved for a generation at least. The Red Ensign appealed to me, because in my early childhood it was used universally and called the Canadian flag. In retrospect I realize it was better to wait for a really distinctive flag.

VE day in San Francisco was an anticlimax. There were no demonstrations and almost no one on the streets in the evening. I went for a walk with Gordon Robertson, and we agreed that for Californians the war was not the war in Europe but the war against Japan, which seemed a long way from over.

A bizarre feature of the San Francisco experience was the appearance of John Diefenbaker. He was not a member of the delegation, but a tourist. He tried to horn in on the proceedings and was a considerable embarrassment to Graydon. Later, when he was prime minister, he tried repeatedly to give the impression that he had been one of the founders of the United Nations.

For me the best thing about San Francisco was the friendship I developed with Gordon Robertson. I had known him casually after he came to External Affairs in 1941. At San Francisco we spent a good deal of time together, and I formed the highest opinion of his intelligence and sense of duty and thought he was someone I would like to work with on a regular basis. And so it was to turn out.

The Japanese Canadians and the Pacific

I had no part in or influence on the decisions made in 1941 and 1942 concerning the people of Japanese origin resident in Canada. The almost hysterical fear so widespread in British Columbia that there might be a Japanese landing on the Pacific coast seemed to me exaggerated. I did not believe that most of the 22,000 Japanese

Canadians were a risk to security unless there was a military penetration by the Japanese. Only a handful were interned as sympathizers with Japan or possible agents. But I knew how hostile many British Columbians were to the Japanese Canadians even before 1941. Most of the Japanese were concentrated in a small coastal area of the lower mainland. The speed of the Japanese advance in the western Pacific increased fear that their advance might not be stopped anywhere, and that fear was soon voiced by the British Columbia MPs in the House of Commons. Mackenzie King feared the hostility might provoke a bloodbath.

Once the United States government declared their Pacific coastal region a security zone from which all residents of Japanese origin were to be removed, I felt that the almost unanimous demand from British Columbia for similar action would not be resisted. Eventually a security zone was established on the coast, and the Japanese residents were moved to the interior of British Columbia, to work camps, or to employment in the sugar beet fields of Alberta and Manitoba. The movement imposed hardship, but the effort to avoid deliberate ill-treatment was largely successful, and the internment seems to have been marginally more humane than in the United States. It was certainly more humane than the hysterical treatment in Britain in 1940 of refugees, many of them Jewish, from Nazi Germany: some of them were shipped off to camps in Canada; one ship was sunk on the way. The risk to the health of those evacuated from the BC coast was minimal, though many suffered psychological humiliation and a sense of isolation. The property of those evacuated was taken over and in some cases sold at market prices. The proceeds of the sales were not confiscated, as is often alleged, but remained the property of the former owners and were put in trust with the custodian of enemy property.

I did not like the action, which those with responsibility felt was necessary as an act of war, but it was certainly less painful than most acts of war. I felt regret but no sense of guilt at the time and later. I did not approve of the monetary compensation recently decided upon. The treatment of the Japanese Canadians was not unique as a war measure, and compensation for one group has already resulted in claims from others. There is plenty of injustice in society today that needs correction; we should not try to correct the injustices of history.

On 4 August 1944, when the war in Europe seemed nearly over and the tide had clearly turned against Japan in the Pacific, the prime minister made an announcement in Parliament of future policy towards persons of Japanese origin in Canada. He divided them into three categories: (1) Japanese nationals who had not been naturalized and who, when the war ended, could therefore be readily deported to Japan; (2) naturalized Japanese immigrants who could have their naturalization revoked for cause; and (3) persons of Japanese origin born in Canada who had a right to stay in Canada and could not be deported for any reason. The prime minister acknowledged the widespread fear in British Columbia of having most of the residents of Canada of Japanese origin once again concentrated on the Pacific coast when the war ended. He added that it would be unwise and undesirable from the point of view of the people of British Columbia and also of the Japanese themselves to allow that concentration to occur again. He stated that for the most part the Japanese residents had remained loyal to Canada, and that no person of Japanese race born in Canada had been charged with sabotage or disloyalty. He said the few persons of Japanese background who had shown disloyalty should not be allowed to remain in Canada after the war, and that immigration of Japanese to Canada should be prohibited, though such a prohibition could not be binding into the indefinite future. The majority who had been loyal should be treated justly and fairly. Not to do so would be acceptance of the standards of our enemies and the negation of the purposes for which we were fighting.

The prime minister went on to outline the measures proposed. The first was to determine through a quasi-judicial commission which persons of Japanese race had been loyal, and which disloyal; the disloyal should be deported to Japan as soon as possible after the war. The second measure was to encourage any persons of Japanese origin who wished to move to Japan voluntarily to do so. All those who had been loyal and who wished to remain should be allowed to stay in Canada, whatever their national status, but they should not be allowed once more to concentrate in British Columbia, and encouragement would be given to Japanese Canadians to move and remain elsewhere in Canada. Even temporary limitations would be undesirable in principle, but as a practical question of policy they might well be inescapable.

The policy was set out later in regulations under the War Measures Act and did involve the compulsory movement of many Japanese from the interior of British Columbia to other parts of Canada. The only protest in Parliament was from MPs who demanded that no person of Japanese origin be allowed to remain in British Columbia. Not one voice was raised in Parliament in criticism of compulsory movement of the Japanese from British Columbia.

The whole issue was to be of direct concern to my brother Tom and later to me. Tom had moved to Ottawa from Winnipeg in October 1942 to deal with the farm labour aspect of National Selective Service in the Department of Labour. Early in 1945 that program was grinding to a halt. The Department of Labour had been charged with the administration of the program of resettling the Japanese Canadians still in British Columbia and arranging passage for those Japanese nationals who chose to return to Japan. Tom was asked by the deputy minister to take charge of the program. He was reluctant to accept and told me he did not approve of the program. My reply was that it was surely better to have someone in charge who would administer it humanely than some racist enthusiast or sadist who might overlook maltreatment or even promote it. He accepted and moved to Vancouver. In British Columbia no one defended the Japanese Canadians, and the postwar program was denounced as too mild.

The feeling against the Japanese in British Columbia was still almost hysterical and was kept aroused by most of the MPs during the election campaign. Ian Mackenzie, the minister for the province, promised that there would not be a single Japanese left in British Columbia once the war with Japan ended. When Tom was asked to comment on Mackenzie's statement, he said his task was to carry out the policy announced by the prime minister, and thereby avoided a direct clash with Mackenzie. It was a source of great pride to Tom that in carrying out his disagreeable task he never had a single unpleasant encounter with any of the Japanese Canadians.

The war with Japan was still raging during the election campaign, and I assumed the prime minister would wish or be required to say something about Canada's part in the Pacific. The question had not been raised in Vancouver, no doubt because he spoke at a dinner rather than a public meeting. I drafted something for his Edmonton speech, but he was reluctant to raise the subject, then or later in the campaign. The government had already announced its limited military program and had made clear that no conscripts would be used, and that the only servicemen employed in the Pacific would be those who volunteered to serve there. Not until the atomic bomb was released over Hiroshima did I understand why Mackenzie King avoided talking about the war against Japan during the campaign.

A question about Canada's part in the war against Japan did arise privately at Edmonton. The government had announced that soldiers overseas who volunteered for the Pacific would be repatriated from Europe before the rest of the troops — a decision that caused serious discontent in the armed forces, where there was widespread feeling that those who had served longest should be brought home first. In Alberta there were members of the legislature who had been elected to represent the armed forces, one of whom was a young veteran named Harper Prowse. He came to the hotel to see the prime minister to protest against the decision to give preference in repatriation to servicemen who volunteered for service against Japan. Instead of seeing Prowse, Mackenzie King suggested that I talk to him. I spent two hours with him and found that, though officially nonpartisan, Prowse had been greatly impressed by the postwar program of the Liberal party and was eager to join in the Liberal campaign. I persuaded him to make no public statement about the recruiting policy and to come out in support of the government. It was not long after the war that

Prowse became leader of the Alberta Liberal party, which he managed to revive for a few years. From the time of the defeat of the Liberal government in 1921, Prowse was the only Liberal leader who made an impact in Alberta.

The election campaign of 1945

Mackenzie King's participation in the election campaign began in Vancouver with a speech at a dinner in the Hotel Vancouver. A part of the speech was to be broadcast live at a specific hour. After VE day he had done some work on my draft, but he was far from satisfied. In the end the speech was completed just in time for Mackenzie King to rest briefly before going to the dinner. The timing worked out accurately, and the half-hour broadcast went well, as did all his broadcasts during the campaign.

The next stop was Edmonton, where the prime minister was to speak at a luncheon. The broadcast was for Alberta only — an appeal to Albertans to give up their eccentric ways and vote for a national party. Bessie, who had come up from Calgary for the day, told me the theme was wrong because Albertans liked to be different. Apparently they still do.

After Edmonton was Prince Albert. The most recent visit by the prime minister to his constituency had been just before the election of 1940, and many of his supporters obviously felt neglected. In the intervening five years there had been no young Liberal recruits, and the CCF, which had won the provincial election in Saskatchewan in 1944, had made serious inroads federally in Prince Albert. Neither the prime minister nor any of his organizers had the slightest expectation that he would lose his seat.

The next stop was Winnipeg. The meeting there was a big one, in the Auditorium. The theme was national unity. Mackenzie King decided to announce that if he was still prime minister, he would ask the new Parliament to adopt a distinctive national flag. He denounced the tactics of the Conservatives, who were advocating conscription for the Japanese war while seeking allies among the anticonscription nationalists in Quebec. It was an effective fighting speech.

The most important broadcast of the campaign was delivered in London. It set out the postwar program, including a commitment to full employment that many, including some cabinet ministers, feared could not be achieved. In substance the speech was the Liberal program circulated to the armed forces on active service. The programs of the other parties were also distributed at public expense. When the election returns came in from the service voter, it was clear that the Liberal program had attracted the largest number. As one of the authors of that program and of the London speech, I was proud that every item in the program was eventually implemented by Liberal governments.

Mother came to London from Port Rowan for the day, and we had time together to talk about Frank. The prime minister took the overnight train for New Brunswick on 4 June. At Sherbrooke we received the results of the provincial election in Ontario, which Drew had won in a landslide. Mackenzie King was depressed by the news, fearing it was a portent of what would happen a week later. The prime minister had been embarrassed even before the Ontario election. He had been greatly relieved when Hepburn gave up the premiership, and encouraged when Harry Nixon, chosen Liberal leader, became premier. Nixon resigned as leader shortly after he lost the election in 1943, and Hepburn manoeuvred himself back into the leadership without a convention's being held. Mackenzie King, who detested Hepburn almost as much as he did Meighen, found it hard to pretend to welcome Hepburn's rebirth. When I told him on the evening of 4 June that I had voted for the CCF candidate in Russell, he was even more upset. I explained that I could not vote for Drew, would not vote for Hepburn and knew the CCF candidate, a young French-Canadian veteran, had no chance anyway. I then asked him if he had voted for Hepburn, and he grimaced as he admitted he had. I felt the score was even. The other meetings of the campaign were at Saint John, Quebec City and Ottawa. In an attempt to win Saint John and southern New Brunswick, Mackenzie King had taken D.L MacLaren, who belonged to an old Tory family, into the Cabinet and had promised to speak at a supporting meeting in Saint John.

There was an enthusiastic crowd at the meeting, but though the Liberals did well elsewhere in New Brunswick, MacLaren did not win.

Mackenzie King dreaded the prospect of the meeting in Quebec City. The campaign in Quebec was a strange one. Cardin had flirted with the idea of forming a group of dissident Liberals who would be covertly supported by Duplessis. Cardin's group would not have supported Mackenzie King. Chubby Power had suggested at an early stage that Liberal candidates call themselves Independent Liberals and, mischievously, that their slogan might be Not Necessarily Mackenzie King, but Mackenzie King If Necessary. As the campaign went on, the Liberal organizers began to realize that most of the voters felt Mackenzie King was necessary, in part because of Bracken's promise of conscription for the war against Japan. In the final two weeks the outlook steadily improved, but the prime minister felt that a great deal depended on the Quebec meeting, at which he and St Laurent were to be the main speakers. It was a good sign when Chubby agreed to be chairman.

The train arrived at Lévis from New Brunswick shortly after noon on the day of the meeting. The prime minister was met by St Laurent and a substantial number of prominent local Liberals, who escorted him across the river on the ferry and to the Château Frontenac Hotel. Mackenzie King promptly went to bed for a rest. About an hour later there was a knock on the door of the suite. I went to the door and found Chubby there, and I warned him that the prime minister was asleep, but as soon as he came in, the bedroom door opened to reveal Mackenzie King in his long underwear. He put his arm around Chubby, greeted him warmly and took him into the bedroom. I could see that Chubby was no more than half sober, and I had grave fears about how he would perform at the meeting.

When we arrived at the Palais Montcalm, the platform was crowded with Liberal dignitaries, but someone insisted I sit at the back corner of the stage. I preferred to be less conspicuous at the back of the room, where I could make a better assessment of the effect on the crowd. Just before the meeting was to start, Wilfrid Lacroix, the MP for Montmorency, who was one of the two so-called Liberals who had spoken in Parliament in September 1939 against the declaration of war and who had later crossed the floor to sit as an Independent, turned up and demanded a place on the platform. I gladly gave him mine; I knew he was such a weathervane that the Liberals must be assured of a landslide in Quebec. Chubby could barely stand on the platform, and his voice was hoarse, but his every word received an ovation, and by the time, near midnight, when Mackenzie King spoke, entirely in English except for a few opening words, the applause was thunderous. The prime minister left Quebec elated for the first time in the campaign.

His final speech was in Ottawa the Friday evening before the election. A half hour of the speech was to be broadcast live as the climax of the campaign. By that time the Tories had so little confidence in Bracken that they had substituted George McCullagh, the publisher of the *Globe and Mail*, to give their final broadcast. I thought that such an outrage that I patterned a draft speech on the Tory publicity, which concentrated on Bracken the Leader. I wrote that Bracken had been advertised like a new breakfast food or a new brand of soap. When he first read my draft Mackenzie King found it much too flamboyant. I begged him to tell me what theme he wanted to emphasize. I sat up most of Thursday night writing a new draft, which I sent to Laurier House in the morning. I heard nothing from Mackenzie King until noon. I was worried the speech would be a fiasco. Finally Turnbull came into my room, just before lunch, and said 'the Chief' would like to see me at Laurier House at 2. I said, 'thank God.'

When I got there, I found he had ignored my overnight draft and had been revising the earlier draft on Bracken the Leader. We worked without a break until after 6, and the conclusion had still to be revised. The prime minister suddenly said he must go off for a rest and would have to depend on me to finish the speech, and I did so. He had a final look at it in bed while I hovered over him, but my recollection is that he did not change a word of the conclusion. He was almost late for the meeting, and the timing was very tricky, to make sure the right section of the speech was broadcast. But all went well, and he spoke with great gusto. I believe that broadcast stiffened the support of many waverers and increased the total vote.

After the Quebec meeting and the Ottawa broadcast I was optimistic that the government would squeak through with a very small majority, but I have never before nor since been so doubtful about an outcome, not even during the six elections in which I was a candidate.

Margaret and I were invited to Laurier House with two or three of the prime minister's close friends to hear the returns. The results from Nova Scotia were highly gratifying, as were those from the other Maritime provinces. A few Independents were elected in Quebec, but not one candidate who called himself a Progressive Conservative. The Liberal victory there was over-whelming. Bracken made substantial gains in Ontario, especially in rural ridings, but in Manitoba, where he had been premier for 20 years, he was the only Conservative elected. Saskatchewan was a bitter pill for the Liberals and especially for Mackenzie King. McNaughton was beaten badly in Qu'Appelle, the riding in which he was born, Gardiner's seat was in doubt, and, worst of all, so was Prince Albert. In the end Gardiner won by a few votes, but the armed services vote defeated Mackenzie King. The CCF had almost swept the province, as Social Credit did once more in Alberta. British Columbia was a mixed bag, with Tory and CCF gains. The Liberals had a majority in Parliament of about 10 overall.

After 10 continuous years in office, 6 of them as wartime leader, it was a tremendous triumph for Mackenzie King — all the greater because the majority of French Canadians had endorsed him despite their bruised feelings over conscription. Equally gratify-ing, the Liberals had won more votes from the armed forces than had any opposition party. The result was a strong endorsement of the postwar program that gave the government a clear mandate for the period of reconstruction.

I had been so deeply involved in every aspect of the prime minister's campaign and in the publicity that I confess I felt some personal satisfaction in the outcome of an election that in April no Liberal had really expected to win. It also was something of a relief to realize that I need not worry about having a job in the immediate future.

Head of the Prime Minister's Office

Immediately before the election, the prime minister's principal secretary, Walter Turnbull, was appointed deputy postmaster general. H.R.L. Henry, his private secretary since 1930, was appointed registrar of the Exchequer court. I anticipated that if Mackenzie King won the election, he would ask me to become head of the Prime Minister's Office.

I had made up my mind not to accept the offer unless the salary matched those of my contemporaries who had remained in External Affairs. It had dragged behind one or two of those who had entered the service after I did. If I became head of the office, I did not want to be described as principal secretary, because every visitor who could not see the prime minister would insist on seeing the principal secretary. I knew I could not receive important visitors, look after the prime minister's engagements, administer the office and at the same time continue the work I had been doing during the war, which had made for a full-time job. I felt I would be of much more use to Mackenzie King as an adviser on domestic problems, a liaison with ministers and senior public servants and a draftsman of speeches, public statements and memoranda on parliamentary and other business. But there must be no doubt that I was head of the office and had the final word in its administration. I wanted to be given the new title of special assistant to the prime minister, without any clear definition of my functions.

When the prime minister asked me to become head of the office, he agreed to those conditions. Gideon Matte, who had managed Mackenzie King's campaign in Prince Albert, became private secretary and receptionist. He was a thoroughly bilingual

French Canadian and proved a useful and reliable contact with the Liberal MPs. Most important of all, I persuaded the prime minister and Norman Robertson to agree to second Gordon Robertson to the Prime Minister's Office. He was to be second-in-command with a new title, secretary of the Prime Minister's Office. He would substitute for me whenever I was absent. That was the beginning of one of the happiest of my official relationships and a wonderful friendship.

I had never found a thoroughly satisfactory personal assistant after William Paterson left the office in 1940. One day I spoke about my need to T.W.L. MacDermot, a wartime recruit to External Affairs. He showed me a letter from Ross Martin, who was in the army overseas. Martin had been at Upper Canada College when MacDermot was headmaster. I was so favourably impressed by the letter from the young major that I resolved to try to get him for the office. Martin was encouraged to compete for a place in External Affairs and, when appointed, was seconded to the Prime Minister's Office as my assistant. That was the beginning of another long and happy official relationship and a deep and lasting friendship.

About a year after I became head of the office, Jean-Louis Delisle, the officer in External Affairs who had replaced Jules Léger as French secretary, felt it was time to return to the department. I asked Ross Martin to look for a young French Canadian in the army who might replace Delisle. He found Michel Gauvin, who came to the office through the External Affairs route as a stage in his remarkable diplomatic career. Gauvin was a tower of strength.

We had an effective and harmonious staff in the East Block always ably backed up by Édouard Handy at Laurier House. Mackenzie King never admitted he was adequately served, but he no longer searched for a superman to head the office. Once or twice he even expressed satisfaction with my work, though complaints were more frequent. I was anxious to give him no legitimate ground for dissatisfaction, no easy feat. There was no way to get firm direction from Mackenzie King or to be sure he would not change direction unpredictably at any moment.

Despite occasional complaints to me and many more to the diary, I believe Mackenzie King found that the postwar Prime Minister's Office operated fairly smoothly. When we could be sure what his wishes were, they were carried out. Being sure required unremitting vigilance and involved a good deal of tension. We continued the wartime regime of having a secretary on duty every day, including Sundays, until 11 p.m., at both the East Block and Laurier House. Except for rare absences from Ottawa, I never went anywhere without leaving my telephone number with the telephone switchboard operator. If I was out of Ottawa and could not be reached, Gordon Robertson's telephone number was always available. The system rarely failed. Margaret believed that Mackenzie King had an uncanny knack of knowing when we were dining with friends or having a party and calling me on the telephone.

I continued the practice, started early in the war, of being unavailable until 10 a.m., but the prime minister called me nearly every working day precisely at 10. In fact I was usually in the office by 9 but never told him that. That interval of one hour gave me a chance to glance at the newspapers and any urgent mail and thereby to anticipate matters he would want to discuss, or I would have to take up with him.

All the secretaries had the strictest obligation to keep me and one another informed of any matter the prime minister was concerned with, so that whatever secretary he spoke to would not be caught by surprise. Memoranda prepared by other members of the staff were clearly identified. I tried to encourage the prime minister to deal directly with whichever secretary had prepared a piece of work, but in that I had only limited success.

Generally speaking, the family took second place to the prime minister. That happened on 5 September 1945, the day before the new Parliament met and the day our second child, Peter, was born. Margaret had gone to the hospital in the morning, and I was anxiously awaiting news of his arrival. I had been hard at work all day on final preparations for the opening of Parliament and then gone to dinner at the Château Laurier with Douglas and Mary

Abbott. We were scarcely seated when I was called to the telephone. Instead of the message I had expected, it was the prime minister. He told me that the governor general had objected to the French translation of the words 'Field Marshal' in the Speech from the Throne announcing the appointment of the governor general designate, Sir Harold Alexander. Athlone said the French translation should be *Maréchal* and not the German *Feld Marschall* used by the translator. I told the prime minister that the governor general was right and the change should be made. Mackenzie King was not satisfied with me as an authority but insisted I consult St Laurent. If he agreed, I should call the Printing Bureau and have the French version of the speech changed. The calls took some time, and I had barely got back to the table when I was called to the telephone again.

That time it was my father-in-law, to say we had a son. The doctor had tried to reach me while I was fussing about the French text of the Speech from the Throne. I finished dinner and then went to the hospital, expecting to find Margaret barely conscious, as she had been for several hours after Jane's birth. Instead she was sitting up in bed smoking a cigarette and as cheerful as I have ever seen her. She challenged me to give up smoking and I have never smoked since that day. Peter was a huge and apparently healthy baby. We did not realize then what a handicap of allergies he would have to live with, or what a great care and anxiety he was to be, especially for Margaret, all through his childhood.

Early in 1945 Margaret and I had decided that once we had another child the house on the Russell Road would no longer be adequate. The Tolmies had moved to Rockcliffe and my brother Tom to Vancouver, and we no longer had close friends as neighbours. We hoped to move to a neighbourhood near more of our friends. We found a semidetached three-storey house on Lambton Road in Lindenlea, on the edge of Rockcliffe, that was close to the Heeneys. They encouraged us to rent it and helped during the move by providing space for Margaret and Peter to stay. Peggy Heeney was greatly attached to Peter and became his godmother. The Lindenlea house was not handsome and had many faults, but it had enough rooms to serve for the next five years.

Jane was just four when we moved. Each morning when I left for work she would walk with me along our quiet street to the top of a slight rise, where she started back. I watched her until she got home. As the first child and the only one for four years she was protected in a way none of the others were.

In addition to the last-minute correction of the Speech from the Throne, the preparations for the opening of Parliament were complicated by an incident I knew nothing of at the time — the defection of the cipher clerk at the Soviet embassy, Igor Gouzenko, who had with him records showing that the Soviets had established a spy ring that included several public servants and one member of Parliament. Gouzenko's defection and its consequences were one of the main preoccupations of the prime minister and the government for most of the next year.

By mid-September it was clear that Mackenzie King was reluctant to spend much time in the House of Commons. I was not surprised when he decided to go to England and leave the management of Parliament and the direction of the government to Ilsley as acting prime minister. He left Ottawa 29 September and took Norman Robertson with him. I was left to manage the office and assist Ilsley. I enjoyed working with Ilsley and recall no serious problems during Mackenzie King's absence, which lasted until mid-November.

There was a prolonged strike against the Ford Motor Company in the fall of 1945, during which the minister of labour visited Windsor and had two meetings in Detroit with Henry Ford II, on which he reported to Ilsley as acting prime minister. I saw Ilsley immediately afterwards. Mitchell had reported that he had concluded his discussion with Ford by telling him, 'in Canada, the King can do no wrong.' When Ford asked what that meant, Mitchell replied, 'I won't tell you, but it is really drastic.' Ilsley could scarcely stop laughing as he told me the story.

On 20 November Mackenzie King was welcomed back in the House after seven weeks' absence. It was not until the following year, when the American columnist Drew Pearson published a report in Washington of the Gouzenko defection, that I learned the main reason for Mackenzie King's visit to England and for the later meeting with President Truman and Prime Minister Attlee in Washington. He felt he should personally advise them of disclosures by Gouzenko that affected all three countries. Drew Pearson's scoop in 1946 would oblige the government to report to Parliament and lead to the detention of the suspects.

Reconstruction

Federal-provincial relations, the surrender of Japan, and the flag

The most difficult problem of postwar domestic reconstruction was the development of satisfactory federal-provincial relations, particularly in the field of taxation. Until that problem was resolved, it was impossible to decide how far to go with expanded federal services for peacetime. During the two years before 1945, a great deal of work had been done on an elaborate plan for the postwar activities of the federal government. It was based on the continuation of tax-rental agreements with the provincial governments on a scale that would permit increased old age pensions, the beginnings of health insurance, and programs for public projects, if needed, to provide employment.

Sandy Skelton, who was coordinating preparation of the plan, discussed the details with me on a regular basis. Once Duplessis was back in office in 1944, I told Sandy that it was not realistic to make any proposal that would depend on amending the Constitution. That judgment was accepted by the planners.

Consequently, the proposals submitted to the cabinet after the election of 1945 were all capable of being carried out without diminishing provincial jurisdiction. What was proposed was the continuation of the wartime tax-rental agreements for the period of reconstruction. The provinces would not resume imposing and collecting income taxes and succession duties. In exchange they would receive guaranteed unconditional annual payments, at a higher level, from the federal treasury. Those tax-rental payments were to be high enough to enable all provincial governments to provide roughly comparable services.

Mackenzie King asked me to sit at the back of the cabinet room to listen to the deliberations on relations with the provinces so that I could discuss them later with him, and I did so for two meetings. I had never seen a cabinet meeting before and was appalled. It seemed to me that most of the ministers paid no attention at all, and that almost no one except the prime minister, Ilsley and St Laurent listened to what anyone else said. Those who took part in the discussion seemed to listen only to themselves. One junior minister, however, did pay close attention, Claxton. I stopped going after the second meeting.

Some days later Mackenzie King asked why I was no longer at the meetings. I told him they interfered with my other work and added that Claxton gave me a brief account after each meeting. I was, in fact, deeply interested in what was being proposed, particularly on the fiscal side. I needed no encouragement to attend the meetings of the Dominion-Provincial Conference on Reconstruction, which met on 6 August to discuss the federal program.

Soon after he became premier of Ontario in August 1943, Drew began demanding a dominion-provincial conference for postwar planning. One of my tasks was to draft replies to his lengthy letters. It was not easy to decide whether to reply to each individual point or to make a summary and deal briefly with the main argument. After several false starts I settled on the second method, though I realized that leaving any point unanswered gave Drew a chance to pretend it had been agreed to. Mackenzie King was able to string out the exchange of correspondence, to make sure that no conference was held until after the fighting had stopped in Europe and the election was over.

It was clear from the opening morning of the conference that Drew and Duplessis had met in advance and agreed to try to discredit the federal program. The prospect of their accepting a reasonable compromise was dim. When it was adjourned on 10 August, it was agreed there should be further sessions in 1946.

Sessions were held from 29 April to 3 May 1946. No agreement was possible with all premiers, and the conference was adjourned indefinitely.

After the adjournment the federal government adopted a procedure similar to that followed in 1941 by offering a separate tax-rental agreement to any provincial government willing to accept. During the prolonged negotiations, carried on mainly by the Department of Finance, I was the usual intermediary with the prime minister. I was also a close confidant of Premier Garson of Manitoba, who was the strongest provincial supporter of the federal program. I participated actively in the negotiation of the agreements ultimately concluded with seven of the nine provinces. By failing to make agreements the governments of Ontario and Quebec lost any share of the federal personal income tax without imposing any of their own. Because not all the provinces had made tax-rental agreements, the federal government withdrew its proposals for social welfare and public investment. The withdrawal was attacked strongly but unsuccessfully by T.C. Douglas, the premier of Saskatchewan, in letters to the prime minister. Preparing draft replies to those letters was one of my duties.

I doubt if anyone, politician or bureaucrat, was more thoroughly familiar with the intricacies of federal-provincial relations from 1945 on than I was. In my view equalization, as federal-provincial fiscal payments were called after 1956, was the greatest domestic achievement of postwar Canadian government. Equalization became the foundation of national unity; it ensured an approach to equal financial capacity among all provincial governments to perform their constitutional functions.

When the conference adjourned for lunch on 6 August, the prime minister informed the meeting that an atomic bomb had been dropped on Hiroshima. The news had reached him just before the time of adjournment. I had no inkling that such a weapon was being perfected, but I realized at once why Mackenzie King had been so reluctant during the election campaign to talk about the war with Japan. I recalled that he had said to me, months before, that a new weapon being manufactured would change the whole character of war. At the time I attached little significance to the remark and made no attempt to find out more about it.

Once it was clear that Japan would surrender, Mackenzie King was eager to be the first, when it happened, to inform the Canadian people. A broadcast was drafted to be in readiness. Word came that surrender was probable Sunday, 12 August. The prime minister met me at the CBC studio at the Château Laurier that morning. He took a suite nearby, and we spent the day writing and revising the speech, with time out for a late lunch and for his siesta. When no word had come by 6 p.m., the prime minister decided to record his broadcast and go to Kingsmere for the evening. It was arranged that the recording would be broadcast as soon as official word came, which by that time seemed highly improbable that day.

I went home to supper. We turned off the radio, which I had been listening to all day. Shortly before 9 the CBC station manager telephoned to say that Japan had surrendered, and that the prime minister's recording was being broadcast. I asked if he was sure and turned on the radio. I heard the rest of the recorded broadcast, which was followed immediately by an announcement that the report of the surrender was false. I tried to reach Mackenzie King at once but was told he had gone out for a walk.

I was debating with myself whether or not I should take personal responsibility for explaining how the prime minister's statement came to be broadcast. I was preparing a statement for broadcast late in the evening on the national news when Mackenzie King telephoned. He had already been told that his recording had been on the air. I expected an explosion, with an attempt to blame me as well as the CBC, but he was exceedingly calm and blamed only himself. I never admired him more. He accepted my advice that an explanation be broadcast on the evening news. I thought the gaffe would never be forgotten, but I was wrong; there were no nasty remarks, and very little ridicule. Within a week nearly everyone had forgotten the incident except for me and, I am sure, the prime minister. The news of the actual surrender was almost an anticlimax for us.

When the new Parliament met on 6 September, the Speech from the Throne announced, among other items, that Parliament would be asked to make provision for a distinctive national flag for Canada. Meanwhile on 5 September an order-in-council had been passed designating the Canadian Red Ensign as a flag distinctive of Canada. That order-in-council remained in force for nearly 20 years, until the government and Parliament finally decided on the design of the flag that was unfurled officially on 15 February 1965.

Soon after Parliament met in 1945 a Flag Committee was set up under the chairmanship of Walter Harris. The committee was revived in the session of 1946 and ultimately recommended the Red Ensign with a gold maple leaf in the fly. That was the design Mackenzie King wanted. But an incipient mutiny developed among a group of French-speaking backbenchers from Quebec who insisted that a distinctive flag could not include the Union Jack. Mackenzie King decided not to proceed with legislation. When St Laurent became prime minister, he decided not to touch the flag question until he felt sure a flag would unite rather than divide the country. The moment did not come while he was prime minister.

I regretted that the flag question had not been settled. One day I mentioned my disappointment to Coldwell, the CCF leader. He replied that he thought it was better to wait until all of us could agree on a genuinely Canadian flag. In time I came to realize that that English-born Canadian had been wiser than I.

Who should be Right Honourable?

Ilsley and St Laurent were included in the British Honours List for the New Year 1946. Both became British privy councillors with the designation Right Honourable. The awarding of those distinctions caused Mackenzie King a good deal of unpleasantness with two other colleagues. The prime minister had an open house at his residence on New Year's Day. I was at home in bed with a slight case of flu. During the afternoon I had a telephone call from one of the secretaries at Laurier House, who read an indignant and almost insulting telegram from Ian Mackenzie protesting that he had been passed over in the Honours List and submitting his resignation from the cabinet. Mackenzie felt that as the senior Canadian privy councillor in the cabinet he had the highest claim to such an honour. Mackenzie King had great difficulty soothing him down and persuading him to stay in the government.

Mackenzie was not the only aggrieved minister. C.D. Howe was in Cuba at the New Year. Upon his return in mid-January he offered his resignation to the prime minister somewhat less belligerently than had his colleague. The prime minister explained to both ministers that membership in the British Privy Council was in the exclusive control of the British prime minister and that he had made no recommendation to Attlee but had felt he could not object when Attlee consulted him. At one stage the prime minister sent me to see Howe to repeat the assurance that the initiative had been entirely British, that he had been surprised when Attlee spoke to him, and that if he had objected, Ilsley and St Laurent would have learned about the recommendation and his objection. I duly carried out my mission, and when I had finished, Howe said, 'Jack, you know that is a damned lie.' He added, 'I would have liked to get that degree.' I thought it characteristic of Howe that he did not pretend it was his wife or children who cared but honestly said he himself was disappointed. In fact, Mackenzie King's diary shows that what he asked me to tell Howe was the truth, as I believed it was at the time.

In May 1946, when the prime minister was in London, Attlee told him he had heard of Howe's disappointment, and offered to have him appointed. That time Mackenzie King got in touch with St Laurent in Ottawa to make sure both Ian Mackenzie and Jimmy Gardiner, the only other 1935 original ministers, would not object. It was an example of St Laurent's persuasive powers that he was able to get both men to acquiesce. Howe was then appointed.

Late in 1946 Mackenzie King had Norman Robertson see Attlee and ask him to include Mackenzie and Gardiner as privy councillors in the Honours List for the New Year 1947. Peace had finally been restored to the cabinet. Mackenzie King had not enjoyed the whole business.

Diefenbaker was the last Canadian minister to become a British privy councillor. When Pearson became prime minister, I persuaded him to have the Queen change the Table of Precedence so that the governor general, the prime minister and the chief justice would automatically be described as Right Honourable without becoming British privy councillors.

Gouzenko and Soviet espionage

On 6 September 1945, the day the postwar Parliament met, the prime minister's life had been complicated by Igor Gouzenko's defection from the Soviet embassy. Although I was unaware of the matter at the time, I had guessed that something serious was afoot because of frequent meetings of Norman Robertson, Hume Wrong and senior officials from the justice department in Norman's office, two doors down the corridor from my own.

News of the defection was kept secret until its appearance in a Washington column in February 1946. By that time the government had appointed but not made public the existence of a royal commission consisting of two judges of the Supreme Court to examine Gouzenko and the evidence he had furnished. On 14 February Norman Robertson told me about Gouzenko's defection and his providing the government with documentary evidence that a Soviet espionage ring existed in the public service and beyond, to include an employee of the United Kingdom high commission and, apparently, a member of Parliament. Robertson added that on the advice of the royal commission the government proposed to have the suspects in the public service arrested the next day and detained for interrogation by the commission. The police had wanted to make the arrests at an early hour in the morning, but Norman had felt that that would look too much like totalitarian methods and persuaded the prime minister to insist that they be delayed until normal working hours. The prime minister was to announce that same day that the government had evidence, of undoubted authenticity, that secret information had been furnished to Soviet agents by employees of government departments or agencies, and that some suspected persons had been detained.

The prime minister's announcement aroused great public curiosity; the Gouzenko affair would clearly be the issue of prime concern when parliament met on 14 March. I was involved in the lengthy preparation of a statement to be made by the prime minister as early as possible in the session.

The most serious question the government would have to answer was what authority existed to permit the minister of justice to have persons arrested and detained for interrogation. New legislation had been substituted for the War Measures Act, which could no longer be used after 31 December 1945. Called the National Emergency Transitional Powers Act, it gave the government no power to arrest and detain persons who were not charged with any offence. The new legislation provided that orders-in-council made under the War Measures Act would continue to be in force until they were revoked. An order-in-council had been made under the War Measures Act on 6 October 1945. Gouzenko's disclosures had indicated that a British scientist, Dr Allan Nunn May, who had been working on atomic research in Canada, would be in London on 7 October and had arranged to meet a Soviet agent to pass on secret information. May was to be arrested on the spot if the meeting took place. The RCMP had convinced the government that if May were arrested, the suspects in Canada should be arrested immediately and kept in custody. The order-in-council of 6 October empowered the minister of justice to authorize such action. The order was made by the acting prime minister, the minister of justice and two other ministers and kept secret even from the rest of the cabinet. May was not arrested, and the power under the order was not used.

On 6 December 1945, during the debate on the new emergency legislation, the minister of justice had been asked by Diefenbaker how many secret orders there were that had not been produced in Parliament, and St Laurent had replied, 'There are no secret orders.' In February 1946 St Laurent was asked by the royal commission to authorize the arrest and detention of the suspects.

He said he had no authority to do so. He was then reminded by counsel for the commission and officials in Justice of the secret order-in-council of 6 October 1945. He used the power given to the minister of justice under that order to have the arrests and detentions made on 15 February 1946. The prime minister and St Laurent both realized that the minister of justice would be accused of having deceived the House by making the earlier statement, that there were no secret orders-in-council.

In his detailed statement in Parliament on 18 March 1946, the prime minister reported that he had left for Washington at the end of September 1945, and that the order-in-council had been passed in his absence to meet the situation in Canada if May had been arrested in London. When May was not arrested, the order remained in abeyance until the authority given by that order was used in February to make the arrests and detain the suspects. Mackenzie King said he doubted very much, though the minister of justice would speak for himself, whether the minister remembered that that order was still in effect when he was asked in the House if there were any secret orders. Mackenzie King confessed that he himself had never thought of it, though he believed he was in the House when the question was asked.

When St Laurent spoke the next day he gave a straightforward reply to a question by the leader of the Opposition about the secret order. He admitted that at the time he was questioned on 6 December, he had had no thought of that order — 'It had entirely slipped my memory.' Bracken then said he was quite convinced St Laurent had not meant to mislead the House. It was a mark of the high regard in which St Laurent was already held that the Opposition made no attempt to accuse him of deliberately misleading the House. There were members who might have been tempted to do so, but Bracken by his generous attitude made it almost impossible for them. Both Mackenzie King and St Laurent were vastly relieved that embarrassment of St Laurent and corresponding loss of prestige did not develop.

The arrest of Fred Rose, the MP for Montreal Cartier, on the evening of 14 March, the day Parliament opened, was a greater sensation at the time, but the government had prepared its defence of the legality of arresting a member when the House was in session, and the action caused the government no embarrassment. But the lengthy period of detention did embarrass the government, as did other aspects of the whole affair. Mackenzie King complained several times to me about the delay in prosecuting or releasing those detained. He felt some impatience that he had no power to do anything about it. I was glad I had no part in the whole affair, except to help prepare such statements as the prime minister had to make.

Travels, tensions and changes

London and Paris

The prime minister was away from Parliament in 1946 from early May until the middle of June, with Ilsley left in charge as acting prime minister and St Laurent as acting secretary of state for external affairs. That time I was in the prime minister's party. The purpose of the visit was to attend a meeting of Commonwealth prime ministers that Attlee had arranged.

We sailed early in May. The party included Norman Robertson, Gordon Robertson, Jean Chapdelaine, who was Norman's assistant and, of course, Handy and Nicol. The conference itself was not really important, and I attended only the final meeting, held in prime minister Attlee's room in the House of Commons. The Australian prime minister had gone home before Mackenzie King arrived and had left the external affairs minister, a man named Evatt, to represent Australia. Evatt was a pushy type, disliked by most of his associates. I was sitting at the table between Mackenzie King and him, and at one point I wrote out in large handwriting a phrase the prime minister might wish to use in the discussion. Evatt read my note and promptly used the phrase himself.

The prime minister stayed on in England after the conference ended. I asked him if I might go to Paris for a few days to meet my brother Frank's friends. I also wanted to visit the de France family. That visit was very emotional for me. Saul Rae, of the embassy staff, literally devoted himself to me full time. He helped to arrange a reception, to which all Frank's prewar friends came. I was deeply moved by the evidence of their attachment to the memory of one who had obviously been an intimate friend. I have had repeated evidence of that devotion over the years, especially in 1978, when I met many of them again after the publication of the new edition of *The Pickersgill Letters*.

Paul de France, who had been married during the war and had two children, was living in Paris. Not only did I meet his wife, Eliane, and the children for the first time, but Saul Rae arranged to take Paul and me to the Château d'Arry for an overnight visit with Paul's parents. It was the last time I saw them. I have always been grateful that I had that farewell visit; for me they were almost second parents.

Saul also took me to see the Grande Caserne at St-Denis, where Frank had been a prisoner for so long. I quickly identified the room from which he and his friend had escaped by sawing through the iron bars. I walked over to the window and lifted out the bars. I noticed that the French sergeant conducting us looked somewhat worried; only then did I realize that several German prisoners had been watching me with obvious interest.

When I got back to London, Handy told me the prime minister had asked for me once during my absence, expressed surprise that I was in Paris and then inquired, 'What has Pickersgill done for me on this trip?' Handy replied that I had done everything he had asked me to do, and the prime minister retorted, 'What have I asked him to do?' I concluded that I was not much use in London, told Handy I hated sea voyages and asked him to find out if Mackenzie King would mind if I flew home. He would not, and I was home by 5 June. Mackenzie King returned by ship and was not back in Parliament until 17 June.

Mackenzie King was highly and unfairly critical of Ilsley's conduct as acting prime minister. Over the year or so previous Ilsley's health had deteriorated from sheer exhaustion. It was clear he was in no position to take on the responsibility the next time the prime minister was absent. Indeed, the strain of the Department of Finance itself was too much for him.

St Laurent as acting prime minister

Mackenzie King went abroad again in July 1946 to represent Canada at the conference in Paris to make peace with Italy. He did not want Ilsley to be acting prime minister, and Ilsley did not want to be. Nor did Mackenzie King want to leave him sitting in the House while another, less senior minister acted for the prime minister. He was even less willing to have Ilsley resign as minister of finance, as Ilsley offered to do. The prime minister solved the problem by persuading him to become head of a Canadian mission that was to travel abroad in connection with the United Nations Relief and Rehabilitation Administration. Lester Pearson was to be second-in-command to relieve Ilsley of most of the responsibility.

Having saved Ilsley from embarrassment, Mackenzie King persuaded St Laurent to act for him during his absence. That decision had a profound effect on the country, on St Laurent and on me, because it was the first step along the road that would end with St Laurent as prime minister. I was to stay in Ottawa to assist St Laurent. I thereby avoided the 'horrors' of Paris with a prime minister no one could please or even satisfy; I was lucky to have escaped the ordeal, described in Mackenzie King's diary in depressing detail.

One of the main achievements of the 1946 session was the passage of the Canadian Citizenship Act. The legislation was piloted through Parliament by Paul Martin as secretary of state, but the prime minister maintained close scrutiny of the bill and agreed to permit Gordon Robertson to help Martin with the actual drafting, under my nominal supervision. Martin was so pleased with Gordon's help that he asked the prime minister if he could offer Robertson a position in his own ministerial office. Mackenzie King flatly refused. He added that he found Robertson a stupid fellow who would not have been much use to Martin anyway. I was greatly relieved, as I relied on Gordon more than anyone else in the office — and never found him stupid.

The session of Parliament proceeded smoothly under St

Laurent's guidance, and he was paid unprecedented compliments by Bracken and spokesmen for the other Opposition groups on the day the session ended. I began to understand why Mackenzie King wanted St Laurent to be his successor. Watching him in action every day, I realized the thorough appreciation he had of every matter to be dealt with in the cabinet. I spent most of my time in the gallery when St Laurent was in the House and was impressed by his capacity to avoid or overcome difficulties in debate. I admired more and more the combination of modesty and self-assurance he displayed, the care he showed for the feelings of others and the loyalty he inspired in those who worked for him.

One day I told him I hoped he would stay in public life and become leader of the Liberal party. His response was that he was too old, that younger men were needed in government. I ventured to express my belief that if he surrounded himself with younger men in the cabinet, he would be a successful leader.

St Laurent knew the prime minister did not want to have to face Parliament when he returned from abroad. Mackenzie King landed at Halifax from Paris and London on 31 August, just as the parliamentary session was proroguing. He expressed deep relief when I telephoned the news that he would not have to meet Parliament — further evidence for me that he no longer derived any real satisfaction from his duties and was too weary to do the job effectively. His judgment that St Laurent would be a competent successor was confirmed for him by reports of St Laurent's leadership in Parliament. He was more resolved than ever to keep St Laurent in public life. I too wanted to do anything in my power to help make him the next prime minister.

All industry and no humanity

But I might have had no chance to help assure the succession. Ross Martin, who had been a white-haired boy in the eyes of the prime minister up to the time of his departure for Paris fell into instant disgrace. Ross had been on duty at the office the evening before Mackenzie King was to leave Ottawa. Handy telephoned me from Halifax to say that the prime minister had complained that Ross had not wished him well when he left the office and had failed to turn up at the train in the morning to see him off. He had told Handy to instruct me to have Ross 'fired.' I sent for Ross at once. He told me he had wished Mackenzie King well when he left the office, had indicated he was saying goodbye in case he did not see him at the train the following morning and had failed to go to the train because he and his wife had been kept awake most of the night by the baby. I told Ross that I would not carry out the prime minister's order; that if he did not want to carry on in the face of the prime minister's displeasure, he was free to take his normal place in External Affairs; and that if he was willing to stay in the office, I would give up my own position before carrying out the prime minister's instruction. When Ross decided to stay and face the consequences, my opinion of him rose.

When the prime minister returned from Europe, his private railway car was sent down to Halifax to bring the party back to Ottawa. I had Martin go along to deliver a bundle of dispatches and other papers for the prime minister to read on the way home. Through some sort of mix-up Martin did not see the prime minister immediately to deliver the papers. When he was received, he told me, he was greeted as coldly as he had ever been in his life. I heard nothing more about firing him, however. I suspect the prime minister had guessed there would be an unpleasant confrontation if I did. Martin never returned to favour, but the prime minister agreed to increase his secretarial allowance at the end of the year, thanks to Handy's plea that I would be relieved and pleased.

Ross was not the only person I was told to have fired. On one occasion in the railway station in New York, the prime minister's private car had been attached to a train for our return to Ottawa. Mackenzie King arrived from visiting a friend just as the train was about to leave. I had been pondering whether to try to hold up the departure or to have the car detached from the train when he came aboard at the last second, breathless, without a word of apology. The chef greeted him warmly and perhaps less respectfully than usual, though I noticed nothing amiss. Afte dinner the prime minister told me the man was drunk and must be dismissed from the service. He was still indignant in the morning when we reached Ottawa. I warned the assistant deputy minister of transport that he might be approached direct by the prime minister, and asked him to do nothing without consulting me. Nothing more was heard of firing the chef.

On another occasion the secretary on duty at Laurier House left a few minutes before 11 p.m. When the prime minister returned well after 11, he rang for the secretary and learned he had left early. Mackenzie King complained to me the next morning and insisted that I check up on all the members of the staff to see how often they were neglecting their duties. Twice later he asked for the report, and I reported that it was not yet ready. I had the records examined for at least a year. The report, when completed, showed hundreds of hours of overtime worked by the staff. In those days there was no overtime pay or days of leave in compensation. I heard no further complaints from the prime minister about neglect of duty. I believe the author of *Industry and Humanity* was shocked and possibly a little ashamed of the exploitation. I once said working for Mackenzie King was 'all industry and no humanity.'

I recall with amusement one Saturday afternoon when I was the only officer on duty. The prime minister was at Kingsmere, dealing with an accumulation of correspondence and memoranda marked for his personal attention. He came across a letter from a close friend with a draft reply that had been on his desk for a week. He telephoned me in some indignation, said the letter should have been shown to him at once and asked who was responsible. I replied that I was. I am sure he guessed I had never seen the letter. He replied that it was a good thing I was responsible, as otherwise I would have had to fire the offender.

Such incidents were not common; they were rare. Generally the office worked smoothly. Although I can hardly remember a word of commendation or satisfaction for work well done, Mackenzie King was capable of acts of concern and even generosity when members of the staff had personal problems or anxieties. He had the most complex personality I have encountered in my life, but I survived for 11 years.

In 1946 I felt the office was well enough organized that Gordon Robertson could manage it whenever I was absent. Once the war was over, I was determined to have holidays from time to time. Margaret and I fortunately had the happiest possible relationship with our parents, and Mother and the Beatties had become close friends. Margaret's parents were very generous when they were in Ottawa about supervising the household and keeping an eye on the children, and so made it possible for us to get away together a few times. We had a wonderful short holiday in the Niagara Peninsula and Norfolk County in 1946 and three weeks in the Gaspé and the Laurentians in 1947.

Mackenzie King was ill in the late winter of 1946-47 and was absent from Parliament a great deal. He was persuaded to go south and spend some time at Virginia Beach, taking Handy and Nicol with him. Before he left Ottawa, I told him I would have the mumps while he was away. He told me not to be ridiculous, mumps was a children's disease. Jane had just had an attack, and as I had never been exposed as a child, I felt I was vulnerable. The first time Mackenzie King telephoned the office from the south, he asked to speak to me. When I said I was in bed with the mumps, he repeated that that was ridiculous at my age. I began to fear it was much worse; the attack was severe, and for at least a week after I was out of bed, I walked up and down the street like a very old man. Alan's birth in 1948 happily proved that I had not suffered the worst consequence.

I had managed, in October 1945, while the prime minister was in London, to get a few days off to go to Winnipeg to speak at the 100th meeting of the History Club of United College, which I had founded in the 1930s. Despite a brief feeling of nostalgia while I was there, I realized I no longer wanted to go back to academic life. Being at the heart of government in Ottawa was far more exciting, despite the tension of being at the beck and call of a bachelor prime minister.

The big shuffle

The first step in making St Laurent prime minister was to keep him in public life. Mackenzie King realized that the only way to tempt him to stay was to make him secretary of state for external affairs. To that appointment St Laurent agreed because he felt it a duty to do his part in finding a way to prevent another world war.

To keep St Laurent, a major cabinet shuffle took place on 4 September 1946, right after the prime minister returned from Paris and London. Ilsley replaced St Laurent as minister of justice. The removal of the burden of Finance gave Ilsley a new lease of life and a fleeting hope that he might become Mackenzie King's successor; he was the only minister who might successfully have challenged the prime minister's goal of having St Laurent succeed him. Abbott, who had repeatedly served as acting minister of finance, was his natural successor as minister; he served with apparent ease and great competence and flair for nearly eight years. Claxton succeeded Abbott as minister of national defence; he was the outstanding minister of that department in the postwar period. Martin succeeded Claxton in Health and Welfare; he remained in that office until the St Laurent government resigned in June 1957, and made a massive contribution to Canadian welfare. The position of associate minister of defence, held by Colin Gibson, was dropped, and he succeeded Martin as secretary of state.

Equally important were changes made the same day in the upper levels of the public service. Norman Robertson, who had been Mackenzie King's closest adviser since Skelton's death in 1941, was exhausted. I believed that Norman with at least half his mind would like to be high commissioner in London. I knew he would be an outstanding success at a time when relations with Britain were still of critical importance. If Mackenzie King had remained secretary of state for external affairs I doubt he would have let Robertson go, but since the under-secretary would be St Laurent's deputy, the prime minister was reluctantly persuaded to let Norman leave Ottawa. The obvious successor to Robertson was Hume Wrong, the associate under-secretary, but the prime minister did not like Wrong and wanted someone he could deal with easily. He chose Pearson instead. Pearson had been ambassador in Washington for a relatively short time. He had mixed feelings about the change, but Mackenzie King was persuasive about the larger scope and opportunities offered by the under-secretary's office. According to the diary, Mackenzie King already envisaged Pearson as an eventual prime minister and told him so.

The most immediate effect of the shuffles in my life was to make me, instead of Robertson, Mackenzie King's closest adviser in the public service, and I continued to be such as long as he was prime minister. I never felt he had quite the same confidence in my judgment as he had had in Norman's.

The changes did little to relieve Mackenzie King's weariness with office, and I became more and more concerned that if he could not persuade St Laurent to seek the leadership, he would cling to office when no longer capable of carrying the burden. I was afraid someone might have to tell him the time had come to retire. One day in 1946 I expressed my concern to Hume Wrong and added that if I had to do it, my career would be ended, and I would be unfit for any other. He retorted that I might be ideally qualified to head a psychiatric institution. Luckily I did not have to bell the cat. I was surprised later by Howe's claim that he had done so.

One day the prime minister told me that he felt he should retire as soon as the succession could be arranged. I neither agreed nor dissented but pointed out that Macdonald and Laurier, whose terms in office he had already exceeded in length, had each left his party virtually in ruins. I said it would be a tremendous achievement if he could leave the Liberal party as strong as it had been at the height of his career. I saw at once that that possibility appealed to him. He told me then that if he could only persuade St Laurent to remain in public life, that objective could be achieved. I realized he was losing no opportunity to persuade St Laurent. He was delighted when, on 1 October 1947, St Laurent told him that he had managed to arrange his personal affairs so as to enable him to stay on and accept the leadership if it was offered.

From that moment Mackenzie King was determined to do his utmost to ensure the succession. But he was also eager to remain prime minister until he had exceeded Walpole's record, and so be able to boast that he had served longer than any other prime minister in a British country. He did both.

No other prime minister in history has left his party stronger at the end of his term, though Pearson left the Liberal party potentially stronger. Both Diefenbaker and Trudeau, consciously or unconsciously, weakened their successors as leaders.

A new immigration policy

I had a small part in the work on the Canadian Citizenship Act, in which Gordon Robertson had such a large share. I had much more to do with the new immigration policy announced by Mackenzie King in Parliament on 1 May 1947. My attitude, influenced considerably by Arthur Lower's views in the 1930s, was conservative. A statement of policy was drafted in External Affairs. I redrafted some of the key phrases with a view to ensuring that the country would not be swamped with immigrants. I was particularly concerned with two questions. One was the way in which to reply to the charge of racial discrimination. I helped draft Mackenzie King's statement that 'Canada is perfectly within her rights in selecting the persons whom we regard as desirable future citizens. It is not a "fundamental human right" of any alien to enter Canada. It is a privilege. It is a matter of domestic policy.' That has remained my attitude since 1947. It is unfortunate that a judgment of the Supreme Court has interpreted the Charter of Rights to give any stranger who sets foot in Canada the right to hearings from which there can be appeals. That judgment is the reason for the huge backlog of cases of persons who have claimed refugee status.

I also had a hand in drafting the statement that 'the people of Canada do not wish, as a result of mass immigration, to make a fundamental alteration in the character of our population' and that 'large-scale immigration from the Orient would change the fundamental composition of the Canadian population.' The statement continues to reflect my opinion.

The reference to the fundamental alteration in the character of our population was distorted in some quarters several years later to mean that the government was determined to maintain the balance between English- and French-speaking Canadians. Because I discussed the phrasing fully with the prime minister, I know that the English-French balance was not in his mind at all. The reference was intended to reassure Canadians, particularly in British Columbia, that the new immigration policy did not mean mass immigration across the Pacific that would make the population mainly Asian rather than European in origin. At the same time the repeal of the law excluding Chinese immigrants was the first step in removing racial origin as a total barrier to immigration. When I became minister of citizenship and immigration in 1954 the immigration law excluded as immigrants all persons of 'Asiatic race.' That provision was removed from the law while I was minister, but the law still permitted selective and controlled immigration. There has never been an open door policy in Canada or, to the best of my knowledge, in any other country.

Immigration had been stopped altogether by the Conservative government in 1930. For a time even some British immigrants were deported merely because they were on welfare. Immigration was a mere trickle after the Liberals came back into office in 1935, and it ended when war came. The new policy announced in 1947 was designed to restore selective immigration primarily from traditional sources. When the change in policy was announced, never in my wildest dreams did I expect one day to be administering both the Citizenship and the Immigration acts.

Paris, Brussels and the royal wedding

The prime minister decided to represent Canada at the marriage of Princess Elizabeth on 20 November 1947 and also to visit France, Belgium and Holland before the marriage and to stay a week or two in England afterwards. I was to accompany him. We travelled from New York on the *Queen Elizabeth*. Our party included Norman Robertson, Handy and Nicol. Georges and Pauline Vanier were also on board, returning to the embassy in Paris, accompanied by their daughter Thérèse, a medical doctor in practice in London. I can rarely recall Mackenzie King more relaxed. The freedom from tension had a good effect on the whole party.

Mrs Gooch, the cook at Laurier House, was also on board, and the prime minister was most solicitous about her welfare, obviously rather worried that she might decide to stay in her native Scotland. On arrival at Southampton we discovered that Mrs Gooch's trunk was missing. Much of the prime minister's time was taken up in trying to have the trunk found. Norman had been persuaded to put one of his pieces of luggage in the hold, and it too was missing, but no one bothered the prime minister about it.

Of even greater concern to me was a piece of luggage I had in the hold that I did not want Mackenzie King to know anything about. Paul de France had had his shotguns taken away by the Germans during the occupation. He had asked me if I could get him one in Canada and bring it to France the next time I came. It so happened that my father-in-law had a very fine gun and had given up duck-hunting many years before. Bob was not interested in the gun. When I told Mr Beattie about Paul's eagerness to have a gun, he gave me his to take to France. I had the gun packed in a wooden case and delivered to my room in the East Block, where it lay on the bookcase. One day the *Time* correspondent, a friend, came into the room to see if I could suggest any likely story for the next week. He saw the wooden case and asked what it was. When I told him, he said, 'Prime Minister's Secretary Takes Shotgun to Royal Wedding' will make a fine story in *Time*.' I countered that it would never appear, but I looked apprehensively at *Time* for the next two or three issues, fearing he might yield to temptation.

All the lost pieces were eventually found. Mackenzie King was vastly relieved when we arrived in Paris to get a message about Mrs Gooch's trunk. I was even more relieved at having got the shotgun brought over incognito from London in an RCAF plane. The Vaniers had a reception for the prime minister while we were in Paris. When Mackenzie King and I arrived, Pauline asked me if

I had found the shotgun. I gave her an apprehensive look. When the prime minister asked, 'What shotgun?' she quickly said: 'Jack was looking after a shotgun for Georges. It was not with the rest of the luggage, and I wondered if it had turned up.' I explained that it had. Apparently it did not occur to Mackenzie King that Georges Vanier, with his artificial leg, was unlikely to have a shotgun in his luggage. Forty years later the shotgun was still in Paul's house in France.

Our day in London, the trip to Paris and our visit there were an unqualified success with no unpleasant incidents. Mackenzie King had his favourite suite at the Crillon, overlooking the Place de la Concorde. The French government had put a private railway car at his disposal for the journey to Brussels. We left early in the morning.

At the station Nicol told me the luggage was not on the car. I thought he meant it had been put in the luggage van, and said we could get it after the train left the station. Mackenzie King was wearing one of his oldest and least fashionable suits, intending to change after taking a rest. But a search of the train revealed that the luggage had been left in Paris. The prime minister was deeply mortified. For the last hour of the journey we sat together. He would look out the window and try to admire the scenery and then come back, in anticipation, to the arrival in Brussels, where Prime Minister Spaak would meet him in a morning coat and a top hat, and he would emerge from the train in his 1908 suit and an old soft hat.

Word reached Brussels about the lost luggage, and one of the embassy secretaries there thoughtfully arranged to take one of us to hire a temporary wardrobe. Queen Elizabeth, as chancellor of the University of Brussels, was to confer an honorary degree on the prime minister at an afternoon ceremony at the university. Handy went off to hire the appropriate costume. The luncheon at the embassy was a tense, gloomy affair, and the prime minister could not imagine what had happened to Handy. As soon as he could get away from the table, he went to a bedroom for a rest while I paced up and down, hoping Handy would arrive before the prime minister had to dress.

Handy appeared in the nick of time with a formal outfit complete with top hat. Nicol took the finery into the bedroom, grumbling that the Chief would never wear it. I stood in the hall expecting Nicol and the clothes to be hurled out of the room. More than 10 minutes passed, and then Nicol appeared, to tell me the Chief wanted to see me. When I went in, I saw him fully dressed, gazing at himself in the full-length mirror. He asked me how it looked, and after a minute's reflection I said, 'Mr King, it looks as though a tailor had made it for you.' It was a surprisingly good fit. He explained that the shirt collar was too tight, but that he had slit it in the back with a razor blade and it had expanded enough. Even the top hat was the right size.

When the time came, we walked across the street to the university, immediately opposite the embassy. The prime minister was taken into the robing room and encased in a heavy gown, which covered him completely from neck to toes. He could just as well have been wearing pyjamas.

The clothes had been rented for the day only, but Mackenzie King discovered that the hat had had to be hired for five days. He insisted I should wear it for the rest of the visit to Belgium and Holland instead of what he called my 'tough hat' which was a soft, black one with a wide, turned-down brim. When we reached London he insisted I buy a top hat, telling me to put it on my expense account. He telephoned his hatter, Lock, in St James's Street, himself. When I went to pick up the hat, I asked if I could try it on. The hatter wondered why I wanted to try on the prime minister's hat, and I explained it was for me. From the look on the hatter's face I realized that in those days of scarcity there would have been no hat if he had not thought it was for Mackenzie King. I did not see how I could put it on my expense account. To get my money's worth I have worn it on every possible occasion since then.

At the official dinners in Belgium and Holland I had several opportunities to talk to officials who had similar status to mine. I was struck by one profound difference between the Belgian and Dutch public servants I met. The Dutch were direct and forthright in their opinions, whereas the Belgians gave theirs only after obvious reflection. It reminded me of the difference I had often noted between American and Canadian officials. I felt that the Belgians, like Canadians, had to think twice because of the two languages and cultures in their country. I confess I found the Belgians more interesting.

All the arrangements worked smoothly for the royal wedding, which Mackenzie King enjoyed prodigiously. I did not tell him that the morning coat I was wearing had been lent to me by Brooke Claxton, who had worn it at his wedding and had outgrown it years before. It was slightly tinged with green and had a few moth holes, which Brooke had covered with black ink. I noticed that many a costume in the Abbey looked rather motheaten. I wore the same morning coat later, to Charles Ritchie's wedding in Ottawa. When Margaret and I were ushered into the same pew as Douglas and Mary Abbott, Doug asked if it was Brooke's morning coat. I replied, 'Yes; what was good enough for Princess Elizabeth is good enough for Charles Ritchie!'

Jim Coyne had told me before we left Ottawa that the growing shortage of United States dollars in our reserves was likely to reach a crisis requiring immediate action in November. He said I should keep that in mind in arranging for the prime minister's return; since Parliament was not in session, it would have to be summoned to authorize whatever emergency measures would have to be taken. He felt and I agreed that the prime minister should plan to be home as early as possible. I made reservations on the first liner to sail from Southampton after the wedding, the Dutch ship *Nieuw Amsterdam*. I told the prime minister what I had done, but he said he would like to stay in England one more week and asked me to get a later reservation, which I did on one of the British *Queens*. He told me to cancel the reservation on the Dutch ship, but that I did not do. When Mackenzie King received word that emergency action must be taken before our U.S. dollar reserves were exhausted, and that Parliament would have to meet, he asked me to try for accommodation on the *Nieuw Amsterdam*. I told him there would be no problem as I had not cancelled the reservation, and he retorted that he had not thought I had.

We duly sailed from Southampton and reached New York on 3 December and Ottawa the next day. Mackenzie King had been sorry to cut short his visit to England, but he was singularly undisturbed by the dollar crisis and by the drastic emergency measures, which were announced by Abbott in a radio broadcast and went into effect immediately, to be authorized retroactively by Parliament. The Opposition tried to make an issue of Abbott's 'budget by radio' without much effect.

Although Mackenzie King hated the prospect of having to face Parliament as soon as he returned, he was much more active and alert in the House than he had been since early 1945. Europe and the royal wedding had been exhilarating for him, and he had returned rested and refreshed. But that was not the whole reason for his better disposition.

The succession

Mackenzie King's preparations for retirement as leader

When St Laurent told the prime minister that he was willing to be a candidate for the Liberal leadership, Mackenzie King decided to retire. After his return from the royal wedding he began to plan for a national convention to choose his successor. He decided to announce his retirement at the annual meeting of the National Liberal Federation, before the new session of Parliament opened in January 1948.

But the plan came close to being derailed. On 18 December 1947 St Laurent made what he thought was a routine recommendation to cabinet, and his proposal provoked the most bizarre crisis of Mackenzie King's career. During the prime minister's absence, while St Laurent had been acting prime minister, Ilsley had represented Canada at a meeting of the General Assembly of the United Nations in New York. The United States had secured United Nations approval for the appointment of a commission to supervise elections in Korea. South Korea was dominated by the United States, and North Korea by the Soviet Union, and elections were intended to unite Korea and give it democratic self-government. Ilsley had been dubious about accepting membership for Canada on the commission, but in the face of intense pressure from the United States he had accepted, with St Laurent's approval. St Laurent felt Canadian membership would be a harmless routine. But the prime minister did not, and feared a third world war might be provoked by interference in Korea. He was taken by surprise at the cabinet, exploded and refused to agree to have Canada become a member.

The resulting confrontation in the cabinet, which threatened to break up the government, is recounted in *My Years with Louis St. Laurent*. A direct appeal was made by Mackenzie King to President Truman to release Canada from its commitment, and despite a personal letter from Truman again urging Canada to appoint a member, the prime minister remained firm. He personally drafted a blunt refusal to Truman, which he read to Pearson on 7 January. Pearson suggested that the draft be considered by cabinet. Mackenzie King refused but agreed it should be shown to St Laurent. Upon reading the draft St Laurent asked me to arrange an interview with the prime minister. He told me he could not back down and still have any authority in the cabinet; he might not be a minister the next day. The prime minister invited him to dinner at Laurier House.

Pearson, Claxton and I all realized how hard it would be for either Mackenzie King or St Laurent to give way. We anxiously awaited word, though I expressed confidence that some compromise would be found. Pearson telephoned me at about 11 p.m. to say that St Laurent had been to see him immediately after leaving Laurier House, and had given him an account of the meeting. St Laurent had made his own position clear to the prime minister, who then seized upon his suggestion that Canada stipulate that the commission should not try to function unless it could operate in the whole of Korea with the concurrence of the Soviet Union as well as the United States. St Laurent had convinced the prime minister that the Soviet Union would not agree, and that the commission would therefore be unable to operate. Mackenzie King had then dropped his objection to the appointment of a Canadian member.

By the end of 1947 St Laurent had clearly demonstrated his capacity to manage the cabinet and to lead in Parliament and, in the acid test of the Korea crisis, had shown he could not and would not be intimidated. Ilsley, the only man who might have challenged him successfully for the party leadership, later pledged his support to St Laurent and thereby virtually assured his succession. St Laurent's skill in resolving the Korean crisis without alienating Mackenzie King or even appearing to have been the victor made the prime minister more determined than ever to have St Laurent succeed him.

Right after the Korean difference was resolved, Mackenzie King had discussions with St Laurent about a cabinet shuffle. St Laurent made it clear that if he became leader, he would not have Ian Mackenzie in the cabinet. The prime minister decided that Mackenzie should be persuaded to resign at once and go to the Senate. He asked Senator Stanley McKeen, the leading Liberal organizer in British Columbia, to secure Mackenzie's agreement, and McKeen asked me to help. He had a dinner in January 1948 at the Château Laurier, to which Margaret and I were invited, to celebrate Mackenzie's recent marriage. The Mathesons, Mrs Mackenzie's sister and brother-in-law, were present. Mackenzie's reaction upon learning the real purpose of the dinner was highly emotional. In the end he was persuaded to accept the senatorship and resign from the government and to do so graciously. I must have made a favourable impression on Mackenzie that evening, because some days later, out of the blue, he told me he had recommended me for an honorary degree from Edinburgh, his own university. I heard no more about that ridiculous suggestion, but was pleased that I had helped towards an amicable solution of an awkward problem.

St Laurent would not be a candidate for the leadership unless C.D. Howe agreed to stay in the government. He said Howe would remain only if he had a real department. The Department of Reconstruction had been amalgamated with Munitions and Supply under the title Reconstruction and Supply, but that department by 1948 had almost no functions and very little staff. Howe was keen to become minister of trade and commerce. J.A. MacKinnon, the minister, was tired, aspired to go to the Senate and would be happy to have a lighter portfolio in the meantime. Milton Gregg was the minister of fisheries; as a holder of the Victoria Cross, he was an ideal choice to succeed Mackenzie as minister of veterans' affairs. MacKinnon agreed reluctantly to take Fisheries, which seemed an odd portfolio for a minister from Alberta. His appointment was ridiculed after the changes were announced; one cartoon portrayed him fishing on horseback. On 10 June J. Allison Glen resigned from the government, and MacKinnon succeeded him as minister of mines and resources.

A minister from British Columbia was needed upon Mackenzie's retirement but none was chosen for several months. The obvious candidate was Jimmy Sinclair, already one of the finest debaters in the House. Mackenzie King had never forgiven Sinclair for his speech in 1940 and set no store by his war service in the RCAF. There was no obvious choice among the Liberal MPs. The prime minister was inclined to choose Tom Reid, the longest-serving backbencher. Reid claimed to have an insight into the Oriental mind and was the most virulent anti-Japanese member in the House. I persuaded Mackenzie King that he should choose Robert Mayhew, the member for Victoria. Mayhew was not brilliant, but he had great common sense and a genuinely liberal outlook. He became the minister of fisheries after MacKinnon. The cabinet changes met St Laurent's wishes concerning both Mackenzie and Howe.

The Liberal party had no tradition for choosing party leaders, but the party had created a precedent after the death of Laurier in 1919 by holding an American-style convention. Mackenzie King had emerged as a leader chosen by the party. But in 1948 the retiring party leader was the prime minister, and the new leader would presumably become prime minister almost automatically. Mackenzie King, not the party organization, decided how the choice would be made: a national convention would be held, patterned on the convention of 1919. The prime minister told his colleagues that he would be completely neutral and would let the convention make the choice. That hyprocrisy fooled no one. His repeated choice of St Laurent as acting prime minister was a sufficient indication that he would regard St Laurent as the most suitable successor.

At the dinner closing the annual meeting of the National Liberal Federation in January, the prime minister announced that his retirement from the party leadership would take place at a national convention to be held in August. To indulge his taste for anniversaries Mackenzie King decided the new leader should be chosen on 7 August 1948, 29 years to the day after he became leader. The preparation of the speech was lengthy, and I was of course involved. Upon concluding Mackenzie King received a prolonged ovation. For once his speech pleased him. His diary discloses that he telephoned me after the meeting and was surprised to learn I had not been there. He never understood my reluctance as a public servant to appear at party functions, however historic.

St Laurent left right after the speech to keep a speaking engagement in Winnipeg. According to his diary, Mackenzie King was 'shocked' to read in the morning papers that St Laurent had said he was prepared to take on the duties of leader provided his doing so would not create division on racial or religious grounds. The prime minister feared St Laurent had raised an issue that might help to defeat him at the convention or in the next election. He wrote that he was greatly distressed and added, 'Of all the men in the world, I have greater regard for St. Laurent than I think for any of the others.' But St Laurent's statement aroused no issue; it had not been made in his speech, but had merely been given as an honest answer to a direct question. St Laurent said and did nothing to promote his candidature. Pearson commented to me that St Laurent should at least say he would regard it as a great honour to be leader of the Liberal party. But I felt his reticence was the right attitude.

The prime minister tried to avoid questions that might divide the party in Parliament or become issues before the convention was held. A most important question of that kind arose in January out of discussions that the minister of finance, officials of his department and officials of the Bank of Canada were having with United States officials relating to the emergency measures taken in 1947 to restore the Canadian reserves of U.S. dollars. Abbott reported to the prime minister that the Americans had raised the possibility of complete reciprocity with Canada. Mackenzie King agreed enthusiastically to have the subject explored further in the utmost secrecy. St Laurent was brought into the secret and at first was favourable. Howe was included later, but the question of reciprocity was never raised in the cabinet. Mackenzie King's diary discloses that he soon began to have misgivings. He discussed his doubts with me. Possibly some of the Toryism of my youth persisted. I was frightened by the political dangers, short- and long-term, both to the Liberal party and to Canada's identity. I was not convinced that reciprocity would be good for Canada, and I encouraged the prime minister in his doubts and misgivings. My attitude may have had some slight influence on his decision in May to have the discussions stopped. By some miracle the secret was so well kept that years passed before it became public.

After St Laurent became secretary of state for external affairs with Pearson as under-secretary, Mackenzie King had growing misgivings that they were too active in the search for collective security. Until the Communist takeover in Czechoslovakia the prime minister seemed to be reverting to his prewar isolationism. His first reaction was to discourage what he felt would be 'interference with the domestic affairs of Czechoslovakia.' His shock over the death of Jan Masaryk, who had remained in office as foreign minister in the otherwise Communist government of Czechoslovakia, affected him deeply. He had met Masaryk and respected him. He wrote that Masaryk's death proved 'there can be no collaboration with Communists.' He began to fear that attempts by Communist parties to overthrow Western European countries might provoke a general war. He was moving towards the view of St Laurent and Pearson that Western Europe and North America must act jointly for their common security. He described 17 March 1948 as 'a memorable day in the world's history.' It began with a meeting of the Liberal caucus, which was adjourned so that the prime minister and all the ministers could listen to a broadcast by President Truman. Truman announced that the military draft would be introduced in the United States, and that the United States would support the already-formed Western Union of Britain, France and the Benelux countries in standing together to resist aggression. Mackenzie King was deeply impressed by Truman's speech and felt he should make a state-ment when the House met at 3 p.m.

He had the ministers meet in his room at the House right after Truman's broadcast. He obtained assurances from St Laurent and Claxton that, in the event of a collective security emergency, conscription would not be required on Canada's part. The cabinet agreed that he should inform Parliament that Canada would support the nations of Western Europe.

Pearson, Heeney and I prepared a statement while the cabinet was meeting. It was revised by Mackenzie King, St Laurent and Claxton and read by the prime minister when the House met. He announced that 'all free countries may be assured that Canada will play her full part in every movement to give substance to the conception of an effective system of collective security by the development of regional pacts under the Charter of the United Nations.' For Canada that statement was the decisive step on the way to the North Atlantic Treaty Organization. I was proud to have had a share in preparing it.

The national Liberal convention

It was soon clear that St Laurent would be opposed as a candidate for the party leadership. Gardiner told Mackenzie King on 21 March that he would stand. The prime minister assured him, hypocritically, that he was taking no sides in the selection of his successor. He was disturbed that Gardiner's candidature might mean a contest in which race and religion would play a part, but they did not.

On 20 April Mackenzie King's tenure as prime minister equalled Sir Robert Walpole's. He was the champion; he had lasted longer than any prime minister in a free country with elected Parliaments. Achieving that record made it easier for him to face retirement, though he still harboured the thought of staying on in the government as a minister.

Martin and his department had been working for weeks on a program for health grants to provide a foundation for nation-wide health insurance. Mackenzie King saw the program as the crowning achievement of his own career. He was able to announce it in Parliament on 14 May. The statement was received enthusiastically by the CCF and Social Credit as well as by the Liberals. According to his diary, he felt the Tories looked dismayed, and told St Laurent he believed the health grants program would probably win the next election. He included a rare word of praise for me in the diary, in saying that I had been most helpful, and that much was owing to my zeal for social reform. When I read that two or more years later, I felt he had given me too much credit: I had not had the zeal for a federal health program that I had for family allowances and decent old age pensions.

Mackenzie King became apprehensive about the outcome of the leadership as the convention drew nearer. Power's candidature did not worry the prime minister, since Power did nothing to promote himself or to encourage anyone else to do so. In May a spontaneous movement developed to encourage Ilsley to become a candidate. Rumours began to circulate that he was considering the possibility, particularly as his health and spirits had improved greatly after he become minister of justice. Mackenzie King was relieved on 28 May when Ilsley had a long talk with him about his future. In part to dispel rumours, he wanted to announce his intention to retire from public life. He and the prime minister agreed on a statement that Ilsley intended to retire at the end of the parliamentary session but would attend the convention to show his continued support for the government and the Liberal party. Ilsley said he felt St Laurent would be the best choice and spoke of him in the highest terms. Ilsley resigned from the Cabinet on 30 June. In my opinion he was the one person who might have presented a serious challenge to St Laurent. His outstanding performance as a wartime minister of finance gave him great prestige, and as the minister of justice he had added to his reputation.

What worried me was not the threat posed by Gardiner but the weakness posed by St Laurent's own diffidence. His doubts were increased by Duplessis's overwhelming victory in the provincial election in Quebec on 28 July. Godbout, the Liberal leader, was defeated in his own constituency, and the Liberal Opposition almost wiped out. I was at Kingsmere working on Mackenzie King's speech for the opening of the convention on the evening of election day in Quebec. St Laurent telephoned me there and asked me to tell Mr King that he was ready to drop out of the contest if the prime minister thought it would be good for the party. I said I knew Mackenzie King would say he was more needed than ever. I expressed my own opinion that if the Quebec Liberals under Godbout had won a decisive victory, St Laurent could have gone back to his law practice without great injury to the country or the party. Instead, I added, the French Canadians in Quebec had kicked English Canada in the teeth, and if the federal Liberals kicked them back by repudiating his bid for leadership, it might be the end of the Liberal party and a disastrous blow to Canada. His reply was 'I have given you a message for the prime minister and I want you to deliver it.' When I reported to Mackenzie King, he said 'Tell St Laurent not to be foolish; I will call him in the morning.' I did not deliver the message verbatim but made it clear that Mackenzie King wanted him to carry on and would confirm that the next morning. According to the diary, Mackenzie King told St Laurent the next morning that he was not discouraged and hoped St Laurent 'did not for a moment think it was affecting his chances in any way.'

After countless revisions Mackenzie King's speech for the convention was finally completed on the afternoon of 3 August and sent to the printers. I was trusted to read the proofs that evening. The next day the prime minister felt so disturbed by Gardiner's tactics in seeking to win 'by all kinds of machine methods' that he decided to take a hand himself. He persuaded Howe, Claxton, Abbott, Chevrier, Martin and Stuart Garson to allow their names to be proposed and, when nominated, to withdraw and announce their support for St Laurent. I had to assist in arranging the charade although I thought it demeaning and unnecessary. Garson, the Liberal-Progressive premier of Manitoba, had already agreed to attend the convention and to nominate St Laurent for the leadership. I had difficulty in persuading him not to refuse to have his name put forward. He finally agreed, only to please Mackenzie King.

At the 1919 convention the leadership candidates had not made direct appeals for personal support but had made proposals for inclusion in the party program. Mackenzie King had intended to have the same procedure followed in 1948, but Gardiner succeeded in having the procedure changed so that candidates could make a direct appeal for support. St Laurent decided he would not make a personal appeal but speak instead on national unity. He asked me to help him with his speech, and I prepared the first draft. Mackenzie King's reaction, as revealed in the diary, was interesting. He noted that St Laurent 'made it plain he had no intention of entering any oratorical contest. Spoke of national unity.' The prime minister 'wished he had wedged in his French between two English speeches' and commented that his concluding with French put him at a disadvantage. He felt St Laurent had 'made it plain he was not seeking the position but the position had come to him.' I didn't think it a great speech but was satisfied with its effect on the convention and felt his attitude compared favourably with Gardiner's advertisement of his own qualities. So apparently did most of the delegates. St Laurent won on the first and only ballot, with 848 votes to 323 for Gardiner and 56 for Power.

I had also drafted a short speech of acceptance of the leadership for St Laurent, which he had changed substantially to give it his own style and vocabulary. He had asked me to prepare a draft of something he might say if he was not chosen, but I had declined and told him I was sure one would not be needed. The speech accepting the leadership was received with great enthusiasm. Mackenzie King spontaneously made a short and moving speech about St Laurent. After 29 years to the day, the Liberal party had a new leader.

7 A New Regime in the Office

St Laurent as party leader

Acting prime minister

When Mackenzie King did not resign as prime minister but decided to remain in office for several months, I was as surprised as everyone else. It was only when I read his diary after his death that I learned he had discussed the plan with St Laurent, on 25 May 1948. St Laurent had agreed that it would suit him better not to become prime minister until after a meeting of Commonwealth prime ministers already planned for London in October. Mackenzie King wanted to go to Paris before the Commonwealth meeting as head of the Canadian delegation to the General Assembly of the United Nations.

The arrangement worked out well. The prime minister went off to Europe in late September, and St Laurent, as acting prime minister, could perform as though he was already head of the government. He was able to learn the ropes and make important decisions without bearing the final responsibility.

Mackenzie King never asked me whether I wanted to stay on in the Prime Minister's Office. On one occasion he commented in an off-hand way that I would be carrying on with St Laurent. That was what I wanted to do, and I was sure St Laurent wanted me. But I could see that if I were not careful, the long delay could be embarrassing for me. I was head of the Prime Minister's Office, and I had to remember Mackenzie King and not St Laurent was my boss. Because of the prime minister's jealousy about respect for his position, I had to be circumspect and sometimes almost secretive about my relations with St Laurent. He naturally wanted to talk to me frequently once it was understood I was to continue as head of the office when he became prime minister.

I was tired after the convention and felt I must get away from Ottawa for a rest. Margaret could not go with me because Alan, who had been born in June, needed his mother. We agreed that I should go to Calgary in August to visit Mother and my sister and should take Jane, not yet seven years old, with me. Her hair, in two long braids I was not skillful enough to maintain, was the only problem. Luckily I found fellow travellers willing to do the chore. Jane was a good travelling companion, and we had a fine holiday.

Mackenzie King noted in his diary on 11 August that, in discussing with St Laurent his plans to go to Paris and London, he had said he would like to take me with him but would not take me if doing so would embarrass St Laurent. He raised the question with me the same day and reported in the diary that I made no comment one way or the other, thereby causing him to feel that I would probably prefer to stay in Ottawa and 'get a foot in' before St Laurent took office. In fact what I replied then, and whenever the question was raised before his departure in September, was that I would do whatever he wished me to do. I realized that any expression of preference one way or the other would be misunderstood. In the end he told me I should stay in Ottawa, and I was vastly relieved. Only when I read the diary did I realize what a tug of war over me, very polite of course, had developed between him and St Laurent. According to the 27 August entry, Mackenzie King yielded 'having much in mind the sacrifices that . . . Mr St Laurent . . . had made . . . at the time of war and coming into the Government.'

One or two of my friends questioned my judgment in remaining in the Prime Minister's Office and said that after 11 years Mackenzie King could not refuse me an appointment that would give me and my family security. I was not tempted and did not consider the suggestions for a moment. I was convinced St Laurent would make a great prime minister, and I had already enjoyed working with him. When Drew became the Tory leader on 2 October, I was more ready than ever to remain with St Laurent.

St Laurent decided to keep in his cabinet all the ministers in office when he became leader. According to Mackenzie King's diary, on 11 August St Laurent raised the question of bringing Pearson into the government. Despite misgivings about Pearson's dynamic attitude in foreign affairs Mackenzie King replied that he would certainly like to see Pearson in public life.

On my return from the west I learned that St Laurent wanted Pearson to join the government and accept the external affairs portfolio. Mackenzie King put on pressure to have the change made right away. Pearson was willing. The problem of choosing a constituency was not great; at least two members were ready to go to the Senate. Algoma East was the choice. To my surprise Mackenzie King was willing to appoint Thomas Farquhar, the MP, to the Senate. Until that time he had invariably refused to recommend anyone who had reached 70, and Farquhar was 73. Farquhar assured us that Pearson would have no trouble winning the seat. In fact neither the Tories nor the CCF nor the Social Credit nominated candidates for the by-election, and Pearson's only opponent was a maverick with no connection with the riding. On 15 September Pearson became the secretary of state for external affairs.

The only concern I felt about St Laurent's leadership was whether or not he had the style and talent to appeal to voters. He had very reluctantly made two speeches in the Quebec provincial election campaign in 1948, and they had not been inspiring or moving.

I was anxious to have an early test in Ontario, and it took place during the Thanksgiving weekend. I had difficulty persuading St Laurent to go to Algoma East. He spent the day driving with Pearson along the mainland shore of Georgian Bay. I was not free to join the motorcade as we had received word the evening before that Mackenzie King was seriously ill in London, and that at any moment St Laurent might have to take his place at the meeting of Commonwealth prime ministers; I had to remain by a telephone in the home of a friend in Espanola. During the afternoon I received word that Mackenzie King wanted St Laurent and me to come to London on 14 October.

At the end of the afternoon Pearson and one or two seasoned campaigners gave enthusiastic reports of the impression St Laurent had made at each stop on the road. I was present at a Thanksgiving supper, with St Laurent and Pearson as guests of honour, in the United Church hall at Little Current, on Manitoulin Island. St Laurent was invited to speak after the meal. In introducing him the chairman laid great stress on the Protestant and Anglo-Saxon complexion of Little Current and the whole of Manitoulin. I was afraid St Laurent might not react well, but I had no need to worry. He began by comparing Little Current with his native village of Compton, in the Eastern Townships, where, when he was young, most of the population was English-speaking, and his home was next door to the Methodist parsonage. He then said that the pie he had eaten tasted just like the 'punkin pie' his mother used to make. One look at the audience convinced me that it did not matter much what else he said. No one had coached him; he had responded spontaneously to the situation. He had completely lost the appearance of stiffness he often showed when he was alone with one or two people and sometimes, at first, with me.

I told St Laurent that we were wanted in London and said that Mackenzie King would expect me to be at his beck and call, that I hoped he would understand when I was not available to him. He understood. Several times I was summoned by the prime minister when I was in the middle of a conversation with St Laurent. I left at once without embarrassment.

The main concern of the Commonwealth prime ministers' meeting was to find a way to keep India in the Commonwealth. St Laurent did not see how that would be possible unless India, like other Commonwealth countries, recognized the Queen as head of state. Mackenzie King convinced him that allegiance to the

Crown was not essential, and that the only bonds necessary to the survival of the Commonwealth were common ideals and traditions of self-government. Once convinced, St Laurent became an effective advocate of the new concept of Commonwealth, but the inspiration had come from Mackenzie King.

St Laurent's unexpected visit enabled him to get to know Prime Minister Attlee and other leading members of the British government. He quickly developed an abiding respect for Attlee. He also met the other Commonwealth prime ministers and got some notion of their attitudes and problems. I had never observed St Laurent at an international conference and was impressed by the easy and effective way he took a leading part in the deliberations. Norman Robertson was of course his main adviser. St Laurent returned to Ottawa on 23 October with even greater respect for Robertson.

After Pearson became the secretary of state for external affairs, St Laurent remained the minister of justice, a portfolio he had resumed in addition to External Affairs when Ilsley resigned at the end of June. There were two problems of cabinet-making: neither Manitoba nor Nova Scotia had a minister.

On the way home from Calgary in August I had spent 24 hours in Winnipeg to find out for St Laurent whether or not Premier Garson would be willing to come to Ottawa as minister of justice when St Laurent became prime minister. Garson was agreeable provided we could find a suitable constituency. That was one of my most difficult problems until a few days before the new cabinet was formed. Mackenzie King had secured Glen's resignation as minister from Manitoba, but Glen was still an MP. He was not willing to resign from Parliament unless appointed to the Senate. There was a Manitoba vacancy in the Senate, but it was the place traditionally reserved for a Catholic, and St Laurent firmly refused to abandon that convention.

A senator from Manitoba, H.A. Mullins, who had once been the MP for Marquette, the constituency Glen represented, was seriously ill. One day in jest I said that if I believed in the efficacy of such prayer, I would be tempted to pray for Senator Mullins's death. St Laurent retorted that it might be simpler to pray for Glen to die! Neither obliged. I had negotiations started to get another member to resign his seat, but when I learned he wanted cash on the barrel-head, I decided, without consulting St Laurent, that we could not take the risk of a scandal. I approached Gib Weir, who had been the chief Liberal whip. He agreed reluctantly to resign and wait for later recognition if no other solution was possible. No one wanted to lose Weir, who was a wise and helpful member of the House of Commons. I was becoming really depressed, when out of the blue I received a telephone call from Mark Shinbane, one of the leading Liberal organizers in Winnipeg. I barely knew Mark and was surprised when he said that he understood St Laurent would like Glen to resign his seat. I agreed. Mark then asked what could be done for Glen. I said St Laurent had offered to have him appointed chairman of the Canadian section of the International Joint Commission. Mark said, 'Glen's resignation will be submitted tomorrow' — and it was. Garson was happy in the constituency of Marquette, which he represented without difficulty until 1957.

The problem in Nova Scotia was quite different. Robert Winters, who had been elected in Lunenburg in 1945, was already an outstanding member and had been an effective parliamentary assistant successively to two ministers. The problem in his case was to find a portfolio. In those days departments of government could be created only by act of Parliament, a salutary requirement that should never have been changed. Fortunately Howe had two portfolios, Trade and Commerce, which had become his main interest, and Reconstruction and Supply, which was a combination of the postwar Department of Reconstruction and the remains of the wartime Department of Munitions and Supply. Howe had recommended that Reconstruction and Supply be abolished, and that military procurement be transferred to Trade and Commerce, but there had not been time to make the change. I suggested that Reconstruction and Supply be given to Winters, that he also be given responsibility for housing, and that he be entrusted with the task of putting through the legislation to establish the Trans-Canada Highway and, when the law was in place, the supervision of its construction. It was a makeshift arrangement, but it served the essential purpose of giving Nova Scotia a minister with a portfolio. St Laurent had felt he would have to make Winters a minister without portfolio, but I argued that Nova Scotia had always been represented by a minister of weight and influence, and that it would be politically dangerous to treat it like a second-rate province. Reconstruction and Supply was a stopgap, until there was time, in 1950, to make substantial changes in the structure of the departments of government.

By the time those arrangements were completed, I had developed a taste for cabinet-making.

Mackenzie King returned from England on 7 November. He arranged with the governor general and St Laurent that he would resign on 15 November, and that the St Laurent government would be sworn in the same day. There were only the two new ministers to be sworn in, and the transfer of office proceeded smoothly.

The union of Newfoundland with Canada

In 1947 and 1948 the public business that interested me most was the prospect that Newfoundland might be united with Canada. Well before the war I had perceived what a shadow was cast over British Columbia's feeling for Canada by the fact that that province was hemmed in by the United States on the north as well as on the south. I realized that if Newfoundland and Labrador were brought in some way into the orbit of the United States, the Maritime provinces and Quebec would be embraced, and Canada weakened.

When the war ended, Newfoundland was still administered by the governor and the Commission of Government established by the British Parliament when Newfoundland had given up both responsible and representative government. In 1946 the British government authorized the election in Newfoundland of a National Convention, to recommend what the future regime of Newfoundland should be.

My first connection with the question of the union was accidental. I had noticed in the press that a man named J.R. Smallwood, the only avowed supporter of confederation with Canada, had been elected to the Convention. Smallwood turned up in the office one day in August 1946 and asked to see St Laurent, who was acting prime minister. Fortunately I recalled Smallwood's name. I welcomed him and explained that St Laurent was detained with business in the House, but that until he was free, I would like to hear more about Newfoundland, that my interest had begun when I was a boy and had developed during the war. I listened for an hour or two and then assured Smallwood that I wanted to see union with Canada and would be glad to do anything I could for the cause.

When the first delegation from the National Convention came to Ottawa from Newfoundland in June 1947, Smallwood was a member, and F. Gordon Bradley the chairman. Bradley was also a confederate. I saw a good deal of Smallwood and Bradley during that long summer of discussions. A cabinet committee sat down at once with the Newfoundland delegation to work out a statement of terms on which Canada would be prepared to receive Newfoundland as a Canadian province. St Laurent was the chairman. I was expected to follow the proceedings and be aware of any points in which the prime minister would be particularly interested.

A statement of terms had virtually been agreed upon when Frank Bridges, the minister from New Brunswick, died suddenly. The prime minister felt that a new minister should be appointed without delay, and a by-election was called in New Brunswick. He insisted that no terms were to be offered to the Newfoundlanders until the by-election was over. The proposed terms, he feared, might be regarded by the Opposition in New Brunswick as too generous, and become an issue that would reopen the whole question of federal-provincial fiscal relations. During the next two months various devices were used to keep the delegation busy, but some of its members showed a good deal of impatience, and Bradley even threatened to go home. The delegates were not, of course, told the real reason for the delay.

Milton Gregg, VC, was chosen as the minister from New Brunswick and the Liberal candidate. His name was suggested by Premier McNair. Gregg had never been a politician, but he was familiar with the House of Commons because he had been sergeant-at-arms before the war. In 1946 he was president of the University of New Brunswick. A rumour started in Fredericton that Gregg was to be the new minister: almost everyone who heard the rumour thought 'Gregg' referred to Frank Bridges's brother Gregory, who was called Greg. A myth was created that Mackenzie King had asked the wrong man by mistake. I can certify there was never any confusion in the mind of either the prime minister or McNair. Milton Gregg was elected with a handsome majority without the question of union being raised. Within a few days the terms to be offered to Newfoundland were settled and published.

The majority of members of the National Convention, who were opposed to confederation with Canada, rejected that option and proposed to the British government that a referendum be held in which the Newfoundland electorate could choose only between continuing the Commission of Government or returning to responsible government. Bradley and Smallwood had already organized a Confederate movement; it promoted a petition, with thousands of signatures, asking the British government to have union with Canada included on the ballot. The British government agreed. Mackenzie King heard the announcement from London that union with Canada was to be on the ballot and said in Parliament, on 11 March 1948, 'Should the people of Newfoundland *express clearly their will* that Newfoundland should enter Confederation, I am sure the people of Canada will welcome them as partners in a larger Canada.'

None of the three options had a clear majority in the first referendum. The Commission of Government was dropped, and a second referendum held, on 22 July, in which the choice was a return to responsible government or union with Canada. The vote was about 52 per cent for union and 48 per cent for responsible government.

Mackenzie King was already beginning to question the wisdom of going ahead with union, and on hearing the broadcast news of the result I feared that he might feel 52 per cent was not a clear enough expression of the will of the people. As soon as I reached the office that morning, I asked Gordon Robertson to work out and give me as quickly as possible the percentage of the vote the Liberal party had received in every election from 1921 on. Only once had the Liberal vote exceeded 50 per cent, in 1940, when it was about equal to the vote for confederation in Newfoundland. I knew Mackenzie King would never admit that the elections he had won did not express clearly the will of the Canadian people. When he telephoned at 10, he asked what I thought of the result. I said it was wonderful. I asked if he realized confederation had received a higher percentage of the vote than the Liberal party had received in any federal election except in 1940. That fact may not have removed all his doubts, but it removed one argument against going ahead with the union. After a cabinet meeting five days later, Mackenzie King noted in his diary, 'Decision reached definitely to regard majority secured as substantial enough to justify the decision to proceed now.' The Commission of Government of Newfoundland was invited to send a delegation to Ottawa to negotiate terms of union.

During the interregnum between August and November the question that most occupied St Laurent's attention was the negotiation with Newfoundland. I had no part in the official proceedings, but St Laurent, Claxton and Walter Harris kept me informed, and Smallwood regularly reported to me on the reactions of the Newfoundland delegation. St Laurent had recognized Harris's qualities in the postwar Parliament and welcomed his appointment in October 1947 as his parliamentary assistant; it was in that capacity that Harris took an active part in the negotiations. He and Claxton were the two politicians most active and helpful during the process, but the main burden of decision rested with St Laurent. He made all the final decisions on the Canadian side, without reference to Mackenzie King, who for most of that period was in Paris and London.

The greatest problem was how to provide the provincial government of Newfoundland with sufficient revenue to provide adequate public services. The fear was that Newfoundland would require so much federal financial support that it would upset the tax-rental agreements with the seven provinces that had been concluded in 1947 after so much stress. St Laurent himself was close to giving up on one occasion. That evening, when he was most discouraged, I said to him: 'If you are responsible for bringing about this union it will be the greatest thing you will ever do as prime minister. If you fail, no matter what else you do, you will have been a failure as prime minister and a failure to Canada.' Those may not be the precise words but they give the correct sense of what I said. The solution was found in term 29 of the Terms of Union, which years later Diefenbaker would try to repudiate.

By the time St Laurent became prime minister, on 15 November 1948, the negotiations were almost completed. The Terms were signed on a date I suggested, 11 December 1948, the anni-

1 April 1949, Parliament Buildings, Ottawa. Gordon Bradley and Mackenzie King completing the Confederation Arch to mark the union of Newfoundland with Canada.

versary of the passing of the Statute of Westminster. Mackenzie King was present at the ceremony as a private member of Parliament.

St Laurent as Prime Minister

The Prime Minister's Office and Privy Council Office

My job as head of the Prime Minister's Office under St Laurent had a happy lack of the tension it had had under Mackenzie King. The new prime minister consulted me about his political problems and gave me his full confidence. My advice was not always accepted, but was considered with care; we were more like partners than master and servant.

The basic organization of the office was not changed, but the way it operated was very different. St Laurent came to the office every morning when he was in Ottawa and worked there all day when Parliament was not sitting. He was always approachable. He liked to leave a clean desk every night, though there were usually official papers to take home to read in the evening. He rarely disturbed the staff in the evenings or on weekends unless some urgent problem arose. The change, according to Margaret, was like having a second honeymoon.

One change was made in the office staff. St Laurent had brought with him, from the office of the Minister of Justice, his private secretary, Guy Sylvestre. I knew it would be embarrassing for Sylvestre to be reduced in rank from head of a minister's office. He agreed to remain private secretary until after the election, when a suitable post would be found for him as soon as possible. A senior position was found, in the Library of Parliament, which led to his long and distinguished career as the first full-time national librarian.

Gordon Robertson remained as second-in-command of the Prime Minister's Office for only a short time. St Laurent had been greatly impressed by Jules Léger, the number two in the High Commissioner's office in London, when we were there in October 1948. St Laurent felt the second-in-command in his office should be a French Canadian. St Laurent asked me, soon after he became prime minister, if I thought Léger would agree to join his staff. I recalled that Léger had promised, when he left Mackenzie King's staff, to return if I felt he was needed. Arrangements were quickly made for him to come as number two in the secretariat. The appointment posed no problem, as Arnold Heeney already had a place for Gordon Robertson in the Privy Council Office. Robertson was still available whenever needed, which turned out to be often, to assist the prime minister on constitutional problems.

Meanwhile a drastic change was on the way in the Privy Council Office. The Department of External Affairs had been without an under-secretary after Pearson became the minister in September 1948. The choice of an under-secretary had been narrowed down to Norman Robertson or Arnold Heeney. St Laurent and Pearson finally decided that Heeney should have the post, and that Norman should come back from London to be clerk of the Privy Council and secretary to the cabinet. I was delighted by Robertson's appointment, both on personal grounds and because the prime minister, I felt, was depending too much on my advice and should have another opinion on important questions of policy. I took all my worries to Robertson, but the close relationship I hoped would develop between him and St Laurent did not.

Léger did not take over the administration of the office; he was an adviser to the prime minister. Ross Martin took over the office management. Michel Gauvin carried on for a time, until Pierre Asselin was discovered in Quebec City and became the ideal private secretary. Gauvin then took up his place in External Affairs to begin his diplomatic career.

Gaining recognition

For the first few months after St Laurent took office, George Drew, the new leader of the Tory party, was expected to win the election anticipated in 1949. I did not believe Drew could win; St Laurent, I was convinced, had already shown he would be an effective prime minister. While acting prime minister he had demonstrated his capacity for leadership in Parliament. But now he had to face a new leader in Parliament and in the country.

The first test of party strength was in a by-election in the Nova Scotia constituency that Ilsley had represented for 22 years. The local Liberal organization was confident of winning, and it was a shock when the Tory candidate, George Nowlan, won by a substantial majority.

The two leaders first confronted each other when Parliament opened at the end of January 1949. Drew appeared to have the advantage. His conduct was flamboyant, his language extravagant and emotional. He had a military bearing befitting the colonel he was, and sometimes sounded arrogant. St Laurent was modest in bearing, moderate in language, candid in expressing himself. He valued brevity, whereas Drew was verbose and pompous. Both leaders were handsome, and both had good voices and fine delivery. Drew was a new face in Parliament; St Laurent had already served there eight years.

Drew ignored the Speech from the Throne and charged the government with undermining provincial autonomy and centralizing power in Ottawa. His speech was obviously designed to influence the vote in a by-election to be held on 7 February in Nicolet-Yamaska, across the St Lawrence from Duplessis's provincial constituency of Trois-Rivières. I began to hear rumours that the Duplessis machine was giving support to the Tory candidate, and that the Liberal candidate was unpopular. I urged the prime minister to intervene. He refused, fearing his intervention might make it appear that the Liberals were in a panic, and do more harm than good. The Conservative candidate won by a small margin. The Tory victory may have been a blessing in disguise. I believe it shook the Liberal organization and the public in Quebec that a French-Canadian prime minister might be defeated. A day or two later a member of the press commented to me that the Liberals might as well give up hope. I replied that I was not worried: given enough time, Canadians would see the difference between pure wool and shoddy.

But Drew's apparent domination of the House had to be ended. I watched for an opportunity and one came at the end of February. Drew had made a speech during the weekend in which he claimed that the Tories were fighting for personal and economic freedom in Canada, and that Canadians were in real danger of losing that fight to the bureaucrats who accepted the basic philosophy of Karl Marx. I urged St Laurent to challenge Drew as soon as Parliament met on the Monday. We worked out a statement in which he demanded that Drew name the bureaucrats he had in mind and produce his proof. Drew waffled and weaselled and then made a personal attack on St Laurent, which the prime minister ignored. St Laurent said he had no apology to make for defending the good repute of the senior civil servants of Canada. From that day it was clear St Laurent was master of the House, though that position was to be seriously strained in 1955 and 1956.

Making sure St Laurent was well and favourably known to the public took a little longer. It was tackled systematically. He decided to give all the broadcasts allotted to the Liberal party in the CBC series *The Nation's Business*. Unlike Mackenzie King he could deliver them himself in both official languages. He gave me the theme, and I prepared a draft. There was no detailed revision: I quickly grasped what he wanted to say, and changes were usually limited to phraseology, to capture his own style. The need to give the same message in French as in English made simplicity and clarity essential. His final broadcast in the spring was addressed to the women of Canada. Against my advice he invited women listeners to write to him. He received hundreds of letters — the office was barely able to cope with the flood — but he insisted on signing every reply.

Rehearsal for the election

St Laurent felt that his position should be confirmed by an election without great delay. Two objectives had to be reached first, and so they were: Canada's membership in the North Atlantic Treaty Organization and the union of Newfoundland with Canada. Years later, in a public speech, I said that only those two achievements captured the public imagination in the election of 1949. I was wrong; something else also captured Canadians, and that was St Laurent himself. He campaigned not as a partisan politician but as the leader of the whole country, and that was how he was accepted.

As well as committing himself to do all the Liberal party's broadcasts, St Laurent decided to travel every weekend to a different place in order to gain recognition. To organize the weekends the Liberal Federation engaged a young man named William Munro. Bill was tireless, imaginative, cooperative and soon utterly devoted to St Laurent and his wife and daughters. We became friends as well as being fellow workers.

Whenever possible, St Laurent liked to have his wife travel with him, preferably by rail in his private car. Life on the car was the next best thing to being at home. One of his three daughters usually travelled with them; in 1949 it was the eldest, Marthe Samson. At one end of the car, beyond the kitchen, was a little bedroom, where I worked and slept, and where I could disappear when I felt the family wanted to be alone.

The first of the weekends was in Niagara Falls. On the way St Laurent told me that he had never learned to dance because his family had lived next to a Methodist parsonage, and his mother had insisted that her children should be brought up as well as the minister's. I persuaded him, with difficulty, to include that story in his speech in Niagara Falls. As I guessed it would, the story got far more publicity than did the rest of the speech, and it resulted in a small flood of personal letters from members of the United Church.

The next weekend St Laurent visited Washington for a meeting with President Truman. He had a practical interest in visiting Truman. Because of an acute shortage of power in Ontario and New York state, their governments wanted the St Lawrence waterway and power development to be started. St Laurent persuaded Truman to give strong support to the project. The talk was easy and informal, and the two men liked and trusted each other from the start. It was St Laurent's first visit to the White House, and mine. I found Truman's blunt and candid manner refreshing and began to realize what a great president he was. The reports of the visit made a good public impression in Canada.

The visit to Toronto included a tour of a public housing project, Regent Park, where St Laurent made a statement supporting public housing, about which he had been until then lukewarm. Massive coverage, particularly photographic, was given in the *Toronto Star* — exposure something like the television would provide today. Harry Hindmarsh, the driving force at the *Star*, was a great admirer of St Laurent and turned the newspaper almost into an instrument of personal publicity for the prime minister from the time of the Toronto visit until the election at the end of June. The reception in Montreal the next weekend was eeually enthusiastic and almost as extensively covered; even more enthusiastic was the reception in Windsor, where Paul Martin's organization demonstrated its pervasiveness and Paul's own popularity. On the train journey there St Laurent's appearances on the back platform drew crowds eager to see the new prime minister; that was the start of 'whistle stop' campaigning.

The final weekend was in Oshawa. The reception was less flamboyant than in Windsor, but just as enthusiastic, with full-scale publicity in the *Toronto Star*. The highlight for me was meeting Michael Starr, the mayor, whose charm and popularity impressed me. I was told he was not committed to any political party. Back in Ottawa I urged the Liberal organization to try to persuade him to be the Liberal candidate in Ontario County, but another prospective candidate, Walter Thomson, had already been approached. I advised a change of candidates, but my advice was not taken. If Starr had accepted, as I believe he might have, the first Ukrainian-Canadian MP and minister would have been a Liberal, not a Conservative, and the fortunes of the Liberal party might have been better in Ukrainian communities all over the country.

At the beginning of the 1949 Easter recess St Laurent left at once for a western tour on the private car accompanied by Mrs St Laurent and Marthe. The railways had put a second car on the train for the press. Bill Munro was in that car to keep the press happy and to make sure satisfactory arrangements for meetings were made at each of the stops. There was usually one nonpartisan engagement and one Liberal function at each major stop. My main task was to make sure St Laurent was provided with written material, usually a series of notes setting out points he could elaborate in speaking. He liked to be well briefed about the places he was visiting, so I found myself undertaking an advanced course in historical and political geography. Munro and I learned on that tour that a lectern was essential if St Laurent was to speak with ease, and we sometimes had difficulty improvising one. Back in Ottawa we had a portable light-metal lectern made, which remained with us during the election campaign. St Laurent also suggested that his notes be triple-spaced, with each sentence a paragraph, so that he could see the sentence at a glance. With a lectern and good lighting he could follow notes or even a text without appearing to be reading. When I became a politician I used the same techniques.

Our whistle stops always drew crowds, many of them children. At Edson, Alberta, where a huge crowd was on the station platform, one sardonic reporter told me the stops were a waste of time because the children had no votes. I retorted, 'No, but their parents have.' It was at Edson that a more friendly newspaperman first called St Laurent 'Uncle Louis,' a nickname I have sometimes been accused of inventing. 'Uncle Louis' had great popular appeal.

The first major stop was at Edmonton, and from there the tour gathered momentum. As we travelled to Vancouver, on to Victoria and back to Calgary, the enthusiasm in the cities and at the whistle stops increased. The high point was Regina, where St Laurent made the best political speech of the tour to a wildly cheering audience. He described many of the supporters of the CCF as 'just Liberals in a hurry.' The phrase had flashed into my mind as I was drafting the notes. St Laurent had hesitated to use it, but I had persuaded him that it might influence waverers. It was picked up and repeated, over and over again, in the press during the campaign. The next day, in Saskatoon, his theme was It's Great To Be a Canadian; an emotional picture of Canada which deeply moved the audience. I believe the brief visit to Saskatchewan turned the tide back to the Liberal party. There was no tide to be turned back in Manitoba; with Garson at his side, St Laurent was merely strengthening its flow to the government. Only one

Tory would be elected in Manitoba, and the CCF membership would be reduced to three. After our final stop, at the Lakehead, where Howe was with St Laurent, we returned to Ottawa on 24 April, all our party feeling that the tour had exceeded every expectation.

The first parliamentary session

Parliament met on 26 January 1949. Much of the broad program set out in the Speech from the Throne was not dealt with because the session was ended on 30 April, and a general election called. The main measures adopted were the approval of the North Atlantic Treaty and the legislation to admit Newfoundland as the 10th province of Canada.

When legislation for the union of Newfoundland with Canada was before Parliament, the Tory Opposition made a formal motion that a new province should not be admitted without prior consultation with the existing provincial governments. St Laurent said there was no precedent for consulting them; the provinces had not been consulted when Parliament approved the unions of British Columbia and Prince Edward Island with Canada or the creation of the provinces of Manitoba, Saskatchewan and Alberta. When the Tories refused to explain what they meant by consultation, an independent member moved to substitute the word 'consent' for the word 'consultation.' The Tories squirmed; they realized that a vote for consent would look like opposition to the union. They all voted against 'consent,' and the steam thereupon went out of the Opposition. No doubt the Tories hoped the opponents of confederation in Newfoundland would rally to their support, and enough of them did to give the St John's seats to the Tories in the general election. But the Confederates in Newfoundland became Liberals, and as the popularity of the union developed, the Liberals held most and later all Newfoundland seats in Parliament for the next 20 years.

On the final day of debate Mackenzie King made a moving speech about the union; it was his last word in the House of Commons.

Two euestions had to be settled before the union took place. One was the representaion of Newfoundland in the cabinet; the other was the formation of a provincial government in Newfoundland. I had a good deal to do with settling both.

A lieutenant-governor had to be appointed to choose a premier to head a provincial government and to call a general election for a provincial legislature. Smallwood never had any doubt about who should be premier, but for St Laurent it was not so simple. He was not entirely happy about giving an aspiring Liberal politician the advantage of being premier before an election was held, and he toyed with the idea that until a legislature was elected, the members of the Commission of Government could serve as an interim government. He consulted Albert Walsh, who had been head of the Newfoundland delegation that had negotiated the Terms of Union. Walsh's advice was that of Bradley and Smallwood, the heads of the Confederate movement that had won the referendum, one should be chosen as premier and the other as a member of the federal cabinet. He added that Bradley did not want to be premier, and that Smallwood should be chosen.

Bradley and Smallwood recommended to St Laurent that Sir Leonard Outerbridge, who had been aide-de-camp to the British governor, be appointed lieutenant-governor. There was doubt that Outerbridge would call on Smallwood to be premier unless instructed from Ottawa to do so. I was concerned about the wisdom of giving all three appointments to Protestants. St Laurent shared that concern, and we both felt that Walsh, if willing to accept the position, would be the best choice as governor. But it was important not to offend Outerbridge, who knew that his name was already under consideration. At my suggestion St Laurent decided to send Walter Harris to Newfoundland to try to straighten out the situation. Harris performed the delicate mission with great skill. Walsh agreed to become lieutenant-governor on 1 April, and at once called on Smallwood to form a government.

St Laurent was ready to have Bradley in the cabinet, but no portfolio was available. Smallwood and I agreed that the appointment of a minister without a portfolio would be resented in Newfoundland and exploited by the anti-Confederates. We felt that the best portfolio would be Secretary of State. The title was impressive, and the minister would have few duties beyond representing the interests of Newfoundland. I told him that J.A. MacKinnon would like to be appointed to the Senate. He could be promised an appointment before the election, resign as minister of mines and resources on 31 March, and remain in the cabinet without a portfolio. Colin Gibson, the secretary of state, could move on to Mines and Resources, and Bradley could be appointed to the cabinet on 1 April. St Laurent asked me to sound MacKinnon out. I did so; he was delighted by the suggestion and asked me to draft his resignation. I drafted St Laurent's acceptance as well. Gibson was pleased to have a more important portfolio. Bradley was sworn in as secretary of state, and Newfoundland had a federal minister with a portfolio on the first day of the union.

The North Atlantic Treaty was approved by Parliament on 28 March after a single day of debate and with only two opposing votes. Once the union of Newfoundland was achieved, on 31 March, there was no longer any reason not to have an election called. Newfoundland, St Laurent felt, deserved to be represented in Parliament as soon as possible. The western tour, Harris told me, had received highly favourable publicity in Ontario. He suggested that I recommend to St Laurent that he call an election at once. I replied that he, not I, was the politician, and that he should make the recommendation himself. He did so, and I was then summoned to join them to draft a statement to announce that Parliament would be dissolved on 30 April and an election held on 27 June.

The election of 1949

Apart from his own tour St Laurent left the organization of the campaign in the competent hands of Claxton and Gordon Fogo. In Quebec the organization floundered, until one day Senator Élie Beauregard appeared in St Laurent's office to offer his services. He had been the highly successful organizer in Cardin's day. St Laurent barely knew him but was at once impressed and accepted his offer. The unobtrusive and effective way in which Beauregard operated appealed to me. After the election I suggested to St Laurent that Beauregard be appointed Speaker of the Senate. While he was Speaker, he only rarely came to see 'the Prime,' as he called St Laurent, but *e* uite often was in touch with me. He was the first person to draw my attention to Guy Favreau, whom he described as a lawyer in St Laurent's class and someone I should keep an eye on for the future.

St Laurent's own tour was to be the central feature of the campaign. The detailed planning was left to me, subject to his final approval. He agreed not to accept any engagements or change any arrangements without consulting me. After talking to Harris and the ministers I planned an itinerary that began in St Laurent's birthplace in the Eastern Townships, went on to the Maritimes, where Liberals held nearly all the seats, and thereafter concentrated on Ontario and Quebec, with its climax a meeting in Toronto. The schedule was published for only one week at a time. The draft plan reserved a week for a return to the west, though I felt another visit there would be unnecessary. As it turned out, St Laurent was stricken with laryngitis and had to take a week off to recover his voice. The western ministers agreed that the campaign was going so well in the west that a visit by the prime minister was not needed. With that week in hand we were able to visit every place on the original itinerary for Ontario and Quebec.

After decades of bachelor prime ministers a family man had a novel public appeal. St Laurent's background and family would be stressed by his opening the campaign in the area where he was born and had spent his early life. The campaign started at his alma mater, St Charles College in Sherbrooke. On the way from Sherbrooke to Compton, his birthplace, he stopped briefly at Bishop's University, in Lennoxville. The day was perfect, the family atmosphere appealing, and the publicity gratifying.

The Maritime tour began the next day. A friendly but un-enthusiastic evening meeting in Saint John was followed by a disastrous one in Yarmouth, where St Laurent, tired by the long drive through the Acadian settlements spoke without vigour or warmth. But our fortunes turned the next day, at the brief stops along the Atlantic in glorious sunshine, where the reception was more and more enthusiastic, and at Lunenburg. There the arena was crowded, the normally undemonstrative Lunenburgers were attracted to St Laurent from the start, and he responded with great vitality. The applause at the close was tremendous. Bob Winters, the minister for Nova Scotia, and Charles Hawkins, the president of the Nova Scotia Liberal Association, were delighted, and I was vastly relieved. More important, St Laurent was enthusiastic. From then on we had no setbacks, through Halifax, Pictou County, and Charlottetown. There I had for the first time to say an emphatic no to J. Watson MacNaught, the member for Prince, who had prepared and advertised an impossibly arduous program. When MacNaught said that cancellation would defeat him, I retorted, better to lose one seat than kill the prime minister. He did not lose his seat, but neither did he forgive me. At Moncton St Laurent made a nation-wide broadcast setting out the program of the government for the next Parliament; to my great satisfaction every item in that program was carried out. The final day of the Maritime tour was in northeastern New Brunswick, Liberal territory, much of it Acadian, and 20 May was almost a triumphal procession.

We knew Ontario would be the principal battleground but realized it would be dangerous to neglect Quebec. No one was sure how much support Drew would receive from Duplessis, or how effective that support would be. Except for a one-day visit to Newfoundland, St Laurent spent the rest of the campaign in those two provinces. The campaign included a circular tour of northwestern Quebec and northeastern Ontario, an area that had never before seen a Canadian prime minister. Most of the constituencies we travelled through first had been held by Liberals in the previous Parliament, and few gains could be expected. Likewise in Montreal, where St Laurent spent Monday, 30 May. The meeting in Cornwall, the centre of Chevrier's constituency, on 31 May was a rousing success.

The next four days, in western Ontario, were the critical period in the campaign. St Laurent agreed to take the offensive against the undercover alliance between Drew and Duplessis, and did so in Owen Sound and Goderich. In Owen Sound, to illustrate how the problem of English-French relations was being exploited in the Tory campaign, he read a leaflet being circulated in western Ontario, that was blatantly anti-French. The press and radio reported the speech sensationally. The ministers in Ottawa were alarmed: Claxton sent me a message that they were afraid St Laurent's line was too extreme and hoped he would moderate his tone. I discussed the message with Harris, who had been at the meeting, and he agreed with me that the speech had been received with enthusiasm and was likely to have a lasting effect. I showed him the outline of the speech proposed for Goderich on the same theme, and he thought it should remain unchanged. Without Harris's endorsement I might have lost my nerve and prepared something different. There was no chance to show Claxton's message to St Laurent until the end of the afternoon; I told him Harris and I thought he should go ahead with the speech as planned. He did not hesitate. After Goderich we felt the theme did not need repetition and decided a different line should be taken. In Stratford St Laurent's theme was more conventional, and the meeting less responsive. In Hamilton, on a Saturday evening, the armoury was packed and the audience enthusiastic even before he began. He was in top form, a politician not a lawyer, and everything he said was cheered.

Good as the evening meetings were in those four days, I felt the daytime campaign was still more effective. If many seats were to be won, St Laurent had to win some of them in that part of Ontario. The itinerary was carefully planned, the timing well arranged, and the weather superb. Harris had supervised the arrangements himself, and every engagement was carried out without a hitch. In those four days from Guelph to Owen Sound to Goderich to Stratford and back to Hamilton, we saw more majorettes and heard more bands than I had imagined existed in the whole of Canada. St Laurent met thousands of people, and everywhere his reception was tremendous. He was welcomed as head of the nation and in his brief informal speeches was almost completely nonpartisan. The publicity was massive and impressive. St Laurent never seemed to tire and obviously enjoyed the excitement. My highest hopes were far exceeded.

I went back to Ottawa convinced that St Laurent was winning Ontario. He went direct to Quebec City expecting to spend the next week campaigning in the city and surrounding district. On 7 June I got word that he had lost his voice. His doctor insisted he must rest for the remainder of the week; all engagements had to be cancelled.

A week later the tour resumed, with days in Montreal, the Montreal district, Renfrew County, and Ottawa, and an evening meeting in Valleyfield. Two days, 17 and 18 June, were devoted to southern Ontario, with a great many whistle stops and large meetings in London, Kingston and Brockville. The momentum of the campaign increased steadily. St Laurent then spent two days in Ottawa, meeting the cabinet and working on his speech for Toronto and his final national broadcast. He also spoke at a public meeting with Mackenzie King sitting on the platform.

Before the campaign had started, I had learned that Drew was having his Toronto meeting in Massey Hall. I had at once insisted that St Laurent's meeting be held in Maple Leaf Gardens. Others feared the place could not be filled, and I had had to threaten a meeting in Maple Leaf Gardens or no meeting at all in Toronto. That meeting was to be the climax. Nothing else was planned for the day so that St Laurent would be fresh. When the time came, he was reluctant to spend the day doing nothing, so I suggested we make a second visit to Drew's birthplace, Guelph, in a constituency the Liberals had an even chance of winning. St Laurent was pleased. I had persuaded Margaret to join me, and in Guelph the Liberal candidate, Henry Hosking, to our amusement, tried to introduce me to my wife, thinking she was one of his prospective constituents. The Liberals won the constituency.

Never before in Canadian history had there been a political meeting like St Laurent's in Maple Leaf Gardens. I was in suspense until we arrived and found the Gardens full to overflowing. Enthusiasm mounted steadily and reached a climax when St

Laurent spoke. The meeting undoubtedly ensured the Liberal sweep in Toronto, which no one, even on election day, had dared to predict. My gamble had paid off.

After Toronto St Laurent visited three constituencies in Quebec the Liberals had not held: Trois Rivières, which he did not win, Nicolet-Yamaska, which he won back, and St-Maurice—La Flèche, gained from the Bloc Populaire, where the meeting at Shawinigan Falls was the most enthusiastic of the whole campaign. St Laurent was spontaneously eloquent and had trouble getting away from people who wanted to shake his hand. His doctor and I, sitting at the back of the auditorium, wondered if his voice would hold out.

On 23 June St Laurent and his party flew to Newfoundland, with a brief stop at Sydney on the way. In those day the flight took almost the whole day, so apart from the drive through St John's from the airport, nothing had been planned for the evening. But such a huge crowd had gathered in front of the Newfoundland Hotel that Smallwood, who took charge on our arrival, had St Laurent appear on the balcony to acknowledge the welcome. The next day was Discovery Day in Newfoundland, a holiday, but not for the prime minister. Smallwood had organized a tremendous motorcade around Conception Bay as far as Carbonear, with numerous stops, where there were long introductions by the premier and short speeches by St Laurent. The motorcade went on until 3 p.m. Everyone but Smallwood was exhausted when I insisted we stop for our picnic lunch. St Laurent was obviously very tired, and I arranged with Smallwood to have Renault St Laurent complete the tour while his father returned to the hotel for a rest before the evening meeting in Bannerman Park. I was concerned about St Laurent's voice, because his speech was being broadcast live in the open air on a national network. But fortunately everything went well.

Except for fuel stops at Gander and Goose Bay on transatlantic flights during the war, that was my first visit to Newfoundland.

In the campaign of 1949 St Laurent travelled to more constituencies than had any previous prime minister. In many places I was surprised to discover that the only other prime minister to visit had been Laurier. St Laurent's instinct throughout the tour was to appeal to all Canadians, not just to actual or potential Liberals. He usually ignored the Opposition. He tried to evoke pride in Canada and to appeal to something distinctive in the history of each place he visited. His travels were more like royal progresses than partisan tours. Apart from the day ending in Yarmouth the reception everywhere was tremendous. The response of the audience was to the leader of the nation. St Laurent's method of campaigning appealed to me, and his example helped me when I became a politician. On tour with him I learned what hundreds of places in Canada looked like and what their political and social outlook was.

After Newfoundland, St Laurent went to Quebec, and I returned to Ottawa, convinced he was winning even in Ontario. On the Sunday morning before the election I had just made an estimate of the seats St Laurent might win, when Mackenzie King telephoned. He asked for my prediction. I said 170 sure, 180 probably and 190 possible. There was a pause; I guessed he was thinking what an impetuous misguided fellow Pickersgill is. He said I had been so close to the campaign that I was overoptimistic. The Liberals won 192 of the 262 seats in the House of Commons, 2 more than my highest estimate. There had never before been such a landslide.

A few days after the election Mackenzie King invited St Laurent and me to tea at Kingsmere. After congratulating St Laurent he turned to me and said he thought I was out of my mind on Sunday, but it had turned out I was too modest.

St Laurent's victory in 1949 was the peak of his popularity. Soon after the election I commented to Stuart Garson that before long the government would be regarded as Goliath and the Opposition as David. Fortunately there was no way Drew could look like David. St Laurent was to win another landslide four years later, and he himself would still be popular in 1957. But by then his government had certainly lost its lustre.

The year after the election

The new Parliament

The new Parliament opened on 15 September. Ross Macdonald of Brantford was elected Speaker of the House of Commons. He had been Deputy Speaker in the previous Parliament and was well liked on both sides of the House. He and his wife, Muriel, were already close friends of the St Laurents. I knew Ross well because of my family connection with Brantford. Both Margaret and I cherished the friendship and enjoyed the hospitality of the Macdonalds for the rest of their lives.

The prospect of a smooth session seemed good. Drew's attitude to St Laurent was in marked contrast to his hostility in the pre-election session. He accepted the result of the election with good grace and refrained from moving the usual amendment of want of confidence, on the ground that the electors had spoken decisively, and that the government was entitled to carry out the program endorsed by the people. Coldwell was even more cordial, but he did move an amendment regretting that the Speech from the Throne had failed to propose legislation to remove the means test from the old age pension.

The old age pension was administered by the provincial governments, and all of them had a means test to determine who was poor enough to receive it. The federal government had paid the provinces three-quarters of the cost on a pension up to $30 a month at the time St Laurent became prime minister, and his government had, early in 1949, raised the limit to $40. But the provinces still had a means test, and the purpose of Coldwell's amendment was to record opposition to it. The amendment was supported by the votes of all Opposition parties after a short debate, concluded in one day. Stanley Knowles, who seconded Coldwell's amendment, was to make the means test the hottest issue in Parliament until its removal in 1951.

Only one question had worried St Laurent when the session began, the provision of federal financial support for construction of a trans-Canada highway. St Laurent had not been happy when the 1948 Liberal convention recommended participation. But the proposal for a highway across Canada had received more spontaneous endorsement from the convention than any other proposal and was generally popular throughout the country.

St Laurent was in sympathy with having a first-class highway that would remove the need for detours through the United

States, but federal intrusion into provincial jurisdiction for roads worried him, even though it merely involved payments from the Treasury to provincial governments. The longest and most expensive sections of the highway would be in the richest provinces, Ontario and British Columbia. To give federal financial assistance on a 50-50 basis to all provinces was diametrically opposed to the concept of equalization; it was easier for the wealthy provinces to find their 50-percent share. That was an objection on principle. But St Laurent was also sure that one province would not participate. Duplessis had repeatedly objected to federal intrusion, even when the intrusion took the form of outright financial grants. Federal action on the Trans-Canada Highway would be represented as more evidence of centralization and a further effort to destroy provincial autonomy.

St Laurent balanced his misgivings against the obvious public demand. He decided that his concern was not great enough to justify opposing the project, and it was not his nature to procrastinate and delay. His misgivings were to prove to have been justified. Quebec had to wait for its share until Jean Lesage became premier. The financial provisions had to be substantially improved to enable the Atlantic provinces to afford to complete the road. But if a start had not been made by the St Laurent government, another decade or two might have passed before Canada had a national highway. I feel he made the right decision. But I too was unhappy with the flat 50-50 sharing formula, and I had a large part in changing the formula to the advantage of the Atlantic provinces in 1963.

During the session almost all the legislation forecast in he Speech from the Throne became law. But the government did not get through the session entirely without scars. The most damaging arose out of a report by the combines commissioner, F.A. McGregor, to the minister of justice about an alleged combine in flour-milling. The combines commissioner was an investigator required to act independently of the government when there appeared to be combines in restraint of trade. The sole responsibility of the minister of justice was to table every report in Parliament within 15 days of its receipt.

Garson tabled the report of the flour-milling inquiry early in November and at the same time informed the House that the combines commissioner had submitted his resignation, which had been accepted. He also tabled the letter of resignation, which implied that Garson had delayed the publication of the report because of pressure from C.D. Howe. In reply to a question, Garson stated that the report had been 'received in his office on 29 December 1948, nearly ten months earlier. The Opposition at once accused the minister of justice of breaking the law by delaying publication of the report and of being bullied into doing so by an overbearing senior colleague. Over the next few weeks an essentially trivial matter blew up into a parliamentary crisis.

Garson's basic mistake had been to tell Parliament that the report had been in his office in December 1948, when what had been received at that time was an incomplete draft of the report, which McGregor had not yet had printed. The report was actually submitted in final printed form only on 29 October 1949 and was tabled almost at once. But the Opposition had by that time made the most of the alleged breach of the law by the minister of justice.

Once I learned all the facts, I urged Garson to seize the first opportunity to make a detailed, consecutive statement, and I helped him prepare one. When it was delivered, the statement was so honest and straightforward that the charge against Garson was soon dropped. What worried me was the great damage done to Garson's self confidence and prestige. Indeed, he never fully recovered from it. Even more serious for the government was that McGregor's letter of resignation had created the impression that Howe dominated the minister of justice and the whole government. That incident marked the beginning of the myth that Howe was the real leader of the government and St Laurent merely a figurehead.

I was deeply distressed by the affair, not merely because Garson, a close friend, had been hurt, but because I felt McGregor, in his zeal, had been unreasonable and wrong in his conclusions. McGregor and I were fellow literary executors of Mackenzie King, a role that required us to meet frequently, and I had difficulty in concealing my disapproval. The whole unhappy experience taught me that trivial matters are more likely to embarrass governments than big ones.

The government shuffle

Bradley had been the only addition to the cabinet before the election, and I certainly had a part in his appointment. After the election St Laurent discussed with me the changes he felt were necessary to strengthen the French-speaking representation. Ernest Bertrand and Joseph Jean were appointed to the bench and replaced by Hugues Lapointe as solicitor general and Edouard Rinfret, the son of the chief justice of Canada as postmaster general. 'Bob' Lapointe, Ernest's son, elected in 1940, served in the army throughout the war and attained the rank of colonel. He had politics in his blood and served in the cabinet with growing distinction and influence while St Laurent was prime minister. Duplessis made a dead set against Lapointe in the election of 1957. He was defeated and never sat again in Parliament, but later he served for many years as lieutenant-governor of Quebec. We were good friends; he had an instinct for public opinion, and I always listened with great respect to his observations. Rinfret had been a good debater after he entered Parliament in 1945, but he proved not to be a good administrator.

The government had three new departments created and two abolished during the first session of Parliament. The stopgap Department of Reconstruction and Supply, of which Robert Winters was minister, was to be replaced by a real department. The unwieldy and misleadingly named Department of Mines and Resources was to be broken up into departments representing their real functions. St Laurent left the task of devising a new structure largely to me. I had the enthusiastic cooperation of Hugh Keenleyside, who when the new immigration policy was announced, had left External Affairs to become deputy minister of mines and resources. Immigration and Indian Affairs were part of the department. Keenleyside suggested that the Naturalization branch, which dealt with applications for citizenship, be transferred from the Department of the

Secretary of State and added to Immigration and Indian Affairs to become a new department, to be called Immigration and Citizenship. I said Citizenship should be put first. The heart of the old Department of Mines and Resources was its authority over the Northwest Territories and the Yukon. The national parks were also under Mines and Resources. In the territories and the national parks jurisdiction over resources was federal. The new department was called Resources and Development. Ministerial responsibility for Central Mortgage and Housing, the National Film Board, and the Trans-Canada Highway were included in the new department, and the Department of Reconstruction and Supply was abolished. The Mines branch, the splendid federal surveying and mapping service and the geological survey could become the Department of Mines and Technical Surveys.

St Laurent agreed, almost without change, and the legislation was duly passed. Winters was to become minister of resources and development, and Keenleyside would continue as deputy minister. Colin Gibson had become minister of mines and resources on 31 March 1949 to enable Bradley to become secretary of state. Gibson could not be expected to accept a fragment of his former department. St Laurent wanted Walter Harris in the cabinet but felt he could not add another minister from Ontario without upsetting the balance. There was a vacancy on the Ontario Court of Appeal, and I suggested to St Laurent that he offer it to Gibson. He would thereby open the way for the appointment of Harris to Citizenship and Immigration. As always, St Laurent was reluctant to suggest to a minister that he retire from the government, but he agreed that an appointment to the highest court in Ontario could not be regarded as a demotion. He decided to make the offer, and told Gibson there was no compulsion on him to leave the cabinet. Gibson was modest about his knowledge of the law and his capacity to be a good judge, but St Laurent pointed out that his experience as minister of national revenue had given him insight into the judicial process, and that his nonpartisan attitude and fair-mindedness would be valuable on the bench. Gibson accepted the appointment, and the new departments were proclaimed on 18 January 1950. Winters became minister of resources and development, and Harris minister of citizenship and immigration. For the time being McCann became minister of mines and technical surveys, in addition to national revenue.

Gordon Robertson, who had helped to draft the Citizenship Act, was ideally qualified to be deputy minister of citizenship and immigration. St Laurent was favourable until Keenleyside pointed out that Laval Fortier was doing an excellent job in the Immigration branch and would be a good deputy minister in an area where French Canadians were in short supply. Fortier was appointed, and Gordon did not become a deputy minister until three years later. The new ministers and new departments strengthened the government.

Alberta had been a Liberal desert since 1921. After MacKinnon became a senator and resigned his portfolio to make a place available for Bradley as minister from Newfoundland, there were no Alberta Liberals in the House of Commons. Although five Liberals were elected in 1949, none had been in the House before, and none had an obvious claim to be minister. St Laurent kept MacKinnon in the cabinet as minister without portfolio to represent Alberta. But he realized that situation could not last, and in December 1950 he took the unprecedented step of asking the five elected members to choose one of their number to be minister. George Prudham was chosen, and became minister of mines and technical surveys.

The Constitution

The Supreme Court of Canada was not really supreme in 1949, as there were appeals from its decisions to the Judicial Committee of the British Privy Council. The Constitution of Canada was an Act of the British Parliament that could be amended only by that Parliament. St Laurent was eager to remove those relics of colonialism, and so was I.

A bill to make the Supreme Court the final court of appeal was passed without difficulty, but the transfer from Britain to Canada of the power to amend the Constitution raised difficult questions.

One of those was how to preserve the safeguards for the use of the English and French languages in the Constitution, when the power to amend was transferred to Canada. In 1943, when the BNA Act was being amended to postpone redistribution until after the war, the Tory Opposition had argued that the provinces should be consulted before the Constitution was amended. St Laurent had replied that redistribution concerned Parliament alone and was not within the jurisdiction of the provinces. He had then been asked whether Parliament alone would have the right to ask for an amendment to the provision of the BNA Act safeguarding the use of the French language in Parliament and the federal courts. Instead of brushing off the question as hypothetical or irrelevant, he had answered candidly that such an amendment would be legal, but that he was not worried about the lack of legal protection because he felt 'the best guarantee of the fundamental provisions of the Constitution' was to be found in 'the good sense and fairness of the Canadian people and of those who represent them in Parliament'.

That answer was repeatedly cited by Tories and nationalists in Quebec as evidence of St Laurent's lack of concern to protect the French language. I persuaded him that the new amending procedure should deny to Parliament or any provincial legislature the right to change the safeguards to the use of the French and English languages in Parliament and the federal courts and the legislature and courts of Quebec. St Laurent himself decided that the rights to separate Catholic schools in Ontario and Protestant and Catholic schools in Quebec existing in 1867 should be similarly safeguarded. Such protection would also apply to the separate schools in Saskatchewan and Alberta and the denominational system in Newfoundland.

Neither St Laurent nor anyone else then in public life felt that Parliament should have the exclusive power to amend the Constitution. There was general agreement that the provincial authorities should have a share in the amending procedure, but about what that share should be there was no agreement.

During the election campaign St Laurent had indicated that the first step in the transfer of the amending power to Canada would be a conference with the provincial governments. That was certainly what I expected would happen. But after the campaign, while he was away on holiday in August, St Laurent sent me a memorandum making the radical proposal that, before holding a conference with the provinces, the government should ask Parliament to seek from the British Parliament an amendment to the BNA Act, to do three things. One would be to safeguard the provisions regarding schools and the French language already in the Constitution. A second would be to give Parliament exclusive jurisdiction to amend the Constitution, except with respect to the minority rights regarding schools and languages and/or in relation to provincial jurisdiction. A third would be to give Parliament jurisdiction as well to make amendments relating to provincial rights or privileges, but provide that no such amendment would come into effect unless and until it was enacted as law by the legislatures of all the provinces. He summarized the advantages of his proposal in these words: 'a) We bring back to Canada the right to amend. b) We do not impinge in any way on the jurisdiction of the provincial Legislatures. c) We leave it to the Courts to say whether or not anything we attempted to do would impinge on a right or privilege of any province. d) We safeguard the school and the language rights.' He also pointed out that any provincial government that refused to adopt an amendment that other provinces wanted would have to bear that responsibility and take any blame there was. Once I recovered my breath, I was excited by his bold, original, and imaginative approach.

Its first advantage was that it would end the damaging campaign that had been waged by Conservatives and nationalists in Québec since 1946, charging St Laurent with indifference to the preservation of the French language. Another advantage was that it would transfer to Parliament the jurisdiction to amend the Constitution in its exclusively federal aspects. And one more advantage was that Parliament would be given power to make amendments to those parts of the Constitution relating to provincial jurisdiction and provincial rights and privileges, provided such amendments did not come into effect until confirmed by all provincial legislatures. St Laurent's plan would have transferred the whole amending power to Canada.

But I felt it would not be wise to have the jurisdiction to make amendments affecting provincial jurisdiction transferred to Canada without first consulting the provincial governments. I was concerned for two reasons. First, I was not happy that every provincial legislature must give positive approval to any amendment related to provincial rights or jurisdiction because I still cherished the illusion that the provincial governments might be persuaded to agree to some less rigid requirement. St Laurent convinced me that, in practice, no provincial government would tolerate having its constitution changed without its consent. We have seen what happened when the Constitution of 1982 changed the Constitution of Québec without the approval of its government or legislature.

My other concern was political. St Laurent had undertaken to consult the provincial authorities about the transfer of the amending power. I felt that if the British Parliament was asked to transfer the whole of the amending power to Canada before the provincial governments had been consulted, he would be accused of failing to carry out a promise and of exceeding his mandate.

St Laurent countered by arguing that his proposal, if adopted, would take nothing away from the provincial authorities, since their consent would be required to any amendment affecting them. But he conceded that his proposed action, if taken in advance of consultation, might be misinterpreted to the disadvantage of the federal government. He agreed reluctantly to drop that part of his proposal until after a federal-provincial conference, but wanted to proceed with the proposals to safeguard rights to schools and the use of the English and French languages and to transfer to Parliament the power to amend the Constitution in the exclusively federal area.

St Laurent correctly anticipated that the Tories would oppose the transfer of that limited amending power to Canada on the ground that no change in the Constitution should be made without consulting the provincial governments.

In reply to the charge that the government was acting in bad faith by exceeding its mandate, St Laurent said that he had never given an undertaking to consult the provincial governments about any matter within the exclusive jurisdiction of Parliament, and that he believed it would be a grave error to subject the exercise of the powers given by the Constitution to the Parliament of Canada, which was composed of members elected in all 10 provinces, to control by provincial governments. He pointed out that the provincial legislatures had the power, under the BNA Act, to amend the provincial constitutions without any reference to the British or Canadian parliaments, and that several provincial legislatures had used that power. He felt that the Parliament of Canada should have similar power to amend its own constitution.

There was no opposition to the proposal to entrench the minority rights to schools and the use of the English and French languages. St Laurent said that he had not been worried by the lack of legal protection in that area, and that he still felt 'the best guarantee of the fundamental provisions of the Constitution' was to be found in the good sense and fairness of the Canadian people and of those who represent them in Parliament. But he believed the constitutional protection being proposed would relieve the anxieties of those who did not share his confidence.

Stanley Knowles proposed a safeguard of popular rights in the form of the entrenchment of the provisions of the Constitution limiting the life of each Parliament to five years and requiring a session of Parliament to be held every year. St Laurent at once accepted the proposal, with the proviso that the life of a Parliament might be extended beyond five years in a period of war or other emergency if not more than one-third of the members of either house of Parliament opposed such an extension.

The request to the British Parliament to amend the constitution was approved, despite Conservative and Social Credit opposition. At the same time St Laurent tabled copies of a letter he had sent to the premiers inviting them to a federal-provincial conference in January 1950 to discuss the transfer to Canada of the power to amend the Constitution in all respects.

The amendment was duly enacted by the British Parliament. The Constitution thereafter contained safeguards for the existing rights to the use of the English and French languages, the existing school systems, and constitutional assurance of annual sessions and the limit on the life of Parliament. The right of Parliament to amend the Constitution in matters of exclusive federal concern was to prove useful on many occasions before it was included in the patriated Constitution of 1982.

St Laurent's relationship with Duplessis was a prime concern in the preparation for the constitutional conference with the provincial governments. After becoming premier again in 1944, Duplessis had treated St Laurent with contempt, as a political amateur. But his attitude changed after St Laurent's landslide in 1949 convinced him he was facing a real professional in Ottawa. Their first encounter after the election was to be at the conference in January 1950.

St Laurent was passing through a period of depression at that time and finding it hard to make up his mind about tactics. I believe that left to himself he would have placed before the conference a simple proposal for an amending procedure. I was afraid that any proposal put forward by the federal government would simply be a target for attack by one or more of the premiers. My suggestion was that he say that the purpose of the conference was to find out what provincial participation each premier wanted in the amending process, and add that it was up to each provincial government, and not the federal government, to say what that government wanted. When the provincial positions had all been stated, St Laurent and Garson could try to achieve a consensus if a consensus seemed possible.

My suggestion did not at first appeal to St Laurent; his own inclination was to be direct and straightforward in approaching

any problem. He described my proposal as negative and uncon-
structive. I agreed but said it was not the federal responsibility to
prescribe the business of the provincial governments. I argued
that almost any amending process agreed on by all the provincial
governments would likely be acceptable to the federal government.

St Laurent finally decided to invite each premier to take the
initiative. He shook off his lethargy and spoke effectively. He said
the federal government agreed that any procedure for amending
the constitution should respect the exclusive powers given to each
provincial legislature. He pointed out that Parliament obviously
had to participate in making any amendment, but that it was for
the provincial authorities to say what part each of them wanted to
have in the case of amendments affecting provincial governments
or legislatures. Such provincial positions would have to be reconciled before the British Parliament could be asked to transfer the
whole of the amending power to Canada. He said he was sure that
sooner or later the people of Canada were going to insist that
somehow means be found to transfer to Canada complete jurisdiction over its own constitution. But it soon became clear that
Duplessis would not put forward any amending formula. He kept
demanding to know what the federal proposal was, obviously
looking for a target to attack.

In the end the conference made no progress, but it did reveal an
amazing change in Duplessis's attitude to St Laurent. There was
no more rudeness. Instead, he said of St Laurent 'you did not try
to force your opinion on anyone; you left the door open for
friendly discussion, and I think that is the basis upon which it is
possible to arrive at definite and just results.' In his closing speech
Duplessis went even further: 'Mr. Prime Minister, if I were to pay
you a compliment I am afraid so many people would be shocked
that some of them might die; and on the other hand it would hurt
your humility. So, in order to save lives and to safeguard your
modesty, I will only express to you in the name of the province of
Quebec our sincere thanks for your courtesies which have been
extended to all the delegates during this conference!' Duplessis
then invited the conference to meet again in Quebec City in the
fall, and his invitation was accepted.

St Laurent was astonished by the almost universal praise in editorials and elsewhere of his statesmanlike attitude, but he had no illusion that one more session of the conference would agree on an acceptable method of amending the Constitution in Canada. No progress was made when the conference reassembled in Quebec City in September, and no date was set for its resumption. Before the end of 1950 St Laurent announced that the constitutional discussions would be resumed at the earliest convenience of the federal and provincial governments. That 'earliest convenience' did not occur while he was prime minister.

Throughout that whole period Gordon Robertson, then in the Cabinet Office, had been working on the constitutional problem with other officials, and he had come much closer than anyone else to finding a possible solution. It is of historical interest that his assistant in the work was Pierre Elliott Trudeau, then a temporary official in the Privy Council Office.

I have often wondered whether I should have dissuaded St Laurent from having his proposed formula for the transfer to Canada of the whole constitutional amending process submitted to Parliament in advance of a conference with the provinces. With his huge majority it would undoubtedly have passed, and the amending procedure affecting provincial rights and privileges been left to be worked out later in Canada. In the light of the unsatisfactory Constitution of 1982, imposed 30 years later by Parliament and nine provincial premiers on the other province, it seems that St Laurent's instinct was probably sound, and that I should not have interfered.

The Red River flood

Nineteen fifty was expected to be a quiet year for the government. No controversial new legislation was planned, and Parliament did not meet until mid-February. Just before the session opened, St Laurent went to New York to speak to the Canadian Society. Mrs St Laurent and their daughter Madeleine accompanied him, and they combined the engagement with sightseeing, shopping, and an evening at *South Pacific*. I was with them, and I watched St Laurent's relaxed behaviour with amazement, remembering

Mackenzie King's state of jitters before every session of Parliament.

But the year turned out other than expected. In early May the Red and Assiniboine rivers reached the peak of the spring flood simultaneously. The floodwaters engulfed about one-fifth of the area of Greater Winnipeg and spread to the rural areas adjoining both rivers. A large part of Greater Winnipeg had to be evacuated. The Manitoba flood excited world-wide sympathy and support for the victims. There had been a similarly spectacular flood in the lower Fraser Valley, in British Columba, in June 1948, and the federal government had eventually made a substantial contribution to the relief of those affected by the disaster and, later, to future flood control. St Laurent's first reaction to the Manitoba flood was to say that the people in the Red River Valley could expect they would be treated in the same way. His matter-of-fact, unemotional statement was not good enough for the public in Manitoba, or for the Opposition in Parliament.

One of St Laurent's weaknesses as a politician was that he could not bring himself to make loud professions of sympathy until he was satisfied that what was called a disaster was not simply a misfortune exaggerated. His tendency to reserve judgment was reinforced on the occasion by the attitude of the premier of Manitoba, Douglas Campbell, a cautious, thrifty farmer who was reluctant to commit his government to spend money unless he was sure it was really necessary. By failing to express enough sympathy for the victims of the flood, both St Laurent and Campbell left themselves open to attack by their political opponents.

Convinced belatedly that opposition and press criticism was hurting the government, St Laurent and Garson visited Winnipeg. There St Laurent was asked by a *Tribune* reporter what federal aid would be forthcoming for the 'little man.' He replied 'Directly, none,' and then explained that federal aid would be channelled through the provincial government to an independent commission appointed by both governments. As it turned out, so much aid was raised by the commission from both governments and public subscriptions that the commission ended up with a surplus that was held in trust for further disasters. But St Laurent's 'directly, none,' taken out of context, was widely represented as indifference on the part of the prime minister. Ironically, the generous but delayed response to the Red River flood marked the beginning of the decline of support in Manitoba for the St Laurent government.

The allegation was aggravated by a charge that the prime minister was more responsive to a disaster in Québec. On 7 May a fire destroyed a large part of the city of Rimouski. The next day St Laurent said that in Rimouski as in Manitoba federal action would depend on whether or not there was a request for aid from the provincial government. Critics in Parliament and in Manitoba accused St Laurent of having responded with more alacrity to the disaster in Québec. When another fire two days later wiped out most of the town of Cabano, Québec, a similar statement regarding federal aid strengthened the impression in Manitoba that Québec was being favoured.

In both provinces the financial assistance given by the government of Canada was exceedingly generous, but a more promptly forthcoming attitude to the Manitoba flood would have been politically expedient.

Korea and NATO

The parliamentary session was almost at an end when communist North Korea invaded South Korea in June 1950. United States troops had been stationed in South Korea since 1945 to defend it from the threat of communist aggression from the north. Resistance to aggression in Korea by American troops alone could have turned the Cold War into a third world war. At that time the Soviet Union was boycotting the United Nations and was not present when the United Nations branded North Korea's attack as an act of aggression and appealed to all members of the United Nations to support a resolution demanding the withdrawal of the North Korean forces.

On 28 June Pearson was asked in Parliament what action Canada would take. He replied that the first step was to confer with other nations. Before committing Canada to any positive action,

Pearson and St Laurent wanted to be sure that restraint of North Korean aagression was, at least in form, a UN operation and not merely an endorsement of the unilateral action being taken by the United States. St Laurent told Parliament on 30 June that any action by Canada would not be war against any state, but Canada's part 'in collective police action under the control and authority of the United Nations.' He said that it was the government's policy to consider making a Canadian contribution, if one would be useful to a UN operation under a UN commander, in order to achieve the end of peace. St Laurent felt, as Pearson did, that unilateral action by the United States would weaken the concept of collective security, and that it was in Canada's interest to insist upon collective action by the UN.

Mackenzie King was disturbed that Canada might be involved in the Korean situation. He invited me to Kingsmere to tell me that he had read his diaries about the Korean difficulty in the cabinet in 1947-48, and that he felt his position on Korea was being vindicated. He asked me to warn St Laurent of the danger of Canadian involvement. I reported the advice to St Laurent, who was not impressed. I learned years later from the diary that Mackenzie King had been warned by a medium at a séance about danger in Korea. A week later Mackenzie King was dead. Ironically, it was at a meeting on Mackenzie King's funeral train that the cabinet decided Canadian troops should be sent to Korea as part of the UN force.

As soon as the original American action to defend South Korea had been transformed into a UN operation, St Laurent and his colleagues showed no hesitation about the Canadian response. The Speech from the Throne opening a special session of Parliament on 29 August announced that Parliament would be asked to provide funds to meet the expenditure to support a brigade, 5000 strong, as a Canadian contribution to the resistance of the North Korean aggression.

Pearson and Claxton dealt directly with the prime minister about Korea, and I was not involved. In the debate only one MP, Paul Gagnon of Chicoutimi, opposed sending troops overseas. Pierre Laporte, then a journalist with Le Devoir, began an article with the question 'Are we to return to the era of Mr. King's lies? Mr. St Laurent had deceived us about Korea — 5000 men who turn out to be 15,000.' I persuaded St Laurent to reply to Laporte's article, one of the rare occasions he corrected a statement in the press. He explained that 15,000 men had to be available to support a brigade of 5000 in the field.

Gagnon in Parliament and *Le Devoir* outside Parliament were not able to stir up any substantial opposition in French Canada to Canada's part in the Korean operation. Their failure was a measure of St Laurent's success in persuading Canadians that world security depended upon collective international action. The fact that the menace was from international communism may have helped. In 1952 Dwight D. Eisenhower campaigned for the presidency of the United States on the promise 'to bring the boys home' from Korea. There was no such demand in the Canadian election campaign six months later. The difference, I believe, was that the American troops were conscripted, whereas the Canadian were volunteers.

The special session of Parliament was also asked to provide funds to support Canadian forces to be stationed in Europe under the auspices of NATO. There was no opposition. For St Laurent the aggression in Korea was an acute threat to world peace that had to be stopped by force, and Canada, by contributing was defending itself. The sending of troops as part of the western defence shield in Europe was likewise a measure for the defence of Canada. The marvel was that under St Laurent's leadership both were done with almost unanimous support in Parliament and the country.

The death of Mackenzie King

When Mackenzie King invited me to Kingsmere to talk about Korea, he also invited Margaret, who could not come because she had no one that day to look after Alan, who was two, and Ruth, who was three months. I asked him if I could bring Jane and Peter with me, and he readily agreed. They were put in charge of the cook while we talked, and then brought into the presence. Peter did a somersault from the door of the drawing room and rose in front of our host with his hand outstretched. Mackenzie King asked for a repeat performance, which Peter readily gave. I had been asked by Margaret to keep it in my head to buy a loaf of bread on the way home. When Jane reminded me that I was to keep a loaf of bread in my head, Mackenzie King looked puzzled, and I hastened our departure. I never saw him again.

He died on the following Sunday, 22 July. St Laurent was at his summer home at St Patrick, and I telephoned him there to report Mackenzie King's death. He decided at once that there should be a state funeral and asked me to have it arranged by the appropriate ministers and officials. Since the Department of National Defence was necessarily involved in almost every detail of the arrangements, I turned at once to Brooke Claxton. Claxton was the most effective organizer in the cabinet, and I knew that once he took charge, no detail would be overlooked. The funeral was elaborate, and the arrangements complicated. Mackenzie King's body lay in state in the Parliament Buildings. There was a cortège to St Andrew's Church for the religious service and from there to the railway station, a special overnight train to Toronto, and the burial the next day in Mount Pleasant Cemetery beside his mother and father.

Mackenzie King had commanded respect, often reluctantly given, but little affection except from a few intimate friends. His death, however, aroused deep feeling everywhere in Canada. It was as though a whole people suddenly realized, at the same moment, that the country had lost one of its greatest citizens, and that a period of history had ended. If there was not an outpouring of grief, there was a solemn feeling of awe.

I felt no real sorrow at Mackenzie King's death. I had seen him regularly after he retired, and had realized that he was failing physically, but what I found sadder was his inability to adapt himself to the inevitable limitations of retirement. He missed the attention and the sense of mission that had sustained him in office. I had known for some time that he would never be happy as a private citizen.

The railway strike

Humphrey Mitchell died four days after Mackenzie King and I was surprised when St Laurent told me he was to have a state funeral. St Laurent felt that such a ceremony would be recognition of the place of organized labour in the national life.

Mitchell's portfolio was not an easy one to fill. There was no other Liberal member of the House of Commons prominent in the ranks of organized labour, nor any obvious candidate outside Parliament. St Laurent made his own choice, so far as I know without advice from anyone. I was surprised when he suggested asking Milton Gregg, but I realized at once that it was the best possible choice. Gregg was not identified with employers or business. His fair-mindedness had already been demonstrated in his dealings with Veterans Affairs, and his genuine humility and lack of pretentiousness would be obvious assets in a minister of labour. Gregg became a trusted and competent minister, and St Laurent was unfailing in his support on every critical occasion. Gregg's place in Veterans Affairs was taken by Hugues Lapointe. Lapointe was a happy choice — a distinguished veteran of actual combat, a colonel and a French Canadian.

Both appointments were made on 7 August. The union leaders had already called a nation-wide railway strike for 22 August. Normally, the main responsibility for dealing with a railway labour dispute would have rested with the minister of labour, but because the new minister had no experience with labour problems, the main burden fell on the prime minister.

St Laurent's first impulse once the strike date had been set, was to call Parliament and introduce legislation to forbid the strike; he feared that the cessation of railway service even for a few days would be a national disaster. There was a danger I felt, that if the strike was not allowed to take place, the public would not realize there was an emergency. Without public awareness, preventive legislation might lack public support, and a law to end the strike might not be obeyed. A brief work stoppage would not be an economic disaster, in my opinion, but would result in enough inconvenience and potential hardship to enlist public support for legislation to restore railway service. St Laurent was concerned about the risk of defiance of a law prohibiting a strike. Instead of calling Parliament at once, he appealed to the union leaders to postpone the strike for 30 days and asked both parties to accept a mediator to make one last effort to reach a settlement through negotiations. The union leaders refused to postpone the strike, the mediation failed, and the strike duly began on 22 August.

St Laurent at once had Parliament called to meet in special session on 29 August. He made one more effort, that time by personal intervention, to achieve a settlement before Parliament met. On Friday, 25 August he and the ministers of labour and transport had a meeting with the presidents of the railways, and on Saturday, with the senior officers of the two labour congresses. On Sunday the parties reported that their efforts had not succeeded in preventing a strike, and St Laurent felt it therefore necessary to find some other way to have service restored. That other way was legislation by Parliament.

The procedure followed in the House of Commons was as unusual as the legislation itself. Normally, when the Commons return to their own chamber after hearing the Speech from the Throne read in the Senate, the prime minister introduces Bill No. 1, called the 'Bill Respecting the Oaths of Office.' The bill is actually a blank sheet of paper, and after it is given first reading, no further action on it is taken. Introducing the bill has the symbolic purpose of asserting the right of the Commons to give priority to their own business over business recommended by the Crown in the Speech from the Throne. I suggested to St Laurent that, instead of treating Bill No. 1 as a formality, the government make it the bill required to restore railway service. The bill could then be debated and disposed of ahead of the usual formalities of a new session. St Laurent liked my idea but asked if Bill No. 1 had ever been used for actual legislation. To my surprise and satisfaction I discovered that Mackenzie King had used Bill No. 1 in 1937 for legislation regarding the succession to the throne after the abdication in 1936 of Edward VIII.

The bill was euphemistically called the 'Maintenance of Railway Operation Act.' If passed, the bill would require the railways and their employees to resume railway service at once, and would give the parties 15 days to reach a settlement or to select an arbitrator, whose decision would be binding. If they could neither reach a settlement nor agree on an arbitrator, the governor in council would appoint the arbitrator. If passed, the bill would require the railways at once to pay their employees the rates of pay the railways had already offered in negotiations. Those rates were to be a minimum the arbitrator could not reduce, but he could fix higher rates for the period of the new contract. His decision was to be final.

All other business was postponed, by unanimous consent, until the bill was passed in both Houses and given royal assent, at 10 p.m. on the second day of the session. St Laurent's speech proposing the bill was one of his greatest displays in Parliament of his skill as an advocate. He said the bill had been drafted to deal with a national emergency. It was not intended to change the regular procedure for reaching wage settlements based on collective bargaining. Departure from the normal procedure was justified only because a prolonged railway strike would bring the economy to a complete stand-still. No other country in the world was more dependent than Canada on railway transportation; a tie-up of rail transportation in the disturbed state of the world at that time could involve serious risk and injury to the cause of peace. He emphasized that the strike was lawful and that those on strike and their leaders were not breaking any law, but that 'insistence upon what may be normally private rights may at times amount to what become public wrongs.' Railway service must be restored, but he hoped that while it was being restored, nothing would be said or done that would rankle afterwards in the minds or hearts of any good Canadians. He welcomed the assurance by the responsible labour leaders that the strikers would obey the law but said there was no reason, and would be no excuse, for enacting a law any more unpalatable than the urgency of the circumstances strictly required.

The strike ended once the law was passed, but the final settlement as required, went to compulsory arbitration by a judge of the Supreme Court appointed by the governor in council.

The railway strike in my opinion caused St Laurent more anxiety even than the conscription crisis of 1944. His anxiety was less about the immediate decision of that labour dispute than about the possible long-term effect of a legislative settlement. He told me one day that he was convinced the survival of the Liberal party would depend largely on its attitude to organized labour, and that he could not make up his mind what its position should be. The traditional Liberal attitude was to support employees rather than employers on the assumption that labour was the weaker party, but he realized that some unions were becoming so powerful they could hold the public to ransom. Neither he nor any other Liberal has yet devised a satisfactory attitude to labour relations.

In a speech of greeting in April 1956 to the newly formed Canadian Labour Congress St Laurent said that one of the problems of bigness was the need to take its power into account. Big governments must recognize the effects of budgets and monetary policies upon the economy, and the impact of defence programs, trade and social security programs, and even works projects. Similarly, giant corporations must take into account the effects of their actions not only on their markets, workers, customers, and competitors, but also on other segments of the economy. In the field of labour a big union in an important sector of the economy had tremendous power at its command and, in using it, must consider the consequences of its actions for the many others it would affect.

St Laurent, a corporation lawyer, had a long and successful experience with labour relations, whereas I had never before had any. It was a privilege to witness the performance of a master, and helpful to me later in my own career.

Relations with the provincial governments

The federal-provincial conference

The agitation for abolition of the means test for old-age pensions became an embarrassment to the St Laurent government in 1950. In the debate on the Speech from the Throne Drew moved to censure the government because it had 'failed to take steps to inaugurate a national contributory system of old age pensions without a means test,' but he did not make a strong attack. Later in the debate Knowles continued his campaign with vigour. St Laurent undertook to have old age pensions discussed at the federal-provincial conference to be held later in the year. He wanted a plan that included compulsory contributions, but Parliament would not have the power to impose contributions without a constitutional amendment, for which the government intended to seek provincial agreement.

A joint committee of the Senate and the House or Commons was appointed to work out a plan. Jean Lesage was the chairman from the Commons and the driving force in the committee. He got unanimous approval for a plan for old age security that to this day has not been fundamentally altered. The plan was devised in large part by St Laurent, who was consulted by Lesage at every stage. Under the plan old age pensions were to be paid by the federal government directly to all persons over 70.

The federal-provincial conference had been called to discuss renewal of the tax-rental agreements, which would expire on 31 March, 1952.

St Laurent himself devised the strategy for the conference and guided its deliberations throughout. The organization was superb. The prime minister set the scene in his opening speech by contrasting the high hopes there had been for lasting peace when the first postwar conference met in August 1945 with the grim international prospect facing the world in December 1950. He concluded by asking Pearson, Claxton and Abbott to outline Canada's place in the world situation, the military response in Korea and western Europe and the financial implications of that response.

He then described the plan for pensions without a means test, to implement which a constitutional amendment would be required. From their statements it was clear that the premiers had been influenced by the campaign against the means test, and that nine of them would support a constitutional amendment. The surprise was the attitude of Duplessis. He reminded the conference that, although the existing old age pension legislation had been enacted in 1927, Québec had not participated until he first became premier, in 1936. He cunningly cited that action by his government as an example of the way Ouébec, in his time, had 'gladly co-operated with Ottawa.' He liked the plan and said Québec would consider a modification of the constitution in a most friendly way, but could not commit the province until an amendment was presented in a satisfactory form.

The Conference met in camera after the opening day. St Laurent himself devised a formula for amending the Constitution to give both Parliament and the provincial legislatures jurisdiction over old age pensions. The formula was acceptable to Duplessis because the amendment would provide that, in cases of conflict between federal and provincial legislation, the provincial law would prevail. No one but St Laurent could have won agreement from Duplessis.

The legal stages were completed in 1951. Since 1 January 1952 old age pensions have been paid to all Canadians over the age of 70. The age was reduced to 65 while Pearson was prime minister.

At the opening of the conference St Laurent also announced that the federal government was prepared to continue tax-rental agreements similar to those in force with 8 of the 10 provinces for another five years from 1 April 1952. He said pressure would not be put on any provincial government to make an agreement, though he felt the public was 'apt to be better and more efficiently served if there is only one authority levying and collecting those taxes which have such an important effect upon our economic well-being.' From the opening day it was apparent that the eight premiers whose governments had tax-rental agreements wanted them renewed, and a strong hint that Premier Leslie Frost was interested in an agreement for Ontario. Despite the cordiality between them, St Laurent could not overcome Duplessis's objection to the tax-rental system.

That conference was the most amicable and most successful federal-provincial conference in Canadian history. All the provincial governments agreed to the constitutional amendment respecting old age security, and 9 of the 10 provinces made tax-rental agreements to last until 31 March 1957. For St Laurent it was a triumph, clouded only by his foreboding that, when Ontario made a tax agreement, it would become intolerable to have taxpayers in Québec pay the same tax as other Canadians while their province was not receiving the same benefits.

The Massey Commission and grants to universities

A commission on the arts had been proposed at the Liberal convention in August 1948 by the University Liberal Federation. Claxton learned that the student Liberals were bitterly disappointed that their proposal had not been adopted by the convention, and promised to take it to the cabinet. Before St Laurent became prime minister, Claxton discussed the proposed commission with me, and I, in turn, discussed it with Pearson, before he went to London for the negotiation of the North Atlantic Treaty. While in London, Pearson saw Vincent Massey, who was there on a visit — possibly looking for a job in England. Pearson advised him not to take on anything until he had seen St Laurent. In a message to me from London, Pearson said, 'The Royal Commission idea which you mentioned, seemed to me to be an imaginative and excellent one and Massey would, of course, be admirable for that work.'

I was sure the very idea of such a commission would have been rejected as ridiculous by Mackenzie King, and I was far from sure how St Laurent would receive it. Claxton and Pearson were able to persuade him that such a commission would be in the public interest as well as being good politics. He was persuaded largely because the commission was to consider broadcasting and the way in which television should be organized in Canada. Aid to universities was also on the agenda. St Laurent realized that the universities were inadequately financed and hoped that the commission could recommend a way to improve their situation. His interest in the the arts was very limited in the early stages; he once told me he was not enthusiastic about subsidizing 'ballet dancing.'

The commission was appointed in April 1949, with Massey as chairman. Unlike many commissions it moved swiftly, and it had completed its work in the spring of 1950. St Laurent was concerned that the government might not be willing to accept some of its recommendations. To keep its report at arm's length, he asked the commission to have it printed before submitting it to the government. Once it was printed, he tabled the report in Parliament and stated that no member of the government had yet read the report, and that he could therefore not say whether or not there would be early legislation on any of its recommendations.

The report recommended federal grants to the universities amounting to 50 cents per capita of the population of each province, to be divided among the universities in the province in proportion to the number of students enrolled in each institution.

It was true that no minister had read the Massey report before it was tabled in Parliament. But N.A.M. Mackenzie, the president of the University of British Columbia, a member of the commission, had discussed the question with me, and I was the actual author of the formula recommended for university grants. St Laurent was not aware of my discussion with Mackenzie until I told him, after the report was published.

Initially St Laurent was reluctant; he feared federal grants to the universities would provoke a new controversy with the Duplessis government. He told me he would rather increase the tax-rental payments to the provinces in order to put the provincial governments themselves in a better financial position to support the universities. I agreed with him in principle that federal grants were not desirable in areas of provincial jurisdiction. But I argued that in the case of universities there were practical considerations that justified direct federal aid. So many university graduates moved out of the poorer provinces to other parts of Canada that those provinces said their taxpayers could not be expected to pay for the university education of young people who went off to live elsewhere. I put the question; Why should the farmers of Saskatchewan pay for the education of the lawyers who come to Ottawa to join the staff of the Department of Justice? St Laurent knew that almost half the lawyers in Justice were graduates of the University of Saskatchewan. Another consideration was that the federal government was, by a wide margin, the largest 'consumer' of university graduates, and the proposed federal grants would not pay the cost even of training essential public servants. After some hesitation St Laurent decided to recommend to Parliament that the grants be made. He explained that since the formula provided the same rate of grant to each province, there could be no suggestion that the grants would interfere in the field of education or with the freedom of the universities.

All the Opposition parties in Parliament welcomed the announcement, as did provincial governments everywhere, except in Québec, where nationalists attacked the plan as intrusion into provincial autonomy. Duplessis accepted a compromise that enabled the Québec universities to receive the grants for one year if the cheques were signed by the Québec minister of finance as well as by the Canadian minister. But after the first year, Duplessis changed his position and forbade the universities to accept the grants. As St Laurent had feared, the grants became another source of grievance against Ottawa.

At my suggestion St Laurent included a requirement that the grants be used for operating expenses and not for capital expenditures; I realized that university administrations sometimes gave preference to new buildings over academic salaries or expenditures on libraries. I knew from my own experience that academic salaries were much too low. The grants helped fill the gap in university revenues that had been left by 1950, when the number of war veterans with fees paid by the federal government was approaching zero.

I was surprised to read recently that Pierre Trudeau had supported Duplessis's opposition to university grants, on the ground that spending federal money on activities within provincial jurisdiction was a perversion of the constitution. After its modest beginning in 1950, federal support for post-secondary education expanded greatly when Trudeau was prime minister, and the support was accepted by all the provinces.

My final period in the Prime Minister's Office

London, Paris and Washington

Before Parliament met in February 1951, St Laurent visited London for a meeting of the Commonwealth prime ministers. He also made an official visit to France. Norman Robertson, Jules Léger and I accompanied him. We flew the Atlantic for the first time in the new official plane, the C-5. We had to refuel in Newfoundland; Gander was closed because of weather, and we were forced to land at the United States Air Force base at Stephenville on New Year's Eve. The senior officers on the base were courteous and attentive, but we had the impression that they did not really welcome the interruption of their celebrations. For our part we found it humiliating to have to land in our own country at an airport totally controlled by the government of another country. When we left Stephenville, St Laurent said some way must be found to make the situation more agreeable for Canadians who worked at or visited the bases in Newfoundland. He had raised the problem with President Truman in February 1949, and official discussions were under way, but at a very slow pace. They were speeded up after our visit.

I believe that that was St Laurent's happiest official visit to London. The prime ministers had no great differences to discuss, and the conference was amicable. St Laurent had genuine respect and admiration for Attlee but was most impressed by Nehru. They had met during the meeting in London in October 1948, but a genuine friendship developed in 1951. I believe it was at that meeting that St Laurent first began to think of visiting India.

But the extracurricular activities rather than the meetings were most enjoyable for St Laurent. He had wanted for years to visit Lloyds Coffee House, the most famous insurance centre in the world, and he was also curious to visit the Bank of England, especially to see the gold reserve, as was I. St Laurent eagerly accepted the suggestion that he should also visit the headquarters of the Hudson's Bay Company at Beaver House. All those visits were arranged by the Bank of Montreal. Renault St Laurent and I accompanied the prime minister, but he was the most interested of the three of us; indeed, he reacted like a bright and eager schoolboy. He also managed to find one or two evenings for the theatre.

I had had an office in the same building with the Canadian gold reserve in 1937 and 1938, but I had not seen it then and still have not to this day.

There was no time for frivolity in the two days in Paris. President Vincent Auriol gave a luncheon for the prime minister, Prime Minister René Pleven gave a dinner, and the foreign minister, Robert Schuman gave a luncheon at the Quai d'Orsay. At that luncheon I had the good fortune to be seated next to Jean Monnet, the leading advocate of European federation, of whom I was already an admirer. I was thrilled to meet him and flattered that he devoted so much of his time to talking to me about his plans for the French economy and his hopes for Europe France was only beginning to recover from the war and the occupation, and it seemed to me that the visit by the French-speaking prime minister of a country with great prestige in the world was a moral tonic for all who met St Laurent. The success of the visit owed a great deal to careful advance preparation and the close attention given to every detail by the Canadian ambassador, Georges Vanier. St Laurent was deeply moved by the cordiality of the welcome.

In September 1951 came a visit to Washington to see President Truman. At their meeting in 1949 St Laurent had stressed to Truman the urgency of starting the St Lawrence seaway and power development. By 1951 the need for power in Ontario was urgent. The federal and provincial governments had reached an agreement on the division of costs. Ontario Hydro had made an agreement for sharing the power with the New York Power Authority. Power development could not start until approved by the United States Federal Power Commission and by the president. Approval of the seaway was being blocked in the Congress. St Laurent intended to ask President Truman to speed up approval by Congress, and if Congress continued to delay action on a joint venture, to get him to acquiesce in the construction of an all-Canadian seaway.

Hume Wrong, the Canadian ambassador in Washington, Norman Robertson and I were with the prime minister when he met Truman at the White House. St Laurent outlined the urgency for Canada of early action and explained that the Canadian government was willing to build the seaway by itself, unless early congressional action could be secured for a joint seaway, which, he tactfully said, would be Canada's first preference. Truman recalled that he had supported the venture since his entry into Congress years before and undertook to make a vigorous new effort to persuade Congress to act. In the words of the joint press statement issued after the meeting, 'The President expressed his strong preference for joint action on the seaway and his hope that the Congress would soon authorize such action, but stated he would support Canadian action as second best, if an early commencement on the joint development does not prove possible.' The result of the visit was both a diplomatic breakthrough and a political triumph for St Laurent. I had no direct part in the St Lawrence Seaway discussions. For me the interesting feature of the visit to Washington, as in 1949, was to see President Truman in action. The evidence of his wisdom and decisiveness impressed me.

The visit of Princess Elizabeth and Prince Philip

Princess Elizabeth and Prince Philip made their first visit to Canada in 1951. St Laurent was concerned that the visit was taking place during a serious illness of the King. He was reluctant to face the complications that would arise if the King should die while the heiress to the throne was in Canada.

St Laurent tried to discourage the visit. When it was first being discussed, he asked me to see the governor general informally to suggest that Lord Alexander advise the King that the visit would be untimely. When Alexander asked me why St Laurent did not advise the King himself, I replied that St Laurent did not wish to restrict the freedom of the King to make the decision; that, constitutionally, the King would have to accept the prime minister's advice. The governor general was the representative of the King, and his advice could be rejected. Alexander agreed to send the advice, and it was disregarded.

The royal visitors arrived in Ottawa on 10 October and stayed until the morning of 12 October. On their first afternoon they visited the Parliament Buildings. Unfortunately and unroyally, they reached the building ahead of schedule. The prime minister and Mrs St Laurent were delayed in traffic, and though they arrived at the appointed time, they were not at the door to greet the royal visitors.

For me that was the most notable incident of the royal visit, and it gave me a certain wry satisfaction. For nearly three years I had tried to persuade the prime minister that nothing embarrassed the organizers of public functions more than having the chief participant arrive ahead of time. St Laurent had a lifelong habit of being more punctual than called for, and my protests had had no effect. Later that afternoon I stopped at the prime minister's residence and commented to Mrs St Laurent that I felt sure the prime minister would now realize why I had so often begged him not to appear before the set time for his arrival. I knew he was listening. From that day, as long as he was prime minister, he was never again ahead of time at any function at which he was the central figure. Nor was he ever late.

The question of subversive activity

Senator Joseph McCarthy's campaign of terror against alleged subversive forces in the United States was at its height in the early 1950s. In a tentative way Drew tried a similar line in Canada. At the opening of the parliamentary session of 1950 he accused the government of failing to take adequate measures to safeguard Canadian institutions from infiltration by communist agents. Drew claimed that the government had already, in 1949, 'had information sufficiently positive to make them decide to change the commissioner of the National Film Board and to have a housecleaning in that government agency.'

The only substance for his charge was a situation that had arisen in the National Film Board. National Defence had doubts about the trustworthiness of some employees of the Film Board and was having films made by a private firm. There had been security screening by the RCMP of all the board's employees, and a few had been deemed security risks.

Winters was the minister responsible for the Film Board. When he turned to St Laurent for advice, Norman Robertson and I were asked to assist him. In addition to the security investigation we felt there should be a review of the administration of the Film Board. We hoped the review might lead to changes in personnel that could be made without injury to individual reputations. We recommended that management consultants be retained. Winters engaged the firm of J.D. Woods and Gordon, and the actual work was done by Walter Gordon himself. Gordon's report was well prepared and paid a high tribute to the work of the Film Board but recommended improvements in its administration.

In March 1950 Winters announced in Parliament that Gordon's report had been completed, and that Arthur Irwin, who had just retired as editor of *Maclean's* had been appointed film commissioner. He also reported that after the security screening of the employees of the Film Board he had assured all government departments including Defence that the board could undertake work of a secret nature. A few employees had been released as not worthy of trust, but none had been charged with wrongdoing. Winters appealed to members of the House not to press for details. To proclaim the employees' names publicly would injure their reputations and their chances of alternative employment. His appeal was successful.

St Laurent took no part in the debate, but his guiding hand was there throughout the crisis. Norman Robertson's advice had been invaluable to Winters, and I had helped him draft and revise his statement. But the main credit for preventing an embarrassing situation from being exaggerated into a crisis belonged to Winters, who performed in Parliament with coolness and good temper and revealed a mastery of parliamentary technique that impressed the House and was the foundation of his reputation as an able minister.

Drew's questions about the Film Board were a legitimate subject for criticism by an Opposition, but he went on to sweeping charges that Communists were 'going on apace and wide open.' Later in the session he concluded that legislation should be introduced so that communist activities in Canada might be made a punishable offence under the Criminal Code. St Laurent replied, in one of his best debating speeches. He agreed with Drew that ideological warfare had been going on for a number of years between communism and what he called 'Christian civilization,' but said that there was no agreement as to the most effective way to deal with communist propaganda. The government had declined to legislate to purge the trade unions of communism and had relied instead on the unions themselves to get rid of 'these obnoxious influences.' The unions, he felt, had done a much better job than could have been done by the police. He thought Canadians generally had been satisfied with 'the autonomous purges' that the labour movement had carried out.

To Drew's charge that the Department of Justice had failed to prosecute foreign-language publications in Ontario sympathetic to communism, St Laurent replied that those publications had already been there when Drew was premier of Ontario. The attorney general of the province, not the federal Department of Justice, had the responsibility for criminal prosecutions, and Drew's government had done nothing about them. He said that he was not criticizing the attorney general, in Drew's day or since, of negligence, but merely pointing out where the responsibility lay. His reply deflated Drew's attack.

St Laurent went on to give his own profession of faith in free institutions in words that deserve to be repeated. He said he had been 'preaching for many months past that the best method of combating communism is to make democracy work as a system benefitting no particular classes or groups, but benefitting all the members of the population.' He felt that the freedom of expression allowed to communist front organizations in Canada was 'the best possible contrast between what happens in a democratic country that is confident of its ability to maintain its democratic institutions, and what is enforced by fear and police in the totalitarian states.'

After the Korean war broke out, St Laurent was asked once more about subversive activity. He replied that the government did not intend to ask Parliament 'to enact any repressive measures against those misguided and, I am glad to say, rather few communists that we have in Canada. We still believe that it is better to meet them and fight them above ground than it is to have them burrow undeground.'

These statements by St Laurent were made spontaneously in debate and ended attempts to introduce McCarthyism in Canada.

I cannot claim any credit for them, but they represented my position, and I was proud of the prime minister.

Wheat for Britain

In 1951 a sharp difference arose between ministers over the final settlement of the postwar agreement for the sale of wheat to Britain. In 1946, largely at Gardiner's insistence, a five-year agreement to sell wheat at fixed prices had been reached between Britain and Canada. The contract stipulated that in the final year of the agreement Britain would 'have regard to' changes that had taken place in world wheat prices over the period of the contract. The farmers had feared that prices would fall after the war, and the agreement was considered a form of price security. Instead, prices had risen, and the farmers had begun to talk about their 'losses.' The British view was that Canada would have insisted on receiving the higher prices if world prices had fallen, and that Britain had no obligation to pay more because world prices had risen. Howe agreed with the British; Gardiner shared the view of the Canadian farmers.

St Laurent thought the Wheat Board had no legal claim, but he felt that both Gardiner and the British minister of food had given the impression to Canadian farmers that the 'have regard to' clause entitled them to some additional payment. He suggested to Attlee and the chancellor of the Exchequer that the British government might consider goodwill in western Canada worth making an additional payment. The British had not borrowed the last $65 million of the Canadian loan for postwar reconstruction and did not need to borrow it. St Laurent suggested that the British use the $65 million as a payment to the farmers. The British debt would be increased, but they would not need cash. The chancellor was adamant that Britain would pay no more.

Gardiner then argued that the Canadian government should make a contribution to the Wheat Board. Howe was opposed, and St Laurent admitted that the Wheat Board had no legal claim. I remember the way he put his position to me: Without some contribution from the government, the farmers would feel cheated. I agreed with St Laurent. He recommended that the federal treasury make a contribution to the Wheat Board of the $65 million of the loan that the British did not want. The cabinet agreed.

An awkward situation ensued. Gardiner made speeches outside Parliament implying that the British had not lived up to their commitment. Howe concluded a statement in Parliament with the words 'I deplore the suggestion that the British government has not played fair with the Canadian people.' Drew thereupon denounced what he called a split in the cabinet and demanded to know which minister, Gardiner or Howe, was speaking for the government. St Laurent replied 'In any government under a parliamentary system all ministers — and I am not speaking of this government in particular — do not necessarily always use the same expressions in communicating their thoughts. . . . If it were otherwise it would be very much simpler to have a one-man government. Our system is cabinet government, and cabinet government involves cabinet responsibility and cabinet solidarity. All members of the government agreed that Britain had discharged its full legal obligation, but that the Canadian wheat growers believed there was a continuing obligation under the "have regard to" clause which had not been discharged in full. For this reason the cabinet had agreed that the government should make a contribution to the Wheat Board. Whatever their views, all ministers were in agreement on the decision.' The rest of the debate was an anti-climax.

After his momentary annoyance Howe accepted, as he always did, the right of the prime minister, when ministers differed, to have the final say. What had looked to the opposition like a cabinet crisis quickly faded away.

A Canadian governor general

The need to appoint a new governor general arose quite unexpectedly out of a visit to Ottawa in January 1952 by Winston Churchill, once again prime minister of Britain. Churchill asked St Laurent's permission to invite Lord Alexander to return to England to become minister of defence in his cabinet. Alexander's term as governor general had recently been extended by the King on St Laurent's advice, but St Laurent felt he should not stand in the way if Alexander wished to accept Churchill's invitation. When Alexander decided he would like to accept, St Laurent advised the King to release him.

St Laurent had no doubt that the new governor general should be a Canadian, and he wanted the appointment made quickly so that embarrassing speculation would be avoided. I believe he had almost made up his mind, even before Churchill's visit, that Vincent Massey was the most suitable Canadian for the office. St Laurent chose Massey partly because of his long association with Britain, as the most acceptable Canadian to make the transition to having a Canadian governor general. Massey, in England on a visit, agreed without hesitation to allow his name to be submitted to the King, and the recommendation was received enthusiastically at the Palace.

St Laurent realized that the appointment of a Canadian would be regarded in some quarters as a weakening of the British connection by a French-speaking prime minister. I was curious as to what he would say to minimize the adverse effect of the appointment. When he announced the appointment on 25 January, he was obviously prepared for the key question, Did the appointment of Massey mean that in future only Canadians would be appointed to represent the sovereign in Canada? He replied that no such conclusion should be drawn, but that he 'would not like to admit that Canadians, alone among His Majesty's subjects, should be considered unworthy to represent the King in their own country.' I breathed a sigh of relief; no self-respecting Canadian could quarrel with that statement. There was no public criticism of Massey's appointment.

Shortly after Massey returned to Canada, I was sent to his home at Batterwood, near Port Hope, Ontario, to discuss the arrangements for his installation, the composition of his official staff, and the finances of Government House. All those matters were settled without difficulty. St Laurent had also asked me to raise with Massey the possibility of doing away with the practice of having women curtsey to the governor general, a practice the prime minister considered out of date and artificial. He told me to assure Massey he was not giving constitutional advice, but simply his personal view. I did my best, without success. Massey asked me to tell the prime minister he felt that the appointment of a Canadian was a big enough departure from precedent, and that it would be unwise for him to change any of the other customary procedures, at least at the beginning of his term — an argument St Laurent reluctantly accepted.

Massey's installation was set for 28 February, the date of the opening of Parliament.

The fuss over 'dominion' and 'Royal Mail'

A favourite Tory charge against Liberals was that they were deliberately weakening ties with Britain and the attachment of Canadians to the Crown. The charge was more damaging when Canada had a French-Canadian prime minister, as Laurier had discovered. In St Laurent's case it did not emerge until 1950. The government had gradually stopped describing the country as the Dominion of Canada in favour of the correct name, Canada, as set out in the BNA Act. Conferences with the provincial governments were being called federal-provincial instead of dominion-provincial. Many Liberals felt the word 'dominion' had a colonial or quasi-colonial connotation, as of course it did. My objection was that there was no French translation of the word, and I felt the country should be described by the same word in both languages.

Many Conservatives considered the word in some mystical way a symbol of the British connection, but the controversy about 'dominion' did not become serious until agitation was raised about the use of the term 'Royal Mail' on letter boxes and some Post Office vehicles. A contractor who collected mail from letter boxes had substituted the words 'Canada Post Office' for 'Royal Mail' on his trucks. It turned out that an over-zealous official in the post office department had advised the contractor that 'Canada Post Office' was legally correct, and that there was no legal authority for using 'Royal Mail.' That trivial incident was blown up by some Conservative critics into a deliberate Liberal plot to undermine the attachment of Canadians to the Crown. A few of the Tory backbenchers even believed the charge was true. But many more thought it was smart politics.

Unfortunately the whole affair was dealt with ineptly in Parliament by the postmaster general, Edouard Rinfret. I believe his handling of it was one reason St Laurent agreed so readily to Rinfret's wish to become a judge.

I was confident there were no letter boxes where 'Royal Mail' had been removed and 'Canada Post' substituted. There was an impressive box labelled Royal Mail just inside the Senate door of the Parliament building. One day I was listening to an indignant protest from a Tory journalist about the insult to the Crown. I persuaded him to go with me to the Senate door. When he saw the words 'Royal Mail,' he was clearly disappointed.

St Laurent took advantage of his press conference announcing the appointment of the governor general to deal with the words 'dominion' and 'royal.' About 'dominion' he said: 'we are a dominion and there isn't anything that I or the Government or Parliament can do about it. Under the BNA Act, Canada is a dominion but the name is Canada.' He added: 'There are some who say the word *dominion* shouldn't be used at all, but they are going too far. It has been the policy of the government to omit the word *dominion* where it is improperly used, but not to take it out of a statute.' He dealt with 'royal' by displaying copies of contract forms still in use in which the post office department required contractors to paint the words 'Royal Mail' and the King's coat of arms on their trucks used to carry the mail. He went on to ask: 'What's the matter with the word Royal? The King is a part of our system of government and it's silly that anyone should be objecting to the word *Royal*.' He explained that to avoid commercial exploitation there were stringent rules about the use of the word 'royal' approved by the monarch himself. The whole trivial fuss was quickly forgotten when word was received of the death of the King.

The death of King George VI

On 6 February, the morning after Lord and Lady Alexander were honoured at a farewell dinner, news reached Canada that King George VI had died during the night.

St Laurent was concerned about what would be the appropriate Royal Style and Titles to be used in the Canadian proclamation of the Queen. Having the Royal Title reflect the equal status of the nations of the Commonwealth had not been settled before the death of the King. Several of St Laurent's advisers, including me, thought Canada should drop some of the obsolete phraseology and specifically include the words 'Queen of Canada.' St Laurent, however, decided that any change from the forms used at the accession of George VI would offend the traditionalists and perhaps start a political controversy. He felt that if no change was made, no controversy could arise. If questions were raised in public, his explanation would be that appropriate changes in the Royal Titles could be discussed by the prime ministers of the Commonwealth countries at their next meeting. The British government itself did not wait for consultation, but changed the Royal Style and Titles when the Queen's accession was proclaimed in London. Once the British had made a change, Canada could follow their lead without criticism, and I realized how wise St Laurent had been.

The new Royal Style and Titles for Canada and for Australia and New Zealand were discussed at the meeting of Commonwealth prime ministers in December 1952. It was agreed that they no longer needed to be uniform. For Canada the new style was 'Elizabeth the Second, by the Grace of God, of the United Kingdom, Canada and Her other Realms and Territories, Queen, Head of the Commonwealth, Defender of the Faith.' Except for the insertion of 'Canada' it was precisely the same as the Royal Style and Titles proclaimed in Britain on the Queen's accession.

St Laurent decided the change should be approved by Parliament early in 1953. He explained to the House that, in the case of Canada, Australia and New Zealand, it had been almost simultaneously suggested by the representatives of the three countries that it would be desirable to retain in the Royal Style and Titles used in those countries 'United Kingdom' as well as the name of their country to indicate that it was the sovereign of the United Kingdom who was recognized as their sovereign. He felt that that was in accord with the historical development of Canada's constitutional relations. Later in his speech he described the evolution of the Commonwealth as an affirmation of the equality of human beings on a universal scale of which Canadians could be proud, just as they were all proud of being Canadian citizens because they can be so and can exercise all their rights as such without forgetting their racial origins and ancestral traditions, and without there being any effort by any of their fellow citizens to make them over into any other kind of Canadian than they happen to be.

Diefenbaker spoke on the bill for the Opposition. The best evidence that St Laurent had succeeded in his effort to make the new Royal Style and Titles, with its recognition of Canada's national status and equality with Britain, acceptable is found in Diefenbaker's speech. He called St Laurent's speech 'a most moving address,' evidence that 'in respect to our system of government and to the unity that is provided by the crown there is no division, there is no diversity of opinion, there is but a common devotion.' When the bill passed later in the day, the members, at St Laurent's suggestion, sang 'God Save the Queen'

St Laurent had been modest in saying the new Royal Styles and Titles had been almost simultaneously suggested by Canada, Australia and New Zealand. I was present at the meeting at which agreement was reached, and the initiative came from St Laurent himself. Through the form adopted he had avoided the accusation of colonialism and at the same time provided a measure of insurance against the charge that a French-speaking prime minister was seeking to weaken the British connection or attachment to the Crown. After that debate the traditional charge against the Liberal party would not be heard again until 1956.

Redistribution

There was no spectacular program to present to Parliament in 1952. The most controversial business was redistribution, the adjusting of the boundaries of constituencies for elections to the House of Commons. From Confederation until the 1930s redistribution had been the most partisan question in Parliament and had taken up the greater part of one session every 10 years, following the census.

Saskatchewan and Manitoba had lost population during the war years and in the 1947 redistribution lost one member each without much agitation. Saskatchewan was to lose three constituencies in 1952, and one of them was to be Lake Centre, represented by Diefenbaker. The constituency had had a small population in 1947 and had been saved because Diefenbaker was the only Tory MP from the province. In 1952 there would have been no way to spare Lake Centre without obvious unfairness. The MPs knew that, but the public paid little attention to the details. It was therefore not hard to gain credence for the charge that the Liberal majority had gerrymandered Diefenbaker out of his seat; it was precisely the kind of cause that suited Diefenbaker best. In a very effective speech in the House, he assumed the role of the underdog. That role he never again dropped, even when he led a government with the greatest majority in history.

There was no other substantial criticism of the 1952 redistribution. I have always felt, and often said, the main credit for the fairest redistribution ever made by Parliament belongs to Walter Harris, who was chairman of the Committee on Redistribution. He had the unwavering backing of St Laurent. But fair though the redistribution was, the charge of discrimination tended to persist, and that was the main reason redistribution by independent commission appealed to me.

8 Member of Parliament and Minister of the Crown

Secretary to the Cabinet

A change of status

St Laurent was 70 on 1 February 1952. He promised his family that he would retire as soon as possible, and he hoped that retirement could be arranged long enough before the next general election to give his successor a chance to establish himself as prime minister. There were growing signs that the popularity of the government was declining, though I am not sure the prime minister realized it. After the session ended in July, he received a memorandum from Claxton describing the serious decline in the government's fortunes and prospects since the 1949 election and indicating the risks of defeat unless the trend was reversed. Claxton's opinion was that St Laurent as leader was the government's greatest asset. St Laurent's reaction to the memorandum and during subsequent discussion in the cabinet was that if his retirement might mean the defeat of the government, he should not retire.

Word quickly spread that the leader would stay through another election. There was even some pressure in the party, by those fearing further deterioration of public support, to have an election before the end of 1952, but St Laurent refused to consider

J.W.P. appointed Secretary to the Cabinet, June 1952. Press photo of family at
550 Maple Lane. Left to right, J.W.P., Ruth, Alan, Peter, Jane, Margaret.

that idea. Instead, he decided to rest as much as possible at his summer home at St Patrick and to embark on a vigorous campaign to restore the fortunes of the government in the fall.

Meanwhile my own status in the public service had changed, as the result of a major shift in External Affairs, which left the office of High Commission in Britain vacant. Norman Robertson was not really happy as secretary to the cabinet, and St Laurent offered to appoint him high commissioner in London. He accepted, and a new secretary to the cabinet had to be found. I had been in the Prime Minister's office for more than 14 years, technically on loan from External Affairs, without the security of a permanent senior public servant. I did not want to remain in the Prime Minister's Office after St Laurent retired. I was not interested in becoming a diplomat. I discussed my future with the prime minister, who asked if I would like to succeed Robertson. He hoped our working relationship would not change if I accepted. Believing St Laurent intended to retire before the next election, I accepted the post gratefully because of the security it offered for my family and for my own future. I was appointed on 2 June 1952.

The shift to the Cabinet Office was a greater change than I had anticipated. Only twice before had I seen a cabinet in action. I discovered how little I knew about the way the cabinet operated. One of my new duties was to attend cabinet meetings. Fortunately for me Gordon Robertson was assistant secretary; he attended the meetings and drafted the minutes, and guided me through the procedures.

Unlike in 1946 I found the meetings exceedingly businesslike; St Laurent hated wasting time. Ministers who served under Mackenzie King and later St Laurent said that Mackenzie King often let his meetings drag on too long but perhaps got a better sense of how the public was likely to view decisions. St Laurent was always familiar with each ministers' proposals, sometimes better informed than the ministers themselves, but he may occasionally have failed to permit enough discussion.

Before meetings St Laurent would go over the agenda and decide, with my help, the order in which items would be discussed. At the meetings he was attentive and rarely impatient. No minister was restrained from presenting his views for fear St Laurent might take offence, but some ministers were probably restrained by fear of appearing ill informed or ineffective. More than any prime minister I have known, St Laurent did not dominate his cabinet by imposing his authority, but by his sheer intellect, his wide knowledge and his unequalled persuasiveness.

Close as I had been to the centre of government for a decade and more, it was a new experience to observe the complex interrelationships among ministers and the way decisions were reached. The House of Commons, as a spectacle, had fascinated me for years, but the cabinet was even more interesting and revealed more of the motives and characters of those in public life. Preparing the agenda for meetings with St Laurent, too, gave me a new insight into policy-making. At the cabinet table I sat on St Laurent's right, slightly back of his chair, close enough for a quiet word or a brief note. And, following up decisions with ministers and departments, in which Gordon Robertson had a large share, increased my familiarity with how the administration of government actually worked.

The secretary was chairman of the cabinet committee on the St Lawrence Seaway. That huge engineering undertaking required the approval of the governments of the United States and Canada, the state of New York and the provinces of Ontario and Québec. For me, that year on the committee was an education. The secretary was also chairman of the Security Panel, which supervised the process of screening public servants in sensitive positions and employees of firms with defence contracts, a subject for which I developed a strong distaste. I was also clerk of the Privy Council, a position established at Confederation. The clerk held precedence as the top public servant, but his functions were largely formal. Until 1939 all draft orders-in-council were considered by the whole cabinet. But senior ministers became so deeply involved in the wartime administration that a committee of the cabinet was set up to deal with routine matters, including the approval of orders-in-council. That practice continued after the war. Except for signing orders-in-council, I did none of the work of the clerk of the Privy Council, which was performed efficiently and conscientiously by deputy clerk, Arthur Hill.

Before the war all government contracts were submitted direct to the cabinet by government departments. I gathered that the main interest of ministers in contracts had been to make sure they were placed in the right constituencies! After 1939, contracts were considered by the committee set up for routine business. Each contract, if approved, was covered by a separate order-in-council. The committee had no staff to examine critically the contents of contracts. When he offered me the appointment, I told the prime minister I felt it was not good enough to have contracts let without the scrutiny of competent officials. Contracts should, I suggested, go first to the Treasury Board for examination, and those approved by the board at each of its meetings could be submitted to the routine committee as a bundle and covered by a single order-in-council. St Laurent accepted the suggestion, and a reform was made that vastly improved the way the government was administered.

I was also given a small but unique task. The coronation of the Queen was to take place in June 1953. St Laurent asked me to take charge of the distribution of the tickets allotted in Westminster Abbey to Canada. I strengthened my own hand by deciding not to go to the coronation. I was so strict in following the table of precedence and making exceptions for no one that a number of tickets were left over. I suggested that we allot two tickets to each university, to which St Laurent agreed. We felt that the universities might, by giving the tickets to wealthy potential benefactors, increase their endowments. Whether or not that happened I never found out, even in the case of Sir James Dunn, who asked Howe to get tickets for him and his wife. Howe told him there was nothing he could do, but he would see if I could do anything. I accepted the challenge, and with Milton Gregg's cooperation, the president of Mount Allison was persuaded to offer the tickets to the Dunns.

When I left the Prime Minister's Office I did not miss the daily attendance in the gallery of the House of Commons, and I readily gave up my association with the National Liberal Federation, which was obviously incompatible with my position as a regular public servant.

The beginning of National television

The Massey Commission recommended that television broadcasting should be started in Canada by the Canadian Broadcasting Corporation and remain under the control of the CBC. St Laurent was unenthusiastic about television and wanted to delay having it in Canada as long as possible. Eventually he yielded, and the CBC was authorized to start stations on an experimental basis in Ottawa, Montreal and Toronto. There was growing discontent with the failure to extend the services, which extension of course would require additional financing from the government. Howe gave the impetus to the wider development. His main interest was not in television but in stimulating the electronics industry. He told me one day that he thought Davidson Dunton, the chairman of the CBC, was dragging his feet, and asked me to talk to Dunton to try to get something moving. Howe professed to believe that Dunton was more likely to listen to me than to him. After speaking to St Laurent, who reluctantly agreed that it was time to move ahead, I arranged to have lunch with Dunton, and at lunch we worked out a plan for the next stage of expansion.

The CBC would establish its own stations in Halifax, Winnipeg and Vancouver, and applications would be received from private operators for stations in other places. Private stations would be required to broadcast CBC mainline programs. Under the plan there were to be no second private stations in any city until country-wide coverage had been achieved.

The range of effective coverage of a station had to be settled to avoid duplication of service. I became an instant expert. I told Dunton TV stations should not be less than 40 miles apart. When he asked how I had arrived at that figure so quickly, I replied that the distance between Toronto and Hamilton was 40 miles, and Hamilton was too big a place not to have its own station.

The cabinet quickly accepted the recommendation that the government finance the establishment of CBC stations in Halifax, Winnipeg and Vancouver. St Laurent announced the decision in Vancouver during his western tour in September 1952, and it was well received.

In November the cabinet accepted the rest of the plan Dunton and I had proposed for nation-wide television coverage. The Speech from the Throne opening Parliament announced that the CBC would receive applications from private operators to serve areas not served by CBC stations. The objective was to make television widely available across the country through cooperation between the CBC and private stations. The policy was received with widespread approval. I have mixed feelings today about having been midwife to Canadian television.

A visit to British Columbia

In the summer of 1952 I made several short visits with St Laurent to the Lower St Lawrence and the Saguenay district. He asked me if I would accompany him on a visit to British Columbia for the annual meeting of the Canadian Bar Association in Vancouver, being held in conjunction with the opening of the new building of the law faculty of the University of British Columbia, where he was to receive an honorary degree

We met at the end of August in Calgary, where I was visiting my mother. On the way to Vancouver we flew over the Crow's Nest Pass to Trail to see the huge smelter of Consolidated Mining. Big industrial undertakings fascinated St Laurent; that summer he had already visited the Alcan Aluminum smelter at Arvida, in the Saguenay region. Three brief stops at towns on Lake Okanagan were also made before we reached Vancouver. Afterwards there was a visit to Victoria and Esquimalt Naval Base, and then a motor trip the whole length of the eastern shore of the island that included an inspection at Chemainus of the largest and oldest sawmill in British Columbia. The tour was completed at Prince Rupert and Smithers. Speeches were made almost everywhere, some short and others substantial. There were a few Liberal functions, which I did not attend, but most were nonpolitical, and I was able to help prepare the speeches for those.

It was easy for me to stay away from Liberal party functions, but it was not possible to avoid discussing partisan problems with members of Parliament who had been in the habit of talking to me while I was head of the Prime Minister's Office. Jack Gibson, the MP for Comox-Alberni, raised the only question of importance. He said the minister from British Columbia, Robert Mayhew, was well liked but, because of his age and the relative isolation of his constituency, Victoria, from the rest of the province, was failing to keep in touch with the party organization, and the members were becoming discouraged. He told me that Sinclair, the brilliant MP from Vancouver North, would leave public life before the next election unless he became a minister. Gibson felt that Mayhew should be replaced by Sinclair without delay. I reminded him that Ralph Campney had cut into his career at the Vancouver bar under pressure to enter Parliament and, like Sinclair, had strong claims to consideration.

British Columbia, in population, had so far outstripped all the other provinces except Ontario and Quebec that I thought, but did not tell Gibson, it was entitled to two ministers, especially since it was so far from Ottawa. I reported Gibson's views to St Laurent and reminded him that in addition to Mayhew's portfolio the office of solicitor general was vacant. He agreed that there should be two ministers, but he had such respect and affection for Mayhew that he shrank from the conventional course of asking Mayhew to resign and accept a seat in the Senate. I had thought of another solution. Canada was now at peace with Japan and was about to restore diplomatic relaions. Mayhew, I suggested, would make an admirable ambassador. St Laurent himself felt that Mayhew, as a former minister of the Crown, would give prestige to the embassy. He gave me the task of persuading Mayhew to consider the new career. At first Mayhew was doubtful about his capacity to fill the post, until I convinced him that the Japanese would be honoured to have a minister of his stature become the first ambasssador after the war. As it turned out, no one could have filled the position more admirably. Mayhew became ambassador on 15 October and Sinclair and Campney were appointed to the cabinet the same day. The two ministers worked together in complete harmony until the end of the St Laurent regime, and there is little doubt that that cabinet shift greatly improved Liberal fortunes in British Columbia.

The visit to the West was enjoyable as well as useful, except for a stop on the way home at the Fort Garry Hotel in Winnipeg, which, unhappily for me, led to a partisan controversy. The affair is recounted at length in *My Years with Louis St. Laurent*. All I need to say here is that I was accused, on the basis of a press report, of causing the demotion of the hotel manager. It was the only time in my 15 years as a public servant that my conduct was attacked in Parliament. I could not have been defended better, but I felt frustrated at being unable to speak for myself because of the silence imposed by practice and tradition on civil servants. After that experience I knew I would never be acceptable as secretary to the cabinet of a Conservative government, nor would I want to serve such a cabinet.

The Senate or Newfoundland

I had another and more compelling reason for being uneasy about remaining as secretary to the cabinet. The more I thought about St Laurent facing another election, the more concerned I became. No one on his staff or available to St Laurent elsewhere had my experience in election campaigns, and there was no one he was so likely to trust to organize his campaign. He needed me, especially as a traffic policeman to keep him from unnecessary pressure.

I went with St Laurent and Abbott to a Commonwealth economic conference in London in November and December 1952. One evening when we were alone, I asked St Laurent if he would like me to travel with him during the election campaign as I had done in 1949. He said the answer was yes, but how could it be arranged? I could not go back to the Prime Minister's Office without a loss of income and security, I said, but there was another possibility. St Laurent, I knew, had undertaken to appoint the government leader in the Senate, Wishart Robertson, to be Speaker if the government won the election. That would leave the position of government leader in the Senate vacant. I had no ambition to be a senator, but appointment to the Senate would enable me to work full time in the election campaign. If the election was lost, a senatorship would provide security for my family. St Laurent agreed to that solution.

The appointment would have to be to an Ontario vacancy. At St Laurent's request I discussed the proposal with the senior minister from Ontario when we got back to Ottawa. Howe was not enthusiastic about having an Ontario seat pre-empted, but said, characteristically, if that was what the prime minister wanted, he was agreeable.

Happily, a unique alternative presented itself. On 31 January 1953 Premier Smallwood came to see me in Ottawa. He told me that Gordon Bradley, the minister from Newfoundland, was in poor health and would like to be appointed to the Senate before the election. Smallwood said he had come to Ottawa to consult me about who would be a suitable successor. I knew few Newfoundland personalities even by repute, and I could suggest only two or three names, none of which he found acceptable. I then raised the question whether there was not someone on the mainland, where many Newfoundlanders were successful in business and the professions, in Toronto, Montreal and elsewhere.

To my utter astonishment Smallwood replied that if I had not become secretary to the cabinet, I would be their man. The very idea seemed to me crazy. He had performed a miracle by bringing Newfoundland into Confederation, but I did not believe he could perform another by getting the people of Newfoundland to accept a mainlander as minister. Newfoundlanders would say, Now that Canada has hooked us, they are telling us there is no Newfoundlander fit to represent them in the cabinet in Ottawa. He agreed that that might be said by a few but added that when he had finished presenting me to the voters, I would not recognize myself.

I was tempted by the rosy picture he painted. I did not tell him about the Senate but admitted I would like to be in a position where I could manage the prime minister's election campaign. I could not consider his proposal if I had to campaign for myself. Unless I could devote myself to travel with the prime minister, I was not interested. He assured me I could be elected without even putting in an appearance in the riding, though he hoped I could manage a couple of days. At the end of the day I would not say yes or no, and reminded him that a minister would not be chosen by him or by me but by the prime minister.

Smallwood made his extraordinary suggestion on a Saturday. I could hardly wait until Monday to report to St Laurent, who had been away for the weekend. He liked the idea. Knowing how hard it was for Smallwood to keep a secret, I said I had warned him that if there was even a rumour, the plan would fail. But by good fortune the secret was kept until mid-May. St Laurent had time to discuss the proposal with Bradley and the other MPs from New-foundland, who all agreed to support me. When the rumour was published in May, the idea was considered so absurd that no one believed it or tried to follow it up.

One warm evening in May I ran into Gordon Higgins, one of the two Conservative MPs from Newfoundland. He had been at a convivial party and stopped to talk to me. I was afraid he had heard the rumour and was both surprised and amused, though not greatly reassured, when he told me that he would be in the Tory cabinet after the election, and that I did not need to worry about keeping my job, as they could not do without my brains.

From secretary to cabinet minister

My final duty as secretary to the cabinet was to assist the prime minister at the meeting of the Commonwealth prime ministers in London, held after the coronation. Mr and Mrs St Laurent left Ottawa on May 19 to travel to England by sea. Howe carried on as acting prime minister until the end of May, when he and several other ministers flew to London. I flew to London later; after taking off from a fuel stop at Gander, I looked down at the white houses in the fishing settlements of the north side of Bonavista Bay and along the Straight Shore and wondered at my audacity in undertaking to return two weeks later to ask the people in that district, which I had never visited and where I knew almost no one, to elect me to represent them in the Parliament of their new country. The prospect filled me with awe.

I submitted my resignation as secretary to the cabinet on 28 April, the day the prime minister began his talks with Bradley about my candidature. The final details about my appointment to the cabinet and my candidature in Newfoundland were to be discussed with Bradley and Smallwood in London, after the coro-nation. Bradley, Smallwood and I met in my bedroom at the

St. Laurent Cabinet 1952-53 with J.W.P. as Secretary — a Karsh photo; Lionel Chevrier was absent.

Dorchester Hotel after dinner on the evening of my arrival and discussed the opening of my election campaign in Bonavista-Twillingate. We agreed that I would go to St John's on 15 June, and that Smallwood and I would meet Bradley's flight at Gander on his return from London on 17 June and drive from there to begin our visit to the constituency.

One pleasant feature of the visit to England was a trip to Oxford. St Laurent had been offered an honorary degree by Oxford University, and I told him I would like to go at the same time and take one of the degrees I had earned years before. The degrees were conferred at a ceremony in the afternoon, and later St Laurent and his party attended a reception at Rhodes House for the Canadian students at Oxford. The rest of the party stayed that night at the leading hotel, but I decided to sleep at New College.

The night was cold and raw, and the floor of the bedroom so tilted that it was hard to stay in the bed; I had very little sleep.

The prime minister and I flew back to Ottawa on 10 June. When the cabinet met on Friday 12 June, I was present in the

J.W.P. admitted to cabinet, June 1953 at press conference in Prime Minister's Office. St Laurent congratulates J.W.P. under portrait of Mackenzie King.

Setting out from Lewisporte on the coastal steamer Glencoe *to start J.W.P.'s campaign in Bonavista-Twillingate, June 1953.*

morning as secretary. Towards the end of the morning I was asked to withdraw. The prime minister then informed his colleagues of the resignation of Alphonse Fournier and Gordon Bradley, who were appointed respectively to the Exchequer Court and the Senate, and of his recommendation of my appointment as secretary of state of Canada in place of Bradley. Just before lunch St Laurent drove me to Government House, where I was sworn into the Privy Council and took the oath as secretary of state. In the afternoon I returned as a minister to the cabinet meeting.

My appointment to the cabinet was a sensation for the press. Years later a friend doing research on the papers of the late Grant Dexter, the representative of the *Winnipeg Free Press* in the parliamentary press gallery, sent me a copy of an extract from a letter Dexter had written to Victor Sifton on 22 May 1953: 'Pickersgill sent me word that he is entering the cabinet as sec of state and assistant to the prime minister. He will take Bradley's seat in Newfoundland and Premier Smallwood has guaranteed his election. Jack will now become an honest man, possessing power properly, but in due course (unless I am greatly mistaken) will land on his face in the street. His constituency is a pocket borough

Meeting at Twillingate on the first night. Smallwood assembled all the children to pronounce the name Pickersgill.

and will go Liberal only so long as the Liberals are in office.'
Luckily for me Grant's prophecy was not borne out. I lasted for 14
years and then left by my own decision at a time of my own
choosing.

Minister from Newfoundland

Introduction to Bonavista-Twillingate

In the morning I had been secretary to the cabinet, sitting between
the prime minister and Howe close to the head of the table; in the
afternoon I was seated at the bottom of the table as the most
junior minister. It did not take me long to realize that my influence
on cabinet had not increased.

The prime minister announced my appointment to the press
and said I would be seeking election in Newfoundlandand, and
Premier Smallwood disclosed that I would be the Liberal candidate in Bonavista-Twillingate, the constituency previously represented by Gordon Bradley. For a candidate to be a cabinet minister
was a great advantage, and my occupation on the ballot was
described as Minister of the Crown. I had never set foot in the
constituency. Smallwood's announcement made it clear that I
could spend only a few days in the riding because I would be
travelling with the prime minister during his campaign.

Most important to me in the campaign was Charles R. Granger,
who had been Bradley's executive assistant. Smallwood and
Senator Ray Petten, the Liberal party treasurer in Newfoundland, felt that Granger's support was indispensable, and I was
relieved and pleased when he readily and generously agreed
to continue as my executive assistant. His knowledge of the
constituency was invaluable, and I can never repay the debt I owe
to his unselfish devotion. Next to Granger my most valuable
supporter was Ray Petten. I have reason to believe that he may
have suggested my name to Smallwood as a possible minister
from Newfoundland. Over the years I avoided many pitfalls
because of his wise and unobtrusive counsel, and his thoughtfulness never failed.

A cannon salute to J.W.P. on Fogo Island.

Two days after becoming a minister I flew to St John's for a couple of days organized by Smallwood for maximum publicity. On 17 June, Smallwood, Granger and I boarded the coastal steamer *Glencoe*. Smallwood had told me that when he introduced me in Newfoundland I would not recognize myself, and after our first stop I realized that he had not exaggerated. The introduction from the deck of the *Glencoe* lasted at least half an hour. I spoke for less than five minutes, and what I said was incorporated into his introduction at the next port of call. The same thing happened at every stop.

At that time it was the custom to salute distinguished visitors with a volley from sealing guns. I was given such a salute for the first time at the public wharf at Twillingate in the late afternoon. No one had warned me, and I was startled and showed it. The gunners were amused and pleased by the effect they had produced. That evening, in the Orange Hall at Twillingate, Smallwood

J.W.P. discussing unemployment insurance for fishermen at Herring Neck.

brought all the children to the front of the hall, sat them down on the edge of the platform and taught them to pronounce my name. More than 10 years later one of those children, Eric Facey, became my secretary.

The whole campaign fell into perspective the next morning at Herring Neck. After Smallwood and I had spoken, while everyone else was gathered around Smallwood, one of the fishermen came up to me and said, 'It was nice of you, Mr Pickersgill, to come here and let us see what you look like, but you would be elected just the same if you had stayed at home, so long as you were Joey's man.' It was also at Herring Neck that another fisherman pointed across to the local fish merchant's premises and asked me why the men who worked there had unemployment insurance and the fishermen who provided the work had not. I explained that fishermen were independent operators, not wage earners, but he was not satisfied by my explanation, and neither was I.

The second night, after dark, the *Glencoe* reached Joe Batt's Arm, on Fogo Island, and was met by a flotilla of all the fishing vessels in the harbour. The boats were flying flags and carrying lanterns, a thrilling sight as they moved towards us in the dark. The fish plant at Joe Batt's Arm was the only building large enough for a meeting. We met in a large room lit by a single gasoline lantern. By that time Smallwood had lost his voice. He had to whisper the words of introduction to Gordon Janes, the local member of the legislature, who then repeated them aloud. Janes tried to abbreviate the message, but Smallwood insisted that he repeat every word. That meeting was the only one at which my speech was not an anticlimax.

Glencoe *arrived at Joe Batt's Arm on Fogo Island at night — a good reception in the dark.*

At Musgrave Harbour, on the third day, one of the local merchants, a celebrated wag, came aboard. He greeted me with the question, 'Do you really think there is no Newfoundlander good enough to sit in the Canadian government?' Fortunately, before I could reply, another Newfoundlander said: 'Shut up, Jim. There are forty thousand Newfoundlanders in Toronto. Surely we can take one Canadian down here!' I did not think I could improve on that answer.

That afternoon I had a long sleep while we rounded Cape Freels, a notoriously rough part of the northeast coast. Charlie Granger woke me just before we reached the wharf at Wesleyville, where a huge crowd was assembled from all the settlements along the shore, from Lumsden to Valleyfield. Smallwood had recovered his voice, and promptly launched into an introduction that seemed to go on forever. I was in terrible fear I would be seasick the moment he handed me the microphone; my fists were clenched so hard that my nails made my hands bleed. I was spared the ultimate humiliation, but my speech was very short.

Wesleyville was to be the last stop on that stage of my campaign. The next morning I was to be picked up by a float plane and taken to Gander to fly back to the mainland to join St Laurent for the opening of his campaign. Though the sun was shining brightly, the sea was too rough for the plane to land. Smallwood persuaded the captain of the *Glencoe* to go several miles off course so that we could land at Hare Bay, which was connected by road to Gambo, a station on the railway. We first made a stop at Greenspond, where Smallwood introduced me from the steps of the post office, and I made a short speech. In his introduction Smallwood called Greenspond his birthplace. I asked him later how many birthplaces he had, since he had told me he was born at Gambo. He admitted that Gambo was true but claimed he had been taken to live at Greenspond before he could remember.

A car was available at Hare Bay to drive us to Gambo. There was no road from Gambo to Gander, and no train until long after the last plane for the mainland that day. The only way to get to Gander was on a speeder on the railway. The speeder was oper-

Last stop on the Glencoe *campaign — at Greenspond.*

ated for the fire patrol by Ernest Stead, who took us and the three mainland journalists who had been with us on the trip the 25 miles to Gander. At one stage a suitcase belonging to one of the journalists fell off the speeder, and his clothes were scattered down the railway embankment. The sight of the premier of Newfoundland scrambling down the bank and gathering up the clothes is one I shall never forget. At Benton, nine miles from Gander, we had to wait until the eastbound passenger train passed us. We telephoned the airport to have the plane for Montreal delayed as long as possible and to have a taxi waiting at the Gander railway station. We arrived at the airport with one minute to spare. As we entered the terminal I heard passengers being called for a plane to Teheran. Gander in those days really was 'the crossroads of the world'; the contrast with the isolation of the coastal settlements we had left a few hours before was almost too great to credit.

I was in Newfoundland again on 2 July, with the prime minister, but we did not set foot in my future constituency. On 19 July I met Smallwood in St John's. We travelled by train to Clarenville that evening, spent the night at the hotel there and started out the next morning by road for Bonavista. The road to Bonavista was the only road of more than a few miles in the whole constituency in 1953.

Our first stop, an outdoor meeting, was at Lethbridge, on Goose Bay in Bonavista Bay. The weather was magnificent, and I thought the sea one of the most beautiful sights I had ever seen. I did not then realize that that spot would be our home for the next two summers. We stopped at every settlement along the shore road to Bonavista for brief meetings and reached a clearing on the outskirts of Bonavista town at about 4 p.m. Every truck in the place and most of the cars were assembled there, with one or two bands, and we began a motorcade through every street and road in that remarkable fishing settlement of 4000 people. In the evening there was an outdoor meeting at which the microphone was snatched out of my hand by a man named Hubert Chard, who denounced Smallwood for the recently established town council. Municipalities were just being started in Newfoundland and were highly unpopular. When Chard concluded, Smallwood took the microphone and announced that the town council would be dissolved. Several years were to pass before Bonavista became a municipality.

We spent the night at the hotel in Bonavista, and the next morning were picked up by an amphibious plane belonging to Bowater's, the company that owned the huge paper mill at Corner Brook. We flew to Glovertown, where I first met Captain Max Burry, the leading businessman of the place. Smallwood and I had our midday meal with the Burrys and then spoke to the crowd that had assembled around the sawdust pile in Burry's shipyard. Burry became one of my most active supporters for the whole of my period in public life and a lifelong friend. Later that day we visited Port Blandford and Musgravetown by plane. Those two days concluded my election campaign in Bonavista-Twillingate. In a radio broadcast I promised, if elected, to return with my wife and one of our children to campaign after the election. Margaret, Peter, not yet eight years old, and I were in Newfoundland four days after the election, and on the regular voyage of the coastal vessel *Glencoe* on 15 August.

For four days we lived on the coastal steamer and visited all the ports of call in the constituency. We disembarked at King's Cove and drove to Bonavista. During the voyage in June, I had got to know the officers and most of the crew. We were given a wonderful welcome on board and soon felt thoroughly at home. We discovered that no one had taken my promise to come back seriously; we were made even more welcome because it had happened. That visit was the beginning of a love affair our whole family has had with Newfoundland ever since.

From Bonavista we drove along the south shore of the bay. We learned that it might be possible to rent Mrs Herman Quinton's cottage at Portland, on beautiful Goose Bay, and did so: our family lived in that lovely place during the summers of 1954 and 1955. We spent a weekend at the Balmoral Hotel at Clarenville, where by chance several members of the fish trades association were also staying. It was under those agreeable circumstances that I first came to know many of the fish merchants of Newfoundland. Charlie Granger was with us throughout the visit to the constituency and at Clarenville, and he made sure we met and talked to everyone we should. Ray Petten met us at Clarenville and drove us to St John's, where we spent a couple of days during which Smallwood had a dinner for the seven members of Parliament and their wives.

I have always believed that my postelection tour with Margaret and Peter to thank the voters was the real foundation of my strength in Bonavista-Twillingate in the five more general elections I won. For my part, I had taken an initial step in understanding Newfoundland.

St Laurent's second general election

St Laurent's tour began in Windsor, Ontario, on 22 June. The campaign was essentially a repeat performance of 1949. The four western provinces were included, and happily there was no week lost to laryngitis. The campaign, less strenuous than in 1949, was still a remarkable feat for a man 71 years old.

St Laurent's main theme was the record of the government. Instead of ignoring Drew as he had done in 1949, he repeatedly contrasted the government's responsible record with the irresponsible promises of the Opposition. Drew had promised to reduce the tax burden by half a billion dollars and to embark on a great variety of costly projects. Later he suggested he would reduce expenditures on defence. St Laurent wanted to deal at once with Drew's program, but I persuaded him that doing so would give Drew too much prominence. To remind the public of the government's record would keep the Tory program in the shade. By taking advantage of every nonpartisan opportunity St Laurent was able to stress his role as leader of the country rather than merely leader of a party.

The opening meeting in Windsor was staggering, organized with all the fanfare Canadians associate with American political meetings. I felt embarrassed by the presence of cheerleaders, but the audience seemed to find it normal and responded enthusiastically. The reception during the rest of that week in western Ontario with bands, majorettes, civic receptions, and many nonpartisan gatherings was as warm as in 1949. The climax was a loudly applauded speech from the deck of a ship in Hamilton Harbour emblazoned with flags and banners.

The second week began in New Brunswick and continued in Prince Edward Island on 1 July, with a late arrival that evening in Newfoundland. That visit was confined to St John's and the Avalon Peninsula, and lasted only one day, but it was more productive than the visit in 1949: the Liberal party won all seven seats. The next day we flew to Chatham, New Brunswick, and went on by train, with whistle stops in northeastern New Brunswick and the Matapédia Valley.

The western tour began in Winnipeg, where St Laurent addressed the Ukrainian-Canadian Convention on NATO and the dangers of Communist imperialism. In Vancouver the prime min-

Campaign 1953 at Calgary. Louis St Laurent with J.W.P.'s sister Jane.

ister opened the Davis Cup tennis match and from a public meeting made his second national broadcast. The next day in Victoria he contrasted Drew's promise to reduce military expenditures with General G.R. Pearkes's demand that defence expenditures be increased. Despite an enthusiastic Liberal meeting, Pearkes was not defeated.

In Calgary St Laurent presented prizes in the evening at the Stampede and spoke briefly during a sudden storm, while the hailstones bounced off his head. There was also a Liberal luncheon. He and I were becoming rather bored with the repetitive speeches, and we tried to liven up the luncheon by replying to an editorial in the *Calgary Herald*, which had been in the form of a bedtime story about hot air and cold facts. I had let myself be carried away and had persuaded St Laurent to include a parody of the editorial: 'And now I have a little bedtime story with a moral. Once upon a time in another land a political party had been out of office so long it was willing to try any kind of hot air to blow its way in. Now it so happened that the government of that other land had not been paying its way and it had not been reducing the debt of the country and it had not been cutting taxes. This political party that had been out of office so long didn't bother about cold facts. Oh no, it just went merrily along promising to balance the budget and reduce taxes. And the people believed them and put them in office. They are now begging the people not to ask them to keep their promises to reduce the taxes. They find they need quite desperately to meet the cold facts of life.' The parody was directed at Drew, but the parallel with Eisenhower's campaign in 1952 was obvious. The American ambassador protested informally to Abbott, and Abbott passed on the rebuke to me. I promised not to do it again. Fortunately the Eisenhower administration did not hold the speech against us.

St Laurent opened the Edmonton Exhibition on 13 July and spoke in the evening at a public meeting, at which he repeated the undertaking already given in Parliament that the government would not permit the export of natural gas until the needs of Canada were met. On his last day in the west, in Regina, he stated that the government was not yet convinced that the building of a dam for power and irrigation on the South Saskatchewan River would justify the cost. No doubt that statement contributed to the Liberal losses in 1953. The Saskatchewan dam became a major issue for the rest of St Laurent's period in office.

At the Lakehead, now Thunder Bay, St Laurent and Howe addressed a Liberal meeting with the prime minister stressing the benefits to come from the St Lawrence Seaway and the virtues of C.D. Howe. I was rather embarrassed by a clamour from the audience to have me speak, the consequence, no doubt, of the novelty of my entry into the cabinet. I sensed at once that Howe was not pleased. I sat stolidly on the platform until the demand ceased. St Laurent and I had agreed from the outset that I would not speak, except in Winnipeg, where Garson felt I should do so briefly because I was a Manitoban.

St Laurent had his first important meeting in Québec at Trois-Rivieres on 17 July after which he campaigned in the province for several days. He had dropped me off in Ottawa, and I flew to Newfoundland for my second appearance in Bonavista-Twillingate. I rejoined him on 23 July at Moncton where he recorded a national broadcast. We went on to Halifax for an evening meeting and the next day drove through the Annapolis Valley and Lunenburg County. There he made a speech on the fisheries, about which my ignorance was profound, and his not much better.

We were in London on 27 July for a public meeting, at which St Laurent's speech, to be broadcast, had to start at a precise time. The meeting began too soon, the chairman concluded the introduction before the broadcast was to start, and I was called on, without preparation, to fill the gap. I surprised myself by holding the audience and was gratified by the applause.

The rest of that week was spent in southern Ontario. I spoke once, very briefly, in the park at Simcoe, in my native Norfolk County, where I took issue with the *Globe and Mail*. A journalist friend who happened to be a Tory told me I was foolish to take on a newspaper, but I said no one in Bonavista-Twillingate had ever heard of the *Globe and Mail*.

St Laurent spent the last week in the Eastern Townships, Montreal and Ottawa, with well-attended meetings. As in 1949 the climax of the campaign was the meeting on Friday in Toronto, at Maple Leaf Gardens. The Gardens were filled, and the audience enthusiastic. St Laurent had no engagements on Saturday, but he made an unplanned visit to Baie St-Paul on Sunday, 9 August, election eve, to reply to a last-minute attack by Frederic Dorion, a former Independent, who this time was appearing as a Conservative candidate. Dorion was defeated.

On election day Margaret and I voted in Ottawa, drove to see Jane at her summer camp in the Laurentians and from there went to St-Lin to visit Laurier's birthplace. We did not get back to Ottawa until the polls in Newfoundland had been closed for more than an hour. There had already been frantic telephone calls with the news that I had been elected overwhelmingly, and that the Liberal party had won all seven seats in Newfoundland. I was pleased, Margaret was relieved, and the whole family was tremendously excited.

The government won 172 seats out of 265 seats, as compared with 192 out of 262 in 1949 — not as great a victory but still a landslide. The best commentary on the election was made soon afterwards by Claxton, who wrote: 'Once again St. Laurent proved to be the star attraction of the whole campaign. I can't help feeling that we Liberals are extremely fortunate to be active in the party at a time when he is our leader. Not only is it inspiring to work with him and his colleagues, but I believe that it is a great privilege to be associated with the Liberal Party in his time.'

The first year in office

On the day I became a minister St Laurent had said that the duties of the secretary of state of Canada were relatively light, and that he planned to call upon me as a junior minister to assist him. The secretary of state's department was in the West Block of the Parliament Buildings, the prime minister's office was across the lawn in the East Block, and my office was directly opposite his, so it was easy to keep in touch. In the fall of 1953 the task of assisting the prime minister was not onerous. The postelection period was quiet. Pierre Asselin, the head of the Prime Minister's Office, had no trouble coping. Our relations were so close that he never hesitated to call me when he wanted advice or reassurance.

St Laurent discussed with me the selection of a minister from Québec to replace Fournier. I had never had any doubt about who it should be. Jean Lesage had been in Parliament for eight years, had been outstandingly useful as parliamentary assistant successively to the secretary of state for external affairs and the minister of finance and was a highly competent debater in the House. St Laurent was a little concerned that there would be no French-speaking minister from Montreal, but he agreed that Lesage was the outstanding candidate for promotion. He decided to accept

Howe's advice about Winters, who was appointed to Public Works. Lesage was appointed minister of resources and development, and Gordon Robertson became deputy minister.

I have always taken satisfaction from part I had in establishing the Lesage-Robertson partnership, which served Canada so well in many ways in subsequent years. I was also happy that R.B. Bryce should be my successor as secretary to the cabinet. St Laurent admired Bryce and had already found him easy to work with.

Ross Martin, who had left the Prime Minister's Office to join the cabinet secretariat, had the main responsibility for preparing and revising the early drafts of the Speech from the Throne. I continued to help with the drafting. My only contribution to the content was a paragraph on the fisheries.

The staff in my office was excellent. Charlie Granger and Audrey McQuarrie looked after Newfoundland; Sybil Rump, who had been my secretary in the Privy Council, was persuaded to become my private secretary; and, to deal with departmental matters, Teresa Maloney from the undersecretary's office joined my staff. No minister was better served. The deputy of the department was Charles Stein, whose title was undersecretary. He was conscientious and a good lawyer, but unimaginative, and our relations were never close.

That year as secretary of state was my least strenuous as a minister, despite the novelty of my being in the cabinet and in Parliament. Having few administrative duties, I began systematically to examine the functions of the department, which had almost no contact with the general public.

I discovered the Patent Office had a substantial backlog because it lacked sufficient staff. The Treasury Board would not approve more because the fees charged did not cover the costs of operating the office. The remedy seemed to me to be to raise the fees to make the office pay its way. That was done, extra staff were hired, and a small burden was removed from the Treasury. The office was still paying its way in 1991. I took similar action in the case of other agencies.

When Stuart Garson was provincial treasurer of Manitoba, he had told me that Canadian patent law created monopolies that kept many prices unduly high. With St Laurent's support I was able to have a commission of inquiry appointed into patents and copyright, headed by Chief Justice Ilsley of Nova Scotia. The other members were Guy Favreau and W.W. Buchanan — a formidable assemblage of brain power in one small commission.

From time to time important inventions were made by public servants in the course of their performance of their official duties. The law was unclear about the ownership of such inventions or the right to exploit them, and the practice varied from one department to another. Howe and I agreed that there should be a crown company to exploit such inventions while safeguarding the legitimate interests of the inventors. Canadian Patents and Development Limited, created in 1954, still exists and has been useful in protecting the public interest.

The secretary of state was the minister responsible for the Queen's Printer. The Printing Bureau was a large industrial operation. The volume of its production had grown rapidly and by 1953 the administration was almost chaotic. Edmond Cloutier, the Queen's Printer, was a past master of improvisation who did his thinking on paper and showered the minister endlessly with memoranda. I soon learned not to read a first edition since I never finished it before a revision arrived. Unless there was a more orderly administration, the Printing Bureau would be swamped. Consultants on management were hired, and their recommendations were accepted as a necessary step towards giving the Printing Bureau an up-to-date structure.

None of the reforms was spectacular, but when I moved on to a new department, I felt the one I was leaving was operating more efficiently.

On 12 November 1953, I took my seat in the House of Commons, where I was to serve for 14 years. When someone asked me what it was like to be an MP, I replied that it was like being inside a goldfish bowl, instead of looking into one. I resolved to look and to listen, and to speak as little as possible in my first session. Since members were not much interested in my department, it was not hard to keep that resolution.

I was aware that there were members, even on the government side of the House, who would not be sorry to see me stumble or even fall on my face. I was nervous, almost to the point of stage fright, before I rose to speak in the House. I discovered that holding the attention of Parliament was actually easier than keeping the attention of university students in a classroom, but I never lost a feeling of nervous tension whenever I had to begin a debate. The first time I spoke was in reply to a question by Stanley Knowles. I said, 'As this is a question concerning the government, I think it would more properly be directed to the prime minister.' I believe that was a suitably modest maiden speech.

My first speech in debate was on a Tory motion to set up a committee to recommend that future redistribution be performed by an independent commission instead of by the House of Commons. Since the secretary of state reported to Parliament for the chief electoral officer, the prime minister suggested that I support the motion on behalf of the government. Donald Fleming spoke for the Conservatives and made extravagant charges of gerrymander ing, dwelling particularly on the disappearance of Diefenbaker's former constituency of Lake Centre. I refuted the charge of unfairness to Diefenbaker at some length. It was perhaps a foretaste of things to come that Diefenbaker had a prominent place in my first partisan speech in Parliament. I argued that if redistribution was to be given to an independent commission, we should get the best possible commission, accept its report, live with it and not bring the matter back into the House.

George Drew had picked out of context some phrases from a speech I had made at the opening of the School of Public Administration at Carleton College. He asserted that my statements were 'a clear declaration of belief in the one-party state.' On those statements he based a vote of want of confidence in the government, to which St Laurent asked me to reply.

I opened by saying I was flattered that Drew had read my speech and even more flattered that he made it the excuse for lacking confidence in the government. At Carleton I had said that politicians lived by keeping their names before the public. I thanked Drew for bringing my name before the House. My agreement with him ended there. At that point Drew interjected, 'Well, sit down.' I did not sit down but went on to a disagree with the leader of the Opposition, and my disagreement covered several pages of *Hansard*. The House listened tolerantly as I gave an almost academic lecture on responsible government. I wanted no one-party state, but as long as the electorate and the members of the House gave the government their confidence, the government had the sole responsibility to govern and to take the blame. That, I believed, was the true parliamentary system, and the 'notion that in some mysterious way the opposition has a share in the responsibility for carrying on government is not.' The duty of the Opposition is to harass the government and to point out mistakes in government policy and performance.

That was my only lengthy speech in the first session. I tried to steer a middle course between the modesty appropriate in a junior member of the government and the desire to get useful experience in speaking, and I survived the first session without landing myself or the government in any trouble. I remember how pleased I was on the last day of the session to get a note from George Nowlan congratulating me on my parliamentary effort — a gesture that was the foundation of a lasting friendship.

After two sessions of Parliament I was still emotionally and psychologically more an official than a parliamentarian. Apart from the cabinet ministers and a few Liberal backbenchers who had been personal friends before my election, my friends were public servants rather than members, and I did not share in the social life of Parliament or the fraternizing in the lobbies. There were still many Liberal backbenchers I barely knew by sight.

I had decided never to get into controversy or debate with backbenchers, a rule I followed during my whole career in Parliament. The leader of the Opposition was my first opponent in debate, apart from one encounter with Donald Fleming.

I had taken the initiative in establishing a caucus of Liberal members from the Atlantic provinces, and I gave it much closer attention than Gregg or Winters did. I was convinced that if I could identify myself with all the Atlantic region, I could serve Newfoundland better.

My task of assisting the prime minister took little of my time, and while St Laurent was on his world tour, none at all. After his return in March 1954, he depended more and more on Bryce, though he never hesitated to call me when he was having difficulty making a decision.

The cabinet shuffle

My apprenticeship ended five days after the close of the 1954 session, when St Laurent made his most important cabinet shuffle. I was no longer secretary of state. Three of the senior ministers, Abbott of Finance, Claxton of National Defence and Chevrier of Transport, retired from the government on 30 June 1954, and two new ministers, George Marler and Roch Pinard, were appointed the next day.

Claxton had become increasingly restive after the election. When the fighting stopped in Korea, several of his friends, including me, urged him to move from Defence to another department. The reason would be to improve his chances of succeeding St Laurent, something that at one time he had hoped to do. In some ways no one was better fitted to head a government. He was perhaps equalled, but never surpassed, as an administrator; he had a thorough knowledge of all parts of Canada; and only St Laurent and Pearson in the cabinet had as great familiarity with the external world or as clear views of Canada's interests abroad. Claxton had the most innovative mind in the cabinet. His talent for political organization was outstanding, and his interest unflagging. But he lacked a light touch, an easy manner and appeal — what is now called charisma. Claxton was a dear friend, and until he retired, I was more constantly associated with him than with any other minister. He was offered an attractive position as Canadian head of Metropolitan Life. When he spoke about

J.W.P.'s most used official photograph.

retirement to the prime minister, St Laurent was not altogether surprised. But he was not happy at the prospect.

It was a greater surprise to St Laurent when Abbott approached him to ask whether he might be considered for appointment to a vacancy on the Supreme Court of Canada. The law required three of the nine judges to be members of the Québec bar. The existing vacancy was likely to create the only chance in Abbott's lifetime for such an appointment. Abbott's prospects of succeeding St Laurent as leader were better than Claxton's. He had headed a heavy department as successfully as Claxton, and though he did not have Claxton's unremitting industry, capacity for organization and roving imagination, he had many qualities in which Claxton was not his equal. He had a facile intelligence, an easier manner, and a felicity and fluency of expression unexceeded in Parliament. He was a more accomplished debater and a better public speaker. One of Abbott's few liabilities was a tendency, not always repressed, to deflate pomposity with flippant and occasionally frivolous interjections in debate. Unfortunately such remarks could be exploited to give the impression that he was not serious, that he did not 'care'; and that impression was reinforced by the apparent ease and rapidity with which he made decisions without seeming to reflect on the pros and cons with becoming gravity. But there was no question Abbott was the favourite to succeed St Laurent as leader.

My relations with Abbott were close, and there were few men whose cool judgment I valued more. Before I entered the government, Abbott warned me that my tendency to make sharp and flippant remarks might be acceptable in private but was apt to harm me in public life. I realized that his advice was sound, and I tried to follow it with, I am afraid, indifferent success.

St Laurent discussed Abbott's future with me. He shared my view that Abbott, though not learned, possessed, in a high degree, a judicial temperament. I remember saying once that if my life was at stake, there was no one I would rather have decide the issue than Abbott.

Chevrier had been a thoroughly competent minister of transport, although while Mackenzie King was prime minister he had operated in Howe's shadow. St Laurent had pulled Chevrier out of the shadow by his firm decision to put him in charge of the St Lawrence Seaway project. Though he was well aware that Howe would have liked to take on the task, he informed the cabinet, in a tone that put the decision beyond discussion, that Chevrier would be in charge.

Chevrier had devoted so much energy to getting the seaway approved that it was not surprising he should want to be in charge of its construction. St Laurent did not want to stand in his way and felt someone else could be an adequate minister of transport. But Chevrier's absence from Parliament would be a serious loss to the government. He was not an impromptu speaker, but no one could speak better from a brief. He was equally fluent in both official languages; he had an exceptionally fine delivery; and once he had mastered his subject, he displayed an unusal capacity to speak with clarity and conviction. He was a splendid colleague, completely straightforward, dependable and utterly loyal. He was torn between the desire to stay in the government and the chance to head the seaway, a choice St Laurent left entirely to him. After much soul-searching he decided to become president of the St Lawrence Seaway Authority. St Laurent realized that the simultaneous departure of three senior colleagues would weaken the government, but he felt it would be wrong to try to dissuade any of them.

The choice of a successor to Claxton was easy. Ralph Campney had been an active and efficient associate minister of defence, and with the fighting in Korea over there was less need for an associate minister.

The choice of a minister of finance was more difficult. Stuart Garson had been acting minister whenever Abbott was absent from Ottawa. His familiarity with government finance went back to 1936, when he became provincial treasurer of Manitoba. No one understood more thoroughly the problems of federal-provincial fiscal relations. But he suffered from two disabilities: his prestige had been damaged by the handling of the flour-milling combine report in 1949, and he lacked the capacity to summarize and simplify a case. St Laurent told me he feared that, with all the business a minister of finance had to bring before the cabinet and Parliament, Garson's lengthy presentations might cause strains that would weaken the government. He also told me that several members and at least one minister, Howe, had recommended Walter Harris. I had to agree that the objections to

Garson were understandable, but neither by background nor experience did Harris seem to me an obvious choice. I would have been happier had I not been consulted. Garson was my oldest friend in public life and I hated to see him disappointed. He was too modest to put forth any claim, but I knew he wanted to go to Finance. My friendship with Harris and my admiration for his ability had grown steadily. His capacity to present a case succinctly and persuasively had been amply demonstrated. He was liked and respected on both sides of the House and trusted by the Liberal backbenchers. I said I was glad I did not have to make the choice. Harris was chosen.

The decision to appoint Harris to Finance left two portfolios to fill, Citizenship and Immigration and Transport. I was astonished when St Laurent told me that Howe was urging him to appoint me to Transport. The suggestion, he said, made him shudder, because if I took on that heavy portfolio he would not dare to talk to me about other things. I was flattered but asked who would then be appointed to Citizenship and Immigration. He told me Abbott had sounded out George Marler, the leading English-speaking Liberal in the Québec legislature. Marler was willing to join the government and to seek election in Abbott's riding. I did not know Marler personally. In my opinion a minister of citizenship and immigration could get a government into more trouble in a week than a minister of transport in a year. Was it fair to a new minister with no federal experience or broad knowledge of the political landscape outside Québec to place him in such a politically sensitive spot? Would it not be an unnecessary risk for the government? St Laurent agreed and asked me to become minister of citizenship and immigration. Because Harris had managed the department with so little trouble for the government, St Laurent, I believe, felt it was not a difficult portfolio. He suggested that I also continue as secretary of state.

I hesitated about holding two portfolios. A day or two later Lesage asked me what I knew of the prime minister's plans. He had heard that Marler was to be the only minister from Montreal. He feared that having an English-speaking minister only would be exploited by the Opposition. He would feel embarrassed if Roch Pinard, the obvious choice from Montreal, was passed over. I advised Lesage to speak to St Laurent but undertook to support the appointment of Pinard. St Laurent was concerned that Pinard's appointment would give Québec more ministers than Ontario. A minister should be appointed from Toronto before long, I suggested, and the position of associate minister of national defence would be available when that time came. Pinard became secretary of state, and I succeeded Harris as minister of citizenship and immigration.

The Pickersgill family in Newfoundland

Smallwood was astonished when I told him of our plan to spend the summer of 1954 visiting Bonavista-Twillingate. In the days of responsible government elected members, nearly all of whom lived in St John's, paid little attention to their constituencies except at election time and the record was not much better after Confederation. But it was imperative for me, not being a Newfoundlander, to know and be known in every settlement in my riding.

I blithely asked Harris to carry on as acting minister for July and August. He gave no hint of the burden and generously agreed. A day or two later Margaret and I left with our four children to spend the summer in the house Mrs Herman Quinton rented to us at Portland, on Bonavista Bay. She put up a cabin on the corner of her large property and took in Charlie Granger and Audrey McQuarrie as paying guests, so I had a staff to help me carry on as minister. During the summer we visited the settlements on the Bonavista Peninsula by road, and many places in the rest of the constituency from the *Glencoe*. Many of the voters saw us at least once. I made one or two visits to St John's and to other parts of the province.

We leased Mrs Quinton's house again for the summer of 1955 and spent part of August that summer travelling in the constituency. The governor general visited Newfoundland while we were there. On the day he passed through nearby Clarenville, the whole family was lined up on the station platform to greet him. Vincent Massey was astonished to see us. At Portland we had a steady stream of visitors, and by the end of the summer the member for Bonavista-Twillingate and his family were becoming well known. Living near one end of the constituency had some disadvantages, since there were no connecting roads except on the Bonavista Peninsula. All that summer I had been admiring a beautiful schooner named *Millie Ford*, anchored at Bloomfield, across the bay from Portland. One day I told Charlie Granger I would like to own that schooner. I believe he thought I was out of my mind, and even I doubted if it was practical. However, 'by coincidence,' a few days later Edgar Parsons, the old skipper who owned the vessel, came to see me and offered to sell her for $7500. Parsons was too old to operate the schooner, and his sons did not have the necessary papers. Max Burry agreed to repair the schooner at his expense and use her for freighting, except when I wanted her for visiting the constituency. It was a good deal, and instead of renewing the lease on the house at Portland, I became a shipowner. By the end of the summer, although the whole family was sad to leave Seven Oaks by the Sea, as the house was called, we looked forward eagerly to the next summer on our own schooner.

In 1956 we went on board the schooner at once for the shortest but most delightful of our three summers in Newfoundland before the election of 1957. We visited every settlement in the constituency from Exploits Island to Cape Bonavista and ended the voyage by sailing through the Narrows into St John's. For several days a writer and photographer from *Weekend Magazine* were on board, and the resulting publicity did me no harm politically. The Soviet minister of fisheries was visiting Canada as the guest of the Canadian minister Jimmy Sinclair. The two ministers and their party flew out from St John's to Valleyfield in a fleet of Otter planes and landed in the sea beside the schooner. Jimmy brought the party aboard for cocktails. Later he told me the Soviet minister could not understand how a Canadian cabinet minister and his family would have such rough accommodation.

Schooner Millie Ford, *1956.*

*Canadian Minister of Fisheries Jimmy Sinclair introduces the Soviet
Minister of Fisheries to the Pickersgill family on the wharf at Valleyfield,
Québec.*

Introduction to the Newfoundland fishery

In the spring of 1954, when Smallwood and I had a serious disagreement over the marketing of Newfoundland salt cod, I became acutely aware of the importance of having first-hand knowledge of the Newfoundland fishery. Smallwood had been persuaded by a self-styled expert on cooperative marketing that the provincial government should establish a salt fish marketing board, to operate like the early wheat pools in the prairies, with initial payments and a final distribution to the fishermen from the annual pool. I had vivid memories of the collapse of the original Manitoba wheat pool and told Smallwood that such a pool would work on a rising market, but that no province had the resources to back it up on a falling market. Unless it embraced the whole eastern Canadian fishery and had the backing of the federal government, a pool could not work. Instead of trying to act on its own, the provincial government, I suggested, should put pressure on Ottawa to take appropriate action to market salt fish. If Smallwood established a provincial marketing board, it would be bankrupt sooner or later. When that happened, I would be expected to lead a federal rescue operation. I said it might be wiser for me to find some other way to earn my living than to agree to face that prospect.

Smallwood reflected on the discussion overnight. The next day, as a compromise, he suggested that responsibility for the marketing of fish should be transferred from the Department of Fisheries to Trade and Commerce. He expressed confidence that Howe could market Newfoundland fish to the satisfaction of the people of the province. He proposed the change in the presence of the minister of fisheries. It was an insult to Sinclair, but he readily agreed to recommend the transfer to the prime minister. When Sinclair and I put the proposal and Smallwood's alternative to St Laurent, he undertook to ask Howe to take the responsibility, which he agreed to do. Howe made a statement in Parliament about fish marketing, giving no hint of any difference between the federal and provincial governments but setting out the change in responsibility for the sale of Newfoundland salt cod. We had coped with an immediate problem, but I was acutely aware of my ignorance of nearly all aspects of the fishery. I resolved to learn all I could as soon as possible.

Before I became a minister, the federal and provincial governments had embarked upon a cooperative program for developing the Newfoundland fishing industry. In the main the provincial government provided financial assistance to fish plants, and the federal government, through the Department of Public Works, constructed wharves, breakwaters and other aids to navigation. Robert Winters, who had become minister of public works in 1953 and who came from a fishing family in Lunenburg, had visited Newfoundland with me in October 1953 to see first hand what was needed, and what was being planned. Winters was well liked by the Newfoundlanders he met, and he readily agreed to repeat the visit in the fall of 1954, when we were both more familiar with the problems.

From the time of my meeting in Herring Neck in June 1953, my prime objective for the Newfoundland fishery had been to extend unemployment insurance to fishermen. As a minister I felt I should confine my advocacy to the cabinet, but I encouraged backbenchers from Newfoundland to speak out in Parliament for the cause. Convincing my colleagues in the cabinet and overcoming the stubborn resistance of the bureaucracy in the Unemployment Insurance Commission was an uphill struggle.

Because of the relatively high incomes and the different character of the British Columbia fishery, unemployment insurance had little appeal on the west coast. Sinclair was at first benevolently neutral and at a later stage a supporter more out of friendship for me than enthusiasm for unemployment insurance. Winters was also neutral. He found no agitation for the change in Nova Scotia and was philosophically unsympathetic, but he did not oppose the measure because it seemed so vital to me. Milton Gregg, the other minister from a fishing province, was sympathetic, but as minister of labour he had constantly to face the opposition of the officials in the commission. Most of the other ministers were at best indifferent, and one or two were opposed.

St Laurent was clearly the key to a favourable decision, and he did not like the proposal for two reasons: one, that including fishermen in an insurance plan would not be actuarily sound, and the other, that it might prompt costly demands from other groups. particularly farm labourers and possibly small farmers. His first objection did not impress me, because the inclusion of fishermen was no more unsound actuarily than the inclusion of seasonal workers had been several years earlier. The second objection was much more difficult to meet.

I had not been successful in finding an acceptable formula in time to have fishermen included when the Unemployment Insurance Act was amended in 1955, and I had been disappointed and discouraged. Unemployment insurance required contributions from employers as well as workers, and the main objection of the officials was that the fishermen were self-employed, and there was no one to pay the employer's contribution. I finally convinced them that that objection could be overcome by changing the law so that the merchants who bought the fish would for insurance purposes be deemed to be the employers.

Once I found that solution, I told Milton Gregg that if further changes to the act were made in 1956 and fishermen were not covered, the situation would be intolerable for me. Some time in July Gregg convinced the government that certain amendments to the act were required for other purposes. Once the act was to be amended, I decided that I could not face the electors of Bonavista-Twillingate again unless fishermen were covered. I did not want to make a private appeal to the prime minister, and I wanted even less to have a confrontation with him in cabinet. I explained my plight to Ross Martin, who was now in the cabinet secretariat, and asked him to explain my situation to St Laurent. He did so, effectively. When Gregg proposed the inclusion of fishermen, St Laurent ground his teeth, as he sometimes did when he felt there was no choice but to do something he did not like, and said he supposed we had to go ahead with the proposal. The decision was made on 31 July 1956.

Gregg proposed his amendments to the Unemployment Insurance Act in Parliament on 6 August. The inclusion of insurance for fishermen was the main feature of the debate. Gregg announced that the plan would permit coverage to begin on 1 April 1957 so that fishermen could make enough contributions in the summer to provide benefits in the off-season of 1957-58. The decision was welcomed by spokesmen for all three Opposition parties, who generously gave me the credit. Gregg joined with the Opposition speakers in expressing gratitude to Sinclair and me for the part we had played in making unemployment insurance for fishermen possible.

Having received all that praise I saw no need to take part in the debate, but I made sure the compliments of the Opposition got wide publicity in Newfoundland. I regarded my part in securing the extension of unemployment insurance to fishermen as my most substantial contribution to the welfare of my constituents and of Newfoundland in general, and evidently the electors had similar feelings.

The Trans-Canada Highway and broadcasting in Newfoundland

There was no continuous road across the province from St John's to the terminus of the ferry to the mainland. The Trans-Canada Highway was begun after Confederation, but progress was slow. I wanted it speeded up; almost the whole gap in the road was in my constituency. Donald Gordon, then head of Canadian National, agreed, at my suggestion, to have the railway operate a rail ferry between Clarenville and Gander to carry motorcars from the eastern to the western sections of the highway. The rail ferry was shortened as the Trans-Canada Highway crept eastwards. The shorter the gap became, the more irritating it was not to be able to drive the whole way.

One day in the summer of 1954 Max Burry arrived at Portland by boat, accompanied by Edgar Baird of Gander and Willis Briffett of Glovertown. They had come to urge me to try to have a national park established in the area between Glovertown and Port Blandford. Under the Terms of Union the federal government was committed to establish a park whenever the provincial government made a suitable site available. I was not particularly interested in a national park and thought at first there were better ways to spend public money. My mind changed when I realized that highways in national parks were built by the federal government. The creation of a national park would shorten the gap in the road across Newfoundland. I made up my mind to try to get the park established in the area the visitors recommended. It was not easy.

A week or two later Smallwood arrived by helicopter and I persuaded him to fly over the prospective site. If a park were established there, I pointed out, a gap in the trans-island highway would be completed at no cost to Newfoundland. Smallwood wanted the road completed but was reluctant to surrender the area in question to the federal government for fear the loss of the timber would jeopardize the prospect of having a third paper mill established, with all a mill would mean in additional employment.

I was able to overcome the premier's natural and prudent reluctance, first, by getting an estimate of the new employment that would result from the establishment of a national park, and then by securing a modification of the rules applying to the cutting of timber in a national park, such as had already been made in one of the parks on the prairies. In June 1955 I persuaded Lesage, the minister responsible for national parks, to fly to Newfoundland to inspect three sites for a park suggested by the provincial authorities. After we had flown over all three, Lesage said that the only one he could accept was the site of what became the Terra Nova National Park. Gordon Robertson, Lesage's deputy, as well as Lesage, was exceedingly helpful, and so, when I appealed to him, was St Laurent. The federal government agreed that the provincial government would have the first opportunity to purchase timber harvested in the park within the limits of good forest management.

I did not want work on the highway delayed until the park was established. Winters, the minister responsible for the Trans-Canada Highway, persuaded the government to agree to reimburse Newfoundland for the cost of any section of the road built in an area that later became a part of the park.

Serious negotiations with the provincial government did not start until 1956. On 12 April 1957 Lesage announced in Parliament that agreement had been reached on the boundaries of the park, that the title to the land had been transferred to the government of Canada, and that the park had been formally established by order-in-council. That was the last day in the life of that Parliament. I was pleased. I was even more pleased after 10 June 1957, because I am sure the new Conservative government would not have established a national park in my constituency. In my years in Opposition it gave me some satisfaction to watch the Diefenbaker government filling in the gap in the most important highway in Newfoundland.

In the spring of 1954 I became involved in broadasting policy for Newfoundland, which was to be a serious problem for me for the rest of my time in Parliament. Contrary to the policy the government had adopted in 1952, the CBC encouraged a campaign for a CBC-TV station in St John's. The corporation's argument was that Newfoundland as a new province needed special attention. When I asked for an estimate of the cost of a CBC station, none was very precise, but it was clear to me that it would end up at more than a million dollars. I felt there were at least a dozen better ways to spend a million dollars of public money for the benefit of Newfoundland. I knew that Geoffrey Stirling and Donald Jamieson, the owners of the private radio station CJON, were prepared to finance a private television station without any cost to the Treasury. I went to Newfoundland to explain to a few influential advocates in St John's why I was not in favour of a CBC station. The money, I explained, was needed more for other purposes, and a private station would in any case be obliged to broadcast CBC network programs.

James McCann, as minister for the CBC, pressed their case vigorously, but the cabinet decided the issue in my favour. CJON applied for a television licence, which was granted in October 1954. The station was of course, in St John's, and its range not great.

In the fall of 1955 the commander of the U.S. naval base at Argentia convinced two U.S. cabinet ministers on their way to a NATO meeting that morale would break down unless there was a television station on the base. One of the American ministers enlisted Howe's support. I opposed the project vigorously, my argument being that CJON already covered part of the base area and with a satellite could cover the whole area and a number of other settlements in Placentia Bay as well. Howe and I argued heatedly in cabinet, until St Laurent suggested the meeting pass on to the next item on the agenda. The subject was never raised again, the Americans did not establish their television station, and a CJON satellite was licensed in 1956. It would have been an affront to Canada, I felt, to have a U.S. television station serving that area of Newfoundland when Canadian broadcasting could be made available.

Administering Citizenship and Immigration

Immigration controversy

I soon discovered that administering Citizenship and Immigration was a major task, filled with opportunities to gain bad publicity. Fortunately Parliament did not meet until early 1955, so I had several months in which to learn how the department operated. Most of my work would relate to immigration.

Canada's immigration policy had always been selective. From the British Isles, including the Irish Republic, Australia, New Zealand, the Union of South Africa and the United States, immigrants were freely admitted as long as they could meet routine requirements. One of St Laurent's early decisions was to add France to that preferred list. In the Nordic countries, Holland, Belgium, Switzerland and Italy, Canada had facilities to provide immigrants with visas, but security screening was added to the routine requirements. In the period before I became minister Germany and Portugal were added to that group. Most immigration was from Britain and Europe.

Immigration from Italy was almost as great as from Britain. I knew that if Italian immigration exceeded British, there would be a public outcry. The Italian ambassador warned me that any discriminatory regulatory measures would be resented in Italy and, more important for us, in the Italian-Canadian community. I managed to contain the number of Italian immigrants by limiting the immigration staff in Italy and refusing to permit them to work overtime. The arrangement was made by word of mouth, with no written record and no offence to the Italian community. It kept the Italian immigration just a little below the British.

But there was no such easy solution to another problem. The law excluded immigration of persons of 'Asian race.' The provision had the ridiculous, though largely theoretical, effect that white and black South Africans could be admitted in the preferred category, but South Africans of Indian origin were excluded as Asians. Gandhi would not have qualified. There was only a trickle of South African immigration, practically all of it white. The government had got around the Asian exclusion with respect to Commonwealth countries by negotiating quotas for India, Pakistan and Ceylon.

But the big problem was over the Chinese. Chinese immigration had been excluded entirely from 1923 to 1947. The Chinese-Canadian community was almost entirely male, and the government had on compassionate grounds agreed to permit the entry of the wives and children under 21 years of Chinese-Canadian citizens. Deciding whether 'children' applied for were really under 21 and really the children of the Canadian applicants was complicated by the absence of vital statistics in China. A further complication was that, for security reasons, no one who was a Communist was admissible. The bar raised no great problem in Eastern Europe, as no immigration was permitted from countries behind the Iron Curtain, but the Chinese wives and children admitted on compassionate grounds had to pass the no-Communist test. The government of the United States admitted no Chinese and was worried that new Canadian policy might provide a back door for agents from communist China.

Many of the Chinese-Canadian applicants were influential in their communities and enlisted the support of MPs and party workers. When representations were from MPs, I insisted on looking at the files myself and replying personally. I wanted to be prepared for questions in Parliament. When the first question was asked I refused to answer on the ground that answers about individuals would be an invasion of privacy. The Speaker supported my position, which I was usually able to sustain.

A number of lawyers specialized in promoting the Chinese applications, often by resort to publicity. One of the lawyers was John R. Taylor, of Vancouver. His legal agent in Ottawa was John H. McDonald, and between them they were responsible for the first serious attack I had to meet in Parliament. Through a sub-committee of the Canadian Bar Association they had stirred up agitation by accusing the Immigration officials of denying the civil rights of Chinese Canadians; they had gained the sympathy of various organizations and enlisted the support of John Diefenbaker.

In September 1954 McDonald saw me to tell me he that he and Taylor would call off their campaign if I would reverse a number of specific decisions made when Harris was minister. McDonald added that if I did not grant their request, I could expect trouble in Parliament. I was shocked and indignantly rejected his approach. His unfriendly warning gave me time to prepare for the kind of attack I would have to face. I soon discovered that all but one of the refusals they wanted me to reverse were applications from Taylor's clients.

The attack began on 15 February 1955, when Davie Fulton moved a vote of want of confidence that charged that the government in its administration of Immigration denied simple justice to Canadians and non-Canadians alike. Fulton tried to drive a wedge between Harris and me by charging Harris with the major responsibility for the mishandling of Immigration. He supported his attack excluslvely on the charges made public by Taylor and McDonald. I knew Fulton was going to be supported by Fleming and Diefenbaker, and I wanted to hear all three before I replied for the government. Fleming obliged, but Harris learned that Diefenbaker would not speak until I did, and persuaded me to go ahead to avoid prolonging the debate.

In my first real test as a parliamentarian I was facing the three most effective debaters in the Conservative Opposition. I had rehearsed my arguments over and over again and spoke from very few notes. Once I got over my initial nervousness, I enjoyed myself, because I obviously had the attention of the House.

Fulton's attack boiled down to this question: Did a Canadian citizen whose application for a relative was refused have the right to be given the reason for the refusal and the right to appeal to the law courts? I replied that the Canadian citizen had the right to apply and to have a decision made by the minister or an official authorized to act for the minister, but that that was the only right he or she had. I explained that one of the reasons for refusing to say why the application had been denied was that immigration officers had to pry into the private lives of the persons applied for, and it was enough of a disability to refuse them admission without revealing their private affairs to anyone else, even a close relative. There was much less reason to give such information to advocates or solicitors, who might use it for other purposes than the advancement of the case of the prospective immigrant. Another reason for withholding information was that information obtained in security screening often came from other countries only on condition that it was kept confidential. I reminded Fulton that Parliament had decided that the admissibility of immigrants was to be determined not by the law courts but by officials and, ultimately, the minister. So long as that was the law, the final decision must rest with someone who was answerable in Parliament to Parliament. I concluded my defence of the department and the former minister by saying that my highest hope as minister was to do as well as my predecessor, because I knew I could not do better

My two-hour defence was, I believe, the longest speech I made in my 14 years in Parliament. It was probably longer than necessary even though my observation of Parliament for many years had taught me that a speech that exhausted the audience often exhausted the subject. Diefenbaker replied immediately with his usual rhetorical flourishes but did not deal with the substance of my argument, as he never did with any.

Harris closed the debate in a very brief speech in which he stated succinctly and more clearly than I had that, under the existing law, no person had a right to be admitted to Canada as an immigrant, and that the ultimate selection exercised by the minister, subject to his responsibility to the House of Commons, had been confirmed by Parliament in the Immigration Act of 1952, with only one dissenting voice, from a supporter of the government. He said that if any member wished to change the system in order to give the right of appeal to the law courts to prospective immigrants or their sponsors, the proper way was to change the law, not to attack the minister or the government for administering the law as recently established by Parliament.

That fundamental difference of approach to immigration procedure persists. Unfortunately, in my opinion, Canada has moved away from the policy of selective immigration controlled by Parliament to a situation in which, by judicial decision under the Charter of Rights, any person who can manage to set foot in Canada can stay until his or her right to do so has been determined, with almost endless appeals to the courts. The result is a huge and almost intractable backlog of residents with no status. If ever there was a case for using the notwithstanding clause of the Charter to enable Parliament to establish jurisdiction to impose a summary procedure, that is the one. The previous legal situation should be restored so that no one who is not a Canadian citizen has a fundamental human right to enter Canada or to stay in the country. Residence of those who are not citizens should be a privilege to be accorded or refused by an administration answerable to Parliament.

The Chinese cases were the most numerous and most difficult. Only the hard cases were brought to my attention, but I dealt with hundreds and perhaps a thousand or more cases in which application was made by a Canadian citizen for prospective immigrants.

It was not total drudgery, because I realized I was dealing with living human beings, but it was harder work than I would ever have as minister of transport.

Changes in immigration

The first change I made in immigration policy was to arrange to have a limited number of women from the West Indies admitted. In May 1955 the Jamaican minister of trade and industry proposed to me during a visit to Ottawa that Canada admit Jamaican women as domestic servants under a form of indenture that would require them to return to Jamaica at the end of their period of service. I replied that I had not become minister of immigration to introduce slavery into Canada, and that anyone coming to Canada for employment while I was minister would be admitted as an immigrant. The minister said he thought Canada was opposed to West Indian immigration. I said I was not opposed to West Indians as immigrants, but I was opposed to admitting immigrants from anywhere to populate the slums. I agreed to consider the admission of a small number of Jamaican women if the government of Jamaica would select them carefully and make sure they had some training. It was later decided Barbadians should also be included. In 1955 the admission of the first 100 women from Jamaica and Barbados was approved. In the next two years the number was increased, and other islands included.

Greece was added as a country with facilities for admitting immigrants. Many of the young Greeks who applied had fought in the civil war on the side supported by the Communist party, and the question of security arose. I decided that applicants below a certain age who had merely been involved in the fighting and against whom there was no evidence they were Communists could be accepted as landed immigrants. I realized that I would be in trouble if any turned out to be communist agents. I have never heard of any who did.

I also ended the automatic exclusion of Armenians and Lebanese as Asians.

In 1956 one ridiculous incident arose. James Gardiner suggested in Winnipeg that Canada should trade wheat to Britain for immigrants. I heard a report of his speech on the morning news broadcast and knew I would have to answer in Parliament that day. Diefenbaker first asked St Laurent how many bushels of wheat he expected would be sold under Gardiner's scheme. St Laurent replied that he had not seen the story and did not expect any wheat would be sold under such a plan. Diefenbaker then asked me what consideration I had given to the weird plan of the minister of agriculture. I answered that, like some other members, I listen to the radio while I am taking my bath in the morning, and that I had heard the report but did not think I was entitled to comment in the House on a statement made outside the House. I had calculated, rightly, that the reference to my bath would result in guffaws and distract attention from my answer. The only result was a cartoon of me in my bath.

Whenever Diefenbaker spoke about immigration, he accused the department and the minister of discrimination. There was some agitation, especially in the universities, for what was called immigration without discrimination. I defended the selective immigration policy in the face of that plausible campaign. I asserted that immigration to Canada from overpopulated countries could not contribute substantially to the reduction of population in those countries. To admit immigrants from any country in such numbers as to create undesirable tensions and strains would not be of benefit to Canada or to the immigrants themselves. I agreed there was discrimination in immigration, but it was my view that once people were admitted, there should be no discrimination. If selective immigration means anything, it means discriminating between one person and another and between one country and another. I added, 'We are going to go on doing that no matter what government is in office.' In recent years I have deplored the reduction of selective standards and the problems that have resulted. I once said that 'selection' was apparently a good word and 'discrimination' a bad word, but that I could find no dictionary that gave the words a different basic meaning.

Canadian babies

Another immigration controversy I brought on my own head.

During the Easter recess in 1955, I made a speech in Victoria on behalf of the MP Frank Fairey, who it happened had been born in England. I repeated the timeworn phrase that the best kind of immigration was the cradle. We all wanted the population to increase, I said, and for purposes of increasing the population I did not believe that an immigrant, no matter where from or how good, was as good as another Canadian baby, because the immigrant had to learn to be a Canadian, and the baby was a Canadian to start with. No one in the audience seemed to find that statement or anything else I said remarkable.

A day and a half later, at the railway station at Calgary, I learned my Victoria speech had become a national sensation. The *Victoria Colonist* had reported that the minister of immigration had said no immigrant was as good as a Canadian baby. The Canadian Press circulated the *Colonist* report across Canada. Some newspapers had pictures of Howe and Sinclair, both immigrants, with reports that Pickersgill had said 'colleagues not as good as Canadian babies.' Spokesmen for various immigrant groups protested in strong terms. The Opposition felt they had a real issue. No speech I have made before or since was quite as great a sensation. Fortunately the *Victoria Times* had reported my statement with the qualifications.

George Hees, the president of the Progressive Conservative Association, attacked my alleged statement in a speech outside Parliament and gave me the first chance to explain what I had really said. In a letter to Hees I wrote that I assumed my speech would find a place in the literature of the Conservative party, and that I was sure he would want the account to be accurate. I repeated the statement as it had appeared in the *Victoria Times*.

The copy of my letter to Hees was useful when the session resumed on 8 April. Drew asked me to amplify my surprising statement. When I replied by reading my letter to Hees, Drew said he regretted I was putting the matter on what he called a strictly political ground. He let me off lightly by agreeing that my statement had not been adequately reported in the press, but he said it had caused grave concern to many people who had chosen

Canada as their home, and reminded me that Sir John A. Macdonald had been an immigrant. Roland Michener minimized the incident by asking me whether I would consider calling my department Citizenship and Propagation. Other frivolous references reduced the unfortunate impression.

Although I got off easily in Parliament, I was anxious to dispel the impression the first report had made. Paul Martin asked me to speak in Windsor at an annual party for new Canadians. There I repeated and expanded to a sympathetic audience what I had said in Victoria. I knew any function Martin arranged would get maximum publicity.

Fulton's attempt to revive the controversy in a later debate was an anticlimax. He accepted my version of the controversial statement but tried to make something of my casual remark to the press in Winnipeg that the whole thing was very silly. I interrupted him to ask, 'Well, isn't it?' Fulton ignored the question and took exception to another remark I had made in Winnipeg, to the effect that I would not have got one-tenth of the advertising if I had been reported as saying something sensible. Apparently, I said, it was a great mistake for a politician to make flippant remarks. 'I recognize it, and every time I do it, I am duly contrite. I find that every time I make a flippant remark, in his presence, the hon. member for Kamloops takes the remark seriously, and I shall try hard in the future to be solemn, if I can. Sometimes it is difficult.'

After that exchange the Canadian baby almost expired from lack of breath, despite one last attempt by Diefenbaker to give it artificial respiration. On balance the baby speech may have done more good than harm, and it certainly made me better known all over Canada.

The Hungarian refugees

My most absorbing task as immigration minister developed suddenly and unexpectedly. In October 1956 a revolt against the communist regime in Hungary overthrew the government. The rest of the world was distracted by the Suez crisis, so it was easy for the Soviet government to rush troops into Hungary to crush the revolt and restore the communist regime. Thousands of those who had revolted, called freedom fighters, fled into Austria, which was overwhelmed by the tide of refugees. In Canada, as elsewhere in the West, there was a wave of sympathy for the Hungarian freedom fighters and a clamour for the country to open its doors wide to receive those willing to come.

The refugees had begun to enter Austria on 4 November. The cabinet gave me virtually a free hand to remove obstscles to their reception in Canada. Two days later the Canadian immigration office in Vienna was directed to give priority to Hungarian refugees and to offer them loans to pay their passages to Canada. Later the cabinet agreed, with some resistance, to waive medical examinations in Austria and have them done in Canada. Those who passed the medical were admitted as immigrants, those who did not stayed in Canada as visitors and received medical treatment. It was soon apparent that there was not enough commercial transport by air or sea to move the refugees, thousands of whom were showing an interest in crossing the Atlantic.

With support from St Laurent and Harris I secured cabinet approval to charter all the suitable aircraft available to speed up the movement of the refugees. The morning after the charters had been arranged one of the ministers, W.M. Nickle, telephoned on behalf of Premier Frost to offer the assistance of the government of Ontario in the movement of the refugees. I asked what kind of assistance they had In mind, and he suggested an airlift. I told him that the federal government had already chartered all the available aircraft; transport was not going to be as difficult as caring for the refugees from the time of their arrival in Canada until they could get jobs to support themselves. To provide temporary reception centres was the most useful thing their government could do. Nickle later advised me that that would be done.

Towards the end of November the Vienna office reported that many prospective Hungarian immigrants were worried about going into debt to pay for their passage to Canada and would not come for that reason. I decided to seek cabinet authority to offer free passage to all refugees who wanted to come to Canada and to cancel all the loans already made. St Laurent was at first taken aback by the proposal. He was properly concerned about the precedent. When I said I feared that unless some country acted quickly and boldly, the refugees would start drifting back to Hungary, his attitude changed at once. He said that if Harris agreed, he would support my recommendation. Harris asked me what I estimated the program would cost. I answered that that would depend on the number who came, and there was no way of telling.

Harris said that that was the right thing to do, and that whatever the cost, he would support me. The cabinet met that afternoon, and the proposal was approved in about half an hour. I announced the decision in the House of Commons that evening and reported that the government had decided I should go to Austria to make sure everything possible was being done to speed up the movement. Such positive action by Canada was needed. The United States, Britain and several European countries had begun to slow down their efforts to receive refugees because of difficulty in finding employment for them. Canada's action helped to turn the tide.

On my arrival in Vienna I found that the immigration office was hopelessly inadequate. No time was lost in securing larger quarters, where there was space to deal quickly with applicants. At my request the Austrian minister of the interior made a camp available exclusively for refugees who wanted to come to Canada. We sent Hungarian-speaking Canadians to that camp to brief the refugees.

The day I arrived in Vienna I learned that the School of Forestry of Sopron University had moved in a body to Austria and were quartered in a temporary camp near Salzburg. They had expressed interest in moving as a unit to a Canadian university. The possibility excited me. I telephoned Sinclair in Vancouver, and in a few hours he succeeded in arranging to have the forestry school affiliated with the University of British Columbia. Through Harold Foley of the Powell River Paper Company he was also able

J.W.P. at a camp in Austria invited the Hungarian Forestry Faculty from Sopron to move en bloc to University of British Columbia.

to arrange to have a lumber camp provided as a reception centre from the time of the Hungarians' arrival in British Columbia until the university term opened in September 1957.

I visited the camp near Salzburg to tell the Sopron faculty and students about the possible arrangements, and they accepted the offer. I found at the camp a number of mining students and a few professors who also wished to come to Canada, and I promised to see whether there was a place for them in another university. A day or two later, from The Hague, I reached the president of the University of Toronto by telephone and asked him if Toronto would receive them. Sidney Smith took a deep breath and then answered without any qualification, 'You can count on us.' I have cherished the memory of his courageous decision and the effective way it was carried out.

On my way home from Vienna I consulted the governments of

West Germany, Holland, Belgium, France and Britain in an attempt to have some of the Hungarians accommodated over the winter in those countries, so that they would not have to be brought to Canada until the spring, when it would be easier to find both accommodation and employment. West Germany and Belgium had labour shortages and wanted to keep all the readily employable refugees. The governments of Holland, France and Britain agreed to my proposal. Holland kept 2000, France 3000, and Britain 5000 refugees through the winter. The arrangements made it possible for Canada to accept a much larger number of refugees.

When I got home in mid-December, I found that the first flush of enthusiasm had faded, particularly in Ontario, where there

J.W.P. with High Commissioner Norman Robertson at his house in London, 1956, on J.W.P.'s return from Vienna to organize Hungarian refugee movement.

were growing doubts about the wisdom of receiving such large numbers of refugees. There was a whispering campaign under way in which St Laurent was accused of encouraging the Hungarian immigration because the refugees were predominantly Catholic. The day I returned to Ottawa, Nickle, the Ontario minister, telephoned to ask me who was going to pay for the reception centres. I was astonished and said so. I had assumed that the Ontario government intended to pay the cost of what they had offered to do. Nickle objected, saying, 'These people are arriving with absolutely nothing, not even an extra suit of under-wear. Who is going to pay for the underwear?' I paused for breath and then said, 'We will.' That telephone call reflected the spirit of the Ontario government's cooperation. When I told Harris about Nickle's call, he explained that the reception of so many Hungarian refugees was not popular in rural Ontario, but added without hesitation that Canada was doing the right thing. The official cooperation from other provincial governments, including Québec was less grudging.

By the time the movement of the refugees was completed, which was not until after I had left office, Canada had received about 35,000 Hungarians, a larger number than any European country and only a thousand fewer than the United States. Of the 35,000, about 600 turned out badly; some of them were Commu-nists who had fled when the uprising started. Most of that 600 eventually went back to Hungary. The great majority of the Hungarians were successful in establishing themselves, and many have achieved eminence in Canadian life. What I did to organize their reception was, I believe, as useful as anything I did in public life. Certainly it was among my most exciting experiences.

The Vienna office reported soon after my return that most countries were reluctant to receive students who wanted to con-tinue their studies before seeking employment. I thought such students would make more useful Canadians. Though our policy was to deal with the refugees on the basis first come, first served, I had oral instructions given to the office to try to get students to the head of the queue each day. Canada consequently received proportionately more students than any other country. To look after the students we had to make elaborate arrangements for their reception by the universities. McGill set an example to the others, thanks in large part to the initiative taken by Senator and Mrs Hartland Molson. Hungarian students were willingly received by almost every Canadian university and in that way were dispersed across the country.

After Suez there was an upsurge of British immigration. I had noted in London in December 1956 there were long queues at the Canadian immigration office. I took action at once to increase the staff and speed up procedures to end the queues. The numbers were so great that commercial transport could not handle all the approved applicants, and a special airlift was arranged that could be extended to France if necessary. We managed to move fast enough to forestall the anticipated criticism that the government was more concerned about Hungarian than British immigrants.

The man without a country

By Christmas the Hungarian and British immigration was moving smoothly, and I felt free to go to a hospital in Toronto for surgery. The day after the operation the deputy minister telephoned me at the hospital to warn me that the *Toronto Star* would carry a sensational sob story about a merchant seaman who called himself George Christian Hanna . He had jumped ship in Vancouver and asked for asylum as 'a man without a country.' As usual with seamen who jump ship, Hanna had been ordered deported. A Vancouver lawyer had appealed the deportation order. The deputy had consulted Harris, as acting minister, and been told to treat the case in the usual way. I smelled trouble and asked why he had not landed him and lost him.

In the next few weeks I became increasingly unhappy as the press and the Conservative Opposition blew that routine case up to staggering proportions. I was tempted to give Hanna a minister's permit to stay for six months just to stop the clamour. Instead of acting on my own I consulted the cabinet. The government was being portrayed as inhuman, and there was always a chance that the deportation order might be quashed by a judge. Though the prospect of his becoming a useful citizen was poor, I hinted at letting the man stay. St Laurent said firmly but quickly, 'Shouldn't you do what is right?' No one else said a word, and I felt I had to let the law take its course. I soon realized I should not have consulted the cabinet but acted on my own.

I was harassed pretty steadily by the Opposition and the press from 10 January, my first day back in Parliament, until a judge decided the case in Hanna's favour, on 26 March. At that point the government could have appealed to a higher court and might eventually have had the decision reversed, but I had had enough. Diefenbaker asked me what I proposed to do about the man. I said that since Hanna was employed and was doing no one any harm, the best course was to allow him to stay in Canada without status. I hoped that he would get on well enough, and that in a few months I would feel justified in recommending that he be admitted as a landed immigrant by order-in-council.

In fact I did nothing more about him, but ironically, two or three years later, the Diefenbaker government deported him, the very man the Conservatives had used to help them gain office. The publicity over Hanna had served them well in offsetting the good effect of the reception of the Hungarians.

The Citizenship Branch

The Citizenship Act was much easier to administer than the Immigration Act. The minister had little discretion. After five years as landed immigrants British subjects and citizens of Ireland were given certificates of citizenship almost automatically on application. All others had to apply to courts of law. Citizenship could not be granted unless a judge recommended the applicant. The minister did not have to accept the recommendation of the court, but in practice recommendations were refused only when the police satisfied the minister that the prospective citizen was a risk to the security of the state. Because police information often came from sources in other countries, the minister usually could not give the reason for a refusal to grant citizenship. Reasons disclosed might in any case damage the employability of an applicant who was refused citizenship

When applicants or friends of applicants persisted in demanding the reason for a refusal and made their demand public, the publicity was usually bad for the minister and the government. Persons refused citizenship could not be deported, so I failed to see how refusal protected national security. I thought the policy was stupid and hoped to have it changed after the election of 1957.

The county courts held the citizenship hearings in Ontario, and courts of similar jurisdiction did so in other provinces. The burden on the courts was not great except in Toronto and, to a lesser degree, Montreal, where there were serious delays in holding hearings. I took advantage in those two cities of a provision in the Citizenship Act allowing the government to set up special citizenship courts. I acted quickly after a visit to a citizenship hearing of the county court in a shabby setting in the basement of the Toronto City Hall, under the stairway. Federal citizenship courts with full-time judges were established in Toronto and Montreal in their own premises, where dignified ceremonies were held with receptions to welcome the new citizens, arranged by voluntary organizations. The IODE in Toronto was especially effective.

Applicants for citizenship born in Soviet Ukraine had on their applications to say they were citizens of the Soviet Union and were not allowed to substitute 'Ukraine.' John Decore, the Liberal MP for Vegreville, Alberta, appealed to me on their behalf. Despite objection from the bureaucracy, especially in External Affairs, I persuaded Pearson to agree that they could declare they were born in Ukraine. In order to gain some credit for the government among the Ukrainian-Canadian community, I had Decore ask me a question in Parliament, and made the announcement where it would get maximum publicity.

There was also a small branch of the department to assist in the social and cultural integration of immigrants into Canadian life. It worked closely with ethnic organizations throughout the country and with the ethnic press. The outstanding official was Andrew E.

Thompson, later to become leader of the Liberal party of Ontario. He had an extraordinary rapport with the ethnic community in Toronto and, indeed, almost everywhere in Canada. Andy Thompson introduced me to the leaders of the various communities, with whom I developed an association that was one of the most agreeable features of my years as minister. Thompson himself had been an immigrant from Ireland. He strengthened his ties with the ethnic community by marrying into the Estonian-Canadian community.

Superintendent-General of Indian Affairs

The minister of citizenship and immigration also had the historic title of Superintendent-General of Indian Affairs, a title brought from New York to Canada after the American Revolution, at the same time that a large number of members of the Five (later Six) Nations came to Canada.

I gradually developed a greater interest in Indian Affairs than in any other branch of the department. I tried whenever possible to visit Indian reserves to see for myself what conditions were like, and it did not take me long to realize the vast difference between reserves in southern Ontario and those in isolated areas in the north. Because of the rapid growth in the population of Indian communities, many Indians, particularly in the north, could not support themselves in their traditional way of life, and unless they were to subsist on welfare, new sources of employment would have to be found. That meant training and education. I felt that the more closely the education of Indians was integrated with the education of other Canadians, the sooner Indians would be able to live and compete on equal terms with and become accepted like other Canadian citizens. It seemed to me that that should be the ultimate goal. I am unrepentantly of that view a quarter of a century later.

I favoured integrated education in areas where it was geographically feasible, and a good deal of progress was made in that direction. All Indians who matriculated and wished to go on to universities or other institutions for post-secondary education had their expenses paid by the department. I insisted that scholarships be established also; my position was that earning scholarships would be a source of pride. A good start was made in the development of opportunities for useful employment in industry by M.R. Jack, who was appointed to find employers ready to hire Indians. He was making substantial progress when the government changed in 1957, and George Hees took him away to be his executive assistant. Unfortunately no successor was found, and the good start was not followed up. I believe that in that area action is urgently needed as it is abundantly clear that more and more Indians cannot gain subsistence from traditional sources, both because of the rapid rise in their population, and because of the misguided discouragement of the use of furs by Greenpeace and other organizations. Action to help Indians get training and the means to seek other employment is the greatest need.

Although the Indian Act had been thoroughly revised in 1951, after Harris became minister, experience showed that amendments were needed. We decided to hold a conference of Indian leaders from all parts of the country before introducing legislation in Parliament. The conference reached a consensus on the amendments to be proposed and was an enlightening experience for me. There was some dissent among the leaders about the amendment to allow Indians to buy liquor legally in any province that would agree to sell it to them. I felt it was discriminatory and demeaning to make something an offence for Indians that was not an offence for other Canadians, and I am still of that opinion. I told the conference that there was no thought, much less an intention, of taking away from Indians any of their treaty rights or traditional rights or anything they felt especially belonged to them, or of using any form of compulsion whatsoever to make them change faster than they were willing to change. G.C. (Slim) Monture, an Indian and one of the most distinguished public servants of his day, told me after the conference that I had made a good impression on the Indians.

The most controversial problem in Indian Affairs arose out of a requirement of the Indian Act of 1951 designed to settle, once and for all, what persons had Indian status. Before 1951 the lists were incomplete of persons belonging to each band who had a right to reside on each reserve. The Indian status of many residents of reserves was in dispute. Harris decided that the lists should be brought up to date by the registrar of Indian bands, a senior official in the department, whose duty it was to maintain a complete list of all persons in Canada with Indian status.

To bring the lists up to date the registrar was required to post the existing list of members of each Indian band in a prominent place on the reserve or reserves. For six months after the list was posted individuals could apply to have names added to or removed from the list. Applicatons to have names removed were called protests. The circumstances surrounding each protest had to be investigated by a commission set up on each reserve for the purpose. The commissions were to present their reports to the registrar, who then had to make a decision as to whether a person in question should have his or her name on the list. The registrar's decisions were final, subject to an appeal to the Courts.

In the case of the Hobbema Reserve in Alberta the Indian status of a number of residents had been questioned in a protest by other residents whose Indian status was not in doubt. After a long investigation the registrar decided that a considerable number of the residents did not have Indian status. Instead of appealing to the courts, as the law provided, the aggrieved residents and their sympathizers appealed to me as minister to restore the rights they alleged had been taken away by the department. As minister I had no legal power to interfere with the decision of the registrar, and the only answer I could give was to advise the complainants to appeal to the courts. Some Alberta newspapers and some Conservatives in the Opposition, led by Diefenbaker, took up the hue and cry in 1957. When I persisted in urging those who were dissatisfied to appeal to the courts, I was portrayed as arbitrary, arrogant and inhumane.

The abuse was hard to take because I believed that the registrar had made a mistake, and that if the case was taken to court, the decision would be reversed. It was alleged that the aggrieved parties did not have sufficient funds to pay a lawyer to take their appeal. Harris and I agreed that in order to have the question settled the government should pay for a lawyer. Since those who had protested were undoubtedly Indians, we felt that it was only fair to pay as well for a lawyer to represent them. The judge reversed the decison as I had hoped, and that was the end of the matter, except for the bad publicity.

I deplore the indiscriminate abuse now fahionable, of the Department of Indian Affairs by many Indian leaders and by the public at large. When I was minister, I said repeatedly that I hoped the day would come when the department and the Indian Act would not be needed and would disappear. I welcomed every sensible advance towards Indians having management of their own affairs, and I still do. But I do not welcome the tendency to try to create a kind of benevolent apartheid for the native peoples, to make them a separate class apart from other Canadians.

The aboriginal population of what is now Canada was probably no larger when the Europeans first settled than at the beginning of the 20th century, when many believed and some hoped that Indians were dying out. Today the Indian population is increasing much more quickly than the rest of the Canadian population. In 1971, the census recorded 313,000 aboriginal people, in 1981, 413,000 — an increase of 32 per cent in a single decade. Unhappily their well-being has not increased at the same rate. But I do not believe that on average it has decreased. The problem is one of the biggest in Canada today, but improvement is far more likely to come from understanding and cooperation than from recrimination an confrontation.

The department and the accomplishments

I was served with efficiency and devotion by my secretarial staff. All of them except Teresa Maloney, who had returned to her senior position in the old department, had moved with me from the secretary of state's office to the new department. I needed a bilingual secretary. Lyone Boult had started her career in the public service in Mackenzie King's office, a young stenographer with almost no English. She had worked mainly for me, and I had taught her English on the side and discovered how able she was. She had married, raised a family and wanted to start work again. She was hired, and filled the bill to perfection. I also needed someone to help with problems arising within the department, and I found two or three young civil servants with promise, to be seconded for a year at a time for that purpose. The experiment was a success. Jack Manion, who some years later moved on to senior positions as a deputy minister and secretary to the Treasury Board, was the ablest.

Charlie Granger concentrated mainly on Newfoundland. From the time Audrey McQuarrie spent the summer with us at Portland, in 1954, I relied more and more on Audrey and her assistant, Shirley Tink. Audrey and Shirley worked with me during the whole of both periods I was minister, and each has had a large part in my working life.

My relations with the deputy minister, Colonel Laval Fortier, were excellent. He was learned in the law and strict in its application. With difficult cases I was sometimes lenient and did not take his advice. The first time that happened I told him I hoped he would always give me his own opinion and never try to guess what might please me. He had a strong will and never failed to recommend what he considered the best course of action, but whenever I decided on a different course, he carried it out loyally and efficiently. We became lifelong friends. He was one of the moving spirits in establishing Le Cercle Universitaire, and he asked me to be one of the founders. Le Cercle was the first dining club in Ottawa to admit women to membership and to permit wives of members to use the club on their own.

I was fortunate in my deputy and staff because the volume of work was as great as I ever had. I presided over the most active period of immigration to Canada except for the years immediately before the First World War. The vast majority of the immigrants were integrated into Canadian life with relative ease and have enriched the country without any fundamental disturbance of our historic political institutions — although I confess that by 1957 I was beginning to be concerned that the numbers might soon exceed our absorptive capacity. Between 1954 and 1957 thousands of immigrants became citzens. Great impetus was given to the education of Indians, and more responsibility given to many Indian bands.

All in all I had few dull moments during my three years as minister in a dynamic department. When the Liberal party went into Opposition, I gave up the portfolio with regret.

Other ministerial activities

Responsibility for other agencies of government

As a minister of the Crown I had responsibility for the Public Archives and National Library, the National Film Board and the National Gallery. Those agencies had no connection with the Department of Citizenship and Immigration, and I dealt directly with them.

The Public Archives was a separate department of government. The dominion archivist was a deputy minister. When I entered the cabinet, the Archives reported to the secretary of state, but when I moved to Citizenship and Immigration, the prime minister let me take responsibility for the Archives with me. I have already referred to meeting Lamb, when Mackenzie King received a delegation Lamb headed and decided he should be archivist. The National Library was in the planning stage, and Lamb and I collaborated in drafting the legislation to establish the Library, which I piloted through Parliament. Lamb became the first national librarian in addition to being archivist. He retained both positions until he retired.

The quarters for the Archives on Sussex Street were inadequate, and a new building was required. I was present at the cabinet meeting at which the site on Wellington Street was chosen. A temporary wartime building housing Howe's office and his department was still on the site. Howe said he liked his office and did not want to move. I said jokingly that problem could be solved by making Howe national librarian; he was not amused, but other ministers were. The site was chosen just the same. Construction did not start until we left office, but Lamb began to work immediately on the plans. The building was already occupied when I became minister for the Archives again in 1963.

The records of departments and other agencies of government had been kept under departmental custody since Confederation. Many were in a sorry state of preservation, and some had been lost. Lamb had worked out a plan for the transfer to the Archives of records no longer current, for sorting, storage and proper management. I embraced the plan enthusiastically and got approval from cabinet for the transfer and for a new building, which was completed in time for me to open it officially.

Lamb was not only a great archivist and an imaginative collector of historical material but a first-rate administrator who left me little to do but sign my name.

I took over responsibility for the National Film Board when I became minister of citizenship and immigration. Albert Trueman, a friend from Oxford days, was film commissioner. I did not interfere at all in the internal administration but confined myself to keeping the budget under tight control. It was while I was minister that the Film Board moved from Ottawa to Montreal. In 1957, when Trueman became director of the newly established Canada Council, I had a large part in the selection of Guy Roberge as his successor. It was an admirable choice. Roberge was still there when I was once more the minister for the Film Board, as a member of the Pearson government. He was so effective that in that office too I had little to do but sign my name.

The ministerial responsibility for the National Gallery was transferred to Walter Harris when he became a minister. The legislation establishing the National Gallery had been thoroughly revised and piloted through the House by him. He had selected Percy Fell, a highly competent businessman, as chairman of the board and had also initiated a major purchase of paintings that gave the institution an international reputation.

I had taken an active interest in the National Gallery from the time of my arrival in Ottawa in 1937. My interest in its administration developed when Mackenzie King persuaded Vincent Massey to become chairman of the board after he retired as high commissioner in London. I in turn persuaded the prime minister to appoint Lawren Harris, my favourite painter, to the board. Before suggesting his name I mentioned the idea to Jim Coyne, who wondered whether the gallery might come to be called the Massey-Harris Gallery. He also wondered whether a 'live artist' should be on the board, and I pointed out that a dead one could hardly qualify. Lawren Harris was appointed, was still on the board when I became minister for the gallery for a second time in 1963, and was very active in its interests.

In 1953 I was delighted to become minister for the National Gallery. My most important task was to find a new director. Alan Jarvis was my choice, and he soon breathed new life into the institution. The choice of the Lorne Building as a temporary home for the gallery was also mine. It was largely because of my persistence that the first woman was appointed to the Board, Mrs H.A. (Bobby) Dyde, a discerning critic and collector of paintings and helpful in administration and public relations. My responsibility for the gallery was truly a labour of love, though its course was not always smooth. It was to be much rougher the second time round.

Acting Postmaster General

I was acting postmaster general during most of the long illness of Alcide Côté in 1953. My duties included dealing with a steady stream of complaints from MPs, to which I replied personally, as I believed MPs deserved word from the minister even though the investigation of complaints and usually the replies were drafted by officials. But I never signed a letter I did not read, and few I did not revise. The officials I had found were better letter carriers than letter drafters.

The deputy postmaster general was my old friend Walter Turnbull, and I was able with his help to have the postal service in Newfoundland improved dramatically. The head of the post office for the province was an old civil servant from Commission of

Government days, trained to say no to any change and resistant to my suggested improvements in service. He was close to retirement age. I asked Turnbull to get the second-in-command a promotion outside Newfoundland and to have the brightest official in the right category moved from the mainland as second-in-command, to be put in charge as soon as the old man could be put out to pasture. The plan worked well, many of the outports were soon receiving mail every day, and service everywhere was substantially improved. Being acting minister involved additional hours of work every week, but what I was able to do for Newfoundland was a reward.

Côté died in August 1955. One burden was removed from my shoulders when Roch Pinard, the secretary of state, was appointed acting postmaster general. Pinard remained acting minister until November while St Laurent looked for a successor. There was no backbencher he wanted to bring into the cabinet, and he saw no alternative to moving Pinard to the Post Office and making Bob Lapointe secretary of state in addition to having him continue as minister of Veterans Affairs.

Pinard, I knew, was not good at administration and had little talent for public relations or dealing with grievances. I did not think the government could afford another fumbler in the Post Office. I made the suggestion that Pinard be left as secretary of state, and Lapointe be asked to take the Post Office as well as Veterans Affairs. St Laurent objected that those two departments would involve a great deal of work, and that Lapointe was reputed to be lazy. I said that Lapointe's father had had the same reputation, but that, in my observation, neither father nor son ever had serious difficulties in Parliament, and each had always seemed on top of his responsibilities. Bob always seemed to know what he was talking about in cabinet and had demonstrated a real feel for politics. St Laurent accepted my view, and Lapointe became postmaster general. He had no trouble in handling the two departments.

A taste of blood

The parliamentary session of 1955 should have been an easy one; no spectacular measures were forecast. But an essentially trivial piece of legislation gave the Opposition the taste of blood. The Department of Defence Production had been created to provide rearmament for the Korean War. The law gave exceptional powers to the minister to provide the sinews of war speedily and without obstruction. Those powers were not opposed when the department was established because it was not permanent. Its life was to expire in 1956. When the Korean War ended, Canadian armed forces were already stationed in Europe as a NATO component. Howe's officials convinced him that the defence production department would be needed indefinitely, and the cabinet agreed.

Legislation was drafted to remove the expiry date in the existing law. When the bill was before cabinet for approval, I noticed that it was in the name of the minister. I said I had never before seen a bill to change the structure of government, or even of a single department, in the name of anyone but the prime minister. Before anyone could say a word Howe struck out minister of defence production and wrote in prime minister. I had raised the point because I felt St Laurent himslf should pilot the bill through the House. But once he introduced it, he turned the management of the debate over to Howe, and I was convinced. St Laurent in his conciliatory way and with his drafting skill would have no trouble in getting the legislation approved, and I suspected that Howe might not. I was reluctant to interfere again by mentioning my concern. The press had already carried stories that the minister had too many arbitrary powers and wanted to keep some he did not need because he liked power for its own sake and because of his contempt for Parliament. I did not, of course, agree with that assessment, but I knew that Howe had no mastery of legal intricacies and relied on officials to say what exceptional provisions were needed in the law. The officials advised him that all the powers conferred by the original legislation were necessary to meet possible emergencies. The Tory Opposition claimed that some of the powers were unnecessary but were retained to satisfy Howe's hunger for power. Howe dug in his heels and a long tug-of-war ensued.

If St Laurent had not been suffering one of his periods of depression, he would have taken over and made concessions and so ensured easy passage of the bill. Instead the debate was dragged on long enough to create a public impression that the government was arrogant, and that Howe dominated the cabinet. Far too late Howe threw in his hand, went off for a fishing trip and told Harris and St Laurent to settle the matter in any way they liked. Once St Laurent took over, he telephoned Drew and worked out a compromise, which, when presented to the House, Drew accepted graciously, and the bill was passed by the time Howe returned. But the Tory Opposition had created the impression that by a filibuster they had forced the government to retreat. They had tasted blood and wanted more, and they were to get it in 1956.

Surplus natural gas

I was only vaguely aware of the oil and natural gas boom in Alberta from 1949 until 1953. The question of where markets should be found for the gas that was surplus to the needs of the province then became a political issue. Transport of gas beyond the province was under federal jurisdiction. Parliament could decide where the gas could be marketed.

I had paid no attention when a company called TransCanada PipeLines was incorporated by Parliament in 1951. The Texan promoters of TransCanada proposed to build a pipeline within Canada from Alberta to Montreal, to be financed by private capital.

Howe announced in Parliament in 1953 that the export of natural gas from Canada would not be permitted until the government was satisfied that there could be no economic use, present or future. for the gas within Canada. When Howe spoke of a pipeline's being started in the near future, I did not realize that a natural gas pipeline would be the dominant political issue in Canada for the next three years. Even when St Laurent repeated the Canada First natural gas policy in a speech in Edmonton during the 1953 election campaign, I did not guess what a controversy would develop.

I did know that natural gas had long been an important source of energy in southwestern Ontario. A cousin of mine had a gas well on the farm next to the one where I was born, and she used her own gas for heating and cooking. The Ontario wells were going dry, and the company that distributed gas wanted to import it mainly from Texas. The producers in Alberta and the Alberta government wanted to export their surplus directly to the United States. That continental system would have been the most profitable for the Ontario distributors and the Alberta producers.

Howe was adamantly opposed to the continental approach, which would have bypassed a potential market in Manitoba and northern Ontario and probably not reached Montreal. Ontario was facing an energy shortage, but Premier Frost did not want to depend on an American source that might be cut off in an emergency. Once Howe had convinced St Laurent that an all-Canadian pipeline could be economically feasible, St Laurent never wavered in his support. Both Howe and St Laurent were prepared to resort to public ownership rather than abandon the idea of an all-Canadian pipeline, though both felt such ownership would be second best.

The promoters of TransCanada PipeLines were a group of rich Texans. It was therefore easy to misrepresent TransCanada as a scheme by an American-born minister to turn a Canadian resource over to American control. The CCF were opposed to a privately owned pipeline and wanted one built and operated by a crown company. The federal Tories had no policy of their own, and there is little doubt their opposition was supported by the interests who wanted to supply Ontario with Texas gas.

The proposed trans-Canada pipeline was a project greater in magnitude, cost and complexity than the St Lawrence Seaway, and it was not altogether an exaggeration to compare it with the original transcontinental railway. Before Parliament was asked to approve the seaway, the government had convinced the public, through speeches by St Laurent and Chevrier, that such an undertaking was in the national interest. The fundamental mistake of the St Laurent government in 1956 was to commit itself to support the construction of the longest pipeline in the world without a campaign explaining to the public both the difficulties and the advantages of such a great national project. In his early years as prime minister St Laurent himself would have taken the lead in such a campaign, and in my opinion he would have made sure the means were available to carry the project to completion. But in early 1956, as in early 1955, he was suffering from depression and lacked the strength and resolution to take overall control from the start. Instead the public presentation of the pipeline project was left to Howe, who had little talent for public relations and little patience for campaigns of persuasion.

St Laurent and Howe did convince Premier Ernest Manning of Alberta that the federal government would not permit export to the United States until Canadian present and future needs were safeguarded. At that point a merger was arranged under the TransCanada name between the Alberta-based company that had wanted to export gas to the United States and TransCanada PipeLines. In addition to the pipeline to Montreal, the new company was to be permitted to build a spur-line from Winnipeg to the U.S. border to export surplus gas.

By that time I had become deeply involved in what was happening. St Laurent discussed developments with me. I was also kept informed by my friend Ross Tolmie, who had been in the Department of Finance during the war. Shortly after the war ended, Tolmie had started to practise law in Ottawa, and Trans-Canada was one of his clients.

The company had originally thought it could finance the pipeline on its own, but complications, mainly about securing permission from the American regulatory authorities to allow gas to be imported at the Manitoba-Minnesota border, made it clear that TransCanada could not raise all the capital needed to build the all-Canadian pipeline without some financial support from government. Without going into the detail, the government of Canada joined with Ontario in forming a crown company to finance a section of the pipeline in northern Ontario. Later a loan from the government of Canada was also needed. The government of Ontario had agreed to the joint crown company on the condition that the construction of the pipeline was started by the end of

1956. Another constraint was that pipe to build pipelines was in short supply. TransCanada had an option on pipe that would expire on 7 June 1956.

The Speech from the Throne in January forecast legislation to facilitate the construction of a pipeline from Alberta to Montreal. The government assumed that the Tory Opposition would not display strong hostility to a project so firmly supported by the Tory government of Ontario. Not much attention was paid to a warning by Diefenbaker on 9 March that the filibuster on the defence production bill in 1955 'would appear a mere skirmish beside the battle we will wage when the Bill regarding Trans Canada Pipe Lines comes before Parliament.'

The unavoidable delays meant that the legislation was not ready for debate in Parliament until the end of the first week of May, and it had to pass all stages in the House by 5 June if construction was to start in 1956.

Because the value of the pipeline had not been adequately explained before the debate began, it was easy to portray what was happening as an attempt by the government, dominated by an arrogant minister, to ram its policy through Parliament without debate. By the beginning of May the government had already lost the battle for public support of the project. In my opinion even St Laurent at his most persuasive could not have presented the government's case for the pipeline effectively enough to penetrate the smokescreen already created by the Conservative and CCF Opposition, who were aided and abetted by the majority of newspapers and broadcasters, reinforced by the new medium of television.

The pipeline filibuster

It was 8 May when Howe introduced legislation to provide financial support for TransCanada PipeLines.

There were two days of procedural obstruction before Howe was able to move the resolution. It was already clear that the Opposition would use every possible parliamentary device to prevent passage of the legislation. The filibuster was to justify

Diefenbaker's forecast and prove a more serious upheaval in Parliament than the conscription debate in 1944. I have already given a detailed account of the proceedings in Parliament in *My Years with Louis St. Laurent*. Here I shall confine myself to the highlights of that turbulent month from 8 May to 5 June. My part in debate was confined to a few interjections, but I was the assistant to Harris as government house leader. We were mainly responsible for strategy and tactics, a role that absorbed much of my time and nervous energy.

Harris had warned the cabinet as early as 1 May that the legislation could probably not be passed by the June deadline without using closure. Closure had not been used since 1932, and no one in Parliament in 1956 had even seen it used. Few understood the closure rule. Closure had never been used by a Liberal government, and when Tory governments had used it, Liberal Oppositions had called it a tactic to stifle debate.

The systematic obstruction on 9 and 10 May was facilitated by Speaker René Beaudoin. Under the rules a decision by the Speaker could not be debated, but only appealed to a vote of the House. Contrary to the rules Beaudoin weakly permitted his decisions to be debated by the Opposition and thereby greatly prolonged the debate.

Harris and I were convinced that the deadline could not be met without closure. We worked out a schedule showing how many days could be allowed for each stage of the procedure and went over it in detail with St Laurent. Howe did not understand the closure rule and left procedure almost entirely to Harris. The government decided not to go ahead with the pipeline debate on 11 May, so that the cabinet could review the situation. Harris read the timetable for completing each stage of the proceedings to the cabinet and explained how closure would work. Some ministers shuddered, but it was left to Harris and St Laurent to decide whether and at what stage closure should be invoked.

The pipeline resolution was called again for debate on Monday, 14 May. The Opposition used up two hours and forced three recorded votes before Howe was able to move the resolution. It was obvious that the opportunities for obstruction were far from exhausted, and were in fact numerous, because unlike in the 1955 filibuster the Tories had the CCF as an ally. Stanley Knowles, with his superior knowledge of the rules, became the real leader of the Opposition from 14 May until 5 June.

Just before Howe rose to speak, Harris and I decided that there was no object in delaying resort to closure. St Laurent agreed, and Harris gave Howe a statement containing the necessary notice. Howe made an excellent and unprovocative exposition of the pipeline project. At its close he turned to Harris, who nodded affirmatively, whereupon Howe announced that he would move closure the next day. Opposition members pretended to be indignant, but they were scarcely able to conceal their satisfaction. Knowles exclaimed, 'The guillotine!' and several members shouted, 'Dictatorship!' The alleged gagging of Parliament was a debating issue that suited them far better than did the merits of the pipeline.

When notice of closure is given, the final vote has to be taken at the end of the next day. Closure was also applied at once to second reading of the bill. Using closure from the start meant that the resolution and second reading took only two days each.

On 23 May the House had reached the committee stage of the bill. We knew it would be the most difficult time: members could speak repeatedly, as often as they could get the floor, on each section of the Bill, and all sections were supposed to be considered before closure could be applied. Harris had worked out a plan for letting the debate go on for several days before closure would be imposed. The plan would have provided up to six days for debate in committee. He suggested to the cabinet that he explain the plan in the House and the cabinet agreed. Harris and I felt that if the plan were explained, press and public would know how much time was available for debate, and the charge that Parliament was being gagged might be lessened. Obstruction in the House all that day prevented the House from getting into committee, and Harris had no chance to make his statement.

Some time between the closing of the sitting that day and the opening of the sitting on 24 May, Howe persuaded St Laurent and

Harris not to have the proposed statement made. It was the only time Howe interfered with procedure. I felt a serious mistake was being made, because neither the press nor the public was given any explanation of why debate had to be limited if the legislation were to be passed by 7 June to ensure the beginning of construction in 1956.

The House got into committee on 24 May, and obstruction began at once. The committee was presided over by the Deputy Speaker, William Robinson. He was one of the best-liked members, fair-minded but with only a modest knowledge of the rules. His mind worked slowly, and he lacked firmness. The Opposition took almost brutal advantage of him, and the obstruction during the rest of that week was relentless.

Not one word was spoken about the provisions of the bill. Robinson himself was exhausted. St Laurent, Harris and I agreed that he should no longer be asked to preside, and that his place should be taken by E.T. Applewhaite, the deputy chairman. Applewhaite was quick-witted and quick on his feet, and no one could push him around.

It was obvious that the legislation could not be completed by the deadline if each clause had to be considered separately. There was a precedent for another method of applying closure in committee of the whole. When Prime Minister Bennett had applied closure in 1932, he had done so before all the clauses of the bill had been considered. That was the most recent precedent, but St Laurent did not believe the precedent represented a correct interpretation of the closure rule. Harris and I persuaded him that the only alternative to using the Bennett precedent was to miss the deadline. He then decided that he would invoke the Bennett precedent himself when the time came, but said he wanted first to make one final appeal for reasonable consideration of the bill.

The weekend before Applewhaite took over the chairmanship of the committee of the whole, I performed my most important role during the filibuster. It was essential, I felt, that Applewhaite should know precisely how the 1932 precedent had worked, how the government intended to proceed, and what objections we anticipated. I briefed him thoroughly and was satisfied that he knew what we were going to do, and that he believed he could maintain control of the committee.

St Laurent made his appeal for reason at the opening of the House on Monday, 28 May. It met a rather friendly response from Drew, but the usual obstruction began and lasted for much of the day. When the House finally got into committee, a non-debatable motion Howe had made the week before had to be voted on. Applewhaite rose to call the vote, and the Opposition at once tried to obstruct. Applewhaite resisted the obstruction successfully, and the motion was passed. No further motion was made by the government, and there was nothing to obstruct. The Opposition was left with no choice but to discuss the pipeline for the latter part of that day, all of 29 May and the first part of 30 May. St Laurent then spoke briefly to make the point that, under the rules, the final vote would not be possible before 4 June, and he offered to have the House sit additional hours to have a thorough debate. He pointed out that if the work of the committee was not completed in the meantime, he would have no choice but to move closure on the whole bill the next day. No progress was made, and St Laurent moved closure on 31 May as soon as the House went into committee.

Knowles raised a point of order, that St Laurent's motion infringed the closure rule. Applewhaite heard Knowles, Diefenbaker and Drew on the point. St Laurent then argued that he did not think the Opposition should question the right of the government to do everything it could, under proper parliamentary procedure, to give every member the opportunity to vote on the bill. On the strength of the Bennett precedent he concluded that the chair should reject the point of order Knowles had raised.

Applewhaite ruled St Laurent's motion was in order, and his ruling was appealed. Shortly after 5 p.m. the Speaker came into the House to call the vote on the appeal. He rose to do so, and under the rules no member is allowed to interrupt him. But instead of calling the vote at once, the Speaker allowed Gordon Churchill to interrupt on an alleged point of order. Harris and I were aghast. For the rest of the day obstruction grew steadily worse, until the house had to adjourn at 10. There was no way to tell what would happen the next day. I walked out of the House with Howe, who said, in deep gloom, 'Our bill is dead.' Harris tried to find out from the Speaker what might be done, but got no satisfaction. He then joined St Laurent, Howe and me in the prime minister's office, and we discussed the situation. I thought I had figured out a way by which, under the rules, the Speaker, if he was firm enough, could gradually get the House back into committee. I offered to see Beaudoin early in the morning to explain my plan. None of them believed I would succeed, but St Laurent finally said we had nothing to lose by trying.

I telephoned Beaudoin early in the morning and he reluctantly agreed to see me. When I arrived at his house, I said we had been baffled as to how the government should proceed to try to get the House back into committee. We had finally worked out a series of motions, and I thought he should be told of them in advance so as not to be taken by surprise. He said that he did not want to listen, that he had made mistakes unfair to the government, and that I could assure the prime minister he knew how to correct them. I was far from convinced, but there was nothing more to do but report to St Laurent and Harris and wait for what would happen in the House.

As soon as the House met on Friday, 1 June, the Speaker brushed aside what was being discussed the evening before and made the statement that at around 5:15 on the previous day he had made a very serious mistake in allowing a point of order and other dilatory motions; that the House should not suffer prejudice or detriment on his account; and that it should revert to its position of 5:15 the day before. He said it was up to the House to decide, and called a vote.

The Opposition raised a disturbance and used various devices to prevent the vote, but for once the Speaker was firm. During the ringing of the bells for the vote there was great disorder on the Opposition side, and taunting back and forth, whlch Harris succeeded in restraining on the government side, though some

Liberal backbenchers began to sing. I was frightened at seeing an orderly assembly turn almost into a mob. As a historian I reflected I was seeing something I had only read about; as a member of the government I realized how fragile the line was between deliberation and disorder, and how easy it might be for disorder to turn into violence. I was far from sure order could be restored. The slow process of taking the vote on the Speaker's proposal relieved the tension a little. There were no negative votes. Drew said that the Conservatives were not voting 'because there is no question properly before the House,' and Coldwell said 'I share that opinion.' By that time, fortunately, it was 1 p.m. and the House adjourned for the luncheon recess. The atmosphere calmed down in the afternoon, and in the evening there was a lively debate, ending with the vote on closure in the committee of the whole.

That day, 1 June 1956, was called Black Friday by the Opposition and the media. The bill was on the order paper for final reading on Monday, 4 June, but it faced another hurdle. Drew had put a motion of censure of the Speaker on the order paper. The rules required that debate on a motion to censure the Speaker must begin as soon as the House opened.

Drew spoke on the motion in a moderate tone, as did spokesmen for the other parties. St Laurent then made a defence of the Speaker in a speech on which he and I had worked during the weekend. He developed his argument from a chronological account of the debate that I had prepared. He agreed with Drew that Beaudoin still had the affectionate consideration and regard of most members. He then argued that, on a highly contentious measure before the House for three or four weeks, there had been demonstrated 'a very firm determination to have the will of the minority prevail over the will of the majority in the house by preventing the majority from having an opportunity to manifest its will in accordance with our constitutional principles.' He said that in spite of the elevated tone of the speeches by Drew and Coldwell it would appear to many observers that the motion of censure was one more attempt to prevent the majority from reaching a final vote on the pipeline measure. Drew objected and expressed regret that St Laurent had made that suggestion. St Laurent replied that not even the prime minister could avoid thinking that each and every move that had been made since the pipeline resolution was first brought before the house was designed to prevent the bill from becoming law. He concluded by saying that a vote on Drew's motion would not create a happy situation, and that he felt members on the government side of the House were entitled to some time to consider it, and that reasonable men, after they had had an opportunity of expressing their views, would feel something had to be done to allow Parliament to carry on its work effectively. St Laurent then moved the adjournment of the debate, and his motion was carried.

Howe then moved third reading of the pipeline bill, and St Laurent announced that he would move closure the next day. Drew and Coldwll spoke, and Harris replied for the government. In my opinion at the time, an opinion confirmed by a reading of it in *Hansard*, his speech was the finest he ever made in the House and one of the unquestionably great debating speeches I had heard in 20 years' observing and participating in Parliament. With respect to publicity the most effective point Harris made was that the pipeline measure had been before the House for three solid weeks, and that Knowles and Fulton had spoken more than 30 times each, Drew and Fleming more than 20 times each, and Coldwell 15 times. If that record represented a gag, it was a new definition of the word.

The bill passed under closure on 5 June, passed the Senate on the 7th and was given royal assent on the day the option on the pipeline would have expired.

In 1975, in *My Years with Louis St. Laurent*, I said that I had never doubted that the construction of the pipeline was worth whatever it may have cost the government and the Liberal party. If the start of construction had not been assured in 1956, Manitoba and, to a greater extent, Ontario would have been forced to turn to other sources of energy. Without the temporary loan to TransCanada the company would probably have disintegrated, and a pipeline from Alberta to central Canada been delayed indefinitely; and the continentalists in Alberta and Toronto would probably have succeeded in having Alberta gas sold in the United States and Texas gas imported into Ontario. I said that northern and eastern Ontario, western Quebec and Montreal might not yet have a supply of natural gas. Howe had the vision to promote a great national undertaking that contributed to the preservation of Canadian independence and the strengthening of the Canadian economy. St Laurent and Harris had the parliamentary skill and the sheer grit to turn that vision into reality. That remains my opinion today.

Parliament recovers

Not only the life of the pipeline had been at stake. Drew's motion to censure the Speaker, which St Laurent had adjourned on 4 June had to be dealt with. The original purpose of the motion had been to delay the vote on the pipeline, and it had failed. The debate was an anticlimax, concluded by Drew on 8 June. The motion was overwhelmingly defeated. In his concluding speech Drew accused me of having encouraged disorder on the Liberal benches on Black Friday. I managed to interject a denial and to add that I had been horrified by the disorder in the House that day.

St Laurent, Harris and I realized there was a real threat to the life of Parliament. Parliament had not yet voted any money to pay for the operations of the government after 31 May 1956. Until all the votes for the expenditures of every department for the year have been voted, the practice is to vote enough money for one or more months at a time to pay the expenses of government. The votes are called interim supply. If the Opposition held up a vote of more money until the middle of June, the government would not be able to pay the civil servants or meet other expenses. The session would have to be ended.

When Parliament is not in session, the law allows the government to use what are called governor general's warrants to authorize the expenditure of money urgently needed to pay its bills. In theory a governor general's warrant could have been used to provide money for one month, and Parliament then called back into session. But the outrage would have been so great that the government could not have faced it. In practical terms, if the Opposition held up granting interim supply until after the salaries of civil servants and other bills could not be paid, the government would have no choice but to have Parliament dissolved, and an election called.

When interim supply was needed, the government in most cases gave no advance notice and asked unanimous consent to proceed the same day. Consent was usually granted. Harris decided to ask for money for the month of June and tried to get consent, but Drew insisted that the government give the 48 hours' notice normally required for any business to be introduced in the House.

We took the refusal of unanimous consent to mean that the Tories and the CCF were going to start another filibuster, to last until the government was not able to pay its bills. Harris gave the necessary notice, and we decided to meet the expected crisis on Monday, 11 June. On that Monday morning there was a gloomy meeting of the cabinet. Everyone agreed that our fate depended on Drew. Howe and I were the only ministers who professed to believe that Drew would not hold up the vote; I don't know about Howe, but I was far from confident. As we left the cabinet I bet St Laurent 25 cents that Drew would cave in. The press reported that Drew had said he intended to stand firm. What changed his mind I don't know; all I do know is that after he had spoken for a very few minutes on Monday afternoon, it became clear that he was not going to hold up the grant of money. Knowles was obviously bitterly disappointed, but he recognized that the CCF alone could not carry on a successful filibuster. The crisis was over. As Drew took his seat at the end of his speech, I moved in behind the prime minister and put out my hand in front of him, and he put a 25 cent piece into it.

Knowles was visibly angry when he followed Drew. He claimed that the government had lost the confidence of the country and should call an election. St Laurent instead made a brief speech about plans for the rest of the session, and the money was voted.

The temperature of the House went down rapidly. By 22 June, St Laurent felt relatively easy about going off to London to attend a meeting of commonwealth prime ministers and leaving Howe as acting prime minister. Until 29 June, Parliament seemed to be performing in a normal fashion. That day the *Globe and Mail* published a translation of two paragraphs of a personal letter the Speaker had written to an elderly journalist, who had published the extract in French in a Montreal newspaper. The story in the *Globe and Mail* was headed 'Critics Falsify the Facts, Speaker's Letter Complains.' In the letter Beaudoin had hotly denied charges allegedly made by Conservative and CCF MPs that he and the Deputy Speaker had abandoned the essential impartiality of the chair and leaned towards the government in their rulings in the pipeline debate.

Drew raised a question of privilege that day. Howe as acting prime minister replied briefly, saying that the fact that an extract from a private letter written by the Speaker was published was unfortunate, but 'to suggest that Parliament should be dissolved because of it is, I think ...' Here he was interrupted by Solon Low, who said, 'Nonsense.' Howe continued, 'The leader of the Social Credit party has used the word, so I will adopt it.' He said a private letter from a Speaker who had recently been upheld by a vote of the House was not an adequate reason to dissolve Parliament. That day was a Friday.

On Monday, 2 July, Beaudoin, obviously upset, announced that he was placing his resignation before the House, to take effect at the pleasure of the House. Howe thanked the Speaker for not pressing his resignation in the absence of the prime minister, who would be back in the House a week later. All of us assumed that the resignation would be accepted.

When St Laurent returned to Ottawa on Friday evening, 6 July, he quickly came to the conclusion that Beaudoin should be persuaded to remain in office, and the cabinet acquiesced. From that moment St Laurent took complete command of the situation and dealt with the crisis as forcefully and authoritatively as he ever did at any time during his years in office. When the House met on Monday, 9 July, St Laurent announced immediately that he had seen the Speaker, who had agreed not to insist on resigning. St Laurent decided without hesitatlon that the publication of an extract from a personal letter did not justify accepting the resignation of a Speaker who had recently received an overwhelming vote of approval in the House. He declared that his confidence in the Speaker was unshaken, and that he knew of no member better qualified than Beaudoin to preside over the deliberations of the House, and believed his confidence was shared by an overwhelming majority of members. He concluded, 'As the one responsible for the leadership in this House, I have expressed that view to Mr. Speaker and I have found that he was willing to subordinate his personal feelings to his duty to Parliament and the country, and to continue in the office in which he has served with great distinction. I am happy to be able to make that announcement to the House.' Surprise reigned; not a word was said in the House in reply.

St Laurent's complete mastery of the House was demonstrated again the next day, when Knowles raised a grievance against the prime minister: 'In addition to the injury that has been done to Parliament in this session a further insult was added yesterday by the Prime Minister.' He urged St Laurent not to close the door to an early dissolution and election. St Laurent replied by reminding the Opposition in general and Knowles in particular that the Constitution did not provide for unanimous decisions by the House of Commons, but for decisions by the majority of its members. For quite a long time the Opposition had tried to create the impression that it was not for the supporters of the government to make decisions, but for the Opposition, and that whenever any proposal was put before the House that the members of the Opposition did not agree with, it was wrong, unconstitutional and a contempt of Parliament not to accept their view.

Once Knowles's grievance was disposed of, the session continued to be presided over by the Speaker, from 12 July to 14 August, in a relatively orderly and peaceful fashion, and a great deal of public business was disposed of. The early restoration of order in Parliament showed that neither the filibuster nor the application of closure did any lasting damage to Parliament. The Speaker and the Deputy Speaker, not Parliament were the real casualties of the pipeline debate.

Equalization

There was a great deal of activity in federal-provincial relations in 1955 and 1956. Public interest was growing in hospital insurance, which was one of the subjects discussed at a conference, held mainly in camera, in April 1955. I was not present and was greatly surprised when St Laurent told me that Premier Frost of Ontario had referred to a speech I had made in Kitchener and protested that the federal government had started a campaign to force the government of Ontario to accept hospital insurance. The *Globe and Mail* had reported that in that speech, to a regional Liberal conference, I had said that Ontario would not have a hospital insurance plan until there was a change of government in that province. Fortunately, Hees asked a question in the House that enabled me to correct the record. I told the House that I had perhaps been the most astonished person in Canada when I read what was attributed to me. I explained that what I had said, in substance, was that health was constitutionally a provincial matter, but that the policy of the federal Liberal party was to assist in provincially administered hospital insurance when the provinces generally were in accord, and that that could not happen until the Ontario government adopted a new attitude.

When Frost made his complaint, St Laurent had the correct version of what I had said, but I have sometimes wondered whether the publicity helped to start Ontario on the road to OHIP. If it did, it was to prove a long, slow road.

St Laurent's main concern in the field of federal-provincial relations was not with hospital insurance but with tax-sharing and equalization. He wanted to find a permanent plan acceptable to all the provinces to replace the tax-rental agreements and the compromise reached with Duplessis in 1954. When the postwar tax-rental system had started, in 1947, Ontario and Québec had refused to make tax-rental agreements but had not imposed any personal income tax, so the tax remained uniform across the country. When Ontario made a tax-rental agreement in 1952, Québec was left in an isolated position. Québec imposed its own income tax in 1954, and St Laurent worked out with Duplessis a stopgap arrangement that substantially reduced the burden of double taxation in Québec, but Québec was still not receiving the benefits other provinces were from tax-rental payments.

During the summer and early fall of 1955 a revolutionary new approach to tax-sharing and equalization of provincial revenues was under discussion. John Deutsch was its main advocate in the Department of Finance, and he convinced me that the new approach would almost certainly end the dangerous isolation of Québec, since no agreements would have to be signed, and no tax fields would have to be rented to Ottawa. The tax-rental payments included a fairly large element of subsidy to the poorer provinces, which subsidy had enabled those provinces to establish and maintain standards of public services approaching those of the wealthier provinces. Under the new plan equalization grants would be substituted for the element of subsidy in the tax-rental payments. The equalization grants would be paid regardless of whether the provincial governments made tax-rental agreements or imposed their own taxes. Under the proposed new tax-sharing plan Québec could therefore continue to impose its own taxes and be eligible for the equalization grant without having to sign any agreement with Ottawa. Since Québec was really a 'have-not' province, it would be entitled to a large equalization grant, which it was not likely Duplessis would refuse, given that there would be no agreement to sign that could be described as infringement of provincial autonomy. St Laurent liked the plan, which might end Québec's isolation.

Some senior officials in the Department of Finance opposed the plan because every provincial government would be free to impose its own tax, and the simplicity and convenience of having the same personal income tax all over Canada would probably disappear. I felt, as Deutsch did, that since Québec already had a different tax, uniformity had already disappeared, and that their objection therefore made no sense. In the face of conflicting advice from his departmental officials Harris did not find it easy to make a decision in a complex field in which he was just beginning to find his feet. I was enthusiastic about the plan and urged him strongly to accept it; he, quite rightly, wanted to convince himself. During his period of hesitation St Laurent became impatient with Harris, the only time that I can recall. He did not show his impatience to Harris, but I knew he expected me to serve as an intermediary. I tried to emphasize to St Laurent how essential it was that the minister of finance not merely be convinced the new proposal was an improvement but feel at ease in presenting it.

Harris made his decision in time to describe the new plan in his budget speech in March 1956, and no provincial government openly objected. A federal-provincial conference in October 1955 found the provincial governments, including Duplessis's, generally receptive to the plan, though all of them wanted a greater share of the taxes than the federal government was willing to concede.

The previous exposure in the budget and the provincial attitude at the conference did not give the Opposition a strong base for attack, and the legislation passed fairly easily.

I sat in the House almost continuously during the debate. I was eager to make one speech on a subject not related to my ministerial responsibilities. It was no doubt largely vanity that impelled me to want to display my knowledge of the problem of federal-provincial tax-sharing, with which I had been directly concerned since my arrival in Ottawa in 1937. I spoke after Harris had assured me that he did not mind my prolonging the debate. My speech was listened to with attention but I am not sure my emphasis on the equalization payments to the poorer provinces was helpful to Harris and the other Liberals from Ontario.

That measure, of fundamental importance to Canada, was enacted by a Parliament in which two Opposition parties had claimed the government was completely discredited. The recovery of normal parliamentary behaviour was a tribute to Harris's skill as house leader and to St Laurent's mastery of Parliament in the crisis. It was characteristic of St Laurent's leadership that he left the management of the debate on equalization entirely to Harris and did not himself say a word during the enactment of a measure for which he was uniquely responsible. The federal-provincial tax-sharing and equalization plan was regarded by St Laurent as his crowning achievement in federal-provincial relations. It is a tribute to him that equalization is now a included in the Constitution.

Suez

That Britain and France were so deeply disturbed by the nationalization of the Suez Canal by Egypt did not really engage my attention until the actual attack on Egyptian territory by Israel, France and Britain on 29 October. There was no warning to Canada or the United States, and the heads of both governments were taken completely by surprise.

The action seemed to St Laurent, as it did to Eisenhower, an act of aggression contrary to the United Nations Charter. Both governments were anxious that the fighting be stopped before it could escalate. At the UN, Eisenhower was ready to join the Soviet Union and other nations in condemning Britain and France as aggressors. Pearson and St Laurent wanted to avoid such a condemnation and find a compromise to end the fighting and restore unity to the free world.

I was in complete accord with Pearson and St Laurent. But I realized that because Canada had questioned the British action, the Conservative Opposition might succeed in portraying the Liberal government in general, and the prime minister in particular, as anti-British. Pearson's remarkable achievement in getting the support of all the free countries for the establishment of the UN Emergency Force might have got general approval in Canada if it had not been necessary to seek parliamentary authority for the expenditures on the Canadian troops serving in the force.

When Parliament met on 26 November 1956, Earl Rowe, the acting leader of the Opposition, condemned the government in extravagant language for failing to support Britain. He aroused St Laurent, who in his reply to Rowe referred to a UN resolution that had been construed, as he thought rightly, as placing some blame on the Israelis, the French and the British 'for having taken the law into their own hands when what had to be dealt with was already before the Security Council of the United Nations.' St Laurent said that Opposition spokesmen seemed to forget that the nations of the world had signed the UN Charter and thereby undertaken to use peaceful means to settle disputes and not to resort to the use of force. He added that he had been 'scandalized' more than once by the larger powers using the veto 'when their own so-called vital interests were at stake' because they were not willing to 'allow this crowd of smaller nations' to make a decision that a larger power claimed affected its vital interests. An Opposition member interrupted to ask, 'Why should they?' St Laurent answered that the smaller nations were composed of human beings just as the larger, and then uttered the fatal words, 'The era when the supermen of Europe could govern the whole world is coming pretty close to an end.'

I shuddered, because I realized at once how the words could be used to paint St Laurent as an enemy of Britain. Howard Green seized on them immediately. He said that St Laurent in his own speech had 'lumped the United Kingdom and France with Russia in his condemnation.' Green said: 'I suppose he considers that all the supermen are in the Canadian government. If they are not all in the Canadian government, then I presume the opinion of this same Prime Minister is that they are in the United States government. Here you have the Prime Minister of France and Prime Minister Eden of the United Kingdom. They do not claim to be supermen.' Working himself up to a climax, Green supposed that 'the Prime Minister of Canada sneers at Sir Winston Churchill as a superman and includes him in his nasty, biting remarks.'

The next day I went off to Vienna. On my return two weeks later I soon realized how widespread a feeling had been created that St Laurent was anti-British. I feared the feeling might be especially strong in Newfoundland. By good fortune I had been invited to speak at the annual meeting of the Newfoundland Board of Trade on 6 February 1957. Every year the speech was broadcast on all the radio stations in the province. When Granger asked me what my subject would be, I said I intended to explain 'the supermen of Europe.' He begged me to let people forget it, but I persisted.

I called my speech 'The Prospects for Peace.' I attempted to put St Laurent's phrase in a broad context: 'Up until 1939, it could still be said with some truth that the world was dominated by the wealth and strength of the European nations, if we include among European nations the nations of the British Commonwealth and the United States. In other words, if I may borrow a phrase, the world of 1939 still looked as though it was dominated by the supermen of Europe. When I speak of the European domination of the world, I do not mean Europe geographically, but all the nations of European stock, including particularly the United States. Throughout this century, there has been a growing resentment in the rest of the world at this domination by Europeans and a growing animosity towards the white races. But during and immediately after the Second World War this resentment and animosity was transformed into an explosive rise of nationalism in every country of Asia and Africa. We are just deceiving ourselves if we pretend that this rise of nationalism is not resentment by coloured people of past domination by Europeans.' I was told, even by Conservatives, that my speech had a favourable effect on opinion in Newfoundland.

St Laurent's alleged hostility to Britin made a greater impact on the public than his and Pearson's solution of the Suez crisis. The impression that he was anti-Britain was not effaced by the favourable publicity surrounding his meeting with Harold Macmillan, who had succeeded Eden as the British prime minister. After meeting Eisenhower in Bermuda, Macmillan met St Laurent and Pearson, to brief them. At a press conference, Macmillan heaped praise on Canada's role and Pearson's part in restoring peace in the world and unity among the Atlantic allies.

Shortly after St Laurent returned from Bermuda, I asked him what kind of man Macmillan was, and he replied: 'You know, I always felt that talking to Churchill was rather like talking to God, though you weren't quite sure that he was listening, and I often felt, when I was talking to Anthony Eden, that he didn't quite understand what I was talking about. But,' he went on, 'I like Macmillan, I could talk to him exactly the same way I can talk to you.'

Several years later, after both St Laurent and Macmillan had retired, I was invited to a dinner at which Macmillan was the guest of honour, and had the opportunity for a conversation after dinner. He talked to me about St Laurent for some time and then asked whether he could telephone him the next day. I was sure St Laurent would be delighted and offered to find out when he would be free to talk. The conversation was arranged, and St Laurent was delighted. I myself became a warm admirer of Macmillan and felt he was the first British prime minister who treated Canada and Canadians as equals, without a trace of condescension.

The deceptive recovery

The parliamentary session began smoothly enough on 8 January 1957. The Speaker had no problem presiding, there were no disorders or filibusters, and a substantial volume of important legislation was enacted. Indeed, the session was a sort of Indian summer for the government.

Drew had retired because of ill health, and Diefenbaker had been chosen leader of the Progressive Conservative party in December 1956. He was less aggressive as leader of the Opposition than he had been as private member. After his first speech as leader I said in a broadcast to my constituents that we had expected he would make a much stronger and more critical speech and were a little disappointed that there was not more in his speech to answer. Rather complacently I added, 'He seemed to be having a hard time finding things to criticize the government for.'

St Laurent seemed to have recovered all his former vitality, and his conduct was dynamic during the session. He was primarily responsible for the decision to double the federal grants to universities and to arrange to pay them through the National Council of Canadian Universities, an arrangement he hoped might remove Duplessis's opposition to the grants in Québec. It did not, but the increase was welcomed in the other provinces. St Laurent took the initiative to establish the Canada Council, which body had been recommended by the Massey Commission. I had a part in its establishment. Maurice Lamontagne persuaded St Laurent that the time had come to act, but while the prime minister was considering action, Deutsch, then secretary of the Treasury Board, and I hit on an idea for financing the council. Two multimillionaires, Sir James Dunn and Isaak Walton Killam, had recently died. It was estimated that the succession duties would amount to about $50 million on each estate. Deutsch felt that it was wrong to put those windfalls into general revenue. I asked why they should not be used to provide a capital fund for the Canada Council in one case and a fund for capital grants to the universities in the other. The universities needed more buildings and other facilities for the arts and humanities. Deutsch liked the idea and passed it on to Lamontagne, who persuaded St Laurent to seek and obtain cabinet approval. At my suggestion Brooke Claxton was appointed chairman of the Canada Council and Albert Trueman director. Their qualities were complementary and they got the council off to a good start.

Other constructive measures were proposed in Harris's last budget. He told me that he did not want to be the first minister of finance to bring in a budget of over five billion, and he did not! He estimated that the surplus of revenue over expenditures would be half a billion and that half the surplus be devoted to reducing the national debt. The other half, he agreed, could be devoted to increases in social security payments.

Harris's preference was to devote the whole quarter billion to higher old age pensions. Lesage was insistent that family allowances be increased as well. I supported Lesage because there was no demand for increased old age pensions in Newfoundland, and an increase in family allowances, I knew, would meet more real needs. In the end St Laurent agreed that both should be increased. The increase fixed for the old age pension was lower than it would have been if family allowances had not also been increased. The six-dollar increase in old age pensions was approximately equal to the rise in the cost of living since the previous increase. The prime minister was not willing to say that the six dollars corresponded to the increase in the cost of living, for fear of creating the expectation that old age pensions would thereafter be tied to the cost of living, and no reason was given for the odd figure. The Opposition charged the minister of finance with stinginess, and considerable harm was done to the government by constant references in the election campaign to 'six-buck Harris.' By clever interpretataion the Opposition succeeded in turning every one of the proposals in the budget from electoral assets into liabilities.

When the election of 1957 was announced on 25 April, members of Parliament and the public felt that the St Laurent government had recovered from the low point of midsummer 1956 and expected the prime minister to march forward to his third victory. Mackenzie King had won two landslide victories and had won by a narrow majority in the postwar election of 1945. St Laurent had won two landslide victories, and the general expectation was that he should do at least as well as Mackenzie King by winning a third election. On the night of 10 June government and country were shocked to discover how wrong they had been, and no one was more shocked than I.

The election of 1957

When the campaign began, the economy was generally buoyant, and the country prosperous, far more so than it had been in 1949 or 1953. There were few complaints about the way the government was carrying on the administration. The good management of finances was praised abroad and acknowledged at home. Some of my friends asked me whether the Liberal government would ever be defeated. I answered that it seemed safe for one more election, but that I felt the public was bored after 22 years and, if there was an obvious alternative, would like to make a change. I had known for years that the strongest governments begin to have symptoms of old age, that people forget past services and turn welcoming faces to something new. But with Diefenbaker as the challenger I could not take the possibility of defeat seriously. I had observed his performance in Parliament from the time he was elected in 1940 and was unfavourably impressed. His histrionics had no appeal for me; his disregard for facts and logic, his lack of a responsible or constructive approach to the problems of government and, above all, his disregard for party solidarity repelled me. I could not believe that his own party, much less the uncommitted voters, would see in him the qualities needed in the leader of a government. One day I remarked rather arrogantly to Harris that if we knew what was good for us, we would lose the election by a relatively small margin, let the Conservatives go into office for four years and then come back for the rest of our lives. But I did not try to make that happen. The cabinet and the Liberal party regarded St Laurent as the platform and the program, and public opinion polls forecast a Liberal victory right up to the eve of the election.

As the election approached, my concern grew about how St Laurent at 75 was going to survive the campaign without someone to manage his tour as I had done in 1949 and 1953. No one with my experience was available to help with his speeches. Three summers in Bonavista-Twillingate with Margaret and children had consolidated my position. With no opponent in sight I believed I did not need to spend much time in my constituency. One day I asked St Laurent if he would like me to travel with him and manage his campaign. He hesitated and then said, 'I think you know, Jack, I would rather have you with me than anybody else, but you are a member of the cabinet and I would be concerned, if you travelled with me, that it might create jealousies.' I had hesitated to make the offer, precisely for that reason, and did not persist.

Once the campaign had begun, reports that St Laurent's speeches were getting little or no response from his audience worried me. Part way through the campaign he sent word that he would like me to join him for a week in Ontario, and I accepted at once. I drafted his speeches that week and felt he was being listened to. Perhaps I should have offered to stay with him longer.

The weekend before election day I had lunch in St John's with my friend Senator Ray Petten, who asked if I thought there was any chance we might lose the election. There was not a chance, I responded. He supposed I was right, but he was worried. On election day I realized that he had sensed what was happening and was trying to prepare me. I had never seen Diefenbaker on the hustings and was not aware that he had caught fire in Vancouver half way through the campaign.

After voting in Ottawa on 10 June, Margaret and I drove to Québec City for the victory celebration planned at St Laurent's house. We arrived at the Château Frontenac at about 6 p.m. The polls had already been closed for over an hour in Newfoundland, and for nearly an hour in the Maritimes. I went into the bedroom of our suite to telephone Granger in St John's to ask about the results in Newfoundland. He reported that I had been elected by an overtwhelming majority and that the Liberals had won the other four outport seats but lost both seats in St John's. That did not surprise me. While we were speaking, I could hear reports on the radio in his room of the results of the first polls in Halifax. We kept talking until there was a further report. Both Conservative candidates in that two-member riding were far ahead of the Liberals. When I went back into the sitting room, where Margaret was talking to the Liberal workers, she gave me a startled glance and asked if someone we knew had died. I answered that we were losing the election: if the Liberal citadel of Halifax was lost, there was little chance of a majority.

By the time we reached St Laurent's house, the Liberals had lost most of the Maritime seats, held most of Québec and been reduced in Ontario from 48 to 20. There was growing gloom in the company, apart from the representatives of the media, who were obviously excited by real news. Some of them could hardly conceal their satisfaction. St Laurent was outwardly calm and unperturbed, but he expressed to me his distress at the defeat of Winters, Gregg, Lapointe, Howe and particularly Harris.

When Manitoba was reduced from 8 to 1, St Laurent turned to me and said, with feeling, that he hoped the Conservatives would elect a few more members than we, so that the government could get out of an impossible situation. I said I hoped so too. Once it was clear that that was going to happen, St Laurent sat down with Chubby Power and me to draft a statement to give on radio and television. The statement pointed clearly towards the resignation of the government. The Tories had 5 or 6 more seats than the Liberals, and the CCF with 25 and Social Credit with 19 could create a highly unstable situation if the government did not resign. St Laurent indicated his own preference in the statement but said that he would consult the cabinet. At the first cabinet meeting after the election only two ministers wanted to stay on to meet Parliament and ask for a vote of confidence; all the rest of us felt we should resign and let Diefenbaker try to form a government. St Laurent was brisk and businesslike and gave no sign of regret or depression. On 13 June he had all his colleagues to dinner at Sussex Street, where we had a photograph taken. I recall it as an enjoyable, almost rollicking evening, where we acted a little like a group of boys just out of school for the holidays.

St Laurent telephoned Diefenbaker to say that as soon as he returned from Prince Albert, the government would resign on whatever day he chose to take over. The date chosen was 21 June. St Laurent planned to leave for St Patrick immediately after Diefenbaker became prime minister and told Diefenbaker that I would act for him in arrangements for shifts in offices between government and Opposition and in arrangements to look after the staff of former ministers who had rights to employment in the public service. Diefenbaker left for a meeting of the Commonwealth prime ministers two days after taking office. He gave Derek Bedson, who had been the private secretary to the leader of the Opposition, the authority to act for him. Bedson, a former Winnipeger, and I performed the task in complete harmony.

The St Laurent record

The conventional judgment a generation later is that the St Laurent years were a period of calm development when Canada had no problems and was an easy country to govern. I challenge that judgment at every opportunity.

Most Canadians living today were not yet born when St Laurent became prime minister in 1948, or even when he left office in 1957. It is not surprising that they do not know what his government accomplished. Here is a partial list of his achievements.

He negotiated the union of Newfoundland with Canada after 28 years of attempts, whereby Confederation was completed. He managed delicate relations with the provincial governments of Manitoba and Québec about federal relief and rehabilitation at the time of the Red River, Rimouski and Cabano disasters. He took the initiative in dealing with Canada's first nation-wide railway strike and pushed conciliation to the utmost limits before asking Parliament for unprecedented back-to-work legisaltion. His government completed three great national construction projects, the Trans-Canada Highway, the St Lawrence Seaway and the natural gas pipeline from Alberta to Montreal. Under his leadership the Supreme Court of Canada became truly supreme with the abolition of appeals to the British Privy Council. The Canadian Parliament won jurisdiction for Canada to amend its own constitution in exclusively federal matters.

St Laurent recommended the appointment of the first Canadian as governor general. He appointed the Royal Commission on the Arts, Letters and Sciences, which recommended federal grants to the universities, nation-wide television and the establishment of the Canada Council. All those recommendations were adopted by the government.

In the field of social security St Laurent's government provided universal pensions without a means test for persons over 70, extended unemployment insurance to cover seasonal workers and fishermen, made legal provision for future federal financial support for hospital insurance and negotiated the plan of equalization of provincial revenues that contributed so greatly to national unity.

In world affairs he and Pearson, in close partnership, had a major role in restoring peace in Korea and at Suez. Committed to support for the North Atlantic Alliance and the United Nations, his government stationed Canadian troops in Europe and used them in combat in Korea without causing protest in Canada. The United Nations Emergency Force, which restored peace at Suez was deployed at Canada's suggestion.

Those were the achievements of a government that balanced the budget almost every year and reduced the national debt substantially. No government since 1957 has had such a record.

9   Coping with Opposition

Opposition: the first phase

St Laurent's resignation as party leader

St Laurent gave no hint to me that he did not intend to carry on as leader of the Liberal party and Leader of the Opposition. I offered to serve him as an unofficial assistant as long as he remained in public life, and he accepted without hesitation. We discussed my financial position and family responsibilities. He asked how much I would need to avoid going into debt and I answered I thought we could keep solvent with another $5000 a year. He asked Duncan MacTavish, head of the National Liberal Federation, to have an allowance paid out of party funds. That arrangement brought my income to just over half what it had been when I was a minister. St Laurent was eager to leave Ottawa to spend the summer at St Patrick. Since it was already clear that Parliament would not meet until October, when it was to be opened by the Queen, there was no reason for him to stay.

It did not take long to complete the arrangements for the change of government. Derek Bedson and I agreed that no future government was likely to last 22 years, and that we should establish some precedents. Under existing practice in 1957, the prime minister, the leader of the Opposition and all cabinet ministers had suites in the Centre Block of the Parliament Buildings for themselves and their staffs. With few exceptions members of Parliament shared a room with another member and had secretarial help provided from a stenographic pool. I persuaded Bedson that that would be a real hardship for former cabinet ministers — what Chubby Power once described as moving from a private car to an upper berth. It was decided each of the former ministers should have a room for himself and an adjacent room for a secretary.

When a minister left office for any reason, his secretarial staff lost their jobs at once. Some of the staff were civil servants on loan who went back to positions in their departments. There was limited protection for private secretaries. Bedson joined with me in arranging with the Civil Service Commission to provide positions for them in the public service comparable with their demonstrated capacity.

As for my own ministerial staff, Charlie Granger, to whom I owed so much, was appointed deputy minister of highways in Newfoundland. Most of the others were civil servants. Because she had worked on Newfoundland matters, I was eager to retain the assistance of Audrey McQuarrie, though I could not ask her to accept the reduced salary of a secretary to a private member. The problem was solved by St Laurent's appointing her to the staff of the leader of the Opposition. Her assistant, Shirley Tink, became my secretary, a position she filled with competence and devotion as long as I was in Opposition.

Once the parliamentary housekeeping arrangements were settled and school had closed at the end of June, the whole family went to Newfoundland, where we stayed until mid-August. Shortly after our return I visited St Laurent at St Patrick. It was a most disquieting experience. He was obviously deeply depressed, and he could rarely be drawn into conversation. He showed no interest in discussing what he would do when Parliament met. Mrs St Laurent and the family were worried, but he made no suggestion during my visit that he might resign the party leadership.

I went to Vancouver for Mother's 80th birthday, which all her surviving children were there to celebrate, and for a day or two I was out of touch with Ottawa. During that time St Laurent announced his intention to resign the leadership. I was not greatly surprised, but I was hurt that I had not been told in advance. Later I learned that his son, Renault, had tried to telephone me. When Renault reached me after the announcement, he said his father was anxious to see me. On returning from British Columbia I went to Québec and spent a day with St Laurent, who was clearly relieved to have made the decision but was still depressed. For that man who had enjoyed unbroken and outstanding success for 75 years, I believe the shock of failure had been almost too great to bear.

At one point he roused himself to say he had been thinking a great deal about what had happened and had come to the conclusion that the defeat was entirely his fault. He could see what mistakes he had made, when they were made, and why they were made. It was characteristic of him, as it was of very few other human beings I have known, not to blame anyone but himself. I did not argue the point, but I remarked that there had been a great difference between his behaviour and Mackenzie King's as prime minister. Mackenzie King, I said, when faced with a problem that looked insoluble, did nothing whatever about it until he was quite sure everybody realized there was a problem; then he found a solution that was not always first-rate, but because it was a solution, people said he was a great statesman. When you saw a problem on the horizon, I told St Laurent, you almost always found a solution before the public and, sometimes, your colleagues knew there was a problem. And the verdict of the Canadian people, in consequence, was that Canada was an easy country to govern, that anybody could do it, and they decided to let anybody try. I predicted that not many months would pass before people would once again be saying that Canada was difficult to govern.

Two decisions were made during my visit. St Laurent asked me to act for him in organizing a national convention to choose a new party leader. If Duncan MacTavish and I agreed about what should be done, we should go ahead. He accepted my suggestion that the procedure in the 1948 convention should be our guide. He was disappointed when we reported that the earliest practicable date was in January 1958. Also, he decided that he would continue as leader of the Opposition. I was relieved that he had himself decided against having an acting leader; I felt, as he did, that the choice of an acting leader would influence the choice of the new leader. He asked me to take charge of the preparations for his part in the debates after the opening of Parliament.

The Queen opened Parliament, a precedent. The Speech from the Throne sparkled like a Christmas tree, with goodies for nearly every important pressure group across the country, including another increase in universal old age pensions, which had been increased earlier in the year.

At the beginning of each session of Parliament the real debate on the Speech from the Throne begins with a speech by the leader of the Opposition, who usually moves an amendment critical of the government. Such an amendment, if adopted, is a vote of want of confidence in the government. The prime minister then has a choice between resigning and having an election called. I was convinced that Diefenbaker would be delighted to have a vote of want of confidence carried so that he could call another election. I had no doubt that in such an election he would win a comfortable majority, instead of having to carry on with his own supporters in a minority. It would obviously not be in the interest of the Liberal party to have an early election. My draft speech for St Laurent said that it would not be appropriate to move the traditional vote of want of confidence, particularly since the government he had headed had recently resigned, and that he had advised the governor general to ask Diefenbaker to form a government. St Laurent agreed with that position and added to the speech that, having decided not to move an amendment expressing lack of confidence, the Liberal Opposition would not support any motion of want of confidence moved by any other party or member. The Liberal caucus agreed to that course. St Laurent's statement assured the government of parliamentary support for the program the Conservatives had put before the electorate.

Our decision not to challenge the government did not prevent us from debating the government's measures vigorously. Debating strength on the Opposition front benches was, on balance, greater than on the government side. In addition to St Laurent, the surviving former ministers were Gardiner, Chevrier, Martin, Pearson, Sinclair, Lesage, George Marler and I, and there were several other good Liberal debaters. The CCF had M.J. Coldwell, Stanley Knowles, H.W. Herridge and Colin Cameron, one of the greatest debaters in Canadian parliamentary history.

Just before the final vote on the Speech from the Throne, St Laurent reiterated his statement that the Liberal Opposition would neither propose nor support a motion of want of confidence.

Pearson becomes leader

The organizing of the convention followed the pattern of 1948. Since most of those who had worked on that convention were still available, the task was an easy one. My part was mainly in the policy committee. I was the main author of the Atlantic resolutions, all of which were implemented by the Pearson government. I prepared the first draft of St Laurent's farewell speech, which was received with great emotion. Pearson was chosen leader with a substantial margin over Paul Martin.

In his speech of acceptance Pearson promised to lead the party to victory 'and soon.' Those two words caused a chill to run down my spine and led to the greatest mistake of my political life. Like many others I interpreted them to mean that Pearson intended to challenge the government at the first chance. That chance came on 18 January 1958, only four days after he became leader. The government had already announced there would be a supply motion that day. On such a motion the Opposition usually challenges the government with an amendment that, if adopted, defeats the government.

In view of his defiant attitude at the convention I assumed that Pearson would feel compelled to propose a want of confidence motion. I discovered that he had neither a motion drafted nor a speech prepared to support it. As I was still being paid by the

Liberal Federation to serve as liaison with the leader of the Opposition, I felt a duty to help him and offered to draft a speech in the spirit of his challenge. The speech Pearson delivered was little changed from my draft. I also drafted a motion of want of confidence, which Pearson used. That motion proved to be a terrible fiasco. I was afraid that if he moved a simple vote of want of confidence, the smaller parties, particularly the CCF, which had already moved one want of confidence motion, might feel compelled to vote for the motion and thereby defeat the government. Pearson's motion, I felt, should be one the smaller parties would not support.

The motion I drafted complained that trade had ceased to expand, investment had been discouraged, and unemployment had risen drastically; that farmers and other primary producers were disillusioned; that relations with provincial governments were in confusion; that the budget was no longer in balance; that there was confusion about defence; and that day-to-day expedients were substituted for firm and steady administration. The motion concluded, 'In view of the desirability, at this time, of having a government pledged to implement Liberal policies, His Excellency's advisers should, in the opinion of this House, submit their resignation forthwith.'

I had been right about one thing: no one in the smaller parties would vote for a motion to restore a Liberal government without an election. But I had completely failed to foresee the ridicule that Diefenbaker would heap so overwhelmingly upon the motion. He admitted that he had listened on the radio to Pearson's acceptance speech at the convention. He said, 'On Thursday there was shrieking defiance; on the following Monday, there is shrinking indecision.' A torrent followed in which Pearson was figuratively torn limb from limb. It was the most brilliant performance I ever heard from Diefenbaker; I doubt if a more effective destructive speech was ever made in Parliament.

The next day Colin Cameron of the CCF said in the House that Pearson's performance would have been quite amusing if it had not been tragic. He recalled Shakespeare, 'Let us sit on the ground and tell sad stories of the death of kings' — even newly crowned kings. He said there had never been such a short period between a coronation and an abdication. We had witnessed a tragic scene the day before. But we had seen something else that was not very pretty to behold. He gave Diefenbaker 'full marks for a magnificent hatchet job.' At that point the Tories applauded, until Cameron wondered if that was the role the prime minister of Canada should play: 'I wondered if he should have rushed with such relish into the abattoir.... When I saw him bring whole batteries of rhetoric, whole armies of guided missiles of vitriol and invective in order to shoot one forlorn sitting duck — a sitting duck, indeed, already crippled with a self-inflicted wound — I wondered if the Prime Minister really believes in the humane slaughter of animals.' Diefenbaker had recently taken up the humane slaughter issue.

The next morning I wondered if the result might be the political slaughter of J.W. Pickersgill. Though neither Pearson nor I ever admitted publicly my authorship of the motion, it was common gossip. In the Liberal caucus I was about as popular as a skunk at a garden party. I did not live down that error of judgment until well after the election of 1958.

The motion was a disastrous beginning of Pearson's leadership. I have since then often asked myself why I offered to help. I had no responsibility to advise Pearson, but after 20 years as adviser to two successive leaders of the party I suppose I had the habit. My intervention certainly did my own reputation no good, although neither then nor afterwards did Pearson ever utter a word of recrimination or blame to me. I went to see him the first thing the morning after the speech to tell him about the arrangement St Laurent had made with the Liberal Federation, and said I assumed it should be terminated forthwith. He neither agreed nor disagreed, but later in the day I saw the president of the Federation and asked to be taken off the payroll.

St Laurent sat as Pearson's seatmate for the rest of the session and on 27 January made a short, effective speech on the legislation resulting from the dominion-provincial conference — Diefenbaker had switched back the title from Federal to Dominion. It was St Laurent's last speech in the House and my last official association with him.

I doubt if, in Canadian public life, there has been a more intimate working association between two men than the association I had with Louis St Laurent from 1948 until his retirement from public life at the beginning of 1958. I watched how easily he assumed authority, and how naturally and willingly everyone associated with him accepted that authority. He clearly had no interest in the exercise of power for its own sake, and he almost never gave orders. He made his own staff, other public servants and ministers feel they were working with him and not for him. He was always ready to give credit to others and seemed to have little interest in getting credit for himself. Because he had never struggled for office or even sought it, unlike most leaders he felt secure in his position and was not preoccupied with any conscious effort to retain office or with any fear of surrounding himself with able men who might become rivals. What I admired most was not his superb intelligence and his judgment, which rarely failed, but his genuine modesty, his lack of concern for his place in history and his complete freedom from meanness or malice of any kind. To me he was the greatest Canadian of our time.

The dissolution of Parliament and the election of 1958

Despite the decisive vote of confidence the government had won on Pearson's motion, Diefenbaker gave increasing signs that he was looking for an excuse to end the life of Parliament. He faced no prospect of defeat when he flew to Québec on 1 February to advise the governor general to dissolve Parliament. He returned to Ottawa to inform the Speaker that Parliament had been dissolved and that the House could no longer sit. In my opinion his action was the closest approach by a prime minister to a claim of absolute power ever made in self-governing Canada. Yet such was the state of the public mind in February 1958 that that virtual coup d'état was not publicly challenged. I discussed the possibility of challenging it with one or two friends, but we all agreed such an action would merely subject us to further ridicule; in any event, my opinion on any question affecting Parliament was not likely to carry weight at that time.

From the outset of the election campaign I was sure that the Liberals did not have a ghost of a chance, and that there would be a fight for Liberal survival, even in Newfoundland. We had lost the two St John's seats in 1957, but had held the other five easily, one by acclamation and mine by 87 per cent of the vote. The surge of Anglo-Saxon Protestant anti-Liberal reaction in the rest of Canada had barely touched Newfoundland in 1957, but it seemed likely to affect the five outport constituencies in 1958, if the Tories could set the British flame alight.

Offended by Diefenbaker, Smallwood decided that new candidates were needed in two of the ridings and arranged provincial appointments for the former MPs in order to make way for the new candidates, one of whom was my former executive assistant, Charles Granger. Apart from appearing at two or three meetings to support Granger, I confined myself to my own constituency of Bonavista-Twillingate. For the first time I had a really serious and prestigious opponent: Gerald Winter was a highly respected merchant in St John's, recently president of the Newfoundland Board of Trade and reputedly assured of a portfolio in Diefenbaker's cabinet. In 1957 I had not held a single public meeting, simply travelled about with my official agent greeting individual voters and talking to small groups whenever they gathered spontaneously, usually on the wharves. I had campaigned frequently on the mainland. But in 1958 I was fighting for my political life. I campaigned as I had not done before and would never have to do again, with meetings in nearly every settlement accessible in the middle of winter. Fortunately the winter was mild, and it was not too hard to get around. I made the same speech at nearly all the meetings, which were exceedingly well attended. My theme was a simple comparison of the characters and achievements of Pearson and Diefenbaker. The organizer of many of my meetings told me they were not like other political meetings, they were like being in church. I was not sure whether I should be flattered, but as he was himself very devout, I knew he meant it as a compliment and believed I was being effective.

The campaign was not without incident. One day I set out from Gander to Fogo Island in a two-seater Bell helicopter. It began to snow at Gander Bay, so we landed in a schoolyard. I went into the school and spoke to the children and appealed to them to ask their parents to vote for me. It was one of the rare times in six campaigns I made a direct appeal for votes for myself — something I always found difficult to do. Shortly afterwards the sun came out and we flew on to Fogo Island, where I had word passed around Fogo town that there would be a meeting at 1 p.m. I then had lunch with one of my main supporters. When we got back to the hall for the meeting the pilot said the weather was closing in and we must get away in seven minutes or we would stay on the island for the rest of the day. The meeting lasted six minutes and was none the worse for that.

As we flew across the water to the nearest point on the mainland of Newfoundland we encountered patches of fog and occasional flurries of snow. The pilot asked me if I wanted to go back to Gander or follow the coast to Valleyfield, where we could refuel. I opted for the coast, thinking the shoreline would be easier to follow and also hoping the weather might clear so that we could fly on across Bonavista Bay to Bonavista town, where I had a meeting planned for that evening.

After refuelling we sat around for more than an hour until the sky seemed to clear a little, and then set out again, following the rugged north shore of Bonavista Bay and then across a stretch of water. It began to snow, and we could see no land except a piece of very flat rock about 150 feet long, on which we landed. After a few minutes the pilot cheerfully suggested that the snow might be followed by fog for a day or two. He was a young Manitoban, slim and apparently healthy; I wondered silently whether I would eat him, or he would eat me.

In ten or fifteen minutes the snow stopped falling, and we could see land, two or three small islands and a stretch of the Newfoundland mainland. I asked the pilot if he knew where we were and found he had no clear idea. I pointed to the mainland and said, with more confidence than I felt, that we were close to St Chads and should head for that bit of coast. Our plastic bubble was partly covered with snow, and the pilot said he must clear it off as soon as possible. I said we could land on the wharf at Eastport. When we got over that wharf I suggested we carry on to Happy Adventure, where I knew there was a telephone in a shop near the wharf.

When we landed on the wharf, the pilot cleared off the snow while I telephoned my agent in Bonavista and told him we would try to get there that night, but to postpone the meeting until the next day. We crossed the south side of the bay intending to follow the shore to Bonavista, but soon encountered a solid bank of fog and had to turn back and follow the railway line across the peninsula to the Trinity Bay shore and start to follow the road to Port Union. I noticed a car below, going in our direction, and thought it might rescue us if we had to land. It was getting dusk, beginning to snow, and there were trees ahead close to the road. We turned back and landed at a clearing I had noticed. After about half an hour the car I had seen earlier caught up to us. I stopped the driver and asked him if he would take us to Port Union. He agreed but wondered if I would be willing to ride in his car and told me to look at the rear. It was covered by a large placard advertising the Tory candidate in Trinity-Conception. I said I would ride in the Devil's car if need be. He duly delivered us to the house of a friend in Port Union, who gave us a hot dinner and drove us on to Bonavista.

In Bonavista I had a conference with my agent and a leading supporter in the town. Both advised me not to have a meeting, predicting there would be trouble. I asked if I would lose votes if I did not have a meeting. They thought not. I asked if my supporters would be ashamed of me if there was no meeting. They looked at each other and then conceded that that might be the result. So I said, 'Let's get the Orange Hall but have the meeting in the afternoon' — before the would-be disturbers had imbibed too much courage.

The hall was packed long before 4, when the meeting was to start. Fortunately, as well as two very noisy drunks, there were a number of schoolchildren at the front of the hall. Farther back were 30 or 40 men wearing blue ribbons inscribed Vote for Winter. I had been told that they had been paid to break up the meeting. I had an amiable chairman who had no idea how to conduct, much less control, a meeting. I had never felt so lonely in my life.

Before I started to speak the two drunks began interrupting the chairman. My supporters, who were a large majority of the audience, began shouting 'Throw them out.' I managed to stop the shouting long enough to point out that Mr Winter had had a meeting at Bonavista at which everyone had listened to him politely and quietly. I begged them all to give me the same kind of hearing.

This appeal managed to quiet my supporters, but the drunks went on muttering. I said, 'These men have something they want to say; I suggest they come up to the platform and make their speeches.' Some of my friends succeeded in getting one of them on the platform, where he was stage-struck and speechless. He left the platform and slunk out of the hall. The other went back half way and muttered to himself for the rest of the meeting.

I started my speech by saying that there were a number of children present, and that I intended, like the minister in church, to speak to the children before I made my main speech. This device clearly aroused everyone's curiosity, and I got a good hearing for a little speech of the most elementary kind on self-government, elections and the right of every citizen to express views freely and without interference or disturbance. I could see that it had some effect, and that I might get through peacefully if I was very brief. I then launched into an abbreviated version of my comparison of the two leaders and the importance of making Mr Pearson prime minister. As soon as I decently could, I stopped and asked everyone to rise and sing 'God Save the Queen,' which I had to lead in my monotone, while inwardly thanking God for saving me from a potential riot.

I flew home from Gander to vote in Ottawa. I did not expect to lose in my own constituency but I did not anticipate an overwhelming victory. When the results were in, Winter had received 4000 votes, and I had over 5000 more than in 1957 — 75 percent of the votes cast. Whatever my position in the party generally, I was sure of a solid base in my own constituency. A day or two after the election I met Diefenbaker in the corridor of the Parliament Building. He stopped and asked me if I was not the only Liberal candidate who had increased his majority. I told him that I had not checked the figures for others, but that I knew I had received 5000 additional votes, and his candidate only 4000 altogether. My own success, however, was small consolation in the light of the overwhelming defeat of the Liberal party across the country.

On election day I spent some time with Pearson in his parliamentary office. I asked whether he had any illusion that we might win the election. He admitted he had none. I believed the best we could hope for was 100 seats and thought about 80 more probable. Few observers predicted the magnitude of the debacle, that Diefenbaker would win 208 seats. The greatest surprise was that the Tories won 50 of the 75 seats in Québec — the first time since 1887 that the Conservative party had won a majority in that province. At the same time it was Québec that had saved the Liberal party from complete annihilation: of the 49 seats we won, 25 were in Québec. Newfoundland was the only province to give the Liberals a majority. In six provinces no Liberal member was elected. Even in Ontario only 14 were returned, none of them in Toronto. Only 5 of the former ministers survived, Pearson, Chevrier, Martin, Lesage and I and Lesage decided shortly after the election to leave Parliament to become provincial leader of the Liberal party in Québec.

Lesage's departure was a substantial loss to our small group. He had become an outstanding debater and was a powerful voice from Québec. He and I had worked together closely even before we became ministers in the St Laurent government, and I missed him very much. Happily our personal friendship was never strained by the differences that developed between provincial and federal Liberals when both of us were back in office.

The family copes with Opposition

Overcoming the shock

After our experience on the *Millie Ford* in 1956, I had had a grandiose dream of a family voyage in 1957 through the Straits of Belle Isle and up the St Lawrence to Montreal. The morning after the election that dream was shattered. With my reduction in income no great voyage would be possible, nor was it even practicable to use the schooner, which required a crew of six. Under the arrangement I had with Max Burry he could use the *Millie Ford* commercially except when we wanted the schooner for our own use. Before leaving Québec that morning I telephoned Charlie Granger in Newfoundland and asked him to get in touch with Max and tell him he was free to look for freight for the summer and beyond.

It would not have been easy to support the family without the allowance St Laurent had arranged for me. Margaret and I had lived through the Great Depression and realized there was no alternative to frugality. We did not ask for sympathy, but Margaret was first hurt and then angry when on our first day back from Québec one of our formerly cordial shopkeepers abruptly asked if she would be able to pay the bill at the end of the month. Happily there were few such gibes. Our first economy was to substitute margarine for butter. That change I pretended was painful to me, because I had won the first prize for butter-making every year at the boys' and girls' fair at Ashern, but I was consoled that nearly everyone used margarine, called butter, in Newfoundland.

We decided in spite of our reverses to go to Newfoundland for part of the school summer holiday. There was of course no government airplane for us, but Charlie Granger's car was still in Ottawa, and he suggested that we drive it to Newfoundland, where he was already installed as deputy minister of highways. So at the beginning of July we left on the first of many motor trips to and from Newfoundland over the next 30 years and more. It was hard work, travelling gypsylike in cars, small boats or the coastal steamer with four children and no headquarters or place of our own. But thanks to the wonderful kindness and help of friends we were able to visit a good part of the constituency and enjoy the experience at the same time. We and our travels were given a great deal of publicity on the radio; everyone knew we had not forsaken Newfoundland. Indeed, that summer cemented our relations with the constituency and increased our affection for Newfoundland. One overriding impression I gained from that visit was how many constituents and other Newfoundlanders who had paid little attention to us while I was a minister went out of their way to be helpful when our luck was down. There is nothing like going into Opposition to show a politician who his friends are.

I was 52 years old when we left office in 1957, and I could not count for long on the stopgap arrangement St Laurent had made with the Liberal Federation. There was a good possibility I might never be in office again. I had the naïve idea of trying to become a lawyer. It was out of the question to think of going to a law school, but I learned that a law degree was not necessary in Newfoundland. In those days in Newfoundland admission to the bar could be gained by being articled to a barrister for a certain period and passing the examinations. Eric Cook, who was a leader of the bar in Newfoundland and also the president of the Liberal association, was a good friend, and I discussed the possibility with him. He told me that, in responsible government days, members of the Parliament of Newfoundland who were articled had not been required to work in the office of their principal but merely to pass the examination. He felt that the precedent would apply to me, and offered to have me articled to him. I accepted his offer and for a few months hoped it might be the eventual solution to my problem. I was duly articled to Eric Cook on 21 September 1957, and from time to time I read some of the books on which I would be examined.

That long-range plan might have continued, had my allowance as liaison officer between the party leader and the Liberal Federation not stopped, at my request, in January 1958. It was not possible to make ends meet on the parliamentary indemnity. Some way had to be found to supplement my income, as neither Margaret nor I had any private means, only some meagre savings.

After the election of 1958 the income problem was met for several years by my fellow literary executors of Mackenzie King. Slow progress was being made on his biography. The time could be shortened, we felt, if someone would read the diaries after the outbreak of war in 1939, pick out the most significant entries and connect them with a narrative that would be a foundation for the biography of the war and postwar years. My fellow literary executors and the trustees thought that I should take on the task experimentally for one year at $5000. I started the work at once.

When MacGregor Dawson, the biographer, died in July 1958, Professor Blair Neatby, who had been assisting Dawson, undertook to complete the biography up to the outbreak of war. By that time it seemed to me that we should let Mackenzie King himself tell the story, through extracts from the diary with a minimum of narrative to link his words. The other literary executors agreed to have me take on that expanded task at the same salary. I decided to call the book *The Mackenzie King Record*. It was hard work for both of us. Margaret did most of the typing of the diary extracts.

Not that I spent most of my time in Opposition on *The Mackenzie King Record*; it provided me with financial independence, but far more of my time and energy were devoted to Parliament and to Newfoundland. What little was left I used to help with party organization and in visits to other parts of Canada spreading the Liberal gospel according to Pearson. I especially enjoyed visiting universities. But Parliament came first.

Parliament sat all summer in 1958 and there was no possibility for the family to visit Newfoundland without me, as we had no place of our own there. That year was the only year since 1953 that Margaret has not spent some time in Newfoundland.

It was a year of change for the family. My sister, Bessie, and my brother Tom both left Vancouver. Mother's health was such that she could not be left alone in Vancouver, so Margaret and I found a nursing home in Ottawa, where she had constant care and lived for the rest of her life. It was not far from our house, and Margaret or I could visit her almost every day, and the grandchildren and our dog, Ginger, quite often. That year too was the first any of our children was away from home for an extended period. Jane went to France by herself to spend the summer with the de France family, Paul and Eliane, at Wacourt; their two eldest children, Guislain, 14, and Agnès, almost 13, would be companions for her.

Putting down roots in Newfoundland

I had won a substantial victory in Bonavista-Twillingate in 1958, but I was in Opposition and knew I could not afford to take my constituency for granted. As soon as the session ended in 1959, all the family except Jane went to Newfoundland. Jane had a summer job in a chemical plant connected with the Price pulp and paper complex in Québec City. That summer marked the end of her life at home. She entered Queen's University in the fall to study medicine and had two more summers in Québec City at the chemical plant.

Mother's 80th birthday, Sept. 3, 1957, at Vancouver. All surviving children and Tom's wife Margaret.

Pickersgill cabin at Traytown — under construction 1959.

In 1959 we began a close association with the Baird family, whose four children were comparable in age with our four. Edgar Baird's family on both sides extended back to the earliest settlement of the northeast coast of Newfoundland. Edgar had served during the war, first in the Newfoundland Forestry Corps in Britain and later in the Royal Air Force. At one period in his service he was sent from Britain to Carberry, Manitoba, to an RAF air training station, and his knowledge of the geography of Manitoba was one of many common bonds between us. Mary Baird was the daughter of an Englishman who had immigrated to Canada and received his theological education in Toronto, where he met his wife, a graduate of Aberdeen University who was a teacher at Havergal College. Mary had been born in Toronto, but her parents had moved to England when she was small. During the war she was employed as a secretary in the Newfoundland government office in London, where she and Edgar met. They were soon married, and their eldest child, William, was born in England shortly before the war ended.

The Bairds settled in Gander in 1948. The first time I met Edgar had been the day he came to Portland in 1955 with Max Burry and Willis Briffett of Glovertown to urge me to try to have the government establish a national park, which had been promised in the Terms of Union, in the area between Glovertown and Port Blandford. Edgar knew the area well and was planning to build a summer place at nearby Traytown, on a lovely sheltered arm of

Alexander Bay. Later that year I met Edgar again in Gander, where he was chairman of the Gander Improvement District, which was developing the townsite. The boundary of my constituency stopped five miles east of Gander. Because of the airport, the railway and later the Trans-Canada Highway, Gander served as the main point of access to both ends of the riding, Bonavista and Twillingate. In 1956 we were well enough acquainted with the Bairds to have their whole family accompany us on the day-long maiden voyage of the *Millie Ford* out of Glovertown. In the summer of 1957, when we were wandering about the constituency like vagabonds, we visited the Bairds at Traytown, where they were camped in a small shack while building their summer house. We were greatly attracted by the site, with its good beach and shallow water, warm enough for swimming. We canvassed the possibility of becoming neighbours of the Bairds, but it was not until early in 1959 that we arranged with Edgar to let us build a place on one corner of his property.

Edgar at that time was in the lumber business. We sent him sketchy plans Margaret and I had drawn up, and asked him to hire carpenters, supply the building materials and get the house started as early as possible in the spring. When we arrived in July, the construction was well under way, but the house was not ready to be occupied, so we took the coastal steamer *Bonavista* on her northward voyage to visit settlements not yet accessible by road. On our return we camped in the house at Traytown as it was being built around us. We also drove to Bonavista town; that was finally possible because the Trans-Canada Highway, through the national park with a short ferry trip across Clode Sound, gave a connection by motor between Traytown and Bonavista.

Traytown was about half way between the two extremities of the constituency and was to prove an ideal headquarters for the member of Parliament. We were comfortable camping in the house, with a wood stove for heating and cooking, water from our own well, a table made of a wooden door on trestles and benches, bunks and beds for everybody. When we left Newfoundland in early September we were already planning the next summer in our completed house.

Opposition in the Parliament of 1958

Liberal strategy and tactics

The strategy and tactics of our party in the House of Commons was my main concern in the first session of the Parliament of 1958. The fact that Newfoundland was the only province to return a Liberal majority, my substantial victory in Bonavista-Twillingate and my being the only former minister from the Atlantic region went some distance to rehabilitate my position in the party.

Pearson had a limited knowledge of parliamentary rules and little interest in learning them. As a professional ball player he undoubtedly knew the rules of baseball and other games, but he never regarded performing in Parliament as a game. I did. I had always been hopeless in sports but was resolved to become an effective debater and a team player.

Pearson wanted the 50-member Liberal Opposition to perform as a team, and welcomed advice on strategy and tactics. The most effective Opposition in the 20th century was led by Mackenzie King and his Liberal colleagues between 1930 and 1935. Power, if not the main strategist for that Opposition, had been its leading tactician. Pearson asked me to find out from him how they had operated. Chubby was generous with his time and advice and lent me his memoranda.

The strategy of that Opposition was to be highly selective in picking issues. They opposed only those government proposals that were unpopular or that involved some issue of principle. Power emphasized that it was essential to work as a team, and for the leader to have a tactical committee of former ministers to decide how the members should perform in the House each day. Backbenchers should be given opportunities from time to time to air local grievances, but there should be no scatter-gun approach. It was of the utmost importance to create a public perception that we had a team capable of governing.

Pearson absorbed the lore quickly. The issues were different, but our methods were similar to those that Power had described and Mackenzie King and his colleagues had followed. Under

Pearson's leadership backbenchers were never ignored. The party caucus was kept fully informed of strategy, on which discussions were often lively. Pearson was once criticized in caucus for not being belligerent and partisan enough. I spoke up and said that, Diefenbaker to the contrary, Canadians did not really like their leaders to be hell-raisers, and expected their prime ministers to speak for all Canadians; the hell-raising should be left to others in the caucus, who would be ready and able to do their part. The other three former ministers and, on occasion, other senior members, such as George McIlraith and Maurice Bourget, met with Pearson nearly every morning to discuss tactics. Maurice Lamontagne and Allan MacEachen, Pearson's senior advisers, were always at those meetings; without them we would have taken longer to convince the public that the Liberal Opposition was a viable alternative government. Lionel Chevrier was Pearson's seatmate and was chosen by him to be house leader for the Opposition. Chevrier was a good choice, approachable and well liked in the House. I was expected to assist him and to act whenever he was absent. We were a good combination: I was interested in detail, and he was conciliatory in presenting an argument. I cannot recall a single occasion when we failed to work together in harmony. Pearson's own leadership in the House was generally limited to broad strategy. It is my opinion that, except for Mackenzie King, Pearson has been the most effective leader of the Opposition in this century.

Our expectations for the first session were modest. In the public mind Diefenbaker was the whole government. We wanted to keep it that way by avoiding attacks on his ministers that would give them a chance to attract favourable attention.

One great weakness of the government was the multiplicity of Diefenbaker's promises. In the 1957 campaign he had made an incredible number of unrealistic or unrealizable undertakings. I thought that one effective way to oppose the government was to keep reminding the public of them. I collected the best press reports and had them reproduced by the Liberal Federation and bound in red in a volume entitled *Diefenbaker's Promises, 1957*. Every Liberal member had a copy, and anyone else who was interested.

We started to use the volume in debate before Parliament was dissolved. After the election I compiled a volume of the 1958 promises. Most of us kept the volumes in our desks in the House of Commons and took them out on every appropriate occasion. They proved to be one of the most effective tools of opposition for the whole period the Tories were in office.

The most damaging of all was Diefenbaker's promise that as long as he was prime minister, no one in Canada would suffer from unemployment. It was made four or five times during the 1958 campaign. Diefenbaker's 'No one will suffer from unemployment' became one of the unforgotten and unforgettable Canadian political phrases, in the same class as Mackenzie King's costly statement in 1930 that his government would not give a Tory provincial government 'a five-cent piece' to spend on relief of the unemployed, and R.B. Bennett's prophetic undertaking in 1930 'to cure unemployment or perish in the attempt.' In 1958 and increasingly through the next four years we made unemployment, which was at the highest level since the 1930s, our basic issue.

I expected the Liberal party to recover and eventually regain office. I believed it would be a mistake to mortgage the future by advocating policies or making promises that would embarrass us when we were again in office. Pearson felt the same way and refused to give undertakings merely to get temporary applause.

Diefenbaker had promised to divert 15 per cent of our imports from the United States to Britain. Pearson, in debate, debunked that self-defeating promise. When the British government proposed a free trade agreement between Britain and Canada, the government's bluff was called, and Diefenbaker's relations with Prime Minister Harold Macmillan suffered a strain from which they never recovered. In the course of debate I pronounced a sort of epitaph on Diefenbaker's 15 per cent diversion of trade to Britain. Once in every generation, I said, the Tory party was able 'to excite the people of this country by stirring up feeling against the United States and by parading a great affection for Great Britain.... We had that in 1911, we had it in 1930, and we have had it again in the last two years.... The pattern does seem to go on.' Each time, when the chips are down, I went on, Britain is forgotten by the Tories.

By the end of that first session the Liberal Opposition had developed an effective parliamentary strategy. We had become competent in debating as a team. Though not himself a great debater, Pearson was clearly captain of the team. As debaters Paul Martin, Chevrier and I were the equal at least of the government front bench, and half a dozen other effective debaters were in the Liberal ranks. The CCF had only eight members, and Social Credit had vanished from the House. We were the Opposition. We were in a good position to take advantage in future sessions of political issues in which there was widespread public interest.

As for myself I had the feel of Parliament in a way I had never had while in the St Laurent government. Despite many — perhaps too many — and varied interventions in debate, I did not seem to bore the House. Without conscious effort to cultivate the press I got plenty of publicity and was frequently the subject of cartoons. Unlike many members on both sides of the House, I was not intimidated by Diefenbaker. I accepted being in Opposition cheerfully and tried to get as much fun as possible out of the relative irresponsibility of being out of office. My hope of eventually being in government again remained high. Diefenbaker would prove he was not an adequate prime minister, and the public would find that out. Our job as an Opposition was to look like a better alternative. I was sure we were on the right road, but I expected the road to be much longer than it turned out to be.

The loss of the Millie Ford

The estimates of the Department of Public Works were being debated on 18 June 1958. In a speech I took the minister, Howard Green, on a hypothetical cruise on our schooner, the *Millie Ford*, along the coast of my constituency from Twillingate to Bonavista. I managed to refer to every wharf, breakwater or other marine work that was being asked for in each outport or settlement. I named over 70 of them from memory. The name of every place in my riding was in *Hansard*. The speech entertained the House and received appopriate publicity in Newfoundland.

The next morning I was telephoned from the parliamentary press gallery and asked if I had a picture of my schooner. I assumed that the picture was wanted to illustrate my speech of the previous evening, but not so. To my horror I was told the *Millie Ford* had been wrecked the previous day in a storm off Cape Race, fortunately with no loss of life. Our family was devastated, but in time we realized that the loss had its consolation: the marine insurance covered the full cost of building a modest summer house at Traytown.

A boat was still essential for reaching many places in the constituency. In succeeding years Ken Goodyear of Grand Falls, a native of Ladle Cove and a good friend, lent us his *Sylvia Joyce,* more modest than the *Millie Ford* but well suited to our needs. Later on Ches Pippy made his luxurious yacht available for a week on a couple of occasions. But as roads were built and the islands connected with ferries or causeways, gradually the whole constituency could be visited without a special vessel for the family.

Broadcasting

The major government legislation of 1958 was the revision of the Broadcasting Act, promised in the Speech from the Throne but introduced only in late August, when the House was getting weary of the long session.

The government was making a fundamental change. Until 1958 the CBC was both the main broadcaster and the licensing authority for private stations; other stations were intended not to compete with the CBC but to complement it. But for several years private radio broadcasters had been carrying on a publicity campaign that it was unfair to have the CBC regulate its competitors. The St Laurent government had resisted, but the campaign had been pervasive enough to win over the Young Liberal Association by 1957. The Tories had included in their program the establishment of a separate agency to regulate all broadcasters including the CBC. With the government's overwhelming mandate and the division in the Liberal ranks, our caucus decided it would be futile to oppose a separate regulatory body. Keeping the CBC free of control by the government in office and answerable only to Parliament was our main concern.

On two basic points my views have not changed since the CBC was established. Public broadcasting is essential if we are to have any Canadian content or any substantial Canadian news on radio or television; it is only necessary to watch the American national channels to see that Canada or anything Canadian is almost never heard or seen. More important, public broadcasting must never become government broadcasting. The only way that can be accomplished is to provide the public broadcaster with financial independence from the government of the day, an independence the CBC had until 1957.

In that year the income from the excise tax on television sets, earmarked for the CBC, was no longer sufficient to finance public broadcasting. A royal commission was appointed under R.M. Fowler's chairmanship to review the structure of Canadian broadcasting and the financing of the CBC. Meanwhile the CBC was provided funds from the Treasury. Fowler recommended that, to assure the CBC's independence from pressure from the government, Parliament should be asked to provide the CBC with a budget for at least five years, a period longer than the life of a single Parliament. Pearson and I were the main Opposition speakers in the debate on the broadcasting legislation. We put the case for financial independence recommended by Fowler. The government refused to accept the recommendation and instead provided for annual grants, subject to the approval of the Treasury Board.

Financial independence for public broadcasting became a part of the Liberal program. It is one of my greatest regrets that no government since 1957 has achieved it. The Diefenbaker, Pearson and Trudeau governments did not reduce the CBC budget, but the danger was there. It became a reality under the Mulroney government, which reduced the CBC grants for operations in the interest of reducing the government's deficit.

On my last day in the cabinet in 1967 a committee was discussing a draft of a new broadcasting act. I made one more appeal for an assured CBC budget for at least five years. Unhappily Judy LaMarsh, who was secretary of state, had a strong antagonism to Alphonse Ouimet, the president of the CBC. To my astonishment she got her bill through Parliament, but instead of giving the CBC financial independence the new act made it a crown corporation: a retrograde step.

'Heads will roll'

Broadcasting disappeared from the parliamentary agenda with the passage of the new act in 1958. To facilitate its passage George Nowlan, the minister reporting to Parliament on the CBC and on the newly created Board of Broadcast Governors, had agreed that a special committee of the House on broadcasting would be established in 1959 and presumably in subsequent sessions. In 1959 the committee caused nothing but embarrassment for the government. The French-speaking Tories were constantly sniping at the CBC, because they believed that Alphonse Ouimet and many of the Radio-Canada broadcasters were not friendly to the Diefenbaker government. A number of western Tories were virtually stooges of the private broadcasters in a campaign to weaken and, if possible, destroy the CBC. Nowlan was the only articulate Conservative who supported the CBC and the principle of public broadcasting. Nowlan in fact got most of his support from the Liberal members of the committee, of whom I was the main spokesman. He was a stalwart defender; without him as the minister, public broadcasting would have been damaged seriously.

On one occasion a Tory member from Québec asked Ouimet a question in French. Because there was no interpreter present, the questioner suggested that Ouimet answer in English. I saw at once what would happen if he did. The nationalist media would report that when asked a question in French, Ouimet, like the rest of the Ottawa establishment, replied in English. I insisted that the reply be given in French. The proceedings of the committee were held up for nearly an hour while an interpreter was found.

Later in the session, when Ouimet was ill and the vice-president, Ernest Bushnell, was acting for him, the government got into serious trouble. In 1959 the CBC had a radio program immediately after the 8 a.m. news called 'Preview Commentary.' Each morning a member of the press gallery was invited to comment on some item in the news. Inevitably some of the commentaries were critical of the government and the prime minister. Bushnell decided on 15 June to cancel the program. Three senior members of the staff of 'talks and public affairs' submitted their resignations and issued a public statement charging that the cancellation of the program was the result of 'clandestine political influence' on the CBC.

Pearson tried to have the ordinary parliamentary business interrupted for an urgent debate. After hearing arguments on the question of urgency, the Speaker refused to accept Pearson's motion. Nowlan was then asked in the question period whether he had made any representations about the program. He categorically denied that he had. More questions were asked the next day. The prime minister replied to each question that it should be directed to the board of the CBC, and refused any comment.

On 19 June, Nowlan made a bare announcement that the board of directors had decided to reinstate 'Preview Commentary,' and that all employees had resumed work except the three who had formally resigned. They wished their resignations to stand until they had appeared before the parliamentary committee. I commented that Nowlan was right and wise in not giving an opinion on the issue, and I hoped no attempt would be made to prevent the committee from finding out the truth.

At the committee F.W. Peers, the supervisor of talks and public affairs, gave a detailed account of the various meetings and consultations in the CBC that had led him and his two colleagues to the conclusion that political pressure had been exerted on Bushnell. It was widely rumoured in the press that the word to Bushnell had been, Unless the program is cancelled, 'heads will roll.' The impression was general that the threat had come directly or indirectly from Diefenbaker. A chance remark Nowlan made to me in the corridor convinced me that neither Diefenbaker nor Nowlan had brought any direct pressure on Bushnell, so I discouraged further attempt in the committee to find out who, if anyone, had told Bushnell that heads would roll. Although it was generally believed that there had been political interference, once the CBC board decided to restore the program, there seemed to be no advantage in pursuing the matter. The resignations and the public outcry were likely to discourage any future attempt at political interference.

The prolonged strike of the French-language broadcasters in the CBC in 1960 was damaging to the government. The government's apparent indifference to the fate of the broadcasters contributed to the impression that most Conservatives were unfriendly, if not hostile, to French Canadians. The Liberal Opposition on the contrary demonstrated interest and concern. That strike was what turned René Lévesque into a politician.

The apparent bias against French Canadians was underlined when the board of the CBC elected one of its own members as chairman in place of Ouimet, who was chairman as well as president. The law clearly stated that the president was also to be chairman of the board. I charged the board with breaking the law and insisted that the House was entitled to have a formal opinion from the deputy minister of justice as to the legality of its action. The government refused. It was widely believed that there had been political pressure on the board to humiliate Ouimet because Diefenbaker disliked him. In 1963, when the Liberals were back in office and I was the minister reporting on broadcasting, I secured a legal opinion that the election of a separate chairman was a breach of the law. Pearson then agreed that Ouimet should be restored to the chairmanship. Years later, when both of us were in retirement, Ouimet told me that he had been in the studio as a courtesy when Diefenbaker made his first public broadcast as prime minister. There was some mechanical problem in the recording, and Diefenbaker turned on Ouimet angrily, denouncing him as a French-Canadian Liberal supporter — a suspicion he evidently never shook off.

Diefenbaker, in my opinion, realized that the CBC was popular. He did not encourage the hostility of many of his backbenchers, but Nowlan alone remained the active defender of the CBC in the government. On one occasion in 1962, in reply to a Tory member who asked the government to interfere with a specific CBC program, Nowlan said that any government that started to interfere with CBC programming would be laying the foundation for either a fascist or a communist state. Public broadcasting owed its independence in the Diefenbaker years mainly to that broad-minded and courageous Tory minister.

The session of 1958 lasted until the end of August and deprived our family of a visit to Newfoundland, but as soon as Parliament rose in September, I went to Newfoundland for a tour of the constituency. I made a second visit in November for the opening of a road in the northeastern corner of the riding that made subsequent visits much easier. While in Opposition I never lifted my pressure on the provincial government to extend the road system, and I had a good deal of success in that effort. I realized more than ever that the support of my constituents was the bedrock of my career, and that their needs should never be neglected. I was a good 'parish pump' politician.

After my tour I wrote to Diefenbaker that I had found that the failure of the cod fishery, the mainstay of more than half the population of the northeast coast of Newfoundland, was of even more serious proportions than earlier reports had led me to expect. I estimated that up to two-thirds of the fishermen would not have enough stamps to entitle them to unemployment insurance which had saved a serious situation in the winter of 1957-58. It was, I wrote, no exaggeration to say that half the fishermen on the northeast coast would be forced to go on welfare in the coming winter unless action were taken by the federal government to treat the situation as an emergency calling for action similar to that taken by the government to assist the prairie grain farmers who had experienced a crop failure that year. Their failure was certainly no more serious for them than the 'crop failure' in the fishery was for the fishermen of Newfoundland. I recommended a way to meet the problem and told him I was sending a copy of my letter to all MPs from fishing constituencies in the Atlantic region and to the ministers of Fisheries and Labour and the minister from Newfoundland. But the appeal fell on deaf ears. The only result was considerable and generally favourable publicity in the media in Newfoundland.

The RCMP in Newfoundland

Two debates in Parliament in 1959 related to Newfoundland, and in both I had a major role. The first developed out of a strike of loggers who cut pulpwood for the paper mill at Grand Falls. From the early days of paper mills in the province both loggers and millworkers belonged to trade unions, which bargained collectively. There was a long history of labour peace in the industry. Wages in Newfoundland were higher than in the Maritime provinces or Québec, where loggers were largely unorganized.

In 1956 the International Woodworkers of America sent organizers from British Columbia into Newfoundland to wean the loggers away from the existing unions. The IWA recruited a majority of the loggers and secured legal recognition as their exclusive bargaining agent. When the new union attempted to negotiate a better wage contract with the Grand Falls paper company, a conciliation board was appointed, and failed to get an agreement. The union called a strike in the winter of 1958-59.

The strike was quite legal, but shortly after it began, a number of acts of violence were committed by supporters of the IWA. Several independent contractors engaged in logging, who had no part in the dispute, were prevented by force from trucking their logs to the mill. IWA supporters raided some of the logging camps and drove out loggers who were not willing to strike. At least one raid made during the night in cold weather forced loggers from the camp to walk without winter clothing a considerable distance to the nearest settlement. Leaders of the IWA also directed strikers to lock themselves in the camps and stay there, using property and provisions belonging to the company.

For the first time violence and lawlessness in labour disputes had been introduced in Newfoundland, and the premier therefore decided to intervene. Smallwood made a province-wide radio broadcast in which he denounced the illegal acts of the IWA and the ensuing violence. He declared that the IWA was useless to the loggers. He invited them to repudiate the IWA and to join a new union, which he himself offered to assist them in organizing. He appealed to the loggers to let him know whether they wanted his help in forming a new union. The response to his broadcast was extraordinary; from all sections of the province there was a tremendous expression of approval for Smallwood.

On the mainland, labour leaders and sympathizers denounced Smallwood's action. The Canadian Labour Congress joined in the outcry. Charges began to appear, especially in the *Toronto Star*, that the RCMP, under their contract to serve as the provincial police, were engaged in strike-breaking.

The first question in Parliament about the strike was raised by Hazen Argue, the house leader of the CCF. He asked Davie Fulton, the minister of Justice, for an assurance that the RCMP was not being used for 'what are commonly called strike-breaking activities.' Fulton replied that the RCMP was carrying out, under contract, law enforcement in Newfoundland under the jurisdiction of the attorney-general of the Province.

Developments followed outside Parliament that almost caused a split in the Liberal Opposition. Pearson received several demands that he repudiate Smallwood. One or two of his advisers urged him to speak out. Pearson was concerned about a letter from Claude Jodoin, the president of the Canadian Labour Congress, that asked for Pearson's clear assurance that the views expressed by such a prominent member of the Liberal party as Mr Smallwood were not the official views of the party. Pearson replied 'the policy in labour matters of the National Liberal Party — for which I speak — is clear and unchanged. It is firmly based on, and will continue to be based on, free collective bargaining.'

Pearson sent Smallwood a copy of the exchange of letters with a covering letter saying he would have preferred not to be involved in the difficulties, which were matters for 'provincial handling.' He said that the pressure on him as national leader had been great, and that he had felt he had to say something at once. He had considered it necessary to state established Liberal policy. He had thought of adding a sentence stating that the dispute was a provincial matter exclusively, and that as national leader he was not concerned with it, but had felt that that would have been interpreted in many quarters as evasion. Pearson sent a copy of the correspondence to the Newfoundland Liberal members. At that point I had a conversation with him. I said I would like to tell him what I would do if I were leader of the national Liberal party. A national leader, I felt, had no mandate to interfere in action being taken by a provincial government within its own exclusive jurisdiction. As a member for a Newfoundland constituency I considered I had the right to support the Newfoundland government and, if necessary, would do so. I did not question the right of individual Liberal members to take exception to Smallwood's conduct, though I hoped none of them would condemn it. But I did not believe a national party could survive if the national leader condemned a provincial Liberal government for action that was entirely within its constitutional jurisdiction. As for myself, I told Pearson I hoped to avoid saying anything at all, and if silence was not possible, to express myself moderately to avoid weakening the unity of the Liberal Opposition.

I hoped our conversation would restrain Pearson from any public criticism of Smallwood, who had already informed me that he proposed to introduce legislation in the House of Assembly to decertify the local unions of the IWA in Newfoundland. When the House approved decertification, the legislation was denounced by the IWA and its supporters and sympathizers inside, and especially outside, Newfoundland. Smallwood was charged with suppressing the union.

That description was not legally correct. Decertification does not destroy or even outlaw a union, it removes the exclusive right of the union to bargain collectively. The exclusive right to bargain collectively is a monopoly given by the legislature to a union with a majority of the employees to bargain with the employer for all the employees, whether they are members of the union or not. The IWA local had been certified as the exclusive bargaining agent once it had recruited a majority of the loggers for the Grand Falls mill. Certification, of course, gave the union no licence to break the law or to take the law into its own hands. The illegal acts of violence were the justification offered in the legislature for the bill to decertify the locals of the IWA. The new law did not end the legal existence of the unions; in fact the union continued to maintain pickets long after the IWA had been decertified. The legislation opened the way for another union to achieve certification if it could recruit a majority of the loggers.

Decertification was not an arbitrary act by the premier or the government of Newfoundland. It was done by an act of the legislature of Newfoundland, which the members of the Opposition as well as the supporters of the government approved without a single dissenting vote. And it had the overwhelming backing of public opinion throughout the province.

At the same time the House of Assembly passed another bill Smallwood had not told me about in advance. The bill amended the provincial Labour Relations Act to permit the Newfoundland cabinet by order-in-council to dissolve any trade union in the province that was the local or branch of a union outside the province in which, in the opinion of the cabinet, a substantial number of the superior officers had been convicted of any heinous crime, such as trafficking in narcotics, manslaughter, extortion, embezzlement or perjury. Fortunately no attempt was made to invoke the arbitrary power given to the cabinet, and the law remained a dead letter. It was, however, highly objectionable in principle, and I would never have been able to defend it.

The Newfoundland strike came up again in Parliament when Fulton made a lengthy and detailed statement regarding the conduct of the RCMP in which he reported on an incident at Badger in which a policeman who belonged to the Newfoundland constabulary, not the RCMP, had been seriously injured. Fulton said that there was no foundation for the charge that the police had been used as strike-breakers and that he was satisfied that the police had acted within the limits of their duty to enforce the criminal law. Pearson accepted Fulton's statement and expressed satisfaction that the RCMP had not been concerned in strike-breaking activities. His reference to the absence of strike-breaking, though perfectly proper, made me vaguely uneasy, because I knew he was under increasing pressure to dissociate himself from the action taken by the government of Newfoundland.

Two days later a rumour was circulating in Ottawa that the government of Newfoundland had asked for reinforcements for the RCMP in the province, and that the minister of justice had refused to send them. When the house met, I asked Fulton whether he had stopped the reinforcements requested. He evaded a direct answer by saying that the authority of the attorney-general of Canada was required before reinforcements were sent, and that that authority had not yet been given. Several exchanges followed, including a question as to whether Fulton had received any communication from the attorney-general of Newfoundland. Fulton replied that he had been in communication with the attorney-general the previous night. I then asked the prime minister if he had received any communication from the premier of the province. Diefenbaker answered, 'The close relationship between the Government of Newfoundland and the honorable gentleman would no doubt provide an answer to his question.' It was widely rumoured that the cabinet was divided over the request for reinforcements. The question would have to be resolved over the weekend.

On Monday, 16 March, Diefenbaker informed the House that the government had replied to two telegrams from the premier of Newfoundland. One telegram asked the prime minister to support the request of the attorney-general that 50 additional RCMP constables be sent to Newfoundland; the other asked the federal government to appoint a judicial inquiry into the labour situation in the province. Diefenbaker stated that while the government had no intention of infringing on matters under provincial jurisdiction, he felt impelled to say, 'The premier of Newfoundland has greatly aggravated the present situation in that province by intervening in a labour dispute in a way which apparently goes beyond the usual role of government.' He added, 'The result, as might have been anticipated, has been a violent reaction on the part of the workers concerned.' He announced, 'Under the circumstances we have concluded that it would be provocative and likely to cause further outbreaks of violence to authorize the sending of further members of the RCMP at this time.' He stated that the RCMP had performed its duty with fairness and efficiency and promised that if they were subject to or encountered intimidation or threats by law-breakers, the government would reconsider its decision. Diefenbaker added that he saw no necessity for a judicial inquiry.

Fulton then announced that he had received and accepted the resignation of the commissioner of the RCMP. L.H. Nicholson had resigned because he considered the refusal to send the reinforcements a clear breach of the contract to have the RCMP police the province. Fulton argued that mere availability of potential reinforcements was not the only factor that he, as minister of justice, had to consider in deciding whether the request should be met. He said that he had also to consider the overall responsibilities of the RCMP and the necessity 'to maintain its full integrity and its ability to discharge that duty on a national basis.' His lengthy and complicated justification was unconvincing.

Pearson immediately expressed regret at the resignation of the commissioner, deplored that there would be no judicial inquiry and said that the terms of the contract seemed clear, but he did not categorically condemn the refusal to send reinforcements. He noted that there were strong differences of opinion about measures taken by the government of Newfoundland and said that, on the basis of information he had received, he would be unable, as leader of his party, to agree with certain of the procedures in Newfoundland or with specific provisions of the provincial legislation. He declined to yield to pressure to be more definite.

Until Pearson made that statement, the five Liberal members from Newfoundland had refrained from public comment. When we met after Pearson had spoken, we were all unhappy about his failure to condemn outright the refusal to send reinforcements and, even more, his reference, which seemed gratuitous, to the measures taken by the government and legislature of Newfoundland. In order to avoid misunderstanding in Newfoundland of our position we issued a statement that set out our support of the government of Newfoundland: 'The Newfoundland Liberal Members of the House of Commons at Ottawa have from the outset supported the emergency action of the Premier, the Government and the House of Assembly of Newfoundland in their determination to uphold law and order and to preserve the continued operation of the pulp and paper industry which provides employment and a livelihood for one-third of the people of Newfoundland.

'The present situation, being a provincial matter, could not, under the rules of the House of Commons, be debated at an earlier date. However, now that it has been brought up in the Parliament of Canada by the Government, we wish to remove any doubt, both in Newfoundland and Ottawa, as to our support of the Premier's stand.'

'We were deeply shocked by the unwarranted and inexcusable failure of the Government of Canada to honour its pledge to provide RCMP reinforcements to Newfoundland during this emergency and we resent, as all Newfoundlanders will resent, the shocking and provocative attack by the Prime Minister of Canada on the action of the Premier of Newfoundland in seeking to maintain law and order in the province, while at the same time refusing to set up the public inquiry that Mr. Smallwood requested so that all the facts might be obtained and placed before the people of Canada.'

All five of us were conscious that our statement might result in a split in the Liberal Opposition. We saw Pearson and showed him the statement before making it public. He asked whether it might result in a split in the party. I replied that it might, but that that would depend on the attitude of others. The criticism in our statement had been directed solely against the government. Pearson asked us to say nothing the following day about a possible split, and we agreed.

The statement was issued at 8 p.m. on 16 March. Shortly afterwards I was invited to go on a television broadcast called 'Press Conference' the next evening. I agreed at once. I woke up at 4 that morning and made a note of every embarrassing question I would ask if I were a member of the panel, and decided on how I would reply to all but one of the them; that question I hoped to avoid. When I told Pearson about the proposed broadcast, he asked me to reconsider and excuse myself. I said that if I did that, I would be considered a coward in Newfoundland; he would have to hope I would say nothing to create any further difficulty.

The *Ottawa Citizen* that afternoon announced, sensationally, that we the Newfoundland Liberal MPs, had formally repudiated

Pearson in our statement, which the paper reproduced in full. It reported that Pearson had known about the statement before it was issued and said that the 'difference of opinion' was 'regrettable' but nothing tragic.

The first question in the broadcast was how wide the split was with Pearson. I said that there was no split at all. Mr Pearson had been quoted in the *Citizen* as saying that there was a difference of opinion about the procedure and the legislation in Newfoundland. I felt that that was almost an exaggeration. Mr Pearson had said only that there were some things he couldn't approve. Those of us from Newfoundland felt we must make it clear that we were supporting the government of Newfoundland in taking action in what we believed to be an emergency.

When asked why we had waited so long, I replied that we felt the situation was a matter entirely for the provincial government and the provincial legislature. The Newfoundland members did not want to take part in a controversy on the mainland.

Asked whether our statement was a repudiation of Mr Pearson and his views, I pointed out that not one word in our statement suggested any thought of repudiation. All five members from Newfoundland were deeply appreciative of the statement Mr Pearson had made the previous day, of the sympathy for and understanding of Newfoundland, he had shown, which were in marked contrast to the attitude of the prime minister and of the spokesman for the CCF.

Asked if there were no real differences of opinion between Mr Pearson and the five Newfoundland members, I replied that I did not think the matter was of any concern to the federal Liberal party. I was not elected, and Mr Pearson was not elected, and neither was any other member of the House of Commons elected, to look after the provincial affairs of Newfoundland. We were elected to the Parliament of Canada to look after federal matters.

Two very important questions, I went on, had come into the federal arena the previous day. One was the question of sending reinforcements to the police ln Newfoundland. On that our whole party was completely united in favour of carrying out the solemn obligation of Canada. And on the question of having an inquiry to bring out the facts, and all the facts, we were also completely united.

One of the panelists asserted that Pearson had said that he did not agree with part of the Newfoundland legislation, and that we had differed with him and said we agreed with the legislation. I said that I did not like the legislation and was sure Mr Smallwood did not like it. There would have been no legislation if almost everyone in Newfoundland had not believed that there was an emergency affecting the economy of the province. The legislation, which decertified two locals of the IWA was not legally necessary. I had with me a copy of the Newfoundland Labor Relations Act and read the section that gave the provincial cabinet power to exclude an employer or employee or any class of employers or employees from any of its provisions.

Asked why there had been new legislation I said that Mr Smallwood had discussed that very question with me. They could have decertified the locals by order-in-council under the existing law, but he had felt that so important a departure from the usual practice should be brought before the representatives of the people in the legislature so that every elected member could express an opinion. Surely it was better to have so important a decision made by the legislature than by the cabinet

When asked what the emergency was, I replied that one-third of the people of Newfoundland derived their living from the pulp and paper industry. The industry's costs were high, and its existence should not be jeopardized. The level of wages of the loggers was higher than anywhere else in Canada east of Ontario, substantially higher. That had been stated over and over again and never contradicted.

Asked whether I would support legislation to decertify a union, I replied that I would not support legislation that interfered with the normal operation of free collective bargaining unless there was a clear emergency. The Liberal Opposition had supported such legislation, introduced by the Diefenbaker government the previous summer, to restore the ferry service to Vancouver Island, because we felt that, with no other steamship ferry service operating there, it was essential to the life of the island. I didn't feel I could refuse to support it, though I didn't like it. I recalled that Mr Pearson had been a member of the St Laurent government at the time of the 1950 legislation to send the railway employees back to work. That had been something very disagreeable for him to do, but there comes a point when the public interest has to be placed first, and that point, we members from Newfoundland believed, had been reached over the loggers' strike.

In reply to the question as to whether Smallwood was trying to protect the mills, I said he was protecting the livelihood of one-third of the people of the province. In the mill at Grand Falls all four unions of millworkers, representing many more men than the loggers who were involved in the strike, all of them belonging to international unions, all of them affiliated with the CLC, all supported Mr Smallwood.

When charged with approving of Smallwood's legislation, I replied 'No, I support the action of the government.' The strike had gone on for 43 days before Mr Smallwood had said a word about it, and during those 43 days many Newfoundlanders had been interfered with by the members of the union as they were seeking to go about their lawful business along the roads of the province.

After some discussion about picketing and violence I was asked if I did not think that the companies had something to do with the action taken by Smallwood. My response was that I was convinced Mr Smallwood took action because he sincerely believed, as I believed, that the industry itself was in jeopardy, that there was a grave danger of one or both of the mills being closed, and that if a mill closed, it might be a long time before it reopened.

Asked if I did not think the IWA had been adhering to the law, I replied: 'No, They were breaking the law. They were flagrantly breaking the law. Members of the IWA were assaulting my own constituents.' One of the panelists then said that according to the law, they could picket and organize without the support of all the loggers. I responded that the law did not allow them to go into a lumber camp in the middle of the night and turn people out into the snow in $-20°(F)$ weather without being warmly clad. I fully supported the view that trade unions, like everybody else, should have to obey the ordinary fundamental law of the country.

It was next suggested that the police had used weapons and clubs against defenceless, unarmed workers. I said that I believed those stories to be entirely untrue; I was convinced that the police had acted in a perfectly proper manner, and that on no occasion had they used force until force had been used by others.

When the chairman of the panel asserted that Smallwood had legislated a union out of existence, I objected that that statement was incorrect, that the IWA still had a legal existence in Newfoundland, that it had headquarters there, and that the headquarters had been protected by the police. People still belonged to the union.

The chairman of the panel then argued, 'But it cannot bargain with the two paper companies.' I pointed out that the union had never had the right to bargain with one of the companies. In the case of the other company, it had been given a privilege, a monopoly, to bargain for all the workers — that was what certification meant. Certification was not a right, it was a privilege. When the union had abused that privilege, it had been taken away by the legislature.

Asked whether the commissioner of the RCMP had been right to resign, I replied that there was no question about that in my mind. I thought the government had acted very improperly; I would hate to be, as Fulton had become, the first minister of the Crown in Canada to break a contract signed by the government.

After some exchanges about whether a contract had really been broken, I said I was convinced that it had, and I explained why. The administration of justice, under section 92 of the BNA Act, was the exclusive responsibility of the province. In Québec and Ontario, where there are provincial police, there could have been no interference by Mr Fulton or Mr Diefenbaker with the administration of justice. But they had presumed to interfere with the administration of justice in Newfoundland by repudiating the contract. Refusing the police reinforcements denied to the province what it had the right to have under a contract with Canada. Under the contract the RCMP was to provide the police necessary to enable the province to discharge its constitutional duty to administer justice.

That broadcast was the greatest test I had faced in my public life. I had persisted, despite the request of our party leader that I call it off. If the effect had been bad, it would almost inevitably have resulted in an open split in the Liberal Opposition in Parliament.

I was vastly relieved when the broadcast ended. I felt it had gone well, and believed it would prevent a split. I told the panelists, as soon as the lights went off, that they had not asked me the one question that would have embarrassed me. The chairman said that he had started to put the question and that I had interrupted and diverted attention to another subject. The question I had feared was my attitude to the second bill passed by the Newfoundland legislature, which would have permitted the cabinet to outlaw any local in Newfoundland of an international union whose leadership was involved in criminal or scandalous activity outside the province. I could not have defended such arbitrary power, and I would not have tried. Fortunately I had avoided the embarrassment.

The reaction to the broadeast was greater than I had dared to hope. I would never receive so much 'fan mail' for a broadcast again in my life. St Laurent telephoned from Québec to congratulate me; even more important, Pearson was completely satisfied. I was warmly received at the Liberal caucus the next day, and we went on, united, to attack the government for its failure to send police reinforcements.

The member of the Newfoundland constabulary who had been injured at Badger died a few days after the broadcast, and the violence stopped quickly, but the public outrage increased.

My belief at the time was that Fulton had intended to send the RCMP reinforcements, and that he had yielded to pressure from Diefenbaker. Donald Fleming confirms that in his memoirs. He says that he gave Fulton his full support, as did a committee of the cabinet appointed to consider the matter, but that in the face of

Diefenbaker's intransigence the cabinet decided against sending the reinforcements. Fleming adds that after the meeting Fulton asked him to join him in telling the prime minister that they would resign if reinforcements were not dispatched at once, but that he himself was not willing to go that far.

I thought at the time that Fulton should have submitted his resignation. I believed that if he had, Diefenbaker would have caved in. Whether or not Fulton would have got his way or had his resignation accepted, it was, and still is, my opinion that his chances of succeeding Diefenaker as party leader and perhaps as prime minister would have been greatly strengthened. Like Mackenzie King I had a good opinion of Fulton, and I was sorry he had not stuck to his guns.

Term 29 of the Terms of Union

The other debate relating to Newfoundland proved even more damaging to the Diefenbaker government. At issue was the obligation set out in term 29 of the Terms of Union. It had been clear during the negotiations that tax-rental agreement on the terms made with the other provinces would not provide enough revenue to make a provincial government in Newfoundland financially viable.

To make the province financially viable, term 29 provided for annual federal grants on a diminishing scale until 31 March 1961 and for the appointment of a royal commission within eight years of the union 'to recommend the form and scale of additional financial assistance, that may be required by the Government of the Province of Newfoundland to enable it to continue public services at levels and standards reached subsequent to the date of union without resorting to taxation more burdensome, having regard to capacity to pay, than that obtaining generally in the region comprising the Maritime Provinces of Nova Scotia, New Brunswick and Prince Edward Island.'

In February 1957 the St Laurent government appointed the commission, under the chairmanship of Chief Justice John B.

McNair of New Brunswick. The appointment aroused high expectations in Newfoundland, especially in the premier. On his visit to Newfoundland during the 1957 election campaign Diefenbaker got off on the wrong foot about term 29, and he never afterwards got on the right foot. He was interviewed on television by Don Jamieson, the leading television broadcaster in Newfoundland, who asked his opinion of the royal commission. Diefenbaker failed to realize, or had forgotten, the connection of the commission with the Terms of Union. He dismissed Jamieson's question by saying there were far too many royal commissions. I was watching the broadcast, and I shall never forget the expression on Jamieson's face; it was the only time I saw him completely at a loss for words.

After he became prime minister Diefenbaker called a conference with the provincial premiers for November 1957. Provision of additional grants to the three Maritime provinces was the only concrete proposal his government made to the conference. Newfoundland was to be excluded on the ground that the province would be taken care of by the recommendations of the McNair Commission on term 29. That excuse was totally irrelevant because the McNair Commission had nothing to do with the fiscal arrangements then in force.

Premier Smallwood was furious at the proposed exclusion of Newfoundland. During the conference Smallwood was in close touch with me. Lamontagne and I helped him prepare a cast-iron case for including Newfoundland in any grants to the Atlantic provinces. Diefenbaker backed down and agreed to include Newfoundland.

The special grants probably got Diefenbaker some support in the Maritime provinces in the 1958 election, but his failure to understand the purpose of term 29 and his unsuccessful attempt to exclude Newfoundland from the special grants incurred Smallwood's hostility, which was mixed with a generous measure of contempt.

The McNair Commission presented its report on 1 May 1958. It recommended that the annual payments of the interim grants to

Newfoundland until 1961 be increased to eight million dollars, and that there be an annual grant of eight milllion thereafter. Smallwood attacked the McNair recommendation as hopelessly inadequate. The question of term 29 was raised in Parliament on 15 August when Pearson asked Diefenbaker about implementing McNair's recommendation. Diefenbaker replied that in view of Smallwood's criticism of its inadequacy, the federal government would have to give the fullest consideration to the matter. When I asked whether that meant no action at the 1958 session, Diefenbaker replied that the lack of support in Newfoundland for McNair's recommendation made the fullest consideration by the government necessary.

On learning of the exchange in Parliament, Smallwood introduced a resolution in the Newfoundland House of Assembly, which was seconded by the leader of the Conservative Opposition and adopted unanimously. The resolution, in the form of a message to Diefenbaker, congratulated him on promising a study of the McNair award and asked the federal government as an interim measure to pay Newfoundland the amount recommended by the commission. Smallwood told me in advance about the resolution. He stressed the urgent need of the province for additional revenue. I suggested to Pearson that the Opposition should support the Newfoundland request. Pearson agreed that I should see Diefenbaker and tell him that if the government would introduce a measure to meet the request made unanimously and urgently by the legislature of the province, the Liberal Opposition would support it and commend the government for meeting the need of the province.

My visit to Diefenbaker on that mission was one of only two occasions I was ever in his office. He told me that he had read the report of the McNair Commission but could make neither head nor tail of it and did not see how the government could act immediately. He then kept me nearly an hour talking about other things. When I got up to leave, I repeated my message and added that if the government did not act, I intended to speak at length in support of Newfoundland's request in the House that day. Diefenbaker repeated his refusal. My speech that day started the confrontation.

A few days after the conclusion of the debate on the RCMP, in 1959, Pearson asked Diefenbaker if the recommendation of the McNair Commission would be accepted before the tenth anniversary of Confederation. Two days later, on 25 March, the announcement came. Diefenbaker said that legislation would be introduced to provide the payments recommended up to 31 March 1962, and that they would be 'in final and irrevocable settlement of the provisions of article 29 and the contractual obligations of the union consummated in 1949.' I could scarcely believe my ears. I turned to Pearson at once and handed him a note on which I had scribbled the words 'final and irrevocable settlement.' In his comment Pearson welcomed the statement that payments were to be in the amounts recommended by the McNair Commission and regretted that the government had not acted sooner. Pearson hoped he was not misinterpreting Diefenbake's statement that no further obligation would exist after 31 March 1962. Such an assumption Pearson said was quite unwarranted.The immediate repudiation of Diefenbaker by Pearson created an issue over Newfoundland between the government and the Liberal Opposition that was to last as long as Diefenbaker was prime minister.

To make doubly sure that there was no misunderstanding, I asked Diefenbaker later that day whether what he proposed was regarded by the government as a 'complete discharge of the obligation under section 29 of the Terms of Union.' Diefenbaker replied, 'That is so.' He added that any consideration in 1962 would be in the context of the larger situation of the nation as a whole. I asked, as a supplementary, 'Does the Prime Minister realize that every person in Newfoundland will regard this as another breach of a solemn contract?' Diefenbaker replied that he did not think I was speaking for all the people. I retorted, 'You will see.'

Parliament adjourned for Easter that day. In Newfoundland the disapproval was universal. The House of Assembly unanimously condemned the federal government's decision, and a majority of the members of the small Conservative Opposition left the party and formed a new group called the United Newfoundland Party. William Browne, Diefenbaker's minister from Newfoundland, was embarrassed in St John's, and the other Tory MP, James McGrath, was known to be considering withdrawing his support from the Diefenbaker government. On his arrival in St John's for Easter, Browne was quoted in the press as saying, 'There are 22 other members in the Cabinet of Canada and I cannot expect to push my opinions down their throats.'

Because of the recess I had no chance to refer to term 29 again in Parliament until the session resumed on 6 April. I raised a question of privilege at once. My point of privilege was that, in view of the collective responsibility of the cabinet, the House was entitled to know whether the minister had concurred in the cabinet decision about term 29. Browne made no reply. The next day I asked Browne to comment on a statement of his, reported in the *St John's Daily News* on 31 March, that he was going to Ottawa 'to tell the Prime Minister of the strong feelings here about his Term 29 decision.' I also asked Browne to report to the House how the prime minister had responded. The Speaker ruled my question out of order. I next asked whether or not since his return from Newfoundland, Browne had made any representations to the prime minister on the subject. Diefenbaker objected to the question, which was also ruled out of order. I then put a third question, as to whether the reason the minister had left Newfoundland so precipitately was that he did not wish to defend his leader. Of course there was no reply, but my questions had served their purpose. They were out of order because they did not relate to the minister's department — he still had no department . The questions might have been in order if I had put them to the prime minister, but my real purpose was to show that the Newfoundland minister would not join in the protest by everyone else in the province.

In a speech on the budget in mid-April I said that the ultimate in bad faith had been seen in Parliament recently, when the prime minister had taken it upon himself 'to alter or seek to alter the terms of the agreement upon which two nations were joined together into one nation.' I recalled telling the House just before the Easter adjournment that every Newfoundlander would regard that as a betrayal. The prime minister had then replied that I could not speak for all Newfoundlanders. Having been in Newfoundland during the recess, I could now speak for 'the Newfoundlanders, all but one of them.' I concluded by saying that there was one other matter about which not only the people of Newfoundland but the people of all Canada were concerned: that when Diefenbaker had taken the side of the law-breakers against those who were maintaining law and order, he had done more to destroy confidence in his government than by anything else he had done or was likely to do, and that it seemed to me that of all the acts of bad faith which would be held against his government that would, for all time, be the worst.

On 13 July the government introduced legislation to provide the McNair grants to 31 March 1962. The minister, Donald Fleming, gave an undertaking that the needs of Newfoundland would be reviewed before that date, at the same time that the equalization payments and Atlantic grants were reviewed. In an immediate reply to Fleming, Pearson pointed out that term 29 was an integral part of the solemn agreement that brought about the union, that no time limit was set by term 29, and that no time limit was set on the payments recommended by the McNair Commission. A review of other payments to the provinces, he insisted, should not reduce the obligation to pay at least the eight million dollars annually indefinitely into the future. When Diefenbaker interrupted to ask whether Pearson interpreted the recommend 'as requiring the payment in perpetuity of the amount in question, $8 million,' Pearson replied that there was no other interpretation of the words 'thereafter, $8 million per annumn.' He concluded by appealing to the government to accept the recommendation of the royal commission 'until both parties to the act of union agree to their change.'

I bided my time until other members from Newfoundland, including McGrath, had spoken, and then asked whether the minister from Newfoundland was not going to speak. Fleming asked, 'What about?' Browne did not rise. I then said that if the minister from Newfoundland was without voice, 'I as the one remaining Member from Newfoundland who had not yet spoken, will certainly not be without voice.' In my speech to refute points made by Fleming I gave a detailed account of the origins of term 29.

At a later stage in the debate Pearson argued that it was the moral and constitutional responsibility of the government to take no action that would interfere with the implementation of term 29 unless the changes made to term 29 were made by agreement between the two parties to the contract. He undertook as follows: '(When) the responsibility is ours again we shall remove this injustice. We shall correct this violation of a contract and we shall make sure once again that the act of union is honoured in all its parts and is carried out as it must be carried out in letter and in spirit.' That undertaking was duly carried out by the Pearson government.

Diefenbaker expressed resentment of Pearson's charge of bad faith in a speech filled with irrelevant observations. I replied that I could not enter into all aspects of his 100 per cent diversion from the subject. When Diefenbaker had no answer to an argument, he shifted the scenery with great skill and produced effects that sometimes took people in until the third or fourth performance.

Diefenbaker then recalled St Laurent's statement in 1949 that a government could not be legally bound to accept the recommendations of a royal commission. I reminded the House that St Laurent had also said it was not necessary to make binding stipulations about what would happen to the report of the commission, because it was expected that men of honour would be dealing with the terms of union, and that the terms would not be interpreted by police-court quibbling.

Term 29 to a Newfoundlander, I said, was the equivalent of the language rights in the Constitution to a French Canadian.

Diefenbaker interrupted to ask whether I remembered that St Laurent had said the language rights could be changed by a majority in Parliament. I said I remembered very well, but also remembered what else he had said, that no man of honour would ever do it. We could not believe any government would fail to respect the Terms of Union with Newfoundland. Pearson interjected that no person of honour would so fail.

No one could believe, I added, that any Canadian government would propose legislation to repudiate the terms of the BNA Act. Yet that was what was before the House that day. That was why every Newfoundlander, except one or two, resented bitterly the action being taken by the Diefenbaker government. I doubted if the government had ever understood the meaning of term 29. I recalled Diefenbaker's broadcast interview in Newfoundland in 1957 in which he had been asked about the McNair Commission and had replied that there were too many royal commissions. Fleming interrupted to ask me to point to any words in the bill that took anything away from Newfoundland. I said there was no fulfilment of an obligation; there was a 'ratting' on the obligation. I added that that was why Fleming had an uneasy conscience about it.

In his memoirs Fleming discloses that he had proposed that the eight million per annum be paid until 1967, but that the cabinet had decided to end the payments in 1962. He also notes that in presenting the legislation he avoided using Diefenbaker's phrase 'final and irrevocable' settlement. He recalls that after the bitter debate in 1959 the storm passed and was succeeded by relative quiet for several years, 'but that it left considerable local damage behind.' That was an understatement: Newfoundland was lost to the Tory party as long as Diefenbaker was its leader.

The loggers' strike and the RCMP reinforcements ceased to be an active parliamentary issue, but the same was not true of term 29. We in the Opposition brought the question up at every available opportunity — and even created some of our own. On 31 March 1960, the eleventh anniversary of union, I appealed to the government to reverse its position. On 2 May, I moved a vote of want of confidence, seeking to censure the government for failing to carry out Diefenbaker's numerous promises of action in the Atlantic provinces. I worked in a charge of repudiation by the government of its obligations under term 29. That time Browne spoke; he claimed that the government had carried out the recommendations of the McNair Commission. I was glad to have Browne on record in defence of Diefenbaker. Term 29 was our best issue in Newfoundland in the election of 1962.

Other parliamentary activities

I lost no opportunity to take part in other debates affecting the Atlantic provinces, especially that on the Trans-Canada Highway. Progress on the highway was very slow, particularly in Newfoundland. In 1962 the final link in the road in British Columbia became passable. Diefenbaker presided at a ceremony there in September that was described as the official opening. The performance aroused indignation in Newfoundland. I protested to Diefenbaker in writing that the route of the highway in Newfoundland had not yet been finally settled.

In March 1959 Alan Jarvis, the director of the National Gallery, resigned. His resignation was the result of the cancellation of a contract for the purchase of a Dutch painting. In 1958 the board of the National Gallery, on Jarvis's recommendation, contracted to buy a painting by Breughel after informing the ministers directly concerned. The ministers apparently believed that enough money was available in the estimates prepared by the Liberal government to cover the cost, and indicated no disapproval. The Treasury Board then discovered that Parliament had not yet voted the necessary funds, and that the contract could not be carried out unless Parliament was asked to vote money specifically for the purpose. The minister of finance refused to ask for such a vote, and the contract had to be cancelled. Jarvis believed that the government had authorized the purchase and was repudiating a contract, and resigned in protest.

Pearson raised the question of the Dutch painting on the National Gallery estimates and brought out the facts. Later in the debate I said that the government had been prepared to buy the picture as long as ministers thought the purchase could be blamed on the previous government, but that when the minister of finance had found he would have to take responsibility for having the expenditure voted in the House, the government backed down. I called such conduct a shocking repudiation of the good name of Canada.

The whole affair would have had little impact on the public if Jarvis's resignation had not taken place at almost the same time as the RCMP commissioner's. The shabby treatment of the gallery by the government alienated a large section of the artistic community.

About one area I was always vigilant: citizenship and immigration. In 1959, the day after the House had passed the Immigration estimates, the government adopted an order-in-council that would have the effect of reducing Italian immigration, though there was no specific reference to Italy. Once the order was made public, there was intense reaction in the Italian community. In the House, I advised the minister, Ellen Fairclough, to admit her mistake and have the stupid and inhuman regulation revoked. A week later Ellen denounced me at length for my description of the order and said that I had done many cruel and inhuman things when I was minister. After dealing at length with my sins she announced that the regulation was being revoked because its purpose was being misrepresented by Liberal propagandists. I thanked her for taking my advice to rescind the order. That clumsy and unsuccessful attempt to restrict Italian immigration helped, of course, to maintain Liberal support in the Italian-Canadian community.

I was less successful in 1959 in another immigration matter. All children born in Canada are natural-born Canadian citizens. When I was first minister I had been responsible for deporting immigrants who had young children born in Canada. Once I realized that young Canadian citizens were being condemned either to exile from their native country or to separation from their parents when the parents were deported, I stopped the deportation of persons with Canadian-born children. When I complained that the Diefenbaker government was once more deporting immigrants with Canadian-born children, Fairclough cited instances in which that had happened when I was minister. I retorted that it was wrong then, and that two wrongs did not make a right.

Under the Canadian Citizenship Act the government had authority to revoke the citizenship of citizens not born in Canada for certain limited reasons. I carried on a running campaign through the Diefenbaker years for the removal of that authority. As minister of citizenship I had, on a very few occasions, used it myself. The most notable had concerned Fred Rose, the member of Parliament mentioned in the Gouzenko disclosures. His citizenship had been revoked only after he had been convicted of espionage and been out of Canada for some time. I had acted with great reluctance, because I realized that the existence of the legal power to revoke citizenship, however rarely used, created a feeling among some who were not born in Canada that they were second-class citizens. I had come to the conclusion that the capacity to revoke citizenship was not a power the government needed to protect the public interest, and that it should be removed from the law.

On the very day in 1958 when Diefenbaker moved first reading of his Bill of Rights, a government bill to amend the Citizenship Act was being debated. I moved an amendment to provide that naturalized citizens should have equality of rights and status with natural-born citizens. I spoke with moderation, and I could never understand why the government did not seize the chance to accept a proposal that would have given all Canadians equal rights as citizens and reflected credit on the government.

Early in 1959 I introduced a private member's bill to give all citizens equality of status. My bill was actually debated. Again I was surprised that the government did not accept a change so completely in the spirit of Diefenbaker's proposed Bill of Rights. I proposed the same bill in every session while the Tories were in office. When the Liberal party was returned to office I was pleased that the Pearson government had legislation passed to end the discrimination.

Diefenbaker's choice of Roland Michener as Speaker of the House of Commons in 1957 was a happy one for Parliament, and his re-election as Speaker in 1958 was generally acclaimed. As Speaker, Michener was scrupulously nonpartisan, scholarly and full of common sense. But in 1959 Diefenbaker began to show his resentment of Michener's insistence that the prime minister, like other members, obey the rules of the House. On 25 May, Pearson raised a question of privilege. His point was that, in replying to a question from a Liberal member on an earlier day, the minister of labour had misled the House. While the question of privilege was being debated, I interjected, 'Deprived of debate by trickery.' My interjection aroused the prime minister, who interrupted the debate to ask me to withdraw the statement. After a couple more exchanges I asked if the prime minister would say what he would like withdrawn. Diefenbaker began to reply with a reference to my 'being about to write the history of Mr. King,' when the Speaker interrupted to say: 'I am afraid the Prime Minister is introducing another point of order in the middle of the first one. The Prime Minister is asking for a statement to be withdrawn. If he would allow me to deal with the first matter, then I would.' Diefenbaker interrupted him angrily, 'Mr. Speaker, will you allow me to finish now?' and continued in defiance of the Speaker. Even some of the Tory members appeared shocked. When Diefenbaker concluded, the Speaker completed his statement on Pearson's question of privilege, which he ruled was not valid.

He then turned to Diefenbaker's question about my interjection and Diefenbaker repeated his demand that I withdraw 'Deprived of debate by trickery.' I said that there was no dispute that we had been deprived of debate. 'Whether it was by trickery or by some other means I imputed no motive to any individual.' If the Speaker considered it was wrong to say the House had been deprived by trickery, I would withdraw the word 'trickery,' but only if the Speaker said so. The Speaker ruled that unless a statement was

offensive by charging a member with some reprehensible conduct, it was not unparliamentary, but added that since the whole
discussion was about the minister of labour, an inference might be
drawn; he would feel much better if I would indicate that I was not
charging the minister with trickery. I replied that I had never
intended to charge him with trickery and was quite willing to
withdraw the word 'trickery' and substitute 'maladroitness.' That
ended the incident so far as I was concerned. I had been anxious
to make sure my behaviour to the Speaker was in sharp contrast
to Diefenbaker's. His defiance was never again quite so blatant,
but his all too obvious resentment of the Speaker's impartiality
continued throughout the years of the Parliament.

The 1959 session had not been a happy one for the government, and there was little constructive achievement to report in
the closing Speech from the Throne. The immigration regulation
that had offended the Italian community, the treatment of Newfoundland, the resignation of the RCMP commissioner and of the
director of the National Gallery, the 'heads will roll' fiasco and
Diefenbaker's rebuke of the Speaker had all hurt the government,
and added to those was the brutal cancellation of the Avro Arrow.
The Opposition was beginning to create an impression that the
administration was not competent, and that the prime minister
often acted impulsively and sometimes vindictively.

More damaging to the government was the background of
unemployment, which had been the main subject of Pearson's
opening speech in the session. The failure to reduce unemployment was the prime public grievance against the government, and
we kept the subject to the fore in debate. The House finally rose
on 18 July, whereupon I joined the family at Traytown.

Liberal revival

A smoother year for the government

The parliamentary session of 1960 was long but easier for
Diefenbaker than that of 1959. No striking legislation was forecast

in the Speech from the Throne, but some useful things were done.

The complete revision of the Canada Elections Act was a constructive measure. R.A. Bell was the spokesman for the Tories, and I was the senior Liberal representative on the committee that worked out the changes. Dick Bell and I were personal friends and worked together in an entirely nonpartisan way. I offered one radical idea that did not find favour in the committee. My proposal was that in election campaigns, expenditures of political parties and individual candidates should be severely limited, and that such expenditures should be reimbursed from the public treasury, not paid out of campaign funds. I believe that that was the first time such a drastic change had been suggested in Parliament. I made it clear that the idea was my own and not yet the policy of the Liberal party.

All the reforms recommended by the committee were accepted by the government and passed by the House. Hazen Argue of the CCF proposed in committee and again in the House that the voting age be reduced from 21 to 18 years. I opposed the change in committee. Later, in the Liberal caucus, Paul Hellyer eloquently supported the lower age, and because I thought no principle was involved, I agreed to support whatever position the caucus favoured.

In the House Pearson announced that the Liberal Opposition would support Argue's amendment. Diefenbaker replied, opposing the amendment. He sought to humiliate me by suggesting that as spokesman of the Liberals in the committee I had now been repudiated by my leader. I spoke right after Diefenbaker to explain my position. Extending the vote to 18-year-olds would, I said, not make Canada more or less democratic. I confessed that in committee I had not supported the reduction in voting age. At the age of 18 I had been a hereditary Conservative; at the age of 21, I had seen the light and become a Liberal. Such a change was not infrequent in western Canada in the 1920s. What was more uncommon in western Canada in those years was another conversion, of a much more distinguished member of the House than I was. While I was advancing, another gentleman was receding. (Everyone knew that Diefenbaker had started out his political career as a Liberal and had become a Tory because he had failed to get a Liberal nomination.) It seemed to me, I continued, there was a tendency, once one had cast a vote, to become more attached to a party than before one had voted. Giving the vote at 18 might cause many voters to remain in their hereditary positions instead of forming more mature views. But I did not think mine a strong argument and had no problem in changing my position. My explanation ended that discussion.

We also supported the government's legislation to give a vote in federal elections to status Indians. When the Indian Act was revised in 1952, that question had been debated but not accepted by the Liberal government. I said that we Liberals were happy to support the Bill.

We also approved the petition to the British Parliament to amend the BNA Act to have superior court judges appointed for life, retire at age 75, as judges of the Supreme Court of Canada already did. But we argued that the retirement rules should apply only to future appointments. Compulsory retirement for judges already appointed for life was, in my view, a breach of the contract on which they had accepted appointment. I felt keenly about that restrospective action, but our caucus generally opposed making it a big issue. When the Pearson government later secured a constitutional amendment to provide for the retirement of senators at age 75, it applied only to future appointments.

In my opinion, and our caucus usually agreed, it was a good tactic for the Opposition to support good measures and get them passed quickly with as little advertising as possible for the government.

In 1960 unemployment continued to plague the country and reduce support for the government. The main debate on unemployment took place on the Labour departmental estimates late in the session. Pearson and Martin demanded that the minister of labour give the House the forecasts of unemployment for the coming winter prepared by his economic experts. The minister of labour, Michael Starr, had foolishly declared in a broadcast in February that the recession was over, and had claimed that the government's policies had provided more jobs than at any earlier time in the country's history. In the debate I said that surely Starr's optimistic forecast had not been made until he had first examined the views of the economic advisers of the government. The House had a right to a straightforward and careful answer to the question Pearson and Martin had already asked. Starr replied that the situation was difficult to assess so far in advance, and that he had in fact received no forecasts. At one point, while I was deploring the level of unemployment, Starr interrupted me to say that he had the greatest confidence in the country, though I seemed to lack it. I did not lack confidence in the country, I said, but in the government. I was sure the country would survive that government as it had survived the previous Tory government, and asked the rhetorical question, Why do we have to suffer Tory governments once in every generation? That and similar remarks at other times prompted the accusation that I had claimed the Liberal party was the natural governing party — a claim never made by me at any time.

Up to late 1960 I felt that we were wearing down support for the government but believed that with its huge majority it would not be defeated in an election.

The Bill of Rights

For Diefenbaker the highlight of the 1960 session was the enactment of his Bill of Rights. In the 1950s it had become a fashion, to advocate a bill of rights for Canada. The question was invariably raised on my visits to university Liberal clubs, and I did not hesitate to say that I was not in favour of a bill of rights. I thought the best bill of rights was the Ten Commandments, and the next best the Criminal Code, with its presumption that an accused person was not guilty until the prosecution proved otherwise. Each of those codes specified wrongs and did not attempt to define rights. All situations could not be covered in a definition of rights.

Despite my misgivings and those of a few other members our Liberal caucus decided that the party could not afford to go on record in opposition to a bill of rights. Instead we would support the bill but seek to improve it in detail and urge amendments to the War Measures Act, which Diefenbaker did not propose to touch. I consoled myself with the reflection that the proposed Bill of Rights would not be embedded in the Constitution but would simply be an enactment by Parliament that could be amended by Parliament at any time.

In the debate I limited myself to a detailed refutation of Diefenbaker's false claim that he had spoken out for the Japanese Canadians during the war. If the prime minister could find anything he had said in Parliament during the years of war in protest against the treatment of Japanese Canadians, I said I would be pleased to be told about it. Diefenbaker tried to weasel out of the situation by asking me if I considered December 1945 in the 'days of war.' I replied, 'No, I do not.' Our exchange did not restrain him from claiming for the rest of his life that he had protested, in wartime, the treatment of the Japanese Canadians. By 1976 Diefenbaker had repeated this myth so often that he probably believed it himself.

My attitude to a bill of rights has not changed. Two decades later I agreed with the views expressed by Sterling Lyon, the premier of Manitoba, at the conference at which 9 of the 10 premiers agreed to the patriation of the Constitution. For me the only redeeming feature of the Charter of Rights, is the so-called notwithstanding clause, which allows Parliament and any provincial legislature within its jurisdiction to set aside a decision of the court. The notwithstanding clause allows the elected representatives of the people and not a majority of the Supreme Court judges — as few as five persons — to decide finally what are human rights.

The Kingston Conference

The most important event in 1960 from the point of view of the Liberal party was the Thinkers Conference at Queen's University in Kingston, organized by Mitchell Sharp at Pearson's suggestion. The conference was not an official Liberal function; a number of those who attended were not members of the party and, in some cases, not Liberals. Among the leading participants were Sharp, Bud Drury, Maurice Lamontagne, John Turner, Bob Fowler, Tom Kent and Frank Underhill, one of the founders of the CCF. To me the most attractive new face was Jean Marchand's; I had not met him before.

Sharp and Drury had been deputy ministers until the Diefenbaker government was formed and in 1960 were engaged in business in the private sector. Neither had been a member of the Liberal party, and neither had Liberal backgrounds. The fact that they later became active Liberals and ministers in the Pearson government helped to give superficial plausibility to the Diefenbaker myth that senior public servants were generally sympathetic to the Liberal Opposition and in many cases were sabotaging the Tory government. In the case of Sharp and Drury and many other prominent Canadians it was, I believe, growing alarm at the incompetence of the Tory government more than the call of Liberalism that attracted them. Pearson was open to new ideas, and the Liberal Opposition was developing new policies. Undoubtedly that was the reason why in most of the mock parliaments in the Universities the Liberals were winning majorities. That was also why Sharp could recruit such an impressive group for Kingston.

Sharp asked me to speak at the closing luncheon and give my impressions. In addition to reacting to the proceedings, I made two or three points on my own. I said there seemed no appreciable dissent among eggheads or among comfortable, liberal-minded, middle-class Canadians about the desirability of maintaining relative independence for Canada. When I was younger, there had still been many Canadians attached to the Empire who did not want independence. In 1960 Canada was a more solid and united country. It would be difficult either to fragment Canada or to persuade Canadians to join another country.

I said that Canadian politicians had to realize that just as French Canadians were indissolubly mixed up with other Canadians and could not get away from the rest of us no matter how many separatists they might generate, so, for better or worse, we Canadians were inseparably mixed up with the Americans. That was the biggest brute fact of our existence. We could have just as much independence as we were willing to pay for. In the 20th century no country had independence in any absolute sense, not even the United States.

I stated that it was increasingly recognized, sometimes reluctantly and almost as a necessary evil, that as far ahead as we could see, we were going to continue to have a dual culture in Canada. I believed that it was wrong to do all the public business in Ottawa in English. There was no doubt that in time there would be a steady increase in the use of the French language in the official life of the country.

I declared that I had no patience with the view that Canadians were superior to Americans. There were times when the United States was resented in Canada, but individual Americans, rarely. I added that though some of us were honest enough to admit Canadians were no better than Americans, we still wanted to have our own national society because it was our own. For me that was sufficient reason. Liberal-minded Canadians wanted that national society to be a liberal society. The Canadian Labour Congress had, I said, replaced the CPR as the greatest aggregation of private power in the country. Instead of trying to stroke the new tiger we had to realize it was a tiger, and like the CPR, which had been pretty thoroughly tamed, it would have to be tamed too. To me the saddest thing about much of modern industry was that a high proportion of those who earned their living in industrial plants did not enjoy their work but got their satisfaction away from the workplace. For workers to have a sense of genuine participation, I believed, they would have to share in the control of the workplace. Most people wanted to work at something they had some creative part in. Another problem was the sharing of income. There was a growing gap between the incomes of industrial workers and the financial rewards of farmers and fishermen. Some way had to be found to shift the emphasis in industry from ever-rising wage rates to the maintenance of real income. We had no answer at all to that problem.

In conclusion I recalled that Mitchell Sharp was a one-time public servant, and that modern efficient government was not possible without brains in its public service. I thanked Sharp for assembling such an impressive conference at Pearson's invitation. The meeting was one of the best examples of the difference between the approach to government of liberal-minded people and hostile-minded.

The Kingston Conference had attracted a group of able Canadians, most of them younger than I. At age 55, I was regarded as part of the old guard. Several participants in the conference were subsequently elected to Parliament, and some became ministers in the Pearson government.

The Liberal rally in Ottawa in January 1961 gave even greater emphasis to youth. Paul Hellyer, the youngest privy councillor, presided. I was not active in the general proceedings but busied myself in making sure that every item in the resolutions of the national convention of 1958 relating to the Atlantic provinces was included in the new Liberal program. The rally was a huge success and stimulated Liberal activity throughout the country, particularly among young people.

By the beginning of 1961 the Liberal Opposition had reason to feel it had reached the great divide in its hard upward climb.

Activities outside Parliament

The Parliamentary session of 1960 dragged into August. Margaret, Peter, Alan and Ruth were already in Newfoundland by 19 July. Jane was back in Québec City at the chemical plant. I skipped the last few days of the session and was in Traytown at the beginning of August. We had a full month in Newfoundland. There were enough new roads to make a car worthwhile, but we still had to visit the northern part of the riding from the sea. Ken Goodyear lent us his cabin cruiser, the *Sylvia Joyce*, for the visits. I met Ken first in 1953, and I saw him from time to time when I was minister. When I was in Opposition he became a generous supporter and a good friend. We had similar trips on the *Sylvia Joyce* for several years, exciting experiences for all of us.

Two events in 1960 gave me a great deal of pleasure. On 1 July the village of Ashern celebrated the 50th anniversary of its founding. Ashern had the unique distinction of providing two cabinet ministers in the federal government at the same time. The central feature of the ceremony was the presence of Stuart Garson, who like me had been in the St Laurent government, and who had earlier been the premier of Manitoba and the member of the legislature for the Ashern area. I had not been back in Ashern since 1935 and was surprised that the village had extended into our farm. The visit evoked nostalgic memories, which I shared with Mother on my return.

The other event was in Newfoundland. The Confederation Building, which was to house the House of Assembly and most government departments, was completed in 1960, and St Laurent was invited to open it. He asked me to go to St John's with him, and I took Alan with us. After St Laurent spoke and cut the ribbon, we went inside, where we were amused to see ourselves among the many other caricatures in the mural painting depicting the history of Newfoundland. I was delighted by the warm welcome St Laurent received as he emerged that day from almost complete retirement.

When I started work on *The Mackenzie King Record* in 1958, the prospect of my carrying on legal studies was remote. In March 1960 I received a letter from Alex Hickman, the secretary of the Law Society, asking whether I was actually serving as a law clerk. He had not raised the question with Eric Cook, with whom I was articled. Eric was indignant and wanted to protest, but I was glad of an excuse to withdraw and did so during the visit to St John's.

I had been working in late 1959 and early 1960 on *The Mackenzie King Record*. The manuscript was already too long for a single volume, and the editor, Francess Halpenny persuaded the University of Toronto Press that the content was too valuable to be cut, and that one volume, to terminate in late May 1944, should be published in 1960. Publication came not a moment too soon, as my salary from the Mackenzie King estate ran only until 31 May. By fall I would need the anticipated royalties. Margaret and I were in Toronto for a party to launch the book on 11 October. Soon afterwards, I went on a promotion tour. At a meeting with the press in Victoria the first question was; What did I think of Diefenbaker's comment? I asked what he had said and was told he had described *The Mackenzie King Record* as the greatest work of fiction of the year. There could, I replied, be no better judge of fiction than Diefenbaker. C.D. Howe told me that the *Record* was the most interesting book he had ever read. Howe's praise did not go to my head, as I realized a book is apt to be more interesting to a reader who is one of the principal characters. Despite the unprecedented price of $9.50 the book sold well, and the royalties improved the family fortunes.

Four provincial elections were held in June 1960. The first was in Nova Scotia, where Premier Robert Stanfield was returned with an increased majority. The leader of the Opposition, the former premier Henry Hicks, lost his seat, as did Gordon Cowan, his most effective colleague. That was the only provincial election campaign outside Newfoundland in which I ever participated, and I did so against my own better judgement. Someone from Ottawa with no close connection with the province might, I feared, be resented and do more harm than good. I agreed to take part only if my concern was reported to Hicks, and he endorsed the invitation. He did so. I spoke at three or four large and enthusiastic meetings and thoroughly enjoyed the experience. My participation did not, I believe, hurt the Liberals, but the results showed it did not help. Believing our fortunes were already rising we Liberals in Opposition were disappointed by Nova Scotia. Our spirits revived a little when the Liberals increased their numbers against the CCF in Saskatchewan the next day, and when not one Tory was elected in Diefenbaker's home province. The Liberals under

Jean Lesage's leadership won a resounding victory in Québec on 20 June, and the outlook improved greatly. Finally, the Liberal defeat of the Tory government in New Brunswick on 27 June made us feel the tide was really turning.

A federal-provincial conference took place in July. Before the conference met, Lesage invited Lamontagne and me to Québec to go over his opening speech. I was consulted about its content but felt my most useful function was to ensure that the English text corresponded as precisely as possible with the French. During the whole time Lesage was Premier of Québec our personal relations were friendly. I never shared the indignation many Liberals felt because Lesage behaved like a provincial politician, sometimes differing with the federal Liberals. His was the outstanding provincial voice in federal-provincial relations, often he was much better informed than the federal ministers, partly because of his wide experience earlier in Ottawa.

At the conference in July, Diefenbaker undertook to maintain the tax-sharing formula set in 1956 by the St Laurent government. At a second conference, in October, the government proposed amendments to the principle of equalization that displeased all the premiers and provided us with one of the contentious issues between Opposition and government in 1961.

A bad government start

The parliamentary session of 1961 actually opened on 20 November 1960. Four new members were introduced. The only Tory elected was Hugh John Flemming. The normally Tory Peterborough was lost to Walter Pitman, the first and only MP elected as a New party candidate while the CCF was transforming itself into the New Democratic party. Pitman was an effective addition to the Opposition in debate. The Liberals held Niagara Falls with Judy LaMarsh, who became a formidable reinforcement. The Liberals won back Labelle, from which the Tory member had resigned to avoid a scandal.

When we were planning tactics for the session I reminded my colleagues that in one session when Bennett was prime minister, the Liberal Opposition had believed that the government had no legislation ready; they had moved no amendment to the Speech from the Throne and had let it pass at once, thereby leaving the government embarrassed with nothing to do. I recommended that we do the same thing, our belief being that Diefenbaker would find himself in the same position. Pearson and the caucus agreed, and no amendment was moved by us. The NDP moved want of confidence, but no Liberal spoke, and the debate collapsed. We had guessed right. The government had no legislation ready.

Fleming had claimed that the government was going to propose urgent action to stimulate employment, but no such action came before Christmas. On the last day before the recess Fleming presented his budget. In his speech he reversed his position by denying that there was an emergency requiring urgent action relating to employment. The debate on the budget began in January. I spoke early, and I contradicted Fleming by asserting that the country and the Opposition felt there was an emergency about unemployment. The subject was so important I proposed to do something I had not done before in the House — 'follow my notes closely,' the traditional euphemism for reading a speech. My statement was couched in colourful and extravagant language about the emergency and the plight of the unemployed. Before I had completed it, Fleming interjected, 'Why can you not tell the truth?' I ignored his interjection and continued to read for a minute or two and then paused and said: 'Mr. Speaker, I cannot go on, sir. I have three more pages, but every word I have just read — and I have read it, sir, I confess it — was uttered in this House by the present Minister of Finance. I used his words because I was not as capable of painting such a vivid picture of doom and gloom as he had done in opposition in 1955 when unemployment was not much more than half as great as it is in 1961.' Fleming did not know how to react, but he was not amused. Ministers and Tory backbenchers barely concealed their amusement. Members on our side of the House did not try.

At a federal-provincial conference in February 1961, the provincial governments were presented with proposals that drastically changed the basis of tax-sharing. The new formula was to be applied to the tax-sharing and equalization arrangements that were to replace for five years those that would expire on 31 March 1962. The proposals were denounced by all the premiers and legislation was not introduced until July. Fleming predicted that the amended proposals would usher in a new era of cooperation on more equal terms. In reply Pearson noted how far short the proposals were from the additional $100 million that Diefenbaker in 1957 had promised to Premier Frost for Ontario. He criticized the change in the basis of equalization. None of the premiers, he noted, was satisfied, not even Mr Frost, though Ontario would fare better than any other provincial government. In my speech I said how pleased I had been in July 1960 to hear Diefenbaker pledge his government to maintain the Liberal principle of equalization, and how depressed I was when it was repudiated. An analysis of the new proposals, I pointed out, indicated a net gain to Ontario of $18 million and a total cost to the federal treasury for all 10 provinces of only $17 million. We Liberals promised to restore the principle of equalization. We did so, of course, when we were back in office.

The new tax-sharing legislation included a grant of the eight million dollars a year awarded to Newfoundland by the McNair Commission, but the payment was to be limited to the five years from March 1962, instead of being provided indefinitely, as McNair had recommended. I repeated the Liberal pledge to have the McNair award paid as a matter of right, and not for a limited period as a matter of grace.

10 Working Our Way Back

Diefenbaker's decline

The Coyne Affair in the House of Commons

What caused the government and Diefenbaker himself the greatest harm in 1961 was what came to be called the Coyne Affair. The affair arose out of a series of speeches James Coyne, the governor of the Bank of Canada, made in 1960 and early 1961 on financial and economic questions. The speeches contained no criticism of the government, but it was clear that they made Fleming largely uncomfortable — and his memoirs have confirmed this — because of criticism by his colleagues that he said nothing publicly to show his displeasure.

Coyne was my closest friend, and Robert Beattie, the deputy governor, was my brother-in-law. Once in Opposition I rarely discussed public affairs with either of them, and even our social contacts were much less frequent. While we were in office as well as in Opposition I took no part in debates on the Bank. I too was uncomfortable about Coyne's speeches, not because of their content but because I did not think a public servant, however independent his position, should make speeches about controversial questions. I was sure the speeches, neutral though they were in tone, would sooner or later result in conflict with the government.

Several Liberals raised questions in Parliament and demanded that the annual report of the Bank be referred to a committee of the House in which the governor and other officials could be examined. Fleming refused. He was provoked into saying that the government did not take responsibity for the opinions of the governor of the Bank contained in its report.

A Parliamentary crisis developed as a result of a meeting of the board of directors of the bank held at Quebec City in June 1961. Coyne told the board that Fleming had asked him on 30 May to resign as governor and that he had replied that he would report that request to the board. After reporting to the board Coyne withdrew from the meeting and gave a written statement to the press. His statement said that Fleming had asked him to resign at once instead of retiring when his term expired at the end of the year. The main reason given by Fleming had been that the cabinet was upset because the board of directors had acted in February 1960 to increase the retirement pension of the governor.

The board had increased the pension only after being assured by the Deparment of Justice that it was acting entirely within its legal powers. Fleming told Coyne that the cabinet felt that, by allowing the board to change the pension provision, he had acted irresponsibly. Coyne stated that he could not ignore or accept that slander on his integrity and would not resign quietly. He felt that it was his obligation for the sake of future governors of the Bank and in the interests of propriety and decency in the conduct of public affairs, to bring the matter into the open for consideration and discussion. He pointed out that at no time had the government expressed disagreement with the operations of the Bank of Canada under his management. So long as he continued as governor he would continue to perform his duties as prescribed by Parliament.

The minister of finance had told him, Coyne continued, that one reason the government wanted him out of the way was that it was preparing certain programs the government thought he would oppose. Coyne called the suggestion mysterious and alarming. He had never opposed government policy and did not wish to do so. It was conceivable, he stated, that it would be the duty of the governor to resign on an important question of policy or to make a strong public stand against some government proposal. But the governor should not resign merely because he was asked to do so. He concluded by expressing the hope that thoughtful consideration and discussion would enable the bank to continue, as in the past, to take appropriate action within its own field in support of the financial requirements and economic policy of the government of the day.

Coyne issued his statement to the press and then returned to the meeting and read it to the board of directors, which passed a resolution by nine votes to one that it was in the best interests of the Bank of Canada that the governor resign immediately.

Coyne's statement burst on Parliament like a bomb. Fleming took the opportunity the next day to make one of his vehement speeches. He described Coyne's statement as defiant and provocative. He would confine himself, he said, to the essential facts, virtually none of which appeared in Coyne's statement. He stressed the government's objection to the increase in the governor's pension and accused Coyne of lacking a sense of responsibility by failing to ensure that the matter was brought to the attention of the government. Fleming informed the House that 'the government would shortly invite Parliament to take appropriate legislative action to meet the needs of the situation.' Pearson made a powerful reply and demanded an urgent debate, which the Speaker agreed to immediately. That was only the first stage of the affair.

I learned of the demand for Coyne's resignation from his press statement in Québec City on 13 June. It was only after learning from that statement of the demand for Coyne's resignation that I felt free to participate in debate on the Bank of Canada. I did not take part in the urgent debate on 14 June; I was satisfied with

Pearson's position and did not think I could add anything useful until Fleming had disclosed what action the government proposed to ask Parliament to take.

The Opposition expected the government to introduce the legislation to deal with Coyne the next day. Instead Fleming brought down his budget. I spoke on the budget on 22 June, and my speech was one of my rougher attacks on the government. There had been a good deal of advance publicity emanating from Tory public relations sources forecasting an expansionist budget that was to be in contrast to the alleged restrictionist policies of the governor of the Bank of Canada. I said that, instead of the promised contrast, the only difference was that Coyne had proposed a program for full employment, whereas the government had a program for the perpetuation of unemployment. At that point Fleming's parliamentary secretary, Dick Bell, asked if I had adopted the governor's program. I replied. 'No, I do not adopt the Governor's programme. I am putting forward my own views. I am supporting the programme of the Liberal Party.' I added that, unlike the government, we had a program.

A Tory MP interrupted, 'Tell us about it.' I replied that I was going to tell the House what the country thought about the budget. After the great expectations aroused by the advance billing, I said, the budget was bound to be an anticlimax. I attributed the publicity to the Tory public relations experts, because its style was succinct and catchy; everyone knew that Fleming had no such style. When misleading, inflated advertising preceded an empty package, I believed, the public felt let down. While listening to the budget speech I had perceived that the government's proposals differed little from what Coyne had suggested in a memorandum to Fleming dated 15 February 1961. Coyne had made that document public on 19 June, the day before the budget. During Fleming's speech I had scribbled on the margin of my order paper, 'Coyne and water, more water than Coyne.' I did not include that phrase in my speech. By coincidence a leading member of the press gallery, Arthur Blakely of the *Montreal Gazette*, had independently used the same phrase in his broadcast on the evening of the budget. In my speech I defied any fair-minded person to go through the budget proposals and find a single item, with one exception, that was not a pale reflection of the memorandum Coyne had sent the minister of finance. Fleming interrupted to say that my statement was silly. I claimed that a friend had gone through *Hansard* to count the number of times Fleming had said 'nonsense,' 'silly' and 'rubbish.' When his count reached 5000, my friend had said he couldn't take it any more. That statistic, I said, was about as reliable as most of the statistics we got from the government.

Of Fleming, I said, this is the Minister who in 1957, in his first press release as minister of finance, said he was going to tackle the tight money situation and end it. Then, a year later, when it was embarrassing, he had washed his hands, like Pontius Pilate, and said the government had no control over monetary policy. When interest rates started to fall again, he said, I did it with my own little hands, and then, when interest rates went up again, there was the Pontius Pilate act: It was the Bank of Canada. We knew that the minister was not a free agent any more. What we had was a one-man government with a lot of little boys running errands. None of them had been running more unpleasant errands than the minister of finance had had to run in the past few weeks.

The evening before my speech on the budget Diefenbaker had said in a broadcast: 'The case of the governor of the Bank of Canada is now out in the open where it can be thoroughly discussed and assessed in the light of the facts.' That same morning he had voted against two motions to provide the House of Commons with the facts out in the open. The prime minister had used his majority to keep those facts from Parliament. I charged that there was one principle of his government — a 'head' every three months. The head of the government has to have heads, one after another. I had just mentioned the RCMP commissioner when my time expired.

If the budget was designed to take the heat off the Coyne affair, it had been a miserable failure. The fate of Coyne was uppermost in the public mind.

On 23 June, Fleming introduced a bill containing only one clause, 'The office of the Governor of the Bank of Canada shall be deemed to have become vacant immediately upon the coming into force of this act.' The debate on the bill began on 26 June. Pearson and Paul Martin both made powerful speeches demanding that Coyne be heard by a committee of the House. I had been outraged when I saw the bill and decided to speak later the same day. By speaking I fell into a trap. I had reached the point in my speech where I asked, since Fleming and Coyne had appeared to be in agreement until the spring of 1961, what had led to Fleming's sudden difference with Coyne? The government had evidently needed a victim to draw attention away from its own difficulties. Maybe the decision was made by the minister? Maybe the prime minister ordered him to do it? I suspected the latter. Coyne must go quickly in order to conceal the facts from the people and Parliament. Did the government come to Parliament and make their case? Did they allow us to perform our functions as an Opposition? Did they allow Parliament to be sovereign? No, they said, We have a huge and servile majority; we will put a bill through this House to take away the rights of this man without letting him be heard.

At that point, Dick Bell interrupted to say that Coyne was in the headlines every day. I asked whether Bell, who was a lawyer, was suggesting that if a man makes a statement in public outside the courts, he should be denied access to the courts. If that was the new doctrine of the Bill of Rights, it was not a doctrine any Liberal could espouse. Bell asked me if I would permit a question. I naïvely said, 'Certainly.' Bell then asked me if I would indicate to the House whether or not I had been in communication with Coyne since 2 June. Too late I knew that I had provided the government with the excuse for a badly needed diversion. Bell said that apparently I did not wish to answer his question, to which I replied: 'It is a very well known fact that I have known Mr. Coyne for thirty years and that he is one of my personal friends. I live in a free country and, of course, I have not denied myself communication with my friends, even under this Tory despotism.'

Fleming interjected triumphantly, 'The bubble is pricked now; now we know.' I made no comment on his insinuation but continued my speech.

Many of the operations of the bank, I said, had to be carried out without publicity, and the governor had respected the requirement of confidentiality 'until the minister fired him, or tried to.' Coyne then felt he had a duty to Parliament and the people of Canada, whose servant he was — 'not the servant of the Government, not the servant of the minister, but the servant of Parliament and the people of Canada' — to tell us that something was wrong and to give us a chance to find out what it was. That was the issue. 'If there is something wrong with the Governor, surely the Government would be delighted to give him a hearing and show he is wrong.' Why was the government so frightened I asked. Why did they not want an inquiry? The answer was that there was nothing substantial to inquire into. They 'want a scapegoat for the past — and what I suspect is a great deal more serious — they want a compliant tool in the office of the governor of the Bank of Canada to deal with their deficits in the future.'

I realized from the moment I had answered Bell's question that I had provided an opening for the government. It was no surprise to me when David Walker, the number one hatchet man in the government, rose to reply to me. He accused me of being 'the confidential adviser of the Governor of the Bank of Canada.' I interjected that I thought I had a question of privilege but 'would simply say that that libel answers itself.' Walker went on to say that I had admitted being 'in constant touch with the Governor' and said that if I would deny it, he would withdraw his remarks. I replied that I had said I had been in touch with him as a friend. Walker interrupted me to say, 'Well, out of his own mouth.' I said that perhaps he would allow me to finish. 'I said I had been in touch with him as a friend of many, many years' ... (and) 'I ... saw no reason, simply because of this action, to alter that friendship in any way whatsoever ... in a free country.' Walker continued in the same vein and concluded by asking the House to pity Coyne, whose advice had been abominable. For that advice, he said, we can only blame members of the Opposition led by the person who would be leader of the Opposition, the member for Bonavista-Twillingate.

I was not ashamed of my speech, but I was not happy that night about the predictable reaction it would evoke. Its immediate effect would be to divert attention in the media from the clear case made by Pearson against the government. That consequence would displease Pearson's staff and members of our party in the House. I feared that Coyne might be hurt if the government could succeed in portraying him as an ally of the Liberal Opposition. I was, moreover, chagrined by my own lack of foresight.

I was completely right about the reaction of the media. The revelation that I had been in touch with Coyne eclipsed the accounts of the rest of the debate, and I was unpopular in the Liberal caucus for several days. But my fear that I might have hurt Coyne's case proved unwarranted; almost no one believed that he was a Liberal partisan, much less that he had been trying to help the Opposition.

The government did not go on with the debate on the bill the next day but reverted to the budget debate. The debate on the bill to remove Coyne did not resume until 4 July, and it continued on 5 July. Diefenbaker was last that day. He made a long discursive speech containing allegations about me, to which I replied briefly on questions of privilege. His final word was that in one of his letters Coyne had referred to a man 'in whom he places reliance.' Glaring across the aisle at me Diefenbaker said, 'I look at that individual now and wonder whether I behold in fact the person who dictated certain portions of those letters. Pearson interjected, 'You do not see him.'

I rose again on a question of privilege. It was 6 p.m., the time of adjournment, and the Speaker suggested that I defer my statement until the debate could be resumed. Both Chevrier and Pearson exclaimed 'No.' Encouraged by their support, I said, 'Mr. Speaker, when one is defamed by the words of the Prime Minister, one should surely be given a second in which to reply.' The Speaker then asked if the House would give me unanimous consent to be heard and to my surprise no one objected. I then said that the charge the prime minister had just made had been made earlier in the debate. 'At that time, I gave a simple and direct answer, which was No. My answer is still No. My reputation for telling the truth in this House, I stand on.' The House then adjourned, but not before Hellyer remarked, 'The Prime Minister plunged to new depths this afternoon.' Later, in the Senate committee on the bill, where Coyne was allowed to appear, he identified the person in whom he placed reliance as Graham Towers, his predecessor as governor of the bank.

As Diefenbaker had not concluded his speech on 5 July, we expected the debate to continue the next day. We were surprised when the government instead called for debate on a Senate amendment to a bill to amend the Customs Tariff Act.

The Senate and the Coyne Affair

None of us in the Opposition could understand that step at first. Under the existing law the minister of national revenue was empowered to fix the value of goods on which customs duties were paid, and an importer could appeal the valuation to the Tariff Board. In 1961 the government introduced a bill that would abolish the appeal and make the minister's decision final. I saw at once that opposition to the abolition of an appeal from an arbitrary decision by a minister was a tailor-made Liberal issue and organized a sustained attack on that one proposal. Our attack got favourable news reporting and editorial attention. There were rumours that the minister, Nowlan, would cave in and restore the right to appeal. I was disappointed when Pearson decided that we should let the bill pass. But what we had failed to do the Senate did, which was to amend the bill to restore the right to appeal and send the amended bill back to the House, where it was available for debate. On 6 July, Fleming and Diefenbaker made furious attacks on the Senate. Fleming challenged the right of the Senate to amend a money bill and declared that the government would not agree to its amendment, and Diefenbaker raised the threat of Senate reform, a prospect unappealing to most senators. Their outburst convinced me they were trying to intimidate enough senators to ensure the passage of the Coyne bill in the Senate which rumour said was no certain thing.

On 8 July the debate in the House on the Coyne bill was resumed, and Diefenbaker took the whole afternoon to complete his speech. It was not one of his best efforts and was interrupted frequently. Paul Martin, Walter Pitman and Doug Fisher made powerful replies, and the bill was passed with all the Opposition members voting against it. The bill then went to the Senate.

Senator Norman Lambert had already warned me that enough Liberal senators were worried about incurring the wrath of the government if the Senate did not pass the Bill, and if Coyne intended to continue as governor of the Bank. Coyne agreed to my informing Lambert that, once he was given a hearing to defend his integrity, he intended to resign. The Senate gave Coyne a full hearing. He gave a straightforward account of his relations with Fleming and responded politely and respectfully to all questions.

Coyne's account to the Senate was markedly different from the account Fleming would give in his memoirs a quarter of a century later. Fleming even then had lost none of his bitterness. His language is extravagant and abusive. Coyne and everyone concerned with the affair, including Diefenbaker, is condemned; Fleming alone was the perfect gentle knight in shining armour. He accuses Coyne of mishandling the record in his presentation to the Senate and of mangling the facts to his own advantage. Fleming pretends that he was not invited to appear before the Senate committee. The committee records show that notices were sent to both Coyne and Fleming and that the committee was prepared to hear them. Notice may not technically be an invitation, but Fleming admits that 'before the Committee had completed its hatchet work, I spoke to Dief and the Cabinet as to whether I should ask to appear before the Senate Committee and I offered to do so if they thought I should. They decided against it.'

In his final summing up Coyne told the Senate committee that he intended to resign as governor once the bill was disposed of. He appealed to the senators to find that he had not been guilty of misbehaviour. When the Senate decided not to proceed with the bill,

Coyne submitted his resignation to the deputy governor. He resigned as a hero in the eyes of the press and the interested public.

The courage of the Senate in refusing to approve the bill to remove Coyne was generally applauded. The Senate also persisted in its amendment to the Customs Tariff Bill, and that bill also failed to pass. The Senate's failure to pass either bill made 1961 a notable year for that institution.

Fleming in his memoirs expresses the belief that public opinion blamed him for the mishandling of the Coyne Affair. My opinion is that Diefenbaker was the villain in the public mind. Most observers, at that time and since then, have judged that the handling of the affair was the greatest single cause of public disillusionment with the government and especially with Diefenbaker. The result of the whole was to make Coyne a martyr and to make the government look both tyrannical and inept. The Liberal Opposition was the political beneficiary, but it would not have been so if we had not found the right issue, punishment without trial, the most flagrant offence under Diefenbaker's Bill of Rights.

Donald Gordon

Donald Gordon's appointment as a director and chairman of the board of CN expired on 30 September 1960. The government took no action to reappoint or replace him. As president he remained in charge of the management of the railway. Diefenbaker undoubtedly regarded Gordon as one of those senior public servants who were Liberal partisans. In his memoirs Diefenbaker discloses that he felt that none of the senior public servants already serving in 1957 was loyal to him except Bob Bryce and Basil Robinson. There was another excuse for failing to reappoint Gordon, an agitation by French-Canadian students and others in Montreal charging CN and Gordon himself with discriminating against French Canadians in choosing senior executives.

By 22 May 1961 no action had been taken on the chairmanship. That day the government had a bill before the House to increase the number of CN directors from 7 to 12. Chevrier and I decided to give the government a hard time. I asked the minister of transport,

Leon Balcer whether or not Gordon was still a director. Balcer replied that Gordon's term had expired, but that the law provided that a director remained a director until a successor was appointed. We argued that the House should not proceed with the bill until it was told whether or not the government intended to reappoint Gordon. All but one of the Tory members who spoke in the debate had attacked Gordon, and the House was entitled, we said, to know whether or not the bill was a device to get rid of him. Never before had the head of CN or any other crown corporation been kept on sufferance for months as Gordon had been. The House should not vote money to pay additional directors until we were told what the government intended to do about Gordon.

After several speeches had been made about Gordon, the chair ruled that references to him were not in order on the bill. I then moved an amendment that one of the new directors should be 'the present President of the Canadian National Railways.' Though the amendment was ruled out of order, the debate on Gordon continued. If the government wanted to keep Gordon as head of the railway I said, they should give him enough support to do the job properly instead of leaving him suspended between heaven and earth.

Another opportunity arose to bring up the Gordon question, on the annual financing bill for 1961, which came up the day after the bill to remove Coyne had been passed by the House of Commons. Chevrier and I joined in attacking the government for its disgraceful attitude to Gordon and the other directors who had been kept in suspense. The day before, I said, we had watched the leader of the government wield the axe against Coyne; now we were discussing the fate of a gentleman who had given long and outstanding service to his country, and who had for nine months and eight days been kept under suspended sentence, not knowing on what day the axe would fall. The prime minister wanted yet another head to roll. We did not question the legal right of the government to replace Gordon, whose term had expired; what Parliament had the right to know before voting additional money to CN was who would be head of the company.

The delay continued until the last day of the 1961 session, when the transport department's estimates were before the House. Balcer then announced that Gordon had been reappointed chairman of the board. I have always believed that public disapproval of the treatment of Coyne saved Gordon's head.

Ministerial problems

Two ministers greatly embarrassed Diefenbaker in 1960 and 1961, both of them from Québec. Henri Courtemanche had first been elected to Parliament in 1949 in the riding of Labelle as one of two Tory MPs from Quebec elected that year. He was defeated in 1953 and elected again in 1957, and, as he was the only French-Canadian Tory with parliamentary experience, Diefenbaker had him elected as Deputy Speaker. After the 1958 election Courtemanche became secretary of state. Rumours began circulating that he was involved in financial transactions that threatened to become scandals. In January 1960 he resigned from the cabinet and the House on the ground of ill-health, but the following day he was well enough to be summoned to the Senate, only to resign in December 1961 in the face of new reports of impending scandal.

A by-election was held in Courtemanche's riding in October 1960. His successor as secretary of state, Noel Dorion, made a speech in the by-election in support of the Tory candidate. The press reported that Dorion had accused the Liberals of trying to 'anglicize' French Canada by bringing over more immigrants from the the British Isles than from any other European country. The St Laurent government, the report said, had used immigration to reduce the proportion of French Canadians for the benefit of the English. He claimed that Diefenbaker had promptly closed the door on English immigration and was trying to offset the Liberal 'anglicization' by fostering immigration from Italy.

In Parliament, I quoted from the report of Dorion's speech and asked the prime minister if Dorion had been speaking for him. Before Diefenbaker could reply, Dorion intervened to say that he had not been reported correctly. He made no correction, nor did Diefenbaker answer my question.

I raised the matter again at the first opportunity. Unfortunately Dorion was not in the House that day. When asked why I was bringing the subject up again, I replied that that kind of speech was a disgrace. 'It is a disgrace for a Minister of the Crown to make this kind of cheap appeal and cheap misrepresentation calculated to promote disunity in other parts of Canada.'

Dorion later denied the report as 'absolutely and completely false.' Whereupon Azellus Denis, a Liberal member, interjected, 'I was there when he said it.' A dispute ensued as to which member was being truthful, in the course of which Denis said there had been 10 witnesses. A group of Liberal MPs had been at the meeting.

Several days later Dorion was asked to table a copy of his speech in the Labelle by-election. Relying on the rules of the House, Dorion replied that his word must be accepted. He was asked why the word of the Liberal MPs who had been at the meeting in Labelle should not be accepted instead of his word.

The question was not pursued that day, but Diefenbaker's embarrassment over Dorion had not ended. During the debate on the Immigration Estimates, in which I was spokesman for the Opposition, I quoted a report of a speech by Dorion in a by-election in Ontario in which he said that Canada had been the victim of mass immigration in 1957 inherited from the Liberal government. Immigration, he claimed, had been chopped down by the Progressive Conservative government. After pointing out that the mass immigration about which Dorion had complained had included the Hungarian refugees, I recalled that in the election campaign in 1957, Diefenbaker had promised to triple the volume of immigration reached by the Liberal government. Now one of his ministers was boasting that the Diefenbaker government had drastically reduced it.

The family and Newfoundland

Activity in Parliament did not take up all my time in 1961. There were changes in the family situation and a dramatic summer in Newfoundland.

My mother died in April. Her physical health had deteriorated in the previous winter, though she remained as alert as ever and keenly interested in public affairs. Her doctor saw signs of an impending stroke and had her go into the Civic Hospital by ambulance on 18 April. I was there when she arrived, and while still in a wheelchair being admitted, she turned to me and said: 'If I have a stroke I hope it kills me. I do not want to linger on half alive.' I said I hoped so, too. When Margaret and I visited her later in the afternoon, she asked me about the welcome given to the Greek prime minister in the House of Commons gallery on the previous Friday. She then began to recite Byron's 'Isles of Greece' from memory. Margaret and I went home with the impression that there was no immediate danger of a stroke. At about 11 p.m. there was an urgent call from the hospital that she was unconscious. We rushed there. Mother did not regain consciousness, and died peacefully not long after midnight. It was just the way she wanted to die.

A year or two earlier Mother had told me she wanted to be cremated and have her ashes placed in the grave where her parents were buried, in the cemetery at Port Rowan where so many of her ancestors and Margaret's and mine were also buried. She had said there was no hurry about the burial, but to pick some convenient time. We were to find a suitable occasion in September 1963.

In 1961 Jane was in Québec City for her third summer. Peter was going to Italy on a pulpwood boat with Bill Baird, on a trip arranged by a pulpwood exporter, who was shipping wood bought from Edgar Baird. By the time the House of Commons had adjourned for the summer, on 12 July, Margaret had already left by train to take Peter and Bill to embark at Carleton, on the south Gaspé coast, and after seeing the boys off to go on to Newfoundland with Alan, Ruth and Alan's cocker spaniel, Ginger.

Walter Dinsdale and W.J. Browne were flying in a government plane to Newfoundland that day to preside at the official opening of Terra Nova National Park, and Dinsdale offered me a lift. I accepted at once, and they agreed to stop at Moncton to pick up

Margaret and the children. The official opening of Terra Nova Park took place the day after we arrived at Traytown. Dinsdale, as minister of northern affairs, presided, and Browne, as minister from Newfoundland, was the main speaker. Premier Smallwood was a guest speaker. A large crowd was present at the ceremony, most of them my constituents. Margaret and I were in the audience. We were mildly embarrassed when Smallwood observed in his speech that he was not an expert in protocol but was surprised to see the founder of the park not on the platform but sitting in the audience. Browne, like anyone else who had to speak after Smallwood, was an anticlimax. He was visibly disturbed and, intending to refer to Dinsdale, who belonged to the Salvation Army, said that Pickersgill was the first member of the Salvation Army who had sat in the Canadian Cabinet!

The next day the new head of the Salvation Army was honoured at a large meeting in St John's. I was invited as a special guest, and spoke briefly. Despite his presence in Newfoundland, Dinsdale had not even been invited. I felt the omission was no accident; it confirmed my view that the vast majority of Salvationists in Newfoundland were still Liberals.

That summer, from June until September, part of Newfoundland was devastated by disastrous fires, the worst and most extensive of which were in my constituency. A quarter of the riding was covered by a pall of smoke. Though the nearest point of the fire was about 20 miles away, we scarcely saw the sun all summer. A friend provided us with a pump and hoses at Traytown to use if the fire reached our settlement. After the fire had subsided along the shore, Margaret, Alan, Ruth, Ginger and I drove through part of the ravaged area and boarded the *Sylvia Joyce* to visit Fogo Island and other places beyond the reach of the devastation. On our way back to the place where we had left our car the *Sylvia Joyce* was enveloped in smoke, and we had to be guided into port by a fisherman in his motor boat. Valuable timber was destroyed that summer, and with it the livelihood of hundreds of Newfoundlanders. The fire reached the boundaries of Gander airport, which one day had to be closed. For a stretch of several miles the Trans-Canada Highway could be travelled only in convoy with police escorts.

In spite of the obvious need for all possible help, the provincial government was reluctant to ask the army to send troops because federal policy required provincial governments to reimburse the federal treasury for the cost of such assistance. Jane, who flew down from Québec City in August for a short visit at a time when Gander was threatened, was horrified that the army was not there. She persuaded me to urge Smallwood to ask the federal government to send in troops. I advised him to ask for help but to give no undertaking to pay, and to sign nothing. Troops were sent promptly on request and fires subsided soon afterwards.

When Parliament resumed sitting in September, I spoke about the fires. I praised the speed with which help had been sent from the navy and air force in late June, and later, when requested, from the army. I said that people in Newfoundland had been surprised to learn that federal assistance was not a national service in an emergency but something for which the government expected reimbursement from the provincial treasury. I appealed to have the help regarded as a national contribution in the emergency in Newfoundland. James McGrath asked if I knew why the government of Newfoundland had waited three months before requesting the help of the army. I said that help might have been offered without waiting for a provincial request; the governments of Québec and Ontario had sent help without waiting to be asked. The overburdened taxpayers of Newfoundland, I insisted, should not have that added burden placed on them. The federal bill for the help was not paid while I was in Parliament and, I hope, has not been paid yet. Assistance from the armed forces in fire fighting, where needed, should surely be a national service.

After we returned to Ottawa in September 1961, Margaret had to visit Victoria after her father had a stroke. The stroke was not severe, but it created uneasiness for her because her parents were so far away from both their children.

Activities outside Parliament

A federal election was expected in 1962, and I was absent from Ottawa frequently in the fall of 1961 to speak at nominating conventions for Liberal candidates. One that stands out in my memory was in Toronto-Rosedale. The candidate chosen was Donald Macdonald, whom I had never met before. I was genuinely impressed and predicted that he would have a great future in the party and, I hoped, in government. My prediction was fulfilled to the point that Macdonald escaped becoming leader of the Liberal party only because of the second coming of Pierre Trudeau in 1980. He was later appointed high commissioner in London by a Tory prime minister, a post from which he retired in 1991.

My most exacting engagement outside Parliament was a television debate with the leader of the NDP, the redoubtable Tommy Douglas, before a live audience in Ottawa. The subject was how political parties should finance election campaigns. Pearson was worried about my tackling so formidable an opponent, and I was not entirely free of apprehension myself. I assumed, rightly, that Douglas would denounce the 'old parties' for raising their campaign funds from large corporations and becoming obligated to them. I agreed that campaign funds should not come from corporations or, I added from trade unions, but that the legitimate costs of parties and candidates in elections should be met by the Treasury. Such a system would, of course, require much more stringent restrictions on how much could be spent and for what purposes.

I believe that was the first time a well-known politician had advocated publicly that revolutionary policy, which I had favoured for many years. I felt the argument went well and was reassured when a number of those in the audience and even more who had watched on television took the trouble to tell me that they felt I had had the better of the encounter. Today, with the vast increase in the cost of federal elections to political parties and the implied obligation to donors thereby created, I am more strongly convinced than ever that legitimate costs of elections should be paid from the federal treasury, that campaigns should be drastically reduced in length, and that exenditures should be rigidly controlled.

Late in 1961 the media were filled with rumours of a sweeeping revamping by Diefenbaker of his cabinet. On 28 December the cabinet met in Quebec City, where the governor general was in residence. There had been rumours in advance that Fleming would be moved out of Finance; the plan was allegedly thwarted by strong representations from financial circles in Toronto. By 27 December it was generally believed that there would be no shuffle, merely the addition of Jacques Flynn, the Deputy Speaker, as a minister in place of Paul Comtois, who had become lieutenant-governor of Québec.

The twenty-eighth of December was a Saturday. The Canadian Press invited me, as the senior Liberal in Ottawa that day, to the press gallery to listen to the report from Québec. When asked for comment, I had a reply ready, which I had rehearsed at the family breakfast table. My comment was that the prime minister had shuffled the cards and dealt himself the same old hand with an extra joker. The comment was published everywhere in the same reports as the news from Québec City, and underlined the anticlimax. Whenever we have met since then, I have greeted Jacques Flynn as the joker. He became one of the few competent Diefenbaker ministers from Québec and was later Tory leader in the Senate.

Many Liberals were saddened by the sudden death of C.D. Howe on New Year's Eve, 31 December 1960. Howe and I had become closer friends after his retirement than when in office. I saw him regularly whenever I was in Montreal, and my appreciation of his contribution to Canada grew steadily. Senator Norman Paterson drove Douglas Abbott and me to Montreal for the funeral. The most impressive tribute to Howe was the presence of Jimmy Gardiner, who, like Howe, had served in the cabinet for the whole 22 Liberal years. At the age of 77 Gardiner had driven himself all the way from his farm in Saskatchewan and he turned round right after the church service and drove back home – a journey each way of nearly 2000 miles, and in the dead of winter. One year later, in January 1962, Gardiner died. Pearson asked me to fly out to Saskatchewan to represent him and the Liberal caucus at the funeral, which was a moving tribute by a large assembly of his lifetime friends and supporters. I felt it ironical that I, who had been the strongest opponent of his cherished dream, the South Saskatchewan dam, should have been chosen to pay the last tribute from the Ottawa Liberals to that redoubtable fighter. But I was glad to pay my personal tribute to a public man who had no interest in the fruits of office and had given bold and unswerving leadership to the public interest as he saw it.

Jack McClelland of McClelland and Stewart decided to publish books on the three political parties at the time the CCF was being transformed into the New Democratic Party, at that stage called the New Party. Stanley Knowles agreed to write the book of that name. Heath MacQuarrie was asked to do *The Conservative Party* and Pearson *The Liberal Party*. Pearson persuaded me to do it, with an introduction by him, so in addition to all my other tasks I produced *The Liberal Party* early in 1962. It was a potboiler derived from sundry sources. A year later an abbreviated version, *Le Parti Libéral* was published in French, translated by my friend David Gourd, with an introduction by Lionel Chevrier. I have never regarded either as a great literary work and have no measure of their effect, if any, on public opinion.

An outside activity that gave me much pleasure was a visit to Québec City on 1 February for Louis St Laurent's 80th birthday. I delivered what was largely a eulogy of St Laurent, in French, at a luncheon at the Reform Club. He was not able to be at the club but, in the afternoon, I shared in the family celebrations.

Later in February, Margaret and I visited Lennoxville, Québec, where I took part in a panel discussion at Bishop's University. The theme was Canadian identity, and I spoke partly in French. In answer to a question I made an observation that aroused wide comment in the media and added subtantially to Pearson's mail. To help him reply to his letters I gave him this memorandum:

'The seminar was organized by the Québec Branch of the National Federation of Canadian University Students for the purpose of discussing the Canadian identity. In the course of the question period following the presentation of speeches and discussions among the panelists I was asked by one of the students if I had any suggestion to make as to how a better understanding between English-speaking and French-speaking Canadians might be achieved. I replied that I had two specific suggestions as to how this understanding might be promoted. My first suggestion was that, over a five-year period, the English-language universities in Canada might try to establish, as a condition of entrance, that all students should be able to read and understand the French language. I added that a parallel requirement on the part of the French-language universities that matriculants should be able to read and understand English would be desirable, though it was less necessary, because practically all French-speaking students had, for economic reasons, to learn English anyway.

'My second suggestion was that French-speaking Canadians elected to the Parliament of Canada should devote less of their energy to concern for the survival of the French language and culture and more to co-operating in the solution of the common problem of all Canadians. I added that survival of the French language and culture was completely assured today, and that what was in question now was the extent of the influence throughout Canada of French-speaking Canadians, and that would depend upon the extent to which they contributed to the solution of our common national problems. In this context I cited the excellent work done by the Hon. Jean Lesage when he was Minister of Northern Affairs.

'Although I was exceedingly careful not to say that I thought students entering universities should be expected to speak French, because I knew how difficult it was, in many parts of Canada, to learn to speak French, the Canadian Press report said the exact opposite. When I got back to Ottawa, I found all my four children very indignant about what I was supposed to have said. However, when I explained what I really had said and pointed out that any intelligent student could easily learn to read French and, with the amount of French that is broadcast and the availability of records, it would not be difficult to learn to understand spoken French reasonably well, and when I added that every university in Europe and every good university in the United States insists on a knowledge of a second language as a pre-requisite to entrance, I found they took a different view, particularly when I reminded them that French was one of the official languages of our country.

'I did not suggest, nor did I mean to suggest, that any external compulsion should be brought on the universities to establish any such entrance requirement, since that would be entirely a matter for the universities themselves. I can hardly imagine that any reasonable person would feel that an understanding of the French language by educated Canadians would not contribute to a better understanding between the two races. I hope this memorandum will convince those who made representations to you that what I said was not wholly unreasonable and it was not illiberal.'

The memorandum still expresses my view.

In the House a French-speaking Tory member from Québec commented on the report from Lennoxville. He said that I seemed to have become an advocate of bilingualism, and that it was the first time he and others had heard me speak on the subject; he thought I should have done so long before.

I could not let that comment pass without a reply. I did not boast about my bilingualism, I said, but from the day I came to work in Ottawa I had never asked anyone to translate any document out of one of the official languages into the other for my benefit. I had always taken the view that if we were to make Confederation work properly, we must seek in every possible and practical way to make it equally easy for Canadians to use either of the official languages in every part of the country. I was no new convert to that view. I added that it had not been easy for me to learn French in the bush in northern Manitoba. If my critic was interested, I could tell him privately how I managed to get my foundation in French, but I would not waste the time of the House by doing so.

The election bait

When Parliament met in January 1962, we all expected dissolution and an election within the year. The Speech from the Throne contained a good deal of election 'bait' but few proposals likely to raise contentious issues — nothing to equal the Coyne Affair, the cancellation of the Avro Arrow, or the resignation of the commissioner of the RCMP. The prime minister got agreement to have the debate interrupted to enable the government to proceed with urgent measures to provide payments to prairie farmers who had suffered from drought in 1961 and to make additional funds available for winter works.

Once the prairie farm item for $42 million had been voted, debate began on an item for $300,000 for a winter works program for fishing settlements in Newfoundland, where the income of fishermen had declined drastically because of decreased catches. The members from Newfoundland, led by Chesley Carter and Herman Batten, argued that that minuscule program compared unfavourably with payments to farmers on the prairies. They recommended an alternative plan, for direct payments to fishermen through the machinery of the Unemployment Insurance Commission. I had spelled out two methods by which payments could easily be made, and my proposals were ridiculed by one or two Tory members and turned down by the minister of fisheries. Parliament, I said, had willingly voted money for the farmers because they really needed it. We claimed correctly that the fishermen needed income support just as much. It was hard to explain to fishermen that the only way they could get help was to sweat it out on road jobs in the wintertime for a total of $20, 'when the western farmer gets a cheque for $200 from Alvin's cheque machine.' Alvin Hamilton was the minister of agriculture. After a prolonged debate the stingy appropriation for fishermen was finally passed. Our protest in Parliament received favourable publicity in Newfoundland.

The Opposition had agreed to interrupt the debate on the Speech from the Throne for those two measures only. Instead of resuming that debate the government proposed to increase the old age pension to $65 a month. Comparable increases were proposed for old age assistance, the blind and the disabled. The Opposition did not oppose the increases, but the debate became increasingly partisan. Diefenbaker made one of his customary discursive speeches, in which he claimed credit for all the social welfare measures of Liberal governments. In his reply Pearson was almost constantly interrupted as the House became rowdier, especially after the prime minister left the chamber. I noted that the prime minister had introduced a totally irrelevant debate about the government's alleged achievements. I was interrupted even more frequently than Pearson had been when I began to correct several of Diefenbaker's inaccurate statements and misrepresentations. I observed, 'Any man who is absent from his office one day out of every two for three months cannot be doing his job, and that is the Prime Minister's record in the last three months of 1961.' I had had someone count his absences to make sure my statement was correct. My statement provoked a flood of angry interruptions from backbenchers protesting that everyone knew what a hard worker Diefenbaker was, that he was always in his office 8 a.m., and so on.

In the course of my speech I asserted that 90 per cent of the flights of ministers around the world could be eliminated without loss to anybody. With equal lack of relevance I said that one of my friends had asked me a few days before, under the Diefenbaker government, has Canada any friend left in the world except Castro? To the minister of trade and commerce, I added, he is a good friend. That reference to George Hees related to the visit of a Cuban trade mission to Canada, during which Hees had referred to the Cuban visitors as 'wonderful customers'. 'You can't do business with better businessmen anywhere.' The exuberance of the minister of trade and commerce had embarrassed Diefenbaker, and we made a point of not letting the government forget their Cuban friends.

My part in those unruly pre-election debates prompted Diefenbaker, while speaking outside Parliament, to say, 'Whenever I need a laugh, all I have to do is mention the name Pickersgill.' The result was one of Duncan Macpherson's finest cartoons in the *Toronto Star*.

Liberal spirits were raised early in 1962 by a Gallup poll indicating that 42 per cent of voters would vote Liberal, and 34 per cent, Conservative. Even more impressive, 42 pe cent expected the

Liberals to win an election, and only 31 per cent, the Conservatives. We decided to continue to stress unemployment as the main issue in the country and to seize every opportunity to give publicity to the Liberal program for creating jobs. The National Liberal Federation had an enthusiastic meeting at the end of January, with St Laurent present to introduce Pearson at the dinner — St Laurent's first appearance at a Liberal function since his retirement as party leader. The meeting concentrated on the program for the coming election.

Once all the legislation likely to help in an election had been passed, the debate on the Speech from the Throne was resumed. It was turbulent and had ceased to serve any purpose when it came to an end under the rules on 22 February. The day before, Hazen Argue, who had been house leader for the CCF and the unsuccessful candidate for leadership of the NDP against Tommy Douglas, announced that he had severed his connection with the New Democratic party, and asked the Speaker to give him another seat. The NDP, in his opinion, was in the control of a small labour clique whose hold on the party was sure to continue and strengthen. Argue declared that he wanted to seek re-election in Assiniboia, and that he expected shortly to make a further announcement about his political future. From the opening of the 1958 Parliament, Liberal Opposition strategy had been to avoid friction with the CCF and to cooperate wherever possible. Pearson had asked me to maintain liaison with Argue to that end. I had come to know him well, and our personal relations had remained friendly, even in 1959, while the CCF carried on an abusive campaign of attacks on Smallwood in support of the IWA in Newfoundland. When he decided to leave the NDP, Argue talked to me about his political future. He made it clear that he wanted to join the Liberal party. I reminded him that when Thatcher left the CCF, he sat for some time as an Independent before announcing he would join our party. I advised Argue to follow that course. Since he had often attacked the Liberal party quite sharply, a period sitting as an Independent would make his conversion more credible. But he preferred to become a Liberal at once. He contested his old constituency as a Liberal candidate in 1962 and won by a very small margin over the Tory candidate. In 1963 he was narrowly defeated by the Tory, and the new Pearson government thereby deprived of an experienced parliamentary champion of the western wheat growers. After losing again in 1965, Argue was called to the Senate and after 1980 he became the spokesman for Saskatchewan in Trudeau's cabinet.

Redistribution and dissolution

After the debate on the Speech from the Throne was concluded, the atmosphere in the House became increasingly unpleasant, except for a marked improvement in tone on 26 March. That day Diefenbaker moved that the House set up a committee on procedure. He made a moderate and constructive speech. In replying for the Liberal Opposition I flattered Diefenbaker by recalling that 26 March 1962 was the 22nd anniversary of his election to Parliament. I said 'The Parliament of Canada would have been a very different place if the Rt. Hon. gentleman had not been elected 22 years ago,' and congratulated him on the tone and temper of his speech.

I went on to remind him of his promise to abolish closure and said that in the light of experience no government in its senses would ever use the existing closure rule again. I suggested that the House repeal the rule at once and pledged Liberal support if the prime minister would amend his motion. Erhart Regier for the NDP objected to my proposal. Diefenbaker, in concluding the debate, accepted Regier's advice not to act before a committee had considered closure. Despite our offer to support abolition of the existing closure rule out-of-hand, I felt that Diefenbaker was prudent not to proceed.

As for amending the rules generally, I occasionally shocked my colleagues in Opposition by seeking to reduce or eliminate rules of the House that could be used to obstruct the business of government. I made those suggestions because I expected to be a member of the government again and favoured changes that would make it easier to govern effectively.

That same day Diefenbaker gave notice of legislation to establish an independent commission to redistribute the constituencies of the House of Commons after each decennial census. When the debate began, as spokesman for the Opposition I stated that the principle of redistribution by an independent commission was completely acceptable to us as it was part of the Liberal program. Establishing a commission and having it carry out redistribution would take a long time. There had been no reason for waiting until the census had been taken to establish the commission. If action had been taken in an earlier session, I pointed out, the commission would have been in place and ready to start its work as soon as the census was completed. In concluding I said that the House should either be assured there would be redistribution before an election or have the matter dropped. If there was to be an early election, there would be no time for redistribution, and the time of Parliament was being taken wantonly and unnecessarily to deal hastily with legislation that should be left to a new Parliament with a fresh mandate.

I said that we should be spending our time doing the business of the country instead of having constant agitation about an election. 'What we have had for the last three months is the spectacle of the Prime Minister of this country, like a little girl among the flowers in the meadow in the summer picking the petals from a flower and saying, He loves me, he loves me not — shall we have an election or shall we not?'

Diefenbaker had evidently picked off the last petal by 17 April, when he announced that the session would be ended and an election called the next day. He wanted the first stage of the redistribution legislation to be completed that day. I refused to let the motion pass without further debate and pointed out that any commission set up would have a year or two of preparatory work to do before it could start the actual redrawing of the boundaries of constituencies. The Opposition would not be satisfied unless the names of the commissioners were included in the bill. Commissioners should not be appointed by the government but by Parliament, to assure the independence and impartiality of the commission.

Two samples of annual Christmas card sent to every household in the constituency.

Diefenbaker replied briefly to my argument. The first stage was completed that day. That was the last mention of redistribution while Diefenbaker was prime minister. I never expected to be the minister to pilot through Parliament a successful conclusion of legislation for independent redistribution.

In announcing the election Diefenbaker told the House that he had originally hoped it could be on 12 September, but that, in the light of the delaying tactics of the Opposition, he had no alternative but to ask the governor general to dissolve Parliament at an early date.

There had, in fact, been no obstruction. Earlier when the Opposition had been charged with obstruction, I had pointed out that backbenchers supporting the government were taking more time in the House than the Opposition, a fact I had checked carefully. Tory MPs continued to take up more time right up to 17 April, when the election was announced. Pearson said that the country would be pleased by the announcement of the election but not as pleased as the Opposition. A few items requested by Diefenbaker were dealt with on 18 April, Parliament was dissolved that day, and an election was called for 18 June.

We made one serious mistake. None of the estimates of expenditures for the year 1962-63 had been voted, and we had agreed to an interim appropriation for five months — which meant that after the election Parliament would not have to meet until the beginning of October.

The election of 1962

Newfoundland and the campaign

The Liberals embarked on an active campaign. We expected to make substantial gains but did not believe we could overcome the huge Tory majority of 1958. I anticipated correctly that I would have an easy time in Newfoundland. The Diefenbaker government was discredited and unpopular everywhere in the province and faced a threat from the Liberals even in St John's. No less important for me, from 1959 on the family had spent most of every summer at Traytown, and our Christmas card, with a photograph of the whole family often taken in Newfoundland, had been sent to every household in the constituency; by 1962 the Pickersgills were well known.

During two periods of campaigning in Newfoundland I visited most of the settlements in my riding, but I had few meetings as my Conservative opponent, Whitfield Bannister, was not active and raised no issues. I did have one exciting day on Fogo Island, where there was a widespread feeling of neglect, mainly attributed to the provincial government and especially to Premier Smallwood, who had ignored repeated requests to visit the island. I travelled from Gander to Fogo in a helicopter and stopped at most of the places en route to a meeting in Fogo town later in the day. After the meeting we boarded the helicopter and had risen 20 or 30 feet when the aircraft began to spin like a top. Almost miraculously, the pilot brought it down safely in the very constricted space where it had been parked. The rear rotor had fallen off the helicopter, so a message was sent to Gander to have a float-plane pick us up at Seldom-Come-By. The rest of the campaign in Newfoundland was much less exciting, and not exciting at all in my riding. Consequently I spent a good deal of time on the mainland supporting other Liberal candidates.

Premier Smallwood caused a flutter in mid-campaign. The minister of finance, Donald Fleming, was invited to St John's to speak to the Rotary Club early in June on the dollar crisis. The club received a grant each year from the provincial government. Smallwood told Rotary that the grant would be cancelled if the club was used for a partisan purpose, so Rotary withdrew the invitation. Smallwood's action was blown up by the mainland press as a denial by the government of Newfoundland of freedom of speech. I was campaigning in Nova Scotia at the time, and Pearson telephoned to ask me to try to do something to ease the situation. I telephoned Premier Smallwood, explained how embarrassing Pearson and other Liberals found the incident, and persuaded him to send Fleming a telegram, which I outlined over the telephone.

Smallwood said that it was charged that his government's refusal to continue grants to the Rotary Club if the club was used as a platform for a partisan speech was a denial of freedom of speech in the province. He continued: 'In order to remove any possible impression that you were denied freedom to speak in Newfoundland, I am authorized by the Newfoundland Liberal Association to say they are prepared to provide, at Liberal expense, the largest available hall in St. John's and travelling expenses if you and your Liberal opponent, Mr. Mitchell Sharp, can come to St. John's to debate the issue of devaluation of the Canadian dollar, which would give you the opportunity to make the speech you intended to make in St John's. Alternatively, if such a visit cannot be arranged, our Liberal campaign committee is prepared to provide a hall in Toronto, at which you and Mr. Sharp can debate the issue of devaluation, and to arrange for a filming of the debate, which film we would undertake to have shown in St John's at a public exhibition.' Smallwood concluded with the hope that Fleming and Mr Sharp, to whom he was sending a copy of the telegram, would accept one of the alternatives, either of which would give the people of Newfoundland an opportunity 'to weigh the merits of this hot political issue ... without dragging the non-partisan Rotary Club into the controversy.' Fleming ignored the offer, but the telegram received enough publicity to prevent any Liberal from repudiating or attacking Smallwood and, what was more important, ended the charge that freedom of speech was being denied.

The dollar crisis

The greatest sensation of the campaign was the devaluation of the Canadian dollar and the return to a fixed rate against the United States dollar. In his budget speech just before Parliament was dissolved, Fleming had reported that the International Monetary Fund wished to have Canada return to a fixed value for the dollar instead of allowing it to float, but was not pressing Canada into hasty action that might be 'premature or impossible to sustain.' He said the government 'would wish the prospects of success to be more assured than they were when the Canadian government made its ill-starred attempts to maintain fixed rates during the years from 1946 to 1950.' Against that background the public was shocked by a sudden reversal on 2 May, when a fixed rate for the dollar was set at 92.5 cents U.S. Included in the Liberal reaction was the circulation of an imitation dollar called the Diefenbuck with 7.5 cents clipped off one corner. It is questionable whether the stunt affected many votes; what really hurt the government was the weakness of the dollar and the lack of confidence in the government.

A sensation in its own right occured on 8 June, when Alvin Hamilton stated that the cabinet had been divided between a 95-cent and 90-cent dollar, and that they had split the difference at 92.5. Hamilton's statement appeared in the press on a Saturday, and Fleming feared that if not repudiated, it would result in a heavy run on the dollar on Monday. Years later, in his memoirs, Fleming recalled that he tried without success to persuade Diefenbaker to disavow Hamilton. Diefenbaker agreed, however, to Fleming saying he had the prime minister's full concurrence, in a statement made on Sunday evening. The blatant division in the cabinet had a profound effect on the voters; we Liberals condemned the lack of cabinet solidarity, but public confidence was destroyed without our needing to say anything.

As the campaign progressed we did not expect to overcome Diefenbaker's strength of over 200 MPs, but I began to hope we might win one or two seats more than the government. In Québec, where we had counted on sweeping victories, our hopes were frustrated by the sudden and unanticipated emergence of Social Credit as a substantial political force. Twenty-six Social Crediters were elected in that province; the Liberals won 35 seats, only 10 more than we had kept in 1958; and the Tories held 14 of the 50 seats they had gained in the landslide.

The Liberals made almost no impression on the prairies but made gains in British Columbia, Ontario and the Maritimes. The minister from Newfoundland, one of the two Tories there, lost his seat. Over all we had 16 fewer members than the Tories. The result was nevertheless a remarkable success for the Liberal party. The Tories had gone down from over 200 to 116. We Liberals at 100 had twice as many seats as in 1958. The survival of the government, which had fallen short of a majority, would depend on the support of 30 Social Crediters or 19 members of the NDP.

The loss of an absolute majority was not the only Tory misfortune. A week after the election, Diefenbaker had to disclose that Canada was facing another dollar crisis. To meet the emergency, Diefenbaker himself announced, on the CBC, a series of austerity measures, which were implemented by order-in-council. The measures included changes in taxation for which the government had not waited for parliamentary approval. Pearson had already been briefed by Louis Rasminsky, the governor of the Bank of Canada, at Diefenbaker's request. To avoid further danger to the Canadian dollar and the national economy Pearson was restrained in his criticism. At the same time he demanded that Parliament be called into session at once.

Secure because the previous Parliament had voted funds to enable the government to finance expenditures until mid-October, Diefenbaker brushed aside Pearson's claim that the government had no right to carry on unless it could win a vote of confidence in Parliament. The prime minister, without a majority, arrogantly stated that the situation should be allowed to cool off, and deliberately delayed the opening of the session until September.

Once it was clear that Parliament would not meet until the fall, the family went to Newfoundland. Jane was already there, in a summer job in the old hospital at Gander. That summer we had visits from Paul de France's elder son Guislain, and from my brother Tom, his wife, Margaret, and their daughter, Clare. We were there for nine weeks, our longest unbroken stay. There was no need for a tour of the constituency, because I had covered it during the campaign in May and June. Nineteen sixty-two was the last time the whole family was together for a summer in Newfoundland.

The minority parliament

The new look of the government and Parliament

The new Parliament finally met on 27 September 1962. Roland Michener had lost his seat, and a new Speaker had to be elected. The government's choice was Marcel Lambert, MP for Edmonton

West. Usually when a Speaker was elected, his nomination was moved by the prime minister and seconded by the leader of the Opposition. On that occasion the nomination was seconded by Leon Balcer, the minister of transport and senior French Canadian in the Cabinet. Balcer may have been chosen by Diefenbaker because Lambert, though a French Canadian, was not from Quebec. Lambert had been combative and partisan in the previous Parliament, and some concern was felt that he might be less impartial than Michener. That apprehension was actually expressed by Lionel Chevrier in seconding Lambert's appointment. It was, in my opinion, not justified by events. Lambert was less judicial in manner than Michener and often brusque, but I felt that once he found his feet, he was fair in his decisions.

The Speech from the Throne read like an election manifesto and was clearly intended to serve as a comprehensive program for the government in a forthcoming election. Very little of the legislation forecast was realized, much of it not even introduced.

Diefenbaker announced the changes in the cabinet that had been made since the election. Fleming had become minister of justice; Fulton, of public works; Nowlan, of finance; Ellen Fairclough, postmaster general; Hugh John Flemming, minister of national revenue as well as forestry; Ernest Halpenny, secretary of state; Paul Martineau, minister of mines and technical surveys; R.A. Bell, of citizenship and immigration; and the newly appointed senator, Wallace McCutcheon, minister without portfolio.

The removal of Fleming from Finance was obviously designed to reduce confrontation in the House. Diefenbaker detested Nowlan but apparently realized he was much more likely to avoid friction with the Opposition.

Fulton's removal to Public Works was clearly a demotion for a minister the prime minister was jealous of. The appointment of Dick Bell to the cabinet was long overdue; during his short time as minister he performed well in a tricky portfolio. The appointment of McCutcheon was a concession to the Toronto business community but added little to the strength of the government.

The Parliament of 1962 was different in character from that of 1958. The government had lost its fighting spirit and a little of its arrogance. The only outstanding new Tory was Gordon Fairweather, from New Brunswick. The Opposition, however, had gained a number of excellent debaters: Allan MacEachen was in Parliament again, as was Arthur Laing, and we had effective additions to our strength in Walter Gordon, John Turner, Bud Drury, Edgar Benson, Lawrence Pennell, Maurice Sauvé, John Munro, John Nicholson, Jack Davis, Donald Macdonald, Lucien Lamoureux and John Stewart.

There was also Richard Cashin, from Newfoundland, who had defeated Browne in St John's West. Cashin was the first Liberal to speak after Pearson on the Speech from the Throne. He did well, but it was his only speech, though he intervened frequently in question period during the short time he was in the House. His election was contested successfully in the courts, and the seat declared vacant on October 25; it remained so until the general election of 1963, when Cashin won with a substantial majority.

Colin Cameron and Stanley Knowles were back for the NDP, and that party had a good new member in Andrew Brewin and an outstanding one in David Lewis. Social Credit was again in the House, with three or four members who quickly became active in debate.

With all the new talent in Opposition and a government that no longer had a majority, the Parliament of 1962-63 became a lively place, though not likely to have a long life.

The first vote of want of confidence

In the debate on the Speech from the Throne Pearson made a powerful speech in which he attacked the government for delaying the opening of the session for three months when it did not have a majority.

On the second day I denounced the government for carrying on government without obtaining the confidence of the House. The government, I said, had anticipated trouble with the dollar in April and had wanted to get the election over before an exchange crisis developed. Hamilton's performance over the dollar had made a mockery of collective cabinet responsibility. He should have been out of the government the next day, I observed, but the prime minister had not mentioned the performance in his own speech at the time. Mine was a good fighting speech, and I was flattered when David Lewis, a great debater, congratulated me enthusiastically.

Tommy Douglas, the leader of the NDP, had failed to win a seat in Saskatchewan, and Lewis was left to be the first speaker for that party. Lewis moved a subamendment to Pearson's motion of want of confidence. When the vote came, we voted for the NDP subamendment, and they voted for Pearson's motion as amended by them. Both votes were 140 to 118, with all the Social Crediters voting to save the government. The government thus won the confidence of the House and was entitled to carry on as long as it avoided defeat. We in the official Opposition wanted another election, which we were confident we could win. We sought every opportunity to challenge the government. Taxation without parliamentary approval still looked to us like a good issue, and we decided to make a determined effort to force the government to produce the legal opinion that they claimed justified their action by order-in-council. On 22 November a motion for the tabling of that legal opinion was debated. The defence of the government was led by Jed Baldwin, the parliamentary secretary to the prime minister, a good lawyer and an able debater. Baldwin quoted a statement I had made several years before that maintaining the confidential character of communications between civil servants and ministers was an essential feature of responsible government.

In reply to Baldwin I said I had more regard for him as a lawyer than for anyone else on the other side of the House. My regard was not diminished when he quoted me as an authority in support of his unconvincing argument. I took back nothing about the confidentiality of communication between civil servants and their ministers, but a legal opinion from the Department of Justice as to the validity of an order-in-council was not a confidential communication. Such opinions had always been producible and sometimes were produced on the initiative of the government. I argued that the case was unique since the government was seeking not merely to legislate but to tax by order-in-council.

Motions for the production of papers were debatable for only one hour each week. That particular motion was filibustered by government supporters week by week for five such hours, the last on 31 January 1963. We never did see the legal opinion, because the government was defeated five days later.

Contempt of Parliament

On 5 November, Pearson moved that the emergency austerity program of tariff surcharges and tight money, introduced on 24 June, should be stopped at once. The passage of the motion would have defeated the government. Robert Thompson, the leader of Social Credit, moved to add to Pearson's motion the words 'and replaced with a policy of debt-free money and constructive proposals to foster balanced domestic economy and balanced international trade.' Thompson's motion posed a dilemma for the NDP. Should they vote with Social Credit and risk defeating the government or vote against the subamendment and be labelled Diefenbaker's saviours? Tommy Douglas who meanwhile had been elected in a British Columbia constituency and taken his seat as leader of the party, without referring directly to the subamendment said in his speech that the NDP would not vote merely to defeat the government and bring on an election.

A special Liberal caucus was held to decide what we as a party should do about the Social Credit subamendment. 'Debt-free money' was the Social Credit name for the kind of monetary system they advocated. Pearson was reluctant to appear to vote for Social Credit 'funny money' but said he would accept the decision of the caucus. Like several other members I argued strongly that we should vote for the subamendment after explaining clearly that we did not believe in 'debt-free money,' but that the combined effect of the amendment and the subamendment would be a vote of want of confidence in the government. We would not as a party vote confidence in the Tory government.

We decided to vote for the subamendment. Paul Martin was chosen to explain our position in the House, where he announced that the Liberals would vote for the subamendment, but that in doing so they would not be voting for Social Credit principles but voting against a government that should be removed in the interests of the nation. When the vote was taken on Thompson's subamendment, which was defeated, the NDP voted with the government, as it did on Pearson's amendment.

The NDP thus made it clear that if Social Credit did not, it would save the government. Like Social Credit, NDP had such fear of an election that we had no hope of bringing down the government unless we could find some issue on which both of the small parties would not dare to vote for the government without entirely losing their credibility. We had little hope of raising such an issue over the government's austerity program, but we lost no chance of continuing to attack, on principle, the government's contempt of Parliament.

Fleming defended taxation by order-in-council by citing as a precedent what he called D.C. Abbott's taxation by broadcast. Abbott back in 1947 had announced in a radio broadcast that the government, which had a majority in Parliament, intended to defend the dollar by bringing certain taxes into effect at once and to ask Parliament to approve them retroactively. When Parliament met, the measures were approved. I drew a contrast between the two cases. The Diefenbaker government had imposed tax changes by order-in-council, but unlike Abbott they had refused to ask Parliament for approval and had claimed that the orders-in-council themselves gave the government legal authority and that parliamentary approval was not necessary. Pearson, I reminded the government, had not objected to emergency action in June, but did demand that the government call Parliament as soon as possible to ask for approval of its actions. We in Opposition still wanted the austerity taxes submitted to Parliament.

We would have fought the battle hard whether or not it could be won, because the Tory claim that the government could impose taxes or increase them without the approval of Parliament, was taxation without representation and a fundamental breach of responsible government.

Spending money Parliament had not voted was another flagrant breach of responsible government, and one not new for Diefenbaker in 1962-63. In February 1958, when he had Parliament dissolved, not one cent of the estimates of expenditure for the fiscal year ending on 31 March 1958 had received the final approval of Parliament. Expenditures for that year were authorized by governor general's warrants, which, constitutionally, are used only in emergencies. There was certainly no emergency when Parliament was dissolved in 1958, 10 days after the government had receied a substantial vote of confidence.

In 1962 Diefenbaker had once more had Parliament dissolved, that time without a single item of the estimates' having been discussed in the House. The Opposition had, unwisely, agreed to vote interim supply for five months. Consequently Diefenbaker, despite losing his majority, had been able to delay the calling of Parliament until September, when the government once more had to ask for interim supply.

A prudent government would have concentrated on getting the estimates voted as quickly as possible. Instead priority was given to other measures, with the result that, in mid-December the government had to ask again for interim supply. Pearson complained about the government's mismanagement of parliamentary business, starting with the delay in opening the new Parliament and continuing with the way government business had been brought forward. The government had boxed itself in and for the first time in history was asking for 10 months' interim supply without there having been voted a single item of the estimates. He accused the government of contempt of Parliament. Pearson felt that the Canadian people were entitled to something better than perpetual interim supply.

Pearson had given one of his most powerful speeches, but he made the mistake of concluding it two or three minutes before 5 p.m., when the debate had to be adjourned to make way for the private members' hour. Diefenbaker had risen to reply, but the Liberal backbenchers applauded vigorously and so took all the time remaining. At 5 o'clock Diefenbaker asked for unanimous consent to speak. Though Pearson indicated he would agree, unanimous consent was not given. The next day the press dwelt on the rude conduct of the Liberal backbenchers and gave little attention to Pearson's speech. The incident offers an example of Pearson's inattention to the details of parliamentary procedure, and also of Diefenbaker's capacity to make himself look like a martyr.

Diefenbaker's excuse for seeking to have the rules relaxed so that he could reply to Pearson that day was that he was leaving the next day for Nassau to meet President Kennedy and Prime Minister Macmillan. The next day Hazen Argue remarked that Diefenbaker's departure had been delayed and wondered why he was not in the House to reply to Pearson, as he was so anxious to do the afternoon before. Later Knowles said that he had agreed with everything Pearson had said, but condemned the Liberals for behaving like an unruly mob. I made a mild disclaimer. I had been distressed that Pearson had not strung out his speech until 5 p.m.; his failure to do so had given Diefenbaker an opportunity to overshadow the speech.

As 1962 closed, it was a time to take stock of what had happened since the election of 18 June. At the end of June the Diefenbaker government had been reeling from its massive loss of seats, which left it without a majority in Parliament. It had had to face the public shock over the dollar crisis and the austerity program. Pearson had, in a responsible way, refused to exploit the crisis for short-term partisan advantage but had demanded that Parliament be called. Diefenbaker's refusal to call Parliament was the most prolonged disregard of a government's responsibility to Parliament since responsible government was achieved in 1848. In one way or another Social Credit and the NDP had evaded chances to uphold the exclusive right of Parliament to impose taxes and vote the money to be spent by the government. The Liberal Opposition alone had defended the rights of Parliament.

But a still clearer issue was developing at the end of 1962. In June 1958 the North American Air Defence Agreement with the United States for the joint defence of North America had been approved, almost unnoticed, by Parliament. The debate was brief; only the CCF had opposed NORAD. No one guessed then that controversy over NORAD would spark a parliamentary explosion over nuclear weapons that would destroy the Diefenbaker government in 1963.

The Liberal position on nuclear weapons

NORAD provided for a joint Canadian-U.S. air defence command. Canada already had fighter aircraft to identify and intercept bombers over its territory. The government had to put those squadrons under NORAD command and replace the aircraft with new and speedier fighters. There were also to be fixed sites called Bomarcs, for launching guided missiles. Both the fighter aircraft and the Bomarcs were capable of being armed with nuclear warheads. Two of the Bomarc bases were to be in Canada. The minister of national defence, General Pearkes, had announced the program for the new aircraft and the Bomarcs on 2 July 1959.

The Liberal policy on nuclear weapons was announced by Paul Hellyer and confirmed by Pearson on 4 August 1960. Essentially it was to get out of roles in joint defence that, to be effective, would require equipping Canadian forces with nuclear weapons.

The question of nuclear weapons entered a more active phase when in September 1961 the minister of defence, Douglas Harkness, stated that the Bomarcs and fighter squadrons could function with conventional arms but would be much more effective and destructive if armed with nuclear warheads. The decision as to whether nuclear warheads would be installed had, he said, not yet been taken. Pearson stated that the Liberal position was unchanged. Canada 'should not be engaged in continental defence ... in a way which would necessitate Canada becoming a member of the nuclear club.'

By 1962 the government had agreed to equip the Canadian air division in Europe with new planes in order for the division to fill a new role as a strike attack force. There was a debate on 20 March as to whether the strike force could be effective without planes equipped with nuclear devices. Pearson and Hellyer concentrated on trying to get Harkness to say whether or not they would be so equipped. Harkness insisted that no decision had been reached, and that none was needed until the strike force was operative. Pearson ridiculed the indecisiveness of the government; he argued that if the U.S. high command had known in 1959 that by 1962 the Canadian government would not have made up its mind to permit the air division to perform effectively, the United States would surely have undertaken the task itself. He was unable to get Harkness to answer the question: Was the NATO command satisfied that the strike attack role accepted by Canada could be carried out with conventional weapons?

Pearson said that Canada would be in a humiliating position if the allies could not count on the country to keep its commitment. He concentrated on trying to smoke out the government. He recalled that the Liberal Opposition had objected to the strike attack role for Canada when it was proposed. Hellyer had said it was the wrong kind of job for the RCAF because it would require nuclear warheads. Against the advice of the Opposition, Pearson pointed out, the government had decided to purchase planes for that role and now refused to tell the House which kind of equipment the RCAF would be given to discharge that dangerous commitment.

How the Bomarcs and aircraft for continental defence and the air division in NATO were to be armed would be a critical question in Parliament in 1963. The cabinet was divided on the issue. But there was a serious risk that the Liberal Opposition would also be divided. The Liberal policy had been on record against arming Canadian forces with nuclear weapons since 1960 and in favour of negotiating Canadian withdrawal from any nuclear commitment to the country's allies. Hellyer, who was defence critic for the Opposition, visited the Canadian forces in Europe late in 1962. He was persuaded that their morale was suffering from the government's reluctance to arm the air division in Europe with nuclear weapons, as it had agreed to do in 1959 and he reported that impression to the Liberal caucus. Pearson, though hesitant about changing Liberal policy, gave the impresssion that he felt commitments must be kept.

I had not been following defence policy closely; Pearson, Hellyer and Drury were the ones active in that field. But at the end of the year I was asked by Pearson to read a paper prepared for him by a commentator on defence. The paper outlined a long-term program that would have obscured the position to be taken on nuclear weapons. When I read it I was apprehensive that it might be used as a basis for a statement of the Liberal position. On 2 January 1963 I hastiiy scribbled out a note for Pearson:

'I have no reason to doubt that this paper contains very good advice to a government in office, but I am sure that any detailed statement of future plans from a politician without the power to carry them out and, presumably, without the secret strategic information on which some of these judgements could alone be made with validity, would simply provide a target for opponents of all kinds.

'But what is far more serious, most of these proposals would be misunderstood by servicemen and would lose votes which may well be decisive in the next election. Moreover I cannot believe any detailed policy that we can possibly formulate can get us any additional support anywhere. Surely we should confine ourselves to taking positions on questions that have to be settled now or should have been settled already, plus general principles only for the future.

'Above all we should avoid suggesting that we are going to try to talk ourselves out of existing commitments (however desirable that might be if we were in office). If we do that, we will be back in another morass almost as bad as the one we are trying to get out of. The average person just cannot grasp subtle and constantly qualified positions and the average MP or candidate can't explain them either. Despite its inherent complexity, surely our position can be explained simply and clearly and positively.

'I believe a speech along the lines of this paper would be an irretrievable political disaster for us.'

The following morning I wrote a further note to Pearson:

'Before leaving Ottawa this morning I thought I should try to be more constructive and ask myself what I thought the Leader of an Oppositioin expecting soon to be a Prime Minister should and/or could say on defence; also what he should not say.

'There is only one defence question that enters the realm of practical politics, viz., nuclear weapons. On that the public condemns the government for vacillation, but those who notice us say we are just as bad. You have already decided what our position must be on existing commitments and there was no dissent in caucus. But let it be said simply and decisively and without any qualifications about trying to get out of it. That I regard as vital. I think it almost as important to put this nuclear weapon issue in the perspective of our total political defence commitment and to make it clear that Canada is not and will not ever become a nuclear power on its own: that our commitment relates exclusively to our position in an alliance for the defence of the continent and of the free world and that our position in the alliance, which we had a large part in forming, depends upon the confidence of the allies, particularly the US in our loyalty and our reliability.

'I am almost equally concerned as a practical politician about retaining the support of the armed forces without which we cannot win an election. For (with dependents) close to a quarter of a million voters are involved and, like other voters, most of them are primarily concerned with their livelihood, and that quarter-million voters in places like Chatham, N.B., North Bay, etc., not to mention larger places like Halifax, are highly sensitive to the attitude of political parties to the forces. Then there are veterans with pride in the three services.

'A Prime Minister has a duty to take political risks and responsibility for reorganizing the armed forces and keeping them up to date. The Leader of the Opposition has neither the duty nor should he be expected to have the detailed strategic and technical information to plan such reforms. His duty ends when he has set out the objectives of defence policy and gives his assurances that a government he leads will pursue those objectives resolutely.

'To envisage distant and hypothetical ends before one has the means of achieving them will, in the field of defence, be almost sure to upset and disturb thousands of voters without the slightest compensating political (or other) advantages that I can envisage.

'It is because I believe this is the one subject on which a wrong course could sink our prospects without a trace that I have written so emphatically.'

I had prepared those documents so hastily because Margaret and I were leaving that day, 3 January, for visits to Paris and London. We did not return to Ottawa until 14 January, and the day after that I left for a week in Newfoundland. I was not back in Ottawa until 21 January, the day the session of Parliament resumed. Only then did I learn that Pearson had defined the Liberal position in a speech in Scarborough, Ontario on 12 January.

I have since then consulted Hellyer about the sequence of events. He has confirmed that the subject of honouring Canada's existing commitments about arming the Bomarcs and the aircraft in Europe with nuclear warheads had been discussed at a Liberal caucus and that at the caucus there seemed to be general agreement that Canada should live up to its commitments. Hellyer is clear that Pearson took no position at the caucus.

My notes to Pearson on 2 and 3 January imply that Pearson had already indicated, at least to me, that he had decided what our position must be on the existing commitments. I was, therefore, not trying to change his mind, but merely to get him to express his position clearly and without qualification. I spoke to Richard O'Hagan, Pearson's press secretary and adviser, who on my return to Ottawa gave me a copy of a memo he had sent to Pearson on 7 January, in which he said:

'Without presumption, I hope, may I say how impressed I was with the points made by Jack Pickersgill in his memorandum to you of January 3 respecting defence policy. It is obvious of course that in elementary political terms the whole question revolves on nuclear weapons, simply and starkly. Will we accept them, and on what basis?

'I agreed entirely with Jack that the answer you give the country must be a model of simplicity and decisiveness, even — and I say this advisedly — at the risk of some over-simplification. We will be hailed or censured not on the subsidiary refinements, however important they may be, but on the central position we adopt, or at least what that position appears to be.

'In defining that position, I hope you will not hesitate to ring a few patriotic bells — not irresponsibly, of course, nor in the chauvinistic sense. Do it rather, as I am sure you will, in a way and as a means of reminding people of what we, as a nation, must do if we are to honourably and adequately serve the cause of freedom.'

Pearson made his announcement on 12 January without

informing Hellyer, who was in Antigua, or, as I learned from Hellyer, Walter Gordon; neither of them knew of his change of position until after the speech. In his speech Pearson said that a Liberal government would carry out the commitment to arm the planes and Bomarcs with nuclear warheads. That speech altered the political landscape and created an issue between the Liberal Opposition and the government that was the dominant theme of the rest of that Parliament.

The announcement of a nuclear policy in Parliament

When the 1963 session opened, Pearson and the leaders of the smaller parties all demanded early debate on defence. Diefenbaker agreed to a two-day debate on the external affairs estimates, which would provide an opportunity to discuss defence as well.

The debate began in the conventional fashion with a speech by the minister, Howard Green, who ranged over the whole field of foreign relations but took no position on nuclear weapons, though he was known to be opposed to their use by Canadian forces. Paul Martin, as the Opposition critic on external affairs, replied to Green. He deliberately avoided the nuclear question, thereby leaving the field open for Pearson. Thompson followed for Social Credit. Tommy Douglas spoke next and made it clear that the NDP was following the CCF line of opposition to Canadian use of nuclear weapons. Not until the end of the day did Pearson take the floor, thereby ensuring that he would be the first speaker on the second day.

Pearson's speech lasted nearly two hours and covered the whole history of Canada's part in NATO and NORAD. He pointed out that as early as 1960 the Liberal Opposition had proposed a change in Canada's role. The change would not have required Canadian forces to be equipped with nuclear weapons. But the government had maintained a commitment for weapons that, to be effective, required nuclear warheads. Those weapons were now being installed, and the time had come to meet the nuclear commitment. 'A Liberal Government,' Pearson declared, 'would honour those pledges made by its predecessor.' While honouring the commitment a Liberal government would seek better and more effective defence roles for Canada in the alliance.

The speech was delivered almost without interruption to an attentive House. The contrast between Pearson's decisiveness and the indecision of the government was clear. Diefenbaker made the contrast more striking by a discursive and inconclusive reply that lasted two hours.

Two points made by Diefenbaker were to arouse controversy. He claimed that, in Nassau, Prime Minister Macmillan and President Kennedy had forecast changes in strategy in Europe that made an immediate decision on nuclear weapons unnecessary, and he implied that negotiations were proceeding actively with the United States about arming the Bomarcs and the new supersonic fighter aircraft for NORAD.

After Diefenbaker concluded, Réal Caouette spoke briefly to declare that the Social Credit MPs from Québec would not support the use of nuclear weapons by Canadian forces.

The debate ended on a Friday. The House and the country were astonished on Monday when the minister of defence gave the press a written statement interpreting the prime minister's speech. Harkness claimed that Diefenbaker had set forth a definite policy for the acquisition of nuclear arms. When Tommy Douglas asked Diefenbaker if that was a correct interpretation, Diefenbaker dodged the question and asserted his own speech was very clear, very direct and very comprehensive and did not require any interpretation.

Despite the obvious disagreement between Diefenbaker and Harkness, we had little hope, because of the position of the smaller parties, of defeating the government on a straight vote to arm Canada's NATO and NORAD forces with nuclear warheads.

The United States intervention

The House went on to other business for the first three days of the week of 28 January. But on the evening of 30 January, the State Department of the United States issued a press release commenting on the debate on nuclear weapons in the Canadian Parliament. Diefenbaker had implied that negotiations about arming the Bomarcs and the fighter planes for NORAD were going well. The State Department asserted, 'The Canadian Government has not as yet proposed any arrangement sufficiently practical to contribute effectively to North American defence.' Since the installing of the Bomarcs had begun in Canada, the statement said, arming them with nuclear weapons had 'been the subject of inconclusive discussions,' and that was equally true in the case of the Canadian jet fighters for NORAD, which would 'operate at far less than their potential effectiveness' without nuclear warheads. About Diefenbaker's claim that the discussions between Macmillan and Kennedy had postponed the need for a decision concerning nuclear warheads for the Canadian air strike force in NATO, the State Department asserted that the Nassau discussions raised 'no question of the appropriateness of nuclear weapons for Canadian forces in fulfilling their NATO and NORAD obligations.' The State Department pointed out that arming the RCAF with nuclear warheads would not make Canada a nuclear power on its own since 'as in the case of other allies, custody of U.S. nuclear weapons would remain with the United States.'

Pearson saw at once that the American intervention could hurt the Liberals, and lost no time in telling the press it was surprising that the U.S. government considered it necessary to issue a statement about the prime minister's speech and the public declarations by the minister of national defence. Questions of Canadian policy, he insisted, should be left entirely for discussion and decision by Canadians.

At the opening of the House on 31 January, Diefenbaker protested the unwarranted and unprecedented intrusion by the United States into Canadian affairs. He saw in the ham-handed intervention an opportunity to represent Pearson as an American stooge, and thus to raise a new issue that would divert attention from the indecision of the government. He said the document bore a striking resemblance to Pearson's speech in the House. When Pearson rose to make a comment on Diefenbaker's charge, a Tory backbencher called 'Go ahead, Yankee.'

Pearson denied that his speech had been worked out in consultation with the U.S. government and called the charge unworthy of the prime minister, 'a cheap and false insinuation.' He reminded the House that as soon as he had heard the broadcast of the

American statement the previous evening, he had objected to interference by the United States. The real issue for Canadians, Pearson said, was 'What are the facts and what is the truth?' Harkness, Pearson stated, had contradicted certain of the prime minister's statements, whereupon Harkness interjected, 'I did not.' The U.S. government, Pearson added, contradicted other statements by the prime minister. He appealed for the facts 'without any further shilly-shallying or delay.' At that point Diefenbaker interjected, 'When are you going back for further instructions?'

The Speaker allowed an urgent debate, and Harkness finally spoke. He denied that he had contradicted Diefenbaker and defied anyone to find anything in his interpretation not contained in the prime minister's speech. We thought that Harkness was buckling under to Diefenbaker, and that for the time being the crisis was over.

I reflected the Liberal frustration in a broadcast to my constituents. One MP, I said, had kept at the centre of the Ottawa stage by failing to speak in Parliament — Douglas Harkness, the minister of national defence. If Harkness said nothing in Parliament, I went on, outside the House he tried to explain away the prime minister's speech by issuing a written 'interpretation' contradicting Mr. Difenbaker's words in Parliament. Old Ottawa hands can remember occasions when public differences between ministers in cabinet had to be patched up by the prime minister; no one can recall a case in which a minister corrected a prime minister and stayed in cabinet.

Everyone was asking whether Harkness would buckle under or resign, I continued. It was hard not to feel sorry for Mr Harkness, who had repeatedly said that Canada's forces should be armed with the most modern and effective weapons. Everybody in Ottawa knows that Douglas Harkness in his heart feels there is only one right and honourable course for Canada.

After the Department of State dropped its verbal bombshell, I went on, the combined Opposition forced a second debate on defence. The prime minister was expected to state Canada's position in the new situation and give Parliament the facts and the truth Mr Pearson had demanded. Instead Mr Harkness replied.

His reply was the greatest parliamentary anticlimax in living memory: debate on the subject of human survival was brought down to the level of a barber shop discussion. Harkness barely mentioned the U.S. intervention. He spent all his time asserting, and trying vainly to prove against the evidence, that his words and the prime minister's meant the same thing, that there was no difference between them. One impression emerged clearly; Harkness had submitted to his chief, and the immediate crisis had evaporated.

The defeat of the government in the House

I could not have been more wrong about the crisis having evaporated. When the House met on Monday, 4 February, Harkness rose to announce his resignation as minister of national defence. He said he had believed when he had spoken that his position was in conformity with Diefenbaker's. Subsequently it became apparent to him that the prime minister's views on nuclear arms and his own were irreconcilable. He had remained in the cabinet, he stated, in the hope of getting the nuclear arms question definitely settled. When that proved impossible, he had resigned on a matter of principle. His honour and integrity, he felt, required that he take that step.

That day's business provided an opportunity for a vote of want of confidence, which Pearson took. His motion read, 'This government, because of lack of leadership, the break-down of unity in the cabinet, and confusion and indecision in dealing with national and international problems, does not have the confidence of the Canadian people.' He phrased the motion in general terms in the hope of securing the support of the smaller parties, which would not be given if the motion dealt with nuclear arms.

Thompson for Social Credit followed Pearson. Before the dinner recess he gave the impression that Social Credit might vote to save the government from possible defeat. When the House resumed sitting after dinner, Thompson announced that Social Credit had reluctantly come to the conclusion that an election would be preferable to prolonging the life of the government. David Lewis followed Thompson. His speech suggested that the

NDP might rescue the government, when he asserted that Pearson had said a Liberal government would carry Canada's existing commitments and then negotiate a way out of them. Hellyer replied to Lewis and, with Pearson's approval, repeated the Liberal position precisely. He quoted Pearson's words that 'the government should re-examine at once the whole basis of Canadian defence. However, until the present role is changed, a new Liberal government would put Canada's armed forces in the position to discharge fully commitments undertaken for Canada by its predecessors.'

Diefenbaker followed Hellyer with a long speech filled with irrelevancies and disparaging references to Pearson. Through the rest of the debate the atmosphere in the House was electric, everyone waited to see whether the NDP would save the government. Douglas was the last speaker. He expressed equal lack of confidence in the Conservative government and the Liberal Opposition, but finally stated that Parliament had been 'reduced to a state of such impotence' that the only answer was to give the people of Canada the opportunity to go to the polls.

The government was defeated 142 to 111. For only the second time since Confederation a government had been defeated in Parliament. There was no minister of national defence and the ministry was in disarray, and two leading members of the government, Fulton and Fleming, had announced they would not seek re-election. Parliament was dissoved the next day, and an election called for 8 April 1963.

The election of 1963

Newfoundland

I had to devote much more time to my own riding in 1963 than in 1962. My Tory opponents in 1962 and 1963 were not a threat, but in 1963 I was challenged by another candidate, Walter H. Davis, who described himself as a true Liberal and a genuine Newfoundlander. He had two aims, to rid Newfoundland of this mainlander and to have a CBC television station established in the province. Davis was striking in appearance and had a commanding presence and a capacity to speak impressively. At the beginning I did not take him seriously, and was surprised to learn that Premier Smallwood was worried about his potential appeal. Without consulting me Smallwood had two succesive statements repudiating Davis and supporting me delivered to every household in the town of Bonavista, where the electorate was the least stable. Smallwood did not offer to speak on my behalf in the riding, nor did I suggest it; I wanted to win on my own. I soon realized that I must have meetings throughout the riding as in 1958.

Davis tried to disrupt those meetings on several occasions. The most amusing was at Salvage in the Orange Hall. The audience refused to admit him, so he placed his car, which had a loud-speaker on top, under a window and gave his speech outside while I was speaking inside. He made a spectacular appearance at my meeting in Bonavista by striding down from the back of the hall after the meeting had started. I insisted that he come up on the platform and make a speech before I made mine. I reached the conclusion that Davis was providing a degree of excitement for audiences but gaining no substantial support.

Davis's demand for a CBC television station in St John's had no appeal in Bonavista-Twillingate, where existing TV reception was poor. What my constituents wanted was a clear picture in their own area, not two stations for the people of St John's. I had not altered the view I had taken when television was started in Canada that alternate service should not be permitted as long as private stations were affiliates of the CBC and broadcast most of its programs. I realized, however, that if we won the election, a Liberal government would have to face the question of a CBC station in St John's, the application for which had been approved by the Board of Broadcast Governors a few days before the election. I have never ceased to be grateful to Don Jamieson, one of the owners of the private station CJON, for his disinterested advice that the political pressure could not be resisted for long, and that I should not commit myself too strongly against a CBC-TV station. I valued his advice all the more in that an alternate station would be harmful financially to CJON and to Jamieson personally. By following his advice I saved myself possible embarrassment after the Pearsorn government was formed and I became the spokesman for broadcasting in the House of Commons.

The winter was mild, and I had little difficulty getting to the main places in my riding. I concentrated on the southern part, especially the Bonavista Peninsula, where Davis spent most of his time. Despite his noisy efforts Davis received about 500 fewer votes than the Tory candidate. I had over 250 more votes than in 1962, about 75 per cent of the total in each election. I took little part in the campaign elsewhere in Newfoundland. None of our members was in any danger of defeat, and Cashin was almost certain to win in St John's West, where Browne was no longer a candidate. Liberal prospects were also good in St John's East. McGrath, the sitting member, had been passed over by Diefenbaker, and Newfoundland had had no minister since the 1962 election. Diefenbaker himself was as unpopular as ever in the province.

The mainland

Half my time during the campaign was spent on the mainland. I crisscrossed Ontario and the Maritimes and got as far west as Edmonton. The French version of my book *Le Parti Liberal* was published in Montreal with considerable publicity.

At the beginning the Liberals expected to win a substantial majority. Most Conservatives I talked to felt they were facing a crushing defeat. In fact they lost only 21 seats, of which more than a third were in Ontario. The prairies were virtually as solidly Tory as before. The Liberals lost Argue's seat in Saskatchewan but won Calgary South in Alberta and Winnipeg South in Manitoba. Neither the NDP nor Social Credit gained anything in the prairies. It was clear that Alvin Hamilton and Diefenbaker himself had a strong hold on the western farmers. Surprisingly, the Tories held 8 of the 14 seats they had kept in Québec in 1962. They lost 4 seats in the Maritimes and their last seat in Newfoundland, where the Liberals had a clean sweep. They lost only 2 in British Columbia. It was a defeat but far from a crushing one for the Tory party.

The greatest single factor in turning potential disaster into mere defeat was the amazing campaign conducted by Diefenbaker himself. His was the last old-fashioned campaign by train, with whistle stops and impassioned appeals directed not to the media but to those who saw him. What denied the Liberals a majority was the continued support for Social Credit members in Québec. Social Credit lost only 4 of the 24 seats they had won in 1962

We emerged from the election with 129 seats out of a total of 265, 4 short of a clear majority. For a short time after the election there was uncertainty as to whether Diefenbaker would resign as prime minister or stay on to meet the new House of Commons and ask for a vote of confidence. When six Social Credit MPs from Québec announced their intention to support Pearson, Diefenbaker decided to resign. Pearson was at once invited by the governor general to form a government. The process took more than a week.

11 Secretary of State and House Leader

The Pearson government

My place in the new cabinet

Pearson sent for me while he was forming the cabinet and told me he had already chosen ministers for three portfolios, Chevrier for Justice, Martin for External Affairs and Walter Gordon for Finance. I could have whichever of the other departments I preferred; and he added he thought I might wish to take Transport. I replied that I would be embarrassed to be minister of transport until several transport problems of special concern to Newfoundland were dealt with. I astonished him by saying my first choice would be to become secretary of state. He replied that it was a minor portfolio without prestige, and that I deserved something better, and asked why I had suggested so modest a post.

I reminded him that two elections had been held during which the constitutional obligation for redistribution was ignored. It would be scandalous not to tackle it immediately. Since we did not have a majority, we could not count on four or five years before another election became necessary. Not only was it our duty to comply with the requirements of the Constitution without delay, but the Liberal party had undertaken to remove the process

J.W.P. as Minister escorting Queen Elizabeth, the Queen Mother in the National Gallery, Ottawa.

from the House of Commons and entrust redistribution to an independent and nonpartisan process. It would take substantial time to set up the appropriate machinery before redistribution itself could begin. The legislation would be complicated and controversial. I doubted if any other member of Parliament was as familiar with the subject and its problems as I, since I had been involved with the two previous redistributions. I did not believe there would be any competition in the party for that thankless task.

We Liberals were also committed to specific and controversial changes in the broadcasting legislation enacted while the Diefenbaker government was in office. Apart from Pearson himself, I had been the main Liberal critic of broadcasting policy in Opposition. I could probably pilot the necessary legislation through Parliament more easily than anyone else available, if I was given the ministerial responsibility. I would not have offered to become secretary of state, I said, if I had not believed Pearson would be willing to give me as well the ministerial responsibility for the

National Film Board, the National Gallery, the Public Archives, and the National Library. In the St Laurent government I had had ministerial responsibility for all those agencies. I assumed I would also, as the only privy councillor from the Atlantic provinces, be given responsibility for the Atlantic Development Board set up by the Tory government shortly before the election.

Pearson had no hesitation in accepting all those suggestions and agreed that, even if the portfolio itself had little prestige or importance, I would have no shortage of responsibility. When I added that I would also like to be the leader of the government in the House of Commons, he was shocked. He asked me whether I did not feel my combative attitude in Opposition would make it difficult for me to secure the necessary cooperation from the Opposition in arranging parliamentary business. I said I hoped he did not think my attitude and tactics in office would be the same as they had been in Opposition. I believed my knowledge of parliamentary rules and procedures equalled that of any of our members. Chevrier had been our house leader in Opposition. As his assistant I had shared in the negotiations behind the curtains since 1958 and had had experience of what was indispensable in making Parliament work.

Since we lacked a majority with respect to our own party members, a majority would have to be created to ensure the passage of every controversial measure. We would have to make sure, as well, that our own members were always available for votes. That task, which would require the almost constant presence of the government leader in the House, would be relatively easy for me since my portfolio would involve few administrative duties. I assured Pearson that my being appointed government leader was not a condition of my acceptance of the office of secretary of state, and that I would not take offence if he decided he would prefer someone else as leader.

I suggested we regard the rest as settled, and that he make no immediate decision about the house leadership. After a day or two he told me he had decided to let me undertake the task for the first session of the new Parliament and see how it worked out. I was pleased and relieved. But it was also desirable to have a

French-speaking member associated with the management of the House. I recommended that Guy Favreau act for me when I was absent from the House and assist me at all times. I had formed a high opinion of Favreau, mostly at second hand. Pearson readily agreed to my suggestion.

When I became a minister I had once again to find staff for my own office. My choice for private secretary was Audrey McQuarrie, who had been appointed to the staff of the leader of the Opposition when the St Laurent government resigned, Pearson generously relieved her. Shirley Tink had served me with high competence and devotion in Opposition. She had worked with Audrey before 1957 and willingly came back to work with her again. Teresa Maloney, who had been seconded from the department to my office while I was secretary of state in 1953-54, was seconded again in 1963 as liaison officer with the department, which she knew from top to bottom.

From my first day as minister I was overwhelmed with correspondence and memoranda and needed an executive assistant as much as I had needed Charlie Granger the first time round. My first and only prospect was Alistair Fraser. I had been impressed by his performance as executive assistant to Jimmy Sinclair during his time in the St Laurent cabinet, and our friendly relations had continued during the Opposition years, when he was secretary to Ross Macdonald, the Liberal leader in the Senate. I sent for Alistair and told him that I had heard he would like to join my staff. He admitted that he would be interested. I then said I had heard his one fault was that he was lazy, and asked if he was. He replied that perhaps no one had tried to find out. If he worked for me, I retorted, he would never have the chance, and hired him. I told him the only way he could imperil his job would be to get his name in the press.

Alistair became indispensable at once in every way. He got no personal publicity, and helped me to avoid much, though not all, unfavourable treatment by the media. He always knew what was happening in the political world and was wise in his advice. When he decided to try his fortunes as a Liberal candidate in the election of 1965, I told him he must find me a successor equally good. He did, in Sandy Morrison. Sandy's support from 1965 until I left the government in 1967 was as competent and indispensable as Alistair's. Despite the knowledge both Audrey and Shirley had of Newfoundland, acquired over many years, I felt I should have at least one Newfoundlander in the minister's office.

Smallwood had introduced me to Edward Roberts, who was still pursuing his brilliant academic career at the University of Toronto. Roberts came to work in my office during the university vacation of 1963, and I began to realize the depth of his interest in public affairs. My admiration for Ed has grown with the years; in my view he has been the ablest man in provincial public life in Newfoundland since the retirement of Smallwood.

I found a successor for Roberts in Twillingate. Eric Facey was a teacher in the high school there who had engaged me in political conversation and plied me with intelligent and informed questions when I had once stayed with his parents. He was enlisted in the summer of 1964, remained in the office until the fall of 1966, when he returned to Memorial University for a year, and came back again in the summer of 1967, my last as a cabinet minister. He was an unqualified success. I urged him to go on to law school, and he did. Since his admission to the bar his life has been a mixture of legal practice and politics, though he has not yet sought election. Eric served me well and helped me to serve Newfoundland.

The Newfoundland flavour of my office was strengthened by the addition of a young man named David Sturge as junior messenger. David was a bright boy with a welcoming manner who helped to make Newfoundland visitors feel at home.

I owe a great deal of whatever I was able to accomplish to my intelligent, hard-working and loyal ministerial staff; to them I cannot measure my gratitude.

Facing the House and securing a vote of confidence

During the campaign Pearson had accepted an unwise suggestion from the party organization that if he became prime minister, the government would be committed to '60 days of decision' once Parliament met. The original suggestion was 100 days, but Pearson rejected that because of Napoleon's 100 days between Elba and Waterloo. Sixty days was in practice even worse. The Speech from the Throne opening the session contained an impressive but scarcely realizable program. Legislation was forecast for the establishment of a department of industry with an area development agency; the recasting of the Atlantic Developent Board; the creation of a municipal development and loan board; amendments to the National Housing Act; the creation of a Canada development corporation; the establishment of an economic council of Canada; amendment of the Department of Agriculture Act to provide for a second minister from eastern Canada; provision of additional federal assistance to complete the Trans-Canada Highway; comprehensive contributory retirement pensions; amendments to the Unemployment Insurance Act; redistribution of representation in the House of Commons; amendment of the Citizenship Act to give naturalized citizens equal status with natural-born citizens; the continuation of subsidies to the railway legislation; and several other lesser measures.

In addition there were bound to be debates on the establishment of the Royal Commission on Bilingualism and Biculturalism, the Columbia River treaty, the establishment of a 12-mile fishery zone and federal-provincial relations.

The session began in a thoroughly conventional fashion on 16 May. Alan Macnaughton, a fully bilingual Montreal lawyer, who had been the chairman of the Public Accounts Committee while Diefenbaker was prime minister, was elected Speaker. Macnaughton proved to be less firm than Lambert and less learned and judicious than Michener. He was inclined to be intimidated by Diefenbaker and too often permitted his rulings to be discussed after they had been made. He was faced with far too many appeals from his decisions in the first session. I became increasingly resolved to do my best to have appeals from the Speaker's rulings abolished — fortunately for me a goal I had already set publicly when in Opposition.

Lucien Lamoureux was chosen Deputy Speaker. He quickly proved himself a splendidly articulate and utterly impartial presiding officer and was later to become one of the really great Speakers. Herman Batten, a Newfoundlander, became deputy chairman of committees. Batten was a firm and imperturbable presiding officer who in due course became Deputy Speaker, and who always retained the respect of the House.

The debate on the Address in Reply to the Speech from the Throne was begun by Diefenbaker, as leader of the Opposition, on Monday, 20 May, in a rambling speech that concluded with a vague motion of want of confidence, which caused us no concern as we were convinced no party in the Opposition wanted another election. If we made sure our members were present for votes, we were not likely to be defeated, even though we lacked a majority.

The first serious threat came on 21 May, on a subamendment, moved by Douglas for the NDP, regretting that the government had indicated its intention to acquire nuclear arms for Canadian forces. We knew that the Social Credit MPs from Québec would support Douglas in condemning nuclear arms. We were greatly relieved to learn that the four Social Crediters from the west would vote with the government and thereby assure us a bare majority. We knew that Harkness would not vote against the acquisition of nuclear weapons, and we hoped some other Tories would abstain. The actual vote was 124 to 113. That was the only division about which we were in any real danger in the first half of the session, except for the risk on appeals from the Speaker's rulings, which did not involve the question of confidence in the government.

The Gordon budget

The session proceeded without difficulty until Walter Gordon presented the budget on 13 June. The content of the budget and, what concerned me as house leader, the way it was prepared aroused a storm in Parliament. Gordon had retained, to advise him, three consultants from outside the public service. Douglas Fisher asked Gordon for an assurance that he and his officials 'alone prepared the budget speech, without assistance of outside consultants or ghost writers from Toronto.' Diefenbaker asked for an urgent debate on the way the budget had been prepared and the flagrant disregard of constitutional practice. The Speaker asked for comments on the question of urgency.

As house leader I said the government was ready to have the matter debated as early as the House desired. The government had planned to have the budget debate begin the following Wednesday but was willing to bring the debate on at once, so the matter raised by Diefenbaker, which related entirely to the budget, could be debated without delay.

Strong objection was made to my proposal. It was argued that the use of outside consultants constituted a separate subject that required urgent debate on its own. Pearson intervened to suggest that the Speaker give his ruling on urgency; he added that if the Speaker's ruling was adverse on the question of urgency, as he felt it should be, the government, to avoid delay, would go on with the budget debate that day. The Speaker ruled that Diefenbaker's motion did not require urgent debate. His ruling was appealed even though the Speaker had pointed out that, under the rules, his decision was final. Thanks to the votes of the Social Crediters the ruling was sustained.

The questioning and raising points of order did not stop there. The House was in an unruly mood, and one day the question peiod went on into the evening. There were rumours that Gordon might resign, and the harassment continued until 24 June, when he made a speech conciliatory in tone. At the conclusion he commented that some members in the House and some people outside had made it plain they would like to see him leave public life. He admitted that he had made mistakes and might make more if he stayed. As long as he remained a member of the House, he would strive to do what he believed to be in the best interests of the great majority of the people of the country. After those comments the attitude in the House improved.

Gordon had in fact offered his resignation and there had been a cabinet meeting at Harrington Lake to discuss the situation. I felt his resignation should not be accepted. I believed that sacrificing a minister who was under fire would be a sign of weakness. Gordon had been accused of no wrongdoing, merely an alleged technical breach of parliamentary tradition. I did not regard the technicality as of the slightest practical importance or what had been done as of the least harm to the public interest. I was relieved when Pearson decided that the resignation should not be accepted and that we should fight back.

Douglas spoke just before the vote was taken on the Tory motion of want of confidence; he said that the NDP would not vote confidence in the government. The party did not believe, however, that people of the country wanted a third election in fifteen months. The NDP believed that the people wanted Parliament to get on with the job of governing Canada. For that reason their members would abstain from voting. The Social Credit members also abstained. The vote was 73 to 113. On the budget itself both small parties abstained once more, and the budget was adopted 119 to 74. The difficulties over the budget reduced the prestige of the government and were a humiliation for Gordon, but the crisis petered out, the government had survived, and it continued to function.

There was a minor procedural crisis on the final day of the budget debate, when Leon Balcer tried to interrupt the regular business to have an urgent debate on another subject. Balcer's demand was rejected by the Speaker, whose decision was appealed. For the first time in 1963 all members of the Opposition parties voted together against the Speaker's ruling, which was upheld by a vote of 108 to 106. The vote would have been tied had not Dr Guy Marcoux, who had withdrawn from the Social Credit caucus and was sitting as an independent, voted to sustain the Speaker. Technically the rejection of a Speaker's ruling is not a defeat of the government, but when the government cannot muster enough votes to sustain the Speaker, its prestige suffers. That vote had been too close for comfort. I was more determined than ever to have the rules changed so that the decisions of the Speaker would be final and not subject to appeal in any circumstances.

I had not spoken in the budget debate, but I wanted to show my support for Gordon, and I was able to do so on his first supply motion. Diefenbaker moved an amendment expressing want of confidence in almost the same words as the Tory amendment on the budget. I raised a point of order that his amendment was an attempt to revive the budget debate, and that it was against the rules to revive, in the same session, a question on which the House had made a decision. After considerable debate the Speaker agreed that the amendments were very similar, but he found one phrase that was different. He therefore ruled Diefenbaker's motion in order but hoped the debate would stick to that one phrase. It did not. The debate lasted only one day. I was the final speaker. For the only time during that session my speech was combative; it contrasted in extravagant terms the irresponsible financial policies of the Diefenbaker government with the prudent and responsible attitude to public expenditure of the new minister of finance. Despite almost constant Tory interruptions my speech was greeted with rousing enthusiasm on our side of the House. Once more the smaller parties abstained, and Diefenbaker's amendment was defeated.

During the budget difficulties I learned that constant vigilance by the house leader was needed if a defeat of the government by accident was to be avoided. I also began to realize as I had not in 1958, that when the smaller parties fear an election, they do their best not to defeat the government. To keep the government's supporters in the House, and in the committee of the whole where snap votes could be called without notice, was the most essential task if defeat was to be avoided. That was primarily the duty of the chief government whip, but I made it one of my concerns also.

The Atlantic Development Board

The Liberal Opposition had objected to the limited scope of the Atlantic Development Board as established by the Diefenbaker government and had undertaken to amend the Tory legislation to make the board effective.

The proposal for an Atlantic Development Board had been in the Liberal program since 1958 and was borrowed by the Tories shortly before the 1962 election. The board represented a formal recognition by Parliament that the four Atlantic provinces had less developed economies and a lower standard of living than the rest of Canada, and was designed to find ways to give additional stimulus to their economic development through federal financial aid. The Liberal program had envisaged a capital fund to be administered by the board, but the Tory measure provided for a board with no capital fund of its own and merely advisory functions.

The Tory Board had been appointed in January 1963, but it had held no meetings before we were in office and had announced in the Speech from the Throne our intention to amend the legislation. I was determined the board should have real powers as soon as possible. On the day after Gordon delivered his budget speech the third item of government business announced for debate was a bill in my name to amend the Atlantic Development Board Act. When the second item was reached, a controversial measure that I expected would take up the rest of the day, I went off to the washroom. I have since then suspected that the Opposition, knowing the item in my name came next, cut off the debate while I was out of the House so that I would be embarrassed by not being present to move my own motion. Gordon moved it on my behalf. Just as the Speaker began to read the motion, I walked back into the House to the applause of our side. The embarrassment ended. As promised, the amending bill would give the board a capital fund to be devoted to specific projects. Although the projects would require the approval of the Treasury Board, we argued that a veto was unlikely to be exercised unless something outrageous was recommended. In fact no project was rejected while I was minister.

I announced that the board would have a capital sum of $100 million, and that we intended to ask all the members of the board appointed by the Tory government to continue to serve. In the bill, Parliament was being asked to increase the membership of the board to make it more representative of the main economic activities of the Atlantic region.

All the existing members agreed to remain on the board. I was able to persuade Brigadier Michael Wardell of Fredericton, the publisher of the *Atlantic Advocate* and the *Fredericton Gleaner*, to resign as chairman but to stay on the board. An Englishman and long-time associate of Lord Beaverbrook in England before coming to New Brunswick, Wardell had been an active and highly partisan Tory propagandist. Despite the objection of one or two colleagues I believed the board would work more effectively if Wardell remained a member. He would be unlikely to be critical of its activities. Though Wardell did not serve his full term, his presence for some time made the board virtually immune from Tory criticism.

On the day before the House rose for the summer recess, I announced the appointment of the six new members of the

Atlantic Development Board and stated that all the members appointed by the previous government had agreed to serve out their full terms and would be eligible for reappointment. I also announced that Ian MacKeigan, QC, of Halifax, would be the new chairman.

The previous government had appointed a full-time director, and I was content to leave him in place — Ernest Weeks, a native of Prince Edward Island. I did not know him well, but quickly developed growing admiration for him. Weeks tackled the job with enthusiasm. He enlisted the warm cooperation of all four Atlantic provincial governments. I took an active interest in the work of the board and Weeks always had ready access to me, as did Slim Monture, the retired director of the federal mines branch and one of the most distinguished of Canadian Indians.

While in Opposition, I once met Monture at Dorval Airport; he was at that time one of the mining experts retained by the United Nations Development Agency. When I asked him where he was going, he replied, 'To Indonesia, where this descendant of generations of North American savages is supposed to give technical advice to members of one of the world's most ancient civilizations.' In addition to having a wonderful sense of humour Monture was invaluable as an economic and technical adviser to Weeks and the Atlantic Development Board.

Diefenbaker's double-cross on indemnities

One piece of legislation I was closely involved with was the proposal to increase indemnities paid to members of Parliament. To induce several potential candidates to accept Liberal nominations Pearson had undertaken privately to have the indemnities for members increased in the first session of the new Parliament. Such legislation would be in the name of the prime minister. Pearson told me he would not introduce it unless I got undertakings from all Opposition parties that it would not be opposed. I had no trouble with Social Credit; most of their members were poor and needed more money. I anticipated difficulty with the New Democrats since some members of the old CCF had opposed increases in the past. To my surprise Stanley Knowles, their house leader, assured me they would all go along. I accepted his word without question, as I always did.

I knew that the majority of the Tories felt increases were overdue. Some of them had resented Diefenbaker's unwillingness to increase indemnities while he was prime minisiter. I told Gordon Churchill, their house leader, that Pearson would not act if there was going to be opposition in the House. He said the question would have to be considered in the Tory caucus. After the caucus he sent me a note of assurance: 'Jack: if you place on Votes and Proceedings the appropriate notices re Indemnity and the other matters so that the normal 48 hours' notice is given we are prepared to pass all stages on Monday.'

It was late July before deliberations with other parties and our caucus were completed. Pearson promptly gave notice of the proposed resolution, and it was debated on Monday, 29 July. The legislation was to increase the indemnity of MPs from $10,000 to $18,000 per year. It was also to provide additional allowances for leaders of smaller parties having 12 members or more, and for the chief government whip and the chief Opposition whip. No change was to be made in the salaries of ministers or the leader of the Opposition. There were to be no pensions for ministers other than what they would receive as MPs, but a prime minister serving for four years or more and his widow would be provided with a pension.

In his speech Pearson stated that he understood the proposed measure had the support of all parties. To the consternation of the Tory benches Diefenbaker announced that he would vote against the increase and, if it was approved, refuse to accept the increase for himself. During Diefenbaker's speech Churchill never took his eyes off me. Several times I put my hand in my pocket as though I was going to take out his note and read it. The temptation was strong; it would have been an immediate parliamentary triumph. But I realized that if the statement was read, I could never hope for decent working relations with Churchill, which were almost essential to effective management of House business. I refrained.

Diefenbaker's defection along with that of six other Tories was regarded as treachery by most of the rest of his party. Their attitude was expressed with great courage and sincerity by a Tory backbencher from western Ontario, W.H.A. Thomas, a loyal and reliable member who rarely spoke. When Diefenbaker concluded his speech, Thomas raised a question of privilege in which he said that normally in the House each party worked as a party, and its leader spoke for the party, but on that occasion Diefenbaker was not speaking for the party.

Diefenbaker and the six were joined in the vote by Réal Caouette and two other Social Crediters. Caouette said he was not opposed to the pay increase but felt family allowances should be increased first. Diefenbaker argued that the proposed indemnities were being increased excessively, and that he had taken particular objection to the provision of a salary for the leader of any party with 12 or more members in the House.

Pearson felt that he had been double-crossed by Diefenbaker, but the real loser was Diefenbaker himself. It was then, and has been since then, my judgement that his action dealt a fatal blow to his leadership of his own party. There was no open revolt but his followers never fully trusted him again. By that repudiation of a caucus decision his effectiveness as leader of the Opposition was permanently impaired.

For me as house leader Diefenbaker's double-cross had one benefit. Churchill was obviously relieved that I had not read his note, and from then on discussing House business with him was easier. I often had to consult him alone, and I invariably went to see him instead of asking him to come to see me.

My working relationship with Eric Winkler, the chief Opposition whip, was excellent. After the session started, he approached me to discuss management of House business. His direct approach pleased me, and I told him I would be perfectly frank with him and tell him whatever I could about our plans, except when the government had decided to keep a particular initiative to itself. I would try never to mislead him, and hoped his attitude would be the same. My disposition, I said, was to accept the word of anyone I was dealing with, but I did my best never to be deceived twice. In the rest of his years in Parliament I found Winkler thoroughly dependable while completely loyal to his own party. Our cooperation behind the curtain helped to facilitate business in what was to become a contentious session.

Resolving the divorce problem

Because there were no divorce courts in Québec and Newfoundland, the only way their residents could be divorced was by private act of Parliament. For many years such divorce bills were introduced in the Senate, and the grounds for divorce were considered carefully by a special Senate committee. The examination was at least as thorough as that in the law courts in the other eight provinces. When the bills reached the House of Commons, they were normally passed in all stages without debate. No House time was wasted.

The procedure changed after two CCF members, Frank Howard and Arnold Peters, were elected to Parliament. In 1958 Howard and Peters started a campaign to give the Exchequer Court (now the Federal Court) power to hear divorce cases from Québec and Newfoundland. Howard and Peters insisted on debating each individual divorce bill when it came to the House from the Senate. Divorce bills could be considered only in one private members' hour a week. From 1961 on those two members succeeded in preventing any divorce bills from passing. Meanwhile the growing backlog of petitions for divorce was causing irritation and, in some cases, real hardship. Favreau and I decided to try to find a device that would remove the irritation.

The government was not willing to confer jurisdiction on the Exchequer Court, but Favreau and I worked out a compromise to give jurisdiction to the Senate to grant divorces. Our recommendation was accepted by the cabinet. A commissioner was to be appointed with the status of an additional judge of the Exchequer Court. The commissioner was to examine the petitions for divorce in the Senate committee, which would then decide whether the divorce should be granted. The drafting of the bill was done by Favreau himself. He did much of the negotiating to secure its acceptance by our own backbenchers and shared with me the discussions with the Opposition parties.

We decided that the bill to give jurisdiction to the Senate should be not a government measure but a private member's bill.

If the bill was sponsored by a private member, no political party would incur the blame for encouraging divorce. We arranged to have Nicholas Manziuk, a Tory MP, introduce the bill. Manziuk was chosen because he had been the chairman of the committee that considered divorces when Diefenbaker was prime minister. The details of Manziuk's bill were not debated, and it passed all stages in a few minutes on 1 August, after Peters and spokesmen for all parties had made congratulatory speeches. I uttered one sentence, and Favreau said nothing, but everyone knew the main credit was his. Favreau's skill in that matter won him the respect of the whole House and a reputation for negotiation and conciliation thoroughly deserved. Peters then agreed to let all the divorce bills before the House pass without debate. I was pleased that that recurrent parliamentary nightmare had been ended in Pearson's first year in office and while I was house leader.

Family activities

Despite the delay over the budget debate Parliament accomplished a good deal by the time we adjourned for a summer recess on 2 August. All but two of the budget bills had been passed. The Department of Industry, the Economic Council of Canada, and the Municipal Development and Loan Board had been established. The Atlantic Development Board had been reconstituted, and 90 per cent of the cost of completing the Trans-Canada Highway in the four Atlantic provinces was already being paid by the federal government. Pearson's announcement on 4 June that the government intended to establish an exclusive 12-mile fishing zone was well received in the Atlantic region. We felt justified in adjourning the session until 30 September after a tumultuous and exhausting year.

Margaret, Alan, Ruth and I went to Newfoundland for the rest of August after a brief stop in Halifax, where I attended the inaugural meeting of the Atlantic Development Board, spoke briefly and withdrew so that the board could get on with its work. We had a quiet time at Traytown and did little travelling because I was very tired. Jane and Peter both went to Europe that summer.

Jane and two fellow medical students from Charleston, South Carolina, were given a passage on a Bowater's ship carrying paper, made in their new mill in the southern United States, to England. Jane had a job for most of the summer at a hospital at Hastings, England. Peter and a school friend got a passage shortly after school closed on another Bowater's ship, carrying paper from Newfoundland to England. Those summer visits for Jane and Peter were made possible by Albert Martin, the head of Bowater's pulp and paper mill at Corner Brook, who had been a staunch friend and supporter while I was in Opposition.

In September, Jane went back to Queen's and Peter entered Bishop's University at Lennoxville; Alan and Ruth in high sohool, remained at home. Margaret had a busy time that fall. Her mother, in Victoria, had become seriously ill and required constant care in a nursing home. Her father, whose health was also poor after his mild stroke in 1962, had a housekeeper, but the arrangement was not a success. A room became available at the nursing home where my mother had lived in Ottawa, and on Margaret's initiative her parents, with some reluctance due to the fear of Ottawa winters, were persuaded to come to Ottawa to live, her mother in the nursing home and her father with us in the 'addition' where he could have comfort and privacy. The nursing home being close by, Margaret could take her father nearly every day to visit her mother. Mrs Beattie lived in the nursing home until her death in January 1966, and Margaret's father with us until his death in August 1965.

My sister, who had been keeping an eye on the Beatties in Victoria, accompanied them to Ottawa in mid-September. She had a special reason for coming. The branch of the Canadian Legion at Port Rowan had placed a plaque in the Baptist church commemorating the local veterans who had lost their lives in The Second World War and had included the name of our brother Frank. A memorial service was to be held on Sunday, 22 September, and I had been invited to unveil the plaque. Members of the family were all included in the invitation. My brother Tom was in Ottawa on business, and he went with me and our sister to the

J.W.P.'s brother Frank in uniform during training in Britain 1942-43 before parachuting into France in June 1943 in SOE. Killed September 1944 at Buchenwald.

service. We decided to take the opportunity to have Mother's ashes buried in the cemetery, and the Baptist minister willingly presided over the burial on the Monday. Both services were moving experiences for all three of us. Ruth was with us, and we spent another day visiting places associated with the family. Ruth reported to Margaret that she had never seen so many cemeteries in her life.

Having her parents in Ottawa put an additional burden on Margaret, who was already bearing more than her fair share of

Memorial to Resistance at Romarantin where Frank landed in France in 1943.

bringing up the family. Margaret's relationship with her father was very close, and I enjoyed his company and his thoughtfulness. The children loved their grandfather and treated him as a friend. The two years he spent with us made us all more aware of what a family can be.

Test of leadership

A threat of paralysis

Until the recess on 2 August 1963 the government had control of the order of business in the House, and my main duty as leader was to arrange the debates on government measures to facilitate their approval by the House. When I got back from Newfoundland in mid-September, my freedom to organize House business was limited by urgent requirements for parliamentary action that had to be met within a limited time.

The first was a split of the Social Credit party into two groups who had quickly indicated that they could hold up all government business until their differences were settled.

The second was that the Canada Pension Plan legislation, already before the House in July, could not be proceeded with because the Québec government had decided to set up its own plan, and the two would have to be reconciled. To avoid frustrating the expectations of old age pensioners the government had decided to have the Old Age Security Act amended to increase the universal pension to $65 from $55 a month and to have the increase included in the October cheques, though the legislation had not yet been introduced.

The third was that a royal commission to investigate charges against the Seafarers' International Union had reported that the leadership of that union and other marine unions were charged with criminal activity, and that until those charges were dealt with, the SIU and the other unions should be placed under a trusteeship.

The fourth and most urgent of all was that the government would run out of funds to pay its bills in September, and interim supply would have to be provided by mid-October to pay civil service salaries and meet other expenses of public administration.

When the House met on 30 September, my position as leader was like that of a person trying to solve a jigsaw puzzle with more pieces than places to put them in.

The Social Credit schism

The Social Credit party in the 1963 Parliament was seriously out of balance. Robert Thompson, the leader, was one of four members, two from Alberta and two from British Columbia. Twenty members had been elected in Québec, all of whom owed their election to Réal Caouette. The split had occurred not over a question of principle but over a dispute about leadership. Caouette and 12 other MPs from Québec withdrew from the Social Credit caucus and formed a separate group with Caouette as their leader. The group called themselves the Ralliement des Créditistes. The Social Credit party under Thompson was left with only 11 members, 7 of them from Québec.

The basic rules of the House of Commons had been made for an assembly with only two parties, one in office and the other in Opposition. Since 1921, however, there had always been a third party in the House, and some privileges were given to it as a courtesy.

In 1935 a fourth party, Social Credit, had emerged from nowhere with 17 MPs, 15 from Alberta and 2 from Saskatchewan, whereas the CCF had elected only 7. Despite their greater number the Social Credit MPs were seated at the far end of the chamber from the Speaker, beyond the CCF. The third party had some procedural advantages over the fourth, the most important being that their spokesmen were recognized in debates before those of the fourth party and had a better chance to raise questions and move amendments.

In 1958 all the Social Credit members had been defeated, and the CCF had been reduced to 8 members. Social Credit came back in 1962 with 30 members, and the CCF by then transformed into the New Democratic party, with 19. The Social Credit leader convinced the Speaker, over a protest from Stanley Knowles, that their larger number entitled them to sit closer to the Speaker and enjoy the advantages of being the third party rather than the fourth. But the split of Social Credit into two groups made the NDP the most numerous of the small parties, and their spokesman, Knowles, claimed that they should have the nearer position to the Speaker. Neither Thompson nor Caouette objected, but they differed sharply about which group should have priority.

Before the session resumed on 30 September, spokesmen for all three had seen the Speaker, who declined to settle the dispute, which he said should be decided by the House.

When the sitting opened, there had been no change in the seating and the two groups of Social Crediters were intermingled. The Speaker took the unusual step of pointing out that two questions had arisen: the first, the order in which the smaller parties should be seated, and the second, whether Caouette's group constituted a recognizable party or merely a group of independents. He said that the Speaker had no authority to answer those questions, and that the House alone could decide. He suggested that the subject be referred to a committee for consideration and recommendation.

Stanley Knowles rose at once and made an excellent speech on the way a similar problem had been settled in 1962. He claimed that the NDP was entitled to precedence because it was now the largest of the smaller parties, and moved that the Speaker's statement and the whole matter be referred to the Committee on Privileges and Elections. Diefenbaker spoke next and once again demonstrated his lack of capacity as leader of the Opposition by insinuating that the split in the Social Credit party was merely a struggle for the salary of a party leader and reminding the House that he had voted against the legislation to provide those salaries. Diefenbaker thus insulted both Thompson and Caouette and annoyed his own MPs by reminding them of his double-cross over indemnities. Pearson spoke briefly to say that we were happy to support Knowles's motion. Both Social Credit and Créditiste groups spoke briefly and agreed to support Knowles's motion. It was adopted without a dissenting voice.

I was greatly relieved and hoped that the House might proceed rapidly with other business while the committee was deliberating.

Delaying old age pensions

The Social Credit dispute having been sent to a committee, I rose and reminded the House that on 2 August no government business had been announced for 30 September. I said we had given notice to the clerk of a resolution to increase the old age pension. We would like to have it dealt with speedily so that the increase from $55 to $65 a month could be included in the October cheques. To do that, the old age security amendment would have to be passed before mid-October. Knowing that there was no opposition to the increase anywhere in the House, I asked for unanimous consent to have the rule requiring 48 hours' notice waived so that the resolution could be debated immediately. Diefenbaker decided to fish again in troubled waters in an effort to embarrass the governemnt because of its inability to go ahead with the Canada Pension Plan, but after a few snide observations he made consent unanimous. Judy LaMarsh then introduced the resolution, and the debate went on acrimoniously for the next three days.

At the end of the first day in announcing the business, I said we would ask for interim supply on Thursday, 3 October.

The Old Age Security Bill got first reading at the end of the day on 2 October and Opposition spokesmen asked me to bring it up as the first business the next day, thereby suggesting that second reading would be completed in a short time. I refused to be seduced, and insisted on asking for interim supply, which could, if the House agreed, be provided quickly; we could then start second reading of the Old Age Security Bill. Refusing to proceed until interim supply was granted gave me a bargaining advantage: no member of the House wanted to be blamed by the old age pensioners for holding up their increases.

The crisis over interim supply

Debate on interim supply took up the whole day on Thursday 3 October and became even more contentious the next day. There were signs that Diefenbaker and some of the Tories thought they might win an election if they could force the government into prolonging the session and having either to use governor general's warrants or to call an election. A filibuster could last long enough to leave the government without funds. That risk was increased when Gilles Grégoire of the Créditistes announced that his group did not intend to end the debate as long as the privileges and elections committee had not remedied 'the ridiculous and illogical situation' prevailing in their corner of the House.

Grégoire had been the whip of the Social Credit party before the split. He knew the rules of the House well, was almost as accomplished in manipulating them as Knowles and was without scruple in doing so. I took Grégoire's threat so seriously that I persuaded Pearson and the cabinet to let me try a big gamble to ensure getting interim supply. The cabinet agreed that I should give notice before 6 p.m. of a motion I could move on Monday that, if adopted, would require that the House not adjourn until interim supply was disposed of, and that all proceedings be dealt with at a single sitting. Since the House might, if such a motion was adopted, have to sit continuously for two or three days, it was closure with a vengeance.

When the motion came up for debate on Monday, 7 October, I said it was being proposed with the greatest reluctance. I reviewed the various developments of the previous Friday, including the agreement of the spokesmen for all parties except Caouette's to grant supply at the end of that day. My statement was based on Grégoire's threat to hold up interim supply indefinitely. Grégoire had said that it rested with certain members of the government to end the failure to recognize his group of 13 members. I said the dispute was not a matter for the government but for the House, which had accepted the Knowles motion to send the matter to the committee. The House could not act until the committee reported. I explained in detail what salaries and other payments the government could not make if the interim supply did not pass both Houses and receive royal assent by the following evening. Unless I could receive assurances that supply would be granted by 10 p.m. that day, it would be my duty to have my motion for continuous sitting voted on.

In reply Gordon Churchill described my action as the most amazing development in his 12 years in the House. He spoke at length about mismanagement by the government and about our record in delaying interim supply when in Opposition. He proposed an amendment that would have suspended proceedings in the House, and instructed the Committee on Privileges and Elections to report within 48 hours. The Speaker ruled the amendment out of order. Churchill appealed his ruling, which was sustained in a vote of 101 to 88. The only Opposition MPs who voted with us were the Social Crediters supporting Thompson.

Thompson then spoke; he attacked Churchill, deplored the fact that if the old age security amendment was not passed, the pensioners would not receive the increase in their October cheques and begged the Créditistes to give up their filibuster. Caouette refused Thompson's appeal and made it clear that they were opposed to granting supply until their demand for recognition as a party was met. To my surprise Douglas announced that he was prepared, if no compromise could be reached, to support my motion so that the business of the country could be continued, particularly the legislation to increase old age pensions. Alexis Caron, who was chairman of the Committee on Privileges and Elections, intervened to say that he would take steps to get the committee to ask permission to sit while the House was sitting, and that, if permission was given, the committee could sit all that evening. A committee in those days could not sit while the House was sitting without the permission of the House. One of the Tory members suggested that Caron's proposal offered a way out of the impasse.

I then got permission to intervene again in the debate, to suggest that the committee meet at 6 p.m. to ask for permission to sit while the House was sitting. Grégoire followed, to say that his group did not want to hold up proceedings but merely to be recognized as a separate party in the House. Another Tory member then suggested that the House could give the necessary permission to the committee to sit without waiting for a request from the committee. I jumped at that sensible suggestion and said that if someone would move the adjournment of the debate, the

House could at once adopt a motion to empower the committee to sit while the House was sitting. That was done, and the crisis was over for that day. The question period dragged on until early evening, but the interim supply was then granted. I had won my gamble, but it had been a close call for the government.

There was a moment of goodwill when the House closed that evening, and I announced that we would go ahead the next day with a bill to increase old age pensions retroactive to 1 October. The Old Age Pension Bill was passed the next day, but our troubles were far from over.

The Seafarers International Union and Hal Banks

The government was not free to get ahead with its own program until the unplanned legislation to establish a trusteeship over the Seafarers Union was dealt with. Diefenbaker had raised the question in a provocative and abusive intervention during the debate on interim supply, in which my conduct as minister of citizenship and immigration in 1953 was attacked, and I had felt obliged to explain how I had become involved in the controversy over the conduct of Hal Banks, the head in Canada of the Seafarers International Union.

In 1962 the Diefenbaker government had appointed Mr Justice T.G. Norris of British Columbia to investigate the charges made outside Parliament about the violent way in which Banks was running the union. The Norris Report fell into the lap of the Pearson government in July 1963. Norris had charged Banks and other officers of the SIU and four related maritime unions with serious criminal offences. The report recommended, in addition to prosecutions, that the five unions should be placed under a trusteeship to manage their affairs.

Pearson and Allan MacEachen first tried to have the unions in question placed under a privately organized trusteeship. In response to a question from Diefenbaker on 30 September, MacEachen told the House that unless a private trusteeship over the maritime unions could be worked out during the following weekend, the government proposed, as recommended by the

Norris Commission, to proceed with legislation to establish a public trusteeship.

I was involved because I had carried out a decision Walter Harris made on his last day as minister of citizenship and immigration. Diefenbaker accused me during the debate on interim supply of embracing Banks and added that Banks had 'friends in government circles.' He asserted that Banks had been accepted as an immigrant because of support he had given to Liberal candidates in elections. During his six years as prime minister Diefenbaker had done nothing about Banks or the SIU except appoint the Norris inquiry in 1962. His insinuations about Banks's being a 'pet' of the Liberal party continued throughout the numerous debates and exchanges on the subject.

The government took advantage of the temporary ceasefire over the place of the smaller parties to introduce legislation for a trusteeship of the maritime unions. Once the party spokesmen had spoken, Diefenbaker accused MacEachen of delaying action. He said someone had tied his hands and added, 'The Secretary of State was one of those who had solicitude for Banks only a few years ago, and it is surprising the solicitude has continued.' I rose at once on a question of privilege, to say that Diefenbaker had made a statement about me that was 'a downright falsehood.' 'I (have) never had the faintest solicitude for Mr. Banks at any time whatever. I have never had any association with him, and have never seen him and never spoken to him in my life.' Diefenbaker retorted that solicitude did not demand personal acquaintance. He claimed that the order-in-council admitting Banks as a landed immigrant had given him the halo of government approval. The admission of Banks, he declared, had prevented his government from deporting Banks. I replied that Diefenbaker, as a lawyer, surely knew that statement was untrue. Any person who was not a citizen could be deported if there were legal grounds for deportation, but Diefenbaker in six years in office had never taken the trouble to look for grounds to deport Banks. Diefenbaker answered that Judge Norris said in his report that once the order-in-council landing Banks was passed, deportation procedures were prevented. I interjected, 'Read the law.' No other member joined him in that dispute between us.

The debate on the trusteeship lasted three days and, on the final day, at my urging, all the Opposition parties agreed to sit on the Friday evening — an unusual concession — and the Trusteeship Bill was passed.

The Créditiste filibuster

By 11 October interim supply, the old age pension increase and the trusteeship had all been dealt with. On Monday and Tuesday of the next week we had won a vote of confidence in the government. On Wednesday the report of the Committee on Privileges and Elections was available, but one of the Thompson Social Crediters refused unanimous consent to debate it without notice, and good progress was made with other government business. The debate on the report of the committee began on Thursday, 17 October.

The report recommended that the New Democratic party be seated next to the official Opposition because their membership was larger than that of either of the other groups. Instead of ranking the other two by their numerical strength, the report recommended that the Social Credit party of 11 members led by Thompson should have precedence in seating over the group of 13 led by Caouette. It did not refer to the latter group by name, questioned whether it should be recognized as a separate party, since its members had not been elected as such and recommended that its legal status be studied by an officer of the House of Commons, who should report to the Speaker.

Knowles began the debate. He argued that the House had no right to determine what the party designation of any group of members or any individual member should be. A group of members had a right to establish itself in Parliament at any time and to call itself a party by any name it chose. Seating parties according to numerical strength, as in 1962 and 1963, should be accepted as a principle. He accordingly moved that the report be sent back to the committee with instructions to recommend that groups in

Opposition be seated according to their numbers. Thompson's spokesman opposed Knowles's motion and argued that Caouette and his followers were a group of independents who had no right to be recognized as a party. When Caouette spoke later, he claimed that all the Social Credit MPs from Québec had described themselves before the election as candidates of the Ralliement des Créditistes, and that his group was the real party, from which the Social Crediters who supported Thompson had seceded. Caouette claimed that the whole matter should have been settled by the government. He added that if the government had given orders to its supporters on the commmittee, the result would have been different. I ignored that observation, as the whole cabinet had agreed that ministers should keep out of the controversy. The debate continued all day.

The Knowles motion was defeated just before the adjournment for lunch next day. Pearson and I hoped the final vote would be taken without further debate. But Grégoire said the group had several members who wanted to speak on the main motion. When the debate resumed later in the afternoon, it became more acrimonious and seemed likely to go on for the rest of the day. Pearson agreed that I should intervene, make a brief speech and move the adjournment of the debate until Monday.

I had thought out carefully what I wanted to say. I knew it was of the utmost importance to say nothing that would offend any group or, if possible, any individual, and to suggest a solution that would seem reasonable to most members and to the public. I must keep my statements simple.

I began by asking the members to realize what we were being called upon to decide. If the House accepted the report of the committee, we would decide that the New Democratic party would be moved forward to the benches occupied at the beginning of the Parliament by the Social Credit party, and that next to the NDP would be members led by the man recognized as leader of the Social Credit party when the new Parliament opened in May. At the far end of the chamber would be the group led by Caouette, which would thereby be recognized as a party. The only point I was seeking to make was that there was a group in the House under the leadership of Caouette, and that that group, which the report described as a group having a leader, if the Knowles motion had been adopted, would have been given seating in the House ahead of Thompson's group.

Knowles had said that the numerical pinciple should be applied, though he had admitted he had argued after the 1962 election for the historical principle. Any member, I said, could conscientiously take either view, but I happened to favour the historical principle. I thought it should have been followed in 1962 and 1963 as in 1935 and 1940, when the CCF had fewer members than Social Credit but was given priority because it had been in Parliament longer. I did not deny the right of any member to take the opposite vlew. The good faith of anyone who favoured the historical principle should not be questioned any more than the good faith of anyone who favoured the numerical principle. For more than 40 years the seniority principle had been followed, and I regretted that it had been abandoned in 1962. The report of the committee recommended that we go back to it since the numerical principle had not worked and was responsible for the present problem.

The hour was 4:20; under the rules we had to go to private members' business at 5. It was evident that the House was not ready to make a decision in 40 minutes. It would, I believed, be to the benefit of all of us to reflect seriously on the question over the weekend, and also on the appearance of Parliament we were giving the public by the prolonged debate. For that reason, I said, I was moving adjournment of the debate until Monday. My motion was carried by 98 to 74, with Thompson's Social Credit voting with the government and the rest of the Opposition MPs against.

On Monday, 21 October I continued my speech and outlined what the House was being called on to decide. In the debate three points, I said, had arisen. One point was irrelevant to the report of the committee; that was the question of the allowance for party leader. Diefenbaker, I thought, had been right when he said that the law had been made by Parliament, and that the law courts, not Parliament, had the responsibility to interpret the law, if any interpretation was needed. The committee had not discussed the question, and there was no reason why anyone else should. I accepted without qualification Caouette's statement that the allowance was not a consideration at all In the matter, and I did not intend to say anything more about it.

The other two questions were, first, the order of seating in the House, which had been dealt with in the report, and second, the recognition of certain members of the House as a group or a party. I was not subtle enough, I said, to understand the difference between a group and a party. It was no business of the House, when any number of members joined together, whether they called themselves a group or a party or something else, as long as they did not try to use the name of an existing party in the House.

The seating could be settled on either the historical or the numerical principle, which I had somewhat disrespectfully referred to on Friday as 'the numbers game.' By rejecting the Knowles amendment the House had decided by a majority not to follow the numerical principle. The problem would not have arisen if the House had stuck to the historical principle in 1962. Knowles interrupted to ask me what position our party had taken at the beginning of the Parliaments of 1962 and 1963. I replied, none. I added that neither the prime minister nor I had taken any position, and that I did not think anyone else was authorized to speak for the Liberal party on the matter. We had taken the view that the organization of the House was the business of the House, and that it was not for the government to tell the House how it should be organized.

On the question of the recognition of groups or parties I repeated that I could not see the difference between a group and a party. The report of the committee had referred to 'the members of the Group under the leadership of Mr. Caouette.' I was then asked to read paragraph 4 of the report, which read 'That the question of the privileges to be enjoyed by the Group under the leadership of Mr. Réal Caouette be referred to the parliamentary counsel of the House of Commons for study and report to the Speaker.'

The fourth paragraph of the report, I suggested, had been superseded by action the Speaker had already taken on one or two occasions, as a courtesy, in recognizing Caouette. Two members interrupted me to say that those incidents were not to be regarded as precedents. I replied that it was only as a courtesy that members of the Opposition, except the leader of the Opposition, who was an officer of the House, were permitted to comment on statements by the government at the opening of the day's sitting. Such recognition had been the practice since 1921, and I thought it too late to change the practice now. Whether the Speaker sought the advice of the parliamentary counsel was a matter the Speaker would have to decide himself in his own good time.

The committee had given advice on two points, namely, the recognition that, in addition to the official Opposition, there were three groups in opposition, and the order in which the groups should sit. That was all that the motion for concurrence was about. There might still be a great deal of argument about the order of seating, but I maintained that that question had been settled when the amendment proposed by Knowles had been defeated.

When the new Parliament was constituted in May 1962, I noted, there was no doubt whatever that a group or party was recognized under Thompson's leadership. There was still a discernible group under Thompson's leadership. Caouette and Grégoire had said it was not for the Liberal party or the Conserative party or the New Democratic party to decide a question affecting the internal divisions of the Social Credit party; that was their business. How they described themselves was their business, and the only thing to decide was the order in which the three groups, other than the official Opposition, should be seated. Of the principles discussed one had been rejected by the House. I concluded by suggesting that it would be a wonderful idea to have a vote, accept the committee's report and get on with the business of the country.

My hope was not realized immediately. As the debate continued, Pearson became impatient, and even I was discouraged. But there was a ray of hope when Caouette asked me whether I could assure his group that they would receive the same consideration as any political party in the House of Commons. That was not my business, I answered, and it would be improper for me or any other member, except the Speaker, to give such an assurance. One of the members of the Caouette group then spoke at some length and moved an amendment that it was not up to any other party to decide which of the two Social Credit groups was the Social Credit party, and that that point should be decided by a majority vote among the Social Credit members. Though that was not a proper amendment at all, the Speaker did not question it, and put the so-called amendment to a vote.

When the bells began to ring for the division, one of our backbenchers told me that Caouette wanted to see me. I told him to tell Caouette that while the bells were ringing, I would be walking up and down the corridor in front of the Speaker's office. Caouette could find me there. Shortly after, I began pacing up and down, and Caouette emerged from the chamber almost breathless. He said that he was as sick of the debate as I was, and that it could be settled in a few minutes once the vote on the amendment was taken if I could solve a problem he had, as leader of the new group. He was overwhelmed with mail and visitors and needed an extra secretary and an additional room. I replied that I had no authority to provide either, to which he retorted that everybody knew I ran the place. I said he was wrong, but that I would be glad to have a word with the Speaker about his problem. He asked if I would really do that. I said yes. He then assured me that after the vote on the amendment was completed, the debate would be ended within 10 minutes.

I was elated by Caouette's assurance, which I reported at once to Pearson. I told him never to ask me how it had been secured. The amendment was defeated. Caouette then made a brief speech, and the report of the committee was adopted without a recorded vote. The result was that Thompson and his group got the place nearer the Speaker, and Caouette got his extra room and secretary and recognition of his group as a party. I had wanted Thompson to get pride of place because his group had been more dependable in supporting the government in close votes than the Créditistes. As it turned out, I had managed to retain the goodwill of both leaders.

The resolution of the dispute between the two Social Credit groups ended the most difficult problem in managing the business of the House in that first session. That it had been resolved without my losing the goodwill of either Thompson or Caouette considerably reduced the risk of a defeat of the government in a close vote.

Thanks to the support of the Thompson western members the government had never been defeated, though on one occasion a Speaker's decision was overruled by a vote of 85 to 83, when the Liberals alone voted to sustain the Speaker's ruling, and all members of the four Opposition parties then in the chamber voted against it. No one suggested that the vote was a defeat for the government, but I felt humiliated. The press reported the next day that I was very angry.

There was always trouble keeping government business moving smoothly and quickly through the House. Grégoire, the house leader for the Créditistes, was a spasmodic and unpredictable troublemaker. He had quickly become a skillful parliamentarian, extremely adept at obstruction. On one occasion, when the government was anxious to conclude a particular measure, he threatened to hold up business indefinitely. I asked one of our backbenchers to find out what he really wanted. It was a Friday, and the report was that Grégoire wanted two tickets to the hockey game in Montreal. I had never been to a professional hockey game in my life and had no idea how to go about getting tickets, but I told my friend to get the tickets for him, whatever they cost. The tickets were got and given to Grégoire, who dropped his filibuster at once and went off to Montreal.

Smoother waters

The government still had a heavy agenda, and by the beginning of November I was uneasy about getting the session completed before Christmas. At my request Pearson made a careful and conciliatory statement about government business, setting out what we hoped to have passed and emphasizing the importance of completing consideration of all the estimates. The statement had a good effect since almost no one wanted to come back after Christmas to complete the session. On 6 December, Pearson gave a revised statement of what business the government wanted to have completed. The list was shorter and improved the prospect of ending the session.

On 12 November, the minister of finance had moved that the House go into committee of supply, and Diefenbaker had moved an amendment that if adopted would have condemned the government for failure to carry out the spirit of cooperative federalism and for neglecting consultation with the provinces before starting programs in their jurisdiction.

I knew that there might be a close vote on Diefenbaker's amendment and that if it was adopted, it would defeat the government. I was relieved when Tommy Douglas moved a subamendment. Douglas's motion struck out the condemnation and urged the government to carry out more fully the spirit of cooperative federalism and to consult with the provinces before announcing programs in their jurisdiction.

Douglas said it was hardly fitting to criticize, much less condemn, a government for a failure to carry out cooperative federalism when the government had been less than seven months in office. Thompson and Grégoire supported the Douglas subamendment.

When he replied, Pearson praised the constructive speeches made by Douglas, Thompson and Grégoire. He concluded by saying that Douglas's subamendment was clearly not a vote of want of confidence but an affirmation of a principle acceptable to the government. The government would be happy to support the subamendment. If the Tory motion as amended by Douglas was accepted, Pearson said there would have to be a new motion for the House to go into committee of supply, which he would ask one of his colleagues to move. That was a rare procedure, used only twice before in the history of the Canadian Parliament, but it was clearly set out in the rules. I had suggested it to Pearson while Thompson and Grégoire were speaking. He then decided to support the Douglas subamendment.

Diefenbaker was taken by surprise, and argued that since acceptance of the original Tory amendment would have defeated the government, the House by voting for Douglas's subamendment would also defeat the government. Diefenbaker asserted that I had advised Pearson badly in January 1958 and had now given him advice that put him in the most difficult position any prime minister had ever been put in in the history of the country. I interjected, 'Read standing order 56.' Diefenbaker went on to argue that any amendment to a motion to go into supply was a vote of want of confidence even if it was amended, and would be so regarded by the Opposition. When the vote was taken on the Douglas subamendment, all members in the House except the Tories supported it. When the vote was taken on Diefenbaker's amendment as amended, every member voted for it. Some Tories then exclaimed, 'Resign.'

The adoption of the amendment wiped out the original motion to go into committee of supply. After the vote the Speaker recognized me, and in order to get the House into committee of supply, I made a new motion for that purpose. There was considerable debate about whether my motion was in order under the rules. The Speaker terminated it by accepting my motion.

Despite the time taken, that unusual use of the rules had enabled the government to avoid defeat and had the good effect of widening the gap between the Tories and the smaller groups. Our hold on the support of the House was strengthened, and my judgement was vindicated.

Redistribution

The procedure necessary to accomplish redistribution was my most immediate preoccupation when the government was formed in April 1963. Even a superficial examination of the election results for 1963 made it obvious that if a redistribution had taken place after the 1961 census, the Liberal party would have won a clear majority. I was under great pressre from our more electorally sophisticated colleagues, particularly Walter Gordon, to act swiftly. My own inclination was to lose no time in making sure we established nonpartisan machinery that would result in a workable organization and fair results. The main advantage of transferring redistribution to an independent, nonpartisan agency would not be in greater fairness but in saving the greater part of one session of Parliament every 10 years.

I had no idea of my own about what shape that fundamental reform should take, so the day the government was sworn in I consulted Nelson Castonguay, the chief electoral officer. I had never met him but had had a high opinion of his father, Jules, who was his predecessor. Nelson seemed just as independent and even more knowledgeable. He soon convinced me that I had taken no easy task.

Castonguay persuaded me that the redistribution by an independent agency undertaken in Australia, a federal state comparable to Canada, was the one to look at. I agreed that he should go there to study it at first hand. He also went to New Zealand, since that country had a long experience of redistributing seats by independent commission. We felt that an examiniation on the spot with the officials who had been involved would be of great value, and so it proved to be.

Castonguay came home persuaded that the task could not be performed effectively or in a reasonable time by a single commission for the whole country. I suggested four commissions, one each for Ontario and Québec, one for the Atlantic provinces and one for the western provinces. But we soon concluded that that plan would have no advantages and several disadvantages over having a separate commission for each province, and the latter scheme was what, after convincing the cabinet, I proposed to Parliament.

The more I discussed with Castonguay the problems involved in setting up machinery for a nonpartisan and objective redistribution, the more complicated and time-consuming I realized it would be. I was resolved not to rush into hasty action, and to have a thorough knowledge of what I wanted to recommend to the cabinet and to Parliament.

The study was not completed until November. Shortly afterwards I introduced a resolution that provided for two bills. One bill was to establish the office of a representation commissioner with a small staff to administer the plan. The commissioner was to be an ex officio member of all 10 commissions, to coordinate their procedures and to provide technical advice. The second bill was to authorize the establishment of the 10 commissions and to lay down the rules for their operations. That bill was intended to provide machinery for all succeeding decennial redistributions. To prevent duplication of debate the one resolution recommended all expenditures to be made under both bills.

When I rose on 26 November to move the resolution, Diefenbaker suggested that we agree to have a general debate at the resolution stage on the whole subject of redistribution. That was precisely what I had hoped would happen, mainly because I wanted to explain the whole plan at once.

I began by describing the attitude with which the government was approaching redistribution, and read a statement that elicited applause from both sides of the House. After it was read, I confessed that the statement was, almost word for word, the statement Diefenbaker had made on the same subject a year earlier, when he was prime minister. Except for the one word 'commission,' which under the plan I was proposing would be plural, there had not been one word in his statement with which I could quarrel. I said that I believed every member would agree with the statement.

The proposed bills were, I explained, government measures in the technical sense that the government alone could propose expenditures. My colleagues and I felt that the collective wisdom of the House should be brought to bear, and that any good suggestions, from any quarter, should be incorporated into the legislation without thought of partisan considerations.

The government was suggesting a separate commission for each province, I reported, because Castonguay estimated that if both bills were adopted in the 1963 session, an election after redistribution should be possible as early as the fall of 1965, but if the legislation was delayed into the spring of 1964, the earliest date for an election under the new redistribution would be the spring of 1966. If there was only one commission for the whole country, Castonguay estimated, the redistribution could not be completed in time for an election before 1968.

We felt that the representation commissioner should be appointed by Parliament to coordinate the work of the 10 commissions and to make sure they operated on a relatively uniform basis. I did not want to hide from the House that my own choice for the new office was the chief electoral officer. It was evident that my suggestion met with general approval, and we agreed that he should be named in the bill to set up the office.

The basic principle of the proposed redistribution was to be representation by population, but the government felt there should be sufficient tolerance to permit a slight bias in favour of rural constituencies. Some consideration should also be given to historical or geographical factors. The representation of the two territories, despite their small population, would be preserved. The senatorial floor, which provided that there must be as many members of the House as there were senators from a province, would also be preserved.

I stressed the importance of fair representation in Parliament as a safeguard of peaceful change of government in Canada, as opposed to shooting the head of government in order to get change, as happened in so many countries. No member in his or her heart, of no matter what party, I was convinced, thought we should try to win elections by rigging the machinery. I believed that we all felt it our duty to make sure the people had a chance to register their opinions, fairly and honestly, by their votes.

In conclusion I repeated words spoken on the same subject by Diefenbaker on 9 April 1962: 'We want to follow the lead which has been taken by almost every nation — certainly by the Commonwealth nations as well as by the Mother of Parliaments — that membership shall be determined fairly by the people.'

Diefenbaker was obviously flattered by being quoted. All members present appeared to approve the tone and substance of my speech, though subsequent Opposition speakers expressed some suspicion of the sincerity of my high-minded approach. Diefenbaker said he had never heard me spreading the charm as I had done that day. He added that it aroused his fears, in direct proportion, as to the probable contents of the bill. His tone was friendly, but he expressed skepticism about the need for 10 commissions and made a plea that smaller population be permitted in widespread rural constituencies than in urban constituencies. He was also concerned about how the commisioners would be appointed. I gave a categorical assurance that the cabinet would have no part in their appointment, and that the method of appointment would be prescrbed by Parliament.

All the speeches were nonpartisan that day and the next. Douglas Fisher, who had been absent the first day, made an impressive speech about constituencies such as his own, with huge areas and small populations. Earlier in the session (12 October) I had spoken on a private member's bill on redistribution and had said that I regarded Fisher as a grassroots egghead. This time we got into a minor dispute about the lack of broadcast coverage in sparsely populated areas. At one point I said Fisher had done what no other member had done, got under my skin. Fisher retorted that on his return to the House he had talked with a gentleman who had observed the proceedings the previous day, and had asked him, 'Did you smell the incense burning, the perfume, and as you came to your seat did you hear the sweet tinkling of bells?' The gentleman had described the day before as 'one of the sweetest, stickiest and stinkiest days he had ever seen in the House of Commons.' Fisher said that that observer had gathered that partisanship had just disappeared and pleasantries reigned.

I did my best to continue the pleasantries and on the whole succeeded. But the resolution did not pass the first day, as several members wanted to get on the record, none of them in opposition to it.

I decided that if the session was to end before Christmas, there was no chance of getting the bill to set up the 10 commissions passed. Pearson accordingly said, on 6 December, that the government would like to have the bill to appoint the representation commissioner adopted but was willing to hold the other redistribution bill over until the session of 1964. The bill establishing the Office of Representation Commissioner and naming Castonguay to the office was passed, and first reading was given to the other bill, to establish the 10 commissions, so that it would be available for study. Given that Parliament had been almost paralyzed until late October, that progress in a substantial reform gave me great satisfaction.

Castonguay's estimate of the time required to get in place the machinery for redistribution by nonpartisan agencies was not exaggerated. The election of 1965 was held before there could be a redistribution based on the 1961 census, and membership in the House was based therefore on the 1951 census. The results in 1965 left little doubt that membership based on the 1961 census would have given the Liberal party a clear majority. I did not stay in Parliament long enough to see the great reform in operation, but I have been gratified to observe how well it has worked.

The end of my house leadership

The session proceeded with more than usual harmony and dispatch. In December the government resolved to devote whatever time was necessary to securing the passage of the estimates of expenditure and money voted for 1963-64. We did not want to run the risk of having to spend money Parliament had not voted, as Diefenbaker had repeatedly done. That objective was achieved by the time the session was ended, on 21 December.

Except for two or three measures the government had postponed because the cabinet was not ready to proceed with them, every priority item on Pearson's list of business had been adopted. None had failed to pass because of weakness of parliamentary management. In addition, all but one or two of the less urgent measures before Parliament had been adopted.

On the last day of the session the House adopted, without debate, a measure to increase the membership of the Exchequer Court by one judge who was to serve as the commissioner to preside over hearings in the Senate committee on petitions for divorce. Arnold Peters, who with Frank Howard had been obstructing those bills for years as a way to get a more judicial system in place, expressed pleasure that the new method of dealing with divorce petitions had reached a satisfactory state and congratulated the government on its efforts. I expressed my appreciation of the help Gordon Churchill, as spokesman for the Opposition, had given in disposing of the divorce issue, which had worried the House for a long time. Tommy Douglas described it as a red-letter day in the history of the Canadian Parliament.

When all the other business had been concluded, I took the unprecedented step of having the item for written questions called, so that all available answers could be given. At the beginning of the session I had stressed to my colleagues the importance of answering written questions promptly. Ministers generally had cooperated. A record number of questions was answered, in most cases speedily.

I had found the house leadership strenuous and exacting. During the whole of the session I had rarely left the chamber. I learned a great deal about the virtues of patience and conciliation. I was able to ensure the passage of most of the government's business without too much obstruction and generally avoided long debates on procedure. I took a great deal of satisfaction in the fact that a motion to extend the hours of sitting had been made only once during the session. Many extensions were achieved by interparty discussions held outside the House or by unanimous concessions actually made in the House to extend the time to complete specific measures. Extensions of time were almost always necessary to complete the work of a parliamentary session, but securing them was often time-consuming and contentious.

Going through Hansard more than 20 years later, I found only one occasion in the session of 1963 on which I lost my composure. On 13 December, I got into a slanging match with Tommy Douglas over a trivial dispute about a CBC news broadcast. The exchange quickly concluded when Churchill said that the secretary of state was wasting the time of the House. I never complained about the length of debates or accused the Opposition or their party spokesmen of obstruction, and I praised them for cooperation whenever it was forthcoming, which it often was, especially late in the session.

On the whole I think the Opposition was better satisfied with my house leadership than our Liberal backbenchers were. Many of them were in Parliament for the first time and were naturally eager to build a reputation for taking part in debates. In order to get business completed I restrained the backbenchers as much as possible, and some of them, I am sure, found the discipline frustrating.

But we had been successful in getting much more government business through the House than I had dared to count on. The attitude of Opposition spokesmen on the last day of the session was gratifying, particularly the tribute from Douglas. He said it had been a remarkable session, which began in uncertain circumstances and could easily have been unproductive. He thought history might show it had been remarkably productive even though no party had a clear majority. He said, 'This has been due to the fine cooperation which has existed in all parts of the House and to the diplomacy and patience of the Secretary of State who has been the leader of the House for the government, and to our patience in putting up with him.' George Nowlan for the official Opposition was a little more restrained. He said that we had started in a rough Parliament in the spring, but that he doubted whether any Parliament had worked better than that one since our return from the summer recess. I was deeply gratified to have the session end so harmoniously.

After such praise from the Opposition I assumed that Pearson was also satisfied with my leadership. At the beginning of 1964, I was surprised when he asked me to become minister of transport, and added that I could not administer that heavy department and remain as house leader. He agreed that I should continue to be responsible for the thankless task of redistribution, which I was anxious to see through to the end.

I was never able to decide whether Pearson felt I was really needed in Transport, or whether he had yielded to pressure from our caucus to have the house leadership changed. I hesitated to ask him. We discussed who should succeed me as leader, and I recommended Favreau strongly. I pointed out that he had been assiduous in his attendance, had developed a feel for procedure and had very good relations with the party spokesmen on the Opposition side. I offered to act as his substitute and assistant whenever required. Pearson agreed, as did Favreau. Favreau and I had been seatmates, and we exchanged seats so that Favreau would be seated next to Pearson.

It was widely asserted later that the additional burden of the house leadership was too great for Favreau and contributed to his difficulties in the 1964 session. I disagree; Favreau's problems did not arise because of any difficulty relating to his leadership of the House, nor did the burden of leading the House leave him too little time to perform his duties as minister of justice, in which office he had succeeded Chevrier when Chevrier was appointed high commissioner in London on 1 January 1964. In my opinion, Favreau was the victim of his failure to appreciate the seamy side of politcal controversy and the capacity of a man such as Erik Nielsen to turn a trivial matter into an apparent scandal.

I was sorry to see Chevrier go. Friends for many years, we had been close comrades-in-arms in Opposition. His long experience, practical judgement and conciliatory manner were precious assets in cabinet and Parliament. His departure weakened the government, especially in the House, where he was a star performer.

Ministerial duties

Though the leadership of the House took most of my time and thought, I tried in 1963 not to neglect my duties as minister of a government department and several agencies. In the three weeks between the formation of the Pearson government and the meeting of Parliament on 16 May, I had an opportunity to become acquainted or reacquainted with the senior officers of the department and the other agencies for which I had to answer in Parliament. My deputy, the undersecretary of state, Jean Miquelon, had been appointed by Diefenbaker. He belonged to a prominent family in the Union Nationale, but I never had any evidence that he was not completely loyal to me. As I planned no changes in the structure of the department and no legislation within its scope, our relations were largely formal, and our contacts infrequent.

Guy Roberge, the head of the National Film Board, a friend of long standing who had been appointed by St Laurent, and with whom I had worked during my years in government until 1957, had my complete confidence. I had no plans for changes in Film Board policy.

My association with Kaye Lamb, the head of the Public Archives and the National Library, had been that of a close friend from the time of his appointment to the Archives by Mackenzie King. Again, I had no thought of any changes in policy, though I hoped to further his efforts to get new and more suitable quarters.

The National Gallery was another matter. During the years in Opposition I had maintained a close relationship with Mrs H.A. Dyde, a friend of long standing, and with the distinguished painter Lawren Harris, both of whom had been appointed to the board of trustees on my recommendation. The trustees, I knew, were almost in revolt, and the staff morale was very low. While we were in Opposition, I had been distressed by the resignations of Percy Fell as chairman of the board and of Alan Jarvis as director. I was resolved to find a replacement for Thomas Maher, who had succeeded Fell, not because he was a Tory worker in Quebec City but because, according to reports that reached me, he took no initiative in promoting the interests of the gallery or even in understanding what those interests were. A suitable replacement had to be found; politically it was desirable that the new chairman be a French Canadian.

Donald Buchanan recommended Jean Raymond, who had been associated with him on the Council on Industrial Design. I knew Raymond slightly and felt he was in every way suitable. He was reluctant to take on the post, but once he was convinced his appointment would be welcomed by most of the other trustees and by the artistic community, he was persuaded to accept. I then went to Quebec City to see Maher, and told him the government wished to replace him as chairman but would be quite happy to have him remain a member of the board. He was naturally resentful and finally decided to resign both as chairman and as trustee. I had no thought of trying to replace Charles Comfort, who had succeeded Alan Jarvis as director. I respected Comfort as an artist and believed he would cooperate willingly with Raymond. I had the full support of Pearson in the reorganization, and the effect on morale was gratifying.

Broadcasting took up very little time in Parliament in 1963, but it occupied a good deal of my own time and thought. I had to deal with broadcasting in the House on 31 May, when Robert Thompson objected to programs by Max Ferguson and others on the CBC. He asked what action I was taking or contemplating to ensure that the CBC did not carry programs obviously harmful to the security and well-being of the nation. I replied that I was sure Thompson and every other member would agree that nothing would be more undesirable than to have the government, or any member of the government, seek to direct broadcasting, the press or any other medium of public opinion. No member of the government intended to attempt such direction. The CBC was reponsible not to the government but to the whole Parliament. The method of assuring that responsibility to Parliament would always be difficult. The best way it could be done, in my view, was to appoint the ablest people to the board of directors and the ablest person to direct the CBC, and to leave matters of broadcasting policy up to the president and the senior personnel while holding them accountable in a parliamentary committee. The CBC, I was sure, would take account of criticism from the public and any member of the House, even a member of the government.

Members of the government, I felt, should not be deprived of their rights as citizens to express their opinions, but the CBC should pay no greater attention to views expressed by ministers than to the views of any other citizen. I was glad to repeat, in office, my total opposition to direction or control of broadcasting by government.

In Opposition I had charged that the replacement of Alphonse Ouimet as chairman of the board of the CBC while Ouimet remained president was against the law; the Broadcasting Act specified that the president also be chairman. I lost no time in getting a legal opinion from the Department of Justice and tabling the opinion in the House. The opinion confirmed my judgement, and Pearson willingly restored Ouimet's position as chairman. Ouimet's authority had been deliberately degraded by Diefenbaker. Ouimet's salary, moreover, had not been increased along with the salaries of others in comparable positions. Pearson agreed readily to end the discrimination.

One decision made by the CBC early in my term as secretary of state had political repercussions. The CBC had two radio stations in Toronto, both broadcasting in English. Ouimet informed me unofficially that the board had decided to convert the outlet with a very small audience into a French station. I offered no objection. There was a loud outcry in letters to the press and, what was worse, from Liberal members from Toronto. More than one member of the Liberal caucus claimed that I was ensuring their defeat in the next election. Since the station's audience was so small, I was reasonably certain that at least 90 per cent of the complaints were inspired by CBC employees, their families and friends. I predicted that as soon as the employees were provided for, the agitation would cease, and it did. On that, as on other occasions, I told the caucus that the test of political durability was a capacity to distinguish between a stiff breeze and a hurricane. I disclaimed any responsibility for the decision of the CBC but said I agreed with it. In Parliament, Fisher asked me whether I had any explanation for the action. I replied that I had received no communication from the CBC on the subject and could provide no enlightenment not already provided by the press. An NDP member asked me whether there had been any pressure from the government to have the change made. My answer was a categorical no. It was, I understood, CBC policy to see that there was radio broadcasting, either private or public, for any significant minority, either English- or French-speaking, in any part of the country. I would be sorry, I said, to see English-language radio broadcasting jeopardized in the City of Quebec and felt that the considerable French-speaking minority in southern Ontario was deserving of similar consideration.

One innovative step I took about broadcasting was to ask the chairman of the Board of Broadcast Governors, the president of the CBC and the president of the Canadian Association of Broadcasters to join in a formal group to advise the government on broadcasting policy. In areas where those three could reach a consensus, I felt, the government would be spared thought and action, and in areas where they differed, if the differences were sharply defined, it would be much easier for the government to make decisions. The group was at once christened The Troika by the media.

All three members of the Troika — Ouimet, Andrew Stewart, the chairman of the BBG, and Don Jamieson, the president of the Canadian Association of Broadcasters — were well known to me. The president of the Association of French Broadcasters, David Gourd, was an old friend who was knowledgeable and wise in his advice to me. But I ceased to be secretary of state before there was time to make changes of policy.

In 1963 I had to deal with the question of whether or not there should be a CBC station in St John's. On 5 April, only three days before the election, the BBG had approved in principle an application from the CBC for a licence. A number of conditions had been attached to the approval, and they had to be met before a formal recommendation was to be made to the government. It was no secret that I had argued in Opposition that alternative TV stations should not be established in any areas until nation-wide service was achieved from single stations The Diefenbaker government had abandoned that policy. Private stations had already been established in Toronto and one or two other places where the CBC had stations. In Edmonton the CBC had been licensed to serve a city already served by a private station. I reluctantly conceded that the pressure for a CBC station in St John's to provide an alternative to the privately owned station could no longer be resisted. Before the new Parliament met in May 1963, I had assured Ouimet that I would support the financing of CBC-TV in Newfoundland but hoped he would insist on extending service through the whole island of Newfoundland from existing facilities in St John's before the CBC embarked on new and expensive construction. I had also told Andrew Stewart of the BBG that I would neither oppose nor delay the carrying out of the decision to approve a CBC licence in St John's whenever it was formally recommended.

After Parliament met, Douglas Fisher, no doubt suspecting that I might try to frustrate the establishment of the St John's station, asked a question of the prime minister about the delay in proceeding with a TV station already approved by the BBG. Pearson replied that he would look into the matter and take it up with the secretary of state. Fisher then asked whether Pearson realized that he had put the question to the prime minister because it was felt the secretary of state had a conflict of interest in the matter. Pearson ignored that observation. The next day I arranged to have Joseph O'Keefe, the MP for St John's East, ask me what was holding up approval of the CBC-TV station in St John's. In view of the uncalled-for reflection on me by Fisher, I said, I welcomed the opportunity to put the record straight. The BBG, I explained, had attached conditions to its approval. The conditions had not yet been met, and therefore no recommendation was before the government. Until the BBG made a recommendation, the government had no legal authority to issue a licence. I was relieved when the licence was issued, on 30 September, just before Parliament resumed its sitting after the summer recess.

In a statement in Newfoundland at the end of August I had said that television service in the rest of Newfoundland was just as desirable as alternate service in St John's. I intended to do whatever I could to see it provided as soon as possible. It was no less important, I said, to give radio broadcasting service to the important and growing communities of Labrador City and Wabush and to tie in that service with broadcasting service in Newfoundland, so that the people of western Labrador would have a constant reminder that they were part of Newfoundland.

If I had remained the minister dealing with broadcasting, the extension of service to the whole province would, I believe, have preceded the erection of new broadcast facilities in St John's. But soon after I ceased to be directly involved, the building in St John's was started, and several years passed before coverage was extended to the whole province.

The establishment of alternate television in Newfoundland made it impossible to resist it elsewhere, once a second licence was applied for, and the BBG decided the market in any place was great enough to sustain two stations. It followed logically that a private network would be necessary to provide programs for the private stations that had previously depended on CBC programs. There was a real danger that a private network would be totally dominated by a Toronto station. That I did not want, and I made the suggestion that the principle of equalization be applied by giving one vote, and one only, to each station belonging to the network. That formula was adopted after I ceased to be the minister reporting for broadcasting.

Fisher introduced a private member's bill designed to ensure the control and regulation of cable distribution of television, which proposal gave me an opportunity to set out my views on broadcasting policy generally. In my speech I recalled that, from the 1920s, when radio broadcasting began, successive governments had been concerned to ensure there would be Canadian radio broadcasting. Because Canada had only one-tenth of the population of the United States, Parliament had repeatedly legislated to that end. The government did not want to see any development, if Parliament could prevent it, that would indirectly undermine the national system of broadcasting. We believed that national control of broadcasting was needed to preserve Canada's existence as a separate country.

The influence of television, I believed, would be far more pervasive than that of radio. Community antenna systems might provide television service in areas, such as parts of Fisher's constituency and mine, which were so remote and sparsely populated that broadcasting from established stations could not reach them; that would be all to the good. But the establishment in large urban centres of community antenna systems linked by cable to broadcasting stations in the United States might circumvent the national broadcasting policy established by Parliament. That threat was under consideration by the minister of transport and by me. If there was to be any effective control of those systems, some amendment of the law would be needed, but we had not yet worked out the kind of amendment we felt would be effective. The policy of the government was to do everything we could to have broadcasting remain, to the greatest degree Parliament could make it, Canadian.

I was sorry to give up being the spokesman in Parliament for broadcasting when I became minister of transport. But I was satisfied that the leadership of the House had not prevented me from discharging my duties as a minister. I had not neglected any parliamentary duties imposed by my ministerial responsibilities.

European interlude

I was very tired when the session ended in December 1963. When Pearson asked me to give up the house leadership and become minister of transport at the beginning of February, there was nothing urgent to keep me in Ottawa in January, and I welcomed the idea of a change of scene for Margaret and me.

Jules Léger had been the ambassador in Italy for almost two years and had suggested more than once that we visit Rome while he was still there. He agreed to have us as guests for a week.

When I told Pearson we were going to Rome he asked me to see the Pope to extend an invitation to him to visit Canada. Jules had no difficulty arranging a private audience for Margaret and me. First I was ushered into his presence alone and greeted warmly. I reminded the Pope that I had met him at a luncheon at the apostolic delegate's house in Ottawa, where I had accompanied Prime Minister St Laurent. He recalled St Laurent clearly but did not pretend he remembered me. His manner was simple, almost diffident. He spoke English with hesitation, and I suggested that we both speak French. That did not work well, and we quickly relapsed into English. The Pope was obviously pleased by the invitation to visit Canada but spoke of the problems of travel. I left with the impression that there would not be a visit while Paul VI was pope. When our conversation was over, Margaret was ushered in to receive a papal blessing, and the three of us were photographed together.

The highlight of our stay in Italy was a visit to Pompeii, at the foot of Mount Vesuvius, and the most astonishing incident was encountering Gordon Mifflin, of Catalina, Newfoundland, and the manager of the Newfoundland Associated Fish Exporters Association, in a hotel in Naples. The Mifflins were one of the leading fish merchants on the northeast coast, lifelong friends of Charlie Granger, and a family we had visited from time to time. Altogether the visit to Italy was a sheer joy, among the happiest holidays Margaret and I ever had.

External Affairs had been in touch with the Ambassador Jean Bruchési to facilitate our visit to Spain, and he had gone overboard. It was emphasized that our visit was unofficial, but he insisted that we be his guests at the embassy. He had heard rumours from Ottawa that I was to become minister of transport and had encouraged the Spanish Department of Transport to put a car with a driver and a guide at our disposal for a tour of the south of Spain with hotel accommodation arranged. I insisted that we pay for our hotel rooms and our meals, but in every other way we were guests of the Spanish government.

That European interlude was exactly what we both needed, as we faced strenuous times ahead.

12   Minister of Transport

Transition to Transport

Adapting to a new role in government

From the day I entered the Prime Minister's Office until I became minister of transport 26 years later, my attention had ranged over the whole field of government. Taking on the responsibility for a great department of state, required a change of focus. Partly from habit, I remained something of a busybody in areas beyond the broad limits of the department. And I had actual responsibilities beyond it. I had to continue to pilot through Parliament the legislation to establish the new method of redistribution, hold ministerial responsibility for the Atlantic Development Board and assist Guy Favreau as leader in the House.

In the Department of Transport I had to cope with a series of difficult local problems in urgent need of attention, and also do a great deal of homework on two country-wide policies for the regulation, where necessary, of both air and rail transport. The government had promised new policies in both fields. I needed almost elementary education in the economics of transport and was resolved not to be pushed to set deadlines, by either colleagues or Opposition. Until I was sure in my own mind that I had them right, I was not prepared to embark on new initiatives.

In meeting my responsibilities I was very well served. The deputy minister was John R. Baldwin, whom I had first met in Paris in 1937, and with whom I had worked, as head of the Prime Minister's Office, while he was assistant secretary to the cabinet. John was no hidebound bureaucrat but an innovative and creative reformer with his feet solidly on the ground. Working with him was a partnership of the closest kind. The assistant deputy, George Scott, I had never met, but I soon learned how knowledgeable he was about every corner of the department, and how wise. Baldwin had gradually accumulated a great deal of talent in the department. He had no reluctance, as some deputies had, to bring other officials with him for discussion of problems and to encourage them to speak their minds.

My staff from the Office of Secretary of State was still intact. Alistair Fraser soon found, in the department, a knowledgeable and highly efficient official, Harris Arbique, to assemble information and draft correspondence relating to transport questions. Arbique was to work with me until I retired from the public service in 1972. I owe him a great deal as an official and a friend.

I was responsible to Parliament for the St Lawrence Seaway Authority and the National Harbours Board. Both were crown corporations; neither was part of the Department of Transport. They reported direct to me, as did Canadian National and Trans-Canada Airlines, though the railway and the airline also maintained a close liaison with the deputy minister.

Two specific problems I started to deal with right after I became minister. One, respecting the TransCanada maintenance base in Winnipeg, was a delicate and lengthy process; the other, requiring a decision whether there should be federal approval for the construction of a provincial bridge across the St Lawrence near Trois-Rivières, was settled easily.

The Air Canada base in Winnipeg

Trans-Canada Airlines (later Air Canada) was established as a subsidiary of CN. The first president, H.J. Symington, maintained his office in Montreal; he was also legal counsel for CN, and from his modest headquarters he handled the financial, legal, medical and purchasing functions of the airline. As its name implied, TCA was originally a transcontinental operation; its traffic headquarters was in Winnipeg, where Gordon McGregor was general traffic manager. In early 1948 McGregor became president of the airline, and in 1949 he succeeded in having the headquarters of the whole operation moved to Montreal. In his book *The Adolescence of an Airline*, McGregor says the logic of the move 'was irrefutable, particularly with the rapid development of Atlantic and Caribbean services having Montreal as their base.' He acknowledges that the decision was unpopular in Manitoba, and efforts were made to block the move by political intervention. He accuses me of going beyond the prime minister's back and letting it be known 'that the move must not be allowed to take place, because it would be bad for Liberal interests in the west.'

I have not the slightest recollection of making any such statement, and I cannot remember knowing anything in 1949 or until 1963 about the details of the move from Winnipeg to Montreal. McGregor's conviction that I had tried to stop the move from Winnipeg may help to explain the tension in our relations after I became minister of transport.

In a parliamentary committee in 1949 McGregor reported that there were some hard feelings locally about the move from Winnipeg, but he told the committee that although it was expedient to move some administrative people east, he could not foresee the transfer of massive units such as 'the main overhaul base' away from Winnipeg. But by 1963, TCA had constructed a new maintenance and overhaul base at Dorval, and there was growing fear in Winnipeg that the maintenance base there would be closed. McGregor described the political agitation over the closing of the Winnipeg maintenance base as the most controversial issue in the history of the airline. Within two months of becoming minister I was plunged into the controversy, with almost no background.

The substitution of larger aircraft was bound eventually to result in an early phase-out of the British-built Viscount

Turboprops, which continued to be maintained and overhauled in Winnipeg. In 1962 McGregor told the parliamentary committee that the Viscount fleet would be reduced rapidly as early as 1966. According to McGregor that statement stirred up tremendous agitation in Winnipeg and became an issue in the 1963 election, 'with both parties implying intervention if elected.' Nor did the agitation diminish after the election. There was unfortunately a failure of communication between TCA and the Prime Minister's Office, and Pearson was unaware of McGregor's forecast. He told the House on 22 November 1963 that 'for at least as far ahead as planning now extends, that is at least ten years, the Winnipeg facilities will continue to be used.'

The government of Manitoba became involved, and on 17 December the prime minister received a delegation from Manitoba, headed by Premier Duff Roblin and including most of the MPs from Manitoba, seeking assurances that the base would continue in operation. In reply to questions in the House later that day, Pearson said he had told the meeting that it was the policy of the government to do everything possible to maintain employment at the TCA base in Winnipeg, and if possible to increase it. On the second day of the session of 1964, 19 February, Pearson said, in reply to a question, that the assurances he had given had been reconfirmed since then in a telegram to the premier of Manitoba.

It was my task to reconcile the irreconcileable. I wrote a memorandum for my own guidance on 18 February: 'It is absolutely essential to the government and, in my opinion, very important to T.C.A as well, that the poisoned atmosphere in Winnipeg should be cleared up. It will never be cleared up on the basis that the maintenance base will be continued in operation until 1973, because it is perfectly obvious that, unless some new dynamic element is introduced into the picture, the operations at the base will steadily diminish, unless the government is prepared to state that idle men should be kept on the payroll at approximately the same numbers employed in November, 1963, when the assurance was given.'

The government had already committed itself to make public a report by the consultants Dixon-Speas, which justified the Dorval base and recommended the closing of the Winnipeg base. The report was to be tabled in Parliament and made available to the premier of Manitoba as soon as certain confidential business information was removed. In my memorandum I stated that the publication of the Dixon-Speas report would arouse another outcry in Winnipeg but that that could not be avoided and might provide a way out of the difficulty. 'In the present political atmosphere in Winnipeg nobody will believe the Dixon-Speas report, which is a report to T.C.A. and not the government. Unless the government has its own inquiry, the Manitoba Government will certainly seek to have a provincial investigation which would create impossible political difficulties.' I wrote that I thought the government should consider the appointment of an eminent businessman from Winnipeg to look at the situation and give an answer to the following questions before we approved the expansion of the base at Dorval:

1 What would be the cost and the advantages of adapting the facilities at Winnipeg for the overhaul and maintenance of the DC-9 without excluding the possibility of some maintenance also being done at Dorval by adaptation and no expansion there?

2 What would be the real additional cost, if any, of doing all the maintenance of the DC-9 in Winnipeg?

3 What additional capacity would have to be provided at Dorval for all the maintenance to be done there?

Every encouragement, I said, should be given to the Bristol company (a Winnipeg firm also engaged in aircraft maintenance) 'to make a proposition to take over the base on terms which would fully guarantee the carrying out of the Prime Minister's assurance of employment there. I do not believe this can be done unless they are guaranteed all the maintenance by T.C.A. and (the department) of Viscounts, and they can also be given an opportunity at least to compete for the business of maintaining the D.C. 9's. It is very important that the proposition should come from

Bristol, and not from us, and that the government should, at first, be very coy about its reception.' The DC-9s were jet planes, of about the same passenger capacity, which were replacing the Viscounts and were to be maintained at the Dorval base. To attempt to solve a political problem in Winnipeg, and just transfer the problem to Montreal, we had to be sure that DC-9 maintenance could be done in Winnipeg without substantial additional cost.

The Dixon-Speas report was available at the beginning of March. I sent a copy to Premier Roblin and tabled it in Parliament. Roblin was in Ottawa on 17 March and put three questions to the prime minister. Pearson put his reply in a press release on 20 March that gave me a mandate to deal with the problem. In reply to the third question Pearson said: 'I entirely agree that it is desirable to have a clear review of the problem. It should be a constructive review directed especially to future development. The federal government will be happy to have the co-operation of the government of Manitoba in carrying out this study, and the Minister of Transport will shortly be discussing with you specific proposals as to how it should be made.'

Gurney Evans, the Manitoba minister of industry and commerce, was the minister with whom I dealt. We had been contemporaries at the University of Manitoba and we trusted each other. After much negotiation, often by telephone, we approved the appointment of D.A. Thompson, QC, as a commissioner to examine the future of the Winnipeg base and related matters and the terms of reference. Both Evans and Roblin accepted that TCA could not continue to use the base effectively once the Viscount fleet was phased out, and that the commissioner should look farther afield. We also agreed that Arthur V. Mauro, the transportation counsel for the Manitoba government, should have a status with the commission that would assure him access to all information. During the setting up of the commission I developed a high regard for Premier Roblin and a confidential relationship based on mutual trust that exists to this day.

Thompson was appointed a conmissioner on 11 June 1964, and the government was given a breathing spell until his report was received and tabled in the House on 19 May 1966. But my warning about trying to solve a problem in Winnipeg and thereby creating one in Montreal proved justified. No notice was taken of the Thompson Commission in Quebec from the time the commission was announced until January 1965, when it was realized that keeping the base in Winnipeg in operation might slow down development at Dorval.

Thompson received several demands for hearings in Montreal, to which he agreed immediately. The Québec government also began to criticize the appointment of a Manitoban as sole commissioner in a matter that affected Québec as much as it did Manitoba. When Premier Lesage himself intervened with a letter to the prime minister, Pearson agreed to have Gordon Robertson, the secretary to the cabinet and Lesage's former deputy minister in Ottawa, intervene by telephone to explain the background to the premier. The intervention was successful. Lesage insisted that he must table his letter to Pearson in the legislature. Robertson discussed the matter with me and reported to Lesage that I felt the best course, if Premier Lesage felt he had to table the letter, might be for him to go ahead without waiting for any reply from the prime minister. We felt that the prime minister could not say anything that would helpfully meet the points Lesage had made, and that there seemed no advantage, therefore, in having a reply to table at the same time. Lesage agreed. That ended the agitation in Québec.

The sequel in Manitoba was an anticlimax. Thompson's report was tabled in Parliament and made public on 19 May 1966. He had warned me that there would be disappointment in Manitoba. I was deeply impressed by the report's factual and fair assessment of the problem and of what might be done to maintain Winnipeg as an important centre of air transport. On the day itself I sent Thompson a telegram informing him that his report would be tabled in the House of Commons that afternoon. I expressed to him my own deep appreciation and the government's for his having undertaken a delicate and difficult assignment. My feeling was that he had set out the whole situation in such a fashion that it would be hard for any reasonable person to disagree in any substantial way.

In the next six months there were numerous discussions between officials of our government and the Manitoba government and several between the premier and me. In a letter of 3 November, Roblin summarized the conclusion we had reached. In my reply I concurred in the summary and, in response to suggestions McGregor had made, added that I had made it clear in our discussions that that statement of broad objectives should not be construed as an indication that the federal government had any intention of issuing directions to the airline, now Air Canada, in areas customarily left to company management.

The Air Canada Winnipeg base was my first difficult problem as minister of transport. It was handled in a way that saved the reputation of the prime minister, preserved the policy of noninterference with the management of the publicly-owned airline and diffused a wave of public indignation in Winnipeg and Manitoba without stirring up a similar indignation in Québec. I was satisfied that I had found my way safely through a political mine field for the governement. What I could not do was end the rivalry between Winnipeg and Montreal, which had begun when McGregor moved from Winnipeg to Montreal in 1949. It continues today in the grievance over the 1986 award of the contract to a Montreal over a Winnipeg firm for the maintenance of the F-18 military aircraft, which later participated in the War in the Persian Gulf.

The St Lawrence Bridge at Trois-Rivières

The government of Québec was in the early stages of constructing a high-level bridge across the St Lawrence River just above Trois-Rivières when I became minister. My predecessor had been told by officials that the bridge would affect navigation in the river in a way that could be corrected only at a cost of millions of dollars. He had been advised not to give federal approval to its construction. The question was still open, and I feared a nasty federal-provincial dispute.

The advice of the officials was not, I believed, sound, but as a layman I was unwilling to disregard the advice of engineers. The only course I could think of was to get an independent opinion, and I suggested the name of an eminent engineer named Lea, who was retained.

After consultation by telephone with the minister of highways of Québec I asked the provincial government in writing to delay letting the contract for construction until our engineer had made his report. The minister agreed. On 19 March in response to a question in the House from a Liberal member, which I had suggested to him, I reported that, just before coming into the House, I had been able to inform the premier of Québec that Mr Lea, the engineer, had made an oral report the previous day; he had indicated that although some difficulties might be encountered as a result of construction, there seemed no adequate reason why the bridge should not be proceeded with.

Under the law no obstruction can be placed in navigable waters without the approval of the government of Canada, but as recent experience in Saskatchewan and Alberta has shown, enforcement of the law against a provincial agency can be acrimonious and litigious. In the case of the bridge at Trois-Rivières, confrontation had been avoided, the bridge was constructed and it has not interfered with navigation.

Later on, while I was still minister, another case arose involving priority for navigation. The city of Montreal had applied for approval of a proposed high-level bridge over the Lachine Canal. Instead of automatically approving a structure running into a cost of several millions, I asked whether there had been any navigation in the Lachine Canal since the St Lawrence Seaway had been opened. I was told that one company in the Lower St Lawrence was shipping its cargo into the lower section of the canal. I asked whether that firm could not abandon the canal for a site in the harbour itself. A site was easily found that suited the shipper, the Lachine Canal was then closed to navigation and the city was given permission to build a bridge at street level at a saving of some millions to the Montreal taxpayers.

The proposed railway in the Gaspé region

In the first question period of the 1964 session I was asked what reasons had led the cabinet to cancel the construction of the proposed railway from Matane to Ste-Anne-des-Monts on the south shore of the St Lawrence. I replied that it was a large question difficult to answer in question period.

A month later I told the House that there was not yet a final decision not to build the railway, which, on the initiative of the previous administration, Parliament had authorized the government to build and CN to operate. The government, I said, felt that the transportation needs and economic interests of the northern part of the Gaspé region could be better served by spending the money on other modes of transportation. I was discussing with the Québec minister of highways a substantial federal contribution to speed up the completion of a modern heavy-duty highway between Matane and Ste-Anne. I added that the government was also considering improvements to harbours and air facilities to serve the region.

Diefenbaker asked whether the government had authority to repeal a statute without an act being passed by Parliament. He wanted to know my views, because I was quite a constitutional expert. I replied that, not being a lawyer, I was not as competent as he to answer the question. I reminded him that he was asking me for a legal opinion, which it was contrary to the rules for a minister to give to the House. Diefenbaker countered that it was an affront to Parliament for a minister to say the government did not intend to follow a statute passed by Parliament.

Later another Tory member asked me to assure the people of Gaspé that the railway that Parliament had approved would be built. He reminded me that authority in the act of Parliament would expire on 31 December. The Tory government, I pointed out, had taken no action to start the railway. When we came into office and examined the project, we found no sound economic justification for the railway. What was needed was improvement in other modes of transportation. Parliament, I explained, did not order the government to build the railway; it gave the governor in council permission to approve its construction. Before we spent $16 million of the taxpayers' money, we felt we should be satisfied that it was being spent to the best possible advantage. There was a great need for the improvement of a local highway, which project did not have as high a priority in the provincial highway program as many others. I said that a federal contribution to speed up the reconstruction of the highway would be far more advantageous to the Gaspé region than a railway. We also intended to recommend to the House that some of the estimated cost of the railway be spent on the improvement of airfields and harbours that would speed up the development of the area.

The next day a Tory member from Ontario asked me on what ground a contribution to the Gaspé highway was justified. No contribution had yet been made, I replied, but I was discussing with the Québec minister of highways a possible contribution and how it would be made. Before a contribution could be made, we would have to come to Parliament and ask for the money.

In a debate on 5 August the subject was raised again by Douglas Fisher. He had been the only member who voted against the bill to authorize the railway. He commended the government for dropping the project but asked under what policy the government was contributing to the Gaspé highway. My reply was that Parliament had decided that $16 million might be spent on improving transportation in the Gaspé area. When we came into office and examined the information available to us, we concluded that the $16 million could be better applied in improvements other than building a railway. For that reason — we did not do anything unilateral — we had made an agreement with the government of Québec to spend $13 million on the highway. We had been told that the government of Québec, which had a timetable for its highways all over the province, could not get at the Gaspé highway project for a number of years, and that it would be greatly speeded up by our contribution. If there were railways that were performing a function rather inefficiently and costing the treasury much money, there would, I hoped, not be too much objection to our closing a railway line and putting something else in its place. It seemed to me that efficiency rather than glamour was the sensible standard, and I hoped to be able to use that standard in dealing with other transportation problems.

We were, I believed, doing something useful instead of something ineffective for a relatively poor area. Our action over the Gaspé railway accurately reflected my general attitude to transport.

The Canadian Coast Guard College

On 5 May 1964 I announced in Parliament that the government had decided to establish a training college for officers for the Canadian coast guard on a site at the Point Edward naval base at Sydney, Nova Scotia, where surplus property had become available. The coast guard had been expanding steadily and was having difficulty finding skilled seamen as officers. In view of the critical shortage anticipated in a few years, the government intended to establish the college as quickly as possible, once Parliamentary approval was received. Actual training, it was expected, would begin sometime in 1965. The first step would be to find a suitable director and to recruit staff.

The idea had come from Captain Eric Brand, himself a graduate of the leading training school in England for officers of the merchant navy, a veteran of the Royal Navy and a long-time official in Canada of the Departments of National Defence and Transport. I had known Captain Brand as a neighbour in Rockcliffe for several years, was aware of his splendid service in war and peace and was impressed by his presentation of the need for a training college.

My announcement was well received by spokesmen for each of the parties in the House, no doubt in part because I had stated that the Marine School at Rimouski, Québec, the new College of Fisheries and Navigation at St John's, Newfoundland and other local institutions that could meet the standards and syllabus requirements of the coast guard would be used to provide basic training in navigation for cadets. Duplication would thereby be prevented.

I lost no time in putting Captain Brand in charge of the planning, and he performed with skill and efficiency. His appointment was questioned in the House on 28 October by the MP for Cape Breton South, Donald MacInnis, who made harassing me a nearly full-time occupation and relished it. He asked whether it was necessary to reach into the ranks of the retired to find an administrator for the college. I replied that no appointment had been made because the college had not yet been established, but that what I had done was to approve a suggestion that, in the planning stage, advantage should be taken of Brand's undoubted abilities and great experience, and that he had been the main initiator of the idea. MacInnis brought the matter up again the next day at a time when I was not in the House, and cited a press release from the Department of Transport, which said that I had announced that Captain Eric Brand, the former director of marine operations in Transport, had been appointed planning officer of the Canadian Coast Guard College. He claimed that there was a complete contradiction between my statement of the previous day and my press release. George McIlraith replied on my behalf that no administrator had been appointed, and that Captain Brand was a planning officer. As the former minister he gave the highest praise to Brand's capacity for the task.

The Canadian Coast Guard College was duly established, and it is a source of pride to me that I had the responsibility for its founding.

In April 1965 the naval base at Point Edward, where the Coast Guard College was located, was transferred to the Department of Transport. The base had space available for other developments. Part of the space was later occupied by Canadian Motor Industries Limited, a Canadian firm created to assemble Japanese Toyota motorcars in Canada. A question had been raised about the use of the word 'Canadian' in the name of the company, and an appeal was made by the promoters to the secretary of state at a moment when I happened to be acting secretary. Since 'Canadian' was not used by any other motorcar manufacturer, I saw no reason why they should not use it. I persuaded the promoters to locate their plant at Point Edward, where it assembled Toyotas for some time. Like some other efforts to attract industry to the Atlantic region, it did not last beyond my time in the government, to my regret.

Averting a work stoppage on Canadian National

As long as coal-fired locomotives were used by the railways, the engines had to be refuelled approximately every 125 miles. The refuelling stops were called divisional points. The use of diesel locomotives substantially increased the distance trains could operate before refuelling and other maintenace were re-quired, and the number of divisional points, needed therefore decreased. CN was about to phase out divisional points, begin-ning with Nakina in northern Ontario and Wainwright, Alberta, on 24 October 1964. There was no great concern at Wainwright, but railway employment was the lifeblood of Nakina, where there was no industry in the town and no agriculture in the area. Eliminating a divisional point was called making a run-through.

I was absent from the House on 22 and 23 October, when the government was urged to direct CN to delay the start of run-throughs. The first request was made by Diefenbaker. Nakina was in Fisher's riding, and he pursued the matter the next day, when the request for a delay could be debated at length. McIlraith, who was acting minister of transport, manfully defended the railway and the measures it was proposing to assist the employees, who would become unemployed. The whole of government time that day was taken up with the subject of run-throughs, and it was apparent that there was great uneasiness in many divisional points throughout the CN system.

I read Hansard at home on Saturday, 24 October, and was worried there might be a work stoppage. A strike was not called by the union, but on Saturday at Nakina, Wainwright and several other places the workers were all sick and did not turn up for work.

On Sunday morning I received a telephone call from Fisher while I was still in bed. My recollection of what happened is that Fisher told me we were going to have the railway tied up. When I asked him what we could do about it, since we could not take over the direction of CN, Fisher suggested an official inquiry by a commission and asserted that if one was appointed the men would go back to work.

After considering the situation I thought I could see a possible way out of a work stoppage. I called the prime minister at 9 a.m. and told him of Fisher's call. If the government appointed a commission of inquiry, I said, Donald Gordon, the head of CN, would resign. But it might be possible to get Donald to recommend that the government appoint a commission. I asked Pearson if I should try, and he agreed.

I telephoned Gordon at about 10 and told him Mike and I were wondering if a work stoppage could be averted if he would send a telegram either to me or, preferably, to the prime minister asking the government to appoint an inquiry. Somewhat belligerently he retorted, 'Do you mean to tell me the government has decided to appoint a royal commission?' I replied that that was the last thing the government would do on its own initiative; it would be interference with the management of the railway. What I was suggesting was a request from the head of the railway to the government for help in solving a problem. After a considerable pause Donald said that he was about to go to church; I recommended that he pray about my suggestion and call me back in the afternoon.

The telephone rang at about 3; it was the prime minister, asking if I had word from Gordon and wondering if I should call him again. My response was that Donald was having a struggle with himself, and that we should wait patiently. At about 4 Donald called to say that he had drafted a telegram to the prime minister and wanted to read it to me. I was relieved, and I was satisfied with its wording but knew I should not make a snap decision. I asked him to read it again, he did so, and after a short pause I said it could not be put better.

The result of the day's doings was reported to the House on Monday afternoon. The president and the prime minister had had an exchange of telegrams. Gordon's telegram stated that if the government was willing to appoint an independent and impartial person to examine the CNR's run-through proposals, the company would not proceed further with its plans until a report arising from such examination could be made. The prime minister's telegram accepted Gordon's suggestion and indicated that the government would appoint such a person to make the desired examinations.

By Tuesday the railway's sick men had all recovered their health, and trains were running again. A week later it was announced that the Honourable Mr Justice Samuel Freedman of Winnipeg would be appointed to conduct the investigation. A year later his report was issued, and railway labour relations had passed another milestone.

Parliament and Government 1964-65

When the second session of Parliament began in 1964, my first duty in the House was to assist Guy Favreau as house leader and to act for him whenever he was absent. That was no great task, though whenever possible I tried to be at his side as he had been by mine in 1963. Our mutual understanding grew stronger, as did my admiration for his character. A friend and long-time associate of Guy's once said that he was a saint. I have known no one in my life with a more completely honest mind. His one weakness, if weakness it is, was that he found it hard to believe others were capable of malice, mischief and evil.

On one of the occasions when both the prime minister and Paul Martin were absent, and I was acting prime minister, Diefenbaker asked me if the announcement by the minister of justice the previous night that he was being relieved as house leader, or wanted to be relieved, had any foundation in fact. I replied that I had seen the television program on which the question was based. The minister of justice, I said, had been asked whether it was possible for him to carry on for any length of time with the multifarious duties he had undertaken; he indicated, as I listened to it, that he was considering asking the prime minister if he might, at a convenient time, be relieved of the position of house leader. That question, I added, was one between the minister of justice and the prime minister about which I could not presume to give an answer.

The next day, when Pearson was back in the House, he was asked whether he had received a request from Favreau to be relieved of his duties as house leader. Pearson replied no and added that they had discussed the matter. He knew, he said, how heavy Favreau's duties were, and how well he was performing all of them, and hoped he would continue. I do not believe that Favreau felt the house leadership a burden at that time. He carried on with no criticism through the first filibuster over the flag.

At the end of October the prime minister told the House that Favreau had asked to be relieved of the house leadership, Pearson had agreed, and asked the president of the Privy Council, George McIlraith, to become house leader for the rest of the session. As McIlraith had been in the house far longer than I, it was the end of my responsibility to assist the house leader.

Favreau had thus fortunately given up the house leadership before his ordeal began. On 23 November, Tommy Douglas asked Favreau a question about two men, Lucien Rivard and another, who were being detained in jail pending a decision on an application for their extradition to United States on a drug smuggling charge. Douglas asked whether any complaints had come to Favreau that persons in high places in Ottawa had sought to bring pressure on the lawyer acting for the United States not to oppose a request by those men for bail. Favreau said he would give an answer later in the day, when the estimates of the Department of Justice came before the House. Erik Nielsen demanded a full explanation at that time. I had heard nothing about a possible scandal, but I was sufficiently alerted by Douglas's question and Nielsen's interest to decide not to accompany Margaret to Québec, where she was to christen a fishing vessel that day. I stayed in the House in my seat at Favreau's side, followed the proceedings closely and intervened briefly two or three times.

In his statement Favreau indicated that the counsel for the United States government, whose name he did not wish to disclose since the police file was still open, had informed the RCMP that he had been under pressure from an official or officials of the government. The commissioner of the RCMP had informed the minister of the allegations, and Favreau had ordered an immediate investigation. When the commissioner reported on the investigation of the officials in question, neither he nor Favreau believed there was sufficient evidence to lay a charge with any prospect of securing a conviction in the courts. If additional evidence was uncovered to convince the police and Favreau himself that there would be a chance of conviction, action would be taken.

Nielsen interrupted to ask whether the report of the investigation had been referred to the law officers of the Crown, and Favreau replied that it was not the practice of the RCMP or the minister to refer such matters to the law officers of the Crown unless the RCMP asked the minister to do so, or the minister felt he needed an opinion. There had been no referral. Douglas was not satisfied and asked Favreau whether any consideration had been given to a judicial inquiry. Favreau said that he and the commissioner were so convinced that there was no possibility of a successful charge being laid that he had not given consideration to such an inquiry, but he opened the possibility that a situation might develop in which an inquiry by a high court judge might be desirable. Nielsen then proceeded to disclose information he claimed to have that Raymond Denis, while in the office of the Minister of Citizenship and Immigration, had offered a bribe of $20,000 to the counsel for the United States not to oppose the granting of bail to Rivard, and that Guy Lord, an executive assistant to the Minister of Justice, had made approaches to the counsel, though there was no suggestion of bribery in his case.

Nielsen's allegations changed the whole atmosphere in the House and created the impression that the government was trying to cover up a scandal, whereas Hansard shows that Favreau was merely trying to avoid sullying the reputations of two former public servants who, because of lack of evidence, had not been charged with wrongdoing. The debate became increasingly heated. The prime minister, who was not in the House, telephoned me at dinner time for a report. I told him a bad impression was being created. I did not tell him how much I regretted that Favreau had told me nothing about the matter in advance. I believed then, and believe still, that I could have helped him draft a statement so forthcoming as to avoid the appearance that information had to be dragged out of him; the whole affair would have ceased to be a sensation after a day or two. Instead a matter in which no member of the government was accused of wrongdoing was exploited to undermine Favreau's career and impair his health.

In the evening the debate was diverted to other questions, including a rehash of the Hal Banks affair. Favreau had no opportunity to answer a question by Douglas as to whether any other person was referred to in the RCMP report of the investigation, except the two already mentioned, Denis and Lord.

The next day, 24 November, when the sitting opened, Guy Rouleau, the parliamentary secretary to the prime minister, rose on a question of privilege to announce that he had already made a voluntary statement to the RCMP that he had made representations about Rivard. He affirmed that he did not exercise or attempt to exercise any undue influence. Meanwhile he had asked the prime minister to relieve him of his duties as parliamentary secretary. Douglas then asked if there was any other person associated with government referred to in the RCMP report, and Favreau replied no one other than Rouleau. Favreau then announced that there would be a judicial inquiry, as recommended by Douglas.

The only significant point that developed out of further questioning was that Rouleau had not informed the prime minister of his intervention until that day. The point led to a question for Pearson by Douglas Harkness, who asked, 'Was he informed by the Minister of Justice in regard to any of the other circumstances of this case prior to those circumstances being brought to the attention of this house yesterday?' To which Pearson replied: 'I was informed by the Minister of Justice of some of the circumstances shortly before his Estimates came before the House. He told me this matter would be before the House during the consideration of his Estimates. He told me the facts of the matter.' That statement was incorrect and was to haunt Pearson and gravely embarrasss Favreau.

The prime minister left the next day for a visit to Manitoba, which had been arranged and advertised some time earlier. That day Paul Martin, as acting prime minister, tabled a copy of the order-in-council appointing Chief Justice Frédéric Dorion of the Supreme Court of Québec to make the inquiry. In the order the name Leo, previously used in the House as Rivard's, was changed to Lucien, the correct name. Douglas claimed that the terms of reference of the commission were inadequate, and asked for an urgent debate. To meet this demand, debate on the estimates of the Department of Justice was proceeded with at once. Nielsen was the first speaker on the estimates; his speech was punctuated by alleged points of order and questions of privilege. There were repeated veiled allusions to other scandals the government was trying to hide, and Nielsen objected to the absence of the prime minister when a question of such seriousness was being discussed. One member interjected that the prime minister was 'campaigning.' Pearson was greatly disturbed by the press reports of proceedings and asked his colleagues to consider whether he should suspend his program and return to Ottawa. After careful deliberation we advised him not to return, as we felt his return would magnify the situation and contribute in no way to quieting the agitation by the Opposition.

The following day, 26 November, Diefenbaker spoke for most of the afternoon; he hinted at many kinds of wrongdoing and deception by the government but made no specific charges. There were repeated suggestions, mainly from NDP members, that the terms of reference of the commissioner be broadened. At the opening of the House the next day Paul Martin announced that the terms had been amended to include a specific reference to the manner in which the RCMP and the minister of justice had dealt with the allegations when they were brought to their attention. That amendment satisfied all Opposition parties except the official Opposition and saved the government from possible defeat on a nonconfidence motion. The debate was much less rough that day, and Nielsen's motion to reduce the estimates of the Department of Justice was defeated 111 to 30.

The next sitting day was Monday, 30 November, and that day the report of the select committee appointed to recommend a design for the Canadian flag came up for debate. Debates on reports of committees have precedence over all other business, day after day, until they are completed or adjourned. That procedural rule created a situation about the Rivard question that was embarrassing for Favreau and for the prime minister.

The embarrassment is recounted precisely as I recollect it in Tom Kent's *A Public Purpose*; having no record of my own, I will paraphrase his. After telling Parliament that he had first heard of the Rivard affair from Favreau the day before Favreau's estimates came up in November, Pearson had left for the West. The following day Favreau had told his colleagues that he had informed Pearson of the bribery charge on the plane returning from Charlottetown on 2 September and had undertaken to report further when the police investigation was completed. Because Pearson was absent during the debate on the Rivard matter, there was no chance for him to make a correction of the date on which he said he had learned about the bribery charge. For that reason Favreau had been unable to reply to repeated charges that he was so eager to conceal the facts that he had not even told the prime minister about the charges.

The prime minister returned to Ottawa on Sunday, 29 November. Kent and Gordon Robertson reported to him at the prime minister's residence, and I also went there, on my own. All three of us urged Pearson to lose no time in apologizing for misleading the House and in correcting the error. We were all convinced that he had really forgotten what Favreau had told him on 2 September. Pearson appeared to agree with us, that he should make the correction at once. I expected him to do so when the House met on Monday and was bitterly disappointed when he did not rise at once on a question of privilege, which the Speaker would certainly have allowed. His excuse was that the motion to approve the report of the flag committee had precedence over other proceedings. That remained the excuse day after day, though each day would make it more difficult to explain why the correction had been delayed.

Pearson never did make the correction in the House, but on 14 December the day before the Dorion Commission was to open its hearings, he took the unprecedented course of writing to Dorion to inform him of the conversation with Favreau on 2 September and to say he had forgotten about it. Dorion made the letter public on 16 December. The following day Harkness raised a question of personal privilege that the prime minister had misled him and the House. Harkness criticized Pearson's delay in correcting his statement. Pearson's reply to Harkness was involved, tortured and unconvincing. Harkness pointed out that the prime minister had not explained his delay and asked the Speaker to consider whether the matter should go to the Committee on Privileges and Elections. Douglas then made a motion to have the matter referred to the committee. The Speaker ruled that there was no question of privilege, and his ruling was appealed and upheld 122 to 109, with the Social Credit MPs of Thompson's group voting with the government.

Kent judges that as the lowest point in Pearson's career. It was certainly the lowest period in my relations with Pearson. One day Margaret remarked that I had lost confidence in the prime minister and should consider resigning. I had considered that possibility earlier, about a situation relating to the flag, but I could not see what purpose would be served by such a protest. I certainly did not want to do anything to help the Opposition defeat the government and give Diefenbaker a chance to get back into office. I realized that Pearson was the best prime minister available and I continued to serve him loyally.

The Rivard affair had injured Favreau cruelly, but the subject remained quiescent until Rivard escaped from the Bordeaux jail, the provincial institution where he was being held pending the extradition hearing. On 4 March 1965 Diefenbaker demanded an urgent debate on the great alarm in all parts of Canada resulting from the slack or careless administration of justice and law enforcement. Diefenbaker knew perfectly well that the escape of a prisoner from a provincial jail did not come within the jurisdiction of Parliament, but he succeeded in creating the impression that the federal government shared the blame for the escape.

Nothing else relating to the bribery charge developed while the government awaited the report of Chief Justice Dorion, which was delivered on 28 June. The report imputed no wrongdoing to Favreau but was critical of his failure to consult the law officers of his department before deciding there was insufficient evidence to justify a charge against Denis and of Favreau's handling of the whole situation.

On his own initiative Favreau talked to me the next morning; he made it clear that he would not continue as minister of justice and must resign immediately. I did not argue with him. He felt that Dorion's criticism of his judgement in failing to consult his senior advisers would destroy his usefulness as minister of justice. I agreed with his view that it would be intolerable for him personally to endure the abuse he would suffer if he remained minister of justice. I predicted that the prime minister would have no option but to accept his resignation, but would urge him strongly to remain in the cabinet and accept another portfolio. He was reluctant to consider that possibility, but I appealed to him not to exclude it. He was, I argued, essential to the government as the recognized French-speaking minister and the leading spokesman for Québec. He agreed to listen to his colleagues and the prime minister when the cabinet met that morning.

The rest of the story is according to Pearson's statement to the House: 'The Minister of Justice this morning submitted his resignation to me. After discussing the matter with him, I have no course but to advise His Excellency to accept it. I do so with very deep regret. My hon. friend remains a man and a Minister of unimpeachable integrity and unsullied honour. He is a devoted and unselfish servant of Canada and of his own province. He entered political life only because he was persuaded — and I had something to do with the persuasion — that he could make a contribution to his country's unity and welfare. I have therefore asked him to continue by considering the acceptance of another post in the administration which would be offered to him. He has written me on this point as follows. I conclude by reading his letter.

' "My dear Prime Minister. Since our talk this morning when my offer of resignation was discussed, I have given very serious consideration to your request, supported by our colleagues, that I continue in the government.

' "As I have already stated to you, it is my view that the conclusions of the report as far as I am concerned, are tantamount to no more than a statement on the part of the Commissioner that, had he been in my place, he would have exercised his discretion in a different fashion.

' "I wish to repeat that my resignation was tendered, not out of a feeling that I had done anything wrong, but because of the feeling that my usefulness as Minister of Justice had been impaired by the situation which had developed.

' "I need not say how deeply moved I am at the confidence which you, Mr. Prime Minister, and my colleagues have shown in me in suggesting that I carry on.

' "Therefore, while I must insist that my resignation be accepted as Minister of Justice, I would be willing to continue to serve in some other capacity.

' "May I take this occasion to say how very grateful I am for your kindness and consideration and for your unfailing support during difficult and, at times, even cruel days. Guy Favreau." '

I am sure Pearson accepted no other resignation with greater reluctance or more distress. For me, it was one of the saddest days of my public life.

All the spokesmen for the Opposition, including Nielsen, commended Favreau for doing the right thing in resigning and praised his probity. But their speeches left no doubt that their tone would have been very different had Favreau not resigned. None of them suggested that there was any impropriety in Favreau's remaining in the cabinet.

Though the rest of his time in Parliament was inevitably an anticlimax, Favreau remained active in debate and did not hesitate to seek re-election in 1965, when he received an overwhelming majority in his riding. He continued as the leader in the government for Québec and had a large share in persuading Jean

Marchand, Pierre Trudeau and Gérard Pelletier to enter public life in 1965. Favreau remained in the House until 3 April 1967, when his health having deteriorated, he resigned from the cabinet and Parliament. He was appointed to the Superior Court of Quebec the following day. His service as a judge was brief. His health continued to worsen, and he died during the summer.

When Parliament resumed its session on 25 September 1967 after a summer recess, Pearson paid tribute to his former colleague. He called Favreau as fine and great-hearted a man, as unselfish and sincere a patriot, as he had ever known in his public life, a man with no trace of meanness or pettiness, a big man in every sense of the word. Warm tributes were paid by spokesmen for the other parties. My own relationship to Guy Favreau was close, and I shall cherish his memory for the rest of my life.

Other alleged scandals followed the Rivard affair and poisoned the atmosphere of Parliament for the rest of my years in public life. None of them affected me in the direct way the agony of Guy Favreau did. My main memory of the scandal-mongering is that it went a long way to diminish the atmosphere of the House and contributed to my decision to leave Parliament and the government in 1967.

The flag

I knew that Pearson had resolved sooner or later to ask Parliament to approve a Canadian flag that did not include the Union Jack or the symbol of any other country, but the flag was not mentioned in the Speech from the Throne. Pearson did not consult the cabinet before his speech at the annual meeting of the Canadian Legion on 17 May 1964. From that day the flag dominated the session of Parliament; until 17 December it was the only item of business on every sitting day.

I watched the report of the Legion speech on television in Bruce Hutchison's company in Victoria. We both deplored that the campaign had been initiated before what was bound to be a hostile audience, with the certainty of bitter confrontation. We feared the flag proposal might defeat the minority government. I was worried about the reaction in Newfoundland and strongly supported Pearson's proposal that whenever Parliament was asked to approve a new flag, the Union Jack should be recognized officially as the symbol of Canada's place in the Commonwealth.

Despite the outcry, the prime minister gave notice on 28 May of a motion asking Parliamentary approval for a distinctive Canadian flag, which also provided that the Union Jack continue to be flown as a symbol of Canadian membership in the Commonwealth and allegiance to the Crown.

There had been rumours that a motion was coming, and they resulted in a misunderstanding in Newfoundland. On 27 May, I was in Montreal. When I returned by train in the late afternoon, Charlie Granger met me at the station. He told me that Premier Smallwood, unable to reach me, had informed him of a report that the government had decided that a new flag was to be substituted for the Red Ensign and that no further official recognition was to be given to the Red Ensign or the Union Jack. He told Charlie that the next day he proposed to introduce a motion in the legislature, to be seconded by the leader of the Opposition, protesting in the most emphatic manner.

Charlie had informed Pearson of the call, and Pearson had asked him to have me get in touch with Smallwood. As soon as I got home, I called Smallwood, who embarked upon a violent tirade about some things being more sacred than friendship or party allegiance. I listened patiently until he ran out of steam. I then told him that if the legislature passed such a resolution, I would resign from the cabinet at once, as my usefulness to Newfoundland would be at an end, but would stay in Parliament and support Pearson. I left no doubt that I meant it, and my statement brought him up short. I then explained that he was misinformed and told him that Pearson's proposed resolution, to be introduced the next day, would give official recognition to the Union Jack. He said he would need some reassurance. I told him to give me 10 minutes to draft a statement; if he approved my draft, I would ask the prime minister to put it in a telegram to him as Premier.

My draft began, 'You have asked for an explanation of the course which will be followed if the flag motion is adopted.' I then cited the words in Pearson's motion and concluded thus: 'We have not yet decided whether there should be a Royal Proclamation to establish the national flag and a separate proclamation to recognize the Union Jack as the symbol of Canada's membership in the Commonwealth of Nations and our allegiance to the Crown, but there is no question of our intention to recommend that both be proclaimed by the Queen.'

When I called Smallwood back, he said that would be satisfactory. I then telephoned the prime minister, reported what had happened and read my draft; he sent the telegram at once after making one or two insignificant changes of words. That was the end of the problem with Smallwood but not the end of my involvement with the flag.

The next evening, 28 May, I left by air for London for a brief holiday with Margaret and Jane, who were to stay on to tour Ireland for a couple of weeks. I had told Pearson about our plans some time earlier, and he had suggested that I might see the Queen to give her a copy of the design of the proposed flag. The high commissioner's office had arranged an audience at Buckingham Palace. I was taken into the same room where I had seen the Queen in 1956 to give an account of the movement to Canada of the Hungarian refugees. I explained the way the government and Parliament were dealing with the flag, of which she had already been informed briefly by cable. I then showed her, and left with her, the design of the flag Pearson favoured. The only comment the Queen made was that she was pleased the design included the colour blue.

On Tuesday, 2 June, I flew home. I could not have anticipated what would happen in Parliament that same day. At the opening of the sitting Diefenbaker had asked the prime minister to tell the House under what circumstances the minister of transport had an audience with the Queen. Pearson replied that I was in England on a private visit and, as is quite normal for ministers of the Crown, had asked for and been granted an audience with the Queen. He added that I had informed Her Majesty of the terms of the resolution about the flag, of which the Palace had been advised by cable. Diefenbaker next asked whether the prime minister had told the Premier of Newfoundland that the minister of transport was going to London to consult with the Queen about the flag resolution. Pearson replied no. Diefenbaker then asked the prime minister to table correspondence between himself and the premier and, in particular, the telegram dated 27 May. He directed Pearson's attention to a press report in the *St John's Evening Telegram* of 29 May in which the premier was reported to have said in a speech the previous evening that the Newfoundland representative in the federal cabinet was in London to see the Queen on the flag issue, and that Smallwood had said he was informed of that by Mr Pearson. Pearson replied that I did not go to London to see the Queen on that or any other matter; I was in London and asked for an audience to inform the Queen of the terms of the resolution on the order paper of the House. Surely, he added, that is a normal and courteous procedure to adopt.

Diefenbaker was not satisfied, and wanted to know what Smallwood had been told that Parliament had not been told of. Another Tory member then asked why the minister of transport went to Great Britain, and why he had an audience with the Queen. Pearson replied that he did not know why I had gone on a private visit, and he added that when I spoke to him about my proposed visit, he had suggested that if I wished to have an audience with the Queen on this matter, it would be quite proper to do so. Caouette later asked Pearson if he had sent me to London after consulting the premier of Newfoundland. Pearson replied that the premier had nothing to do with the royal audience, nor had he made any effort to have anything to do with it. A Tory member then asked whether I had gone to London at government expense or my own, and Pearson said he would find out. Diefenbaker returned to the fray, to ask whether the prime minister would table his telegram of 27 May and other correspondence. Pearson said he would ask about Smallwood's telegram and would be glad to table his own telegram to Smallwood. The next question was whether I had travelled on a commercial flight or a government plane. Pearson replied that I would be in the House the next day, 3 June, and would answer. Diefenbaker interjected, 'A man on a mission.' Later Pearson evidently received a note from his office: he told the House he had just been informed that I had gone to England on a Trans-Canada Airlines commercial flight, accompanied by my wife and daughter, and that I was returning alone that day. He added that I had bought my own tickets, and that the visit had been arranged long before the question of the audience with the Queen had arisen.

The next day Pearson informed the House that on my return I had told him that I had bought tickets for my wife and daughter, but that like all my predecessors as minister of transport, I was provided with transportation by TCA and had used the transportation so provided. He added that because my visit was a personal one, I had submitted no account to the Treasury for any expenses incurred. I had asked Pearson to make that explanation to ensure that the record was straight and avoid any suggestion that he had misled the House.

That day Pearson tabled his telegram to Smallwood of 27 May. Diefenbaker asked whether he would table communications from Smallwood. Pearson replied that a request had been made by telephone, and that that was the only correspondence dealing with the matter. There had in fact been no telegram from Smallwood about the resolution on the flag, but Pearson did not report that Smallwood had written to him on 11 May suggesting that Canada should have two flags, a distinctive Canadian flag and the Union Jack or the Red Ensign to symbolize membership in the Commonwealth and allegiance to the Crown. Pearson had not replied until 25 May. In his letter he had explained the manner of recognizing the Union Jack. If Pearson had replied promptly to Smallwood's letter of 11 May he would have received the reply before the misunderstanding arose. Smallwood would not have protested, I would not have threatened to resign, and Pearson would not have needed to send the explanatory telegram. A tempest in a teapot would have been avoided.

The debate on the flag resolution actually began on 15 June, was interrupted on 17 June, resumed on 30 June, was adjourned on 3 July, resumed on 12 August and continued off and on for the rest of August and from 1 to 10 September, when the prime minister announced that a special committee would be appointed to consider the design of the flag.

In a speech on 1 September, Diefenbaker asserted that the prime minister had not made clear before the elections of 1962 or 1963 what he meant by a distinctive flag. I was acting prime minister that day, and I felt that Diefenbaker's statement should be corrected at once. I pointed out that on the program called 'The Nation's Business' on 21 January 1960 Pearson had said, 'We must agree on a distinctive national flag which cannot be mistaken for the emblem of any other country and which is accepted as such by the Canadian people.' Pearson had been asked for a clarification of that statement, and on 27 January 1960 he had issued a statement from the Office of the Leader of the Opposition. I quoted the whole statement, but it can be summarized in this passage: 'Whatever action parliament might take in regard to a Canadian flag, I believe that the Union Jack should be accepted by Canada as an emblem to be flown on all occasions which are concerned with our commonwealth association and our status as a monarchy with the Queen as the head of the commonwealth.' That position, I said, was accepted by the Liberal party, was the position we took in the election of 1962, was in our literature then and was repeated in our literature in 1963, from which I quoted: 'Within two years of taking office a new Liberal government will submit to Parliament a design for a flag which cannot be mistaken for the emblem of any other country. When adopted this will be the flag of Canada. The union jack will be flown on appropriate occasions as a symbol of our membership in the commonwealth.' I went on later to say I would tell the leader of the Opposition 'why there is unity in the Liberal party on this question. It is because we did what has been done time and again in the history of this country. It was done at Charlottetown, Québec and at the Westminster Palace Hotel and was embodied in the British North America Act. We agreed on a compromise that was set out in the program that we honestly and straightforwardly put forward to the Canadian people in two elections. We said we wanted a

Canadian flag that was Canadian, and we wanted to fly the Union Jack or a flag containing the union jack, to symbolize our association with the Commonwealth and our monarchical character and devotion to the Crown. I said that position was honourable, it was loyal and, above all, Canadian.'

Rereading it more than a quarter of a century later, I feel it was one of the best debating speeches I made in Parliament. I had had no intention of speaking until Diefenbaker made the statement that Pearson had not made the Liberal position clear before the elections of 1962 and 1963, and that consequently the government had no mandate to propose a distinctive Canadian flag.

The flag committee, whose final report recommended the design adopted for the flag, did not report until the end of November. On 9 December, Leon Balcer recommended to the prime minister that closure be used to end the debate. Churchill said Balcer was not speaking for his party, but the cabinet decided to follow Balcer's advice. McIlraith, as house leader, announced on 11 December that closure would be invoked the next sitting day, which was 14 December. The flag was approved by a vote of 163 to 78. All but one or two members who voted against the flag were Tories, and the only Tories who voted for the flag were French-Canadian MPs. The report on the Union Jack was approved, without closure, by a vote of 185 to 25. Diefenbaker was absent for the vote. The design of the Canadian flag adopted was not the design I had shown the Queen but the flag that flies today as the emblem of Canada. It was raised officially on 15 February 1965.

Redistribution

I felt I had made a good start on the legislation for the new system of redistribution at the close of the 1963 session. The House had given first reading to the Bill, so its contents would be public, and Parliament had created the office of representation commissioner and, in the act itself, appointed Nelson Castonguay as the first commissioner. I had the bright idea of forming a study group drawn from interested members of all five parties in the House.

The members of the group had no authority to commit their parties or even themselves. I reverted to my earlier academic manner and conducted the group like a university seminar. Castonguay was always present to assist. The result was that when the debate started on the new bill on 10 March, a number of members were familiar with its contents.

In the 1963 debate I had gained another asset: for once Diefenbaker was on my side. In my opening speech in 1964, I repeated my previous statement that the principle of having redistribution performed by independent commissions instead of by the House was the only point on which the government insisted. No question of confidence would arise on any other change, and, I myself had an open mind. Any proposal that the House convinced me would improve the legislation, I would support. Members of our party including ministers would be free to vote as their judgement dictated. Diefenbaker interrupted me to commend my attitude.

From the informal discussion I had learned which questions were likely to raise differences. The first was whether there should be one commission for the whole country or one for each province. The second was the composition of the commission or commissions and the method of appointing commissioners. The third was the extent to which constituencies might have a smaller or larger population than the average for their province. That was called tolerance and was expressed as a percentage above or below the average.

To my surprise Nielsen was the first speaker for the Tory opposition. He made a nasty, mean-spirited, partisan speech that obviously displeased many in his own party and everyone else in the House. Knowles then spoke in a high-minded fashion, as did most of the other speakers in the debate on second reading, during which it became clear that I had correctly diagnosed the points of difference.

In the debate on the individual clauses the provision for a commission for each province was adopted reasonably quickly. When the clause involving the composition of each commission and the method of choosing the commissioners was reached, the debate became contentious and at times heated. The bill provided for four members of each commission. The representation commissioner was to be a member of all 10 commissions. The chief justice of the province, or a judge of his court designated by him, was to preside, and the other two commissioners were to be appointed, one by the prime minister and one by the leader of the Opposition. Knowles objected that that method would involve at least the appearance of partisanship and be a reflection on the smaller parties. He proposed an amendment designating senior provincial officials as commissioners. I objected that Parliament did not have constitutional jurisdiction to compel provincial officials to serve. The wrangling went on for parts of five days, and the government decided to postpone the debate after 23 April. It was clear that the legislation would not be passed in time to apply to an election in 1965 or, probably, 1966 and there was no longer the same urgency.

The bill was called again for debate late in the day on 14 September. I proposed that the House postpone consideration of the contentious clause and several other clauses that might lead to lengthy discussion, and get on with the less contentious of the more than 30 clauses. That procedure was agreed to, but the debate did not continue because I fell ill.

My heart was out of rhythm, a condition caused by extreme fatigue, according to the series of doctors who examined me. I was put in hospital for a week and confined to the house for four more weeks. I used the telephone hardly at all until my heart began to beat regularly, after five days. Thereafter I received no incoming calls and was able to set my own priorities. Often during the five weeks that I was absent from Parliament I felt that I was accomplishing more by having control of my own time at home than I would by being at the office, where much of my time would be pre-empted by others. But I had begun to miss the House when I reappeared on 28 October, after being absent since 25 September.

My absence had been so prolonged that the prime minister had decided to ask Allan MacEachen to proceed with the Redistribution

Bill on 20 October. To my surprise, in that one day MacEachen was able to get all the clauses I had described as not contentious passed.

Included among them was a clause that I had feared might be opposed. I was determined that the commissions, not Parliament, should have the final word. In Britain, Parliament was able to amend the recommendations of its commission and occasionally had done so. I realized that the House should have some say before the final boundaries were drawn. A procedure was devised whereby a draft map of the revised constituencies from each provincial commission should be laid on the table of the House of Commons. If at least 10 members signed a request, each report could be debated but not voted on. Subsequently the report would be sent back to the commission with the record of the debate. The commission could then decide whether or not to make any changes. Whether the commission made any change or not, the boundaries would be established in a final report from which there was no appeal. To ensure that redistribution would be free of any partisan bias, I felt from the start, the final word should be left to each independent commission. I was relieved that the House had accepted that position.

The Bill was not called for debate again until 30 November. Debate began on the composition of the commissions. There was no objection to the chief justice of the province as chairman and the representation commissioner as a member, but differences continued over how the other two commissioners should be appointed. During my absence I had given careful thought to that question, and I finally decided to recommend that they be appointed by the Speaker of the House of Commons.

I had meanwhile had a private talk with the Tory whip to try to find out what that party really wanted. He could give me no advice but told me that Diefenbaker had authorized Eldon Woolliams to speak for the party. Woolliams was one of the most partisan and articulate Tory backbenchers, a lawyer who frequently took part in debates on legal questions. I saw him, and he spoke to me frankly. He assured me that the Tories would support my suggestion concerning the Speaker if I would agree that the tolerance be raised from 20 to 25 per cent. Remembering Diefenbaker's double-cross of his party on sessional indemnities, I asked him if his assurance could be counted on. Woolliams exclaimed, without mentioning Diefenbaker's name, 'You don't think the s.o.b. would double-cross me.' I decided to take the risk. The alliance with Woolliams lasted for two days of debate, and the bill emerged with the Speaker designated to appoint two commissioners in each province and a tolerance of 25 per cent above or below the average population of constituencies for the province. I was not concerned about the size of the tolerance as I was sure the independent commissioners would feel bound to stay as close to the average as possible.

When the bill received third reading on 16 November, I had the satisfaction of realizing that I had succeeded in getting Parliament to approve a great reform in the system of representative government. I had no other major legislation as a minister before Parliament until after the election of 1965.

Outside Parliament

From February 1964 to the beginning of April 1965 Parliament sat in every month except January 1965, in what was the longest session up until that time. The new session started two days after the 1964-65 session ended, and went until 30 June. Nevertheless I had time to travel a great deal, largely thanks to an official aircraft to which I had first claim as minister of transport. I made certain rules for the use of the aircraft by a minister: it was not to be used for trips to Montreal or Toronto except in a real emergency, and each time it was used the minister's own department had to absorb expenses the equivalent of the commercial fare and thereby somewhat reduce the cost to Transport. I used the plane frequently on weekends during the marathon sittings of the 1964-65 session and did not hesitate to use it for trips to Traytown. I found the plane a good place in which to catch up on office work. I gave a lift to an MP from the Atlantic region for whom it would speed up a visit. I liked, whenever possible, to have at least one Tory passenger as insurance against questions in Parliament.

In 1964 a number of airport terminal buildings were completed. Most of them I opened myself, and I was present at all the ceremonies. The first was Edmonton, a building of impressive design. But I was concerned to learn that it was 20 miles from the city centre, and that the existence of an airport in the very heart of Edmonton used by commuter flights between Edmonton and Calgary, would keep the use of the new airport well below capacity. Despite expert assurances that the city centre airport met safety standards I also had occasional nightmares about a crash. The biggest opening was of the new air terminal at Toronto on 28 February. The prime minister was to declare the building officially open, and I was to preside and introduce him, until I had a sudden inspiration. Red Kelly, one of the stars of professional hockey, was the Liberal MP for York West, where the airport was located, and I decided to ask him to introduce Pearson. Kelly's participation made the ceremony much more newsworthy. Premier Smallwood happened to be in Ottawa the day of the opening, and I asked him to fly down with Kelly and me. On the way Smallwood, who was even less knowledgeable about hockey than I, asked Red whether he was still playing hockey. Red told me afterwards that he had been tempted to ask Smallwood whether he was still premier of Newfoundland. The opening was a gala occasion, and the name Pearson was later given to the airport.

That summer there were openings at Sault Ste Marie, Victoria and Kamloops. The Victoria airport was so far from the city that I wondered how much it would be used, given that the ferry service to Vancouver was so attractive, and the overnight service a real time-saver. The Kamloops airport was named for Davie Fulton's brother, a wartime casualty of the RCAF. At every ceremony there was some kind of stunt; at Kamloops, for example, I performed on horseback, and luckily the horse was docile. In August, I also attended the opening ceremonies in Newfoundland of two causeways that connected New World Island with the island of Newfoundland.

There were only two terminals to open in 1965, at London and, on 14 May, at Fredericton, the first new airport for the Atlantic regional service. Two days later the site of a proposed civil air terminal at Goose Bay, Labrador, was examined and approved.

I had strong pressure from various groups in St Catharines , Ontario, to improve the airport there, and was able to have it done quickly. One day in September 1965, I flew from there to the Toronto Island airport in five minutes, thereby avoiding a 100-mile drive on a busy highway. I was also pressed by the city authorities and other groups in Hamilton to preserve an air training runway at Mount Hope, which I helped to turn into the Hamilton airport, of which use could be made as an alternate for Toronto for smaller planes.

Whenever I was in Vancouver I visited the site of the Vancouver terminal, on which the city was impatient to have construction speeded up. I spent two days in that city visiting, from the air and the ground, every transport facility — harbours, airport, roads and bridges and ferries to Vancouver Island. At the end of the visit I had a clear picture of the whole transportation pattern of Greater Vancouver. I did a similar tour of the Niagara Peninsula, with special attention to the Welland Canal; of the Saint John, New Brunswick, region and of Halifax-Dartmouth. All my life I have disliked dealing with plans or problems in places I have never seen. As minister of transport I felt a need to see what I had to deal with from the air and on the surface. By mid-1965 I had vastly expanded my visual knowledge of airport and harbour facilities and felt I could cope with the officials on nearly equal terms.

I had other occasions for travel, apart from official openings. In 1964, I addressed the Chamber of Commerce in Corner Brook, Newfoundland, and met with the town council in Stephenville. The visit made a good impression, as there was some feeling that the minister for Newfoundland was neglecting the west coast of the island. I was commodore of the annual regatta in Kelowna, BC, Premier W.A.C. Bennett's home town, to which the Liberal mayor had invited me in order to have a Liberal overshadow the premier for a day. In the parade I rode in the first car and Bennett in the second. Margaret and I were in Newfoundland for the visit of Princess Mary, the Princess Royal, for whom I was minister in attendance at her inspection of the Newfoundland regiment and at morning service in the Anglican cathedral; we dined on the royal yacht *Britannia* and were present at a ceremony at the university at which the princess and Pearson received honorary degrees. Whenever it was convenient, I took one of our children on my travels, to expose them to new places. With Alan I visited Hudson Bay, thereby fulfilling a childhood dream, and Churchill. Peter and I had a trip to Jamaica, on which we really became acquainted, and which began our family's connection with the West Indies. Later Margaret and I visited Freeport, Grand Bahama, with the Tolmies, and Montego Bay, Jamaica. After we returned I suggested to Gordon McGregor that TCA examine the possibility of direct service to Freeport; after investigation by their traffic experts, the airline began to serve Grand Bahama.

I had transport business in both Paris and London. I took Alan with me to Paris on 15 April, where Jules Léger had just become ambassador to France, and George Ignatieff was ambassador to NATO, where the headquarters still was. Alan and I were provided with splendid accommodation by both families. We also visited the de Frances in Picardy. It was Alan's first visit to Europe. I saw the French minister of transport to explore the possibility of securing landing rights for Air Canada in Guadeloupe and Martinique and was given some encouragement, but years passed before that objective was realized. On my last evening in Paris, François de Laboulaye joined Jules and me at the embassy after dinner; he was just back from Moscow. François and I had become friends when he was in a junior position at the French embassy in Ottawa, and it was a pleasure to renew our friendship. Later he became ambassador to the United States; he is the ablest French diplomat I have known. From 22 to 26 April, I was in London, staying with the Chevriers. The day I was to leave London I had an appointment with Roy Jenkins, then minister of transport, which delayed me until after Air Canada had departed. There was a seat on BOAC, where my seatmate turned out to be

Max Aitken, Lord Beaverbrook's son. We had a pleasant conversation, and I formed a much better impression of him than I had done of his father. I was in Paris again from 17 to 21 June for the annual air show. That time I took Ruth, for her first visit to Europe.

I had an unusual experience in mid-June. The closest village to the hamlet where I was born was called Langton; it had become a centre of tobacco farming in Ontario. The local priest had decided that Langton had been named for Stephen Langton, the archbishop of Canterbury who led the barons in forcing King John to sign Magna Carta in 1215. He organized a celebration of the 750th anniversary to which he invited the premier of Ontario, John Robarts. The Liberal MP for Norfolk, J.M. Roxburgh, said he would not let the Tories take over my birthplace and had me invited as a second guest of honour. Robarts and I headed the processsion. I told him that my father, a Tory, had been a member of the township council in Langton at the time I was born in nearby Wyecombe. It gave me a feeling of pride to look at the township records and several documents my father signed. To get to Langton I had flown to Brantford airport, where I was picked up by a cousin, Hazen Pickersgill, and his son, Donald, neither of whom I had met before. I persuaded them to divert a mile or two off the main road to visit graves in the cemetery at Bookton, the place where our Pickersgill family had first settled in Canada. They were impressed by my knowledge of the family background.

We had some time in Traytown that summer. While we were in Newfoundland, Parliament was dissolved and an election called for 8 November. We had arranged to have Paul de France's daughter, Agnès, come to live with us to learn English. Agnès arrived on 20 October while I was campaigning in Newfoundland, and I was not able to welcome her until the weekend. She lived as a member of the family during a troubled six months for Margaret, who had to undergo two big operations on 20 November. Fortunately Margaret had recovered sufficiently for us to arrange a Caribbean visit to St Martin, Saba, Antigua and Barbados in December.

One day the Air Canada manager in Barbados took us to call on the prime minister, Erroll Barrow, whom I had already met in

Ottawa, and who had made a lasting impression on me. At Barrow's house we met Kenneth R. Patrick, already heavily involved in business and politics in the West Indies. Both Barrow and Patrick were to have a large part in my life for the next few years, as was the Caribbean.

The election of 1965

High expectations

The 1965 session of Parliament had been adjourned on 30 June to meet again on 27 September. The record of legislative achievements in 1964 and 1965 was impressive. The new flag, the new system of redistribution by independent commissions, the integration of the armed forces, the Canada Pension Plan, the provision for the reduction of eligibility for universal old age pensions year by year to age 65 and other improvements in welfare, a new labour code, better provisions for farm credit and a beginning of crop insurance, the 12-mile fishing zone in coastal waters, the auto pact with the United States, the Columbia River Treaty and peacekeeping in Cyprus were the highlights of under three years of Pearson government. But records rarely win elections.

The standing of the government in the Gallup poll had risen in 1965. Walter Gordon and those advising him, including Keith Davey, believed the government could win a majority in an election. Gordon began canvassing the possibility with Pearson and some of our colleagues in midsummer. A successful election would give the government a life expectancy of four or five years instead of one or two. In Newfoundland there was nothing more to win; all the seats were held by Liberals, and I had no fear that any would be lost. Most of the ministers were either indifferent or doubtful as to an election, a few strongly opposed. I knew Pearson hated elections and was not sure he really liked being prime minister. He would have liked to achieve a few more reforms, especially in the health field, but he could not see a real chance to complete his agenda in a year or so.

What finally convinced him, as me, was a technical consideration. Once the redistribution of seats in the House of Commons under the new system reached a certain stage, there would be a period of about five or six weeks during which an election would no longer be possible in the existing constituencies, and the new ones would not be sufficiently organized. Since we did not have a majority, there was always a risk of defeat in Parliament. I felt that it would be irresponsible to allow a situation to arise in which a government defeated in Parliament could not have an election held at once. With a government with a majority that would not have mattered, but then there would have been no excuse for an election. I explained the hypothetical situation to the cabinet, and enough of the ministers who favoured an election used the argument to put more pressure on Pearson. He satisfied himself, by consultation with experts, that I had described the technical situation correctly. I have always believed that that consideration tilted the balance. Whatever finally decided him, Pearson had Parliament dissolved on 7 September and an election called for 8 November with the old electoral map still in place, and Scarborough constituency with a larger population than the whole of Prince Edward Island.

I had no worry about my own seat. Diefenbaker had joined the hue and cry against the seal hunt and thereby added substantially to his unpopularity in Newfoundland. I was confident we could hold the other six seats in Newfoundland, though St John's East was vulnerable, expecially when W.J. Browne, hoping to return to Parliament, resigned from the House of Assembly to become the Tory candidate. All the seats were retained by the government with substantial majorities. Despite my confidence I made appearances with the candidates in every constituency, but I was free to campaign a good deal in other parts of the country. I visited, I was told, more constituencies than any minister except the prime minister; my travels included every province from Manitoba east.

My executive assistant, Alistair Fraser, decided to seek election and resigned to do so after finding a first-rate replacement in

Sandy Morrison. Late in the campaign I spent a whole day with Alistair in Pictou County, Nova Scotia, but that day was not enough to elect him. He subsequently became clerk of the House of Commons without a word of dissent from the Opposition and served in that high office with great distinction.

George and Margaret McIlraith were with us in Newfoundland when the election was called. As minister of public works McIlraith was more important to Newfoundland, especially the outports needing wharves and breakwaters, than were most ministers. The government had decided to bring St John's Harbour under the jurisdiction of the National Harbours Board. I took advantage of McIlraith's visit to have a ceremony marking the transfer, a popular move with the business community.

I found that I was as much an asset in 1965 as I had been a liability in 1958. One of the staff members of the Liberal Federation somewhat deflated my importance in telling me that I was more willing than any other minister to go wherever they asked. I suspect I was often sent to be a token Liberal minister in hopeless ridings. In the best calculation I can make from my records, I made some contribution to the campaign in over 30 constituencies. Not one of them was gained from the Opposition and 16 had been held by the Liberals before the election. At least I knew more about many parts of Canada than I did before the election.

One notable visit arose out of bitter complaints from prairie wheat exporters that the railways were not providing enough boxcars to move wheat to the Lakehead to satisfy hungry importers abroad. Mitchell Sharp and I went to Winnipeg for a meeting on 27 September with the railway officials and representatives of the wheat exporters, and our efforts resulted in some improvement of the situation. But the Liberals made only a slight dent in Tory support in Manitoba.

Pearson visited St John's on 30 September. In 1963 Smallwood had insisted on introducing Pearson and had completely overshadowed him. In 1965 I insisted on introducing the prime minister and having Smallwood thank him. There was no anticlimax.

The defeat of both Liberal MPs in Prince Edward Island left the province without a minister, and once more I became the Liberal spokesman in Parliament for that province. When Alex Campbell won the provincial election and became premier in 1966, we developed a close relationship and a lasting friendship.

I was in Montreal on 10 October for Bryce Mackasey's nomination in Verdun. When the election was called he had invited me to be guest speaker, and I had agreed. Later on he was the first MP to perceive the rising star, and he asked me if I would object to his inviting Pierre Trudeau as well. I said he could substitute Trudeau without offending me, but he insisted he wanted both of us. I believe that was the only time I ever spoke from the same platform as Trudeau outside the House of Commons.

An unpleasant episode and no majority

I was in Newfoundland in the middle of October when I was confronted with the one disturbing situation for me during the campaign. Dr Guy Marcoux, one of the Social Credit MPs who had stayed with Thompson and opposed Caouette's group, published a book containing allegations against the six Social Credit MPs who had announced after the 1963 election that they would support a Liberal government if Pearson became prime minister. Marcoux hinted that I had been involved in payment for their support. Pearson and others were disturbed, and I received frantic telephone calls. I urged callers not to panic and said I would make a statement at once and follow the matter up in Ottawa on the weekend.

My statement issued on 13 October read: 'I do not wish to make any contribution to political gossip by making any comment on the press reports about Dr. Marcoux's book except to say, categorically, that, to my knowledge, no money was paid or offered to any Member of Parliament or anyone else in connection with the incident the book refers to.'

Sensational stories appeared, and I was asked to appear on the CBC program 'This Hour Has Seven Days.' After returning to Ottawa I read the main press reports, which confirmed the telephone report I had received in Newfoundland: the only wrongdoing alleged by Marcoux was that someone bribed or tried to bribe someone else. In a telegram to Alphonse Ouimet, the president of the CBC, I repeated my statement that I had bribed no one, had tried to bribe no one, had no knowledge of any bribe at the time and had seen or heard no evidence of any bribe since then. So much for the connection of my name with the only allegation of wrongdoing in the book. Dr Marcoux, I added, had suggested that I was engaged in some kind of plot to persuade some of his fellow Social Credit MPs to support the formation of a Liberal government. I denied that I was involved in any plot but said there would surely have been nothing wrong with trying to persuade members to support a Liberal government, as long as no improper inducements or pressures were used. I asserted that I had no contact whatever with any Social Credit MP at that time. I informed Ouimet that if anyone had the courage to charge me with wrongdoing in connection with the incident, I would take whatever action the law permitted. I declared that in my 12 years in public life I had consistently refrained from publishing gossip or any other form of scandal-mongering and would not have any part in spreading Marcoux's political propaganda; accordingly I was declining the CBC invitation. I expressed the hope that the CBC had no intention of linking my name with any improper conduct. I made the full text of my message to Ouimet public.

I had already telephoned one of the leading barristers in Toronto, Joseph Sedgwick, and secured his agreement to act for me if there was need. I knew him only slightly, but his brother, Harry Sedgwick, a private broadcaster who had served the government in public information in wartime, was a friend. The Sedgwick brothers were known Conservatives. I felt that choosing a Conservative to act for me, if required, would increase my credibility. Fortunately there was no follow-up, so far as I was concerned, and no evidence in the election results that Marcoux's book had harmed any party except the two Social Credit groups, which both shrank in 1965. Marcoux dropped to fourth place among the five candidates in his riding, and the Liberal who was elected won twice as many votes as the runner-up. No more was heard of Marcoux.

I was back in Ottawa from Newfoundland to vote on 8 November, fully expecting we would have a majority, though not a large one. In fact we missed the majority by 2 seats; we won 131 compared to 129 in 1963. Our losses were 2 each in Ontario, Manitoba and Alberta, 2 in P.E.I. and 3 in Nova Scotia. If we had held the Maritime seats or even those in Nova Scotia, we would have had a bare majority. We had gained the 1 seat in the Northwest Territories and 9 in Québec. The most notable change in the new Parliament was the appearance of Jean Marchand, Gérard Pelletier and Pierre Trudeau, who were dubbed by the press the Three Wise Men. The return of Bob Winters to public life and his election in an Ontario riding was almost equally newsworthy.

The government would still have to be vigilant to avoid an accidental defeat, but no party in Opposition wanted another election, and the government was much less vulnerable in direct confrontation. The election underlined the danger of calling a premature election, without a specific issue, merely to ensure a longer period in office.

Aftermath

There was a substantial cabinet shuffle after the election. Two days after it was over, Walter Gordon, who had been its leading advocate in the cabinet, resigned from the government on the ground that he had misled the prime minister about the prospect of winning a majority. Whether he expected his resignation not to be accepted is a question that will never be answered.

Mitchell Sharp was appointed acting minister of finance. Until Sharp became minister a week later, there was suspense about whether Pearson would accept Gordon's resignation. Sharp also remained minister of trade and commerce until 3 January 1966, when he was succeeded by Robert Winters. There is an unresolved question about Winters. When Pearson asked him to become a candidate for Parliament, Winters had the impression that at some stage he would follow Gordon in Finance. When Gordon resigned, and Sharp succeeded him, Winters was obviously not happy. That may be why he did not become minister of trade and commerce when the general shuffle took place on 17 December.

The two defeated ministers, Harry Hays and Watson MacNaught, had to be replaced. Hays had been minister of agriculture and the only Liberal MP from Alberta. There was no Liberal MP from Saskatchewan, and Roger Teillet, the only MP from Manitoba, was not a farmer and had no agricultural background. He remained in Veterans Affairs. The minister of agriculture had therefore to come from Ontario or Québec. I was shocked when Pearson chose J.J. Greene, who represented the mainly rural Renfrew South, but who had been born and educated in Toronto; there were some farmer MPs in Ontario and Québec, and a city boy seemed an odd choice.

Bill Benidickson had gone to the Senate in July 1965, and MacNaught had succeeded him, though Mines and Technical Surveys was an odd portfolio for a P.E.I. member. Lawrence Pennell succeeded MacNaught as solicitor-general at that time and retained the portfolio after the election. Jean-Luc Pépin replaced MacNaughton in Mines and Technical Surveys in the December shuffle. Pennell and Pépin both added strength to the cabinet. The shuffle was made larger when Pearson asked Maurice Lamontagne and René Tremblay to resign; he presumably hoped to remove from the cabinet the odour of the furniture charges, which unfairly clung to them. Lamontagne was replaced as secretary of state by Judy LaMarsh, who was demoted from Health and Welfare because of differences over the Canada Pension Plan. Judy was not happy in her new portfoio and developed a feud with Ouimet, the head of the CBC. Judy was replaced by Allan MacEachen at Health and Welfare, and Allan, by John Nicholson as minister of labour. Nicholson's move to Labour made Citizenship and Immigration available to Jean Marchand, the only newly elected MP to be appointed in the shuffle.

Jean-Pierre Côté succeeded Tremblay as postmaster general. His appointment was the only one on which I had any influence. Six months before, when Cardin succeeded Favreau as minister of justice, I had told Pearson that too much attention was paid to francophone Liberal intellectuals who read *Le Devoir*: they had about as much weight with the public as members of the NDP had in English Canada. He asked me whom I would recommend, and I said we needed someone who represented mainstream attitudes. Though I barely knew him personally, I said, I had been impressed in caucus by Léo Cadieux, who had the additional merit of having been a codirector of public relations for the army from 1941 to 1944 and correspondent for *La Presse* on active service in 1944. His appointment as associate minister of national defence in succession to Cardin was well received. In December 1965 Favreau and I discussed the appointment of postmaster general and recommended Jean-Pierre Côté, for the same reasons that Cadieux had been chosen. Côté had more limited education than Cadieux but was blessed with an exceptionally engaging personality. He had the additional merit of being the son of a postmaster. He was a good minister with plenty of common sense who ended his career as lieutenant governor of Québec.

That major cabinet shift was completed by the appointment of John Turner as a minister without portfolio. Pearson asked Turner to assist me, which he did, to my profit and pleasure, until he was given a portfolio in April 1967.

The return of Winters raised a question about my seat at the table. Pearson, like St Laurent, had the ministers placed around the cabinet table in their order of priority as members of the Privy Council. In 1963 Chevrier had sat on the prime minister's right, and Martin on his left, and so on, down to the bottom of the table, where I had taken a seat in 1953. In 1963 I had been third from the top, and when Chevrier left the cabinet to become high commissioner in London, Paul Martin took his place at Pearson's right, and I was at Pearson's left. Winters, though five years younger, was nearly five years my senior in the Privy Council. I asked Pearson whether Winters should not take my place, and I move over, next to Martin. His answer was no, I want you to stay where you are, and Winters can sit on the other side, next to Paul.

I was pleased by the decision because my proximity to Pearson enabled me to pass a note to him unobtrusively and to intervene more easily in debate. I intervened more frequently than most ministers on matters outside my ministerial responsibility. I once

Pearson Cabinet after 1965 election and Walter Gordon's resignation. Front row left to right: Allan MacEachen (NS); Arthur Laing (BC); Mitchell Sharp (ON); J.W. Pickersgill (NF); Paul Martin (ON); L.B. Pearson, (PM); Robert Winters (ON); Paul Hellyer (ON); George McIlraith (ON); Lucien Cardin (PQ); Hedard Robichaud (NB).

Second Row left to right: Jean Luc Pepin (PQ); Léo Cadieux (PQ); Maurice Sauvé (PQ); Guy Favreau (PQ); Judy LaMarsh (ON); Roger Teillet (MAN); C.M. Drury (PQ); J.R. Nicholson (BC); E.J. Benson (ON); L.T. Pennell (ON).

Back Row left to right: John N. Turner (PQ); J.J. (Joe) Greene (ON); Jean Marchand (PQ); Jean Pierre Coté (PQ).

asked Pearson if he minded; his answer was that my interventions were usually helpful, but that he would not want two of me in the cabinet. Pearson had neither liked nor admired Mackenzie King, but their intuitions were similar. Quite often when he made a decision, I would say, 'That is what Mackenzie King would have done.' One day Paul Martin said to me, 'I wish you would stop referring to Mackenzie King, Mike is beginning to like it!'

Of the new ministers, two, Larry Pennell and Jean Marchand, became very close friends of mine. I soon regarded Pennell as my counsel in personal as well as official matters. He was so fair-minded, so modest yet wise and so utterly trustworthy that I confided many of my worries to him. His early departure was a loss to public life, but he was almost destined to become the great judge he proved to be. Marchand had attracted me since the Kingston Conference. I enthusiastically supported Favreau in his effort to persuade Marchand to enter public life. In the House and in cabinet we found we were compatible, and we soon established a warm friendship that lasted for the rest of his life.

John Turner I saw nearly every working day when we were both in Ottawa; he removed many burdens from my shoulders, particularly in receiving delegations, replacing me at meetings and giving those he talked to on my behalf the confidence that their messages would get to me when he could not dispose of their problems himself. I missed him when he was given a portfolio of his own.

13　A Minister at Work

Tasks in the new Parliament

Concentration on transport and Atlantic development

My first two years as minister of transport were mainly a learning experience. When I was given the portfolio, I was of course aware that effective means of transportation were the glue that held Canada together. But I had only the sketchiest notion about the operations of the different modes of transport and their relations to one another and to government. By the beginning of 1966 I knew what many of the problems were and was eager to get on with the constructive job of making improvements where needed. I found plenty to do. Looking back on the record, I can see that I was devoting most of my time from the end of 1965 to transport and to the Atlantic Development Board and less and less to the general activities of the government and to the Liberal party.

The Liberal party was portrayed by the press as divided between the nationalists, personified by Walter Gordon, and the continentalists, personified by Mitchell Sharp. Actually the differences between Gordon and Sharp were both slight and subtle. I was not interested in magnifying them, and my attention to party policy became increasingly marginal. The alienation of the west from the Liberal party was in my view more serious and harder to bridge. Western interests were not neglected. No other subject claimed as much attention as wheat did in Parliament and in the cabinet. In all my years associated with prime ministers and later in Parliament, the West, especially the prairies, got more consideration than Ontario or even Québec. It was a source of mild irritation to me that the concerns of the Atlantic region, where the Liberals maintained a good share of support, were of little interest to most of my colleagues, whereas any western agitation was a minor or even a major crisis.

Looking back I can see too that the poisonous atmosphere of alleged scandal in Parliament, which destroyed the usual civilities of public life between 1964 and 1966, was reducing my appetite for Parliament itself and driving me unconsciously into the transport corner. I have reread many of the debates on various aspects of transport and on the Atlantic Development Board while I was minister and have been pleased to discover that they were largely free of rancour or malice. It remains some satisfaction to me to realize that I often gained the concurrence of both sides of the House. I am vain enough to believe I became an effective parliamentarian.

The big tasks in Transport concerned the railways, the airlines and the seaway. There had been suggestions that the department was too big for one minister, and that there should be a separate department of civil aviation. During the debates on the estimates in February 1966 I made the case for having all forms of transport under federal jurisdiction coordinated. I said there was no other country with 20 million people that depended so much for its standard of living on exporting a large proportion of its products to the rest of the world and, in so many cases, to competitive markets, and no other country in which the cost of transportation was such a large part of the cost of living of almost every person in the country.

I told the House that I had sent a note earlier that day to the leader of the Opposition to the effect that I hoped he would recover from the shock when I told him that I agreed more with his views on transportation than with those of anybody else who had taken part in the debate. He had said that we had to change, that we could not leave things as they were, that we had to be up to date. He was indicating, I said, that we must have modern transportation; in other words, when services become redundant, they must be discontinued.

I went on to point out that there were only two ways we Canadians could pay for transportation, and that we had to pay for part of it one way and part of it another way, if we were to have a sane and viable policy. Transportation must be paid for either by the users or by the taxpayers, and no matter which way it was paid for, the cost of manpower, resources, capital and know-how would have to come out of the sum total of what we produced. If the amount we expended on transportation was too high in

Manitoba University Alumni, Montreal, March 1967. Left to right, J.W.P., Minister of Transport, Norman MacMillan, President of Canadian National, Hugh Saunderson, President of University of Manitoba, Ian Sinclair, President of Canadian Pacific.

relation to the rest of the expenditures of the country, we would be not richer but poorer. That seemed self-evident.

As for the proposal for a separate department of civil aviation, I said that my own opinion — and it was no mere desire on the part of an old man to hang on to his empire — was that all forms of transport should be integrated and the redundant and wasteful eliminated as far as possible. If we did not have one department of government and one minister to direct the coordination, I did not believe it could be done.

To the same end I had concluded that the separate regulatory bodies over transport — the Board of Transport Commissioners, the Air Transport Board and the Maritime Commission — should be amalgamated as a transport commission, and that the commission should be relieved of its regulatory functions over communications.

Communications, I felt, also should be separated from the Department of Transport. Jurisdiction over communications — technical location of broadcasting channels and sites for stations, the regulation of telegraphs and telephones under federal jurisdiction, weather forecasting and the whole range of wired and wireless communications — should become a separate department. To work towards that goal, shortly after I became minister I had asked the deputy minister to have a plan worked out for the segregation of all those functions so that a separate department could be set up quickly whenever the government could be convinced it was necessary — a goal achieved not long after I ceased to be minister.

The Atlantic Development Board

Of all my responsibilities the one closest to my heart was the Atlantic Development Board. The first meeting of the expanded board was held in Halifax on 6 August 1963. I was present at the opening session and spoke about how the government envisaged the work of a board composed entirely of residents of the region. In the years I was minister there was never the slightest division on partisan lines, and there was the utmost cooperation with the provincial premiers, two of whom were Tories, and two Liberals. It was through the work of the board that I began my association with Robert Stanfield, which in our days of retirement has developed into a close friendship. I had an amiable relationship with Walter Shaw in P.E.I., and a warm working relationship with Louis Robichaud, even before he became premier, as well as a deep admiration for his record of modernization and reform of the institutions of New Brunswick. As for J.R. Smallwood, he had welcomed the board with open arms.

Not every project worked out, but the board's contribution to the regional economy was substantial. I was deeply sorry to see it abandoned after I left the government in favour of departmental administration of regional development from Ottawa. I believe that it was a mistake that contributed to a sense of alienation in the Atlantic provinces.

That the board had got off to a good start was clear from the answer to a question in Parliament on 15 August 1964 in which I said that projects estimated to cost well over $50 million had been approved for assistance from the Atlantic Development fund, and that some 30 more were under consideration.

The new chairman, Ian MacKeigan, welded the board together well. Ernest Weeks, the director, and Slim Monture, his main adviser, were imaginative and dynamic. They showed great capacity to use the experience, realism and local knowledge of the economy of the members of the board. I was kept fully informed, and felt we were forging a lively partnership between the government in Ottawa and representatives of the economies of the Atlantic provinces.

The two largest projects to which the board was already committed in 1964 were the Mactaquac power development on the St John River in New Brunswick and an equally substantial hydro development at Baie d'Espoir, on the south coast of Newfoundland. I was asked in the House to justify $20 million grants to each project, and expressed the conviction that power from both would be urgently needed in their respective provinces by the time construction was completed. I regret that a project for a power cable between New Brunswick and Prince Edward Island proposed by the board did not get started.

The board also set aside $10 million for assistance to trunk roads in the four provinces in addition to the 90 per cent share of the cost of completing the Trans-Canada Highway. The Atlantic region did not feel neglected by the new government.

By mid-1966 all but $10 million of the $100 million in the fund of the Atlantic Development Board had been committed to specific projects. On 27 June, I introduced legislation to add $50 million more to the fund. The short debates that day on the resolution and the next day on the bill were virtually love feasts. Speakers for both the Tories and the NDP praised the work of the board; their only criticism was that the additional sum was not great enough. Not the slightest exception was taken to my statement that though I had shown a keen interest in the work of the board, which had to deal with two provincial governments that were of our political persuasion and two that were not, the board's activities had kept above party politics and treated all provinces alike. That opinion was confirmed by Melvin McQuaid, who had been appointed to the board by the Tory government and kept on by us. McQuaid had resigned to contest and win election to Parliament in 1965 in Kings County, Prince Edward Island. I was glad of that vindication of my decision to retain the Tory appointees when the board was enlarged and funded in 1963.

Transport objectives

The prime goal of the Pearson government in transport was to find some way to eliminate the subsidy the Diefenbaker government was paying the railways to prevent an increase in railway freight rates. That subsidy had reached $100 million, an intolerable burden on the Treasury in those days when balancing the budget was still taken seriously.

One good thing the Diefenbaker government had done was to appoint a royal commission on transport headed by M.A.

MacPherson of Regina, which produced one of the finest reports of any commission in my time. The Tory government had been at work on legislation based on the report designed to remove the subsidy by annual installments over a period of years. My predecessor, George McIlraith, had introduced a bill to that end in 1963, but there had not been time to proceed with the measure in that session. I inherited the problem when I became minister of transport.

In Opposition the Liberals had maintained that civil aviation policies, such as they were, were inadequate to meet the problems of expanding air transport, and had undertaken when in office to implement a revised air transport policy. Setting that policy was to be one of my main problems as minister.

The St Lawrence Seaway Authority was a crown corporation, and the minister of transport had no responsibility for the administration of the seaway, in which the Welland Canal had been incorporated. The minister reported to Parliament on the seaway, however, and had responsibility for changes in its mandate. The Welland Canal had become a traffic bottleneck and my predecessor, McIlraith, had been persuaded that it should be twinned, to provide separate upstream and downstream channels. There was also the controversial question of the level of tolls on the seaway and the Welland Canal.

The minister was also the spokesman in Parliament for the National Harbours Board, another crown corporation. The government had no thought of any change in the structure or functions of that board, but problems were frequently to arise about individual harbours, both within and without the jurisdiction of the board.

But the heaviest tasks were railway legislation, air transport policy and the future of the Welland Canal.

Railway legislation

A poor start

I was ready to proceed early in the session with legislation modified slightly from the 1963 bill of my predecessor and, with the optimism of ignorance, had inserted a provision in the bill fixing 1 July 1964 as the date it would come into effect. Because the government gave priority to other business, my legislation was not reached until 24 September. On that day several other items were given priority. I anticipated that they would take all day, and had no notes with me, but, unexpectedly, the other items passed quickly, and the resolution preceding the railway bill was reached in the late afternoon. In describing what was planned I spoke entirely from memory and made one of the best speeches of my parliamentary career. It was in that speech that I expressed the often-quoted, and sometimes misquoted, opinion that over the years railways in Canada caused almost as much emotion and certainly as much controversy as flags, and almost as much as language. My speech was listened to without interruption, with close attention and in a cooperative atmosphere. At the end of the day there had been one speech from a member of each party, the resolution was adopted and the bill was given first reading.

The following week I went into the hospital, and I was not back in the House until the end of October. The session not completed by 18 December was adjourned until 16 February 1965. The House took until 2 April to complete business already under way, and it would have made no sense to proceed with a complicated bill that would involve lengthy debate and sharp differences.

During the question period on the opening day, 16 February, I was asked when I expected to proceed with the railway bill. I replied that I wished to discuss with Opposition spokesmen whether there could be agreement to have the subject matter of the bill referred to the railway committee without debate, because we had no hope of getting it passed in that session. Sending the subject matter of the bill to a committee killed the bill for that session but made its contents public and open for discussion by members and other interested parties.

At the close of the sitting on 18 February I moved second reading, and without debate McIlraith moved an amendment that the subject matter of the bill be referred to the railway committee. As a result there were some useful sessions in committee: they revealed weaknesses that could be dealt with before legislation was introduced in another session.

The new legislation

The Speech from the Throne opening Parliament on 18 January 1966 forecast a bill to amend the Railway Act that had been modified in the light of consideration in the previous Parliament and public discussion in the intervening period. There was so much competition for time in the House that my legislation was not reached before Parliament adjourned for the summer in mid-July, and I did not expect to get started until the late fall.

Parliament was called back on 29 August to end a railway strike. When the prime minister asked for urgent consideration of his bill to restore railway service, spokesmen for all the Opposition groups demanded to see the Railway Bill at the same time, and the government agreed. Both Pearson 's bill and mine were given first reading. One reason the strike had occurred, Pearson said, was that the railways were prevented by law from taking action that would increase their revenues. Their inability to increase freight rates had resulted in subsidies from government amounting to more than $100 million a year. To correct that situation the government had introduced my bill dealing with railway matters, which Pearson hoped would be debated as soon as his bill was passed.

On 1 September, after an acrimonious three-day debate, Pearson's bill passed, at 5:30 p.m., and I was obliged to go ahead with my speech on second reading of my bill, which was described officially as a bill 'to define and implement a national transportation policy for Canada, to amend the Railway Act and other acts in consequence thereof and to enact other consequential provisions.' When enacted, it would be the National Transportation Act.

I spoke on the bill for more than an hour and a half and was listened to for most of that time with close attention. After an interruption from and a light-hearted exchange with the prime minister, I said that Pearson's bill had dealt with the crisis; mine was to deal with its root causes. I referred to an editorial in that morning's *Globe and Mail* entitled 'Can Politics Be Kept Out of Transportation?' There was only one place in Canada, I said, where anybody could be so divorced from the realities of Canadian life as to write an editorial with that title. That was the city of Toronto, and perhaps only in the editorial offices of the *Globe and Mail*. Anybody who knew anything knew that there would have been no Canada without transportation, and no Canadian politics without Canada. I hoped the day would never come when some editor in an ivory tower in Toronto was able to take politics out of transportation.

At that point Mitchell Sharp rose on a frivolous question of privilege to say that he understood my politics, but that I should do justice to the great city that he, as one member, represented. I retorted that others, like Sharp and myself, who had found it necessary for economic, social or other reasons to be transplanted from Winnipeg, had found there were better places to go than Toronto. Hellyer interjected, 'I object.' Stanley Knowles then raised what he called a point of order to ask: 'Is it not a well-known rule of this House that no matter should be brought before Parliament by the government unless there is cabinet solidarity? Should we not adjourn until there could be a cabinet meeting on this?' When I replied that I had said nothing up to then, the Opposition hooted in agreement.

The frivolity was creating a good feeling in the House, which was what I had hoped for. I became more serious and admitted that there was a germ of truth in the *Globe* editorial. There were two kinds of politics in transportation. In one kind, in our collective wisdom, plus a certain amount of distributive foolishness, we tried in the House, despite partisan considerations, to get some kind of consensus as to what would be suitable to bind the country together from Bonavista to Vancouver Island. In the other kind of politics, which undoubtedly the editorial writer had in the back of his mind, we were all tempted, no matter what place we represented, to place the selfish interest of individuals, groups or sometimes even regions above the broader interests of the whole community. That kind of partisanship and that kind of politics we must try to keep out of our consideration of the measure, if collectively we were to achieve something really useful for the country.

By that time I had managed to achieve the kind of sympathetic atmosphere that had existed in the standing committee that had considered the 1964 bill. I had attended all of its meetings and was to find that having so many members familiar with the contents of the earlier bill was a substantial advantage in debate on the new bill.

The bill was one of the longest ever dealt with by Parliament and was not without complexity. Getting it accepted would be the greatest task of my legislative career and the greatest test of my capacity as a parliamentarian. I decided, as far as possible, to use the technique that had worked with the redistribution legislation.

Early in my speech I took advantage of an interruption to say that the broad principles of the bill were endorsed by the government and were government policy, and that on those policies we were staking our lives. The terms of the bill, I thought, were much better than those of the previous one. We owed many of the improvements to the members of the previous Parliament and to individuals and groups who had made representations to the parliamentary committee and to the department. I did not think the bill was perfect. I believed improvements could be made when the bill was sent to committee. I would not consider I was retreating if a member of the Opposition was able to produce a better idea, and I accepted his, rather than mine; I would like to feel I was wise enough to use his brains.

Since 1959 the cost to the Treasury of the railway wages had increased from $20 to $100 million. The government felt that the process could not go on without grave danger to the Canadian economy and to the well-being of all Canadians. Changing the situation would not be easy for any of us. I had no illusions that it would be easy to get the bill through the House, although I had the impression that because we in the House were elected to represent all Canadians as well as our own constituencies, and because we rubbed shoulders a good deal of the time, we tended to have somewhat wider horizons than many of our fellow citizens who would be making representations about the legislation before it was passed.

I explained that the bill was described as the National Transportation Act rather than the Railway Act because passage of the bill would create a Canadian Transport Commission to regulate all modes of transport under federal jurisdiction and to replace the Board of Transport Commissioners, the Air Transport Board and the Maritime Commission. I had concluded that it was of the highest importance to have one unified body to look at all modes of transport, compare one with another and, when considering the regulation of one, take account of what was happening in the others and determine whether we were getting the best value by spending public money on railways, for example, or whether it would be better to scrap a branch of a railway and concentrate on a highway or an airline.

The debate on second reading took up most of the time of the House until 8 September. Diefenbaker closed the debate for the Opposition. I opened my reply by saying that I agreed with a great deal of what had been said that afternoon by the leader of the Opposition. I commended his government for having appointed the MacPherson Commission and for laying the foundations for the present bill, foundations I hoped they would not attempt to sap. The contents of no other Bill had been more carefully studied by two successive governments, and I paid tribute to the previous government.

Second reading was adopted without a recorded vote, and the bill sent to a special committee. It was not back in the House until 20 December.

At the close of my speech on second reading I said I had hoped to include a provision in the bill to end the exemption from municipal taxation enjoyed by the CPR on its main line. The CN and other railways paid municipal taxes, as did the CPR on all its other lines. In the case of the CPR main line, I had discovered, the situation was complicated. The perpetual exemption from local taxation on its main line was included in the contract of 1881 between the company and the Crown. The best legal advice of the government was that that contract was a part of the Constitution of Canada and of the constitutions of Manitoba, Saskatchewan and Alberta and could be changed only by the British Parliament.

I had persuaded the presidents of the CPR, Buck Crump and his successor, Ian Sinclair, that it would be a fine gesture for CPR to agree voluntarily to follow the example of CN and make grants in lieu of taxation to municipalities on their main line. They had agreed to do so, one-third each year, in three successive annual stages, starting when the bill before the House became law. I tabled a letter from Sinclair giving that undertaking. The concession did not make everyone on the prairies love the CPR, but it was received with appreciation by the municipal authorities in Winnipeg, Regina, Calgary and all the smaller places on the main line, and had the effect of encouraging CPR to develop its urban properties and thereby contribute even more to municipal revenues.

The National Transportation Bill

The debate on second reading of the National Transportation Bill took almost a full week, but a bill with so many contentious clauses that must be approved or amended would, I knew, not be completed in one week. In addition to two days in December 1966, the detailed consideration of the clauses took up most of the time of the House from 9 January 1967, with a debate on third reading on 27 January. The proceedings on the bill filled almost 2 of 12 volumes of the Hansard for the session, a session that lasted even longer than that of 1964-65, the previous record for length.

I play no games, but I confess I regarded the proceedings in Parliament partly as a competitive sport in which I played to win. My son Peter once told me that I was the most complete team player he knew. That pleased me, but I did not regard winning as overcoming the other side in debate. For me what counted was not the number of players I could wound but success in getting the final decision we wanted. I tried to persuade our political opponents that what we were seeking to do was tolerable or, better still, right.

Before the new bill was introduced, I had studied the problems of transport and the solution proposed, and had discussed them with officials and experts who had far longer familiarity with them than I had. The bill I introduced had become my own. I knew it was far from perfect, but I believed that what it proposed was as much as Parliament could reasonably be expected to approve. I realized, for example, that the prairie MPs would filibuster endlessly if every railway branch line in the wheat-growing areas could be considered for abandonment. I discussed the problem one day in Winnipeg with the head of the Manitoba Wheat Pool, W.J. Parker, a personal friend. He asked why we did not take a positive approach and decide which branch lines must be retained for a fixed period of years. The railways could apply to abandon the rest, but that did not necessarily mean abandonment would be approved. In a flash I saw that he had solved the problem for me, and said so. A map of the protected branch lines was prepared and published. Opposition to the bill was reduced substantially.

Ministers piloting legislation through Parliament usually had officials sit in front of them when the clauses of a bill were being considered in committee of the whole. I did not follow that practice, not out of vanity but because I felt it was better to admit at once that I could not make up my mind about proposed objections or changes and to have the decision delayed so that I could consult my advisers without wasting the time of the House. In Parliament as in life I had discovered that the frank admission 'I don't know' is far better than any kind of bluff or prolonged wrangling.

Many changes made in the clauses of the bill I proposed myself; most of the rest came from members of the Opposition. I tried never to disparage or ridicule their suggestions but to discuss them seriously and either explain why I could not accept them or give full credit to the member who made the suggestion. The long debate was carried on almost without rancour. On third reading the Tories decided to vote against the bill. Churchill described the way the bill had been handled in these terms: 'No bill in my experience has pursued a more tortuous route than this one. It was introduced and then withdrawn, It was reintroduced and then withdrawn. It was reintroduced in September and referred to a committee. It was amended 60 or 70 times in that committee. I have the greatest sympathy for the legal draftsmen who prepare bills for this House. I understand something of the nature of that difficult work. They must have been driven frantic by the instructions received from this minister. A bill that has to be amended to that extent at the committee stage must have been very badly conceived in the beginning.

'Not content with the amendment in the committee, we had amendment after amendment in committeee of the whole house. No bill has suffered more amendment in the course of its progress through the house than this one. No bill has had more words expressed about it by the Minister piloting it through the house than this one. If there is a page in Hansard dealing with this bill on which the Minister did not make himself heard, it is an exception. This will stand as a record for all time, and I hope as a guide to other Ministers to take a different course of action. But this Minister is verbose, has to be very active and likes to wear himself out in the process. Of course we assisted him in so doing.

'He may now rest on his laurels, but I do not want him to be carried away and think he has accomplished something that is simply wonderful, because I think it is a very bad example of how to put legislation though the House of Commons and I hope nobody else will imitate it.'

In the course of the debate Opposition members had frequently predicted that I would be banished to the Senate once the bill was passed. Early that day there had been a jocular suggestion that Churchill might go with me. When Dick Bell later asked Churchill whether the House would be lonely without me, Churchill replied that some members might be lonely for me, but that he had got the impression that I might like to have him go too. Churchill concluded his speech by saying 'We have been performing here, faithful, honest and hard work, and although this session has lasted now for 195 days I challenge anyone to say and be believed that we have been spending our time wrangling and indulging in ineffective debate. The minister and I can exchange a few humorous remarks without becoming bad friends. He has my respect. I do not like all the things that the minister does, but we have been doing honest and hard work which should be recognized in this country.'

The vote on third reading was 70 to 53. There had been no attempt by the Opposition to mobilize their forces to defeat the bill or the government. I had the impression of a general feeling, which all those who had participated shared, that we had done a service to the country.

I did not escape unscathed in the proceedings in the committee; that experience I want to recount.

The most controversial proposal in the bill was a requirement that the new Transport Commission make a study of the Crow's Nest Pass freight rates on the carriage of grain for export to determine their effect on the costs and revenues of the railways. The Crow's Nest rates were, for the grain growers of the prairies, Magna Carta. The bill did not propose to change the rates; we said they were inviolate, and I repeated over and over again that there would never be any attempt to change the Crow rates by any government of which I was a member. The MacPherson Commission had decided the rates resulted in a loss to the railways, which the commission fixed at $20 million. The commission recommended a payment by the government to the railways of that sum annually. There was such a provision in the bill I introduced in 1964.

After much discussion in the interval I decided that the calculations of the alleged loss were out of date and should not be put into legislation. I realized that there was widespread belief on the prairies that the railways were losing nothing by carrying grain. Any assumption on the part of the government that there was a loss would be politically harmful. Instead we put in a provision that a study be made to determine whether there was a loss, and if so, how much.

In my speech closing the debate on second reading I said that the Crow rates not only were not touched in any way, but were guaranteed indefinitely by the legislation. Jack Horner, the main

Opposition spokesman for the wheat farmers, asked me, if the Crow rates are guaranteed forever and a day, why is there a particular clause in the bill saying that a three-year study will take place? I replied that that was a very simple question to answer. MacPherson said that the Crow rates were costing the railways a considerable sum of money, and he was asking the government to pay $20 million to the railways because of the losses. But we were not willing to agree that there were losses. We wanted to have a three-year study to find out, and if it was found that there were losses, then the Transport Commission might recommend to the government that something be done about those losses on the part of the railways, but the commission could not recommend that anything be done about the Crow rates themselves.

When the clause came up for discussion, Opposition spokesmen repeatedly asserted that the Crow rates were remunerative to the railways, and that no investigation was necessary. I repeated that I had refused to put in the bill the assertion that there was a loss to the railways, but that I did not regard it as an article of faith that there was no loss. I honestly admit, I said, that I am ignorant; I do not know, I am entitled to find out what the facts are, and the people of Canada, the taxpayers of Canada, are entitled to find out what the facts are. That is all that clause does; it substitutes fact for faith. If the honourable gentleman's faith is justified, he ought not to object to the facts.

An amendment was made to strike out the part of the clause requiring the study and was carried 59 to 58. I was of course embarrassed, though no one suggested a question of confidence in the government was involved. I asked that debate on the rest of the clause be postponed until I could consider its implications. I pointed out that the amendment had removed the provision that fully guaranteed the Crow's Nest rates. I did not imagine, I said, that that was their intention in moving the amendment. If we allowed the clause to stand, I could give consideration to the effect of the amendment and perhaps have something drafted that would ensure that the members opposite, by their votes, had not destroyed the Crow rates. The postponement was agreed to.

The law officers, draftsmen, officials and I worked furiously over the weekend and came up with an elaborate and complicated amendment to another clause. In essence it would permit the railways to apply to the Transport Commission to investigate the revenues and costs of the carriage of any commodity where the rates were fixed by law. The amendment would have made it possible, after two years had passed, to begin an investigation of the effect of the Crow rates.

The amendment was challenged on the ground that it was seeking to reopen, in the same session of Parliament, a question already decided in that session, a procedure contrary to the rules. I maintained that I was proposing a different question. The point of order was discussed at length. The chairman of the committee, Deputy Speaker Herman Batten of Newfoundland, waited until the following day to decide whether or not my motion was in order. In a lengthy ruling he decided that the new proposal was substantially different from the proposal that had been defeated. Horner exclaimed, 'Shameful ruling,' and repeated, 'A shameful ruling; a partisan ruling.' Churchill then said the committee was grateful for the care and attention the chairman had given to the ruling but added, 'Regretfully I must appeal the ruling to the Speaker.'

The Speaker delayed his ruling until the next day. He said he had read all the arguments in committee and asked whether the minister of transport had anything to add. When I realized that I was the only one to be allowed to speak, I felt sure the Speaker would reverse the decision of the chairman. In addition to arguing that the proposed amendment was different, or sufficiently at variance, to be in order, I pointed out that removal of the clause from the bill had also removed guarantees of the Crow and other rates established by law, something I did not believe the Opposition wanted to do. The Speaker then, in the most considerate language, reversed the decision of the chairman. There was no applause or gloating by the Opposition, and no suggestion that the government had been defeated. Batten was the one member most affected; several of his friends, including me, had great difficulty in persuading him not to resign as Deputy Speaker.

I spoke at once to propose consideration of an amendment that would restore the protection of the grain rates, and I asked for unanimous consent to move it. I admitted that my proposal was a direct reversal of the amendment passed the previous week and was therefore, under the Speaker's ruling, even more out of order than the amendment I had moved previously. That is why I hoped I would have unanimous consent. It was certainly never the intention of the government at any time to endanger in any way the rates on any grain products. I appealed to members to overlook the fact that the House had taken an opposite view the previous Wednesday and to allow me to move my amendment. I was asking not for unanimous approval of the amendment but merely for unanimous approval to move it.

Churchill commended me for the rapidity with which I had been able to produce another amendment, within about 20 minutes of the Speaker's ruling against the previous one, and suggested that rather than being asked to give unanimous consent at once, members should have an opportunity to study the proposed amendment. He added that a little later that day the minister might repeat his request and perhaps at that stage unanimous consent would be forthcoming.

After Churchill spoke, I felt certain that the Opposition was grateful to me for pointing the way out of an error that would have haunted them. I was confident that I would get unanimous consent after reflection. Meanwhile the atmosphere in the committee was greatly improved by an intervention by Horner, who said he was recorded in Hansard as using some words in the heat of the debate that he now wished he had not used. He apologized to the chairman and said he would not like Batten to consider them to be as harsh as they sounded at the time. I spoke right after Horner to say how pleased I was; in the consideration of the bill, about which he felt very strongly and to which he had applied himself with great diligence, he had revealed to us a new side and gained new stature and new respect in the House. I hoped the chairman would feel that the amends were complete, and that all of us on both sides of the House had absolutely undiminished confidence in his impartiality.

Before the House rose at 6 p.m. I was given unanimous consent to have the amendment moved. After some alterations in the language of the amendment it was adopted. The debate in committee was completed shortly after 11 that evening, and the bill received third reading the next day, 27 January.

My own verdict on what we had accomplished was expressed that day in these words: 'I do not pretend for one minute that this Bill is perfect. I do not pretend that we may not want to make some amendments to it quite soon. But I think it is about as good a measure as we could have agreed upon collectively at this particular time.' I also said: 'I think it would have been most ungracious of me in light of what I sometimes think were the many quite undeserved and charitable things that have been said about me at various stages during the course of this long debate if I did not acknowledge, in turn, the very genuine appreciation, occasionally perhaps slightly mixed with irritation, that I have felt throughout the passage of this Bill, both in the standing committee and in the committee of the whole in this House. I do think, the whole record taken together, we can all feel that we have, perhaps not in speed but pretty well in every other respect, given a fair example of how Parliament ought to work in producing good legislation.'

Alvin Hamilton, the Opposition official critic, who had been helpful, added, 'Mr. Speaker, my last words will be to join with the Minister of Transport in emphasizing as well as I can that when Parliament does do a good job, as it has done with this transportation bill, the country should know about it.

The accomplishment

The National Transportation Bill was duly adopted by the Senate without amendments and given royal assent. As the sponsor I had persuaded the House to approve its 90 clauses, many of them in improved form. Only one provision asked for in the bill had been denied. The railways were much more disappointed than I was about the denial of a requirement to study the effect of the Crow and other rates fixed by law.

The Act achieved several things in the public interest. Indirectly it restored the possibility of negotiating wages by collective bargaining. The breakdown of collective bargaining had resulted in the strike and the emergency action by Parliament to set wages by legislation. Collective bargaining had broken down because the Diefenbaker government had frozen freight rates and in effect subsidized wage increases by the railways. That process continued in the first three years of the Pearson government, because there had not been parliamentary time to deal with the railway legislation.

The drastic act of ending the railway strike created an atmosphere in which reform was acceptable. Railway freight rates had been set by an independent quasi-judicial board since early in the century. The new act allowed the railways, wherever there was an alternative mode of transport available, to set their own freight rates, and at the same time it gave the protection of a maximum rate to captive shoppers who had no alternative way to ship their products. The railways were encouraged to compete for traffic with other modes.

The railways continued to be required by law to carry grain for export from Canada at the Crow's Nest rates without provision for any loss in carrying that traffic, except for losses incurred on branch lines they were required to keep in operation. The Treasury was required to reimburse the railways for those losses. Most of the prairie network of branch lines was required to operate until 1975. The railways could apply to abandon the unprotected lines, but if the Transport Commission decided they were still needed, the Treasury would cover the losses.

The railways were free to apply for the abandonment of any passenger train service. If the Transport Commission decided that such services were still in the public interest, 80 per cent of the losses on such services would be met by the Treasury. Some incentive was thus left to the railways to make passenger service more efficient and less costly.

In return for meeting those specific losses, the so-called wage subsidy was to be reduced in annual instalments until it disappeared.

Competition and the freedom to set prices for all passenger and most freight services, except grain for export, were expected to provide the railways with enough revenue to enable them to have adequate income to restore collective bargaining.

The government was resolved not to treat the railways in isolation but to look at all modes of transport under federal control in an integrated fashion; that was the reason the Board of Transport Commissioners, the Air Transport Board and the Maritime Commission were amalgamated into the Canadian Transport Commission.

Two broad changes were achieved. First, the railways had in most respects, the freedom to compete for traffic and profits that other business operations had. Second, through the Transport Commission the national treasury was to be protected from duplication in and the undue expansion of transport services at the public expense; such protection was the basic task of the new Canadian Transport Commission.

Air transport policy

Basic principles

When I became minister of transport I had only the sketchiest idea of the questions to raise in formulating air transport policy. I believed it made good sense to have a single air carrier for both trans-Canada mainline service and international service, and that, as a monopoly, it should be publicly owned. After 10 years in Newfoundland I had practical experience of the importance of having mainline service supplemented by a regional scheduled carrier and also of the need for what came to be called third-level air carriers.

The decision of the Tory government to permit Canadian Pacific to have any part in trans-Canada air service had been, in my opinion, a mistake. I was resolved to limit CP Air to the one flight each way between Vancouver and Montreal that they had been allowed, until I was familiar enough with the whole field to make sound decisions.

I was fortunate to have the best possible teacher. The deputy minister, John Baldwin, when he was in the Privy Council Office in wartime and afterwards, had, jointly with Escott Reid of External Affairs, drafted the civil aviation policy. He had subsequently been chairman of the Air Transport Board and deputy minister to C.D. Howe as minister of transport for air before becoming deputy for the whole Department of Transport. No one else in Canada was so well informed about every aspect of civil aviation and its relation to other modes of transport. Baldwin was my indispensable guide.

One decision I had already made on my own. Trans-Canada Airlines, which was just being renamed Air Canada, should not be faced with competition or restrictions that would result in deficits of the kind Canadian National Railways had faced over the years; Air Canada should be protected from being put 'in the red.' That decision was based on my lifelong awareness that CN had been created at the end of the First World War to rescue bankrupt railways and had been an almost incessant drain on the Canadian treasury and the taxpayers. Competition, I was determined, should not be allowed to develop to the point where Air Canada would be put in a similar deficit position.

I had learned from the agitation in St John's over television broadcasting how easy it was to arouse discontent with a monopoly and to generate a demand for a choice of service. The Diefenbaker government had created an appetite for choice of service by permitting CP Air to have one flight daily each way between Montreal and Vancouver.

It did not take me long to decide that there must be efficient regional carriers to supplement the mainline service. One great, single carrier, or even two, could not perform all scheduled air service satisfactorily. Mainline headquarters were too remote from the regions. For a regional scheduled carrier to operate effectively, its headquarters had to be in the area of its operation. Anybody who had been a politician in Newfoundland when there were very few roads, as I had been, and who had seen how dependent a region could be on air transport, would know that a regional service could not be effectively provided from Montreal.

By early April I had worked out with Baldwin and other officials a statement of three principles on which I proposed to base air transportation policy:

1 In the international field, air services provided by Canadian air lines should.serve the Canadian interest as a whole; these services should not be competitive or conflicting, but should represent a single integrated plan, which could be achieved by amalgamation, by partnership or by a clear division of fields of operations.

2 In the domestic mainline field, while the principle of competition is not rejected, any development of competition should not compromise or seriously injure the economic viability of TCA's mainline domestic operations, which represent the essential framework of its network of domestic services. In other words, there must not be the kind of competition which would put TCA into the red; and, in the event that competition continues, the Air Transport Board should ensure an opportunity for growth to both lines above this basic minimum.

3 In formulation of policy based upon the foregoing point, a reasonable role for regional air carriers providing scheduled and regular air service must be established; this role must provide for a relationship between the regional air carriers and TCA (and any other licensed mainline transcontinental carrier) which will give the regional air carriers a reasonable chance to operate without government subsidies.'

Since TCA was a subsidiary of Canadian National and CP Air of Canadian Pacific, I invited the presidents of all four companies to meet with me and Baldwin on 27 April 1964, and I gave them, in confidence, copies of the statement of three principles.

Donald Gordon of CN I had known since I arrived in Ottawa. I had a deep appreciation of the resolution and skill he had displayed as chairman of the Wartime Prices and Trade Board. I had joined with Norman Robertson in urging St Laurent to appoint him head of CN. Gordon knew well how government operated, and our relations were excellent after I became minister, though I have learned since then that he initially expressed some apprehension. I first met N.R. (Buck) Crump during the first railway labour dispute after the war, when the government had to intervene to prevent a strike. I developed at that time a high regard for his sense of responsibility and his decisiveness in a crisis. Our relations became excellent. Grant McConachie, the president of CP Air, I had met once while we were in Opposition. I had been attracted by his charm but had gained no impression of his capacity. I had never met Gordon McGregor, to the best of my recollection, before I became minister and was unaware of his bias against me, which I have already mentioned in my account of the Winnipeg base controversy. In *The Adolescence of an Airline* he claims that, under the new administration of a party traditionally favourably disposed to TCA, he had expected to have clear sailing, until he found that political expediency apparently came foremost in the minds of Jack Pickersgill and his successor as minister of transport. McGregor wrote later that it was typical of me that though I might feel it correct to return to the one-carrier principle, I considered it politically untenable and therefore dismissed it from further consideration.

The main question to be answered at the meeting with the presidents was whether both carriers or only one was to operate on the mainline transcontinental service. I did not, in fact, rule out returning to a single mainline carrier. Indeed, later in 1964, Max Bell, a large shareholder in CPR, approached me with a proposal for the purchase of both airlines by a new private company. I told Bell that I would be willing to put a proposal before the cabinet for a merger of both companies into a new one. The government, I said, would not permit a private monopoly of mainline air services but would consider a merger with some governmental participation in ownership. I heard no more of the proposal, which he told me he had discussed with McGregor before he saw me. The only monopoly I would have considered was one that was basically public. But in one sense McGregor's phrase 'political expediency,' he described my attitude correctly. I believed that the prime purpose of air transport was to serve the public, not to maximize the profitability of one airline, even if it was owned by the government.

In reply to a question at the meeting, I assured the CPR president that the government had no intention of legislating CP Air out of existence. I expressed my strong opinion that there should be no direct competition between Canadian carriers on international routes and the hope that the carriers could work out some division of the international field by consultation between themselves, rather than by direction from the government. I did ask the airlines to sell the services of the other Canadian carrier on international routes they did not serve, instead of influencing passengers to use foreign air lines, as both of them were doing.

It was already apparent that CP Air was filling its one plane each way every day, though that situation was helped by a lower fare than Air Canada's for economy seats and a higher one for first class. First class on CP Air appealed to those who were willing to pay more to satisfy their distaste for public ownership. I told the presidents that unless the airlines adopted equal fares voluntarily, I would ask the government to compel them to do so.

I was eager to have the two airlines themselves work out arrangements based on the principles I had laid down. I put no pressure on them to act swiftly because of other more urgent demands on my own time.

Public discussion of air policy, I thought, would be useful and I decided to inform Parliament of the statement of principles. On 30 April, I arranged to have a Liberal MP ask me a question. The Speaker decided that the answer was not urgent, and that the question should be put on the order paper. Instead the questioner put it down for reply after 10 p.m. At that time an experimental procedure was in effect that permitted a member who did not get a question answered at the opening of the sitting to bring the question up again at 10, the normal time of adjournment. The questioner was allowed to elaborate the question for seven minutes, and the minister or his parliamentary secretary to reply for three minutes. Though it was not written into the rule, it was clearly understood that no other member would interrupt. The practice worked reasonably well for some time and gave some backbenchers a little more scope. But that evening my questioner was interrupted by another member, raising what he called a question of privilege, which the Deputy Speaker ruled out of order. An altercation ensued, and the seven minutes allotted to the questioner were exhausted. I was not able to reply to the two short paragraphs the questioner had uttered, but managed to say for the record that I had not been allowed to speak.

I accepted an invitation from the CBC to read my answer on television. In doing so I provoked a debate on a question of privilege when the House opened on 1 May. There were, in fact, two alleged questions of privilege raised, one by Erik Nielsen and the other by Tommy Douglas. It was alleged that I had committed a flagrant affront to the House by making a statement of policy outside the House. Douglas argued that my answer was in reality a statement of policy that should have been made at the opening of the sitting, when a representative of each party had the right to comment. In defence I described my answer as a very tentative stage in the formulation of a policy that had not yet been made, and said I had hoped to avoid taking up the time of the House with a mere progress report. I had made that report public only after I was prevented from delivering it in the House. I took no other part in the debate, which involved Diefenbaker, Pearson and spokesmen for other parties. After Knowles had made a moderating speech, the Speaker ruled that there was no question of privilege, merely a statement of grievance. His decision was appealed, and all members except the Tories voted to sustain his ruling. I realized that it would have been wiser merely to make my statement at the time when spokesmen for other parties could comment. Certainly I had saved no time of the House.

No progress was made in establishing policy in 1964. The first step came on 25 April 1965, when CP Air finally agreed to raise its economy fare to equal Air Canada's, and Air Canada raised its first-class fare to the CP Air level. CP Air was prevented from filling its economy section by cream-skimming, and Air Canada had some net benefit.

During the debates on the transport estimates in September 1964, I was accused of procrastination and delay in arriving at an air policy. I reminded the House that Mackenzie King and C.D. Howe had taken at least a year and a half in wartime to work out a policy for civil aviation, which had worked well for 20 years. I was more eager to ensure that my policy would work for 20 years than to meet a deadline of 30 September or 31 October. What we wanted was a policy right for the country; if it took two or three extra months to get it, it would be wiser to take the two or three extra months. I believed that the framework announced on 1 May, with which I had found very little quarrel in any part of the country, was the right framework within which to work out the policy. The two airlines, I reported, had been asked to hold discussions to see whether they could come up with agreed recommendations within the framework. On some points they had already reached agreement. A number of the conflicting difficulties outside Canada had already been removed. The greater the measure of consent and agreement on policy we could get, the more likely it was to work smoothly and effectively.

Dividing the world

Policy on international services was the easiest to achieve. It was evident that the two airlines would not present a united proposal to the government on their own initiative. In April 1965 I invited McGregor and McConachie to my office and told them it was time to agree on a clear geographical separation, with Air Canada having all points north of a line through western Europe and CP Air all points south of it. I thereupon excused myself to go to the washroom, where I stayed for some time.

McGregor and McConachie decided to stay with the status quo, including leaving Amsterdam to CP Air. I never told McGregor that if there had not been agreement, I intended to take Amsterdam away from CP Air. I did not get around to announcing the agreed division of international routes in the House of Commons until 1 June 1965, when I described it as similar to the division of the world outside Europe between Spain and Portugal by Pope Alexander VI. The division served well enough for many years after my retirement.

The conclusion announced was that each each carrier should continue to serve all the points it now served, and that the geographical areas now served by each should be defined and extended so that practically the whole world would be open to service by one airline or the other. CP Air would serve the whole Pacific area, the whole continent of Asia, Australia and New Zealand, southern and southeastern Europe and Latin America. Air Canada would serve the United Kingdom, western, northern and eastern Europe and the Caribbean. The only exception to that clear-cut division was that CP Air would continue to serve the Netherlands.

The division accounted for the whole world except Africa and the United States. For the time being neither airline was contemplating service to any part of Africa, and the question of service to that continent was left aside until some practical question arose. In the case of the United States, where negotiations for a new bilateral agreement were going on, once they were completed, a decision would be made as to which of the new points was to be served by each airline.

The scope of regional air carriers

At the meetings with the four presidents in April 1964, I had explained that there would have to be a proper balance between the one or two mainline carriers, whichever there were going to be, and the regional carriers. It was important, I said, to get that balance in such a way that, as far as possible, the users and not the taxpayers would pay for the service, though there might be air services so essential that they would have to be provided even if subsidies might be needed, in areas where there was no alternative means of transport. I warned that that balance would not be easy to reach.

The regional policy was not announced until 20 October 1966. It provided that regional carriers would continue to provide regular operations into the north, where Air Canada had none and CP Air only a few, in the far west. The policy envisaged limited competition on mainline routes by regional carriers in segments where it was helpful for local route development. It also forecast the transfer to regional carriers of some secondary routes operated by Air Canada or CP Air. A larger role for regional carriers in domestic and international charter services was forecast. Greater cooperation between mainline carriers and regional carriers was to be developed in a variety of fields, ranging from technical and servicing arrangements to joint fare arrangements and other suitable areas of cooperation. There were to be temporary subsidies for regional carriers. Subsidies would be continued only if the carriers were able to develop and maintain an adequate volume of traffic, and there would be firm control over their financial structure. Regional carriers were to be assisted technically by the Canadian Transport Commission to explore the possibility of a joint approach by regional carriers for the acquisition of new aircraft.

The regional policy was new and untried and proved far from easy to implement. Over the years of my involvement as minister and as president of the Transport Commission it was to be substantially modified in the light of experience. But at least we had a policy for the first time.

Mainline service

The extent to which mainline transcontinental service was to be divided between Air Canada and CP Air was the most difficult question. It was not answered except for my 1964 assurance that competition was not rejected, but that any development of competition should not compromise or seriously injure the economic viability of Air Canada's mainline domestic operation. If competition continued, there should be an opportunity for growth to both lines beyond the single daily flight of CP Air.

Despite what I believed was the clarity of my language in 1964 about an opportunity for growth to both airlines, I do not doubt that McGregor honestly interpreted my statement to mean that no extension of the competition would be permitted. I was sure the travelling public would exert pressure for more competitive flights, and that it was up to me to make sure any increase of competition by CP Air did not impair the economic viability of Air Canada's operations.

I decided that expert advice was needed on the point, and on John Baldwin's advice the department retained Stephen Wheatcroft, a British consultant who had advised George Hees on the original application of CP Air for mainline service, to advise us whether or not additional competition would impair the economic viability of Air Canada.

McGregor was upset over the employment of Wheatcroft. A sharp difference ensued between us over a letter McGregor sent to me demanding that Wheatcroft's report be shown to Air Canada for comment before it was made public or acted on. I decided that our relationship would become impossible if it was not more clearly defined. I called McGregor to Ottawa and told him that I wanted the letter withdrawn and destroyed. If it was not withdrawn, I told him, either I would cease to be minister of transport, or he would cease to be head of Air Canada. I said I was not trying to run the airline, and he was not going to run the department. The letter was withdrawn, and a mild and respectful request for consultation was substituted. My confrontation with McGregor is described in Philip Smith's account of the first 50 years of Air Canada, *It Seems Like Only Yesterday*. It was the sharpest of the few confrontations I had with a public servant or a colleague.

Wheatcroft's report indicated that the CP Air service on the Vancouver-Winnipeg-Montreal-Toronto route, limited to a once-daily round trip, had not produced either major improvements in efficiency or new traffic but had resulted in wider public satisfaction because of the choice offered. It had effected some diversion of revenue from Air Canada, but had not prevented Air Canada from maintaining a profitable position. Wheatcroft found that because of expected future growth on the transcontinental route the role of CP Air could be expanded, both in the frequency of flights and in the number of points that might be served, without injury to the ability of Air Canada to maintain a profit. Accordingly he recommended that CP Air be allowed to expand its operations in a manner that would permit it to share in the future traffic growth on the route.

The government policy, based largely on Wheatcroft's report, was announced on 27 March 1967. It stated that the government had reached the conclusion that it was in the public interest to permit an increased role for CP Air on the transcontinental route, but that that role must be clearly defined in such a way as to protect the future economic position of Air Canada and ensure that under competent management the airline would be able to maintain a profitable position.

Air Canada had a major role to fill in providing domestic services of a wide variety and, in addition to the heavily travelled transcontinental route, must maintain a substantial number of other domestic services, some of which were not in a profitable position. Moreover Air Canada's capital requirements for new aircraft would be substantial. It was therefore necessary to ensure Air Canada a large portion of the trancontinental market, the most profitable domestic market in Canada, so that it could continue to maintain less profitable domestic routes, where necessary, in the public interest, and to develop the funds necessary for the substantial expansion that faced it, both domestically and internationally.

After considering all those factors the government had decided that the Air Transport Board should be authorized to allow CP Air to double its present capacity that year on the transcontinental route. For the future the board was being authorized to allow CP Air to increase its transcontinental services until it was providing approximately 25 per cent of the total transcontinental flights by the year 1970, and to expand its services thereafter in a manner that would permit it to continue to provide 25 per cent of such capacity.

As long as I was minister or president of the Transport Commission, that policy remained in force, and CP Air competition did not compromise or seriously injure the economic viability of Air Canada, much less put it into 'the red.' CP Air tried to get authority to do cream-skimming by serving only Toronto/ Vancouver on some flights, but that was not permitted in my time. CP Air also tried to persude me that it should be allowed to extend its mainline service to Halifax. I answered that that would be done over my dead body; I knew it would impair the regional service in the Atlantic provinces. I said the airline might have embarrassed me by asking for St John's instead of Halifax, but my flippant observation did not tempt it.

McGregor writes that I had declared in 1964 that as long as I was minister of transport no government action would be taken that would be detrimental to TCA's interests with respect to its transcontinental services. What I actually said was that competition would not be allowed to injure Air Canada's economic viability. As I look back on the record, it seems clear to me that while I was minister, I made sure that competition from CP Air did not reduce Air Canada's economic viability.

International air transport

Negotiations for bilateral air transport agreements with other countries were conducted officially by External Affairs in consultation with the Department of Transport. As minister I was involved in two of them.

Late in 1965 agreement in the United States negotiations had been reached on all but two issues. We wanted a Canadian carrier to serve Winnipeg/Chicago, then served only by an American airline. The Americans wanted Chicago/Montreal, then served only by Air Canada. I suggested that both be agreed to. I felt confident that since Chicago/Montreal was more valuable than Winnipeg/Chicago, the Americans would agree to my suggestion, but the negotiators could not reach agreement. Pearson was going to Washington at the end of the year to visit President Johnson. I asked him to try to settle the problem directly with the President, and he did so. To my surprise the President said the United States would drop its request for access to Montreal from Chicago if we would drop ours for access to Chicago from Winnipeg. Pearson agreed, and the new agreement was signed early in January.

I was mildly embarrassed because I had unwisely said publicly in Winnipeg during the 1965 election campaign that we had a good chance of getting access to Chicago for Air Canada. I was later accused in Winnipeg of misleading the public.

After the agreement was reached, I asked the U.S. ambassador why they had made a choice so unfavourable to the United States. He replied that they were sure they would get access to Montreal without having to concede anything in return, because the additional service would be needed during Expo 67 in Montreal. I made sure they did not.

The other important negotiation was with the Soviet Union. McGregor had visited the U.S.S.R. with a group of Canadian businessmen in 1964 and had had talks there with the head of the Soviet airline, Aeroflot, who had shown interest in service to Canada. In reporting to Pearson, McGregor suggested that an agreement for reciprocal service might help to improve East-West relations, though it was unlikely to be profitable for Air Canada at least in its earlier stages. Pearson had McGregor talk to me. If Canada could negotiate a bilateral agreement, he proposed Montreal/Moscow service would be started provided the government would meet the expected losses in the first few years. I agreed to put the proposal to cabinet but said I would not recommend it, as I did not believe it could ever become profitable.

A little later McGregor approached me again to report that Air Canada had revised its calculations and was willing to bear the initial losses itself, as they believed the service would quickly become economically viable: the service would draw American traffic since there was no service between the United States and the U.S.S.R. I put the case to the cabinet, which approved negotiations with the U.S.S.R. The negotiations bogged down over a Soviet demand for onward flights from Gander to Cuba. At that point I was asked by External Affairs to intervene personally in the negotiations. I told the Soviet team that we would agree to give them onward rights to Cuba only if they would give us the right to overfly Siberia to Japan.

While we were negotiating, the U.S. government, which did not want us to permit Soviet access to Canada, intervened. President Johnson sent Averell Harriman to Ottawa to see Paul Martin as secretary of state for external affairs to protest onward Soviet flights to Cuba. Paul asked me to join him and his officials in meeting Harriman, who virtually forbade us to permit the Soviets to fly on to Cuba and expressed distaste for Soviet service to Canada. Paul replied calmly but firmly, taking note of the American representations but giving no hint of our reaction. He then asked me whether I wished to say anything. What I said was that Harriman had used the kind of language I assumed the Soviet government used to the Polish government, but it was not the kind of language I expected to hear used by the United States to Canada.

Harriman then asked Paul and me to move away from the officials into his bedroom, where he told us that he had been instructed to convey the message he had read without altering a word, but clearly implied that we should not anticipate any retaliation if we did not accept the advice. I told him that the negotiations with the Soviets were at a deadlock over access to Cuba, that the Soviets were keen to reach an agreement for service to Canada, and that I did not think our condition, which I did not disclose, would be met. He could report that to his government, and that, while taking American concerns into account, we would act in our own best interests. Shortly afterwards the Soviets dropped the demand for Cuba, and agreement was reached.

I found negotiating with the Soviets tough and slow, because the negotiators had to refer every point at issue back to Moscow. On balance, though, I did not find them as tough as some negotiations with Canadian trade unions into which I had been drawn.

I had predicted that the American traffic to Moscow on which Air Canada counted would not last long. The service to Moscow was started in 1966. I had forecast that the American ideological scruples would soon vanish. Pan-American and Aeroflot did not take long to establish reciprocal Moscow/New York services, and Air Canada's American traffic to Moscow disappeared. The losses on the service were so great that Air Canada had to stop its service, though Aeroflot continued flying to Montreal and, during fuel stops at Gander, exchanging passengers for Cuba with Cubana airline.

Harriman's intervention was not the first attempt by the United States to interfere with Canadian international operations. An American company had the contract for providing garbage disposal service to foreign aircraft that stopped at Gander for refuelling. In 1964 that company submitted the lowest tender for similar service at Halifax. Before the contract was let, the company informed the department that they had orders from Washington not to service Cubana airlines. I was informed promptly, and I directed the deputy minister to inform the American company that they would get no contract for Halifax, and that their contract at Gander would not be renewed, unless they serviced Cubana and any other airline the Canadian authorities permitted to land at Gander. I cautioned Baldwin to prevent any leaks while the U.S. presidential election campaign was under way. A few days later Baldwin was advised that there had been a misunderstanding; the American company would service Cubana.

My other experiences in the field of international bilaterals were less important. The British were almost constantly seeking access to additional points in Canada without having much to offer in return. The Netherlands government was eager to get access for KLM to Toronto in addition to Montreal. We stood firm because Holland had nothing to offer in return. The Dutch gave notice of termination of the bilateral; that would have excluded CP Air from Amsterdam. Before the termination date arrived, the Dutch proposed that both airlines carry on as before. They never got access to Toronto, and neither did any other foreign carrier while I was minister unless something equally valuable was secured in return. I offered a switch from Montreal to Toronto to Air France knowing full well they would not dare to drop Montreal. The Icelandic authorities approached me about a stop in Toronto on the flight of Icelandair to Chicago. Iceland was not a member of the International Air Transport Association and was providing bargain-rate cream-skimming operations between the United States and Europe with a terminus in Luxembourg. Service to Europe via Iceland would give no advantage to Canada. In refusing them I said it would have been much harder to refuse if they had asked for Winnipeg, which was probably the largest or second-largest Icelandic city in the world. They were not tempted.

In bilateral negotiations I kept two cardinal points in mind. One was that more than half the passengers flying into and out of Canada were Canadians, and that Canada's prime goal should be to have the capacity and the landing rights to carry at least half the traffic. The other was that the heaviest international air traffic was generated into and out of Toronto, so access to that city should not be given to an airline of any country unless the country offered access to its best traffic point in return.

Changing the guard at Canadian National and Air Canada

Donald Gordon had been reappointed chairman of CN for three years in 1963, and the question of a further reappointment in 1966 had to be considered. In 1966 Donald would be 65 years old; he had told Pearson he would like to retire even before that if certain tasks could be completed earlier. As the date approached, he hinted to me more than once that he should perhaps stay on if the government approved. I brought the decision to a head by saying that he was free to talk to the prime miinister, who would probably agree, but that I would not recommend an extension of his term. He was clearly shocked and asked why. My answer was that he would want another career; he would not want to stop at 65. I said that Donald Gordon, unlike most men at 65, would be employable with choices, at 66, less so; and at 67 no one would want him, and there would have to be retirement. He thought about my observations briefly and then said he would not stay. I asked him to remain on the Board, but he replied that he would prefer a clean break.

A suitable successor was available in the vice-president, Norman MacMillan. MacMillan was a graduate of the University of Manitoba; unlike Ian Sinclair, who had been one of my students for a year, MacMillan had been most prominent in the university when I was at Oxford. But I was not unaware of his academic standing. He nearly always accompanied Gordon to see me, and I developed confidence in him and, later, admiration for him. The transition was smooth, and MacMillan performed superbly.

Gordon McGregor was also 65 in 1966, but in my opinion there was no obvious successor. McGregor's health was failing, and there was no question of another career for him. His candidate for the succession was Herbert Seagrim, by chance another Manitoban. I had never got to know Seagrim: McGregor rarely brought him or any one else to meetings with me, and the once or twice we met he had little to say and seemed too deferential to his boss. The Air Canada management, I felt, needed some fresh air from the outside. I told McGregor to go ahead with his plan to make Seagrim executive vice-president, but to tell him there was no presumption that he would succeed to the top job. I persuaded McGregor to stay on for another year while I could consider the decision further. I also did not like it that McGregor and Gordon were retiring at the same time, since Air Canada was technically a subsidiary of CN. Before a year was up, I had ceased to be minister of transport, and the problem was left to my successor. I have often wondered whether I did not make a serious mistake in resisting the appointment of Seagrim, but there are no second chances.

Water Transport

Tolls

The legislation to establish the St Lawrence Seaway Authority would not have been approved by the cabinet and introduced in Parliament if there had not been a provision for the collection of tolls to pay for its operation. For the federal government there were strong budgetary reasons why the waterway should be self-supporting. Carrying out the commitment to finance the operation through tolls was complicated when the government, instead of having the whole seaway in Canada, accepted the belated offer of the United States to construct two of the canals on the international section of the St Lawrence. Under the agreement with the United States a review of the tolls at stated intervals was required. That provision limited Canada's capacity to fix the tolls independently and the United States authorities dragged their feet.

The Welland Canal was capable of handling deep-sea ships without enlargement and was exclusively under Canadian control. Transit of the Welland Canal had been free until the seaway was opened for traffic. Tolls were then imposed on the Welland, and opposition from vested interests of course arose. During an election campaign Diefenbaker announced that the Welland tolls would be removed. He failed to realize, I was told, that the microphones were still open, and went on to exclaim, 'That should get their votes.' It did not; Liberal candidates won most of the seats in the Niagara Peninsula. Removing the toll was one of the few promises Diefenbaker kept. To reduce the burden on the Treasury I was determined to restore tolls, or user fees in some form, on the Welland traffic.

User fees were restored, but they were not called tolls. In its annual report the Seaway Authority suggested another name, 'lockage fees.' The lockage fees would be phased in over a period of five years. The government accepted the suggestion. In putting it to Parliament I pointed out that the operation and maintenance of the Welland had cost $9 million in 1966, a significant sum. The lockage fees would rise progressively, from $20 per lock for the current navigation season to $100 in the 1971 navigation season. They would not cover the full operating costs but would make a sizeable contribution. I concluded by recalling that the Welland canal, although entirely within Canada and built and operated by Canadians, was open to all the ships of the world. To continue to ask the Canadian taxpayer to be the sole provider when more than 50 per cent of the cargo moving through the Welland was of non-Canadian origin was difficult to justify. Those who profit most directly, the users, would quite rightly be asked to bear a share of the financial burden. I had no difficulty in getting approval in the House.

A couple of days later Diefenbaker asked whether I had received a protest that the lockage fees were discriminatory against

Ontario steel production, and whether the government would reconsider. I admitted that I had received a protest and had given it careful, indeed agonizing, consideration. I had concluded that the government would not be justified in continuing free passage. Diefenbaker then asked whether it was a final decision, or whether my heart might be softened enough to provide for an agonizing reappraisal. I replied that I did not think any decision in this vale of tears was ever final. I reminded him that decisions were sometimes made in connection with the Welland Canal without much consideration of any kind. It gave me some satisfaction to remind him that taking off the Welland tolls had not won him the seats.

Major changes in the Welland Canal

By 1963 there were serious delays in passage through the Welland because traffic had greatly increased. McIlraith had undertaken that the government would construct a second channel so that upward and downward traffic could be separated; the process is called twinning.

During the year before I became minister, the Seaway Authority received a proposal for a system of computer traffic control that would speed up traffic almost as much as twinning and at a much lower cost. The Authority recommended that alternative to me; I saw the engineer who was promoting the computer system and was impressed. I then asked each of the three members of the Authority to speak for himself in making a recommendation. All three without hesitation recommended traffic control. I accepted their recommendation, though I knew my decision to abandon twinning would be attacked by the retiring engineer in the transport department, who was highly regarded. Despite his protests, supported by others, the cabinet agreed to drop twinning in favour of the use of computers. In the spring of 1966, I reported to Parliament that the new facilities had reduced substantially the average time required to travel the canal and had consequently brought savings to the users.

There were also substantial delays in seaway traffic because of the number of highway and railway bridges that had to be opened for the passage of each ship. The canal passed through the city of Welland and cut it into two more or less equal parts. The Seaway Authority had worked out a plan to enable the canal to bypass the city. The bypass would be costly, and I did not want the cost to rise because of land speculation. I authorized the Seaway Authority to prepare, in the greatest secrecy, the documents needed to file for expropriation of the land necessary for the new channel. The documents were available for filing when the Land Titles Office opened on a Monday morning. I saw Pearson and Mitchell Sharp, the minister of finance, together during the weekend, and they gave me their assurance that they would make certain my proposal was approved by cabinet. The precautions prevented the cost of the land from rising in anticipation of construction.

Larger ships were being constructed for grain handling on the Upper Great Lakes, and it was possible that the Welland might have to be enlarged to permit their passage. The new channel would be wide enough for them. Land was also expropriated for a possible new channel below the escarpment to carry such ships. Such a costly undertaking has not been needed, but the land acquired was a good investment. When I announced that major construction program, the expropriations were already under way. The actual cost was $188 million.

The Welland bypass was not the whole program. Arrangements were made with the Ontario government to have highway bridges over the bypass sufficiently elevated that they would not interfere with traffic on the canal and to have a single tunnel constructed to carry all railway traffic crossing the canal. The speed of transit was thereby vastly improved, and the consequent savings to users far exceeded the cost of lockage fees. Lift bridges no longer delayed most motor and railway traffic in the Niagara peninsula; all three modes, water, road and rail were made speedier and safer. In addition a major obstacle to the integration and growth of the city of Welland was removed. The government had every reason to be proud of the transformation in the transit infrastructure of the Niagara region.

An unhappy wage settlement

My relations with the Seaway Authority were excellent, and I had the greatest confidence in Pierre Camu, who succeeded to the presidency early in my time in office. The one fly in the ointment was over the handling of a labour dispute.

Grain traffic was heavy in 1965 and 1966, and it was in the national interest to keep the channels of transport open. Traffic through Montreal had been stopped by a longshoremen's strike in May 1966, which was ended by the personal intervention of the prime minister on 14 June. In March a dispute began between the Seaway Authority and the union negotiating for the workers on the seaway. The workers on the Canadian side had lower wages than those on the American side and wanted parity. After the usual preliminaries, with a strike date set for 17 June, the minister of labour, John Nicholson, appointed Senator Norman Mackenzie as mediator. Mackenzie held a meeting with the union negotiators in the Château Laurier at which he asked Nicholson and me to be present for the opening. I agreed reluctantly; I really represented the Seaway, not the union. Nicholson and I withdrew after the introduction of Mackenzie. Before attending the meeting I had received a promise from Mackenzie that he would make no commitments until he had reported to Nicholson and me. I was tired and went off to rest in a hotel bedroom. Not long afterwards I had a telephone call from Mackenzie to tell me that he thought the union had a good case, and that he had told the negotiators he would recommend to the government that their demands be accepted.

I thought it appalling for a mediator to listen to only one side in a dispute; I was outraged and said so. But I did not see how the government could accept another interruption of grain traffic just a day or two after one had been ended. I called Mitchell Sharp, who was even more concerned about the moving of grain than I was. We agreed that the government could not face another strike, which if the report of the government's own mediator was rejected, would almost certainly be long and next to impossible to end by legislation. Mitchell agreed that I should recommend to the cabinet that the Seaway Authority be directed to implement the mediator's recommendation. We had a glum cabinet meeting. One minister asked whether the Authority could not accept on its own. My reply was that if I was president of the Authority, I would resign rather than accept voluntarily a wage settlement about which I had not even been consulted, much less allowed to make my case to the mediator. I said the government itself must take the responsibility, and in the light of all the circumstances I recommended that we direct the Authority to implement the mediator's recommendation. I had never taken responsibility with greater distaste, and the government accepted with even greater reluctance. I was told later that even the union negotiators were shocked; they had never expected or even hoped that their full demands would be met. An inflation-breeding decision had been made, but I continue to believe that the alternative would have been worse.

The decision was never criticized or even discussed in Parliament. The NDP would not criticize a decision in favour of organized labour, and the Tories evidently feared the wheat farmers. But it was a bad day's work.

The National Harbours Board

My relations with the chairman of the National Harbours Board, Howard Mann, were always smooth. As minister I of course had responsibility for any change in the functions or scope of the board. I introduced one change in making the board responsible for dredging the St Charles River as part of Québec Harbour, and I arranged to have the administration of St John's Harbour in Newfoundland taken over by the board. My main relations with the board related to Vancouver Harbour, which was rapidly becoming the busiest in Canada. I had been involved with arrangements to ensure that all three railways, CN, CP and Pacific Great Eastern (now British Columbia Railway), owned by the provincial government, should have effective access to the harbour, particularly for the shipment of grain.

But my most memorable involvement was in a complicated problem regarding the export of coal to Japan. The Diefenbaker government had started to subsidize, on an experimental basis, shipments of coal to Japan for steel production, and contracts were later arranged on a regular basis between two coal mines in the Crowsnest Pass and one on the main line of the CPR in Alberta. There were still subsidies being paid in 1966, but the government was eager to get transportation and shipping costs reduced in order to eliminate the subsidy. One of the mines in the Crowsnest was acquired by the Kaiser interests, and a scheme was worked out with the B.C. Social Credit government of W.A.C. Bennett by which Kaiser would export coal provided the coal was moved by rail to the international boundary, carried by an American railway to the coast and then moved back into Canada for shipment from a long wharf to be constructed in the province at Roberts Bank, just north of the American boundary. The freight rate would be lower than the CPR was charging, and the federal subsidy could therefore be reduced. The B.C. government would build and own the wharf.

When Kaiser and Bennett discovered that there would not be federal approval for a railway line from the mine across the international boundary to the American railway, they proposed to overcome the difficulty by building the connecting railway to just short of the border, so that it would be entirely under provincial jurisdiction: if the American railway did not cross the border, it would not be subject to Canadian regulation. One proposal was to leave a gap of about one inch between the rails through which the international boundary would pass. I regarded the proposal as ridiculous and was resolved to prevent Canadian coal produced under subsidy from being transported through another country when the CPR had facilities available.

My parliamentary secretary, Jim Byrne, was the MP for East Kootenay, where the Crowsnest mine was situated, and he was afraid my tough stand would upset the sale and deprive the miners of employment. I put pressure on the CPR to match the American freight rate and to get running rights on the long wharf being built at Roberts Bank so that the coal could be moved directly from the freight cars into ships. In order to make sure the whole operation would be under federal control I persuaded the cabinet to extend the boundaries of Vancouver Harbour from the mouth of Burrard Inlet to the international boundary.

It was not long before federal subsidies were no longer needed, and other mines, including one owned by Canadian Pacific, were sharing in the expanding Japanese market, with the freight charges being paid to a Canadian railway.

The Caribbean

Guyana

In Opposition I had followed with interest the founding of the federation extending from Jamaica to Trinidad of all the British Caribbean colonies, and deplored its break-up. Not long after the Pearson government was formed, I met Errol Barrow, the premier of Barbados for the first time and expressed my regret at that failure. He explained that communications were not good enough, and industry and commerce not developed enough to make cohesion possible, though he saw it as a long-term goal, particularly in the eastern Caribbean. Jamaica he thought too far away to be a helpful senior partner. My own experience was to convince me that his judgement was sound, and that conversation also convinced me that I was talking to a leader in the making.

By December 1965, I had visited Jamaica, Grand Bahama, and St Martin and had made a brief stop in Antigua, so the region was not totally strange to me when I next saw Barrow, at his residence in Barbados during my first visit there, with Margaret. It was at his house that I first met Ken Patrick and learned of his substantial business interests in the Caribbean, particularly in Antigua and St Lucia. He became a guide to the region and a close friend.

My first official connection with the Caribbean began when I was chosen to represent Canada at the ceremony in May 1966 establishing Guyana, the former British Guiana, as an independent member of the Commonwealth. Margaret and I flew there.

J.W.P. making a Canadian presentation of an Inuit carving to Forbes Burnham, Prime Minister at the celebration of the Independence of Guyana, 1966.

Guyana was unique: geographically a part of South America, it belonged politically and socially to the British Caribbean.

The population was almost equally divided between blacks originally from Africa and East Indians brought in as indentured labour after the abolition of slavery. When limited self-government was achieved, the People's Progressive Party dominated the legislature, and Cheddi Jagan, its leader, an East Indian, became premier until the party split, mainly along racial lines. In an ensuing election Forbes Burnham, a black, became premier. Burnham, like Jagan, was a champion of independence, but within the Commonwealth; Jagan inclined towards close ties with the Soviet

Union. Canada's main interest in Guyana was the extensive operations of Alcan, which owned and operated mines there from which it derived much of its supply of bauxite. In my five days there I learned a great deal about the country. The Canadian high commissioner was my one-time cabinet colleague, Milton Gregg, recently married to Erika Deichmann, widow of the well-known Danish-Canadian potter and herself a potter, who became a lasting friend. Margaret and I were guests of the Greggs.

The British Governor was to continue as governor general until David Rose, of East Indian origin with an English wife, succeeded him. Rose was a wise and experienced man who could have been a useful confidant and adviser to Burnham had he not been killed by a falling stone while going through a doorway in Whitehall. The ablest minister in Burnham's cabinet was a Jamaican of East Indian origin, known to everyone as 'Sonny' Ramphal. He was later to become secretary to the Commonwealth in London. a position from which he retired in 1991. The ceremony of transfer from Britain to an independent Guyana was completed at midnight on 26 May by the lowering of the Union Jack and the raising of the Guyanese flag while Burnham and the leader of the Opposition, Jagan, embraced. It was a moving occasion. I confess I did not expect the new nation to escape serious racial conflict, but Burnham, who remained head of the government as prime minister and, later, president, when Guyana became a republic within the Commonwealth, maintained order and civil government, though elections were not won without dubious tactics. Burnham was a strong supporter of West Indian federation and helped to form a Caribbean free trade area with Barbados and Antigua.

The Canadian-Commonwealth Caribbean Conference

I cannot recall precisely how the decision was made to have a Canada-Commonwealth Caribbean Conference in Ottawa in July 1966; the first suggestion might have come from me. The notion was accepted with enthusiasm by the prime minister. All the ministers from the Atlantic Provinces were keen, particularly Bob

Winters, the minister of trade and commerce, whose father had carried fish to the West Indies in his schooner.

All the Commonwealth states in the Western Hemisphere were represented at the conference, which generated a great deal of goodwill and some positive results in both trade and aid. The idea of a free trade area was discussed, but no positive steps were taken to explore the question thoroughly. I referred to the existence before Confederation of the monetary union between Newfoundland and Canada and suggested that we should explore the feasibility of a wider monetary union with the countries of the Commonwealth in the Caribbean. I still regret that the idea was not examined seriously. I was in favour of having some permanent machinery established to follow up the meeting, but no minister had a specific mandate to organize such a government agency. I believe an opportunity was lost. The most lasting result was a closer coordination of transport and aid for airport development, which I pursued actively both as minister and, later, president of the Transport Commission.

Independence and statehood

By the time an official presence in the Caribbean was called for again, Pearson had tacitly recognized me as the minister most interested in the area. I was chosen to represent Canada at the ceremonies of independence for Barbados. That island was readier for independence than any other part of the British West Indies. It had been an English colony from the beginning; it had not changed hands during the wars of the late 17th and the 18th centuries. It had the best-educated population and a long tradition of public order and substantial self-government. In Barrow it had the ablest political leader in the Caribbean. He had served in the RAF during the war; he had had part of his training in Prince Edward Island and was well disposed to Canada.

Nothing could have exceeded the warmth of our welcome in Barbados or the smooth organization of all the ceremonial functions. The exchange of the Barbadian flag for the Union Jack was the same moving experience we had had in Guyana. Rapport with

Barrow was established in a way that I believe served both Canada and Barbados well.

While we were in Barbados, I was given an invitation to make an official overnight visit to the Dominican Republic. On arrival I was carried off to the presidential palace to greet the president. Our ambassador, George Hampson, had an evening reception in my honour in the embassy garden. At the reception I was seated on a dais with the president on one side and the papal nuncio on the other. I suggested that we converse in French, which was our only common language. I was surprised and gratified to find that I was more fluent than either of them. In fact we had little to say to one another.

A half-way stage between colony and independence, called associate statehood, had been worked out in Britain for Antigua, Dominica, Grenada, St Lucia and St Kitts-Nevis-Anguilla. They would have internal self-government with Britain retaining responsibility for defence and external relations. Statehood ceremonies were arranged for late February and early March 1967. I was

Official visit to the Dominican Republic by J.W.P., 1 Dec., 1966. Left to right; J.W.P., the President of the Republic, the Papal Nuncio and Canadian Embassy Officer.

the official Canadian representative to all of them, accompanied by Edgar Benson, then minister of national revenue. The
ceremonies in Antigua and St Kitts were on the same day, so
Benson went to St Kitts in my place. We were charmed by St Lucia
and dazzled by the beauty of Grenada. I had met all the premiers
at the Ottawa conference and Vere Bird of Antigua even earlier.

By November 1967, when Dominica was ready for statehood, I
was no longer in the government, and Donald Macdonald was
the official representative of Canada, but Pearson arranged for
Margaret and me to go as well. We flew ahead of the Macdonalds
and stopped in Barbados for a couple of days at the Paradise
Beach Club, where Prime Minister Burnham of Guyana also
happened to be staying. I had a pleasant luncheon with Barrow
and Burnham. We went on to Trinidad to stay with the high
commissioner and Mrs McKinney, who arranged a day trip for us
to Tobago, a beautiful island that seemed to me a miniature
Jamaica in topography. McKinney had a dinner for us with Prime
Minister Eric Williams, a most successful occasion. McKinney
was also high commissioner to Dominica and we flew there with
him and Mrs. McKinney.

Family activities and other travels

The year 1966 was on the whole less strenuous for Margaret and
me than the previous one. I made visits connected with my duties
to Quebec City, Vancouver, Victoria and St Catharines, on which
I took Agnès de France and Eric Facey, and to London, accompanied by Margaret. Ken Patrick took Peter and me to Antigua for
three days' sailing in his new cabin cruiser, and I took Alan and
Jamie Benidickson to Jamaica at Easter. Jane and Ruth had a youth
hostel tour of Europe in the summer, and in the autumn Jane and
Margaret travelled in Europe and the Middle East, one of the
highlights of Margaret's life. We were twice at Traytown, and we
spent a wonderful family Christmas in Antigua in a house lent to
us by Ken Patrick. From Antigua, Jane and I flew by Bermuda to
Gander, where she was to begin medical practice on 1 January,
and where I had a speaking engagement.

Centennial year was more active. I gave centennial lectures at Waterloo Lutheran (now Wilfrid Laurier) University and the University of Victoria and took part in a discussion at Carleton University. I took Alan Boyd, the U.S. secretary of transportation, to a sod-turning ceremony for the Welland Canal diversion. I had speaking engagements in Juneau, Alaska, Yellowknife and Vancouver, and Transport engagements in the Isle of Wight, Paris and Seattle. Margaret and I attended the installation of Roland Michener as governor general, and we participated actively in centennial functions across the country. I received honorary doctorates from three universities, Memorial, Manitoba and Bishop's, the last one at the ceremony at which Peter was awarded his BA degree, and at which St Laurent honoured us by his presence.

We were present at the opening of Expo 67 and various luncheons with heads of state and during the visit of the Queen. I was the minister in attendance on the Queen Mother during her visits to Charlottetown and St John's. We were at Traytown, preparing to fly to Ottawa for the state dinner for De Gaulle, when the French president made his triumphal tour from Quebec City to Montreal, climaxed by the shocking 'Vive le Québec libre!' We first heard of his outburst in a telephone call at 3 a.m. from an indignant Saskatoon resident who said I was the only cabinet minister he could reach to protest. I asked him if he thought De Gaulle should have said 'Québec pas libre,' and hung up the receiver.

In addition to, or in the course of the official responsibilities Margaret and I had trips to Montreal, where we spent a weekend with my brother Tom and his wife, Margaret; London; and France, where we saw the de Frances. We also made an extensive aerial tour of the north from Alaska to Baffin Island, a splendid experience. It was a special pleasure to have Paul and Eliane de France come to visit us in Ottawa and to take them to Expo, on their first and only visit to North America. For the last days of their stay, during which I had pressing engagements, they were the guests of Frank and Thérèse Lafferty in Montreal, who also had my sister, then known as Jane, as their guest that year. Such hospitality in Montreal during Expo was by no means rare, and added something to the happy spirit of the centenary.

14   A New Role in Transport

Leaving public life

Considering a new career

By 1967 I had completed the three major reforms I had undertaken as a member of the Pearson government. Canada had a new
method of redistribution of constituencies entirely free of partisan
pressure. Legislation was in place to reduce the growing subsidies
of railway wages, greatly limit the regulation of railway freight
rates and establish a regulatory body to coordinate all modes of
transport under federal jurisdiction. A new civil aviation policy
had been formulated.

I had no legislation to bring forward in the new session of
Parliament, which did not open until 6 June and was to adjourn on
7 July until late September to provide a recess for ministers and
MPs during Expo. There were always plenty of administrative
problems for the minister of transport, but there were no big new
projects. There could be no better time to retire with the likeli-
hood of ensuring a smooth transition in the cabinet.

Until 1967 I had given little thought to my personal finances.
The member of my staff who looked after my banking and other
financial chores asked me one day if I would like to know what
my financial future would have been if I had remained clerk of the
Privy Council or a deputy minister. She made the calculation and

reported that my pension as a public servant would have been twice as much. At that time there was no pension whatever for ministers, and a meagre pension for MPs. I had no debts, but no private means. If I ceased to be a minister, I would be virtually a pauper, even if I stayed in Parliament as a private member. So early in 1967 I began to think of seeking a new career in order to establish financial security for myself and my family.

Once the National Transportation Act was passed, the urgent task for the minister was to see that preparations were made to enable the Canadian Transport Commission to function fully from the day it was set up. Regulations for its operation had to be drafted and approved in advance, a large task requiring highly skilled legal talent. Prospective commissioners had to be recruited to fill the new positions on the commission. The act permitted the appointment of one or more commissioners before the commission itself was established, amd it was desirable, in my view, to decide first who would be president. In early May I decided that John Baldwin would be the most suitable choice. I spoke to him and found he was willing.

During the following night I woke up and was suddenly struck by the thought that becoming president of the commission might solve my own problem. By morning I had decided to see Baldwin at once to tell him about the result of my overnight reflections. He was younger, had long been a senior public servant and would have a substantial assured pension. I compared my precarious position with his and told him I intended to see the prime minister to find out whether he would have me appointed, if I was still of the same mind when the time came to set up the commission. If I was not, I would recommend John. He received my decision sympathetically and, I felt, without much disappointment.

I saw Pearson the same day. He was greatly surprised, but readily agreed. He told me that he would have been more reluctant to agree if he had not already decided to retire himself as soon as the centennial celebrations were over. I warned him that it would be highly embarrassing to both of us if any word leaked out before I had made my final decision; fortunately none did. I had already made up my mind to leave the cabinet and parliament. When Pearson agreed to recommend me, I decided to accept.

The first step was to find a senior vice-president. The vice-president could exercise all the powers of the president and would make the final decision on points of law arising in drafting decisions that the commission would have to make in its quasi-judicial function. Under the act the vice-president had to be a lawyer; I wanted an eminent lawyer, a legal scholar and a French Canadian. There would have to be an adequate salary; it was my opinion that a qualified lawyer could not be found for less than $35,000 which was higher than the salary of any deputy minister. The prime minister and the president of the Treasury Board agreed.

Having secured their agreement I approached L.J. Pigeon, who had been legal adviser to the Québec government when Lesage was premier, and who had a high reputation as a legal scholar and draftsman. I had never actually met Pigeon, but I was impressed by his attitude when we had a long talk about the commission, and I offered him the vice-presidency. He was obviously interested, but he later declined, after calculating what the retirement pension would be and deciding that it would not be adequate. It was lucky for him that he refused, as Pearson not long afterwards had him appointed a judge of the Supreme Court of Canada.

The next person whose name came to my mind was Pierre Taschereau. I had met him once or twice casually but did not really know him, though his wife, Yseult, the daughter of Laurent Beaudry, was a long-time friend of Margaret's and mine from our early days in Ottawa. Pierre had recently left the legal department of CN to join a leading law firm in Montreal. I consulted Norman MacMillan, the CN president, who said that Pierre was not only the best French-Canadian lawyer he knew but the best lawyer he could think of. He predicted that Pierre would not be interested but agreed that there was no harm in trying. Shortly afterwards I was spending the night in the private railway car at Windsor Station in Montreal and invited Taschereau to see me in the morning. After I had outlined the position and made my offer, I quickly asked him not to make an immediate decision, and said I would be disappointed if he said yes immediately and insulted if he said no without taking time for reflection. He undertook to think about it during the weekend, telephoned me on Monday or Tuesday to say that if the offer was still open, he would accept.

I could not have done the job of president wihout the benefit of Taschereau's devoted support and wise counsel. Working with him I gained one of my dearest friends. He produced a legal and administrative structure, and when the commission was in operation, his knowledge of transport and his capacity for administration were as invaluable as his knowledge of the law.

Ceasing to represent Newfoundland

I had been elected MP for Bonavista-Twillingate six times in 12 years with overwhelming majorities. I had to think about facing a seventh election in a year or two, if I planned to stay in Parliament. Almost everyone told me after my sixth election that no one could ever defeat me in Bonavista-Twillingate, but I was sure that if I stayed on too long I would be defeated as I grew older, and the majority of the voters grew younger.

I thought long and hard about ceasing to represent Newfoundland in the cabinet. I knew that many Newfoundlanders would regret my departure. But in the light of what had been accomplished during my 14 years as an MP and my more than 8 years as a cabinet minister, I did not think I could be fairly accused of deserting Newfoundland or of lack of devotion to the people in my constituency.

One of the most noteworthy achievements was the completion of the Trans-Canada Highway from Port-aux-Basques to St John's as quickly as possible after the Pearson government came into office and the 90-10 cost-sharing program came into effect. I watched the progress with pride on each visit to Newfoundland. Smallwood had signs along the highway reading We'll Finish the Drive in 65. Thanks to Mr. Pearson. Few provincial politicians gave the government of Canada similar credit for federal support. And finish the drive in 1965 they did, with a substantial reduction in the time taken for travel on any part of the Trans-Canada.

By late 1967 most of the outports on the northeast and west coasts of Newfoundland were connected with the Trans-Canada Highway by local roads, and the roads along the gulf shore to the Straits of Belle Isle were well under way. Most of the inhabited islands were connected by ferry to the road system. The roads were provincial, but they had received substantial federal help from one program or another as a result of constant pressure from me and other MPs. The ferries to the islands greatly reduced the need for expensive service by the coastal boats in addition to providing more frequent service.

The Atlantic Development Board had promoted the hydroelectric development at Baie d'Espoir, which in turn made the electrification of the island of Newfoundland feasible. A road between the Trans-Canada Highway and the power plant at Baie d'Espoir was ending the isolation of a substantial section of the south coast, previously served only by marine coastal service.

Ferry service had begun across the Strait of Belle Isle to the most easterly settlement in Québec, a stage in opening a back door to Newfoundland along the Lower St Lawrence and access by road to the Labrador side of the strait as far as Red Bay.

The ferry service between Port-aux-Basques and North Sydney had been expanded steadily. A terminal for civilian air service had been established at Goose Bay, and a road constructed from there as far east as the historic settlement of Northwest River.

Gander had been greatly stimulated when Eastern Provincial Airlines there acquired Maritime Central and became the recognized carrier for the Atlantic provinces. Chesley Crosbie and his family were the main owners of Eastern Provincial Airlines, and in A.J. Lewington they had an efficient and imaginative manager. Jim Lewington was a great help to Margaret and me; we have remained friends and summer neighbours on the shore of Bonavista Bay in our retirement years.

The harbour of St John's improved substantially after I arranged to have its administration entrusted to the National Harbours Board.

The passenger service on the Newfoundland railway had disappeared amid lamentations, many of them phoney, and been replaced by an efficient bus service operated by the railway on the hard-surface Trans-Canada Highway. Freight service on the railway was already becoming obsolete, but I did not want to see it disappear until adequate highways were in place to meet traffic needs. I felt and still feel that since the government of Canada accepted the responsibility for the railway at Confederation, the federal treasury had a moral if not a narrowly legal responsibility to maintain adequate highways for freight service across the island if the railway was closed. I hope that some day that responsibility will be assumed by the federal government.

Newfoundland had come a long way since the establishment of Terra Nova National Park had closed the gap in the road across the island. I was satisfied that the province had not been neglected while I was minister of transport.

Smallwood was still obsessed with his dream of a third paper mill at Come by Chance. My friends who were knowledgable kept me skeptical that there was enough wood for a mill in that location. John Shaheen, an American promoter with big ideas, had undertaken to promote the third mill. Instead he came up with a new objective for Come by Chance, an oil refinery. Building a refinery would require federal cooperation in the provision of a dock. The deep waters of Placentia Bay could be navigated by large tankers, and the project was technically feasible. I was not involved in the financing of the refinery.

In the course of discussions about the dock Shaheen retained Richard Nixon, who had a legal practice in New York between his first political career and his second. Shaheen brought Nixon to Ottawa to see me as minister of transport. I was not an admirer of Nixon but was curious to meet him and gave a luncheon for him. To my surprise I found him well informed about world affairs and moderate in his views. We also discussed the domestic scene in the United States and the leading personalities in Washington. He professed great admiration for Lyndon Johnson. I did not invite the prime minister to lunch, but took Nixon to see him briefly afterwards; my recollection is that Pearson had not met Nixon before.

I was consulted less about the oil refinery than I was about the project to develop the vast potential hydroelectric power at Churchill Falls, in Labrador. My connection with the project began when Robert Winters took over in July 1963 as chairman and chief executive officer of Brinco, the company inspired by Smallwood and entrusted with the development of Churchill Falls. When we were in the cabinet together, and indeed, from the time Winters became a minister, we had a close relationship and often discussed his serious problems; Brinco could not develop the falls until there was agreement between Newfoundland and Québec, and Winters sought consolation from me about his difficulties in getting the two premiers, both prima donnas, to agree and stay in agreement. He and I had both served in the cabinet at Ottawa with Jean Lesage, the premier of Québec, and my unique relationship with Smallwood was also helpful in preventing a total breach several times. Two examples: when Hydro-Québec bought a minority interest in Brinco without Lesage's telling Smallwood, much less seeking his approval, anger erupted; when Smallwood said Lesage was so arrogant he made De Gaulle look humble, Lesage was not amused.

I was most helpful in another area. At that time hydro power producers owned by the provincial governments were agents of the Crown and not subject to federal taxation, but privately owned corporations had to pay corporation income taxes on their profits. Not only was that anomaly inequitable, but the financial advisers of Brinco in New York calculated that federal taxation would increase the cost of Brinco power beyond the cost for which Hydro-Québec could produce power on one of the undeveloped rivers in Québec. I was able to arrange meetings for Smallwood with Pearson and Walter Gordon, where he could put the case for removing the federal tax to make the huge development possible. I used what influence I had to the same end. Fortunately power in Alberta and Nova Scotia was produced by private corporations, and there was pressure from both provincial governments, especially Alberta, for the removal of the federal tax, so action, when taken, was not solely for Newfoundland.

Winters decided to return to public life in 1965, and I was astonished when he proposed that I should replace him as the chief executive officer of Brinco. I could not imagine myself as a business executive, did not regard the proposal as serious and gave it no consideration. Two years later, when I decided to leave public life, Winters told me that he had been serious, and that I had made a great mistake in not accepting an offer that would have made me financially secure for life. But I had no desire to be a tycoon and have no regrets.

The only serious strain over policy in my relations with Smallwood after I became minister of transport arose over a decision by the Wabush Mining Company to establish a pelleting plant near Sept-Îles for the iron ore from Labrador. Smallwood had bullied the Iron Ore Company to build its pellet plant at Labrador City, and he tried to do the same with Wabush, saying that iron ore would be sent out of Labrador to be processed elsewhere over his dead body. Wabush held its ground and insisted that the ore would be shipped out of Canada without processing unless the plant was built on tidewater. I had to persuade Smallwood that he would have to acquiesce, or he would jeopardize federal support of much greater importance to Newfoundland. But it was not easy, and I regarded the incident as a warning for the future.

During my years of association with Smallwood I always recognized that there could be only one king in Israel. That did not bother me, but I sensed that Smallwood felt I was no longer as responsive as he would have liked.

A difficult situation developed when by-elections were called to fill the vacancies in the House of Commons created in 1966 when Smallwood persuaded Charlie Granger to resign from the House and join his government as minister for Labrador, and Chesley Carter was appointed to the Senate. Without consulting Charlie or me Smallwood announced that Ken Goodyear's son, Terry, would be the Liberal candidate in Grand Falls-White Bay-Labrador. Charlie soon realized that there was such resentment on the part of many voters in Grand Falls and Gander at being taken for granted that the election might be lost. Without consulting Smallwood we decided to call a convention to choose a candidate, and young Goodyear lost to Andrew Chatwood, who won the election. Similarly, Smallwood wanted Don Jamieson to be the candidate in Burin-Burgeo to succeed Carter, and so did I, but I told Jamieson we should have a convention. I attended the convention without Smallwood's being invited. He would be displeased, I knew, but I telephoned him the day after the convention to say how well it was attended, and what a fine reception Jamieson had received. My report got cold, monosyllabic acknowledgment. For some time afterwards, I was told, Joe talked about Pickersgill Liberals and Smallwood Liberals. That did not worry me, as I was confident the pique would blow over the moment he wanted me to do something for him in Ottawa, and it did.

What worried me was that some of the ventures Smallwood was promoting were dubious, and that a clash over substance would occur sooner or later. I felt that he was entitled to some advance warning of my personal plans, so, on 15 August, at the official opening of the Baie d'Espoir hydro project, I told him what I was considering. I said I had not finally decided but made it clear that it would be hard to dissuade me. He was shocked and at once told me that if I merely wanted to leave Parliament, he would make me an adviser to the provincial government on terms more favourable than I could expect as head of the commission. I was not tempted. I had found it relatively comfortable to work with him in an equal relationship, but nothing would have induced me to work with him as a subordinate, though I did not tell him that. I had really made up my mind by then, but I did not give him my final decision until we were together again, at the opening of the shipyard at Marystown. He tried once more to take me up to the top of a high mountain and offer me everything I could see, but I convinced him that my decision was firm.

Resignation

The need for financial security was not my only reason for deciding to leave public life. My health seemed good, and my capacity for work had not diminished, but the heart flutter in 1964 had been a warning. While there were urgent tasks to perform, and there always would be in Transport, I could not slow down. Someone described the president of the Transport Commission as the Czar of Transport, and the word had caught on even before the commission was established. In fact the creation of the commission did not take one function away from the department, and I knew that the burden would not be as great in the commission, especially as the act conferred on the senior vice-president the capacity to perform all the functions of the president. But my sons call me Czar to this day.

I had developed a distaste for the atmosphere in the House of Commons, though I realized that it might improve after the deposition of Diefenbaker as party leader and his replacement by Stanfield. My impact on public and party policy was already declining, and looking ahead, I could see that the decline was bound to continue, particularly if I continued to carry the heavy responsibility for Transport.

Pearson was about to retire, and I did not believe that Paul Martin was likely to succeed him. Any other new leader would be younger than I, and I was sure that if I remained in the cabinet, I would be an embarrassment to the new leader no matter how good our personal relations might be. I knew far more about how a prime minister should perform than a new leader could possibly know at the start. Mackenzie King had told me more than once that as long as Sir Lomer Gouin and W.S. Fielding, both much older and more experienced, were sitting one on each side of him, he did not feel he was really prime minister, and I did not want to be in that kind of position. There was always a chance that the new leader might not keep me in the cabinet, but I doubted that I would be discarded, at least at the beginning.

I had enough negative reasons for leaving public life. On the positive side the opportunity to see whether the new agency of government I had had such a large share in designing would work well in practice, and how well I could direct it, was an attractive prospect.

By the beginning of September, Taschereau, who had become vice-president at the beginning of July, had the regulations drafted and other preliminaries planned. I gave Pearson my decision and told him I would like the act proclaimed, and my appointment made, before Parliament met again on 25 September. I gave him my letter of resignation on 5 September; it read:

Dear Mike:

Some time ago, I discussed my possible retirement from public life with you and you were good enough to assure me that if I wished to be president of the Canadian Transport Commission when the time came to set it up, you would recommend my appointment.

As you are aware, the work preparatory to setting up the commission is now largely completed and it will be possible to proclaim part one of the National Transportation Act by mid-September with the assurance that the commission can then begin to function immediately.

After a good deal of reflection, I have come to the conclusion that, if you are still of the same mind, I would like to become president of the commission. The position is one which I believe I can fill adequately, and which will give me the opportunity of continued public service for several years. While a demanding and responsible position, it would not involve the same pressures as there are upon a minister of the crown. Though my general health seems to be excellent, I have, as you know, found these pressures very great in the past three years.

I believe it would be in the public interest at this time to have a younger man assume the portfolio of transport and, happily, in the government and in the ranks of your supporters in the House of Commons, there are several who could fill that office as well as I can.

One of the main reasons I agreed to leave the public service and enter public life in 1953, was that I was persuaded by Mr. St Laurent and Mr. Smallwood that I could make some contribution to a smooth transition of Newfoundland from its earlier status to a full integrated Canadian province. Not only has confederation now been almost universally accepted in Newfoundland, but there are happily several men active in public life today who could represent Newfoundland effectively in cabinet.

My main reluctance, therefore, in leaving public life is that, in doing so, I shall be breaking that close association I have had with you, in opposition and in government, since you became the leader of the Liberal party. While we have not always seen eye to eye on every public question, I have never faltered in my conviction that our party made a happy choice for Canada in 1958. I have been proud to be associated with you and our other colleagues in the government of our country, and in the indispensable work you have done to strengthen the foundations of a united Canada, which I believe history will recognize as the greatest of your many public achievements.

Despite my reluctance to sever this relationship which has been a happy one for me, I feel that I should accept the opportunity for somewhat less strenuous public service offered by the presidency of the Canadian Transport Commission and, if you agree, ask you to accept my resignation as Minister of Transport as soon as it is convenient for you to have the Commission established.

In doing so, I want to express my deep appreciation of your unfailing understanding and support of my efforts in public life as one of your supporters, and my gratitude for your friendship.

Yours ever,
J.W. Pickersgill

Presumably he advised the governor general and received his approval before he replied on 11 September:

Dear Jack:

I have already told you with what great regret I received your letter of September 5 indicating your desire to retire from the government and your willingness to accept the presidency of the Canadian Transport Commission, an appointment which I discussed with you some time ago.

While I know that this appointment is a most important and responsible one and will give you a further opportunity for public service, I cannot help but feel sad at the thought that it will mean your departure from the cabinet and from the political life of our country where you have played such an important role for so many years.

I don't suppose there is anybody who is in a better position than I am to appreciate the value of the contribution you have made as a member of the government; to our party when we were in opposition, especially in its parliamentary activities, and to the Canadian public service before that. No one knows better than I do, how much you have given of your great knowledge and outstanding talent; of your energy and your devotion, to the service of this country.

We have been colleagues for more than thirty years in public service and I have valued our close collaboration only less than I have the friendship that has grown up between us as we worked together.

My great regret at your departure, however, is reduced but not removed, by the assurance that our friendship will continue, as well as that close personal association which I value so much.

All the best in the days ahead,

As ever,
L.B. Pearson

He said that he would inform the cabinet on 18 September. I knew that I would be accused in some quarters of creating a 'cushy' job for me, so I told Pearson that I did not want the appointment to give me any immediate financial advantage. I calculated that my income as a minister and an MP, with the tax-free allowance, was about equivalent to $40,000 a year, and that I would not want more than that.

At a certain point in the Cabinet meeting Pearson asked me to withdraw. When I was called back into the cabinet he told me that my resignation as a minister had been accepted, and that I had been appointed president of the Canadian Transport Commission. He did not mention the salary, but it had been fixed at $40,000. I was told later that one or two ministers had said it should be $50,000, but that Pearson had explained why I did not want a higher figure. Regret was expressed by my colleagues.

At midnight on 18 September 1967, I ceased to be a cabinet minister and a Member of Parliament. The next morning I was in improvised quarters in the Birks Building on Sparks Street as president of the commission wondering what I should do first. I knew that what I would miss most was not the cabinet or Parliament but having an aircraft at my disposal.

When Pearson announced my resignation and appointment in Parliament a week later, the comments from spokesmen of the other parties were friendly. Diefenbaker had ceased to be leader of the Opposition and was not in the House, but I felt he paid me the greatest compliment when he said later, 'Parliament without Pickersgill will be like Hell without the devil.'

The Canadian Transport Commission

The transition

Taschereau was well named Pierre: he was the rock on which the Canadian Transport Commission was founded. He had drafted the rules of practice and procedure for the new commission. On the day the commission was established, the Board of Transport Commissioners, the Air Transport Board and the Maritime Commission ceased to exist, and their members became members of the Canadian Transport Commission. Taschereau had a clear idea of how those bodies could be fused into one structure under the direction of the president and vice-president. For me, adapting to a judicial role, his guidance was vital. From the beginning, as vice-president in charge of the administration of the commission, he demonstrated quiet, even-handed firmness. He was the final authority in the commission on legal questions, and in the exercise of that authority he reminded me of St Laurent. I spent my first day as President with him; it was the start of a harmonious and happy association and a cherished and enduring friendship.

The Commission met for the first time on 20 September. Most of the commissioners from the old bodies I knew only slightly, three or four not at all. I realized that the process of assimilation would take time and patience. At the meeting, the members of the former bodies became members respectively of Railway, Air and Water Transport committees charged to carry on the business already under way in the former boards, according to the rules and procedures each had followed. The new rules of practice and procedure, adopted that day, would apply to new business. Motor Vehicle and Commodity Pipeline committees were also established and directed to look ahead for the functions they might be required to carry out. Provision was also made for a Review Committee to be set up if and when needed.

J.W.P. and Judy LaMarsh presenting locomotive to Museum in Ottawa.

Three Commissioners were appointed at the same time I was. David Jones, from a law firm in Winnipeg, who had impressed me during a presentation to the committee of the House on the National Transportation Bill was appointed to the Railway Committee. A.P. Campbell, from British Columbia, was appointed to the Water Transport Committee. Both Jones and Campbell later became chairmen of those committees. Laval Fortier, my deputy when I was minister of citizenship and immigration, was made chairman of the Motor Vehicle Transport Committee and also a member of the Air Transport Committee.

Harris Arbique, who had assisted me so effectively with ministerial correspondence about transport questions, was appointed secretary of the commission on my recommendation. He was the Chief Administrative Officer of the Commission, a function he performed admirably. Audrey McQuarrie moved to the Commission with me as my private secretary. She recruited the personnel needed to make a small but harmonious and efficient office. Audrey was thoroughly accustomed to my way of working and made sure I was free to do my job without distraction. My gratitude to her is unbounded.

At the start the headquarters of the Commission was in a building on Sparks Street, separate and apart from the offices occupied by the component entities, which were each in a separate building. It was obvious that the commission could not operate effectively as a unit until it was under one roof. It was not until 31 October 1968 that the commission was quartered at 275 Slater Street in a new office building. In the interim the headquarters had been moved to the Centennial Towers, where the Board of Transport Commissioners had been before the commission was set up. The Centennial Towers contained a courtroom that the commission took over and continued to use as long as I was President.

The most urgent task of the commission was to examine the existing railway costing regulations and to revise them, where necessary, to determine the financial support required from the government to meet the losses of the railways on those operations being maintained as a public service. That was the primary purpose of the national transportation legislation.

I made it clear that I would not take part in revising the costing regulations, and that I did not intend to participate in the regulation of telecommunications, which would be the responsibility of the vice-president, until such time as the government saw fit to establish a separate department of communications. I informed the commissioners that the vice-president would be responsible for the day-to-day administration of the commission, and that as president, I would concentrate on action needed to implement the policies laid down in the legislation and from time to time by the government or the Department of Transport.

I had no intention of being a mere figurehead, but I was resolved not to work at the break-neck pace I had maintained as minister of transport. My first duty, as I saw it, was to learn how the regulative and judicial task had been performed by former agencies, and what changes were needed to carry out the new law. I had also to shake off my partisan skin and learn to behave like a judge. Above all I had to divorce myself from any connection or any appearance of connection with the activities of the Liberal party. As long as I was president of the commission I never entered the gallery of the House of Commons, and visited the Parliament Building only when I had official business with the minister of transport. I have been in the gallery of the House only once since I resigned in 1967, and that was on a day when I was showing visitors around Ottawa.

I was not even consulted about the choice of my successor as cabinet minister for Newfoundland. There were two obvious possibilities in the House, Richard Cashin and Don Jamieson. I was glad Pearson did not ask my opinion as I would have found the choice as difficult as he did. When I told Charlie Granger, who was then in the provincial cabinet, about my intention to leave the cabinet and Parliament, I predicted that Pearson would consult Smallwood, and that he would advise Pearson to invite Charlie to be minister and a candidate in my old riding of Bonavista-Twillingate. I suggested that Charlie make up his mind in advance, but I refrained from offering him any advice. My prediction proved correct. Granger became minister without portfolio and the Liberal candidate in the by-election. Before the by-election could be held, Smallwood had a by-election called in the provincial constituency of Gander, which Granger had vacated. As I feared would happen, the Liberal candidate lost Gander to the Tories. I was then worried that Charlie might not win Bonavista-Twillingate and was vastly relieved when he did.

Two social occasions marked my departure from the cabinet and Parliament. Three days after my resignation the government of Newfoundland gave a dinner as an expression of appreciation of my services to the province. Those services were not undervalued in a speech by Smallwood. I was asked what would please me most as a recognition of my years as a Newfoundland MP and minister. My suggestion was the establishment by legislative action of an annual postgraduate scholarship bearing my name. That was done; the scholarship is still awarded every year. On 15 November the Speaker of the House of Commons gave an official dinner for Margaret and me to commemorate my years in Parliament.

On 24 November, Margaret and I were in Sorel, where she christened a new ferry for the Newfoundland service named *Ambrose Shea* for one of the two Newfoundlanders who were present at the Quebec Conference in 1864 which laid the foundations of Confederation. The premier of Québec, Daniel Johnson, was also at Sorel, to open a new building in the Marine Industries complex. Margaret and the premier stood side by side for about two hours shaking hands with a stream of visitors. She was delighted by his wit and charm.

Those three social occasions were as close as I ever came to partisan politics in the years I was president of the Canadian Transport Commission. I have never once had the slightest nostalgia for cabinet or parliament.

Learning on the job

At the beginning of 1968 I wanted to get the Research Division established as soon as possible. The creation of a research function for the commission was my own conception, and I was eager for its birth. I started in 1967 to look for an eminent Canadian with an academic background in transportation studies to be director of research. Unfortunately transportation was not a subject much studied in Canadian universities, and the few experts in the field were already employed. During the drafting of the national transportation legislation I had been attracted by Ray Cope, a relatively junior member of the drafting team in the Department of Transport. I asked John Baldwin whether he would be embarrassed if I invited Cope to join the commission. He shared my high opinion of Cope, who I found was willing to join the commission to work on organizing a Research Division. He was duly appointed, and joined the Commission on 15 February 1968. Cope worked out a structure for the division and began to recruit staff, partly Canadian and partly British, who proved competent or better. I was well satisfied and arranged to have Cope appointed vice-president from 1 January 1969.

Recalling my experience with the Atlantic Development Board, I felt the Research Division could be strengthened by contact with a group of interested citizens from every region of the country. At my suggestion the minister of transport appointed a 15-member advisory council to assist the Research Division in determining priorities for study. The council members were drawn largely from universities and industries that were heavy users of transport. We had two enthusiastic meetings in 1968, at which Cope and I were present.

By the end of 1968 the Research Division had a staff of 23, of whom 16 were professionals. I felt that a good beginning had been made in a novel experiment. Unfortunately a good deal of frustration developed largely because the planned scope of the Research Division was not adequately explained. The advisory council had to be allowed to die, because of limits placed on the scope of research. But my hope of an independent and permanent entity available for research into transport problems and opportunities faded away. I still believe the concept was a good one, and I was disappointed. The Research Division continued to do valuable work directly related to the regulatory functions of the commission and other chores entrusted to it from time to time by the minister of transport.

In Washington at the beginning of April, Taschereau, the accompanying staff and I met the heads of the various regulatory agencies of U.S. transport. We returned from Washington satisfied with Canada's progress in railway policy. Their rail freight rates were still regulated, and their passenger trains were much less efficient and even less lucrative. There was no coordination of rail, air and water transport. We felt, for once, that Canada was ahead of the United States.

Because of my experience in Newfoundland I took a special interest in regional and local air services. I had no direct knowledge of air operations into and within the north, so in June, accompanied by Margaret, I made an on-the-spot examination of northern air services. The vast empty land was no longer just on a map, but inside my head. I felt I had some background for coping with the problems of northern transport. Hearings in Yellowknife to consider applications for air services had been fixed for the week of 10 July and I decided to preside myself. Afterwards, I returned to Ottawa until the hearings resumed in Frobisher Bay on 24 July. Margaret went with me. We flew from Gander to Goose Bay and then along the Labrador coast, my only sight of the magnificent grandeur of those northern stretches. The hearings lasted the rest of that week. I had successfully completed my first judicial experience and found the process fascinating.

In negotiating with Public Works for space in a new office building on Slater Street, we had asked for the top two floors, which were considered the most prestigious. Atomic Energy Limited was also seeking new quarters. As a crown corporation it had the right to rent its own quarters, and it refused to rent through Public Works unless it could have the top floors. George McIlraith, who was still minister of public works, appealed to me to take space lower down to prevent a bureaucratic nightmare, and I readily agreed. I never understood why the top floor gave the occupant greater prestige. When we were moving in, the question of drapes for the windows of my room arose. Evidently my choice would determine the relative quality of the drapes for the other commissioners. I refused to have any drapes at all; I said I thought windows were to let in light, not to shut it out. I was told that my decision had embarrassed the secretaries of the other commissioners. It became obvious to me that I was not aware of the intricacies of the bureaucratic social world.

The only change in the composition of the commission in 1968 apart from Ray Cope was John Magee, who because of his background was appointed to the Motor Vehicle Committee.

One important structural change was made in November, when the International Transport Policy Committee was established. Gerald Morisset was finding it increasingly difficult to make decisions as chairman of the Air Committee, and the consequent delays were becoming embarrassing to the commission. I had a high regard for Morisset, who was knowledgeable about air transport, and I was not willing to demote him. I hit on the idea of having an International Transport Committee, with no regulative function, to have a watching brief on bilateral air negotiations and transborder transport by rail, water and road. I outlined the proposal to Gerry and asked him to become chairman of the new committee and to continue to serve on the Air Committee. He accepted, I thought with relief. I then appointed John Belcher, who was decisive and knowledgeable, as chairman of the Air Committee, where he served effectively until his retirement.

There were important changes in the transportation environment in 1968. Gordon McGregor insisted on retiring as head of Air Canada before mid-year, and Norman MacMillan, the head of CN, replaced him in an acting capacity while the government decided on the succession. When the decision was made, the post was divided between a chairman and a president. The new Chairman was Yves Pratte, an outstanding lawyer from Québec, who also became chief executive officer, and the president was John Baldwin, the long-time deputy minister of transport. It was to prove an unhappy combination for both incumbents and a bad experience for Air Canada. Baldwin was succeeded as deputy minister of transport by Gerald Stoner. I had got to know Stoner when he acted for a time as secretary to the cabinet; he had performed well in that capacity.

I find I made no fewer than 17 speeches in 1968, nearly all of them related in one way or another to transport.

Through 1968 I was learning on the job, discovering the scope of my duties as president and working to put the pieces together to make an effective team. By the beginning of 1969 I was, I believed, ready for an active role in the discharge of the functions Parliament had entrusted to the commission.

I soon discovered that the commissioners were being asked by the media to explain their decisions in the same way ministers were asked by the media to explain their policies. My own response to such requests was to point out that decisions made by the commission were judicial, and that judges were never called upon to explain their decisions. I stressed that point to all the commissioners. But I realized that we could be saved embarrassment by having an information officer to brush aside questions about our judicial decisions and to answer factual questions about our administrative activities. In the spring of 1968 I was invited by Ben Ward of the Canadian Press to attend the parliamentary press gallery dinner. Ward was the transportation reporter for Canadian Press, and I had been favourably impressed by the quality of his reports in the newspapers. When he told me the Canadian Press intended to transfer him to Toronto, where he was reluctant to go, I said we needed a public relations officer and asked him to apply. He won first place in a public service competition and was appointed on 1 October. Ben was not bilingual, so I insisted that his assistant must be. The first assistant was a French immigrant who left for a position elsewhere in the spring of 1970. Landon Stewart, who was thoroughly bilingual, had just completed a year of postgraduate work and was looking for a job. Landon was the daughter of William Stewart, head of the Canadian Press in Montreal, and his wife, who was the sister of my first wife. She applied at my suggestion and was appointed in June 1970. I was pleased that the position had been filled by an anglophone: it would serve as evidence that bilingual in the public service did not mean francophone only. Landon decided in the fall of 1971 to return to university to complete her postgraduate work.

Ben Ward was a tower of strength to the commission, both positively, by making sure of his facts, and negatively, by preventing a great deal of misunderstanding of the work of the commission. I regarded him as the most effective public relations officer in the public service and was not surprised when after 10 years at the commission he was recruited by the Department of Finance. We developed a warm friendship, which ended only with his death in 1992.

Highlights of 1969

When one of the commissioners died in January 1969, I had no difficulty in persuading Paul Hellyer, then minister of transport, to have Frank Lafferty, a son-in-law of St Laurent, appointed. Frank was a chartered accountant and a tireless worker who became invaluable to the commission. By 1969, I really knew all the commissioners and had begun to size up their varied abilities. Once we were all in the same building, it was easier to shift commissioners from one committee to another to make sure that each served at all times on more than one. I attached great importance to giving all the commissioners exposure to more than one mode of transport, with a view to promoting our task of harmonizing and coordinating services. I decided to concentrate my own activity in two areas, railway passenger service and regional air carrier development.

The withdrawal of the mainline railway passenger service in Newfoundland required CN to substitute motorbus service. The buses covered the distance in half the time, the service was available to many settled areas along the Trans-Canada Highway not served by the railway, and the number of passengers increased from the beginning. But the substitution received no praise, and the withdrawal of the trains evoked noisy charges of attack on the heritage of Newfoundland, mainly from those who had rarely, if ever, used the trains once the Trans-Canada Highway had been completed. All the commissioners realized that the outcry would be just as great or even greater elsewhere in Canada. But as we studied the problem, most of us were shocked by how small a part of the cost of railway service was paid for by the passengers, and how great were the losses that would have to be paid for by taxpayers.

As a former minister I was acutely aware that the commission would have to remember that all our decisions could be appealed to the cabinet. If the hue and cry was great enough, our decisions might be reversed, and if that happened often, the usefulness of the commission would be greatly impaired. The risk, I felt, must be taken into account as we made our decisions. In fact, no decision of the commission was changed by the cabinet while I was president, but not as many passenger trains were allowed to disappear as was warranted.

After Don Jamieson succeeded Hellyer as minister of transport in 1969, I suggested to him that the regional air service policy needed revision to give the regional carriers access to metropolitan centres. As a Newfoundlander, Don knew how essential the regional carrier was to satisactory service. Despite some opposition from Air Canada we worked out together a substantial amendment of regional air policy, and later, in 1970, I applied myself assiduously to having the policy implemented by the commission.

The British government was pressing Canada hard to give BOAC access to ports of entry to Canada in addition to Montreal and Toronto. I felt strongly that in that field there should be genuine reciprocity: Canada should not give more profitable access to the airline of another country than that country gave to Canada's. External Affairs felt Canada should at least talk to the British, and I was asked to take on the task. Margaret and I flew to London on 31 October, where we took up residence at the Savoy, and I began talks with the British at an official level. The British officials referred to the talks as negotiations; I insisted that they were merely discussions about whether or not there was anything to negotiate. I told them that I had no authority to negotiate, but that if they could offer any advantages to Canada comparable with what they wanted from Canada, I would report to the government on the prospects of any satisfactory ageement. Britain had nothing substantial to offer. The only profit I derived from the exercise was an agreeable week in London, with visits to the theatre, and my discovery of the luxury of having a telephone in the bathroom.

On 8 November, I went to Brussels to meet Jamieson, where he was to represent Canada at a Conference on the Law of the Sea. Howard Darling, the chairman of the Water Transport Committee, had talked to me about the conference, which was to deal with oil pollution caused by tankers. He persuaded me that oil pollution was a particular hazard to Canada, with its long coastline and the risk of oil leaks even in the Arctic. I reported my impressions to Jamieson and persuaded him to attend the conference as minister, and he asked me to be with him as a consultant. We took a strong line and had considerable influence in the adoption of a resolution for the establishment of an international fund to provide adequate compensation for damages. The Brussels conference was as positive as the London discussions had been usefully negative. Jamieson and I also went to Paris to see the aerotrain operating on a test rail line.

I made at least 10 speeches in 1969, all related to some aspect of transport. The most noteworthy were to American audiences; each of them was arranged by the head of an American railroad who was enthusiastic about the deregulation of freight rates by Canada, and who became a fan of mine.

The big event in the transport world in Ottawa was the change of ministers. I had recommended Hellyer as my successor to Pearson and had been pleased when he was appointed. I had hoped and expected he would bring the same innovative energy to Transport that he had shown in National Defence. I was disappointed when he gave his main attention to the chairmanship of a task force on housing and left many of his responsibilities to James Richardson, a minister without portfolio designated to assist Hellyer. I had been friendly with Richardson, a fellow Winnipegger, and remained so, but as a minister he was a headache for me. He had some odd notions about regional air policy that he kept trying out on me, always insisting that the government needed a new air policy. He never seemed to realize that I had devised the existing policy and felt that all that was needed was some additional scope for the regionals; an idea he seemed incapable of grasping, much less of getting implemented.

I regretted Hellyer's resignation from the government, but I welcomed the appointment of Jamieson as minister. I had lasting gratitude for his support and valuable advice during my years as a politician representing Newfoundland and knew he was thoroughly aware of the problems of transportation, particularly in the air, in his native province. Our relations were cordial during my years at the Transport Commission, but I tried never to use our friendship to embarras him with unsought advice.

The president's year in 1970

There were a number of changes in the membership of the commission in 1970. Darling resigned on 20 February to become a consultant. I viewed his decision with mixed feelings; he was knowledgeable, especially about water transport, and had made a substantial contribution by his advice on oil pollution on the high seas, but he was uncompromising in his opinions and, in my view, always stubborn and often wrong. I appointed A.P. Campbell as his successor as chairman of the Water Committee. Campbell had a wealth of understanding of marine transport and a detailed knowledge of the British Columbia coast. He was modest, a good listener and an excellent team player; my appreciation of him as a colleague grew steadily, and I learned a good deal from him. Two former members of the Board of Transport Commissioners left the commission when they reached the age of retirement, and a former member of the Air Transport Board died near the end of the year. There was only one new appointment in 1970, R.M. March from Nova Scotia.

The Review Committee was set up late in 1970 under the chairmanship of the vice-president. Its function was to review decisions of other committees when dissatisfaction was expressed that might lead to appeals to the courts on points of law, or to the cabinet. The committee became active in 1971.

The government had a bill before Parliament to empower the Canadian Transport Commission to regulate telegraph and telephone tolls for the private wire services of federally chartered companies. Before the bill was introduced, the subject was considered by a cabinet committee of ministers and officials. I was invited to appear before the committee, which was presided over by Eric Kierans, the minister of communications. Unlike public services, which were not competitive, private wire services were offered by more than one company. I pointed out that they were highly competitive and in my opinion needed no regulation of their rates. I asked what public interest regulation was supposed to protect and expressed the opinion that the objective should be clearly stated, if Parliament was to impose such regulation. I got no answer to my objection except an astonishing statement by Kierans that the existence of the power to regulate would have a good moral effect. I assured the committee that the CTC, if given the responsibility, would do its best, but that I hoped it would not be imposed on us. Kierans assured me that if an act was passed by Parliament, it would not be proclaimed without previous notice to the commission. One day in July 1970 I learned from a newspaper report that the act had been proclaimed, to come into effect in August. That was my only experience of a mixed cabinet committee of ministers and officials, and I was horrified. It seemed to me that having officials of other departments pawing over projects that were within the scope of a specific minister was a dilution of responsible government and an unwarranted extension of bureaucratic influence. I was glad such mixed committees had not existed in my day in government.

One decision of the commission in which I took no part, because my participation might have been regarded as a conflict of interest, was the denial of an application from the Kootenay and Elk Railway and the Burlington Northern in the United States to connect their lines between British Columbia and Montana to enable Burlington Northern to carry Canadian coal through the United States for shipment to Japan from Roberts Bank, just north of the border in Canada. I had fought that outrageous proposal hard when I was minister of transport, and I rejoiced when the application was denied. The decision was appealed to the Supreme Court. In 1971 the court upheld the decision, the matter was finally put to rest, and the profit for carrying Canadian coal for export to Japan continued to be earned in Canada, not the United States.

I was involved in negotiations and hearings for much of 1970. Margaret, Ruth and I went to Antigua and Barbados in February, and I went on alone to Trinidad to meet Prime Minister Williams to facilitate the conclusion of negotiations for a bilateral air agreement permitting Trinidad's airline, BWIA, to operate to Canada. Margaret and I flew to Jamaica on 27 March where I presided over negotiations of a bilateral air agreement for exchange of services between Canada and Jamaica and an agreement between Air Canada and Jamaica to establish Air Jamaica with assistance from Air Canada personnel; it proved a happy relationship. We returned from Jamaica on 4 April, and the following week I was in British Columbia to hold hearings on air services in the interior.

The most extensive and controversial hearings were on an application by CP to withdraw the transcontinental train, the 'Canadian,' from service. I decided to preside at the hearings and to open them in Winnipeg on 17 August. My right to preside was challenged by counsel for the unions of the employees, on the ground that I had demonstrated partiality for CP and was in a conflict of interest. The evidence of partiality was a speech I had made at Montreal on 9 June, in which I had said, 'The public generally, and business men specifically, must come to realize that it is just as moral and just as praiseworthy to operate a railway, an airline, or trucking firm at a profit as it is to make a profit manufacturing motor cars or packing meat or making steel.' I adjourned the hearing to consider the charge, and when it resumed, I ruled that there was no evidence of partiality for the railway. My ruling was appealed to the Superior Court, and I adjourned the hearing until the case was heard in that court. My friend Dick Hunter, who was a leading counsel with the most prestigious law firm in Winnipeg, was retained to act for the commission, and won the case. I was able to resume the hearings in Calgary on 23 August. What I remember most clearly was the appearance before the hearing of Peter Lougheed, who had recently become leader of the moribund provincial Conservative party. I was attracted by his manner and impressed by the clarity of his presentation, with which I did not agree. I subsequently followed his career with great interest and growing admiration. When Stanfield resigned as leader of the federal Tory party, I said publicly that if I was a

Tory, I would crawl on my stomach to Alberta to beg Lougheed to be leader. Unhappily for the party, I was not a Tory. The hearings continued in Vancouver on 26 August, Ottawa on 29 August and Regina, Winnipeg and Thunder Bay in October. I agreed, with great reluctance, to a decision that the service should be continued, with recommendations designed to reduce the public expenditure to meet the substantial losses.

In September I presided at hearings of an application by Transair, the regional airline based in Winnipeg, for access to Toronto by way of Kenora, Dryden, Thunder Bay and Sault Ste Marie. The hearings began at Thunder Bay and continued in the Soo and Kenora, where we stayed over the weekend and I drove to Clearwater Bay to look at Highbrow House — for the only time

Negotiation of Air Bilateral between Canada and Jamaica at Ocho Rios, Jamaica, and recognition of partnership between Air Canada and Air Jamaica. J.W.P. was head of Canadian Delegation.

I have seen it since 1939. The house looked as solid as when it was built, and the view was as beautiful. We concluded the Transair hearings in Winnipeg and in due course approved the Transair application despite opposition from Air Canada.

A year of change, 1971

The most important event in 1971 was Taschereau's leaving the commission on 31 July and the appointment of his successor. Pierre told me early in the year that Norman MacMillan had approached him about the possibility of his returning to CN as vice-president. It was obviously a bigger and more exciting job than being number two in the commission. I had not at that time thought of retiring early; I would not reach the retirement age of 70 until 1975, so there seemed no prospect that Taschereau would succeed me at an early date as president. I told Pierre I could not and would not try to stand in his way, though I would miss him greatly. All I asked was that he should not leave until a suitable successor could be found. MacMillan readily agreed to have the appointment delayed until that happened.

After a day or two of reflection, I knew whom I would like to have succeed Pierre. Guy Roberge had impressed me by his performance when he was head of the National Film Board. He had gone to London to be the *agent-général* for the Québec government when Bobby Lapointe was obliged to give up that position to become lieutenant-governor of Québec. Before he went, Guy had assured me that he would come back to Ottawa if he was really needed. I wrote and asked him to see me the next time he was in Canada, but gave no hint of what I had in mind. He found a reason to come home soon after he received my letter. I told him that I had no power to choose Pierre's successor, but that I believed my recommendation would probably be accepted. Guy was obviously interested in the job, and he was anxious to be back in Canada before his children had been absent so long they would no longer feel Canadian.

When I approached Jamieson, he was very cooperative, and we soon got the formalities completed so that Taschereau could retire on 31 July and Roberge succeed him on 1 August. It took Guy a few weeks to become familiar with his duties, but no change could have been smoother. He was not as learned a lawyer as Pierre, but he had a greater familiarity with all parts of Canada and a wealth of knowledge that never ceased to astonish me. We became close friends in our work and in retirement and were in touch nearly every week when we were both in Ottawa. Guy's death left a gap in my life.

Two new commissioners were appointed in 1971, J.B.G. Thomson and L.R. Talbot. Thomson was from Saskatoon, a lawyer, a farmer and a pilot who owned his own plane. When Belcher retired in 1972, I appointed Thomson chairman of the Air Committee, where he served most effectively, I was told, until his life was almost shattered by a family tragedy. Talbot was a lawyer in the Department of Transport, where he was underemployed; I happily concurred in a proposal from Jamieson that he be appointed a commissioner and he served well.

By 1971 I felt that the commission was well integrated, and that the personnel was of a slightly higher calibre than in 1967. I paid close attention to the performance of the commissioners and continued to shift them around from time to time.

Country-wide hearings were held that year on CN's application to withdraw the 'Supercontinental.' I did not feel compelled to preside at the hearings as I was already familiar with their case, which practically duplicated the CP application. The CN application was denied, and the train became eligible for subsidies, though some recommendations of economies were made. By 1971 the railways had applied for withdrawal of almost all the passenger services in the country. The CN losses alone were greater than the original $100 million of general subsidies paid to the railways in 1967. I felt increasingly that we should be making more rapid progress. But we were restrained by public opposition and the widely held myth that the railways were deliberately trying to destroy passenger service. The truth was that when CP put the 'Canadian' into service, it was one of the finest trains in the world. Crump never ceased to be proud of the train and did not want it removed. CN had tried several ways to make passenger service more attractive; some of them increased the number of passengers but also increased the losses. The MacPherson Commission had recognized that passenger trains in Canada were obsolescent when not obsolete. Yet myth is often stronger than fact, and the taxpayers are still paying half a billion dollars and more every year to preserve that myth.

Better progress was made in 1971 in rationalizing air services. I presided over a hearing in Chicoutimi, conducted almost exclusively in French, which resulted in Air Canada's stopping service to Bagotville and leaving Québecair as the sole carrier. In August I was in Goose Bay for a hearing that ended Air Canada's service and left Goose Bay to Eastern Provincial Airways. On 15 September, Nordair inaugurated service between Hamilton and Pittsburgh. On 1 and 2 October I held hearings that permitted EPA to withdraw service from Summerside, P.E.I. In December hearings in Windsor, Ontario, at which I presided, approved an application from Nordair to add Windsor to its Ottawa/Hamilton service, despite Air Canada's opposition.

CP Air reached its limit of 25 per cent of transcontinental service in 1970, but its attempt in 1971 to limit some flights to Vancouver/Toronto was frustrated when the airline was required to serve both Vancouver and Montreal on all flights.

A speech I made to the National Defence Transportation Association of the United States at Minneapolis so impressed the audience that I was invited to go to Hawaii in 1972 to speak at an International Transport Pacific seminar.

By the end of 1971, I was finding myself tired at the end of each week. I seemed to have no capacity to work at a slower pace, and the possibility of retirement began to have some attraction. Early in 1972 I asked my brother Tom to calculate what my probable income would be on retirement, and he persuaded me that I did not need to remain on the job until 70.

Retirement

The CTC achievement that gave me the greatest satisfaction in 1972 was the appointment of Anne Carver as a commissioner. I had felt for some time that at least one woman should be appointed to the commission. One Sunday morning I said to Margaret, 'Surely I know one good woman, meaning someone with suitable qualifications.' Out of the blue I thought of Anne Carver, whom I had known since 1938, and who, upon her retirement from the public service, had a high reputation as an economist. I telephoned and asked her if she would be interested, and she called later to say she would be pleased to accept an appointment. I was shocked that it took the government several months to accept the recommendation; the appointment of a woman would obviously be helpful politically. When I retired half a year later, Anne had already proved to be one of the abler commissioners and one of the easiest to work with. In my years of retirement she has become an even closer friend.

Once I had decided to retire, I presided over no hearings on which decisions might have to be delayed until after I left the commission. But I ended my tenure in a blaze of glory with a tour of the northwest — Whitehorse, Dawson City and Inuvik. Dawson City was an indulgence for Margaret and me, but the visit to Inuvik was serious business. Against the advice of at least one of the members of the Air Committee, I had decided to have a pre-hearing session of several conflicting applications for air service in the north to see whether or not they could be sorted out and reduced to the point where they could be disposed of sensibly . During the hearing I was acutely ill for a day, and one of the other commissioners had to preside in my place. We received enough evidence to settle all the differences when we got back to Ottawa, and I felt my decision to hold the hearing had been amply justified.

I sent my resignation to the prime minister for acceptance at the convenience of the government at any time up to the end of August, and Jamieson told me it would be accepted on 31 August. John Belcher was retiring on 31 July and he told me that he had chosen that date to give him one more full year of service. There was a retirement allowance for each full year of service, but nothing for a fraction of a year. I had paid so little attention to the terms of my employment that I lost something like a thousand dollars by not waiting until 18 September, when I would have completed another full year. I was ashamed to admit my ignorance by suggesting a change of date. I made no recommendation of a successor. My choice would have been Guy Roberge, but I had heard rumours that someone else was being considered, and I did not want to risk the humiliation of having my recommendation ignored.

My last meeting as head of the commission was held on 31 August, and I went to Newfoundland the next day. Alan met me at Gander with the news that Parliament had been dissolved, and that E.J. Benson had been appointed president of the CTC. I was not surprised, but was sorry it had not been Roberge.

I felt that the performance of the commission had been creditable, though we had not accomplished as much as I had hoped. I thought that much more railway passenger service should have been discontinued, but my greatest regret was the comparative failure of the Research Division, for which I had had such high hopes. I had begun to feel the constraints of being an official after being a minister. I could have carried on competently, I believe, as an administrator for the three more years the law allowed, but I doubted that I could have continued to summon imagination and the energy for innovation. In my years of retirement I have never missed the extra income and never doubted that the decision to retire was the right one.

Other memories of the commission years

In addition to my official travels in the North, to Washington and to Pittsburgh for a speech designed to stimulate interest in a trans-border flight for Nordair and other brief travels for speeches or for weekends in Newfoundland, I travelled a great deal in 1968, probably more than in any subsequent year at the CTC.

Apart from my work the most memorable event for me in 1968 was the Liberal convention that chose Pierre Trudeau as leader of the party. Although I avoided contact with the Liberal organization, I watched the proceedings on television with avid interest. I was glad Jean Marchand refused to be a candidate and agreed with the reasons he gave. Marchand was second-in-command to Pearson as the acknowledged Liberal leader from Québec. I felt that his defeat, if he had become a candidate, would have been a body-blow to the Liberal party. I did not feel that way about Pierre Trudeau. He was not the Québec leader, and was much more of a novice in the political world. His failure to win would not have been an affront to French Canada. As the contest progressed I reached the conclusion that if I had been at the convention, I would have supported Trudeau, and I still think he was the best choice, despite the misgivings I later developed about his conduct of government. But I was glad I was not free to participate.

I had lunch with Pearson at the prime minister's residence twice in 1968, but we did not mention the succession. On the day Trudeau replaced Pearson as prime minister, the governor general gave a luncheon in Pearson's honour, at which I was present. Trudeau consulted me about whether or not he should call an immediate election. I was not able to give him a firm opinion. He never sought my advice again on any subject — which for me, was not a grievance, but a relief. I have never wanted to have an avuncular role.

One of my happiest memories of 1968 is of a dinner at the British High Commission in Ottawa in January in honour of Harold Macmillan, who was no longer prime minister. It was on that occasion that he asked me about telephoning St Laurent, and I arranged for the call. Macmillan's thoughtfulness increased my admiration for him.

In August, I visited St Laurent at St Patrick, and I took his grandson, Stephen Lafferty, with me. I found St Laurent in good spirits and full of interest in what was going on. In November my Oxford friend Bill Luttrell turned up in Ottawa on a business visit. We had lost touch for many years, and it was a great pleasure to renew our friendship. I recall another visitor I had in 1968, because of the prominence he has attained in recent years. Jacques Parizeau came to see me to discuss the regional air carrier Québecair, about which he was advising the Québec government. I thought the provincial government was entitled to my opinion, and I gave it frankly to Parizeau. One other prominent Canadian I met for the first time that year was Maurice Strong, who invited me to lunch, urged me to write about my career and offered financial help, which he subsequently gave me when I was working on *My Years with Louis St. Laurent*. I remain grateful for his encouragement.

In 1969, I concentrated on the commission and paid little attention to public affairs generally. I recall a few specific social occasions. Jules Léger had ceased to be ambassador to France and was back in Ottawa as a deputy minister. Guy Roberge was home from London on a visit, and the Légers had a small dinner for Guy, to which Margaret and I were invited. On 8 March, Walter Harris was in Ottawa, and I persuaded him to fly with me to Quebec City to visit St Laurent, a happy occasion for all three of us. Margaret and I had, on various visits to Antigua, become friends of the governor and Lady Jacobs. Sir Wilfred Jacobs was in Canada on a private visit, and I persuaded Mitchell Sharp, who had succeeded Paul Martin at External Affairs, to ask the governor to spend a couple of days as guest of the government at the hospitality house at Rideau Gate, where I was host at an official luncheon on 23 April. In 1992 Jacobs was still in office in Antigua, now as governor general, since independent status has replaced statehood. Our friendship with him and his congenial wife has grown as our visits to Antigua have continued.

Donald Gordon's funeral on 7 May 1969 was an impressive close of a life devoted to public service of great benefit to Canada. I mourned Donald as a friend and congenial fellow worker in the field of transport.

Pearson and I lunched together occasionally in those years, and on 4 February 1970, I was asked to thank him for a speech he gave at the Canadian Club. Our friendship became much closer in his years of retirement. We were together at a testimonial dinner in Vancouver on 9 April for our common friend, Bruce Hutchison, at which Mike was the main speaker. Margaret and I were in Toronto for a dinner given by the University of Toronto Press for Mike and for me on 29 October 1969. The third and fourth volumes of *The Mackenzie King Record* were in the last stage of preparation.

Margaret and I were at the funeral of Bishop Reed of Ottawa on 4 March. Ernest Reed and I had been at the University of Manitoba at the same time as students but had not actually met there. He and his wife, Vera, had become good friends of both of us; his death was a personal loss. He was one of three clergymen who have been special friends. Another was Bishop Abraham of Newfoundland, and the third is Reverend J.A. Davidson. Jock Davidson is a cousin of Margaret's and a more distant cousin of mine; all three of us are descended from Elizabeth Stacey, who was born in Detroit in 1784. Jock was a United Church minister in Kingston when Jane was there as a student. The Davidsons provided her with a second home, for which all of us remain deeply indebted. The Davidsons live in retirement in Victoria, where we had a happy meeting early in 1992.

Arnold Heeney's death in 1970 was a source of great sadness for Margaret and me. He was a dear friend, whom I count among the greatest public servants of my time.

In 1971, I became a Companion of the Order of Canada, an honour that I accepted with some hesitation because, while in the government, I had opposed the establishment of the Order. In February, I was in St John's for the funeral of Ches Pippy, one of my most generous and helpful supporters during all the years I was an MP. I paid a visit to Churchill Falls as a guest of the Brinco company from 21 to 23 August and was given a tour of inspection by William Mulholland, who after the construction was completed, became head of the Bank of Montreal. I was impressed by the magnitude and complexity of the development and also by the fact that, unlike so many big operations, it was being built within the estimated cost. In mid-October, I was invited to the installation of a new president of the University of Winnipeg by Sterling Lyon, later premier of Manitoba, and asked either to participate in a panel to discuss China or to be its moderator. I said I knew nothing about China and felt my ignorance would be less apparent if I was in the chair. It was always interesting for me

University of Toronto Press, October 29, 1970. Left to right, L.B. Pearson, Marsh Jeanneret, publisher, and J.W.P.

to visit the institution where I had taught for eight years and to see how it had flourished since the 1930s.

Occasions I remember in 1972 were a dinner at the National Arts Centre to celebrate the centennial of the Public Archives, with which I have had such a long association, both public and personal; the official opening of Churchill Falls by Premier Frank Moores of Newfoundland, at which he paid a glowing tribute to Smallwood, who was not present; and, to mark my retirement from the commission, a buffet given by Guy and Marie Roberge on 25 August and a farewell party at the Arts Centre on 30 August.

As a memorial to W.C. Clark, the great wartime deputy minister of finance, a trust had been established to finance a series of lectures on public affairs, to be given annually across the country.

I was chosen to give the lecture in 1972. I prepared two lectures, 'Responsible Government in a Federal State' and 'Bureaucrats and Politicians.' I reread them recently and was gratified to find that they seem relevant even today. I used them on more or less alternate occasions, according to which I felt more suitable to the place of delivery. My lectures took me to Vancouver, Edmonton, Halifax, Toronto and Winnipeg; to Regina, where Premier Allan Blakeney invited me for a talk at his office in the Legislative Building; to Ottawa, where Jules Léger and Gordon Robertson were present, one to introduce me and the other to thank me; and to Quebec City, where I stayed at Government House with Bobby and Lucette Lapointe and gave my lecture in the room that had been the chamber of the legislative council until the council was abolished on Jean Lesage's initiative. Paul Tellier, now head of CN, recently clerk of the privy council and secretary to the cabinet at Ottawa, was there as a senior official in the Québec public service. He took me to see the premier's office in what was called the Bunker, where I met Robert Bourassa for the first time. The final Clark lecture was delivered in St John's, shortly after my retirement.

Family activities

Margaret and I had more time for travel during my years at the commission, and Newfoundland remained as much a part of our lives as when I was an MP. We had visits to the Caribbean; to London, France, Brussels and Copenhagen; to parts of western Canada, including a trip to the Queen Charlotte Islands with my sister, Jane, and her husband, Ken Seaborne; and to Hawaii. Alan and I were in France In 1968 and 1970, and our daughter Jane and I in France and the Netherlands in 1968. Some of my travels were connected with transport: in addition to speaking engagements there were visits to several experiments, such as an experiment in the generation of tidal power in Brittany, a look at the port of Rotterdam, and a crossing of the English Channel in the new Hover-craft. Margaret and I were present at ceremonies in Athens inaugurating the CP Toronto/Athens service. We had several opportunities to see members of the de France family — Paul and Eliane and their daughter, Diane, Guislain and his wife, Roseline, and Agnès.

In 1968, I had a letter from Agnès de France about her cousin, Arnaud de Gouville, who wanted to find a situation in the public service of another country, as the accepted alternative to doing military service. He was one of the top graduates of the school to train candidates for admittance to the French public service. I had no difficulty in finding him a post in the Transport Commission, which he took up in January 1969. He proved an outstanding recruit to the Research Division, with his high intelligence and prodigious appetite for learning. He was soon doing courses at Carleton and, later, some teaching there. From the commission he went to jobs in Toronto and Montreal, and eventually he became a landed immigrant. He was always a welcome visitor in our house, and over the years I developed a great affection for him.

In 1970, Alan and I called on a man named Jean Boucher in Vence, near Nice, who had written to me about meeting Frank during the worst period of Frank's internment. He had been hurt that Frank had not mentioned in letters to us his surreptitious gifts of food at Montreuil in 1941, when Frank was almost starving. Alan and I drove to Romorantin, in the Loire Valley, near where Frank and Macalister had landed by parachute in June 1943, on the property of a man named Jean Charmaison. We had alerted him that we were coming, and arrived to find that he had organized a luncheon party of the local survivors of the Resistance. It was a moving experience. We were photographed later by the memorial, on which the names Pickersgill and Macalister appear.

One day in 1970, in a drive from Traytown to Salvage, Margaret and I discovered an abandoned cottage at the end of the road. Margaret later bought it for $100 and restored and enlarged it. We have spent part of every summer since 1974 in that little house, which has the finest view in Newfoundland.

In the fall of 1971 Jane was well established at Thunder Bay as the medical officer of health. She had given up her medical practice in Gander in 1968, spent a year in the Faculty of Arts at

Carleton University and subsequently attended the University of Toronto School of Hygiene. Thunder Bay was the place of her choice; she described it as the most scenic place in the world that was not on the sea. Peter had been married to Lisa Young in 1968; in 1971 he was in his final year as an architecture student at the University of British Columbia, and Lisa was teaching. Ruth was a student at York University, and Alan had graduated from Memorial University in the spring. Both Alan and Ruth had spent some

View from table at Margaret's house, Salvage, where much of this book was written and revised.

time in the Interlangue school in Paris, where their French had improved considerably.

When I retired I realized that I had given more time and attention to the family during the previous five years than during my years as a politician and in the Prime Minister's Office. Margaret and I had travelled more, and I had not worked evenings and weekends. But I still had had deadlines to meet, and I hoped my time would be entirely my own in retirement.

15 An Active Retirement

The view from retirement, 1972-82

The first task

Once I had decided, early in 1972, to retire before the end of the year, I gave a good deal of thought to what I would do without the discipline of regular employment. One task I had set for myself was to write a book about my association with Louis St Laurent. It was not to be a biography; Dale Thomson, one of the secretaries in the Prime Minister's Office until the end of St Laurent's career, had already written one. My book was to be an account of my relations with St Laurent from our first meeting until he left public life in January 1958, the happiest time of my working life.

At Christmas 1968, St Laurent sent me a copy of Thomson's biography, with the inscription 'To my most devoted and loyal friend Jack Pickersgill with highest esteem and best wishes, Louis St Laurent, Québec, Christmas, 1968.' I value nothing I own more than that inscription. I was also deeply touched when, during the course of the last conversation we had, shortly after his 91st birthday, St Laurent said, 'You know, Jack, I believe you and I together were able to accomplish a good many things for the public good that neither of us could have done by himself.'

On my first day of retirement I went to Newfoundland to join Margaret for a brief respite before settling down to write. I started to work as soon as we returned to Ottawa. From the outset I had a research assistant who also served as a secretary. Landon Stewart returned to the Canadian Transport Commission in June 1972 to a temporary job to sort my papers for transfer to the Public Archives. On my retirement she agreed to become my research assistant on an experimental basis. Landon carried on until my research was completed in August 1974. Her competent and conscientious help eased my transition to private life.

A grant from the Ford Foundation enabled me to rent a two-room office in which to do my writing and otherwise manage the project. When the university term ended in the spring of 1973, I offered Ruth a job as assistant to Landon. After Landon left, Ruth carried on alone as my secretary until *My Years with Louis St. Laurent* was ready for publication in March 1975.

The death of Pearson

The last time Margaret and I spent together with Mike and Maryon Pearson was the evening of 20 October 1972, the day of Trudeau's second election. The Pearsons had declined Trudeau's invitation to watch the returns at his headquarters; they preferred to watch television at home and asked Margaret and me to join them. The Liberals did not win a majority, and had only two members more than the Tories under Robert Stanfield. Mike was clearly relieved that he had stayed at home.

That evening he seemed in reasonably good health. About a month later I saw him briefly and was shocked by his appearance. As we were going to Antigua for a week, I decided that if I hoped to see Pearson alive once more, I should do so before we left. I saw Mike in his bedroom, sitting up in bed working on his memoirs. We both knew it was our last meeting. By the time of our return from Antigua, Pearson was too ill to see visitors, and two days after Christmas he died.

Before the funeral on 31 December, Pearson's body lay in state in the Parliament Building in a coffin draped in the Canadian flag. The funeral in Christ Church Cathedral was impressive. The weather was cold with rain, and I did not go to the cemetery, near

Wakefield, where Pearson was buried close to Hume Wrong, and where Norman Robertson joined them later.

My association with Pearson's death did not end with the funeral. The question of a suitable memorial arose early in 1973. Shortly after Pearson's death Walter Davis of Newfoundland, who had tried to purge me from public life in the election of 1963, turned up in Toronto without having consulted the Pearson family, to enlist support for the establishment in Canada of a United Nations University as the principal memorial to Pearson. Davis succeeded in arousing the interest of a number of prominent Torontonians, many of them friends of Pearson. At the same time Senator Hartland Molson and Senator John Nichol, both close friends of Pearson, were seeking to establish a foundation for a memorial with the blessing of the family.

Maryon Pearson and her son, Geoffrey, were distressed by those apparently competing initiatives and asked me to try to bring the groups together as a single body. I agreed to undertake that delicate task. Fortunately the head of the group in Toronto was Rt Rev. Ernest Howse, a former moderator of the United Church who had been a classmate and friend of Pearson's in their university days. I had known Dr Howse, who was a Newfoundlander, and felt I could talk freely to him. We worked out a letter for me to send to him for discussion with his group. When Davis heard of my connection, he told the *Toronto Star* that I had been appointed liaison between the government and the Pearson Memorial Foundation he was trying to establish in Toronto. The *Star* story upset Senators Molson and Nichol, who were about to begin to raise an endowment.

I had to make a public statement that I did not represent the government, but had been asked by the Pearson family to try to ensure that only one group would seek to create a foundation, and that Walter Davis had acted wituout consulting the family. In January and February, I spent a good deal of time talking on the telephone to Dr Howse, Molson, Nichol, Geoffrey Pearson and many others, and finally I got Davis out of the picture and arranged for a meeting in March of a single body drawn from the

Toronto group and those associated with Nichol and Molson. When Davis withdrew he announced that as he knew from experience, there was no point in trying to fight Jack Pickersgill.

The meeting of the united group on 16 March went well. The Pearsons had meanwhile decided a world college was their choice as a memorial, and the advisory group concurred in that objective and offered support for the foundation. Once agreement had been achieved, with harmony and goodwill, on the memorial desired, my task was completed, and the task of establishing an endowment for the L.B. Pearson College of the Pacific was headed by Nichol, the main founder of that flourishing memorial. Lord Mountbatten, the president of the International Council of the United World Colleges, visited Ottawa in September 1973, when the establishment of the Pearson College seemed assured. Margaret and I were at a small dinner for Mountbatten at Government House to mark the occasion. I have been one of the many patrons of the college from the beginning.

The death of St Laurent

St Laurent's death followed just half a year after Pearson's. Margaret and I were in Newfoundland in July 1973 and for once had gone off on an excursion without letting any of the family know of our plans. When Alan heard the news in St John's he tracked us down that evening at Marystown, in the Burin Peninsula. I was back in Ottawa late the next night. The following day I spent at the office making arrangements by telephone for the trip to Quebec City to attend the funeral and the burial at Compton. Walter Harris and I agreed to share a room for the night at the Château Frontenac so that we could have time to reminisce. I flew to Quebec City in the evening.

The state funeral at the basilica on 28 July was well organized and impressive, and the crowds on the streets were large and responsive. Harris returned home after the funeral, but I drove in the cortege to St Laurent's birthplace for the burial. Stanley Knowles and Senator Muriel Fergusson were in the car with me. It was a beautiful afternoon, and for the whole 100 miles or more the roadside was lined with men, women and children paying their tribute to one of their own. Every person in Compton seemed to be at the cemetery.

I was flattered that the *Globe and Mail* used as St Laurent's obituary, without attribution, part of a speech I had made several years earlier at Fort William with the title 'the Greatest Canadian of Our Time.' Reflecting afterwards on the funeral and the mourning for St Laurent, I felt more pride than sorrow. When I had last seen St Laurent the previous February, it was clear to me that he was tired of living, frustrated by the difficulty of remembering names in conversation and hesitant in speech though not in thought. We had talked of Pearson's recent death and his place in history. At one point St Laurent had said, 'Mike had the courage to do things that needed to be done, and that I did not dare to tackle.' He was thinking, I am sure, of the flag and the recognition of the two official languages, but also of the place Canada had gained in the world under Pearson's leadership. But although I was beginning to appreciate how great a prime minister Pearson had been, for me St Laurent remains the greatest Canadian of our time.

Back in Ottawa on 30 July, two days after St Laurent's funeral, I attended a memorial service at St Andrews Church for J.M. Macdonnell, who had just died. Jim was the Conservative MP I respected most in my time in Parliament, and we had become friends. He was the finest kind of conservative, attached to tradition but not stubbornly resistant to change, a champion of human freedom, the soul of loyalty and a genuine believer in responsible parliamentary government. His death, so soon after those of two great prime ministers with whom my life had been so closely linked, caused me to reflect that the political world to which I had belonged was vanishing.

The election of 1972

Parliament was dissolved on 1 September 1972, the first day of my retirement. In my retirement I was free to resume an active role in public life, but I had no interest in doing so. In the election of 1972 I supported the Trudeau government passively. I believed nation-wide political parties were essential to good government, but I did not believe that a Tory government under Stanfield would be a disaster. The Liberal slogan for the election fo 1972 was The Land Is Strong. I felt those words contained no appeal for support of a Liberal government. My son Peter did a prophetic cartoon of two Indians paddling a canoe labelled ominously 'The Land Is Strong but It's ours.'

Apart from the Official Languages Act, which I approved strongly, I had not been impressed by the achievements of the Trudeau government during the years 1968 to 1972. Trudeau's lack of interest in good administration and his poor judgement of the suitability of men and women for membership in the cabinet and high administrative posts I deplored. One of his aims I shared: I had since 1949 been a supporter of every initiative to patriate the Constitution.

My first reaction to the proclamation of the War Measures Act in 1970 had been one of shock. But then I asked myself what position I would have taken if I had still been in the cabinet. I decided I would have supported the decision but with great reluctance. It was the word 'apprehended' that weighed in the balance in my mind. I recalled that the War Measures Act had been invoked in 1939 in apprehension of war two weeks before Canada was at war. I had been alarmed by the acts of violence in Montreal in 1970 and much more by the widespread demonstrations, which threatened to move into the streets, and by the apparent lack of confidence by prominent citizens that law and order could be maintained. I felt that the apprehension of insurrection was warranted, since no lesser security measure existed.

Proclaiming the War Measures Act in itself does not confer any specific powers, but merely permits the law to be suspended or changed by order-in-council made by the government of Canada. I telephoned a friend who was an influential senior official to suggest that the order-in-council empowering the attorney-general of Quebec or of any other province to detain persons without warrants or charges should specifically give all persons detained access to legal counsel. I learned that the order-in-council had already been made. I was sorry, but there was nothing more I could do. I took some comfort from the fact that Frank Scott, probably the most outstanding defender of civil liberties in Canada, agreed with me that resort to the War Measures Act was justified. But the wholesale and undiscriminating use of detention certainly was not.

What disturbed me most about Trudeau was his contempt for provincial governments in Quebec regardless of party. He did not seem to realize that the aspirations for provincial sovereignty-association or even outright separation could not be kept in check unless one provincial political party asserted that the legitimate ambitions of francophones in Quebec could be satisfied within the Canadian federation. The Liberal party led by Robert Bourassa was the only one that took that position. When Bourassa won the election of 1970 with an overwhelming majority, ordinary common sense should have told Trudeau that he should do everything he could to support and bolster up the Bourassa government. But common sense was one quality Trudeau lacked. In 1968 he had talked about applying Cartesian logic to government. I recall saying at that time that if government could be provided by geometry, government itself would not be needed. And between 1968 and 1970 Canada had very little government, though plenty of musical chairs in the bureaucracy. In 1971, I had been disappointed that the patriation of the Constitution had come so close without being achieved. I did not blame Bourassa for the failure any more than I did Trudeau. Claude Castonguay was Bourassa'a ablest minister, and his objections weighed heavily with the premier. With a little more flexibility, I felt, those objections could have been met. An additional effort by Trudeau might have achieved agreement, and I felt he had given up too easily. I resented Trudeau's contemptuous abuse of Bourassa and the impression he gave that the Canadian federation had no provincial champions in Quebec, and that Ottawa alone would fight separation.

Trudeau never seemed to grasp, as Pearson had, the ambiguity of Québec's position within Canada. As a province with a substantial minority that was not French-speaking, Québec was a province like the others, needing no special treatment. But as the one province with the bulk of the French-speaking population of Canada, Québec, many French Canadians believed, had another function: it should be recognized as a distinct society, if the French language and culture were to be preserved. Trudeau felt that the presence of French Canadians in Ottawa should be sufficient to uphold French distinctiveness in Canada. He failed to understand that French-speaking Canadians generally were at a real disadvantage in the federal public service, in commerce and in industry, and that a new generation in Québec was determined to remove those disadvantages. Perhaps because he had been bilingual all his life and perhaps because he had not had to earn his living, Trudeau never appreciated emotionally the mixed sense of grievance and ambition in Québec. Bourassa did, and on that question I have always been on his side, even though at times he has taken specific steps of which I could not approve.

As a Liberal, I was mildly pleased that Trudeau remained prime minister of a minority government. I hoped he would give more attention to administration and begin to realize that one duty of the leader of a political party is to maintain the party organization. There was much activity for a year or two after the election, but I do not believe Trudeau ever appreciated what the historical function of a political party was, or, how helpful party morale could be to good government.

Newfoundland after Smallwood

The provincial election in Newfoundland on 28 October 1971, which resulted in a virtual tie, was a shock to the public and to Premier Smallwood. I watched with fascination from Ottawa the manoeuvres of Smallwood and the Tory leader, Frank Moores, one to retain and the other to gain the premiership. I was relieved when Smallwood resigned on 18 January 1972, and Moores became premier. It was clearly past time for a change of government and a change of leadership of the Liberal party.

Joe called a Liberal convention for early February, and Edward Roberts was chosen leader. I was delighted. Roberts lacked Smallwood's charisma, but he had already demonstrated outstanding capacity for administration and the ability to win a constituency and secure the continuing support of his constituents. He was becoming known to the wider provincial electorate. There was not, of course, the slightest hope that the Liberals would win the election called for March 1972. Moores won a sweeping victory, but Roberts had a nucleus of members, performed well in the legislature and set about vigorously building a party organization. His most serious problem was Smallwood, who was not in the House of Assembly, but who began to seek a come-back the moment there were signs of a Liberal revival.

In January 1974, Roland Michener was succeeded as governor-general by Jules Léger. The Légers decided to make a state visit to Newfoundland for the 25th anniversary of the union with Canada. There was to be a dinner given by the provincial government on 1 April. Smallwood, though no longer Liberal leader, was already planning a Liberal dinner for the same day. After repeated discussions on the telephone during which I urged Joe to hold his dinner on 31 March, the official anniversary, he refused to change his date. I told him I would not affront my friends the Légers by failing to attend the official dinner in order to go to a rival partisan ceremony. He resented my decision. I never got a clear account of how his rival dinner went in St John's, but the government dinner at Memorial University was a glittering occasion. Joe should have been present.

Later in 1974, Smallwood was determined to try to regain the leadership of the Liberal party. He managed to get a leadership convention called to challenge Roberts's leadership. I was officially a delegate but had no intention of going to the convention and could have ignored it altogether. But I was convinced that it would be bad for Newfoundland, for the Liberal party and for Smallwood himself if he became leader again. I was ready to do what I could to help Roberts, but I was not sure whether anything

I might say would help him or arouse sympathy for Joe. I consulted two or three persons whose political feel I appreciated. The opinion I received was that some of Joe's old supporters might resent my intervention, but more Liberals would be impressed by my judgement. I discussed the question with my son Alan, who was working actively for Roberts. He said Ed was making a mistake by behaving like a candidate rather than a leader. That was my clue as to how to intervene. When asked by someone in the media whether or not I was going to the convention, I said no, I was going to British Columbia. When asked whom I would support if I went to the convention, my reply was, 'I would support the leader of the party; I have always supported the leader of my party, federal or provincial.' Whether my statement influenced a single delegate I will never know, but it certainly outraged Smallwood. In Victoria I watched him on television denouncing me for ingratitude.

It was obvious that there would be an estrangement, and I regretted it, but I was pleased that Edward Roberts remained leader of the Liberal party.

The election of 1974 and Stanfield's retirement

Until late in 1974, I had worked steadily at *My Years with Louis St. Laurent* and paid only casual attention to the activities of the government and even less to Parliament. Believing as I always have that a vigorous Opposition as well as a vigorous government provide the greatest prospect of good government, I had deplored the way in which Diefenbaker had sabotaged his successor, Stanfield, by encouraging division in the Conservative party. In spite of that handicap, I felt, Stanfield had done well in the House. When he made an issue of wage and price control in the election of 1974, which was provoked by the NDP defeat of the Trudeau government in the House, I was of two minds about the question of controls but continued to give my passive support to the Liberal candidate. I would not have been upset if the Tories had won. I encountered Stanfield a day or two after the election and said to him, 'Whatever you do, Bob, don't quit.' He retorted that if that was my advice, he should probably retire at once.

I was sorry he did resign as I could see no one in the party likely to be a successful leader, barring Premier Lougheed of Alberta. Of those who sought the leadership my preference would have been for Joe Clark. I had liked the tone of one or two of his speeches, but, I did not meet him until late in 1975, in Edmonton, where I was promoting my book. Clark approached me in the lobby and introduced himself. He told me he was about to go upstairs to a meeting to announce his candidature for the leadership of the Tory party in succession to Stanfield, and I said I supposed he did not want me to come with him. I did not tell him that if I had been a Tory, I would have supported him, though I did not think he had the ghost of a chance of winning.

In January 1976 the Rideau Club had a dinner for Bob Stanfield at which I was happy to be chosen as one of the speakers. I have never ceased to regret that he did not stay on as leader; he would have made a good prime minister. I was as surprised as Joe Clark himself was when he won the leadership on 22 February.

The paralysis of air transport

In 1976 the airline pilots and air traffic controllers went on strike to oppose allowing French-speaking pilots to communicate in French with French-speaking traffic controllers in airports in the province of Québec. The strike leaders claimed that the use of any language but English would imperil safety in the air and alleged that, in every country in the world, English was the only language used for communication between pilots and traffic controllers — a practice adopted to increase safety in flying. That claim either was based on inexcusable ignorance or was a barefaced lie. But the hint of a threat to safety in the air aroused fear in the public mind. There was widespread sympathy for the strikers among English-speaking Canadians, and strong feelings by French-speaking Canadians that the strike was another attempt to treat them as second-class citizens and to degrade their language.

Nowhere in the media was there an attempt to expose the false claim and report the truth. I knew that French pilots did not communicate with the Paris airport in English, and I was confident that Russian-speaking pilots did not communicate with the Moscow airport in English. I collected accurate information about the language of communication in all the countries in Europe and in other countries where Canadian airlines operated, and put it in a letter to the *Winnpeg Free Press*. That paper did not publish my letter until I complained to their correspondent in Ottawa.

For the only time while he was prime minister, I offered advice to Trudeau. I told an official in the Prime Minister's Office that the issue behind the strike was 'the worst threat to national unity since the conscription crisis' of the First World War. I know my comment was passed on to Trudeau because he used those exact words in Parliament the next day. I said that the 'big lie' should be exposed by the prime minister, and that the use of French as well as English for air traffic control be permitted wherever it was feasible.

The strike lasted for nine days; it paralyzed scheduled air traffic within, into and out of Canada before the ugly situation was straightened out, the use of French was permitted where safety was assured, and air traffic resumed.

The attempt to prevent the use of the French language left a scar. Despite the fact that the governor general, the prime minister, leading cabinet ministers, the commissioner of the RCMP and the chief of the defence staff were French Canadians in 1976, many in Quebec felt the strike had once more demonstrated that French Canadians had to struggle to get a fair deal in Ottawa. There is little doubt that one result was an increase in support for the Parti Québécois that contributed to their victory in the provincial election later in the year.

I was discouraged that not one investigative reporter in the media had exposed the false claims on which the strike had been based, and that it had not been easy for a former minister of transport to get publicity for the facts.

The Parti Québécois victory

Bourassa won the election of 1970 with a comfortable majority, and, despite all the problems over the War Measures Act, his government was returned in a landslide in 1973. The Liberal party alienated many of the anglophone voters in Quebec by legislation limiting access to English-language schools, and the Union Nationale was thereby enabled to stage a revival in predominantly English-language ridings. That split among those voters opposed to sovereignty enabled the Parti Québécois under René Lévesque to win 71 seats with 40 per cent of the vote, reduced the Liberals to 26 seats with 34 per cent and gave the Union Nationale 11 seats with 19 per cent. Bourassa lost his own seat. Towards the end of the campaign I had begun to fear that the PQ would win the largest number of seats, but I had not expected the party to win a majority and so substantial a one as that.

Why Bourassa called an election in 1976, after only three years, without a program, has never been explained. Shortly after the election, Jean Lesage told me that Bourassa had not asked his advice. When he saw Bourassa after the dissolution was announced, he said, 'Bob you have called an early election without an issue, and you will lose.'

I have never believed that Lévesque, despite all the talk of sovereignty, really wanted to break up Canada, and never thought his party would do so then or later. It is my opinion that the real steam behind the sovereignty movement was the demand for the predominance of the French language in Québec. That predominance was secured by Bill 101.

The resurrection of Trudeau

Looking back at my diary for December 1979 and January 1980, I am surprised to find how little reference I made to political confusion after the defeat of Clark's government. I was sure the Tories expected, at the start, to repeat the 1957-58 experience, when Diefenbaker led a minority government into a landslide. In 1958 the Liberal party had had a leader. In 1979 Trudeau had resigned the leadership, and no successor had yet been chosen. I watched with interest, from the sidelines, the manoeuvring that followed, when Donald Macdonald seemed within a hair's breadth of being called on to fill the gap, until Trudeau was drafted, with an appearance of reluctance on his part.

I took no part and had little interest in the campaign. I hoped Trudeau would win because of the forthcoming referendum in Québec. I thought it would help during René Lévesque's referendum campaign to have a French-Canadian prime minister in Ottawa. But I continued to feel that 15 years of Liberal government had been enough, and I believed that the country could have survived a few years of the Clark government.

The main advantage I saw in the resurrection of Trudeau as prime minister was that his return to office was evidence that French Canadians were not excluded from the highest office in the country. Trudeau was living proof that independence for Quebec was not essential for French Canadians to have opportunities for successful careers.

After the election the Liberals had 147 seats, only 2 west of Ontario. The lopsided House of Commons obliged Trudeau to have senators in the cabinet to represent the three westernmost provinces. The membership in the House of Commons underlined the alienation of the west from the Liberal party and the government of the day.

My interest was rekindled when Parliament met on 14 April with Pierre Trudeau prime minister once more. The following day Lévesque announced that a referendum would be held in Quebec on 20 May seeking a mandate for the government of Québec to negotiate sovereignty-association with the rest of Canada. The question was even wordier and more complicated than Mackenzie King's question in the plebiscite of 1942, but in the popular mind the issue was independence for Québec.

I did not believe that Lévesque really wanted Québec to become a foreign country; he wanted Québec to have a different status — more legislative and administrative power — from that of other provinces. But in the campaign the lines were joined sharply within Québec, and considerable resentment and some anxiety developed outside Québec.

Never at any time did I believe that Canada would break up, but I hoped the negative vote would be larger, and the question of a special status for Québec postponed for another generation. I knew a 'yes' vote would be the beginning of prolonged discussions, largely to the exclusion of other public business. On the evening of the voting it was soon clear that there would be a majority of 'no' votes, fairly evenly distributed over the whole province, with a few remote areas strongly for the separatist option and the non-francophone areas strongly against. I noted in my diary that I felt 10 years younger.

Even before the referendum of 1980 I said privately that Bill 101, by giving priority to the French language in law as well as in fact, had weakened the case for sovereignty, as I believe it did. I took Lévesque at his word on the night of the referendum, when he indicated that the battle for sovereignty was not over but would be dormant for many years.

The result of the Québec election of 1981 was a shock. As the date approached, I became increasingly apprehensive that Lévesque would win. He had put sovereignty aside in the election campaign, and he undertook to make the best of the position within Canada.

The PQ victory on 13 April did not stop Trudeau from pressing ahead with efforts to patriate the Constitution. I followed all his twists and contradictions with close interest and I had frequent discussions with Gordon Robertson about the developments. Gordon had retired amicably when Clark became prime minister. Trudeau, to my surprise, made no effort to bring Robertson back into office, but left him free to behave as a private citizen.

I was shocked and almost horrified by Trudeau's threat to ask the British government to put legislation before their parliament to patriate the British North America Act to Canada without any consideration of the views of the provincial legislatures whose constitution the BNA Act also was. I would not have been shocked if he had followed the formula St Laurent considered in 1949, which would not have changed the existing constitution but merely provided for its amendment within Canada — but not by Parliament alone.

The proposal for the Canadian Parliament by itself to ask not merely for patriation but also for amendment to the Constitution affecting the jurisdiction of provincial legislatures outraged at least 8 of the 10 Premiers and forced a reference to the Supreme Court. The court rendered a decision that I still regard as bizarre.

Liberal decline and defeat, 1974-79

From the moment Trudeau had a majority in Parliament again, the fortunes of the government declined, and Trudeau himself became more and more isolated from his ministers. His indifference to administration continued. He allowed John Turner and Donald Macdonald successively to leave and failed to appreciate how much their departure weakened the government. Jean Marchand ceased to have any influence though his judgement of public opinion was needed more than ever.

I was reminded forcibly of the profound change in the western attitude by one sad event in Winnipeg on 7 May. Stuart Garson died, almost forgotten. I was told his wife, Emily, hoped I would attend the funeral and I did so. Garson was the politician I had known longest in my life and one of the friends and associates I cherished most. His career in Ottawa had not lived up to promise, but I never forgot the skill with which he managed to hold the Manitoba government and caucus together when John Bracken, a Liberal Progressive, left the premiership to accept the leadership of the Conservative party and change that party's name to Progressive Conservative. In the election of 1945 Garson had kept the Liberal flame alive. Without the 10 Manitoba MPs, Mackenzie King would not have had a clear majority in that postwar election. In 1949, when Garson was himself in the St Laurent government, the Liberals won 12 seats. In my opinion Garson was by a considerable margin the ablest of all the premiers of Manitoba and by far the most effective of all provincial premiers in working out the postwar federal-provincial tax-sharing arrangements, which resulted in equalization, the real glue of Confederation. I have known other public men with almost total devotion to the public welfare but none more than Stuart Garson. Nevertheless, the public memory had faded in his years of retirement. Garson's last years were saddened for family and friends by his own complete loss of memory.

By 1977 there were only three Liberal MPs from the Prairie provinces; in the prairies Liberalism had become a third party. The contrast with the days of Mackenzie King and St Laurent was startling. As a Manitoban I found the political scene in Manitoba depressing. But Liberal prospects continued to decline as the Parliament of 1974 dragged on into its fifth year.

Parliament was dissolved in late March 1979 and the election set for 22 May 1979. Towards the end of the campaign Walter Harris and I went to Maple Leaf Gardens in Toronto for Trudeau's meeting. The Gardens was filled, but there was no enthusiasm, even though Trudeau's speech, unlike many of his, had some content. I began to fear that the Liberals were losing the election despite the unexciting performance of Joe Clark. After the TV debate on Sunday, 13 May, though Trudeau put on the best performance, I felt more sure that the Tories were winning. On election day the Tories were just a couple of seats short of a majority. Trudeau gracefully conceded defeat and announced that he would advise the governor general to call on Clark to form a government.

Joe Clark became Prime minister on 4 June. His cabinet was unimpressive. Doubt began to be expressed in the Liberal party about Trudeau's future, and there were signs that his stock was waning after eleven years as a leader. I was not surprised when he announced that he was retiring as leader of the Liberal party.

Margaret and I went to Barbados on 1 December for two weeks. On the morning of 14 December we were shocked, and at first incredulous, to hear the radio report of the defeat of Clark's government in Parliament. We went home the next day to find the political world in a state of confusion. Parliament was going to be dissolved, and an election called. The Liberal party was without a leader.

The patriation of the Constitution

At the federal-provincial conference to discuss the patriation to be requested from the British government and Parliament, Lévesque, I felt, should have been taken at his word when he declared that sovereignty was not dead but would not be an issue for many years, and that Québec must make the best of its position in Confederation. Instead of his statement being put to the test a deal was worked out in a shabby way behind his back by the other premiers and accepted by the prime minister.

My own position was so uncertain that I was glad I no longer had a voice in the cabinet. I was 100 per cent for patriation, not only out of national pride but out of fear that there might be changes in Britain that would result in British interference with the Canadian request. Some British MPs were starting to monkey around with the subject. I was strongly opposed, however, to having the rights or prerogatives of provincial legislatures amended or restricted without their consent.

I was also opposed to the insertion of a bill or charter of rights into the Constitution. I did not believe that having the final decision as to the law of Canada left to as few as five elderly judges was compatible with the country's system of parliamentary responsible government. I agreed with the position taken by Sterling Lyon, the premier of Manitoba, and was pleased when a number of the premiers insisted on the so-called notwithstanding clause, which left a final voice, though one difficult to use, to the elected representatives of the people.

Balancing the advantage of patriation against my objections to the specific proposals to change the Constitution I would have supported the patriation, but sadly and reluctantly. In my diary I noted, 'A remarkable triumph for Trudeau, but, I fear, isolation of Québec.' I thought the argument used by Trudeau and others that Québec was not isolated, since 74 out of 75 MPs from Québec were supporters of the government, was specious and cheap. The almost unanimous condemnation of the action by the members of the Québec legislature of both parties was a far more accurate reflection of opinion in Québec on a provincial issue.

Margaret and I were on Parliament Hill for the proclamation by the Queen of the Canadian Constitution. There was heavy rain while the Queen spoke, and the scene was cheerless. We went on to the West Block for a luncheon for the Queen, at which Margaret and I were at the head table and had some amusing exchanges with Prince Philip before going in to lunch. In the evening there was a dinner given by the Liberal caucus. For me it was not a joyful day.

I was relieved that the government of Québec, while continuing its protest, accepted the legality of the new constitution. The question in my mind, as in many others, was when, how and whether the grievance could be redressed, and a reconciliation brought about. But most politicians outside Québec were unconscious or unconcerned that a deep wound would continue to fester until effective measures were taken to heal it. Substantial changes took place in the political scene in Québec and elsewhere in Canada before the problem was tackled nearly five years later at Meech Lake.

Private pursuits

Travels, visits and visitors

Our house on Maple Lane East in Rockcliffe suited us so well, even when we no longer had children living at home, that Margaret and I gave no thought to moving. Our rule was to spend part of the summer in Salvage, usually the whole of July and August. Nineteen seventy-six was the first year we drove to Newfoundland and back. We often varied the route, and we became familiar with most of the main roads across Québec and the Maritimes and one or two in New England. We have never failed to go to Newfoundland in the summer. Margaret had done all the driving and I felt that her health was such that she would suffer from driving both ways in 1991. I wrote to Agnès de France to ask if she would like to come to Canada to help drive us to Salvage and was surprised and delighted when she agreed. She was an excellent driver and travelling companion, and all of us enjoyed a visit that reinforced the bond between our families.

Our love of travel has taken us on numerous trips since my retirement. We have seen many new parts of Canada. We have visited Mexico, Lisbon, Amsterdam, Ireland, Italy, Greece, from which a brief visit to Ephesus enabled me to set foot in Asia for the only time in my life, Iceland, where the people seemed oddly familiar, like Manitobans who had never gone to Gimli, and, Peru. I made a special visit to Wacourt in 1979 to commemorate 50 years of friendship with Paul de France. We have kept in touch with the Luttrells and other friends on visits to England and Scotland, and with other members of the de France family on visits to France. Good health has allowed us to continue travelling, though with an interruption in 1992.

One of our most ambitious visits was in 1976, to Australia and New Zealand. It was beyond our means to pay the full cost of such a trip, so I hit on the idea of selling in advance a report of our impressions, which I persuaded the *Financial Post* and the *Globe and Mail* to accept. On our return the *Vancouver Sun* also provided a market. I also arranged with the Australian Institute of International Affairs to speak at several meetings. Margaret and I agree that that was the greatest travel experience of our lives. There were innumerable parallels with Canada. The relationship of New Zealand to Australia was an image of Canada's to the United States, and the parallel between Tasmania and Newfoundland was particularly striking. The visit to those two countries contributed to our understanding of our own as no other visit outside Canada could.

Another great experience, in 1987, was a visit to Ashern to celebrate it 75th anniversary; 1912 instead of 1911 had been chosen as the founding year. My sister, Margaret and I hired a car in Winnipeg and drove. I had not been in Ashern since the election of 1963, and Bessie, as my sister had been called in Ashern, had been away for much longer; Margaret had never visited the interlake country. From a hamlet of 100 when we lived there, Ashern had become a substantial settlement of over 300 and was a relatively flourishing community. There had been little immigration since the 1920s, and intermarriage had created a population of second- and third-generation unhyphenated Canadians. Bessie and I met many of our contemporaries and found most of the family names familiar.

In early retirement I had to visit Toronto frequently to see my publisher and often for other reasons, and Margaret and I made an arrangement that added ease and pleasure to the visits. In 1972 George Ignatieff retired from the diplomatic service and became provost of Trinity College, Toronto; we were present at his installation. At about that time we reached an understanding with George and Alison that we might stay with them at the Provost's lodge when we were in Toronto, and they with us in 'the addition' at Maple Lane when they were in Ottawa. The arrangement worked well as long as George remained provost; on both sides we felt free to come and go without any of the usual constraints of hospitality.

When Bruce Hutchison was in Ottawa in 1974, Margaret urged him to stay with us on future visits, He did so, every year until 1991, when, at the age of 90, he did not feel equal to the journey, I learned more during Bruce's annual visits about what was going on in Ottawa than I did all the rest of the year.

We were growing concerned about leaving our Ottawa house unoccupied during our summer visits to Newfoundland. Robert Bothwell of the University of Toronto and John English of Waterloo University, friends of ours, suggested that we have as a tenant Constantine Brancovan, a professor at Manchester University in England who taught a summer course in Russian history at Carleton University. Constantine was a Romanian whose family had got out of Romania after the Communists took over, and he had been educated at Oxford and Harvard. He was our tenant for every summer but one from 1978 until 1991, a happy arrangement on both sides.

Paul de France sent me a piece from *Figaro* of 2 June 1984 about a Harold Pickersgill who lived near Caen, in Normandy; he had landed in France on D-Day and after the war had returned and married a local woman. I wrote to him, received an invitation and was able to visit in 1986 and 1988. I had sent Harold a copy of *The Pickersgill Letters*. Harold had been brought up in Scotland, as his speech revealed, though his father was from Yorkshire; Harold and his wife, Minette, were charming, and we became good friends. Margaret was with me on our second visit which was very pleasant.

Another new friend, M.F. Perutz, I wrote to after reading a piece by him in the *New Yorker* in 1985 that referred to Mackenzie King. Perutz was one of the many British residents of German and Austrian origin who, during the invasion threat of 1940, were rounded up and interned; most of them were refugees from the Nazi regime, and many were Jewish. The British government had asked Canada to receive and detain some of those unfortunates, and the ones Canada accepted were quartered in prisoner-of-war camps. Perutz had written about that first stay in Canada. He was a leading British scientist, a Nobel Prize winner. He came to Ottawa in 1987 and proved one of the most interesting guests of our later lives, a wonderful conversationalist with wide interests, great public spirit and exceptional intelligence. Margaret and I felt a real warmth for Max and were glad to visit him and his wife and daugher in Cambridge the following year.

Books

From early in my retirement I was associated with various literary endeavours. As a member of the C.D. Howe Foundation I became involved with the preparation of Howe's biography. William Kilbourn had been chosen as biographer, but his progress was so slow that the members of the foundation wanted to terminate his contract. I felt that such an action would end his goodwill to no purpose and recommended finding a collaborator as joint author. Robert Bothwell, whose work I admired, was my suggestion. The members of the foundation agreed that W.J. Bennett, the president, should interview Bothwell and appoint him as joint biographer if Bothwell and Kilbourn would accept that arrangement. They did so, and the biography was published by the University of Toronto Press in 1979.

The first edition of *The Pickersgill Letters* was long out of print. In March 1977, Jack McClelland of McClelland and Stewart agreed to bring out a revised version if George Ford was willing to undertake the venture. By the time the book was finished, George had uncovered the full story as far as it will ever be known. The book first appeared in 1948 but was soon out of print. A revised and enlarged edition was published in April 1978, with the additional title *The Making of a Secret Agent*. I went to France to distribute copies to as many of Frank's friends as I could meet, and I was deeply touched by their continued devotion to his memory after so many years.

In 1984, Mackenzie King's literary executors took advantage of a visit to Ottawa by Kaye Lamb, the original chairman of the literary executors, to make a formal presentation at the Archives of the Mackenzie King papers to the Crown. At the same time we declared that the task of the literary executors had been completed.

Early in 1978, three years after the publication of *My Years with Louis St. Laurent*, I began to feel the urge to start writing again. I made an outline of a book that would trace my concept of Canada from childhood to show how I had gradually formed a picture of the whole country geographically, historically and politically. I began the work but put it aside when I was approached by Fitzhenry & Whiteside to do another book, a short work on St Laurent that would be part of a series of booklets about Canadian public figures, designed primarily for secondary school students. I found it harder to write a book of 60 than of 300 pages and spent many weeks refining the text. *Louis St. Laurent* was published in 1981. It pleased the St Laurent family more than my larger book. Later a French translation was brought out in Montreal.

Beginning in 1978 I had also been working on an account of the Liberal years in Opposition under Pearson's leadership. Bruce Hutchison encouraged me in the project, and by 1985 I had made enough progress to persuade Robert I. Fitzhenry to discuss publication with me and my son Peter, who was interested in doing some of the illustrations. Fitzhenry told me he could not undertake the book without a sharing subsidy, which I was in no position to provide. Later that year the University of Toronto Press, which earlier had said it would require a subsidy, decided to risk publishing the book without one. *The Road Back* was launched in November 1986. It was beautifully produced, but sales proved to be poor. There were several books by politicians that fall.

From there I returned to the manuscript about my life, and I got down to steady work in 1989, I intended to terminate the narrative at the end of Mackenzie King's time as prime minister; I thought a brief epilogue would cover the later periods, about which I had already written. I took no steps to arrange for a publisher: I was 84 years old, and the prospect of my living long enough to finish the book was uncertain. But on 7 April 1989, I received a spontaneous offer of financing. I advised Fitzhenry, who had several times expressed an interest in publishing what he described as an autobiography if there was a sharing subsidy, that I was prepared to make a commitment if the text satisfied him. Margaret and I began to revise and had completed the draft by March 1990. Fitz was pleased with the text but insisted that it should not stop at 1948; he said I could surely 'gut' *My Years with Louis St. Laurent* and *The Road Back*, fill in the subsequent period and make a book that would cover my whole life. I agreed without enthusiasm, and as I laboured to write, I was not always certain whether the deadline I was trying to meet was the book's or my own.

The Constitution

Revival of political interest

I continued to be a lukewarm Liberal, far from happy about the performance of the Trudeau government. In three of the four provinces in which I took the closest interest, Newfoundland, Manitoba and Québec, the fortunes of the Liberal party were dismal in the early 1980s. Only in Ontario did I see a glimmer of hope. I began to take a closer interest in provincial party fortunes in Ontario after David Peterson was chosen leader of the Ontario Liberal party.

I followed the struggle for leadership of the Tory party in 1983 with great interest. I was shocked when Joe Clark decided a two-thirds vote of approval for his leadership in January was insufficient and called a leadership convention. When the convention was held in June, I guessed that Brian Mulroney would win, but I was surprised by the close vote and did not foresee his landslide of the next year.

Trudeau was wearing out his welcome even within the Liberal party, and I felt that, having exceeded Laurier's years as prime minister, he was unlikely to contest another election. I was not surprised by the announcement of his intention to resign the leadership of the party. Though I was free to do so, I decided not to take any part in the leadership campaign or to express a preference for any candidate. In fact I had no preference, though I was convinced that the choice was between John Turner and Jean Chrétien.

Turner had been almost an associate minister with me in Transport until given a portfolio of his own. I owed him a measure of gratitude and valued our association. I had never forgotten Chrétien's decision to resist provincial temptation and to remain in Ottawa, about which he had asked my advice when we were still almost strangers. I felt that he had acquitted himself well in government and was impressed by his public appeal. Both men were friends, and I was glad I had decided not to attend the convention, and was not forced to make a choice.

One statement I made in the press was that the new leader should not call an election as soon as he became prime minister, but give the public at least a full session of Parliament to see how he performed in office. I was sorry that advice was not followed. Delay would not have enabled the Liberals to win an election, but it would have made their defeat less overwhelming.

Turner in my opinion made a greater mistake the day he was chosen leader, on 16 June 1984. I expected him to recognize Chrétien as his principal lieutenant in the tradition of Mackenzie King with Lapointe and St Laurent with C.D. Howe, and had a sense of foreboding when he failed to do so. I was appalled by Trudeau's legacy of patronage. His utter disregard for the future of the party that had given him 15 years of the highest office in public life was unforgivable.

I was in Newfoundland for most of the election campaign of 1984, cast my vote at Salvage on 4 September and watched Mulroney's landslide on television at Gander. The Liberal party, reduced to 40 members, had a long way to go to recover.

That year and the next, 1985, were years of profound political change. Mulroney was prime minister. Lévesque announced his intention to retire as premier of Québec. Peter Lougheed announced his impending retirement as premier of Alberta, and David Peterson became premier of Ontario, thereby ending 42 years of unbroken Tory government. Robert Bourassa made an amazing comeback as leader of the Liberal party of Québec and in December 1985 became premier.

Meech Lake: stage one

There is a widespread myth that Prime Minister Mulroney stirred up a crisis over the Constitution. In a speech during the election campaign of 1984 he said he would like to help remove the grievance in Québec over being left out of the 1981 agreement to have the Constitution patriated. But it was Premier Bourassa of Québec who started the process that resulted in the Meech Lake Accord. Bourassa took the initiative at a meeting of provincial premiers in Edmonton in 1987. The other nine premiers were sufficiently impressed by his proposals to ask Mulroney to call a federal-provincial conference of first ministers. Mulroney became involved only when he agreed to the premiers' request by calling a meeting at Meech Lake.

A unanimous agreement was reached at Meech Lake and made public. Any interested person could read it and voice objections. A few did, but there was no public outcry. The Meech Lake agreement was subject to review by the first ministers when it was put in legal language. That review took place in the Langevin Block in Ottawa in June 1987, and the premier of Québec agreed to several modifications suggested by premiers and experts. Unlike the Constitution of 1982, which was accepted by nine premiers acting on their own, the Meech Lake agreement had to be approved by all the provincial legislatures within three years after the first legislature approved it.

While the meeting was in progress at Meech Lake I had a conversation with Robert Stanfield in which we both expressed skepticism that agreement would come out of the conference. Having had long experience of federal-provincial discussions, we knew how rarely far-reaching agreements were achieved. We were astonished that agreement was reached so quickly at Meech Lake and when the terms were made public, surprised that Bourassa's conditions for approval of the Constitution were so moderate and so reasonable. Thirty people were holding an informal discussion on 6 May 1987 during which Stanfield and I were the only two who expressed unqualified approval. One clause or another provoked objections, though most of those who expressed opinions later came round to the view that the agreement, though imperfect, would end the grievance of the government of Québec without weakening the federal government or affecting adversely the government of any other province.

I was present when Premier David Peterson spoke at the Ottawa Canadian Club on 7 May in explanation and strong support of Meech Lake. It was the first time I had heard Peterson speak, and I was impressed by his simple, straightforward style and the clarity of his exposition of a complex subject. It was the beginning of a close relationship and a warm friendship between us.

Much of the criticism of Meech Lake was of the proposed recognition of Québec as a distinct society, which, it was claimed, would give one province a special status. But the language of the agreement clearly did no such thing. In an off-hand comment to the press Peterson said that any grade four student knew Québec was distinct from the other provinces.

But one universally known and highly influential critic had not yet reached grade four. Pierre Trudeau was so eager to condemn Meech Lake that he could not wait to denounce it even until the agreement was put in revised and legal language. Trudeau condemned the accord by twisting and distorting its provisions and saying Canadians could say goodbye to the dream of a single Canada, bilingual and multicultural. If the accord was adopted, we would have two Canadas, each defined by its language. But he was not content with attacking the accord; he made the most abusive attacks against the heads of government in Canada ever made by an actual or former prime minister. Special venom was reserved for Premier Bourassa, who was accused of espousing the cause of the Québec nationalists. Trudeau said 'That bunch of snivellers should simply have been sent packing and been told to stop having tantrums like spoiled adolescents.' He accused the political leaders of wanting courage and flaunting their political stupidity; he said it would be difficult to imagine a more total bungle.

Trudeau claimed that Canada had had since 1982 a constitution binding on the provinces, under which a united front of all 10 provinces could not have forced the federal government to give ground. He claimed that the federation was set to last a thousand years. Only one eventuality had not been forseen: that one day the government of Canada might fall into the hands of a weakling. That had happened in the case of Mulroney, who with the complicity of 10 provincial premiers had become the author of a constitutional document which, if accepted by the people and their legislators, would render the Canadian state totally impotent and design it eventually to be 'government by eunuchs.' The truth was that every provision of the Meech Lake Accord had been proposed at one time or another by Trudeau as prime minister in his spasmodic attempts to patriate the constitution.

The accord, as put in legal language, was modified to remove the slightest possibility of the reduction of Parliament's constitutional powers. But it would have reduced the capacity of the government and Parliament of Canada to use the spending power to intrude deeply into provincial jurisdiction. That intrusion, under Trudeau's long reign, made a large contribution to the uncontrolled increase in the national debt and the consequent drastic decline of the purchasing power of the Canadian dollar. Not only was Meech Lake, in which all 11 heads of government were brought into harmony, almost a miracle in itself; its adoption would have removed a grievance in Québec that nourished separatist sentiments. Meech Lake could have removed the Constitution from active politics for a generation or more.

Trudeau was determined to sabotage Meech Lake, and I decided to do whatever I could to help prevent such a disaster. His long diatribe had appeared in the *Toronto Star* and other papers on 27 May, a full week before the revised Meech Lake Accord was agreed to by 11 first ministers on 3 June. My reply appeared in the *Ottawa Citizen* on 16 June. It was almost as long as Trudeau's and was given almost a page of coverage.

I pointed out that Superman had swooped down on the collection of 'weaklings' and 'snivellers' who had conspired at Meech Lake 'to render the Canadian state totally impotent' even before the accord was put into final form. In abusive language he had denounced, as destroyers of their country, a prime minister who had received a greater mandate to speak for Canada than he himself had ever been given, a premier of Quebec who had an overwhelming mandate to speak for Québec, and the nine other premiers, to whom misguided 'nobodies' had entrusted the governments of their provinces.

What was Superman's case for his extravagant, almost hysterical outburst I asked. He charged that by recognizing Québec as a distinct society the country was henceforth to be two Canadas. To reach that conclusion he omitted the words expressly recognizing that Québec society included an English-speaking minority, and that the other provinces included French-speaking minorities. Even more shocking was his assertion that the accord would give Québec 'a constitutional jurisdiction the rest of Canada does not have.' He reached that conclusion by deliberately leaving out the substance of the paragraph limiting Parliament and the provincial legislatures to the exercise of their respective powers. The accord gave the Québec legislature no constitutional jurisdiction beyond what it already possessed.

I went on to deal, point by point, with Trudeau's other objections. I recalled that since 1982 the voters of Québec had chosen a government overwhelmingly opposed to any form of separatism. In 1987 the time seemed ripe to try to remove the grievance of 1982 and to secure the full acceptance of the Canadian constitution by the provincial authorities of Québec. If the Meech Lake Accord was approved by Parliament and all the legislatures, that would be achieved.

I said that as a Liberal I was proud of the Liberal premiers who supported the accord so wholeheartedly, and that as a Canadian I was proud of the statesmanship of the prime minister and the 10 premiers. I was pleased that Trudeau had failed to intimidate the leader of either Opposition party in Parliament. I agreed with John Turner's view that the acceptance by Québec of the constitution was to be 'on the right side of history.' I went on, 'One would have expected a really big man to express gratitude that his own substantial constitutonal achievement in patriating the constitution was being completed in so united a fashion. Instead he has used his great prestige to try, by distortion and misrepresentation, to sabotage the Accord.' I warned that if the moderation, common sense and patriotism of Bourassa were rebuffed, and the goodwill of all his fellow premiers was dissipated, a generation or more could pass before the timing was right again. If the Accord, in its legal form, is incorporated in the Constitution, the government of Québec will cease to be reluctantly submissive and become a full participant in Canada's constitutional development, thereby crowning Trudeau's achievement in patriating the constitution.

The legislature of Québec approved the agreement on 23 June 1987, thereby setting a constitutional deadline for approval of 23 June 1990. Seven other legislatures, including Newfoundland's, approved Meech Lake, notwithstanding Trudeau's dire warnings. In Manitoba and New Brunswick there were elections, and new governments and premiers were still considering the question.

Meech Lake: stage two

An ardent supporter of Meech Lake, I made a formal submission to the combined committee of the Senate and the House of Commons on the accord on 20 August 1987 and to the separate Senate committee on 18 November. In the latter I addressed myself primarily to the objections raised by the new premier of New Brunswick, Frank McKenna.

The political situation then changed in Manitoba. Premier Howard Pawley, one of the authors of Meech Lake, lost an election before he had submitted the acccord to the legislature. The new premier, Gary Filmon, a Tory, did not have a majority in the legislature, and the leader of the Opposition, Sharon Carstairs, a Liberal and a devotee of Trudeau, was vociferously opposed to Meech Lake. Filmon, hoping no doubt for support from the NDP, put a motion on the order paper of the legislature to approve the accord. Then the whole political atmosphere in Canada was changed by a decision of the Supreme Court on the validity of Québec's Bill 101, the charter of the French language in Québec. In essence the court decided that the Québec legislature could make laws to promote the use of the French language and culture but did not have the power to prohibit the use of the English language. In Québec there were demonstrations of outrage at the decision, and, despite the resignation of most of the anglophone ministers, the government of Québec went ahead with a ridiculous proposal to forbid English commercial signs on the outside of buildings but to permit them inside. It was resented by most anglophones living in Québec, among them the three of our children who lived in the province. But the harm caused by Bill 178 outside Québec was far greater. The view of the misinformed majority was that while French was being promoted in every other part of Canada, English was being prohibited in Québec. Bill 178 undoubtedly contributed substantially to the destruction of Meech Lake. Its immediate effect was the angry withdrawal on 19 December 1988 by Premier Filmon of Manitoba of his motion for the approval of the Meech Lake Accord.

Deeply distressed by Bill 178, I did not allow my feelings to discourage me from trying to persuade others that the adoption of the accord was in the interest of all Canadians. On 24 March 1988, I made a presentation to the meeting in Ottawa of the committee of the Ontario legislature at the urging of my provincial member, Gilles Morin. In August 1989, I wrote a lengthy article dealing with the objections raised in Manitoba and persuaded the *Winnipeg Free Press* to publish it even though the paper was at that time unfriendly to Meech. I thought that as a former Manitoban I might have some influence.

But my greatest concern was about the attitude of the new premier of Newfoundland. Immediately after the Liberal party won the provincial election in April 1989, Clyde Wells stated at a press conference that his government might ask the legislature to rescind the approval given earlier to Meech Lake. Meech Lake had not been an issue in the provincial election. I did not take the threat seriously until October 1989, when Wells made speeches at Osgoode Hall, at York University and at Memorial University in St John's. In both speeches he distorted the literal meaning of the distinct society clause as giving Québec unique legislative powers to protect and promote its status. His statements were a reflection of Trudeau's. Wells threatened to ask the Newfoundland legislature to withdraw its support for the accord if there was no indication that the federal government was willing to have changes made to meet his objections.

I did not know Clyde Wells. I assumed that, as a novice head of government, he might be interested in the views of a former Member of Parliament for a Newfoundland constituency who had been associated with prime ministers in handling constitutional questions since December 1937. I prepared a memorandum dealing with the points raised in his speeches and had it passed on to him with the message that I would be willing to discuss the subject with him if he wished. He sent me word that he would see me a few days later when he was in Ottawa on public business. He received me in his hotel for half an hour, during which he gave me a lecture on provincial finances without mentioning Meech Lake, much less my memorandum. He said he would keep in touch, but I never received further word. When I read the press release Wells issued on 20 October 1989 and his open letter to the prime minister, I understood why we had had no discussion in Ottawa. It was clear that he was an implacable opponent of the accord, that he believed he already possessed the truth and had nothing to learn.

The prime minister had a first ministers' meeting on the economy on 9 and 10 November 1989. Inevitably Meech Lake came up for discussion. Wells declared that he could not support the accord without amendment. He got into a sharp exchange with the prime minister, in which he contrived to appear as David overwhelming Goliath. Figuratively punching the prime minister in the nose earned Wells a flood of letters from the redneck anti-Québec element across Canada, which response convinced him that he knew the mind of the country better than those who had been active in public life for years. At the close of the meeting the new premiers of Manitoba and New Brunswick joined Wells in insisting that there must be amendments to the accord before they could support it. Wells did agree not to ask the legislature of Newfoundland to withdraw its approval immediately.

On 25 September, Premier Bourassa had won a landslide victory for the second time. The poor showing of the Parti Québecois indicated that there was no growth in separatist or sovereignist support, and that Meech Lake would remove the grievance.

In November, Robert Stanfield approached me about working out a joint reply to the position Wells had taken in his letter to the prime minister in October. I agreed enthusiastically. We spent until the beginning of January 1990 drafting an open letter to Wells, which we were satisfied dealt accurately with every point raised in his open letter to the prime minister. Our letter was delivered to Premier Wells on 10 January. He replied at even greater length on 15 January, and we replied in turn late in February. I enjoyed working with Stanfield and was impressed by his legal scholarship, clarity of mind and objectivity. I had over the years found him increasingly friendly, but at the end of that experience I felt we had become close friends.

That was the only positive effect of our open letters. Both newspapers in St John's almost totally ignored them, as did television. Any influence they might have had on opinion in Newfoundland was lost by their not being given greater attention in the media. As for the premier, they only strengthened him in his attitude.

The action Wells took in using his majority to have the legislature rescind its approval of the accord removed any doubt that he was determined to destroy the work of the prime minister and the 10 premiers. Among those in public office in 1989 and 1990 Wells made himself the leader in that work of destruction.

The first ministers met in May and June 1990, and, on 1 June, I telephoned Premier Joe Ghiz of Prince Edward Island, whom I had never met, to suggest a formula for membership in a reformed and elected senate. He put my suggestion to the meeting and attributed it to me. I regretted the mention of my name; the suggestion would have carried greater weight as coming exclusively from Ghiz. I had already been told that Ghiz was the most knowledgeable and cooperative of all the premiers in the formulation of the accord.

When Stanfield and I were working on our open letters to Wells, Lowell Murray, the government leader in the Senate, had arranged to have the transcription and distribution done for us, and I had come to know him through Stanfield. He became a channel through which I brought suggestions about the Constitution to the attention of the government. Murray passed on a request to me from the prime minister to write an article on Newfoundland as a distinct society, which Murray arranged to have published in the *Globe and Mail* on 4 June. That day I had a telephone call from *Le Devoir* asking my permission to publish a French translation. I was flattered, and agreed.

Premier Peterson was in touch with me more than once during that crucial meeting of first ministers, but I had no part in his spontaneous gesture in the meeting of first ministers, the offer to give up seats in the Senate, which brought the meeting to an apparently successful conclusion on 9 June. In my diary I noted that I was 'vastly relieved but a little worried about Newfoundland,' with that damned asterisk that Wells had placed beside his signature.

The destruction of Meech Lake

I had good reason to be worried about Newfoundland. Wells had agreed to put the question of approval of the accord to a referendum or to a free vote in the House of Assembly. On 11 June he announced that there was not time to hold a referendum. He decided instead to adjourn the legislature so that the members could consult their constituents before having to vote. He encouraged the premiers and the prime minister to visit Newfoundland to address the legislature. The premiers of Ontario and Saskatchewan responded, as did the prime minister on 21 June.

When Mulroney left St John's that night, he has said that Wells assured him that the vote would be taken the next day. Wells has not denied that he gave the assurance, but has said he cannot remember. He has said that he telephoned the premier of Manitoba and learned that the Manitoba legislature had adjourned until after 23 June without taking a vote and had thereby killed the Meech Lake Accord. Wells has said that he telephoned Lowell Murray on the morning of 22 June to indicate that he did not intend to have a vote taken in the House of Assembly; a vote, he felt, would hurt Newfoundland without saving the accord. What Murray's reaction was, and whether or not the vote would have been taken if Murray had telephoned again, is a question that can never be answered. For me it is irrelevant. I believed then and believe still that the assurance Wells gave to the prime minister should have been honoured, and that his failure was an act of bad faith.

According to information I had from Newfoundland, there were some Liberal MHAs who felt the accord was good for Canada and Newfoundland, and who were courageous enough to have voted for approval in a genuinely free vote such as Wells had promised. If the vote had been held, the accord might, I believe, have been approved by one or two votes. It was a humiliation of the membership of the Assembly to deny them the opportunity to represent their constituents that they had been promised.

Having adjourned the legislature, Wells rushed off to Calgary, where the convention was meeting to choose a new leader for the Liberal party of Canada. In Calgary, Wells was embraced by his mentor, Pierre Trudeau, and photographed embracing Jean Chrétien, a photograph Chrétien described in an interview in 1992 as one of his liabilities as leader.

I watched and listened intently to Premier Bourassa's broadcast on 23 June; for me it was an act of high statesmanship. I was impressed that the flag of Canada was clearly visible over his left shoulder. I wrote to him in July: 'In my view your greatest service to our country in this crisis was the splendid broadcast you made when the Accord was repudiated. Many expected recrimination and a call for vengeance. Instead there was a constructive approach which envisaged a continuing future for the whole country. Not least important symbolically was the red maple leaf behind your shoulder.' In his acknowledgment Bourassa said, 'You may rest assured that I deeply appreciate your kind and encouraging gesture.' I have not hesitated since then to communicate with Bourassa whenever I felt I had something helpful to say, and my interventions have invariably been welcomed. I count him a friend and believe he regards me in the same way.

The Liberal leadership convention

I had honoured John Turner most of all for his unequivocal support of Meech Lake despite the misgivings of some members of the Liberal caucus in Parliament and the division within the party inspired by the hostility of Trudeau. When John announced his retirement from the leadership in 1989, I was deeply concerned that the party would be split over Meech Lake. I had watched the NDP convention that chose Audrey McLaughlin as leader, and felt the divisions disclosed in that party were bad for its health. I feared that the Liberal convention would disclose even graver division, particularly as the party organization, with stupidity or malice, had set the date for the election of the new leader on the day Meech Lake would expire if not approved by all the provinces.

On 31 December 1989, I had written a memorandum on the Liberal leadership in which I began: 'The dismal performance at the NDP convention could be equalled or surpassed at the Liberal convention unless great care is taken to avoid mistakes. The NDP had no new ideas and no attractive presentation of old ones. They had no candidate with any real appeal. They humiliated their former leader over Meech Lake.' Later I said, 'The Liberals have one asset the NDP lacked. They have one, and only one, leadership prospect with popular appeal. Chrétien could probably win the leadership in a bitter contest but, if he cannot unite the party, he would have little hope of winning an election.'

Strife over Meech Lake I identified in the memo as the most serious threat to unity, and I said it could easily be avoided.

Knowing how difficult it would be for Chrétien, as one of the main architects of the Constitution of 1982, to talk about its imperfection, I wrote: 'I do not recommend that Chrétien become a supporter of Meech Lake. That would not be credible. His statement was wise that the Liberal party in Parliament had given its verdict and Meech Lake was therefore *not* an issue for the national party. Meech need not become an issue. The convention should not take any position on the attitude of provincial parties which are still debating the issue, and Chrétien certainly should not. The Liberal party should not miss a golden opportunity for SILENCE, and do everything possible to get on instead with current problems. Making an issue of Meech Lake would be a humiliation of the present leader as it was of the retiring NDP leader. Humiliating the retiring leader would not contribute to party unity.... I could not support a candidate for leadership who had the poor judgement to make Meech Lake an issue or failed to put a damper on any attempt to make it an issue.' I offered other advice, but neutrality on Meech Lake was my prime concern.

I was invited by one of Chrétien's supporters to sit on the platform when Chrétien was going to announce his candidature for the leadership. I knew he was to give a lecture on the Constitution the next day at Ottawa University, and I told the supporter that I would not give an answer until after the lecture. The lecture was a hostile academic critique of Meech Lake obviously not written by Chrétien and not in his style. It made me very sad. On the morning of 18 January I called his office to say I would not appear on the platform to endorse Chrétien and could not support him for the leadership. Chrétien called me in the evening to ask me to reconsider. We both spoke in the most moderate fashion. After a brief exchange I said, 'Jean, you are not going to change my position, and I am not going to change yours, but I hope our difference will not affect our friendship.' It has not.

I was so deeply involved with Meech Lake that I paid little attention to the Liberal leadership campaign and never entertained the idea of attending the convention. I noticed a statement by Sheila Copps that Trudeau had told her that if Chrétien supported

Meech Lake, he, Trudeau, would see that Chrétien did not get the leadership. I expected a denial from Trudeau, but none came that I ever saw.

It was common gossip in Ottawa in mid-June that Chrétien was doing his utmost behind the scenes to influence his supporters to do what they could to have Meech Lake approved. I was sure the gossip was correct, and I spoke to him on the telephone on 18 June to urge him to come out publicly in support of the accord. He indicated that he hoped it would be approved, but did not feel a public statement at that stage would help. He did not resent my call.

I watched the convention in Calgary on television whenever I could take my attention away from the televised debates on Meech in the Manitoba and Newfoundland legislatures. I was sure Chrétien would win, but I thought Paul Martin, Jr, and Sheila Copps deserved great credit for maintaining a good atmosphere and endorsing Chrétien's leadership. Much the best speech at the convention was John Turner's farewell, probably the greatest speech of his life.

The end of an era

Family milestones

Once I had cleared my office, published *My Years with Louis St. Laurent* and reached the age of 70, I felt retirement was real, and I devoted more time to my private life.

When I retired, I had two brothers and one sister living. Tom had retired at 65 from Central Mortgage and Housing and was in a consulting partnership in Toronto. My sister, Jane, and her husband, Kenneth Seaborne, had retired in Victoria, and Jane's twin, Walter, who had become a high school teacher after wartime service in the army, was teaching in Mission City, in the Fraser Valley. Tom, Jane and I were close friends; Walter had gone his own way, and we had less contact with him.

In 1974, Tom and his Margaret spent Thanksgiving with us. It was Tom's last visit to Ottawa; by December inoperable cancer had been diagnosed. In order to see Tom while he was alive, Jane and I met in Toronto in January 1975, where we spent a hilarious evening with Tom reminiscing about childhood and student days. We had a more sober lunch the next day. Jane and I cherished the memory of that visit. Tom died on 25 February 1975.

On 28 June 1981, Jane telephoned that she had just received word of Walter's sudden death. After retirement he had continued to live in Mission City. His death was a shock, and we felt sorry for his widow, Effie.

Jane's husband, Kenneth Seaborne, died on 24 September 1982. He was a First World War veteran, considerably older than my sister. I admired Ken and his devotion to Jane, and the more I learned of his career the greater had been my respect for his achievements. In October, Margaret and I attended a memorial service for Ken in Victoria, for which I helped to draft a tribute that was read by their daughter, Kate, originally called Nora.

My 80th birthday was in 1985, and for me the big event of the year was a dinner given in my honour on 20 June by John Turner. John thought the guest list should be based primarily on personal friendships, but I told him that as leader of the Liberal party he should not contemplate so elaborate a function unless it was to be an obviously Liberal celebration. I preferred to have as guests those who had been associated with my career as a public servant and a politician, and he accepted my view. There were more than 100 present, among whom Pierre Trudeau and Jean Chrétien were conspicuous. Robert Bourassa, not yet premier again, had been invited at my suggestion; I did not expect him to attend, but I was agreeably surprised to receive a personal letter of regret. In my speech at the dinner I stressed the Liberal character of the occasion. Turner's gesture was one of the greatest honours of my life.

Margaret's 75th birthday, in 1989, was celebrated by an extended family party at a fashionable restaurant in Gatineau called L'Eau Vive. All the children were present except Jane, who telephoned from Gander. Tom's widow, Margaret, and Mary Beattie, Margaret's sister-in-law, were there, as were Hélène Tolmie, Margaret's longest-standing friend in Ottawa, and Peter and Ross Martin, neighbours as well as dear friends. Margaret described the occasion as one of the happiest of her life.

Also in 1989 was a celebration of our 50th wedding anniversary, held on the deck of our house by the children, who performed as hosts. There were about 100 guests, many from outside Ottawa, including my sister from Victoria and Tom's Margaret from Toronto. It was the last time George and Alison Ignatieff were in our house. Alison's loss of memory was noticeable, the only sad note the whole day. Margaret and I felt the party was a festival of friendship.

The Queen described 1992 as *annus horribilis*, and I feel I could describe that year the same way. My sister died after a long and unsuccessful struggle with cancer. Her death came during one of my three periods in hospital, in Newfoundland and in Ottawa, with the painful disease shingles complicated by an accident in which my skull was fractured. There were, necessarily, delays in completing the text of the book on my life. The year would have been even harder to bear without the marvellous support of the family. Margaret was constantly vigilant.

Our children have confirmed and strengthened our appreciation that they are all our friends, and as we have grown older, their friendship has taken on an increasingly protective quality. We see Jane and her family every weekend when we are at Salvage, and the other three children live close by, across the Ottawa River in Québec.

Jane, established at Thunder Bay as the medical officer of health, came to Newfoundland for a holiday in 1977 and there renewed her friendship with the Baird family, in particular the elder son, Bill. She had known him for 20 years, but it was not until that summer that a spark struck. They were married in May 1978 in Ottawa, with both families present. They settled in Gander, where Bill already was the town engineer, and Jane became the medical officer of health for central Newfoundland. We turned the house at Traytown over to them, and they use it for most weekends. In 1979, Thomas John Baird was born, and in 1981, William Alan Frank Baird.

Peter graduated in architecture from the University of British Columbia in 1972, and he and Lisa returned to live in Ottawa. Peter was already doing cartoons and finding a good market for them. He decided not to practise architecture, apart from occasional freelance work. Lisa worked briefly in the Prime Minister's Office and subsequently returned to teaching. They have a summer home near Salvage and a house in Pointe Gatineau, Québec.

Alan served in the federal public service in St John's until 1980, when he was transferred to Ottawa. In 1985 he moved into a town house in Hull.

Ruth was married to Garth McKane in 1973. They subsequently bought a house in Farrellton, just beyond Wakefield up the Gatineau River, from which Garth commutes to work in Ottawa. They have a son, Michael, born in 1984, and a daughter, Madeleine, called Maddy, born in 1987. Ruth is concentrating on being a mother.

Old and new involvements

In late June 1982, Margaret and I flew to Newfoundland for what proved to be the outstanding event of the year for me. I had been invited to be the main speaker at the 25th anniversary of the establishment of Terra Nova National Park. The premier and Smallwood were also invited. I was not surprised that Premier Brian Peckford did not appear, but I was astounded by Smallwood's being there and even more by his speech. He not only described me as the founder of the park but reviewed the whole 14 years I had been an MP and attributed everything good that had happened in Newfoundland in that time to me. I waited apprehensively for a sting in the tail, but there was none. Needless to say, he made my speech an anticlimax, but I was so glad that the coldness between us had suddenly thawed that nothing else mattered. There was a ribbon to cut, and I had Smallwood and our grandson Baird hold the scissors with me. I had regretted more than I realized the breach in our relations after our long priod of working in partnership and was very pleased it had ended. Later ln the summer I called at Smallwood's office in St John's and we had a long reminiscent talk, as old men should.

Jules Léger died in 1980, and there was a dinner in Hull in May 1981 to mark the establishment of a chair at St Francis Xavier

University in Antigonish as a memorial to him. At that dinner I met Brian Mulroney for the first time. I was one of the sponsors of the legislation in Parliament to establish the Jules and Paul-Émile Léger Foundation to provide a solid base for Cardinal Léger's many charitable endeavours. I was one of the members of the foundation from the outset, and in 1982 our daughter Jane, as a resident of Newfoundland who is also a medical doctor, was chosen to be a member. Neither of us has contributed much to the work of the foundation, but we have faithfully attended the annual meetings in Montreal and been impressed by the efficiency, courtesy and bilingual competence of the officials. Listening to Cardinal Léger once a year while he lived was an inspiration. Our friendship with Mme Léger remains as warm as ever, and our meetings keep alive the close association Margaret and I began with Jules and Gaby over half a century ago.

In 1982, I was given an honorary doctorate by the University of Winnipeg. That same year Margaret and I attended a moving commemoraton of the 25th anniversary of the reception at the University of British Columbia of the complete forestry faculty of Sopron University. Jimmy and Kathleen Sinclair joined us for the dinner; it was the last time I saw my old colleague.

In 1989, I was awarded an honorary doctorate by Carleton University. It was conferred by my old friend Gordon Robertson, the chancellor. My speech to the convocation, which was entitled 'Canadian History Is Not Dull,' was one of my best.

In January 1990 the Writers Development Trust had a dinner at which there was a debate on whether or not the immediate postwar period had been the golden age of Canadian policy and diplomacy. Charles Ritchie and I supported the affirmative. The negative was argued by John Fraser, the editor of *Saturday Night*, and Hugh Segal, who was either about to join or had just joined the Prime Minister's Office. The debate was presided over by Robert McNeil of 'The McNeil-Lehrer News Hour' and was great fun.

In June of that year there was a rollicking picnic in celebration of the 50th anniversary of the Five Lakes Fishing Club, at which the three surviving founding members spoke — Ross Tolmie on

Ken Eaton, Bob Bryce on Clifford Clark and I on Donald Gordon.

I was invited to address the annual convention of the Non-Prescription Drug Manufacturers Association of Canada in Vancouver in September 1990. I was puzzled as to what might be an appropriate theme for drug makers but reassured when told that the other speakers would be John Kenneth Galbraith and Hugh MacLennan, the author of *Two Solitudes*. As it turned out MacLennan was too ill to travel and died soon afterwards; I never got to meet that great Canadian. I had had previous meetings with Galbraith. The theme of the convention was the greying of Canada, a recognition that the rise in the average age of Canadians was good for the drug manufacturers. I called my speech 'The Aging of Canadian History'; it was a companion piece to my speech at the Carleton convocation. It ended with a profession of faith that Canada has not reached the decay of old age, that the country 'will continue aging as a tolerant and peaceful society, in which human welfare is a deep and common aim.'

In 1991 the School of Public Administration of Carleton University began a series of annual public lectures. I was the first lecturer — not inappropriately, since I had been involved in the founding of the School and had been the speaker at its opening in 1953. I used the text of that 1953 speech again, knowing that few if any in the audience would have heard the original. The lecture was well received, and afterwards the series of annual lectures was named after me.

One initiative in particular has helped me maintain contact with friends in Ottawa and occasional visitors. Paddy Sherman of Vancouver, who moved to Ottawa in 1982 to publish the *Ottawa Citizen*, was a member of the Round Table, the Vancouver discussion club that had been started after the First World War; I had often been a guest. Paddy broached the idea to several friends of forming a Round Table in Ottawa. I was enthusiastic but felt that, unlike Vancouver's, Ottawa's Round Table should have women members, individuals chosen on their merit. We agreed, and after drawing up a list of persons to be invited, we began the Round Table early in 1985. The group meets every Wednesday, except in July and August. Most members are not young, and many have retired. I am now the oldest member. I sometimes describe the Round Table as a collection of extinct volcanoes, but it has been lively and stimulating. For me and others it has become the principal event of the week.

The passing of friends

I have occasionally remarked that more and more of my friends are in cemeteries; there have been frequent bereavements.

In 1977, I received a cable from Paul de France with the tragic news that Arnaud de Gouville had been killed in a motor accident in Africa. His work had not been confined to Canada; he had been involved in World Bank projects in Bolivia and West Africa. His death ended a most promising career and was a loss to Canada.

Jean Lesage died in 1980. I attended the funeral in Quebec City and a reception afterwards at Government House, where Jean-Pierre Côté, the lieutenant-governor, received me warmly. The gathering might almost have been a Liberal caucus; it was on that occasion that I had my first conversation with Robert Bourassa. I was happy to be among those paying tribute to Lesage, who had been one of the three or four greatest French Canadians of the century and one with whom I had enjoyed a lasting friendship.

The death of David Lewis in May 1981 left another gap in my political generation and marked the end of a friendship that had spanned partisan lines.

My deepest grief was for my brother-in-law, Robert Beattie, who, in failing health from 1982, died suddenly in January 1987. His death was a blow to Margaret and the whole family. Bob had the finest brain in Ottawa, and he applied it, almost without rest, to the most difficult problems of finance. As an author of the plan of equalization of federal-provincial tax-sharing, he is associated in my mind with John Deutsch, who died more than 10 years earlier, and with the beginning of my own participation in federal-provincial and constitutional affairs.

Another veteran of the war and postwar years and a close friend for half a century, Davidson Dunton, died in 1987. We had worked together when he was head of the Wartime Information Board and head of the CBC and had had frequent contact when he was president of Carleton University and till the end at the Round Table.

In January 1988 Arthur Lower died in Kingston at the age of 98, deaf and almost blind. We had been academic colleagues for 8 years and friends for approaching 60. He had taught me more Canadian history than any other person and had inspired many hundreds of students.

Later that month Guislain de France telephoned that his father had died. Paul had been unwell, and though his death was a relief to the family, it was a loss to all of them, as it was to me. I had telephoned greetings to Wacourt on New Year's Day, and Guislain told me the call had given his father much pleasure. Ours had been a close, 60-year friendship; Paul had been more like a brother than just a friend.

My classmate in university days, Stanley Laing, died in February 1989. He was the last of our class with whom I had maintained a connection. Another, Norval Hunter, had died some two years earlier. King Gordon died two days before Stan. I met King after my return from Oxford, when I occasionally spent weekends at the pulp mill at Pine Falls, where King was the United Church minister and shared a house with Norval. For several years the Gordons were neighbours of ours here in Ottawa.

Our stay at Salvage in 1989 was saddened by the news in August of George Ignatieff's sudden death. Margaret and I attended a memorial service in Convocation Hall at the University of Toronto in September. After the service we spoke to Alison, who recognized us. I was impressed by the care their son Andrew took of his mother that day. On my next visit to Toronto, in June 1992, I went with Andrew to see Alison, who realized I was a friend but did not know who I was. I was glad she seemed content, and struck again by Andrew's devoted attention. Alison died a few months later.

A classmate of both Manitoba and Oxford days, Ruth Reid, Escott Reid's wife, also died in 1989. Escott and I had been born in 1905, had matriculated at Oxford in the same year, had joined External Affairs in the same period and had often been closely associated, not in our work but in our careers.

More and more the political world to which I had belonged was vanishing. Walter Turnbull, the head of the Prime Minister's Office through most of the Second World War, died in May 1990. Brooke Claxton, Douglas Abbott and Lionel Chevrier, all veterans of Mackenzie King's day, were gone; I especially mourned Chevrier, who had been a comrade in Opposition and a devoted friend.

In June 1991, Guy Roberge died as a result of a cancer that he had believed was under control. I had visited him several times and each time found him weaker but still following events, especially those relating to the Constitution. I was always impressed by the vast range of his knowledge and the sanity of his judgement, and I miss our discussions deeply.

The death of Bud Drury also that year and of Paul Martin in 1992 removed two of the few links left with my former public life. Only Allan MacEachen, Paul Hellyer and Mitchell Sharp were left from the Pearson government, and only Walter Harris from the St Laurent government.

The break with the past was even more complete in Newfoundland. Senator Eric Cook, the president of the Liberal party when I entered politics in 1953 and a stout friend, died in 1986. Don Jamieson died later that year.

But the great break came with the death of J.R. Smallwood. A Smallwood Day had been held in Gambo, his birthplace, in August 1991. Margaret and I had turned up, to Smallwood's surprise; he was obviously delighted and kept me at his side for the rest of the day. His death in December was not unexpected. Smallwood's funeral was unprecedented in Canadian history. It was held in the Roman Catholic basilica, with the archbishop present to give a tribute. The service was presided over by the president of the United Church Conference. The Anglican church, the Presbyterian church, the Salvation Army and the Pentecostal church all had spokespersons. The prime minister and the premier of Newfoundland made well-crafted and appropriate appraisals of Smallwood's unique contribution to Newfoundland and Canada.

Seeing Canada Whole:
A Memoir
Conclusion

Writing this book has taken longer than I anticipated. Before I started I had already published books about my relations with two prime ministers, St Laurent and Pearson. What I felt was needed was to write about my early life and my relations with Mackenzie King. I had edited Mackenzie King's wartime and postwar diaries, but in the edited volumes of *The Mackenzie King Record* he had spoken for himself and there was little about my relations with him.

When I reached the year 1948 in the draft of this book the publisher persuaded me to add the St Laurent and Pearson periods, and I then decided to include my twenty years of retirement.

It took even longer to agree on the title. I had thought of calling the book *Seeing Canada Whole*. That title appealed to me because it could apply equally to history and geography on the one hand, and to the politics and government of Canada on the other. The book is about my experience of both. We were unsuccessful in finding a better title, and in 1993 the publisher suggested that I go with my original inclination. *A Memoir* is added to the title so that the book will not be mistaken for a travel guide.

I had planned to finish writing the book in 1992, but 1992 proved to be a difficult year. In the spring my sister had a serious illness, which led us to visit her in Victoria, and which, until her death in November, caused us much anxiety. We went to Newfoundland later than usual that year. In July and early August, I worked on the manuscript with Margaret. Quite suddenly in late August I became ill and went to the Gander hospital, where the illness was diagnosed as shingles — a serious case, which delayed our return to Ottawa until mid-September. Back home I again resumed work on the book, but late in October I had a fall that fractured my skull and sent me to hospital in Ottawa until early in the new year.

During those interruptions in my work I reflected on my attitude to political developments since I left Parliament in 1967. Though I had no part in the selection of Pierre Trudeau as Pearson's successor, I continued, as a Liberal, to support the Liberals in every election. I could have no active role as long as I was president of the Canadian Transport Commission, and my support was passive after my retirement in 1972. The one issue I was keenly interested in was Trudeau's effort to patriate the British North America Act.

The resurrection of Trudeau as prime minister in 1980 after his first retirement was living proof that Québec did not need to be independent for a French-speaking Canadian to have a long and successful career in federal politics.

Trudeau's intervention may have been decisive to the defeat of sovereignty-association in the Québec referendum. On the night of the referendum René Lévesque indicated that the battle for sovereignty was not over but would be dormant for many years. I took him at his word. Lévesque's second successful election did not stop Trudeau from pressing for patriation.

I was shocked and almost horrified by Trudeau's threat to ask the British government to put legislation before their Parliament to patriate the BNA Act without formal approval of the provincial governments, whose legislative constitutions the BNA Act formulated. The suggestion to have the federal Parliament alone ask for patriation of the Constitution affecting the jurisdiction of the provincial legislatures outraged at least 8 of the 10 premiers and forced a reference to the Supreme Court as to the legality of the procedure. The Court rendered a decision I regarded as bizarre, because never in the past had amendments to the BNA Act affecting provincial constitutions been solicited without the approval of every provincial authority; it opened the way for the exclusion of one or more provinces.

I felt the earliest opportunity should be seized to secure the approbation by Québec of the new constitution. I welcomed the initiative of Premier Bourassa and the subsequent agreement of all the first ministers at Meech Lake. I thought Meech Lake as amended by the heads of government in Ottawa was historically sound and wholly admirable.

I had deeply resented Trudeau's intemperate attack on the Meech Lake Accord before it was finally drafted, and I published a detailed public refutation of his attack. I worked later with Robert Stanfield to try to overcome the dissent of Premier Wells of Newfoundland. I earlier made submissions to the committees of Parliament and the Ontario legislature in defence of Meech Lake. All this activity delayed my work on this book.

I took no active interest in the working out of the Charlottetown Accord, which I felt was a ramshackle document much inferior to Meech Lake. But when all the provincial governments supported it before the referendum, my vote was cast in favour. The rejection of the Charlottetown Accord did not depress me. I was glad that the majority of the votes in all the provinces except Québec were not on one side, with Quebec on the other.

The BNA Act was never the total constitution of Canada. It was a long-term design to unite all the colonies of British North America. The first of July 1867 was the natal day of Confederation. We celebrated that date as Canada's 125th birthday in 1992. But the roots of the Canadian nation go into history long before 1867. The Canadian Constitution, as it has developed historically, is made up of precedents and British statutes and other legal instruments relating to Canada as well as to some of the practices of New France. The oldest elected Legislative Assembly in what is now Canada was established by Britain in Halifax in 1758. The Nova Scotia colonial government was modelled on the governments of the American colonies before the Revolution. New France was treated differently. Its name was changed to Québec in 1774 by the British Parliament. Unlike Nova Scotia, Québec was not given an elected Assembly, but the Roman Catholic religion was tolerated, as was the official use of the French language.

After the American Revolution, loyal colonists gave up their homes to preserve their allegiance to the British crown. They left the former colonies in thousands. Many of these refugees, including my own ancestors, settled in Upper Canada. In 1791 the British Parliament enacted legislation to divide the 1774 Province of Québec into two provinces, which were named Lower and Upper Canada. Lower Canada was the former New France and Upper Canada was to become Ontario. Both of the Canadian provinces were to have elected Legislative Assemblies, as well as Legislative Councils and Executive Councils appointed by the governor. The Assembly was the pattern for the House of Commons, the Legislative Council for the Senate, and the Executive Councils for the cabinet. The Legislative Council as well as the Assembly had to pass bills before they became laws. Lower Canada retained its special position with respect to the French language, the Catholic religion and the civil law of New France.

For me, the free elections of 1792 in the Canadas were the beginning of modern Canada. In 1992, we should have celebrated 200 years — not just 125 years — as a country based on a French-English partnership.

The Assemblies in the Canadas were elected in 1792. It was not long before some members in each Assembly began to demand that the executive must have the support of the Assembly. Reformers led by Joseph Papineau in Lower Canada and William Lyon Mackenzie in Upper Canada maintained sympathetic correspondence about their demands for reform and self-government. Both started armed rebellion in 1837. The rebellion ended quickly in Upper Canada and lasted a little longer in Lower Canada. Both Papineau and Mackenzie went into exile.

After the rebellions the British government sent Lord Durham to Canada to investigate the disorder and recommend appropriate action. Durham reported that official recognition of two languages was the main cause of trouble in Lower Canada. He recommended the union of the two Canadas into one province, with English as the sole official language. His report suggested that self-government was a legitimate objective, and that the Executive Council should eventually be required to have the confidence of the Assembly.

The British Parliament united the two Canadas into one Province of Canada, with English as the official language. It was anticipated that the use of the French language would gradually die out. Instead, the Assembly, with more English- than French-speaking members, took the initiative in restoring French as a permissible language in debate — one of the noblest acts of Canadian political history. Reformers in the Assembly under Robert Baldwin and Louis-Hippolyte LaFontaine united in a single political party. By 1848 the Reform party had gained control of the Executive Council of the Province of Canada, thereby achieving what was called responsible government. Nova Scotia also won responsible government in 1848. In the Province of Canada, John A. Macdonald and most of the Tories, joined by George-Etienne Cartier and a group of French-speaking members, endorsed responsible government.

Responsible government accordingly became an unwritten part of the Constitution of Canada after Confederation. There was no mention in the BNA Act of a prime minister, a cabinet or a leader of the opposition in the House of Commons. Yet after Confederation all these were essential features of the Constitution of Canada, patterned on the British Parliament.

Responsible government enables the prime minister to get a decision from Parliament rapidly. A government measure can always be brought to a vote — by closure if necessary. When a government measure is defeated, the prime minister has a choice between resigning or asking for the dissolution of Parliament and a new election. This procedure makes the changing of governments possible in Canada in a short time. By contrast, when the President of the United States is in conflict with the Congress, which often happens, that conflict can continue for months or even years because the Congress is elected for a specific term and cannot be dissolved. The Canadian system is far more flexible. In emergencies, governments can reach decisions much more easily. Canadian responsible government is, I believe, the most satisfactory system for a people who want a peaceful, orderly but dynamic system of government. Having the cabinet as the only formal government and an official Opposition as a potential alternative government makes changes of administration simpler to bring about and provides a source of public pressure on government. Responsible government is, in my opinion, the most valuable part of the Canadian Constitution.

As a public servant and, later, a politician I always supported recognition of the equal status of the two historic official languages. That recognition is, I believe, essential to the maintenance of a united Canada.

Since the defeat of the Charlottetown Accord, I discern a declining sense of urgency about changing the Constitution of 1982. Leaders of movements for sovereignty in Québec still claim that, in a referendum there, sovereignty would win. They imply that a majority for sovereignty in Québec would automatically divide Canada into two countries. They fail to realize that sovereignty, if it means independence for Québec, could not be achieved legally without the consent of the Parliament of Canada and all the provincial legislatures. To reach an orderly agreement to break up Canada would be so difficult, if not impossible, that the public in Québec and elsewhere in Canada would come to feel it would be better to make changes within Confederation.

My faith is unshaken that Canada will endure for as long as any of us can foresee. I believe that most Canadians, inside and outside Québec, will wake up one day from their rosy dreams or disturbing nightmares to look around the world and discover there is no large country anywhere more peaceful, more orderly and better governed than Canada. Our self-government has been achieved by political parties of English- and French-speaking Canadians combined in the same causes and able to gain office through ballots not bullets.

The union of the Canadas in 1841 expanded into the federation of 1867. Confederation had reached the Pacific by 1871. Prince Edward Island and Newfoundland had been united with Canada in 1873 and 1949. The creation of modern Canada was one of the greatest peaceful political achievements in human history. The time will come when Canadians inside and outside Québec will be content to live in the real world and enjoy this vast and rich land where peace, order and government are better than in most countries and as good as in the best.

I was recently asked whether or not, if I had to do it again, I would go into public life. I have no regret at having entered Parliament in 1953. The opportunity was unique. The prime minister wanted my help in the general election campaign. I was ready to take the risk of defeat in Newfoundland. The prospect of representing a new province had a great appeal. Going into the cabinet before being elected reduced the gamble. I did not have to come to Ottawa if elected; I had already lived in Ottawa for 25 years and had no desire to live elsewhere. I believed that I could represent a constituency a thousand miles away.

I was elected with overwhelming majorities six times in the first 12 of my 14 years in Parliament. I was an active and effective parliamentarian, as John Diefenbaker testified after my retirement by saying, 'Parliament without Pickersgill will be like Hell without the Devil.' I had a close association with Premier Smallwood that I believe served Newfoundland well. Newfoundland became a second home for Margaret and me and all our children, and still is.

Two things would not have happened if I had not been in the government. One was the provision of unemployment insurance for fishermen, which preserved the self-respect of a generation of in-shore fishing families. The other was the provision of a place in Canada for 35,000 Hungarian refugees, who became exemplary citizens.

I was never bored by Parliament. I would try again.

And so, while not fully recovered from a disabling illness, I end the writing of this memoir of my long life. I could not have completed the book without the constant and creative assistance Margaret has given me during this final stage. The largest contribution to the recovery of my health has been her uninterrupted vigilance and the devoted care of all our children.

The friendship of our children for their parents and for each other has been a great reward for Margaret and me. Despite two great wars and some personal sorrows, mine has been a happy life. The half century of living with Margaret has been the supreme experience of that happy life.

Index

Praise for *Cranky Uncle vs. Climate Change*

"People are always asking me, "What's the best source for debunking the claims of climate change deniers?" Now I have an easy answer: buy a copy of John Cook's new book, *Cranky Uncle vs. Climate Change*.

Prof. Michael Mann
Author of *The Madhouse Effect* and *The Hockey Stick and the Climate Wars*

"This rare book answers many of your pressing questions, such as what to tell your crazy Uncle Joe when he insists at Thanksgiving dinner that climate change is a liberal hoax. Thank goodness for this book!

Prof. Naomi Oreskes
Author of *Merchants of Doubt* and *The Collapse of Western Civilization*

"This funny and factual walk through climate science and its impacts—and common arguments against them—will leave you informed, recharged, and excited to see the sequel: "*Cranky Uncle vs. Climate Solutions.*" I can't wait!

Prof. Katharine Hayhoe
Texas Tech University

"Because the book is so humorous and well written, it's easy to forget that you're learning a lot of climate science as you read it. I highly recommend it.

Prof. Andrew Dessler
Texas A&M University

"*Cranky Uncle vs. Climate Change* is a fun way to learn about climate science and the psychology of denial. Come for the cartoons; stay for the science!

Dana Nuccitelli
Author of *Climatology vs. Pseudoscience*

"*Cranky Uncle vs. Climate Change* turns climate skeptics into foils for Cook's main mission of educating climate novices—witty, sardonic, enlightening, and engrossing.

Prof. Michael Oppenheimer
Princeton University

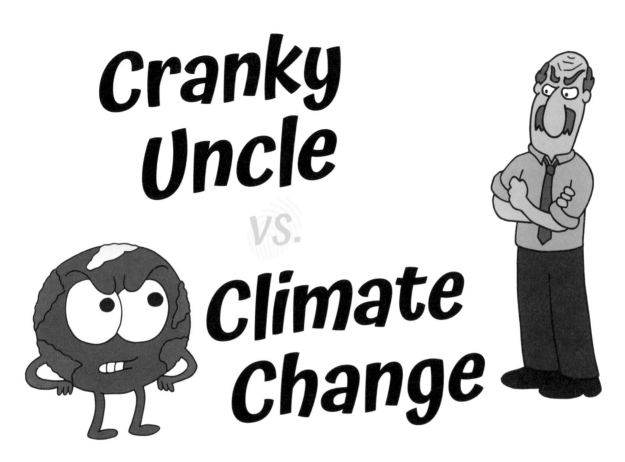

Cranky Uncle vs. Climate Change

How to Understand and Respond to Climate Science Deniers

DR. JOHN COOK
Founder of SkepticalScience.com

CITADEL PRESS

Kensington Publishing Corp.
www.kensigntonbooks.com

CITADEL PRESS BOOKS are published by
Kensington Publishing Corp.
119 West 40th Street
New York, NY 10018

Graphic design by John Cook and Wendy Cook.

All Kensington titles, imprints, and distributed lines are available at special quantity discounts for bulk purchases for sales promotions, premiums, fundraising, educational, or institutional use. Special book excerpts or customized printings can also be created to fit specific needs. For details, write or phone the office of the Kensington sales manager: Kensington Publishing Corp., 119 West 40th Street, New York, NY 10018, attn: Sales Department; phone 1-800-221-2647.

ISBN-13: 978-0-8065-4027-6
ISBN-10: 0-8065-4027-3

First trade paperback printing: March 2020

10 9 8 7 6 5 4 3 2 1

Printed in the United States of America

Electronic edition:

ISBN-13: 978-0-8065-4028-3
ISBN-10: 0-8065-4028-1

For references and more information, see http://crankyuncle.com

To my dearest Wendy,
whose editing, design, support, and love
made this book possible.

Contents

Why so controversial?

EASY. IT'S A HOAX!

Evidence for global warming

WHAT EVIDENCE?

5 Denying science   109

How does climate science get attacked?

THEY HAVE IT COMING!

6 Responding to science denial   141

What do we do about climate denial?

NOTHING, REALLY.

x

Cranky Uncle

vs.

Climate Change

Making sense of climate science denial

We are bombarded with information about climate change. On the one hand is a mountain of facts and scientific evidence that human-caused global warming is happening. This has led to overwhelming expert consensus, with 97% of climate scientists agreeing that we're causing climate change.

On the other hand, we are also confronted with a huge pile of myths casting doubt on climate science. Fake news can make people disengage from real news, so misinformation is a problem that can't be ignored.

We need to deal with misinformation. But how? By shining disinfecting daylight on the techniques of denial. When we learn how we're being misled, misinformation loses its power.

Cranky Uncle vs. Climate Change explains how the climate issue became so controversial, exposes the flaws in misinformation, and shows how we can respond to science denial.

HOW DID CLIMATE CHANGE GET SO **CONTROVERSIAL?**

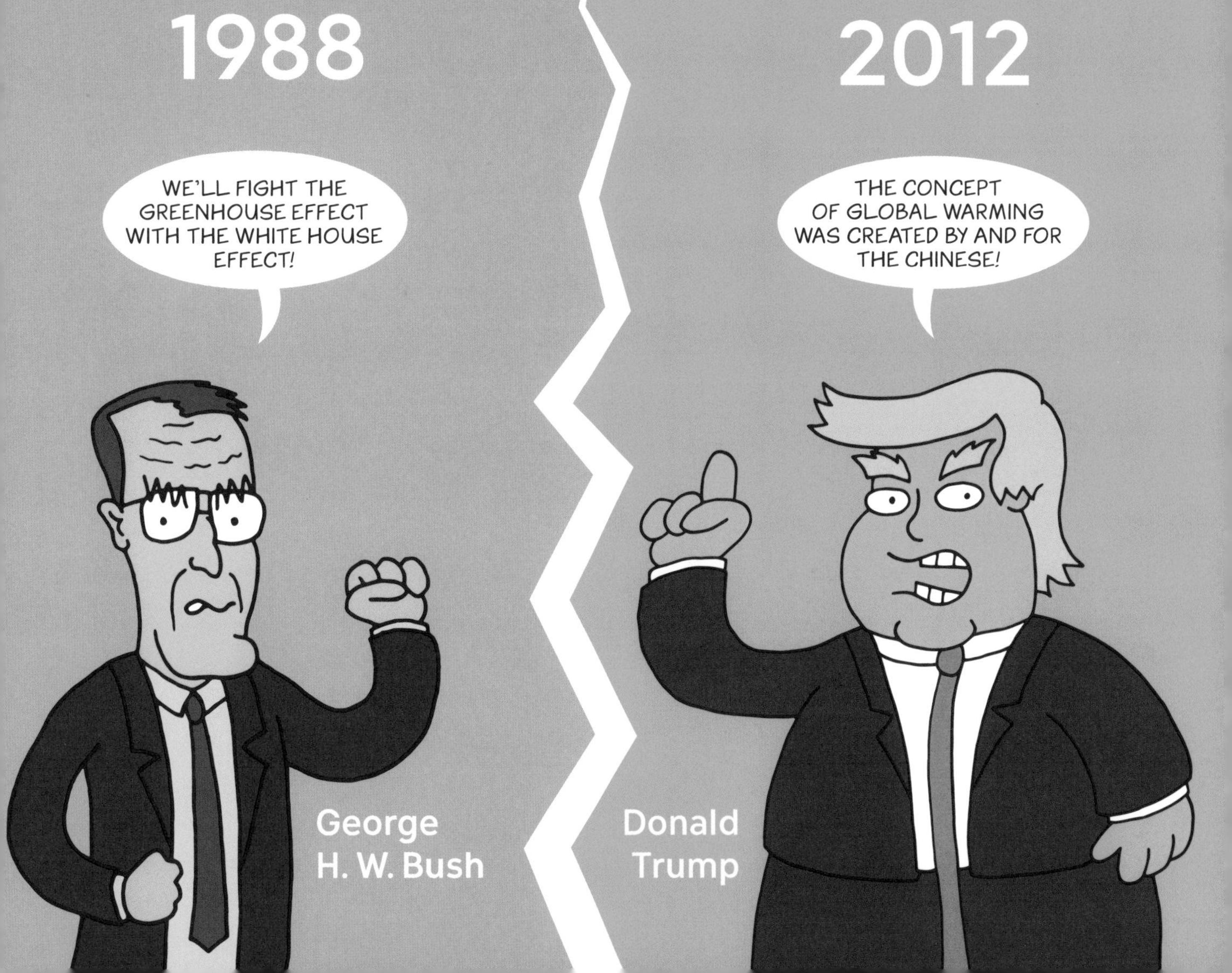

Climate change: A perfect psychological storm

Our human brain is poorly equipped to deal with a threat like climate change. Over millions of years, we've evolved to avoid life-threatening dangers like predators jumping out of bushes. We've survived by quickly detecting and avoiding immediate, short-term dangers.

In contrast, global warming is a slow-motion disaster happening on a global scale. Our brains aren't built to respond to planetary crises stretched out over a lifetime. It should come as no surprise that people have trouble appreciating just how dangerous climate change is.

On top of all these difficulties, we are also being hit with a massive wave of misinformation about climate change. Vested interests, political polarization, the global nature of climate change, and misinformation combine to form a perfect psychological storm, preventing people from accepting climate science and supporting climate action.

MISINFORMATION CAMPAIGN

VESTED INTERESTS

LOBBYISTS

PSYCHOLOGICAL DISTANCE

POLARIZATION

From the public's point of view, the tsunami of misinformation looks like scientific controversy. We hear experts and contrarians on TV or social media spouting jargon and assume scientists are still undecided on basic questions, like whether humans are causing global warming.

This veneer of controversy conceals the fact that our scientific understanding of human-caused global warming is built on more than a century of research. Scientific confidence is strongest when many different lines of evidence all point to a single conclusion. That's what we observe with climate change.

Unique patterns matching human-caused global warming—otherwise known as human fingerprints—have been observed all over our climate. This body of evidence has resulted in overwhelming agreement among climate scientists.

The scientific consensus on climate change

Since 1990, the Intergovernmental Panel on Climate Change (IPCC) has brought together the world's top climate experts to assess the scientific research into climate change. They regularly issue a new report summarizing the latest scientific understanding of climate change.

As the evidence continues to accumulate, the IPCC's confidence that humans are causing global warming has grown stronger. In 1995, the IPCC first concluded that humans were influencing global climate. The latest IPCC report, published in 2013, says it is now "extremely likely" (that means 95% confident!) that humans have caused most of the global warming observed since the mid-20th century.

Based on all the evidence summarized in the IPCC reports, there is overwhelming scientific consensus, with 97% of climate scientists agreeing that humans are causing global warming.

97% of climate scientists agree that we're causing global warming

Not only has there been scientific consensus on climate change for decades, there used to be political consensus as well. In the 1980s, George H. W. Bush—head of the Republican Party—pledged to fight climate change.

So how did a bipartisan issue turn so partisan? The story begins in the late 1980s. Three physicists began attacking the science linking smoking to cancer, the reality of acid rain, the severity of the ozone hole, and global warming. In short, they tried to discredit any scientific evidence showing that industries were harming the public's health or the environment.

Why did these scientists turn against science? While the obvious suspect is money, it turns out their motives run deeper. They subscribed to a belief system called free market fundamentalism. This ideology holds that capitalism and personal freedom are inextricably linked. Even a small action like a tax on tobacco could be the start of a slippery slope of ever-increasing regulation, leading to government controlling every part of our lives.

The controversy about climate change is not about the science. It's about how much the government should regulate the marketplace to protect the public. Believers in free markets dislike the implications of the science, so they deny there is a problem in the first place.

> IF WE DO NOT CAREFULLY DELINEATE THE GOVERNMENT'S ROLE IN REGULATING… DANGERS, THERE IS ESSENTIALLY NO LIMIT TO HOW MUCH GOVERNMENT CAN ULTIMATELY CONTROL OUR LIVES.

S. Fred Singer

SLIPPERY SLOPE FALLACY

Slippery Slope

The slippery slope fallacy argues that taking a small action will eventually lead to major (and often ridiculous) consequences. It falsely assumes that one thing inevitably leads to another.

> IF YOU DON'T DO A PH.D.…

> …YOU'LL END UP LIVING ON THE STREETS IN TORN JEANS!

The actual argument my dad used when I was thinking about getting into cartooning.

> " This is not a scientific debate; it's a political debate. But it's a political debate being made to look like a scientific debate.

Prof. Naomi Oreskes
Harvard University

An unholy alliance between ideology and industry

As political conservatives led the charge against climate science, they had powerful allies in the fossil fuel industry, whose profits depend on the continued burning of their product. Since the early 1990s, fossil fuel groups have poured billions of dollars into groups to cast doubt on climate science.

In earlier decades, the fossil fuel industry's own scientists had found that burning fossil fuels causes climate change. But rather than act on the science, these companies invested in misinformation. They poured billions of dollars into conservative groups who appear to be more credible messengers than industry spokespeople.

This partnership proved to be highly effective. Over several decades, they transformed climate change into a polarized public debate: a perfect storm fueled by an unholy alliance.

What fossil fuel knew vs. What fossil fuel did

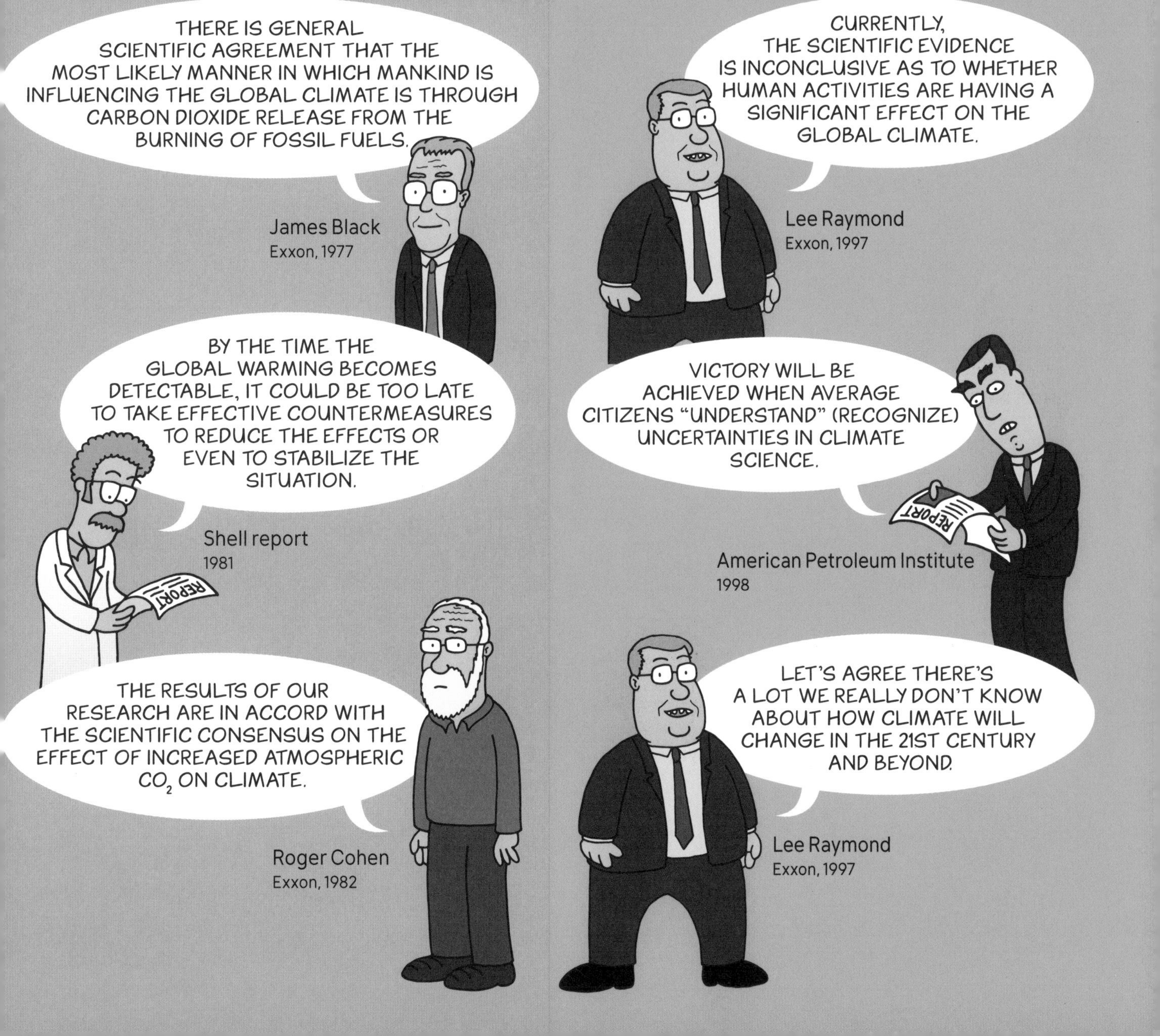

The tobacco playbook of selling doubt

How did conservative think tanks attack the science? They sold doubt. They emphasized uncertainty. But let's give credit where credit is due. Climate misinformers didn't invent this strategy. They borrowed from the tobacco industry, who used the same strategies to cast doubt on the scientific research linking smoking to cancer.

Not only did the fossil fuel industry use the same techniques as the tobacco industry, they even used some of the same people! The three physicists who first cast doubt on the link between tobacco and its health impacts also began casting doubt on all manner of environmental impacts from industrial activity.

Reusing the same strategies with the same people—never let it be said that the merchants of doubt didn't recycle!

The misinformation campaign has been all too effective. Over the last few decades, Americans have become more polarized about climate change. While acceptance that global warming is happening has increased among Democrats, Republicans have been moving in the opposite direction.

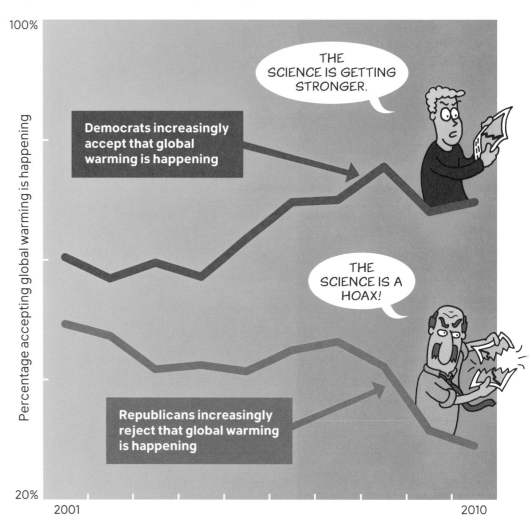

Climate change has become so polarized that political affiliation is now the strongest factor influencing people's views on this topic. How and what we think about climate science is driven more by who we vote for than by education, income, gender, or age. Unfortunately, climate change has become tribal.

IRONY ALERT!

Failing to act on climate change because of a fear of government intervention will lead to climate impacts that will require strong government interventions in response.

Psychological research shows that the misinformation campaign has made a deep impact. This was demonstrated in a study in which people were presented with a message about climate change followed by possible responses. When conservatives were presented with a solution involving regulation, they rejected the science. When presented with a solution involving nuclear power, they accepted the science. Whether they accepted the science depended on whether they accepted the proposed solutions to climate change.

For most people, this kind of science denial happens at a subconscious level. But it's most publicly demonstrated by Donald Trump, for whom subtext becomes text. He explicitly explains that his position on how much humans are causing global warming is based on how much it's going to cost his companies.

What our leaders say matters. When our political leaders promote misinformation, public acceptance of climate change shifts accordingly. Imagine what it might look like if Donald Trump publicly supported climate science rather than attacked it...

TRANSLATION:
My position on reality depends on how much it's going to cost me!

The telltale characteristics of science denial

Skepticism is a good thing. Science and skepticism go hand in hand. A genuine skeptic considers all the evidence before coming to a conclusion. Science denial, on the other hand, works in reverse.

A **GENUINE SKEPTIC** considers the evidence...

THEN

...comes to a conclusion.

THE EVIDENCE INDICATES...

A **SCIENCE DENIER** makes up his mind...

I DON'T BELIEVE IT!

THEN

...denies inconvenient evidence.

How do you tell the difference between genuine skepticism and denial? Science denial has five telltale characteristics—argumentative techniques designed to convey the appearance of ongoing scientific debate when there is none. They can be summarized (and more easily remembered) with the acronym FLICC:

F Fake Experts   L Logical Fallacies   I Impossible Expectations   C Cherry Picking   C Conspiracy Theories

The five characteristics of science denial are seen in all movements that deny a scientific consensus, whether it be human-caused global warming, biological evolution, or the link between smoking and cancer. Understanding these techniques and fallacies is critical to identifying and countering misinformation.

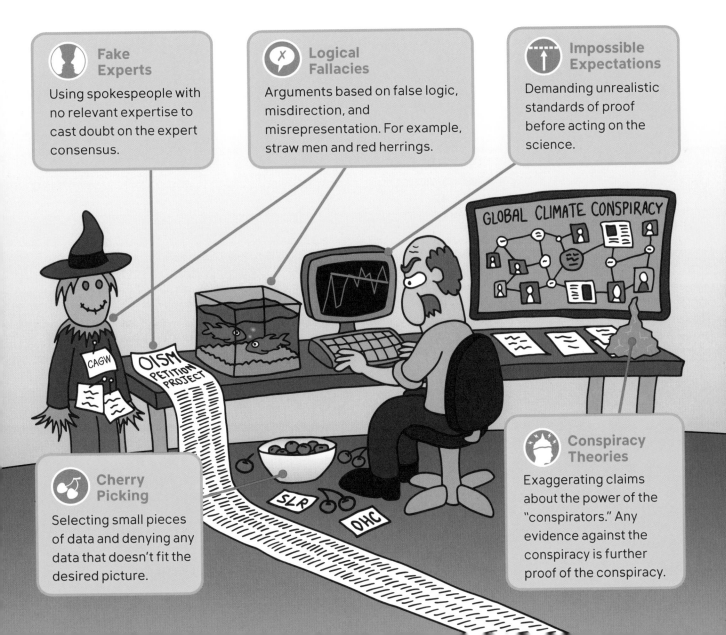

Fake Experts
Using spokespeople with no relevant expertise to cast doubt on the expert consensus.

Logical Fallacies
Arguments based on false logic, misdirection, and misrepresentation. For example, straw men and red herrings.

Impossible Expectations
Demanding unrealistic standards of proof before acting on the science.

Cherry Picking
Selecting small pieces of data and denying any data that doesn't fit the desired picture.

Conspiracy Theories
Exaggerating claims about the power of the "conspirators." Any evidence against the conspiracy is further proof of the conspiracy.

Understanding the five techniques of science denial is key to identifying and responding to misinformation.

Fake experts are people who convey the appearance of expertise without possessing any actual relevant expertise. They're often used to confuse the public about expert agreement. The tobacco industry mastered this strategy in the 1970s. In fact, their title for this misinformation campaign was the Whitecoat Project.

Our psychological biases make fake experts a powerful strategy. We tend to think people whom we agree with have greater expertise than people we disagree with. That means deniers tend to dismiss statements by climate scientists while paying attention to contrarian voices.

Fake Experts

MMM... SOOTHES THE THROAT!

Fake debate and media false balance

Journalists typically cover contentious issues by giving both sides equal attention. This works fine in politics or arguments of opinion. It doesn't work so well with science and fact.

Climate deniers exploit false balance by promoting a handful of contrarians, raising them to equal prominence with climate scientists. The public are left with the impression there's a 50:50 debate among experts, rather than the 97% scientific consensus.

Ironically, the journalistic practice designed to prevent bias has resulted in the public being misled about climate change.

TONIGHT, WE'LL BE TALKING TO A SCIENTIST ABOUT THE SOLAR SYSTEM...

...TO BALANCE HER VIEWS, WE'VE INVITED A MEMBER OF THE FLAT EARTH SOCIETY.

Logical Fallacies

Logical fallacies are false arguments leading to an invalid conclusion. There are a number of different logical fallacies; here are just a few that are commonly found in deniers' arguments.

Ad hominem
Dismiss an argument by attacking the person.

> THERE ARE MANY INDICATORS SHOWING THAT OUR PLANET IS WARMING.

> YOU'RE WACKY!

Non sequitur
The conclusion isn't supported by the premises (a.k.a., jumping to conclusions).

> WE'RE EMITTING HEAT-TRAPPING GASES, SO WE'RE CAUSING WARMING.

> CLIMATE ACTION COSTS ME MONEY... THEREFORE WE ARE NOT CAUSING WARMING.

Red herring
Distractions that have nothing to do with the argument.

> THE BALANCE OF EVIDENCE TELLS US THAT HUMANS ARE CAUSING GLOBAL WARMING.

THWACK!!

Impossible expectations demand unrealistic standards of proof before acting on the science. Uncertainty is an important part of science. However, deniers exploit uncertainty by promoting the misconception that science is about absolute proof.

Impossible expectations are also accompanied by lowered expectations— uncritically accepting contrarian positions on little or no evidence.

Impossible Expectations

Cherry picking involves focusing on select pieces of data while ignoring anything conflicting with the desired conclusion. How do you tell the difference between misleading cherry picking and appropriate examples? Someone is cherry picking when their conclusion comes from a small selection of the available data and that small selection conflicts with the full body of evidence.

Cherry Picking

Conspiracy theories are created when science deniers accuse the world's scientists of a massive, global conspiracy. Of course, such a huge conspiracy is utterly implausible. Imagine scientists from all over the world trying to fake the overwhelming amount of evidence for climate change...

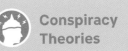

Conspiracy Theories

"SCIENCESPLAINING"

When nonscientists condescendingly lecture scientists about how to do science.

What a global climate conspiracy would look like

The stages (or states) of climate denial

Climate denial arguments can be grouped into categories such as "it's not real," "it's not us," or "it's not bad." These are often thought of as stages of denial. For example, we think a logical person would change their position from "it's not real" to "it is real but it's not us" as the evidence builds up. But this is not how deniers work.

Deniers are more like an agent in *The Matrix* who can dodge bullets by shifting instantly from one position to the other. Similarly, deniers jump from one position to another depending on whatever evidence comes their way in the moment.

On Monday, they're denying that global warming is happening. On Tuesday, they're conceding that global warming is happening but is caused by the sun. On Wednesday, they're back to arguing that global warming is on hiatus. Coherence is not a concern. Ultimately, every argument ends with the same conclusion: "Therefore we should do nothing."

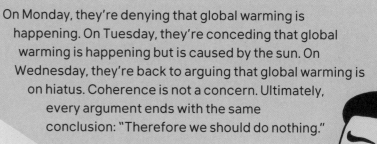

Tens of thousands of warming indicators

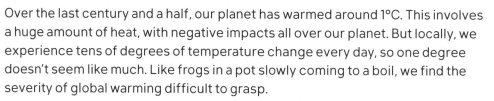

Signs of global warming are being observed all over our planet. Thermometers measure surface warming. Buoys sunk to ocean depths measure heat building up in our oceans. Ice is melting across our planet, with ice sheets crumbling and glaciers retreating. Spring is coming earlier. Sea levels are rising. Species are migrating to flee warming temperatures. Even tree lines are shifting!

Over the last century and a half, our planet has warmed around 1°C. This involves a huge amount of heat, with negative impacts all over our planet. But locally, we experience tens of degrees of temperature change every day, so one degree doesn't seem like much. Like frogs in a pot slowly coming to a boil, we find the severity of global warming difficult to grasp.

Psychological distance

We think of something as psychologically distant if we're not directly experiencing it.

The notion that global warming is some far-off, distant threat is an insidious but prevalent misconception. It arises in part from the way we maintain psychological distance from our fears.

Psychological distance manifests in different forms—thinking that global warming is happening in the distant future, that it's happening in far-off places (this misconception perpetuated by clichéd images such as polar bears), that climate impacts are hypothetical and uncertain, and that the impacts are happening to communities different from us.

In reality, global warming is already happening and affecting all parts of society, in every corner of the world. As President Obama often reminded us, global warming is happening here and now.

Global warming at four atomic bombs per second

Scientists have measured the amount of heat building in the oceans, warming the land, warming the air, and melting ice. They find our planet is building up heat at a rate of four atomic bombs per second.

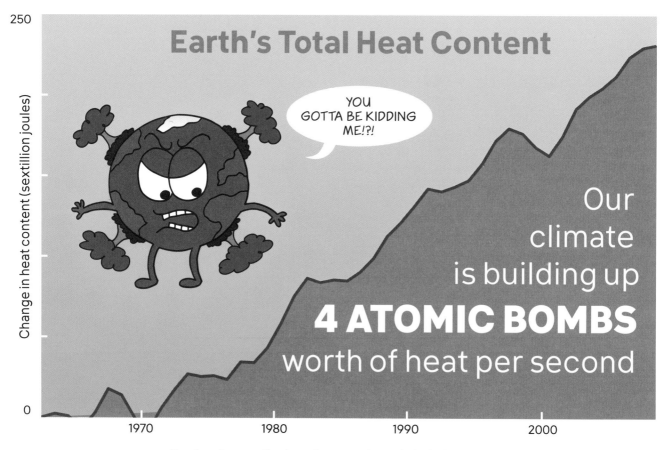

Deniers ignore the fact that our planet is building up heat by focusing on small pieces of data while ignoring the rest of the evidence. They argue that global warming stopped or slowed down since 1998. How can surface warming have slowed down if the planet is still building up heat?

While heat steadily builds up, the temperature jumps up and down from year to year. Heat is constantly sloshing between the ocean and the atmosphere. This is driven by ocean cycles like El Niño (Spanish for "the little boy").

El Niño sloshes heat between the ocean and the atmosphere, causing the surface temperature to jump up and down from year to year.

Temperature change (°C)

0.75

−0.5

1980   2010

Because the temperature varies from year to year, it's possible to find short periods during long-term warming when it looks like warming has paused. But this is cherry picking the data and fails to look at the big picture: our planet continues to build up a huge amount of heat.

WHAT DO YOU MEAN WE'RE SINKING? I'M MOVING UPWARD!

Does cold weather mean the sun doesn't exist?

Global warming doesn't stop cold weather from happening. It means we see *more* hot weather and *less* cold weather. Across the United States, the proportion of hot record temperatures has been increasing; over the last decade, there have been twice as many hot records as cold ones.

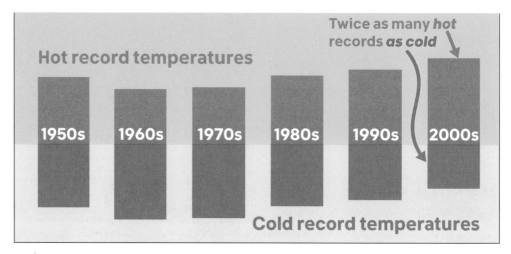

However, every time it gets cold, you hear the refrain: "What happened to global warming?" This argument commits the fallacy of impossible expectations. Global warming doesn't mean we'll never get cold days. It means hot days will be more likely and cold days will be less likely.

The "cold weather" argument—a form of cherry picking—also ignores that the planet as a whole is warming.

Our planet is thinning on top

Arctic sea ice extent (the area of open ocean with at least 15% sea ice coverage) has steadily been declining over the last few decades. This is especially obvious when we look at the sea ice extent minimum in September, after the summer melt period.

The Arctic is changing dramatically. It has been warming nearly three times faster than the global average. The sea ice cover is only half as big as it was 40 years ago.

The amount of sea ice is affected by many factors, such as shifting winds, cloud cover, water vapor, and heat transported via ocean currents. Its extent varies by location and year, but the long-term decline is clear.

When the sea ice extent sets a new record low, it sometimes rebounds the next summer. Deniers jump on these brief events, claiming that the sea ice has recovered. This is cherry picking and ignores the clear long-term trend. It's like giving up on dieting because your weight fluctuates from day to day.

MY WEIGHT WENT UP FROM YESTERDAY...

...DIETING IS USELESS!

"The top of the world is the canary in the climate coal mine.

Prof. Katharine Hayhoe
Texas Tech University

OH NO, I'M THINNING ON TOP!

MAYBE IF I COMB OVER CANADA...

Glaciers are melting

Glaciers are shrinking across our planet, losing about 150 billion tons of ice each year. Glacial retreat has accelerated over the past two decades. Some glaciers are now smaller than during any time in the past several thousand years. This is of great concern in parts of the world where glaciers act like water towers. They build up water in the winter, which gets released downstream in the summer.

One myth cites growing glaciers to argue that global warming isn't happening. But the vast majority of the more than one hundred thousand glaciers in the world are shrinking. This myth cherry picks the few glaciers that aren't shrinking.

Why aren't all glaciers shrinking? While warmer air melts ice, it also causes more moisture in the air. This means more snowfall in some regions. So each individual glacier reacts differently to warming, with most shrinking but a rare few growing. Ignoring this complicated relationship is an oversimplification.

Ice loss is greatest from the largest ice sheets on the planet—in Greenland and Antarctica.

Greenland: The worst bait and switch in history

The Greenland ice sheet is losing over 300 billion metric tons of ice every year. That's roughly the weight of two Mount Everests per year!

Greenland loses ice when icebergs break off the end of glaciers. Melt water lubricates the base of these glaciers, speeding up their flow into the ocean. Greenland is losing ice at an accelerating rate.

At the same time, Greenland is gaining ice in its interior. Warming leads to more moisture in the atmosphere, which means more snowfall. Nevertheless, the ice loss at the edges is greater than the ice gain in the middle.

Deniers cherry pick ice gain in the middle of Greenland and ignore ice loss at the edges. This is like arguing that drinking diet soda means fast food is having no effect on our waistlines.

Another Greenland-related myth is the argument "Greenland used to be green." What's this about? Around 1,000 years ago, explorers from Scandinavia and Iceland settled in southwest Greenland. The ice sheet is at least 400,000 years old, so the island today would've been fairly similar to when it was first named Greenland.

If the island was essentially a huge ice sheet, why was it called Greenland? In short, good marketing. To persuade his people to settle there, Erik the Red promoted the new land as the promise of a better life. However, hospitable parts of the island would have been limited.

The claim that "Greenland was green" argues that Greenland was warmer in medieval times, implying that modern warming must be natural, too. It's false to say that our planet was warmer in medieval times. While some regions in Greenland may have had temperatures comparable to now, the planet as a whole was colder than today.

Today's global temperature is warmer than any time over the last 1,000 years, including during medieval times when Eric the Red gave Greenland its name.

41

Confusing Antarctic sea ice and land ice

Antarctica is split into West and East Antarctica. If all the land ice in West Antarctica melted, it would raise sea levels by 7 meters. The East Antarctic ice sheet is the biggest land ice mass in the world. If it were to completely melt, sea levels would rise around 65 meters.

West Antarctica began to lose ice in the 1990s. Its ice loss is accelerating, and is now losing around 100 billion metric tons per year. East Antarctica is losing ice at the edges but is balanced by more snowfall in the middle. So the East Antarctic ice sheet is stable for now.

Overall, Antarctica is losing many billions of metric tons of land ice per year. Deniers who argue that Antarctica is gaining land ice are cherry picking the data. They focus on ice gain in the middle of East Antarctica and ignore other ice loss elsewhere in the continent.

Antarctic sea ice is more complicated. The area of sea ice around Antarctica has been slightly increasing over the last few decades. How can this happen when the area has been warming?

There are a number of possible contributors. A leading suspect is wind blowing from the continent. This pushes ice away from the coastline, creating open water, which allows more sea ice to form. This wind has been increasing, creating a sea ice factory along the coastline.

Another possible contributor is fresh water melting from the Antarctic ice sheet. Fresh water freezes more easily than salt water.

The Antarctic sea ice increase has been used to argue that global warming isn't happening. This is an oversimplification, ignoring the multiple factors driving Antarctic sea ice trends. It's like bingeing on fast food after exercising and wondering why you're not losing weight.

> Sea level rise is like a creeping catastrophe.

Josh Willis
Jet Propulsion Laboratory

Shifting the goalposts on sea level rise

All the heat being absorbed by the oceans is causing thermal expansion. Warmer water takes up more space than colder water. This is one reason for sea level rise. Another contributor is melting land ice. The Greenland and Antarctic ice sheets are losing hundreds of billions of metric tons of ice every year, and it's going into the oceans.

Combining tide gauge measurements with satellite data, we've found sea levels steadily rising over the last century, and getting faster over time. The rise is so steady that it's very difficult for deniers to claim that sea level rise isn't happening. This hasn't stopped them from trying, though! They'll often cherry pick short periods where sea level rise temporarily stalls in order to cast doubt on the long-term rise.

In fact, sea level rise is so difficult to ignore that an alternative denier response is to instead argue that it's not accelerating. Rather than deny it's happening, they accept sea levels are rising but move the goalposts by denying that the rise is getting faster over time.

Moving the goalposts

Implicitly accepting the reality of sea level rise but transitioning to argue that it's not accelerating is a way of distracting from the reality of sea level rise.

The sun is not our get-out-of-jail-free card

Over the last few decades, the sun has been getting cooler. What if it keeps cooling? The sun has been cooler before. In the 1600s, the sun went through a period of low activity at the same time as the "Little Ice Age".

What would happen to future global warming if the sun's output decreased to these same levels? The drop in sunlight would only offset about one decade's worth of global warming. Compared with greenhouse warming, the sun is a minor factor.

So why do we hear some people argue that we're heading into an ice age? This misrepresents how much the sun affects climate change. Greenhouse warming is the main driver of modern climate change. The sun is not our get-out-of-jail-free card. Winter is not coming.

47

We are causing all of global warming... and then some!

Scientists have conducted many studies quantifying how much human activity has contributed to recent global warming. Across these various studies, a consistent picture has emerged. We have been causing around 100% of global warming since 1950.

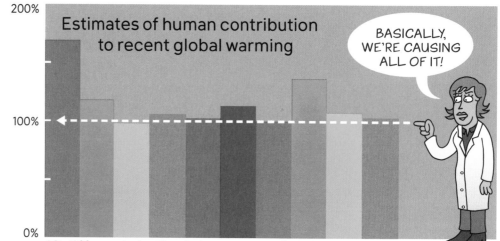

Estimates of human contribution to recent global warming

BASICALLY, WE'RE CAUSING ALL OF IT!

10 different studies into causes of global warming

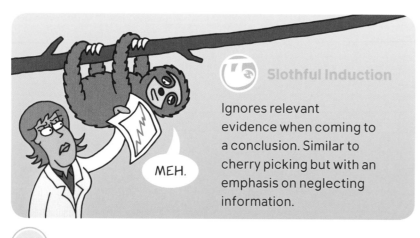

Slothful Induction

Ignores relevant evidence when coming to a conclusion. Similar to cherry picking but with an emphasis on neglecting information.

MEH.

In fact, our best estimate is we are causing slightly more than 100%, with natural factors contributing a slight cooling effect. We are causing all of global warming... and then some!

If climate change was a murder mystery, it would be an open-and-shut case. The lines of evidence for human-caused global warming are numerous.

THE OVERHEATED CLIMATE
A SCIENTIFIC WHODUNNIT

54

Why is the Keeling Curve so curvy?

In 1958, Charles Keeling began measuring atmospheric carbon dioxide (CO_2) levels in Mauna Loa, Hawaii. He found CO_2 rising and falling from year to year. This graph became known as the Keeling Curve.

This yearly cycle is due to CO_2 moving between the atmosphere and vegetation. In spring, plants convert CO_2 into foliage. In autumn, the leaves fall and rot, emitting CO_2 into the atmosphere.

Keeling also found that over time, the amount of CO_2 in the air was increasing. All our fossil fuel burning is causing a rise in atmospheric CO_2.

We've upset the natural balance

Over thousands of years, atmospheric CO_2 levels remained relatively steady. Nature was in balance, with natural emissions equal to natural absorptions. Humans upset the balance during the Industrial Revolution, when we began burning fossil fuels. This sent large amounts of CO_2 trapped underground as coal, oil, or gas into the atmosphere. Now atmospheric CO_2 has increased to levels not seen in millions of years.

Deniers try to minimize our role in disrupting the carbon cycle through a crafty piece of cherry picking. They argue that human emissions are small compared to natural emissions. For example, humans are emitting around 33 billion metric tons of carbon into the air every year, while nature is emitting around 740 billion metric tons of carbon.

This argument ignores that natural emissions are balanced by natural absorptions. Each year, nature emits approximately 726 billion metric tons of CO_2 but also absorbs close to the same amount.

By failing to consider the full picture, this cherry pick distracts from the fact that human CO_2 emissions have upset the natural balance. It's like boasting about your gambling wins while ignoring your losses.

Spring denial!

Failing to consider natural absorptions means ignoring when trees take in CO_2 to grow leaves.

We win the belching contest

Humans are emiting billions of metric tons of CO_2 into the atmosphere every year. As you'd expect, it's causing atmospheric CO_2 to increase.

Nevertheless, deniers persist in claiming that the recent rise in CO_2 is all natural. For example, geologist Ian Plimer falsely claims that "one volcanic belch" can match a whole year of human CO_2 emissions.

Ian Plimer
Mining geologist

When scientists add up all the CO_2 being emitted by land and underwater volcanoes, it comes to 310 million metric tons per year—less than 1% of human emissions.

In other words, humans emit around 100 times more CO_2 than every volcano combined on the planet. In a belching contest, humans win hands down!

To appreciate the negligible impact that volcanoes have on atmospheric CO_2, we can look at the largest volcanic eruptions over the 20th century. They have had no discernible impact, while humans continue to steadily add CO_2 to the atmosphere.

> We have not had levels of CO_2 at 400 parts per million by volume in 800,000 years of history.

Prof. Lonnie Thompson
Ohio State University

Cutting down on carbs

Scientists observe even more evidence that we're causing the rise in carbon. There are several types of carbon, including the lighter carbon 12 and the heavier carbon 13. Plants prefer the lighter carbon 12. Fossil fuels come from ancient plants, so burning them means we expect to see more of carbon 12 than carbon 13 in the air. That's exactly what we observe.

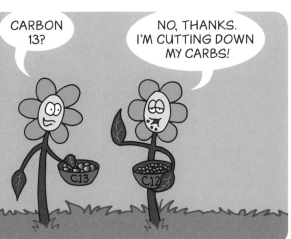

It's a trap!

Different types of radiation have different wavelengths. Visible light from the sun has a short wavelength and is called shortwave radiation. Infrared heat emitted by the Earth has a long wavelength and is called longwave radiation. Longwave radiation gets blocked by greenhouse gases.

LOW ENERGY!

SHORT STUFF!

Why does CO_2 matter? It's a greenhouse gas that traps heat. It's like a blanket wrapped around our planet keeping us warm. Sounds comforting, right? Not necessarily. Adding extra CO_2 to the atmosphere is like throwing on another blanket. Too many blankets and things get uncomfortably warm.

We can understand the greenhouse effect in three easy steps. First, greenhouse gases allow visible light—sunlight—to travel freely to the Earth's surface. Second, the Earth absorbs sunlight, warms, and glows with infrared heat. Third, this infrared heat is radiated from the Earth's surface, but greenhouse gases trap the heat, stopping it from escaping to space. This is how the greenhouse effect warms us. It lets sunlight in, then traps heat on the way out. It's a trap!

In the 1820s, physicist Joseph Fourier first proposed that something in the atmosphere caused a warming effect. Over nearly two centuries, scientists have conducted experiments, taken measurements, and improved our understanding of how greenhouse gases cause warming.

NOT ANOTHER BLANKET.

IT'S WHAT THE SHAREHOLDERS WANT!

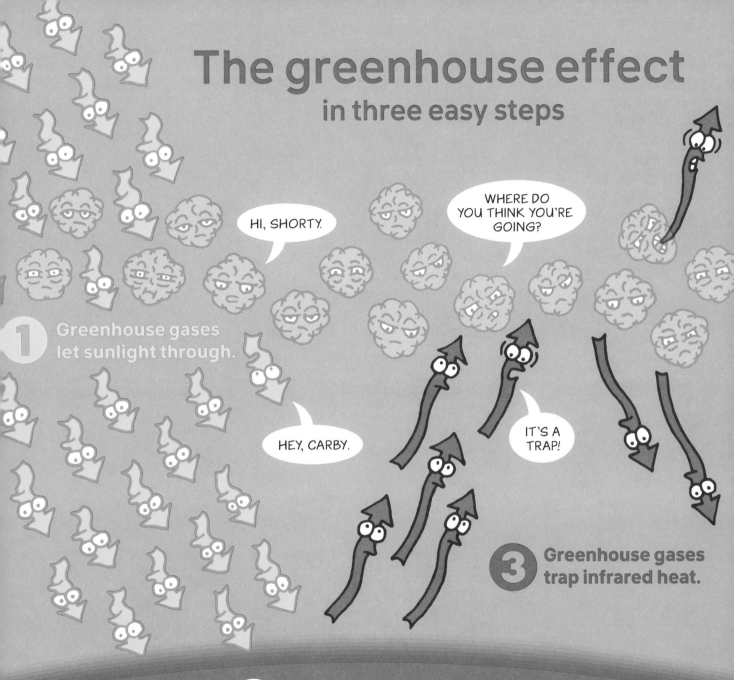

Climate science: A brief history

A small amount can go a long way

The warming effect of CO_2 has been confirmed by many lines of evidence. Aircraft and satellites have measured less heat escaping to space at the exact wavelengths that CO_2 absorbs energy. The greenhouse effect is a measured reality. Without it, we wouldn't be able to live on the Earth's surface.

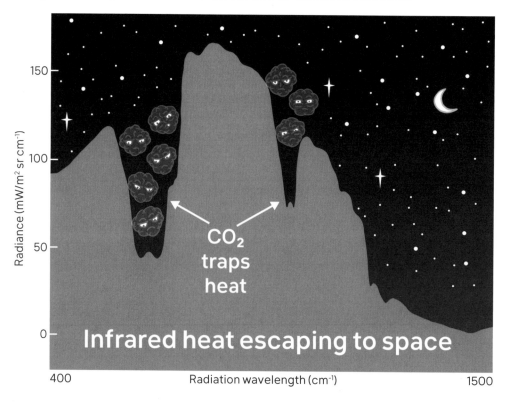

Nevertheless, some people reject even basic physics like the greenhouse effect. One myth argues that as CO_2 is such a small percentage of the atmosphere (400 parts per million is equivalent to 0.04 percent), it can't have a significant effect.

This is a red herring. The fact that CO_2 is a small percentage of the atmosphere is irrelevant. Small amounts of an active substance can have a strong effect.

Other myths downplaying the greenhouse effect

There are a number of myths about the greenhouse effect designed to cast doubt on our role in causing global warming. Some myths play on human psychology, others distort the science.

The laws of physics tell us there is a greenhouse effect, and we've measured it. But some people still can't accept that the greenhouse effect exists. In an ironic twist, they appeal to the laws of physics, claiming the greenhouse effect violates the second law of thermodynamics.

This is a law of physics saying that heat flows from hot to cold, and not from cold to hot. The myth argues that the greenhouse effect requires heat flowing from the cooler sky, where greenhouse gases trap heat, to the warmer surface.

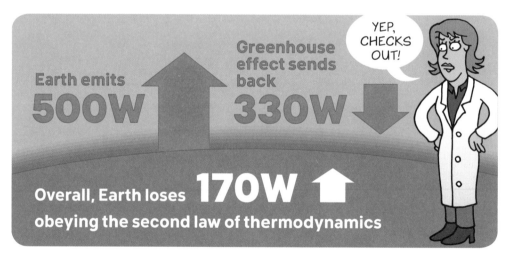

This myth misrepresents the second law. The law says that the overall flow of heat should be from hot to cold. That doesn't prohibit some heat from flowing in the other direction. The Earth emits around 500 watts of heat. The greenhouse effect sends 330 watts back to Earth. This means that overall, Earth is radiating 170 watts to space. Heat is flowing from hot to cold. But the greenhouse effect does send some heat to warm the Earth.

Another myth is that because CO_2 is invisible, it's therefore harmless. After all, if we can't see it, how can it be a problem?

Greenhouse gases like CO_2 are invisible to sunlight. (This is why we can't see them.) Sunlight is able to pass through the atmosphere and warm the Earth's surface. The warm Earth radiates infrared heat, which is blocked by greenhouse gases. CO_2's invisibility is a key feature of the greenhouse effect.

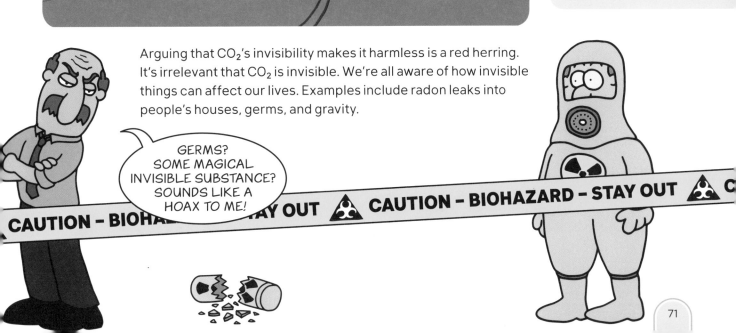

Arguing that CO_2's invisibility makes it harmless is a red herring. It's irrelevant that CO_2 is invisible. We're all aware of how invisible things can affect our lives. Examples include radon leaks into people's houses, germs, and gravity.

History's first global warming myth

History's first ever global warming myth began in 1900. Swedish physicist Knut Ångström conducted an experiment in which he shone infrared heat through a tube of CO_2. The CO_2 blocked some of the heat. But when he increased the amount of CO_2, the amount of blocked heat didn't change. He concluded that the greenhouse effect was saturated and that adding more CO_2 to the atmosphere wouldn't cause global warming.

Ångström's mistake was thinking the atmosphere was the same as a single tube of gas. In reality, it's made up of multiple layers. Low in the atmosphere, the air is thicker and the greenhouse effect is saturated. High in the atmosphere, the air is thinner and the greenhouse effect isn't saturated.

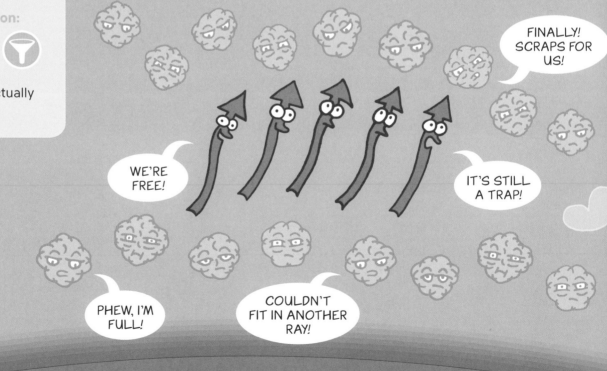

When we burn fossil fuels, the CO_2 we emit gets stirred by winds and mixes through the atmosphere. The greenhouse gases higher in the atmosphere are blocking more of the heat that is radiating out to space.

We now have aircraft, satellites, and observatories measuring heat escaping to space. These measurements find that the greenhouse effect is getting stronger.

THE GREENHOUSE EFFECT IS SATURATED!

I ARGUED THAT BEFORE A CENTURY OF DATA PROVED THE GREENHOUSE EFFECT. WHAT'S YOUR EXCUSE?

I JUST INVENTED THE FIRST GLOBAL WARMING MYTH!

Knut Ångström

IF THE INTERNET EXISTED RIGHT NOW, I'D HAVE GONE VIRAL!

Arguing for a saturated greenhouse effect oversimplifies our atmosphere. One can forgive Ångström for making this error in 1900. But anyone repeating Ångström's mistake, after a century of scientific research confirming the increased greenhouse effect, has no excuse!

THAT WAS EASY!

OH!

Water vapor is an amplifier, not a control knob

Emitting CO_2 causes some initial warming. With this warming, evaporation increases and more water vapor is added to the atmosphere. As a greenhouse gas, that extra water vapor causes further warming. This leads to extra evaporation, leading to more warming—a reinforcing feedback loop.

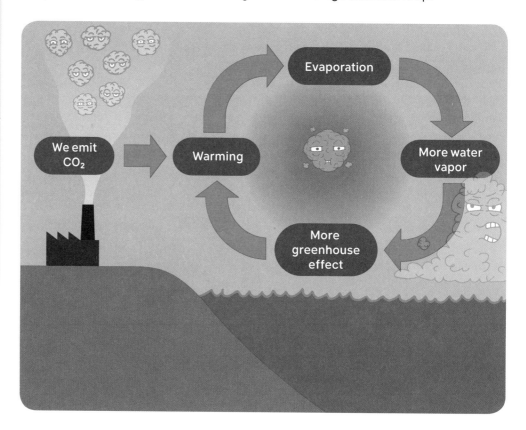

It's important to clarify that while water vapor amplifies warming, it doesn't cause the initial warming. This is because the amount of water vapor in the atmosphere depends on how warm the air is. If extra water is added to the atmosphere, before too long it falls as rain or snow.

Some deniers argue that CO_2 isn't a major problem because water vapor is the most powerful greenhouse gas. This misrepresents how water vapor influences climate. Water vapor doesn't drive climate change, it amplifies it. For current global warming, CO_2 is the control knob that initially started it.

> Saying water vapor is a more important greenhouse gas than carbon dioxide is like saying the amplifier in a sound system is more important than the volume dial for producing the sound.

Prof. Adam Sobel
Columbia University

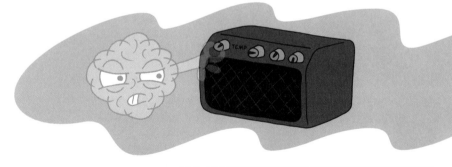

🔥 **IRONY ALERT!**

Citing water vapor as a reason not to worry about CO_2 warming has it backward.

Water vapor is a big reason why our climate is so sensitive to CO_2 warming.

Climate and sun moving in opposite directions

In 1859, John Tyndall discovered that greenhouse gases trap heat. He also predicted what greenhouse warming would look like.

IF WARMING WAS CAUSED BY GREENHOUSE GASES, THEN WINTERS SHOULD WARM FASTER THAN SUMMERS...

...AND NIGHTS SHOULD WARM FASTER THAN DAYS.

PROBABLY BECAUSE OF ALL THE EXTRA BLANKETS!

John Tyndall
Physics professor

> The contribution of solar variability to the temperature trend since 1987 is small and downward.

Prof. Mike Lockwood
University of Reading

Why this pattern? At night, the Earth's surface cools by radiating heat to space. More greenhouse gases in the air mean less heat escaping to space and less cooling at night. Similarly, extra greenhouse gases reduce the cooling that happens in winter, when the Earth's surface receives less sunlight.

At night, the surface cools by radiating heat to space.

More greenhouse gases in the air slow down night cooling.

Over 150 years later, scientists have observed the exact patterns that Tyndall predicted. Winters have warmed faster than summers, and nights have warmed faster than days. These are just two of the observed climate patterns confirming human influence on global warming.

Despite strong evidence, one myth claims the sun is causing global warming. This myth is based on cherry picking. It looks at times in the Earth's past when temperature and solar activity moved in the same direction. But this ignores all the data that clearly rules out the sun.

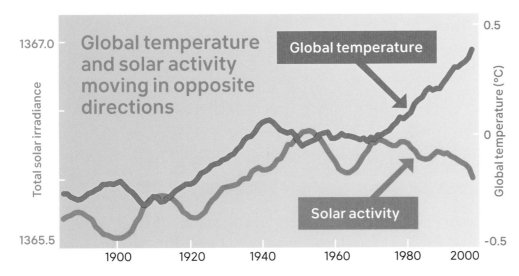

In the last few decades, global temperature and solar activity have moved in opposite directions. Temperatures have warmed at the same time that the sun has cooled. Ignoring the latest information can lead to a completely wrong conclusion!

FACT

Human fingerprints in the daily and yearly cycles confirm greenhouse warming and rule out the sun.

MYTH

"The sun is causing global warming."

FALLACY

Cherry picking: Ignores the last few decades of data showing solar activity and global temperature moving in opposite directions.

We are unique in the solar system

Over the last 50 years, the sun's output has decreased slightly: it is radiating less heat. The sun is not causing recent global warming: decreasing solar activity has had a cooling effect.

One myth is that the sun must be causing climate change because other planets are also warming. However, the entire solar system isn't warming. Of the one hundred bodies in our solar system, only six planets or moons have been observed to be warming. Some, like Uranus, are cooling.

Ironically, deniers who are convinced that other planets are warming are often skeptical that our own planet is warming. The evidence for Mars warming is based on two snapshots of the planet taken 22 years apart. Compare this to the mountains of evidence that the Earth has been warming over the last few decades.

We also know the sun is not warming the solar system because the sun's output is decreasing. For planets that have warmed, factors besides solar activity are likely to be the cause of the warming.

The planets farther away from the sun have much longer orbits than Earth, so climate change may be seasonal. For Neptune, whose year lasts 165 Earth years, temperature changes over a few decades is like our weather change from one month to the next.

Warning from the past: Climate is a cranky beast!

Throughout Earth's history, there have been periods when climate changed dramatically. Over the last million years, our planet has transitioned from ice ages to warm periods then back again. This dramatic ice age cycle has been caused by subtle changes in the Earth's orbit.

The past sends us a clear message: our climate is highly sensitive to small changes in heat. Over tens of thousands of years, slight changes in the Earth's orbit have affected how much heat the Earth received. Slight nudges can push the planet in and out of ice ages.

Right now, we're not giving climate a gentle nudge. We're hitting it with a big stick! Human fingerprints are found all over our climate system. That's why climate is currently changing faster than it has for hundreds of thousands of years.

> " Past climate change shouts out to us that, far from being self-stabilizing, the Earth's climate system is an ornery beast which overreacts to even small nudges.

Prof. Wallace Broecker
Columbia University

Cranky Uncle VS. Cranky Climate

But past climate change can be misinterpreted. One myth is that climate has changed naturally in the past, so current warming must be natural as well. This argument commits the fallacy of jumping to conclusions. It's like arguing that murders don't happen now because people died of natural causes in the past.

We're emitting billions of metric tons of heat-trapping greenhouse gases into the atmosphere every year. Everything we have learned from past climate change warns us that our planet will react strongly to all the extra heat we're adding.

HUMANS HAVE DIED NATURALLY IN THE PAST...

...SO THIS DEATH MUST BE NATURAL!

🔥 IRONY ALERT!

Deniers claim past climate change tells us human-caused global warming is not a problem. What the past is really telling us is that our climate is sensitive to changes in heat, including the heat caused by our greenhouse gas emissions.

They look at the beast baring its teeth and think it's smiling. In truth, it's a warning.

OH LOOK, HE'S SMILING AT ME!

FACT

Past climate change tells us that climate reacts strongly to changes in heat, including heat trapped by greenhouse gases.

MYTH

"Climate has changed throughout Earth's history, so modern warming is just natural variation."

FALLACY

Jumping to conclusions: Just because climate has changed naturally in the past doesn't mean it's natural now.

Climate and CO_2: A reinforcing feedback

We know from over 150 years of scientific research that greenhouse gases trap heat. More CO_2 causes global warming. When it gets warmer, the oceans release CO_2. This is because warmer water can't hold as much dissolved CO_2.

So more CO_2 causes warming, and warming causes more CO_2 to be released—a reinforcing feedback.

In the past, when the Earth warmed due to factors like changes in the Earth's orbit, this caused the ocean to release more CO_2. The extra CO_2 in the atmosphere added even more warming. This reinforcing feedback was strong enough to pull the Earth out of ice ages.

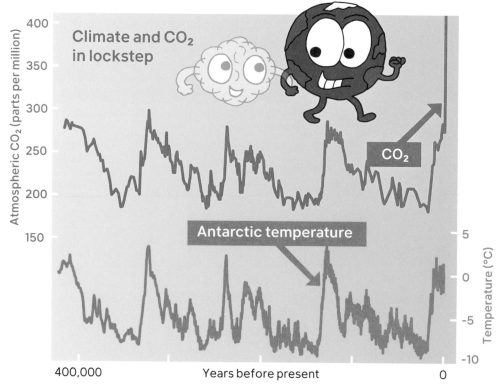

One myth has arisen based on ice core records. Deniers argue that CO_2 rose after warming, therefore CO_2 mustn't cause warming. This argument commits the logical fallacy known as false dichotomy.

The ice core record tells us that more CO_2 causes warming and warming causes more CO_2. Both options are correct.

The false dichotomy fallacy is like arguing that either chickens lay eggs or chickens come out of eggs, but both can't be true.

The CO_2 lag doesn't disprove its warming effect. On the contrary, the ice core record provides evidence of a reinforcing feedback that amplifies the warming caused by our greenhouse gas emissions.

Human fingerprints rule out the usual suspects

Scientists observe many different patterns throughout our climate. Most of these patterns rule out natural factors like the sun, volcanoes, or internal variability (e.g., ocean cycles) as the main cause of recent global warming. The one factor consistent with all observed climate patterns is warming caused by greenhouse gases.

I'D RECOGNIZE THAT GREENHOUSE GAS ANYWHERE!

	CO₂	SUN	VOLCANO	INTERNAL VARIABILITY
Winters warming faster than summers	✓	✗	✗	✗
Cooling upper atmosphere	✓	✗	✗	✗
Rising tropopause*	✓	✓	✓	✗
Less heat escaping to space	✓	✗	✗	✗
More heat returning to Earth	✓	✗	✗	✗
Nights warming faster than days	✓	✗	✗	✗
Pattern of ocean warming	✓	✗	✗	✗
Land warming faster than oceans	✓	✓	✗	✗

* The tropopause is the boundary between the lower atmosphere and upper atmosphere.

Many lines of evidence tell us we are causing global warming. Human fingerprints are found all over our climate. How serious are the impacts from climate change?

DENYING
CONSEQUENCES

Climate change has impact on nearly every aspect of society

Global warming is having negative impacts across society and the environment. Melting glaciers threaten the water supply for one-sixth of the world's population. Hundreds of millions of people are affected by increased coastal flooding. Warming causes migration of disease-bearing insects like mosquitoes.

To distract from the negative impacts of global warming, deniers cherry pick the beneficial impacts and ignore the full picture. They claim some regions far from the equator may become more productive in agriculture due to global warming. But this ignores that other regions will suffer from excessive warming and that the overall impact on agriculture will be negative.

In addition, there are some climate impacts that have no upside, such as sea level rise and ocean acidification.

Only focusing on global warming's benefits and ignoring the many negative impacts is as valid as promoting smoking as a weight-loss strategy.

Climate goes extreme!

> COWABUNGA, DUDE!

Every weather event is affected in some way by global warming including the buildup of heat, more moisture in the atmosphere, and rising sea levels. A direct impact of the extra heat is more intense and frequent heatwaves.

Warming also accelerates evaporation of water from the ground and water sources. As the ground dries out, drought intensifies and fire danger increases. Extra evaporation also puts more moisture into the atmosphere, and warmer air can hold more water vapor. Both these factors result in heavier downpours. The warmer oceans also provides additional energy for hurricanes, making them more intense.

Weather is somewhat unpredictable, like rolling dice. Global warming increases the occurence and/or strength of many types of extreme weather. It's like drawing extra dots on the dice, increasing the odds of a higher roll.

People often ask: "Was a specific weather event caused by climate change?" That's the wrong question. A more appropriate question is: "Are weather events being *affected* by climate change?" The answer is yes, global warming is increasing the occurence and/or strength of extreme weather.

How our greenhouse gas emissions influence extreme weather

Deke Arndt
National Oceanic and Atmospheric Administration

Heatwaves are getting hotter and more frequent

Heatwaves are getting hotter, lasting longer, and happening more frequently. Globally, heatwaves are happening five times more often due to global warming.

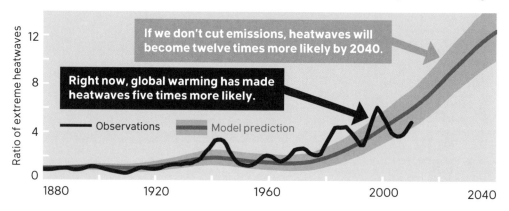

Ratio of extreme heatwaves

If we don't cut emissions, heatwaves will become twelve times more likely by 2040.

Right now, global warming has made heatwaves five times more likely.

—— Observations   Model prediction

12
8
4
0

1880   1920   1960   2000   2040

The number of heatwaves is predicted to increase in the future. If we don't reduce greenhouse gas emissions, heatwaves will become twelve times more likely by 2040.

CLIMATE WAS MORE CHILL BEFORE GLOBAL WARMING.

YEAH, HE'S BEEN ACTING LIKE A REAL JERK LATELY!

Deniers try to distract from the increasing risk of heatwaves by arguing that they have happened in the past, so today's heatwaves are not influenced by global warming.

This argument commits the fallacy of jumping to conclusions. It's like arguing that humans were dying of cancer long before cigarettes were invented, so smoking doesn't cause cancer. The science is sending us a clear message: Heatwaves have happened throughout history, but global warming is increasing the frequency of heatwaves now and that risk will increase further in the future.

FACT

The risk from heatwaves is now five times greater due to global warming.

MYTH

"Heatwaves have happened before, so heatwaves now are normal."

FALLACY

Jumping to conclusions: Just because heatwaves happened before doesn't mean we're not influencing them now.

93

Hurricanes are getting intense

Hurricanes cause storm surges that can result in devastating coastal flooding. These storm surges are made more destructive because of the additional sea level rise caused by global warming. Sea level rise caused an extra $8 billion in damage during Hurricane Sandy.

Global warming is also adding more moisture to the air, causing heavier downpours and more flooding. Wind speeds are getting stronger as hurricanes scoop up more energy from the warming oceans.

Deniers ignore global warming's influence on hurricanes by pointing to periods with low hurricane activity. This is a red herring. Global warming makes hurricanes more intense but not more frequent. Focusing on the number of hurricanes distracts from the fact that they are getting stronger.

After the devastating impact of a hurricane, a common refrain from deniers is that it's too soon to talk about climate change. But that's exactly when we should be talking about how climate change is making weather more dangerous for everyone.

95

Plants need food *and* water

Plants need the right amount of water to flourish. Global warming disrupts the water cycle, causing some regions to become wetter and experience flooding and other regions to become drier and experience drought. Both floods and droughts harm plants' ability to grow.

Plants also need a comfortable temperature range. When it gets too hot, crop yields go down. Extreme heatwaves are particularly hard on plant growth.

One myth ignores the negative impacts on plants, arguing that global warming will be good because "CO_2 is a plant food." This argument oversimplifies how plants grow. While plants do need CO_2 to grow, this is only one aspect of what they need to flourish. This myth is like saying humans need calcium, so all we need to eat is ice cream.

We need to consider CO_2 *and* water. Negative climate impacts outweigh the small benefit from extra CO_2.

CO₂ is a hard-core pollutant

A pollutant is any substance that causes harmful effects. We have overwhelming evidence that too much CO_2 is harmful—heating the Earth, intensifying extreme weather, raising sea levels, and acidifying the oceans.

Unlike local pollutants, the harm caused by CO_2 covers the entire planet. It lingers in the atmosphere for thousands of years, while most local pollutants don't last anywhere near that long. The U.S. Environmental Protection Agency concluded that CO_2 should be regulated as a pollutant because its climate effects pose a clear danger to public health and welfare.

GLOBAL DOMINATION!! BWAH HA HA!

WOAH, THAT DUDE IS HARD CORE!

One way deniers avoid the seriousness of climate impacts is to claim "CO_2 is not a pollutant". Quibbling over the technical definition of the word *pollutant* is a red herring. It's an irrelevant point that distracts from the fact that CO_2 is changing our climate and causing harm.

FACT

A pollutant is any substance that disrupts the environment; CO_2 does that by trapping heat.

MYTH

"CO₂ is not a pollutant."

FALLACY

Red herring: Quibbling over the technical definition of the word *pollutant* is a distraction from the negative impacts of global warming.

🐟 **Red herring**

A red herring is a smelly, smoked fish used to throw tracking dogs off the scent.

In arguments, red herrings are irrelevant points distracting from the heart of the discussion.

THIS SHOULD THROW THEM OFF THE SCENT!

Polar bear survival depends on sea ice

Polar bears need sea ice to survive. To hunt seals, they need a platform of floating sea ice. The problem is that Arctic sea ice is melting. Polar bears have to swim long distances to reach the sea ice. This is threatening polar bears' ability to hunt and their very survival.

Not all of the Arctic is the same. In some regions, ice melts and refreezes each year, with the ice-free season getting longer because of global warming. In other regions, ice is more persistent throughout the year. Polar bear populations are dwindling in the Arctic regions where the ice melt is strongest. The link between global warming, the ice melt, and the threat to polar bears is clear.

Deniers argue that polar bears are not in danger from global warming because there are more polar bears now compared with the 1970s. This claim is an oversimplification, ignoring that other factors also influence polar bear survival.

Polar bear hunting was common in the 20th century. Over one thousand bears were killed each year, and populations were shrinking. However, between the 1950s and 1970s, a number of countries passed laws to restrict hunting. This helped polar bear populations to recover.

Common-sense laws have removed one threat to polar bears. But now we are threatening their survival with human-caused global warming.

FACT

Polar bears need sea ice to hunt, so melting sea ice threatens their survival.

MYTH

"Polar bear numbers have increased, so they're in no danger from global warming."

FALLACY

Oversimplification: One threat (hunting) has been removed, but it was replaced with the ever-increasing threat of melting sea ice from global warming.

Ocean acidification: Global warming's evil twin

> BWAH HA HA!

Around 30% of the CO_2 we emit is being absorbed by the oceans, making the water more acidic. Once CO_2 dissolves into ocean waters, a number of chemical reactions take place. Most important, carbonate ions get converted to bicarbonate ions. This is a problem because marine animals and plants (such as those that create coral reefs) build their skeletons and shells out of carbonate ions. Ocean acidification means they have fewer building blocks to work with.

> WHERE DID ALL OUR BLOCKS GO?!

One denier myth argues that acidification is not an issue because the ocean is not currently acidic. This argument is a red herring. What matters is that the oceans are changing to become more acidic. Focusing on whether ocean waters are mostly alkaline or acidic is a distraction.

This is like pouring cold water into a hot bath and calling it "cooling". The bath may not be cold straight away, but the temperature is going down. In the same way, the oceans may not become mostly acidic, but they are becoming more acidified as they absorb our CO_2 emissions.

> HEY, YOU'RE MAKING THE BATH COLDER!

> THE WATER IS STILL WARM SO QUIT GRIPING!

FACT

Ocean acidity has increased by 30%. This makes it hard for marine species to build their skeletons and shells, threatening coral reef ecosystems.

MYTH

"Oceans aren't actually turning into acid yet, so acidification is not a concern."

FALLACY

Red herring: Arguing about the absolute value of ocean acidity distracts from what really matters—that ocean chemistry is changing rapidly and becoming more acidic.

The current rate of acidification is faster than at any time since dinosaurs became extinct 65 million years ago. At that time, volcanic eruptions and a meteor impact caused rapid climate change, wiping out 75% of the world's species. Coral reefs were devastated, with many species going extinct.

Deniers argue that coral reefs have recovered from past extinction events, so they'll recover from modern global warming. This argument is a misrepresentation, ignoring that it took millions of years for coral reefs to recover after a mass extinction event. Scientists believe we are currently driving another mass extinction event that will take a similarly long time for recovery.

FACT

Coral reefs will suffer permanent damage from global warming and ocean acidification.

MYTH

"Coral reefs can recover like they have in the past."

FALLACY

Misrepresentation: It took millions of years in the past for coral reefs to recover from mass extinction events.

Global warming's evil twin

Global warming damages coral reefs when the water gets too hot. Acidification is causing even more damage.

For this reason, ocean acidification has been labeled the evil twin of global warming.

IF OCEAN ACIDIFICATION IS THE EVIL TWIN, DOES THAT MEAN GLOBAL WARMING IS THE GOOD TWIN?

WASN'T ME!

NO, YOU'RE BOTH EVIL.

PLOP

Feedbacks are not our get-out-of-jail-free card

When we emit heat-trapping gases into the atmosphere, the world warms. But it doesn't end there. A number of feedbacks occur in response. Some magnify the warming, while others suppress the warming. What's the overall effect?

> "The Earth is not going to break its own fever.

Kate Marvel
NASA

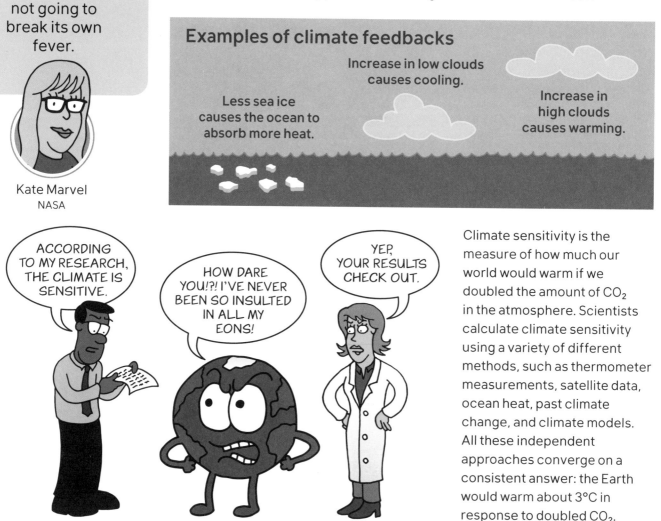

Examples of climate feedbacks

Increase in low clouds causes cooling.

Less sea ice causes the ocean to absorb more heat.

Increase in high clouds causes warming.

ACCORDING TO MY RESEARCH, THE CLIMATE IS SENSITIVE.

HOW DARE YOU!?! I'VE NEVER BEEN SO INSULTED IN ALL MY EONS!

YEP, YOUR RESULTS CHECK OUT.

Climate sensitivity is the measure of how much our world would warm if we doubled the amount of CO_2 in the atmosphere. Scientists calculate climate sensitivity using a variety of different methods, such as thermometer measurements, satellite data, ocean heat, past climate change, and climate models. All these independent approaches converge on a consistent answer: the Earth would warm about 3°C in response to doubled CO_2.

The direct greenhouse warming from doubled CO_2 is around 1°C. After various feedbacks have taken effect, the final amount of warming is 3°C. In other words, after we've added up all the amplifying and dampening feedbacks, the overall effect of reinforcing feedbacks is to triple the direct warming from CO_2.

One myth argues that climate sensitivity is low and there'll be little warming from our CO_2 emissions. This myth cherry picks from the different methods used to estimate climate sensitivity. It only looks at isolated studies and ignores the full body of research conducted by the rest of the scientific community.

A more complete picture of climate sensitivity can be found by considering the entire body of research by the scientific community, not just isolated studies.

FACT

Many lines of evidence point to our climate being highly sensitive to changes in heat.

MYTH

"Climate sensitivity is low."

FALLACY

Cherry picking: Ignores all the independent evidence for high climate sensitivity.

Feedbacks vs. runaway feedback

One misconception is that reinforcing feedbacks inevitably result in runaway feedback. This isn't always the case; if the feedback is small, eventually it levels out and stops having an effect. Bank interest is a reinforcing feedback but is never big enough to runaway.

Species can't keep up with climate change

When the environment changes, species have to evolve to survive. These evolutionary changes take thousands of years. However, because we're causing rapid climate change over decades, species are having trouble keeping up.

When climate changes too quickly, species go extinct. Throughout Earth's history, there have been five mass extinction events in which most species became extinct. In each case, rapid climate change was a contributing factor.

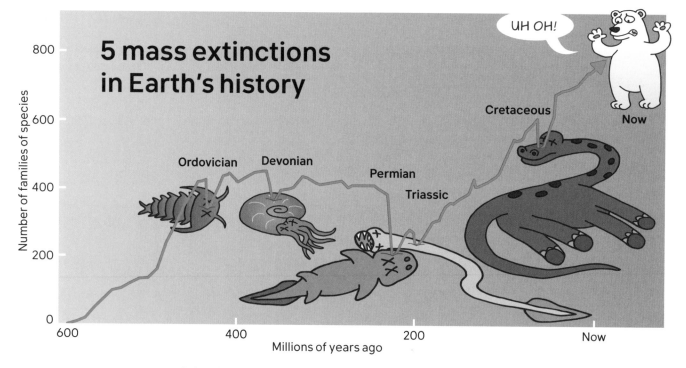

5 mass extinctions in Earth's history

Number of families of species

Ordovician Devonian Permian Triassic Cretaceous Now

UH OH!

Millions of years ago

Scientists worry that we may now be entering the Earth's sixth mass extinction event. Over the last 500 years, extinctions have been happening at least as fast as the previous five mass extinction events. These extinction events usually take hundreds of thousands to millions of years. If we lose all currently threatened species, the current mass extinction event will happen over centuries.

One myth is that species will simply be able to adapt to the Earth's changing climate. This commits the fallacy of jumping to conclusions. Just because species can adapt in some conditions doesn't mean they can adjust to *any* new situation.

There's a limit to how quickly species can adapt to environmental changes. In past mass extinction events, over three-quarters of the world's species became extinct.

We are now changing the climate so fast that species are already struggling to keep up. If we keep burning fossil fuels the way we are now, more than 40% of species could go extinct by the end of this century. We are only in the early stages of the sixth mass extinction event. We can still change course and prevent many species from going extinct.

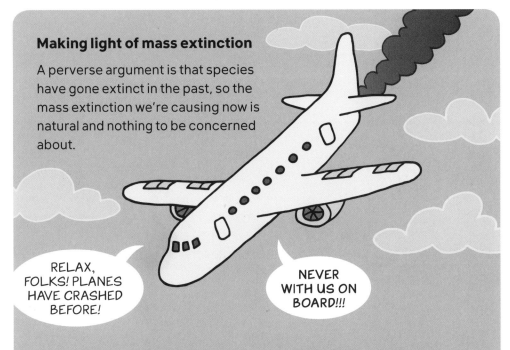

Making light of mass extinction

A perverse argument is that species have gone extinct in the past, so the mass extinction we're causing now is natural and nothing to be concerned about.

RELAX, FOLKS! PLANES HAVE CRASHED BEFORE!

NEVER WITH US ON BOARD!!!

Just because it's happened before doesn't mean it's something we want to go through now. Plane crashes have happened before, but no one ever wants to be in one.

FACT

Species become extinct when climate changes too fast for them to adapt. Currently, species are becoming extinct at similar rates to past mass extinctions.

MYTH

"Species can adapt to climate change."

FALLACY

Jumping to conclusions: Just because species can adapt to gradual climate change doesn't mean they can adjust to the rapid climate change happening now.

Standing (and marching) for science

Science is under relentless, intense attack. This has inspired hundreds of thousands of people around the world to take to the streets and stand up for science. But the recent barrage is only the latest chapter in a longer misinformation campaign. Climate science has been attacked for decades.

Galileo vs. the church: Which is the science denier?

Science has been attacked since the time of Galileo (an Italian scientist in the 1500s), whose evidence-based approach became known as the scientific method. Using a telescope, Galileo collected evidence that the planets revolve around the sun, challenging a 1,000-year-old understanding of the universe. In response, the church attacked his science. Their ideology, based on a literal interpretation of the Bible, placed the Earth at the center of the universe.

Deniers like to promote the myth that they're like Galileo, challenging conventional wisdom. But deniers are more like the medieval church, rejecting scientific evidence that threatens their worldview. Just like Galileo's critics, they attack scientific data, sow public doubt, and seek to restore outdated beliefs.

Who are the real alarmists?

The Intergovernmental Panel on Climate Change (IPCC) assesses and summarizes the science on climate change. Since 1990, they've produced five reports. Every sentence of each summary report is rigorously scrutinized, and the world's governments have to agree on the report. Consequently, the IPCC reports tend to be quite conservative.

In previous reports, they've underestimated how much greenhouse gases we've emitted. IPCC predictions of Arctic sea ice melt have been much slower than the actual ice melt. Sea level rise has accelerated faster than any of the climate models predicted.

New scientific findings, published after an IPCC report, have been twenty times more likely to be worse than the IPCC predictions. The IPCC has been systematically underestimating climate impacts.

Climate scientists and the IPCC are often accused of being alarmists, exaggerating the dangers of global warming. This myth cherry picks rare examples where the IPCC overestimated climate impacts. They tend toward underestimating climate impacts—the polar opposite of being alarmists.

Climate scientists are accused of exaggerating climate risks...

...in reality, they're twenty times more likely to *underestimate* climate risks.

Despite uncertainty, we're certain there's a problem

To a scientist, the word *uncertainty* means something different than it does to the average person. For nonscientists, uncertainty conveys ignorance, as if the scientists don't know what's going on. For a scientist, uncertainty means a range of values around a best estimate. For example, the climate response to doubling CO_2 in the atmosphere is estimated to be between 2°C and 4.5°C with a best estimate of 3°C. While we expect 3°C warming, we might get less or more.

Climate deniers argue that because there's uncertainty, we shouldn't act. But just because we don't know the exact amount of danger doesn't mean there's no danger. Uncertainty means that the climate impact might be even worse than our best estimate.

Arguing "don't act until we have certainty" is like being told there are a range of possible side effects from drinking poison but drinking the poison anyway.

How deniers manage risk

The consensus on the 97% consensus

A number of studies have quantified the level of scientific agreement on climate change. In 2009, a survey by Peter Doran found that 97.4% of publishing climate scientists agreed that humans were changing global temperature. In 2010, Bill Anderegg analyzed public statements about climate change. He found 97–98% agreement among the most actively publishing climate scientists that humans are causing global warming.

In 2013, I led a team of researchers analyzing 21 years of scientific papers about global warming. Among relevant climate papers, 97% affirmed the consensus. Three different studies all found overwhelming scientific agreement.

The scientific consensus has also been endorsed by many scientific organizations around the world, such as the American Geophysical Union, European Geosciences Union, Royal Meteorological Society, and Australian Bureau of Meteorology. The National Academies of Science from eighty countries have all affirmed human-caused global warming.

Deniers argue that there's no scientific consensus on climate change because thirty-one thousand science graduates signed a petition rejecting the consensus. This argument appeals to fake experts. The only requirement for the Petition Project is an undergraduate degree in any kind of science. Only 0.1% of the signatories are climate scientists. Asking for nonexpert opinion on a complex topic is like asking a computer scientist to perform heart surgery.

Studies quantifying the percentage of climate scientists who agree humans are causing global warming.

100% Naomi Oreskes 2004

97% Peter Doran 2009

97% William Anderegg 2010

97% John Cook 2013

91% Bart Verheggen 2014

93% Neil Stenhouse 2014

97% Stuart Carlton 2015

This argument also misleads by using the technique of magnified minority. More than 10 million people have earned a science degree since 1971. That means that only 0.3% of Americans with science degrees signed the petition.

Citing thousands of dissenting nonexperts to cast doubt on consensus is an age-old technique, perfected by the tobacco industry in the 1970s.

How deniers maintain the consensus gap

Frank Luntz
Republican strategist

Climate deniers have been trying to cast doubt on the scientific consensus for decades. Why attack the consensus? Republican strategist Frank Luntz conducted market research and found that people's opinions on climate policy depended on whether they thought experts disagreed about human-caused global warming. Luntz advised Republican politicians to cast doubt on the scientific consensus.

Decades of misinformation have taken its toll. The public mistakenly think 67% of climate scientists agree on human-caused global warming. The chasm between public perception and the 97% consensus is known as the consensus gap.

Over a decade after Luntz's insight, social scientists began researching how people think about consensus. They identified that public perception of consensus is a "gateway belief." Once people understand that there's scientific consensus, they're more likely to accept that climate change is happening and requires action. Social scientists recommended that scientists should communicate the overwhelming expert agreement on human-caused global warming to correct the misconception that scientists disagree.

Communicating the 97% consensus has begun to undo the damage of misinformation campaigns. Over the last 5 years, public awareness of the scientific consensus has steadily increased.

This has led to a new argument from the same deniers who have claimed there is no consensus: now they argue we shouldn't talk about consensus. Deniers want to convince the public that experts not only disagree on climate change but also stop scientists from clearing up this misconception.

The case for human-caused global warming isn't based on the 97% consensus; it's based on scientific evidence (described in the chapter Denying Responsibility).

Nevertheless, the public often rely on expert opinion to guide their views on complicated topics like climate change. This is why deniers target expert agreement and why it's important to communicate the 97% consensus among climate scientists.

THERE IS NO CONSENSUS

DON'T MENTION CONSENSUS

A confirmation of hockey sticks

In 1998, Michael Mann, Ray Bradley, and Lesley Hughes constructed a record of Northern Hemisphere temperature going back 600 years. They used a variety of sources, including ice cores, ocean sediments, cave deposits, tree rings, and boreholes as indicators of temperature change. They found that current global warming was unprecedented over the past 600 years. The graph was dubbed the "hockey stick".

Since 1998, many studies using different data and methods have independently confirmed that current temperatures are unprecedented over at least the last 600 years. The largest study, involving sixty scientific institutions, collected data from all over the globe. They found the same hockey stick, with the last few decades being the warmest in at least 1,400 years.

There are many lines of evidence that humans are causing global warming. The hockey stick is just one small piece of a much larger picture. Nevertheless, the original 1998 paper has been intensely attacked by deniers. The first critique of the hockey stick was by Canadian mining engineer Steve McIntyre, who claimed that the hockey stick contained statistical flaws. This kind of nitpicking of statistical methods is known as the blowfish fallacy.

> There are now dozens of hockey sticks and they all come to the same basic conclusion. The recent warming does appear to be unprecedented as far back as we can go.

Prof. Michael Mann
Penn State University

Blowfish fallacy

The red herring fallacy is used to distract from important scientific findings. The blowfish fallacy is a special type of red herring. It involves laser-focusing on a small methodological aspect of scientific research, blowing it out of proportion in order to distract from the bigger picture. If you persuade people to focus hard enough on specific details, they can miss the gorilla in the room.

AAH! THEY'RE PRICKLY!

Statistical nitpicks of the 1998 study distract from two decades of subsequent research that confirms the same result. Many studies have established that we're currently experiencing the warmest temperatures in thousands of years.

Getting medieval on climate change

Medieval times were around a thousand years ago, lasting from 900 to 1150 A.D. Temperatures at this time were relatively warmer compared with the earlier Dark Ages and the later Little Ice Age. This period is called the Medieval Warm Period.

The warmer temperatures were a combination of several natural factors. Solar activity was slightly higher during the Medieval Warm Period. There were also relatively few volcanic eruptions. Volcanoes send tiny particles into the atmosphere that reflect sunlight and cause temperatures to cool. The combination of a warmer sun and less active volcanoes caused warmer medieval temperatures.

On average, temperatures during the Medieval Warm Period were similar to those during the mid-20th century. Global warming in the second half of the 20th century took us above medieval temperatures.

The myth about the Medieval Warm Period being warmer than now commits the fallacy of cherry picking. It falsely assumes the whole planet was warmer then or compares medieval temperatures with today's temperatures at a single location. Some individual locations may have been warmer in medieval times. But other locations were cooler. When averaging out temperatures over entire regions, medieval times were cooler than today's climate.

We also know that the Medieval Warm Period was cooler than now because sea levels were lower. If global temperatures were warmer in medieval times, more ice would have melted, causing higher sea levels. But this never happened.

Jumping to conclusions

The medieval argument is a precursor to another climate myth we've already examined—the argument that natural factors warmed the climate in the past so natural factors must be warming the climate now. This commits the fallacy of jumping to conclusions. We know the sun and volcanoes caused medieval warming. These same natural factors are currently having a cooling influence. The only way to explain recent warming is to include heat-trapping greenhouse gases.

Climate models' reliable track record

Climate models simulate how our climate works by dividing the Earth, oceans, and atmosphere into a three-dimensional grid. They use the laws of physics to calculate aspects such as temperature and rainfall in each grid box and to simulate how the aspects change over time.

Prof. Wallace Broecker coins the term *global warming.*

Climate models have made many predictions that were subsequently confirmed by observations. In the 1960s, scientists correctly predicted that warming would increase the amount of water vapor in the atmosphere. In the 1970s, Prof. Wallace Broecker (who coined the term *global warming*) predicted that climate would warm due to rising CO_2 levels. In 1975, climate models predicted that the Arctic would warm faster than the rest of the planet, in part because of decreased reflectivity due to melting ice. In the 1980s, scientists predicted that the land surface would warm faster than the ocean surface.

Models have correctly predicted many other aspects of climate change, such as Arctic sea ice melt, sea level rise, and the geographic pattern of global warming. This gives us confidence in using these models to predict future climate change.

Climate deniers attempt to cast doubt on climate models by arguing they're not perfect and can't be trusted. This myth commits the fallacy of impossible expectations. Climate models aren't the real world; they're simulations of the real world and so cannot be perfect. As the statistician George Box said, "All models are wrong, but some are useful."

> A computer simulation that's able to exactly reproduce all of reality: that's not a climate model. That's the Matrix.

Kate Marvel
NASA

One example of impossible expectations is demanding that models make perfect short-term predictions. The problem is our climate is influenced by unpredictable factors like ocean cycles and changes in the sun that can cause short-term warming or cooling. However, these short-term factors average out over time, making reliable long-term predictions possible.

Our confidence in climate models' ability to predict the future is based on their reliable track record. By relying on the laws of physics, climate scientists have used models for decades to make accurate predictions.

FACT
In the 1970s, most climate research predicted warming due to increasing greenhouse gases.

MYTH
"Scientists in the 1970s predicted an upcoming ice age."

FALLACY
Misrepresentation: Portrays the ice age research in the 1970s as consensus when there wasn't overwhelming agreement at the time.

What were scientists predicting in the 1970s?

In the 1970s, global temperature hadn't changed much for several decades. It had even cooled slightly. Nevertheless, most climate research published in the 1970s predicted that global warming was just around the corner. The number of papers predicting global warming was increasing. The reason: we were emitting more and more amounts of heat-trapping greenhouse gases into the atmosphere.

From the late 1970s, global temperatures did start to increase, just as climate scientists expected. Scientists made a prediction based on physics and were proven correct.

Deniers try to cast doubt on climate science by arguing that in the 1970s, scientists were predicting global cooling or an upcoming ice age. This myth misrepresents the scientific position in the 1970s. A small number of papers in the 1970s speculated that under certain conditions, global cooling might happen.

In 1974 and 1975, *Time* and *Newsweek* magazines published articles warning about a possible oncoming ice age. But *Time* and *Newsweek* are news magazines, not scientific journals. In scientific papers, the growing majority of research indicated oncoming global warming.

1975

"We do not have a good quantitative understanding of our climate machine and what determines its course."

U. S. National Academy of Sciences and National Research Council

The most comprehensive study in the 1970s was the 1975 report by the U. S. National Academy of Sciences and the National Research Council. The noncommittal statement in 1975 stands in strong contrast to the current position of the U. S. National Academy of Sciences (see right margin).

ANOTHER IRONY ALERT — Some deniers still predict an upcoming ice age to this day!

NOW

"The scientific understanding of climate change is now sufficiently clear to justify nations taking prompt action."

U. S. National Academy of Sciences

Distinguishing between weather and climate

People often mistake weather for climate. What's the difference? Weather is the state of the atmosphere at a single place and time—for example, the temperature, cloud cover, and wind speed right now where you live. Climate is the average weather across a region over a long period of time.

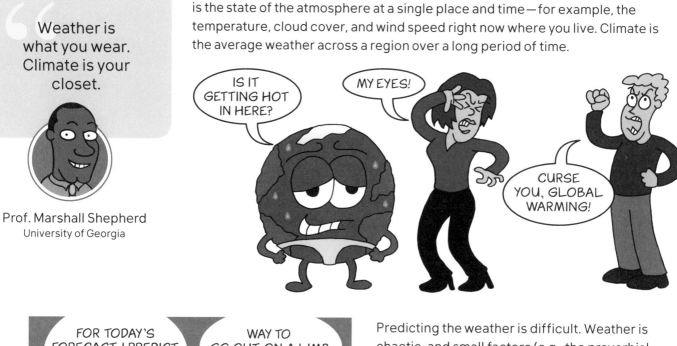

Predicting the weather is difficult. Weather is chaotic, and small factors (e.g., the proverbial butterfly flapping its wings) can have big effects.

Climate models are different. They don't predict the weather on any specific day. They predict the average weather over decades across large regions.

For example, it's hard to say exactly what the weather will be next Tuesday. But we know on average, summer is going to be warmer than winter. The average climate is easier to predict than the weather on specific days.

One climate myth tries to cast doubt on climate models by arguing that since weather predictions often get it wrong, we can't trust climate predictions. Using weather predictions to cast doubt on climate predictions is a red herring. Just because weather models don't always get things right doesn't mean we can't trust climate models: comparing the two is like comparing apples and oranges.

You can't accurately predict the roll of a single die. But you can predict with confidence the result of a million dice rolls. A casino can't predict a single roll at the craps table, but they know that at the end of the day, the dice will average out in a predictable way.

Stolen emails shine light on conspiratorial thinking

In 2009, climate scientists' emails were stolen and published online. Quotes were taken out of context and published online. Deniers used these quotes to promote the conspiracy theory, dubbed "Climategate", that scientists had faked the evidence for global warming. This is absurd given that the evidence for warming includes the melting of billions of metric tons of ice and global sea level rise.

Nine separate investigations across two countries independently evaluated the stolen emails. Every investigation unanimously concluded that nothing in the emails affected the science. Conspiracy theorists assumed that each investigation was part of the conspiracy.

Traits of conspiracy theorists

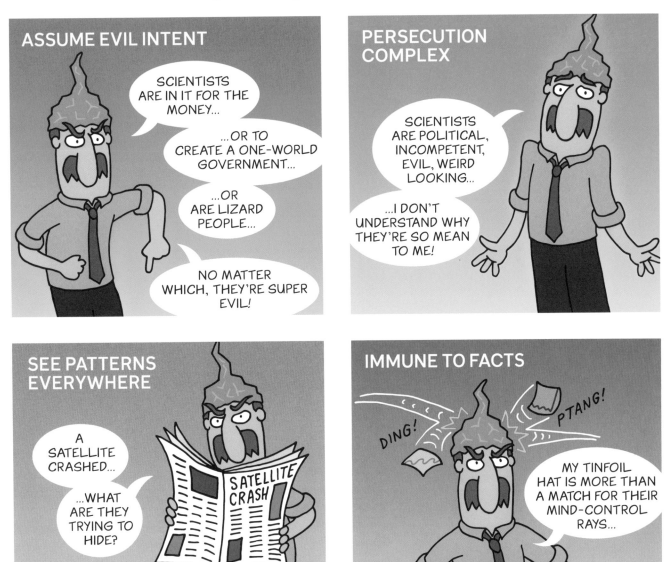

Confusing "Mike's trick" with "hide the decline"

Prof. Phil Jones
University of East Anglia

One of the most used denier techniques associated with Climategate is the technique of quote mining.

> **Quote mining**

Quote mining is taking excerpts of someone's words out of context. This is a form of the straw man fallacy, distorting their original meaning to misrepresent their position. Often this is a form of personal attack, used to make the person look bad.

WE AREN'T CAUSING *MOST* OF GLOBAL WARMING. WE'RE CAUSING *ALL* OF GLOBAL WARMING!

SCIENTISTS SAY WE AREN'T CAUSING MOST OF GLOBAL WARMING!

The most quoted Climategate phrase comes from an email by climate scientist Phil Jones talking about two different scientific techniques: "Mike's trick" and "hide the decline."

What is Mike's trick?

The "trick" refers to the technique (i.e., a clever mathematical device) of plotting thermometer data in the same graph as past temperatures reconstructed from indicators like tree rings and ice cores.

Reconstructed temperature...

...in the same graph as...

Thermometer measurements

THAT'S IT!?!

THAT'S IT.

What is "hide the decline"?

"Decline" in this quote refers to a decline in tree-ring growth since the 1960s (Keith refers to Keith Briffa who published tree ring research). Normally, tree rings track closely with temperature: tree rings are thicker when it's warmer. But for some trees in the Northern Hemisphere, tree rings declined after 1960, even though temperatures warmed. The decline in tree growth was caused by less sunlight reaching certain regions due to local pollution. The divergence between tree rings and temperature is an issue that has been publicly discussed in scientific papers since 1995.

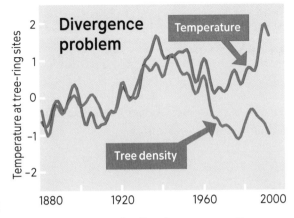

So "Mike's trick" and "hide the decline" have nothing to do with each other. But deniers confuse the two, often referring to "Mike's trick to hide the decline." Deniers are imagining conspiracy theories about ordinary scientific techniques being discussed in public journals.

FACT

"Mike's trick" has nothing to do with "hide the decline," which refers to a decline in tree-ring growth.

MYTH

"Scientists tried to hide the decline in global temperature."

FALLACY

Conspiracy theory: Belief that scientists are hiding something arising from quote-mining emails, taking sentences out of context without understanding the science being discussed.

Can you change your cranky uncle's mind?

A common question is: "What do you say to change a denier's mind?" A more appropriate question is: Who should we focus our communication efforts on?

When someone rejects science for ideological reasons, the chance of changing their mind is very small. In many cases, science-based messages are ineffective and can even be counterproductive. In other words, there are some cases where deniers can respond to scientific facts by believing in the science even less!

This happens across a range of issues. Anti-vaxxers respond to debunkings of vaccination myths by doubling down on their opposition to vaccination. When Republicans were shown evidence that WMDs were not in Iraq, most refused to change their mind. Only one out of fifty was convinced. Those are the kinds of odds we're facing when trying to persuade a science denier!

When we think science threatens our ideology, we may respond in a biased way. This can happen at a deep psychological level, so we often don't even realize we're being biased. When science denial causes someone to lie to themselves, it's practically indistinguishable from deliberate lying.

What are some of the ways that biased thinking causes the five traits of denial (FLICC, see page 16) to appear?

We tend to think people who agree with us know what they're talking about. Deniers think dissenting voices have more expertise than mainstream climate scientists, so they rely on **fake experts**.

Biased thinking can cause us to commit **logical fallacies**. For example, focusing on an opponent's weaker arguments while ignoring their stronger arguments leads to the straw man fallacy.

Disconfirmation bias is our tendency to resist evidence we don't like—leading to **impossible expectations**.

The flip side of disconfirmation bias is confirmation bias: our tendency to put more weight on information we like. This results in **cherry picking**.

Conspiracy theories are inevitable if you disagree with the global community of climate scientists. How else do you explain the world's scientists coming to conclusions that you disagree with?

TRANSLATION
"You have **my** taste in music."

Climate deniers are a small but vocal minority

Research has found there are six different ways that people think about climate change. The groups are defined as alarmed, concerned, cautious, disengaged, doubtful, and dismissive. (While this is based on the American public, similar types of analysis have been done in other countries, such as Australia and India.)

The majority of people—those in the alarmed and concerned groups—accept the reality of climate change. The dismissive group, though a tiny proportion of the population, have a disproportionately large influence. The misinformation they promote is having a significant, negative influence on the general public.

IRONY ALERT

Pluralistic ignorance VS. False consensus effect

51% of Americans are concerned or alarmed about climate change. But they are unaware they're in the majority. This misconception is known as **pluralistic ignorance**.

9% of Americans are dismissive of climate change. But they think they're a much bigger group than they really are. This misconception is known as the **false consensus effect**.

The minority who reject climate science can be especially influential. We saw this in 2017, when Donald Trump appointed climate deniers to many positions of power in his administration. In 2015, half of the U.S. Senate voted for a motion that humans were not causing global warming.

Another vocal source of climate misinformation is conservative media. Radio, newspapers, websites, and cable TV are releasing a firehose of falsehoods that reach millions of people.

> It is not so much the fanaticism of the small minority of active deniers that concerns us, but the vulnerability of the majority to their influence.

Prof. Clive Hamilton
Charles Sturt University

This steady stream of misinformation is not stopping any time soon. It threatens to drown out or undo efforts to educate the public about climate change. So it's important to understand the impact of misinformation in order to develop ways to stop it from influencing people.

Why it's dangerous to ignore misinformation

In order to counter misinformation, we need to understand the impact it has. The most obvious is causing us to believe things that aren't true. But the insidious and dangerous aspect of misinformation is its potential to cancel out accurate information.

When presented with conflicting pieces of information, we often don't have the ability to tell which is fact and which is fiction. In these cases, we can disengage and stop trying to find out the truth. Misinformation can stop us from understanding and accepting the facts.

This is a big danger of fake news. Misinformation doesn't have to be convincing or coherent to be effective: it just has to exist. By presenting people with conflicting information, deniers can reduce the effectiveness of scientific facts.

Misinformation and information are like matter and antimatter. When the two collide, there is an explosion of heat. Afterward, nothing remains.

This has huge consequences for scientists and educators. It's not enough to just explain the science. We might go to great pains to make our science as clear as possible, only to find our best efforts undone by a myth. We ignore deniers at our own peril.

This also tells us how to respond to misinformation. People need to be able to discern the difference between fact and fiction when faced with conflicting information. We need to give them the tools to resolve the conflict.

By explaining the techniques used to distort the facts, the conflict can be resolved. This is like exposing the sleight of hand behind a magician's trick. Once people see the technique behind a misleading argument, that argument loses its influence. Explaining the misleading tricks of denial is called inoculation.

> "When you're designing a debunking, you can use two sets of supporting explanations: one telling people why the fact is true and one telling people why the myth is incorrect.

Prof. Ullrich Ecker
University of Western Australia

Inoculation is the key to eradicating denial

In the medical world, inoculation has eradicated diseases (such as smallpox) by exposing people to a weak form of a disease. This helps build up resistance so that when we encounter the real virus, we don't get infected.

The same principle applies with misinformation. If we encounter a weak form of misinformation, we build up resistance and are not influenced when encountering real misinformation.

An inoculating message warns us that we might be misled by false arguments, then explains the techniques used to distort facts. It can also explain the motivating factors driving the sources of misinformation (e.g., fossil fuel companies' desire for profits).

Inoculation is about increasing critical thinking skills—teaching people to identify attempts to mislead them. If enough people are inoculated, we can achieve herd immunity and eradicate science denial.

Prebunking vs. debunking

Preemptively countering misinformation before people come across it is more effective than trying to undo the damage afterward.

How do we respond to misinformation? An effective debunking requires three elements: fact, myth, and fallacy.

While facts alone are not enough to counter misinformation, the fact is still the most important part of a debunking. Ideally, the facts should be more concrete, simpler, and "stickier" than the myth.

If you're talking about a myth (in order to debunk it), warn people that you're about to say something false before mentioning the myth. This puts them on guard, so they're less likely to be influenced by the myth.

Last, you need to help people resolve the conflict between fact and myth. You can do this by explaining the technique or fallacy that the myth uses to distort the facts.

FACT
Communicate simple, sticky facts.

WHY CAN'T I CATCH A BREAK?!

2014, 2015, AND 2016 WERE THE HOTTEST YEARS ON RECORD...

Full debunking on page 32

MYTH
Warn people before mentioning the myth.

...BUT ONE MYTH ARGUES THAT COLD WEATHER DISPROVES GLOBAL WARMING.

FALLACY
Resolve the conflict between fact and myth.

THIS IS LIKE SAYING NIGHTTIME DISPROVES THE SUN.

AN OBJECT IN MOTION STAYS IN THE SAME MOTION UNLESS A FORCE IS APPLIED TO IT.

AN OBJECT'S ACCELERATION DEPENDS ON THE FORCE ACTING ON THE OBJECT AND THE OBJECT'S MASS.

FOR EVERY ACTION, THERE'S AN EQUAL AND OPPOSITE REACTION.

Three laws of science communication

In 1686, Isaac Newton presented his three laws of motion, describing how objects move when a force is applied. Similar principles apply to moving an audience, summed up by these three laws of science communication.

INEFFECTIVE COMMUNICATION WILL CONTINUE TO BE INEFFECTIVE UNLESS WE CHANGE OUR APPROACH.

1st law of science communication

Communicating the science of climate change hasn't been as effective as it should be, with public acceptance shifting very slowly. A significant contributor to this is decades of misinformation. New approaches are needed—not only teaching the science of climate change but also understanding our audiences, embracing creativity, and inoculating against denier myths.

INSANITY IS REPEATING THE SAME ACTION AND EXPECTING A DIFFERENT RESULT!

IS THAT REALLY YOUR QUOTE?

NAH, I'M JUST HERE BECAUSE IT ANNOYS NEWTON!

2nd law of science communication

Newton's second law of motion says we need to apply a force to accelerate an object. Forcefulness is not what's needed to propel science messages. We need to make our science sticky if we want it to go viral. This can be achieved by making science messages simple, telling compelling stories, and using metaphors to make the abstract concrete and meaningful to people.

"The key to science communication: simple clear messages, repeated often, by a variety of trusted voices.

Prof. Ed Maibach
George Mason University

3rd law of science communication

When science communication has impact, expect pushback. The forces of the status quo will not go quietly into the night. Decades of misinformation have created widespread misconceptions about climate change. Deniers are determined to maintain that state of confusion.

Not only do climate deniers promote myths about climate science, they also personally attack climate scientists, trying to cast doubt on scientific research.

"When you say things of consequence, there will be consequences. But the alternative is to be inconsequential.

Katie Orenstein
The OpEd Project

151

Breaking the spiral of climate silence

While most people are concerned about climate change, many of us never talk about it with family and friends. The main reason is pluralistic ignorance: we don't realize most people are also concerned about climate change. When we don't voice our concern, we reinforce the misconception of pluralistic ignorance, causing a spiral of silence. Debunking the misconception that most people don't care about climate change is important to break climate silence.

Another reason we don't talk about climate change is we worry we'll be made to look stupid. Understanding the fallacies in climate misinformation empower us to speak up, knowing we can respond if we encounter denier arguments. But it's also important to remember that deniers are a vanishingly small minority.

People expect pushback when they talk about climate change. But despite the third law of science communication ("with impact comes pushback"), people rarely encounter pushback in everyday conversations. There is a gap between expectation and reality.

Expectation

People expect pushback if they talk climate.

Reality

People receive very little pushback when they talk climate.

What we do and say matters

To avoid the worst impacts of climate change, we need to stop adding heat-trapping gases to the atmosphere. That means transitioning from fossil fuels to clean energy. This is a complete transformation of our society that is already happening!

How can we as individuals contribute to this monumental change? By helping build the social and political momentum required. We achieve that with one simple action—talking about climate change. Talk to our friends, our family, and most important, our elected officials. When politicians realize voters care about climate change, they'll care about the issue, too.

We can also contribute to climate action by reducing our own carbon footprint. Personally acting to solve climate change allows us to walk the walk, making our talk more powerful.

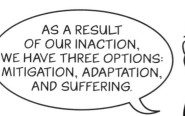

It's important to recognize that climate change is not binary. Our choice is not "suffer climate change" vs. "avoid climate change." We are alreadying experiencing climate change. The only question is how much more. Climate change is literally a matter of degrees. Mitigation today means less suffering in the future.

What we do now matters. Every bit of climate action we take reduces the climate impacts we experience down the track. When we talk about climate change, we add to public awareness and crucially important social momentum.

Prof. Lonnie Thompson
Ohio State University

This book examines the problem of climate science denial. It's unfortunate that some deny there's a problem when we really need to be talking about how to solve it. There is no single magic bullet to address climate change: many solutions all offer valuable contributions. This is a complicated, difficult discussion that has been delayed because of science denial.

As the reality of climate change becomes more difficult to ignore, deniers are grudgingly making the transition from science denial to solutions denial. Ultimately, the denial of climate change is driven by aversion to the solution. Now that the denial of the problem is becoming untenable, many myths and false arguments casting doubts on climate solutions are becoming more prevalent.

But *Cranky Uncle vs. Climate Solutions* is another topic...

Fact-myth-fallacy summary

Global warming is happening

FACT	MYTH		FALLACY
Over recent decades, our planet has been building up heat at a rate of four atomic bombs per second.	"Global warming stopped in 1998."		**Cherry picking:** Ignores all the evidence telling us the planet is building up heat.
Global warming has made hot days more likely.	"It's cold, so global warming isn't real."		**Impossible expectations:** Global warming doesn't mean no more cold days. It means cold events are less likely to happen.
Arctic sea ice is in steady retreat, losing half its coverage in only 40 years.	"Arctic sea ice has recovered."		**Cherry picking:** Looking at only a few years of sea ice data ignores the long-term decline in sea ice.
Glaciers across the planet are shrinking at an accelerating rate.	"Glaciers around the world are increasing."		**Cherry picking:** Picking a handful of growing glaciers ignores the vast majority of glaciers that are shrinking.
Greenland is losing two Mount Everests of ice every year.	"Greenland is thickening in the middle."		**Cherry picking:** Ignores the accelerating ice loss at the ice sheet's edges.
The Greenland ice sheet has been around for hundreds of thousands of years.	"Greenland used to be green."		**Misrepresentation:** Paints a false picture of the state of the Greenland ice sheet over history.
Antarctica is losing 100 billion metric tons of ice per year.	"Antarctica is thickening in the middle."		**Cherry picking:** Ignores the accelerating ice loss at the ice sheet's edges.

FACT	MYTH	FALLACY
Antarctic sea ice is affected by different contributors such as wind, which acts like a sea ice factory.	"Increasing Antarctic sea ice disproves global warming."	**Oversimplification:** Ignores that factors other than warming are increasing Antarctic sea ice.
Sea level has been rising steadily over the past century.	"Sea level rise is exaggerated."	**Cherry picking:** Looks at short periods where sea level rise is flat compared with the long-term increase.
Even if solar activity dropped, it would only slightly delay global warming.	"We're headed into an ice age due to a cooling sun."	**Misrepresentation:** Overstates the role of solar activity on climate change; it has a minimal effect compared with greenhouse warming.

We're causing global warming

FACT	MYTH	FALLACY
Humans have caused all of global warming since 1950.	"Humans haven't contributed much to global warming."	**Slothful induction:** Ignores research into how much humans are contributing to climate change.
The carbon cycle was in balance. We have upset the CO_2 balance.	"Human CO_2 emissions are tiny compared with natural CO_2 emissions."	**Cherry picking:** Ignores how nature absorbs CO_2, balancing natural emissions.
Humans emit one hundred times more CO_2 than volcanoes.	"Volcanoes produce more CO_2 than humans."	**Misrepresentation:** Volcanic emissions are only 1% of human emissions.
A strong warming effect from CO_2 has been directly measured in a number of different ways.	"CO_2 is a trace gas and has a weak effect."	**Red herring:** Although CO_2 is a small percentage of the atmosphere, it has a large effect on global warming.

FACT	MYTH	FALLACY
Greenhouse gases trap some (but not all) heat escaping to space and radiate it back to Earth.	"The greenhouse effect violates the second law of thermodynamics."	**Misrepresentation:** The second law is about the net flow of heat and doesn't stop some heat flow from cold to hot.
CO_2's invisibility is a key feature of the greenhouse effect.	"CO_2 is invisible, therefore harmless."	**Red herring:** CO_2's invisibility has nothing to do with how effective it is.
Emitting more CO_2 means more heat being trapped in the higher atmosphere where the air is thinner.	"The greenhouse effect is saturated."	**Oversimplification:** Considers the atmosphere as a single layer when it's actually multiple layers.
Water vapor provides a reinforcing feedback, making climate even more sensitive to our CO_2 emissions.	"Water vapor is the strongest driver of current global warming."	**Misrepresentation:** Mistakes water vapor as a climate driver when it is actually a feedback.
Human fingerprints in the daily and yearly cycle, confirm greenhouse warming and rule out the sun.	"The sun is causing global warming."	**Cherry picking:** Ignores the last few decades of data showing the sun and the climate moving in opposite directions.
Earth's climate change, caused by humans, is unique in the solar system.	"Other planets are warming due to the sun."	**Slothful induction:** Fails to consider conflicting evidence, such as cooling planets.
Past climate change tells us that climate reacts strongly to changes in heat, including heat trapped by greenhouse gases.	"Climate has changed before, so modern warming is natural."	**Jumping to conclusions:** Just because climate has changed naturally in the past doesn't mean it's natural now.
More CO_2 causes warming. Warming causes more CO_2. Together, this is a reinforcing feedback.	"CO_2 lagged behind temperature in the past, disproving CO_2 warming."	**False dichotomy:** Presents a false choice between two options when both are true.

Climate impacts are serious

FACT	MYTH	FALLACY
Climate change will impact all aspects of society, including agriculture, health, infrastructure, and the environment.	"Warm periods are good for people."	**Cherry picking:** Ignores all the negative impacts of global warming.
The risk from heatwaves is now five times greater due to global warming.	"Heatwaves have happened before, so heatwaves now are normal."	**Jumping to conclusions:** Just because heatwaves happened before doesn't mean we're not influencing them now.
Ocean heat is fuel for hurricanes, making them more intense.	"Hurricanes aren't linked to global warming."	**Red herring:** Distracts from increasing hurricane intensity by focusing on the number of hurricanes.
Plants need the right amount of water to flourish; climate change upsets that balance.	"CO_2 is plant food."	**Oversimplification:** CO_2 fertilization is one factor affecting plant growth, but negative climate impacts outweigh any benefits.
A pollutant is any substance that disrupts the environment; CO_2 does that by trapping heat.	"CO_2 is not a pollutant."	**Red herring:** Quibbling over technical definitions distracts from negative climate impacts.
Polar bears need sea ice to hunt, so melting sea ice threatens their survival.	"Polar bears have increased and are not in danger."	**Oversimplification:** One threat (hunting bears) was replaced with the growing threat of melting sea ice from global warming.
Ocean acidity has increased by 30%, making it hard for marine species to build skeletons and shells and threatening coral reef ecosystems.	"Oceans aren't turning into acid, so acidification is not a concern."	**Red herring:** Arguing about the absolute value of ocean acidity distracts from the fact that ocean chemistry is changing rapidly and becoming more acidic.
Coral reefs will suffer permanent damage from global warming and ocean acidification.	"Coral reefs can recover like they have in the past."	**Misrepresentation:** It took millions of years in the past for coral reefs to recover from mass extinction events.

FACT	MYTH	FALLACY
Many lines of evidence point to our climate being highly sensitive to changes in heat.	"Climate sensitivity is low."	**Cherry picking:** Ignores all the independent evidence for high climate sensitivity.
Species become extinct when climate changes too fast. Species are now becoming extinct at similar rates to past mass extinctions.	"Species can adapt to climate change."	**Jumping to conclusions:** Just because species can adapt to gradual climate change doesn't mean they can adjust to the rapid climate change happening now.

The scientific consensus is overwhelming and robust

FACT	MYTH	FALLACY
Galileo overturned an ideological worldview with scientific evidence, making him more like climate scientists, not deniers.	"Climate deniers are like Galileo, opposing a consensus."	**Misrepresentation:** Deniers are more like Galileo's critics, who rejected science that threatened their ideology.
Scientists are twenty times more likely to underestimate climate impacts, than exaggerate them.	"Climate scientists are alarmists."	**Cherry picking:** Selectively looks at when the IPCC overestimated climate change and ignores underestimates.
Scientific uncertainty means a range of possible values around a best estimate, so climate impacts might be worse than expected.	"If there's scientific uncertainty, we shouldn't act."	**Jumping to conclusions:** Just because we don't know the exact amount of danger doesn't mean the danger doesn't exist.
97% of climate scientists agree that humans are causing global warming.	"Thirty-one thousand scientists dispute human-caused global warming, so there's no consensus."	**Fake experts:** Using non-climate scientists to portray the impression of ongoing scientific debate where there is none. **Magnified minority:** Thirty-one thousand is only 0.3% of all U.S. science graduates.

FACT	MYTH	FALLACY
Many studies have confirmed the original 1998 hockey stick.	"The hockey stick is broken."	**Cherry picking:** Ignores over a decade of research confirming the hockey stick.
While the Medieval Warm Period saw unusually warm temperatures in some regions, globally, the planet was cooler than now.	"It was warmer during medieval times."	**Cherry picking:** Focuses on the hotter regions, while ignoring cooler areas.
Models have made a number of successful predictions based on fundamental physical principles.	"Climate models are unreliable."	**Impossible expectations:** No model is perfect, but they are useful tools that reproduce the past and provide insights into the future.
In the 1970s, most scientific research predicted warming due to increasing greenhouse gases.	"Scientists in the 1970s predicted an upcoming ice age."	**Misrepresentation:** Portrays the ice age research in the 1970s as consensus when there wasn't overwhelming agreement at the time.
Climate models simulate climate, which is weather averaged over time.	"Scientists can't predict weather, so we can't trust climate models."	**Red herring:** Confusing weather with climate distracts from the fact that short-term weather predictions are irrelevant to climate predictions.
Climategate reveals the conspiratorial nature of climate deniers.	"Climategate revealed a conspiracy among climate scientists."	**Conspiracy theory:** Deniers interpret everyday scientific discussions as global conspiracies.
"Mike's trick" has nothing to do with "hide the decline," which refers to a decline in tree-ring growth.	"Scientists tried to hide the decline in global temperature."	**Conspiracy theory:** Belief that scientists are hiding something arising from quote-mining emails, taking sentences out of context without understanding the science being discussed.

The fallacies of science denial

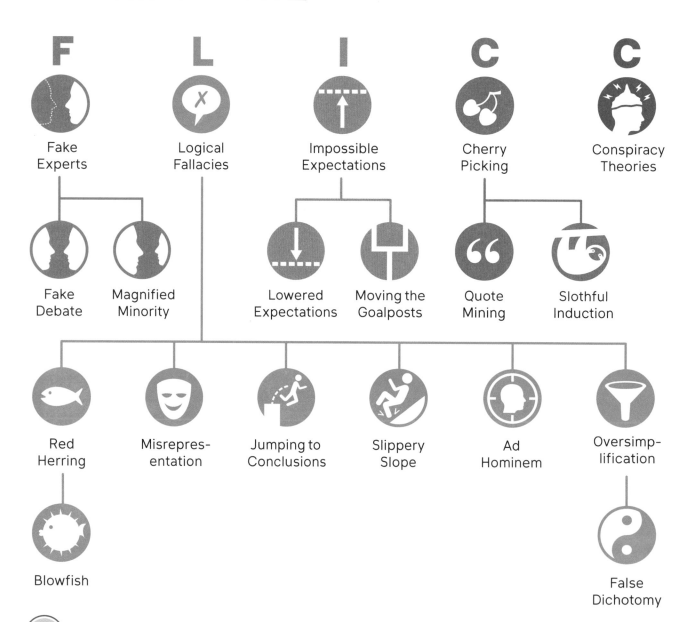

Acknowledgments

Thanks to the following people, whose feedback and support helped make this book possible:

Aaron McCright (Michigan State University)

Adam Sobel (Columbia University)

Ben Santer (Lawrence Livermore National Laboratory)

Bärbel Winkler (Skeptical Science)

Bob Henson (Wunderground)

Briony Swire-Thompson (Northeastern University)

Carrie Finn (University of Queensland)

Constantine Boussalis (Trinity College Dublin)

David Piepgrass

Deke Arndt (National Oceanic and Atmospheric Administration)

Ed Hawkins (University of Reading)

Ed Maibach (George Mason University)

Eric Rignot (University of California, Irvine)

Genevieve Guenther (EndClimateSilence.org)

Isabella Velicogna (University of California, Irvine)

Jason Box (Geological Survey of Denmark and Greenland)

Jennifer Francis (Rutgers University)

Josh Willis (Jet Propulsion Laboratory)

Kasha Patel (NASA)

Ken Rice (University of Edinburgh)

Kristin Timm (George Mason University)

Michael Mann (Penn State University)

Naomi Oreskes (Harvard University)

Pascal Diethelm (OxySuisse)

Peter Jacobs (George Mason University)

Sander van der Linden (Cambridge University)

Sarah Myhre (University of Washington)

Scott Mandia (Suffolk County Community College)

Simon Donner (University of British Columbia)

Susan Hassol

Wendy Cook

Yoram Bauman (standupeconomist.com)

About the author

John Cook completed an honors degree in physics at the University of Queensland, Australia. While contemplating his degree, he often drew cartoons in the margins of his physics notes.

After graduating, he spent a decade as a cartoonist and graphic designer. However, he never strayed far from science and spent his spare time reading climate research and debunking misinformation.

In 2007, Cook founded SkepticalScience.com. He began exploring how to combat science denial and completed a Ph.D. on the cognitive psychology of misinformation.

He found that inoculation, or explaining the techniques of denial, was the key to neutralizing misinformation and that parallel argumentation was a powerful way to put it into practice. This inspired him to bring together his two careers, using parallel arguments in the form of cartoons to explain the techniques of science denial.

Cook is currently a research assistant professor with the Center for Climate Change Communication at George Mason University, where he focuses on combating fake news and misinformation by conducting research into using critical thinking to inoculate against misinformation.